Horace between Freedom and Slavery

Publication of this volume has been made possible, in part, through the generous support and enduring vision of *Warren G. Moon*.

Horace between Freedom and Slavery

The First Book of *Epistles*

Stephanie McCarter

THE UNIVERSITY OF WISCONSIN PRESS

The University of Wisconsin Press
1930 Monroe Street, 3rd Floor
Madison, Wisconsin 53711-2059
uwpress.wisc.edu

3 Henrietta Street, Covent Garden
London WC2E 8LU, United Kingdom
eurospanbookstore.com

Printed in the United States of America

Library of Congress Cataloging-in-Publication Data
McCarter, Stephanie, author.
  Horace between freedom and slavery : the first book of Epistles /
Stephanie McCarter.
       pages cm. — (Wisconsin studies in classics)
  Includes bibliographical references and index.
    ISBN 978-0-299-30570-3 (cloth : alk. paper) —
    ISBN 978-0-299-30573-4 (e-book)
1. Horace—Criticism and interpretation. 2. Horace. Epistulae. Liber 1—
Criticism and interpretation. 3. Epistolary poetry, Latin—History and
criticism. I. Title. II. Series: Wisconsin studies in classics.
    PA6411.M334 2015
    871′.01—dc23
                                                  2015009227

to

DANIEL, RORY, *and* EDITH

Contents

Acknowledgments   ix

Abbreviations   xi

Introduction   3

1 The Dilemma of *Libertas*: *Epistles* 1.1   25

2 Horace the Student: Inconsistency and Sickness
in *Epistles* 1.1, 1.8, and 1.15   43

3 Horace the Teacher: Poetry and Philosophy
in *Epistles* 1.1 and 1.2   67

4 *Nil Admirari*: The Moral Adviser of
Epistles 1.4, 1.5, 1.6, and 1.12   93

5 *Otia Liberrima*: Horace, Maecenas, and the Sabine Farm
in *Epistles* 1.7 and 1.16   124

6 The Limits of Rural *Libertas*: *Epistles* 1.10, 1.11, and 1.14   161

7 Moderate Freedom and Friendship: *Epistles* 1.17 and 1.18   190

8 Moderate Freedom and Poetry: *Epistles* 1.3 and 1.19   226

Conclusion: Freedom and Publication
in *Epistles* 1.13 and 1.20   256

Notes   275

Bibliography   333

Index   349

Index Locorum   355

Acknowledgments

This book started life as a doctoral dissertation completed in 2007 at the University of Virginia, where I could not have asked for a more vibrant Classics community or a more generous group of colleagues and friends. I am especially grateful for the many years of encouragement and support provided by K. Sara Myers, who directed the dissertation and has provided invaluable guidance on a number of other projects along the way. Special thanks are due to the other members of my doctoral committee, John Miller, Tony Woodman, and Dan Devereux, who provided much helpful feedback and criticism. I am indebted also to Jenny Strauss Clay, Edward Courtney, Elizabeth Sutherland, and David Rohrbacher for teaching me a great deal about Horace. Over the years I have received the benefit of having many an *utile exemplar* in the field of Classics. In addition to those already listed, these include especially Christopher Craig, Susan Martin, David Tandy, Anne Groton, and Jane Crawford. I am deeply thankful for these teachers and mentors.

I have had a great deal of support at Sewanee: The University of the South during the writing of this book. In particular I would like to thank Christopher McDonough for being a model of collegiality and an ideal departmental chair. This project would not have been possible without a sabbatical leave generously endorsed by John Gatta, Dean of the College. I have been fortunate to teach Horace's poetry to so many talented students at Sewanee, and I can think of no greater reward for what I do than to have students share my love for this wonderful poet.

I owe great appreciation as well to the members of the University of Wisconsin Press. Patricia Rosenmeyer, Raphael Kadushin, Matthew Cosby, Amber Rose, and Adam Mehring have guided the book through the various steps with immense professionalism and kindness. The Press's readers generously offered many helpful suggestions. All remaining errors are of course my own.

My family has given me an immeasurable amount of love and support not just during this process but throughout my academic career. No note of acknowledgment can sufficiently express my gratitude to my mother, Sandra McCarter, my father, Carl McCarter, and my brother, Chris McCarter. Finally, I thank my husband and fellow Classicist Daniel Holmes, whose feedback, love, and encouragement made the completion of this book possible. I dedicate this book to you and to our beautiful children, Rory and Edith.

Abbreviations

Whenever I abbreviate the names of ancient authors and their works, I use standard abbreviations, as I do for journal titles in the bibliography. Other abbreviations are used as follows:

LSJ   Liddell, H.G., R. Scott, and H.S. Jones. 1940. *A Greek-English Lexicon*, 9th ed. Oxford: Oxford University Press.

OLD   Glare, P.G.W. 1982. *Oxford Latin Dictionary*. Oxford: Oxford University Press.

RIC I² Sutherland, Carol H.V., and Robert A.G. Carson. 1984. *The Roman Imperial Coinage*, vol. 1, 2nd ed. London: Spink and Son.

SVF   von Arnim, Hans. 1903–24. *Stoicorum Veterum Fragmenta*. Leipzig: K.G. Saur.

Horace between Freedom and Slavery

∞ Introduction

THE HORACE WE FIND IN THE FIRST BOOK of *Epistles* is a man torn between the claims of competing spheres.[1] Ensconced in the private seclusion and freedom of the countryside, he sends out his poetic missives to friends and associates in order simultaneously to defend his absence from and maintain his ties to the city and its elite. The letters enact a compromise between Horace's presence and absence, and in being sent they open up a path between two ways of life, neither of which fully holds his allegiance. It is the persona's profound ambivalence toward public and private, engagement and withdrawal, independence and obligation that this book addresses. This ambivalence is central to four areas: philosophy, location, friendship, and poetry. In each of these spheres the speaker longs above all for freedom, and this study examines through close readings of the poems how Horace carefully negotiates, over the course of the collection, what degree of freedom works best for someone who wants to remain engaged while retaining independence.[2] The letters explore what sort of freedom befits a successful poet and associate of Maecenas—or any ambitious man in 20 B.C.E., when the Augustan principate is in full bloom and the role of traditional *libertas* is in question.[3] (As my argument will show, the persona projected in these poems *is* an ambitious man, proud of his poetic and social accomplishments.) The transition from republic to empire forms an important background against which we can analyze Horace's focus on freedom in the *Epistles*. The freedom ultimately formulated in these poems exemplifies the *aurea mediocritas* famously coined at *Odes* 2.10.5–6. It is a path between the truculent, Republican *libertas* represented by Lucilius (but downplayed by Horace) in the *Satires* and the servile obsequiousness so often attributed to imperial courtiers by later writers. In this introduction I lay the groundwork for my reading of *Epistles* 1 by first examining the idea of "moderate freedom" in its historical context, connecting it directly not only with late Republican and Augustan ideology but also with later imperial thought. Horace's reconfiguration of *libertas* reflects the political transformations to *libertas* taking shape during the early Augustan principate. I next consider how Horace carefully constructs poetic personae both for himself and his addressees, and I give an overview of my approach to one of the most tangled and complicated questions of the *Epistles*: Horace's use of philosophy. Finally, I provide a brief overview of my argument, focusing on its organization.

THE *EPISTLES* AND *LIBERTAS*

The preoccupation with *libertas* is not new or unique to the *Epistles* among Horace's writing, but in them it takes on a new urgency.[4] In the *Satires*, especially in the programmatic satires 1.4 and 1.10, *libertas*, manifested as freedom of speech, plays a key role, and Horace's formulation of freedom in these poems has been read as a response to Octavian's rise to power and to the appeals to *libertas* made by all sides in the dramatic upheavals of the first century B.C.[5] In Horace's satiric poetry, *libertas* is a trait that must be toned down since it has the potential to become unwarranted abuse or *licentia*, lack of restraint. The representative of unmitigated *libertas* is Lucilius, Horace's satiric model, whose invective (*aerugo mera*, "undiluted malice," 1.4.101) he tempers and moderates. Horace's taming of Lucilian *libertas* is politically significant since Republican partisans aligned their own uncompromising freedom with that practiced by Lucilius in his vituperative satires.[6] As DuQuesnay has shown, Horace thus harmonizes his satiric program with the larger aims of Octavian, who strived to align himself with appropriate *libertas* while connecting his enemies to its unmitigated extreme, *licentia*: "His . . . redefinition of Lucilian *libertas* as something morally responsible invites the inference that the Triumvirs are opposed not to true *libertas*, which is traditional and responsible, but rather to license, the irresponsible, malicious and divisive exercise of freedom with which true *libertas* is wrongly confused by those who oppose them."[7] The *Satires* thus situate the rule of Augustus within the old values of the *mos maiorum* and align him with true *libertas*, a term that had been propagandized by various factions in the late Republic, with devastating results.[8] Kennedy has pointed out, however, that the overt political associations of the word *libertas* are avoided in the *Satires*, "with its delicate political connotations being mediated principally through discussions of the less sensitive term *aequitas*, through coded readings (presented as 'literary' comment) of the 'free' and 'outspoken' aristocrat Lucilius, and through remarks on the social constraints upon Horace as the son of a freedman."[9] As part of this redefinition of *libertas* Horace divests his satire of the invective *ad hominem* attacks that he attributes to his literary model (1.4.100–103) and sets up the circle around Maecenas as an ideal environment for the exercise of this new humane and moderated liberty, with its frank criticism among *amici* and lack of competition (1.5.39–42; 1.9.48–52).

In *Epistles* 1 Horace resumes the theme of freedom from his earlier hexameter works and expands upon it. Here too the conversation about freedom, which takes place across the book, relates to Augustus only obliquely, though his presence is felt in almost every poem.[10] The Horace of the *Epistles* wrestles much more strenuously with freedom than the Horace of the *Satires*, and he only grudgingly dissociates himself from extreme *libertas* as he gradually charts a course between it and slavery, a middle path that will constitute a kind of freedom that is at once both deeply traditional and a response to the unprecedented ascendency of the *princeps*. The freedom that he will espouse furthermore has a much sharper "imperial" outlook than what we find in the *Satires*. It is designed for a new political age so as to enable his addressees and himself not only to live well but also to gain prominence without asserting independence too forcefully or forfeiting it too slavishly. The *Epistles* therefore occupy a pivotal position in Rome's transformation from republic to empire.

The definition of ideal *libertas* as a mean between extremes emerges only gradually in the course of the collection but is expressed conclusively in the opening of the antepenultimate poem, 1.18. Though I examine this poem in detail in chapter 7, it is worthwhile to glance at this passage now in order to understand how it draws extensively on Roman political ideas about freedom. Addressing Lollius, Horace acknowledges the young man's tendency toward excessive independence (*liberrime Lolli*, "most free Lollius," 1) and encourages him to curb such excess not by rushing to the opposite extreme but by adhering to the mean:

> est huic diversum vitio vitium prope maius,
> asperitas agrestis et inconcinna gravisque,
> quae se commendat tonsa cute, dentibus atris,
> dum volt libertas dici mera veraque virtus.
> virtus est medium vitiorum et utrimque reductum. (1.18.5–9)[11]

> There is a vice opposed to this one and almost worse: rustic harshness that is unbecoming and severe, which recommends itself with closely cropped hair and black teeth while wanting to be called undiluted freedom and true virtue. Virtue is a mean between vices and removed from both.

Though Horace has in mind here the patron-client relationship, the moderate freedom he espouses, especially through his use of wine imagery (*mera libertas*, "undiluted freedom"), has a strong political undertone. The discussion that follows situates Horace's moderate *libertas* within a larger constitutional debate unfolding in the final years of the Republic and the early years of the Principate.[12]

We must, however, bear in mind the caveat repeatedly made by scholars that freedom during this period, just as it is today, was a complicated idea that did not lend itself to simple or straightforward definitions.[13] At its most basic level, to be free was simply not to be a slave.[14] Such a sharp dichotomy, however, fails to admit the various shades of freedom that were possible in the Roman mind.[15] Neither does it adequately take into account how the Romans applied the concept to their political lives.[16] Arena has recently provided a succinct definition for political freedom during the Republican period: it is "a status of non-subjection to the arbitrary will of another person or group of persons."[17] Such *libertas* can be possessed by both individuals and states and is best maintained when all citizens are equally subjected to the protective and punitive force of law.[18] To quote Cicero, *legum . . . omnes servi sumus ut liberi esse possimus*, "we are all slaves to the law, so that we can be free," *Pro Cluentio* 53.146. These are the aspects of freedom—non-subjection to arbitrary will and equal subjection of all citizens to the law—that were considered threatened during the crises of the late Republic.[19] With the rise of Augustus, the state and the individuals within it became subjected to his arbitrary will as he rose to a position above the law, and the traditional definition of *libertas* consequently could not remain intact.[20] Freedom now became closely aligned with the *pax Augusta* and was bestowed by the largesse of the *princeps*. Augustus thus became the chief guarantor of freedom for the Roman populace, which, because of his stabilizing influence, was no longer subject to the violence propagated by powerful individuals claiming to champion *libertas* at any cost.[21]

Libertas was a political slogan exploited throughout the first century B.C., with different factions repeatedly accusing their enemies of attaining to tyranny and thus threatening to reduce the state and the individuals within it to slavery.[22] Since this is well-worn territory, a few examples suffice to illustrate this phenomenon. Cicero, who claimed to have freed the state from the tyrannical aspirations of Catiline,[23] was himself accused of threatening *libertas* by executing the conspirators without trial. Upon his exile in 58 B.C., Clodius had his house razed and an altar to *Libertas* erected in its place.[24] Julius Caesar considered his own freedom as well as that of the state threatened by his political enemies and put himself forth as a champion of liberty against their impending tyranny.[25] He in turn was accused of *dominatio* and assassinated in the name of *libertas*, which as an ideal became especially associated with those fighting for the Republican cause in the ensuing civil wars.[26] At Philippi, for example, *libertas* was the watchword of those fighting on the side of Brutus and Cassius.

To their enemies these Republican partisans are exemplars not of freedom but of *licentia*, of *libertas* taken to an extreme, unbridled neither by the rule of law nor by the *mos maiorum*.[27] In *Odes* 3.24 Horace himself attributes the crises and civil wars of the late Republic to *licentia* and calls upon Augustus to check such excesses and thereby to earn the title *pater urbium*, "father of cities":[28]

> o quisquis volet impias
> caedis et rabiem tollere civicam,
>   si quaeret PATER VRBIVM
> subscribi statuis, indomitam audeat
>   refrenare licentiam. (25–29)

Whoever desires to remove unholy slaughter and civic madness, if he wants "father of cities" to be inscribed upon his statues, let him dare to bridle untamed license.

Similarly, in *Odes* 4.15 Horace includes the restraining of *licentia* as one of the measures Augustus has undertaken to restore the *mos maiorum*, the foundation of Roman expansion:

> tua, Caesar, aetas
>
> fruges et agris rettulit uberes,
> et signa nostro restituit Iovi
>   derepta Parthorum superbis
>   postibus et vacuum duellis
>
> Ianum Quirini clausit et ordinem
> rectum evaganti frena licentiae
>   iniecit emovitque culpas
>   et veteres revocavit artis,
>
> per quas Latinum nomen et Italae
> crevere vires, famaque et imperi
>   porrecta maiestas ad ortus
>   solis ab Hesperio cubili. (4–16)

Your age, Caesar, has brought back rich produce to the fields and has restored to our Jupiter the standards snatched from the haughty posts of the Parthians and has closed the doors of Janus Quirinus, free of wars, and has applied reins to license, which was transgressing the proper boundary, and has called back the ancient arts through which the Latin name and Italian strength grew and the fame and majesty of the empire were extended from the sun's western bed to his [eastern] risings.

Later, in the *Dialogus de Oratoribus*, Tacitus will have Maternus associate *licentia* with the volatile political period of the late Republic, a period that fostered the arts of oratory but not the arts of peace:

> Non de otiosa et quieta re loquimur et quae probitate et modestia gaudeat, sed est magna illa et notabilis eloquentia alumna licentiae, quam stulti libertatem vocant, comes seditionum, effrenati populi incitamentum, sine obsequio, sine

severitate, contumax, temeraria, adrogans, quae in bene constitutis civitatibus non oritur. (40.2)

We are not discussing a topic born of leisure or peace or one that rejoices in uprightness and restraint, but that great and remarkable eloquence that is a foster child of license, which fools called liberty. It is the companion of civil war, the stimulus of an unbridled populace, without obedience, without sternness; it is defiant, rash, overbearing, and it does not arise in well-governed states.

What Rome has lost in unbridled liberty, argues Maternus, it has gained in stability and security. Whereas license is the concomitant of civil war, real *libertas* contains a measure of deference, *obsequium*, a word used by Horace in his definition of moderate freedom at *Epistles* 1.18.10 and to which we will return shortly.

Unless checked, immoderate license, in both Greek and Roman thought, leads ultimately to the eventual loss of freedom and the rise of tyranny. The descent from unbridled democratic license to tyranny famously finds expression in Plato's *Republic* in a passage translated by Cicero in his *De Re Publica*, and the formulation of extreme liberty found in these texts must be kept in mind when approaching the *Epistles*. Both Plato and Cicero use a wine metaphor very similar to the one used by Horace (*mera libertas*, 1.18.8) to describe the liberty greedily drunk by the democratic populace when there is no aristocratic or monarchical element powerful or responsible enough to curb the people's license. For Plato, who notes at *Rep.* 8.560e5 how readily lawlessness (ἀναρχία) can be mistaken for freedom (ἐλευθερία), democratic license is fostered by demagogues, "bad cupbearers," who dispense ἐλευθερία to the people too liberally, like unmixed wine:

ὅταν, οἶμαι, δημοκρατουμένη πόλις ἐλευθερίας διψήσασα κακῶν οἰνοχόων προστατούντων τύχῃ, καὶ πορρωτέρω τοῦ δέοντος ἀκράτου αὐτῆς μεθυσθῇ, τοὺς ἄρχοντας δή, ἂν μὴ πάνυ πρᾷοι ὦσι καὶ πολλὴν παρέχωσι τὴν ἐλευθερίαν, κολάζει αἰτιωμένη ὡς μιαρούς τε καὶ ὀλιγαρχικούς. (*Rep.* 8.562c8–d4)

Whenever, I think, a democratic city, thirsting for freedom, obtains bad cupbearers as commanders, and becomes excessively drunk on that undiluted wine, it punishes its leaders if they are not entirely meek and do not provide abundant freedom by reproaching them as brutal oligarchs.

According to Plato, the "undiluted" freedom of a democracy eradicates all distinctions between individuals, creating rampant equality between unequals, such as father and son, citizen and foreigner, men and women, slaves and freeborn, man and beast (8.562e–563d). Amid such unmitigated ἐλευθερία, the citizen's soul becomes so "soft" (ἀπαλὴν) "that, if someone should offer any slavery at all, it becomes angry and does not tolerate it," ὥστε κἂν ὁτιοῦν δουλείας τις προσφέρηται, ἀγανακτεῖν καὶ μὴ ἀνέχεσθαι (563d5–7). Such an immoderately free people refuses to be subject even to the laws "in order that they may have no master at all," ἵνα δὴ μηδαμῇ μηδεὶς αὐτοῖς ᾖ δεσπότης (563d8–e1). Excesses, Plato's Socrates suggests, lead directly to their opposites (563e9–564a1), and so too much freedom, termed also "license" (ἐξουσία, 563e8 and 564d2), engenders too much slavery: ἡ γὰρ ἄγαν ἐλευθερία ἔοικεν οὐκ εἰς ἄλλο τι ἢ εἰς ἄγαν δουλείαν μεταβάλλειν καὶ ἰδιώτῃ καὶ πόλει, "for excessive freedom is likely to turn into nothing other than excessive slavery both for the individual and for the city" (564a3–4). This occurs when immoderate freedom and license create fertile ground for civil strife and the eventual rise of a tyrant who poses as a champion of the people, a process that Plato traces through the end of Book 8. For Plato, the extremes of freedom and slavery collapse upon one another, and in the *Epistles*, too, it will be those who aspire to uncurbed freedom who ultimately exhibit the most slavish qualities.

In Cicero's *De Re Publica* 1 a similar process unfolds, this time described by Cicero's spokesman Scipio, who fully acknowledges his debt to Plato. Scipio adopts Plato's wine imagery to describe the "undiluted freedom" (*meraca libertas*) of the democratic populace:

'Cum enim' inquit 'inexplebiles populi fauces exaruerunt libertatis siti, malisque usus ille ministris non modice temperatam sed nimis meracam libertatem sitiens hausit, tum magistratus et principes, nisi valde lenes et remissi sint et large sibi libertatem ministrent, insequitur insimulat arguit, praepotentes reges tyrannos vocat.' (1.66)

"When," he said, "the insatiable jaws of the populace have become parched by thirst for liberty and it, employing evil cupbearers,[29] has thirstily drunk not moderately tempered but excessively undiluted freedom, then the people censures, accuses, and blames the magistrates and chief men, if they neither are meek and mild nor administer liberty to them in abundance, and calls them despotic kings and tyrants."

Following Plato, Cicero's Scipio repeatedly stresses the immoderate *libertas* and *licentia* fostered by such an environment: *plena libertatis esse omnia* ("all things are full of liberty"), *tanta libertate* ("such great liberty"), *infinita . . . licentia* ("infinite license"), *nimia licentia* ("excessive license," 1.67–68). Under these conditions servitude and tyranny easily arise: *nimiaque illa libertas et populis et privatis in nimiam servitutem cadit*, "and that excessive freedom falls into excessive slavery both for populations at large and for individuals" (1.68). Cicero, however, not only offers a translation of the Plato passage but reworks it to apply to the late Roman Republic of the first century B.C.[30] For Scipio, the best preventative measure for such *meraca libertas* is not the ideal state of Plato but

the carefully mixed constitution of the traditional Republic, which—continuing the wine metaphor—tempers and moderates pure democratic freedom by
incorporating strong aristocratic and monarchical elements, as if adding water
to wine. He strongly advocates *id quod erit aequatum et temperatum ex tribus
primis rerum publicarum modis*, "that which will consist equally of and be tempered by the three main types of republics," 1.69. Freedom, as Gregory shows, is
"a term of invective for Plato, but not for Cicero. While rejecting the Athenian
version of liberty, which he (like Plato) equates with anarchy, Cicero stops short
of discrediting the concept itself. He may wish to keep the concept in reserve,
since a modified version of popular *libertas*, balanced with the *potestas* of the
magistrates and the *auctoritas* of the senate, will figure as one element in his
ideal constitution."[31] The mixed constitution therefore becomes crucial for the
maintenance of moderate liberty.[32]

The advocacy of a moderate *libertas* that avoids the extremes of *licentia* and
servitus is certainly not restricted in Latin literature to Cicero's *De Re Publica*.
In the *Pro Flacco* Cicero similarly criticizes the immoderate license fostered by
the Athenian Assembly: *illa vetus quae quondam opibus, imperio, gloria floruit
hoc uno malo concidit, libertate immoderata ac licentia contionum*, "that ancient
[country], which once flourished in wealth, empire, and glory, fell because of
this one evil: the immoderate liberty and license of its assemblies," 16. In *Pro
Plancio* 94 he claims that his own sense of *libertas* rests on moderation: *liber-
tatemque quam tu in me requiris, quam ego neque dimisi umquam neque dimit-
tam, non in pertinacia, sed in quadam moderatione positam putabo*, "and the
liberty which you seek in me, which I never have lost and will never lose, I judge
that it rests not on defiance but on a certain moderation." Livy, too, extols the
benefits of moderate freedom, characterizing the multitude as being drawn to the
extremes either of slavery or of domination rather than the true path of freedom, which lies between these: *ea natura multitudinis est: aut servit humiliter
aut superbe dominatur; libertatem, quae media est, nec struere modice nec habere
sciunt*, "This is the nature of the crowd: either it is submissively a slave or it
haughtily dominates. They do not know how to construct or possess liberty,
which is a mean, with moderation," 24.25.8. In 34.49.8, Livy has Titus Quinctius
Flamininus recommend the path of moderate liberty: *libertate modice utantur:
temperatam eam salubrem et singulis et civitatibus esse, nimiam et aliis gravem
et ipsis qui habeant effrenatam et praecipitem esse*, "They should employ their
liberty with moderation: when tempered it is a source of health both to individuals and to states, but when excessive and unbridled it is grievous to others
and dangerous to the very ones who have it." If we apply such thinking about
freedom to the context of the late Republic, with its competing strong men each
claiming to champion the liberty of the people, the constitutional collapse that

led to the rise of Augustus could be viewed as the product not of true, moderate freedom, but of the extreme *licentia* that was jeopardizing it.

By championing moderate freedom in the context of Augustus's Rome, Horace situates the principate within the traditions of the *mos maiorum* and suggests that it provides a moderate, stabilizing degree of freedom removed from the volatile extremes of license and servitude that contributed to the Republic's demise. Augustan *libertas* is paradoxically both deeply old-fashioned and yet undeniably new. Augustus's extraordinary power put him in the position of exerting his arbitrary will over the Roman state and thus undermining the traditional definition of *libertas*, which, as we have seen, was guaranteed by equal subjection to the law. Fears nicely sums up Augustus's unprecedented position:

> His absolute power rested upon clearly articulated and legally transmitted constitutional and juridical forms. Yet despite its constitutional facade . . . the commonwealth of the Roman People was now properly a *regnum*—a dictatorship; it was the antithesis of the republican concept of Liberty. Now one man, because of his power, stood above the law of the commonwealth. Compliance with the law was the hallmark of a good emperor; but such compliance was voluntary. If the emperor obeyed the law it was because he chose to obey. . . . The emperor became the font of law.[33]

As Fears goes on to point out, after the advent of Augustus *libertas* "underwent a startling and profound metamorphosis."[34] Augustus fashioned himself as the chief guarantor of *libertas* and thus put an end to competing interests fighting in its name. He yoked his bestowal of *libertas* firmly to that of *pax*, a connection carefully cultivated on a coin issued in 28 B.C., eight years before the publication of *Epistles* 1.[35] One side of the coin lauds Augustus as the *Libertatis Populi Romani Vindex*, the "Protector of the People's Liberty"; the other side depicts the goddess *Pax* trampling underfoot the sword of civil war.[36] Augustus himself highlighted his role as protector of *libertas* in the opening sentence of the *Res Gestae*, in a phrase that echoes the legend on the obverse of the coin: *rem publicam a dominatione factionis oppressam in libertatem vindicavi*, "I delivered the republic, which had been oppressed by the domination of a faction, into freedom."[37] He restored the Roman people's liberty, of course, by bringing an end to the civil wars and inaugurating a new era of peace, the *pax Augusta*. To quote Galinsky, "the excess of *libertas* had degenerated into license (*licentia*); the reaction to it is the redefinition of *libertas* in terms of *securitas*."[38]

Many of the strands we have been tracing—moderate freedom, the mixed government as the best guarantee of such freedom, and Augustus's yoking of liberty and peace—are brought together in Cassius Dio's highly positive assessment of

Augustus, composed in the early third century A.D.[39] According to Dio, Augustus's incorporation of monarchy into the Roman state introduced a sorely needed stabilizing force that ensured the survival of freedom. The death throes of the Republic are thus attributed to excessive democratic license:

> διά τε οὖν ταῦτα, καὶ ὅτι τὴν μοναρχίαν τῇ δημοκρατίᾳ μίξας τό τε ἐλεύθερόν σφισιν ἐτήρησε καὶ τὸ κόσμιον τό τε ἀσφαλὲς προσπαρεσκεύασεν, ὥστ' ἔξω μὲν τοῦ δημοκρατικοῦ θράσους ἔξω δὲ καὶ τῶν τυραννικῶν ὕβρεων ὄντας ἔν τε ἐλευθερίᾳ σώφρονι καὶ ἐν μοναρχίᾳ ἀδεεῖ ζῆν, βασιλευομένους τε ἄνευ δουλείας καὶ δημοκρατουμένους ἄνευ διχοστασίας, δεινῶς αὐτὸν ἐπόθουν. (56.43)

> And so they missed him terribly not only for these reasons, but also because, by mixing monarchy with democracy, he protected their freedom and additionally provided order and safety, with the result that, without democratic audacity, on the one hand, and tyrannical violence, on the other, they lived in moderate freedom and in a monarchy without terror, being ruled by a king without being slaves and inhabiting a democracy without sedition.

One of Augustus's chief accomplishments here is the creation of ἐλευθερία σώφρων, "moderate freedom," which stands between the extremes of pure democracy (total freedom) and pure monarchy (total slavery). Such tempered freedom, embodied by the mixed constitution provided by Augustus, guaranteed order and peace, whereas total freedom promoted violence and constitutional disarray. Such moderate freedom is, according to Dio, a safeguard against servitude. The freedom attributed by Dio to Augustus's reign looks suggestively similar to the kind of *libertas* Horace will espouse in the *Epistles*, which enables one to stand between the extremes of either *mera libertas* or *obsequium plus aequo* and which promotes friendship and concord over wrangling and quarrels (cf. esp. *Epistles* 1.18.1–20). Horace's moderate freedom therefore can be closely aligned with the *libertas Augusta* that was taking shape while the first book of *Epistles* was being composed.

In standing somewhere between total freedom and slavery and in being guaranteed their *libertas* by the beneficence of the emperor, Augustus's subjects occupy a position not unlike that of a freedman, whose independence has been bestowed by a patron and whose position in society was always viewed as neither entirely free nor yet that of a slave. Patterson draws a clear parallel between the freedom provided by Augustus to his subjects and that granted to a manumitted slave by his former master:

> Augustus had as his ultimate model of freedom the patron-freedman relationship. Like the good master, he had used his power wisely, first to control and then to liberate the Roman people. It is important to understand that Augustus saw his interaction with the Roman people as something that moved between the two

relationships of master (-slave) and liberator (-freedman). . . . Having freed the
Roman people, Augustus felt that he had established a new relationship which
replaced the *imperium* of the warlord and slave master, a relationship in which
both parties—patron and freedman—had privileges and duties. It was his duty
to protect and care for his people . . . and to guarantee their personal liberty in
exactly the same way that the patron protected and cared for his ex-slaves.[40]

Augustus himself seems to configure his relationship with the Roman populace
in this way both on the coin of 28 B.C. and in the introductory sentence of his
Res Gestae, cited above, where he is described as the *vindex* of the *libertas* of
the Roman people. Roller has shown that this phrase evokes a specific form of
manumission, the *manumissio vindicta*:

> The phrase *vindicare in libertatem* describes a juridical procedure whereby a per-
> son called (for these purposes) an *assertor* or *vindex libertatis*, asserts in the pre-
> sence of a magistrate, a slave, and the slave's master, that the slave is in fact a free
> person who is being illegally held in a servile condition. If the evidence is persua-
> sive . . . the magistrate adjudges the slave free. The procedure was commonly used
> in a symbolic mode, at the master's instigation, as a way of manumitting slaves
> whose status was not actually in doubt (the *manumissio vindicta*). Augustus's
> usage here, however, implies that the Roman state was indeed being held illegally
> as a 'slave' to its 'masters,' and that Augustus, by serving as a *vindex libertatis*, re-
> stored it to its properly free condition.[41]

In granting freedom to the entire state Augustus performs on a grand scale the
same kind of *beneficium* that the individual slave receives upon manumission,
and in doing so he places the state in a position of obligation to him. Mouritsen
has nicely examined the paradoxical nature of the patron's gift of freedom.[42]
Quoting Publilius Syrus's maxim that "to receive a favor is to sell one's freedom"
(*beneficium accipere libertatem est vendere*, *Sent.* 48), he states that "the position
of freedmen was therefore always regarded as one of dependency, the irony
being that by accepting freedom they also surrendered a major part of it. The
very gift of *libertas* made them subject to the lasting authority of their benefac-
tors. Manumission was for that reason an ambiguous symbol of freedom." The
primary duty owed to his benefactor by the freedman was *obsequium*, "compliance," which "represented a compromise between his emancipated status and
the patrons' claim to exercise continued authority."[43] Freedmen who failed to
offer their patron the expected *obsequium* were accused of *licentia*.[44] If Augustus's citizens take on the intermediate status of *liberti*, then appropriate *libertas*
can be understood as observing the proper degree of *obsequium* toward the
emperor and avoiding the extremes of *licentia* and *servitus* in relation to him.
Horace certainly has such a formulation of *libertas* in mind in the opening of

Epistles 1.18, where he is especially concerned with the exercise of *libertas* by a client toward his patron—a relationship similar to that between a freedman and his former master or between a citizen and the *princeps*—and urges the client to avoid the extremes of *mera libertas* and *obsequium plus aequo*.[45] For Horace an excess of *obsequium* is just as bad as an excess of *libertas*, and so the observance of the mean protects *libertas* as much as it limits it.

The opening of *Epistles* 1.18 has much in common with a passage from Livy, in which Philip V of Macedon condemns his former subjects, the Thessalians, for acting toward Rome, which liberated them from his rule, as bad freedmen: they were behaving toward their liberators not with *libertas* but with *licentia*. This passage is a significant parallel since it draws a direct comparison between the employment of freedom by a state and by freedmen and since it employs the same wine metaphor used by Horace:

> insolenter et immodice abuti Thessalos indulgentia populi Romani, velut ex diu-
> tina siti nimis avide meram haurientes libertatem: ita servorum modo praeter
> spem repente manumissorum licentiam vocis et linguae experiri et iactare sese
> insectatione et conviciis dominorum. (Livy 39.26.7–8)

> [He claimed that] the Thessalians insolently and immoderately abused the indul-
> gence of the Roman people, just like those who, after a long thirst, drink unmixed
> freedom too greedily; that, in the manner of slaves manumitted suddenly and
> unexpectedly, they were testing the license of their voice and tongue and were
> showing off by abusing and insulting their masters.

Livy's Philip here plays on stereotypes commonly associated with newly freed slaves who, because of their unfamiliarity with liberty, do not yet know how to employ it with moderation.[46] Like Horace's overly critical client in *Epistles* 1.18, such a freedman is said to drink *mera libertas*, "undiluted freedom," the same wine metaphor used also in Cicero's *De Re Publica* (*meraca libertas*). In Livy it is applied to the freedman who does not observe the proper *obsequium* toward his benefactor and who exercises his *licentia* as harsh, unmitigated free speech. Horace's use of the phrase *mera libertas* therefore has a number of important political and social connotations. It alludes to both the excessive political free- dom curbed by Augustus in the interests of peace and the unmitigated harsh speech bad freedmen stereotypically exercised toward their patrons. Since the social practice of manumission metaphorically applies to the relationship be- tween Augustus and the Roman populace, excessive resistance to or harsh criti- cism of the *princeps* might be described as *mera libertas*. It is not insignificant, then, that the collection opens and closes with allusions to manumission, with Horace in 1.1 occupying the status of the liberated slave and in 1.20 that of the liberating master. The moderate freedom formulated in the *Epistles* is embodied by the figure of the freedman. Horace had associated himself with the freedman's status as early as *Satires* 1.6 by describing his father as a *libertinus*, a claim he will echo in the closing poem of the *Epistles*: *me libertino natum patre*, 1.20.20.[47] However, the epistolary Horace initially chafes against this status and only progressively comes to accept it with equanimity.

Horace's formulation in *Epistles* 1.18 of *libertas* as free speech that should be exercised with restraint toward one's social superiors significantly anticipates later articulations of freedom under the Empire, particularly those found in Tacitus.[48] This is by no means to suggest that *libertas* as the exercise of free speech within the patron-client relationship is new to the imperial period, but the emergence of an emperor at the top of the social pyramid added a layer of complexity to this cultural practice. The patron-client relationship in the *Epistles* in many ways stands by proxy for the relationship between Augustus and his subjects, and Horace's instructions on how to be a successful client apply equally to being a successful citizen of Augustan Rome. In *Epistles* 1.17, for example, the patron-client friendship is described as "associating with kings" (*regibus uti*, 13 and 14) and "pleasing the foremost men" (*principibus placuisse viris*, 35), and there is no denying that the chief of these *reges* and *principes* was Augustus. When Horace speaks of his own successful friendships with the city's elite in *Epistles* 1.20.23 (*me primis urbis . . . placuisse*, "I pleased the foremost of the city"), we must certainly count Augustus among this group.

In Tacitus the emperor is the ultimate target of free or fawning speech, and the degree to which he allows criticism is a good measure of his beneficence.[49] Again and again we find excessive *libertas* configured as overt censure of the regime and extreme *servitus* as obsequious and distasteful flattery. The latter, in fact, is for Tacitus the more pronounced during the Empire: *sicut vetus aetas vidit quid ultimum in libertate esset, ita nos quid in servitute*, "just as the former age saw what was the farthest extreme in liberty, so we have seen what is the farthest extreme in slavery" (*Agricola* 2.3). Tacitus establishes the antithesis between Republican *libertas* and imperial *servitus* early in the *Annals*. In its very first line the establishment of the consulship, and thus the Republic, by Brutus in 509 B.C. is yoked so clearly to freedom that *libertas* and the Republic are scarcely distinguishable: *libertatem et consulatum L. Brutus instituit*, "Lucius Brutus established freedom and the consulship," 1.1. With the advent of Augustus, *servitus* became the dominant means for men to ingratiate themselves with the *princeps* and thus rise to prominence: *ceteri nobilium, quanto quis servitio promptior, opibus et honoribus extollerentur ac novis ex rebus aucti tuta et praesentia quam vetera et periculosa mallent*, "The rest of the nobles—according to how much each was prepared for slavery—were exalted by wealth and offices and preferred the safety of the present rather than the dangers of the past since they had been enriched by the new circumstances," 1.2. To Tacitus the security of the Empire has as its concomitant the servitude of the Roman people, and those who are willing to render themselves slaves enjoy the greatest financial and political success. Slavery is therefore the easiest and most crowded route to distinction in the Empire: *Romae ruere in servitium consules, patres, eques*, "At Rome there rushed into slavery the consuls, the senate, the equestrians," 1.7.

How, then, is one to gain distinction in imperial Rome while eschewing servile flattery? The opposite extreme is hardly more attractive and is much more dangerous. Again and again those who find themselves in opposition with the emperor must pay for—or demonstrate—their *libertas* through suicide.[50] The first of these is Cremutius Cordus, who during Tiberius's reign finds himself charged with the crime of praising the Republican heroes Brutus and Cassius and thereupon ends his life by starvation. Tiberius's reign therefore constitutes a turning point for free speech insofar as tolerance of it is severely restricted and so free speech itself becomes an instrument of political defiance. Between such dangerous displays of freedom and abject servitude lies a far more preferable path, a middle one exemplified by men such as Marcus Lepidus and Agricola.[51] In his assessment of the former's successes he praises such a mean: *sit aliquid in nostris consiliis liceatque inter abruptam contumaciam et deforme obsequium pergere iter ambitione ac periculis vacuum*, "there is something in our own judgments that allows us to travel a path free from ambition and danger between uncompromising stubbornness and shameful obsequiousness" (*Annals* 4.20). Public success under an emperor is therefore achievable through the careful exercise of *moderatio*, which is the avoidance of extremes such as *contumacia*, associated with excessively harsh speech, and *obsequium*, associated with slavish flattery:

> Domitiani vero natura praeceps in iram, et quo obscurior, eo inrevocabilior, moderatione tamen prudentiaque Agricolae leniebatur, quia non contumacia neque inani iactatione libertatis famam fatumque provocabat. sciant, quibus moris est inlicita mirari, posse etiam sub malis principibus magnos viros esse, obsequiumque ac modestiam, si industria ac vigor adsint, eo laudis excedere, quo plerique per abrupta sed in nullum rei publicae usum ambitiosa morte inclaruerunt. (*Agricola* 42.3–4)

> In truth Domitian's nature was quick to anger, and he was as unrelenting as he was secretive. Nevertheless he was mollified by the moderation and prudence of Agricola, because he was not calling forth fame and death either through obstinacy or through a useless display of liberty. Let those whose custom it is to admire illicit things learn that it is possible for great men to exist even under bad emperors and

that compliance and moderation, if industry and energy are present, result in the same degree of praise as the many who by courses that were dangerous but of no use to the Republic became famous through an ostentatious death.

This moderate path that avoids "useless displays of *libertas*" and admits a degree of *obsequium* becomes for Tacitus the most prudent path to success in the Empire.

Horace's middle path between *mera libertas* and *obsequium plus aequo* serves as an early exemplar of such ideas. Like Tacitus, Horace is concerned with *libertas* as it is exercised in one's public life, which is represented by a wide range of people, places, and activities. In order to achieve public distinction for himself without slavishly losing his autonomy, Horace must exercise the appropriate degree of freedom toward, for example, poetic models, philosophical models, the city, Maecenas, and ultimately Augustus. For Horace, as for Tacitus, the key to achieving the correct degree of independence will be moderation, and throughout the *Epistles* this virtue will be consistently coupled with adaptability. Horace's goal in formulating such freedom, both for himself and his addressees, is to chart a new path to distinction that is appropriate for the new imperial age in which they find themselves.[52] This helps to explain why Horace chooses his addressees, apart from Maecenas, not from the upper echelons of Roman society, but from its second tier.[53] A number of the addressees are working their way up, occupying important positions in the staffs of famous men but not counting themselves among the city's *principes*.[54] The Horace of the *Epistles* is keenly interested in helping such men achieve prominence with their integrity and autonomy intact.

For the Horace of the *Epistles*, however, the transition from undiluted freedom to the middle path is a difficult one that he repeatedly resists. When we first encounter him in *Epistles* 1.1, we find unbending insistence on *libertas*. That insistence borders on hostility toward his *amicus* Maecenas.[55] The freedom that opens the collection is one for which compromise and moderation are scarcely possible. In *Epistles* 1.1.4 Horace justifies his adoption of epistolary poetry by claiming that his age is no longer the same (*non eadem est aetas*). As Freudenburg notes, *aetas* "may touch on not only his ageing, but on changes in 'the age' in which he now finds himself living."[56] The *Epistles* are, perhaps even more than the *Odes*, Horace's poetic response to the age of Augustus. Horace's instinctive response in the *Epistles* to this age is one of resistance and refusal to abide any diminishment of his independence, which in his eyes would be tantamount to slavery. Rather than try to take part in the public life of Augustus's Rome, Horace is tempted simply to opt out entirely. Over the course of the collection, however, he comes progressively to accept moderate *libertas*, and as he does so he rises in status from lowly freed slave to patron and master in his own right.

Before turning to the issue of Horace's epistolary persona, one more aspect of Horace's moderate freedom needs elucidation. The title of this book suggests that Horace, in opting for something *between* freedom and slavery, is ultimately less than free. But we must remember that moderate freedom *is* still freedom, though different in degree from absolute autonomy. Moderate freedom cedes a degree of mastery to others, but submitting to complete mastery at the hand of others amounts to slavery. The dichotomy between total freedom and total slavery is in many ways equivalent to that between mastery and slavery, and Horace will frequently connect "being free" with "ruling."[57] In accepting a compromise to his freedom he simultaneously circumscribes his own sphere of mastery. He can ultimately involve himself with a number of potential "masters" and yet remain free. These masters include Maecenas, poetic and philosophical models, urban life, Augustus, and we his readers and critics. By yielding to some degree of mastery at the hands of another, Horace departs markedly from Republican ideals. Cicero, for example, has his Scipio forcibly state that *libertas* is utterly incompatible with having a master: what Scipio champions is *libertas, quae non in eo est ut iusto utamur domino, sed ut nullo*, "freedom, which does not mean that we have a just master, but that we have no master" (*De Re Publica* 2.43). For Horace a compromise will be possible. Yet at every point of compromise Horace retains a degree of autonomy so as never to yield himself entirely. His adoption of the mean is in many ways designed primarily as a way to protect his autonomy even as he negotiates away part of his freedom.

HORACE AND THE ADDRESSEES: THE EPISTOLARY *PERSONAE*

In the preceding section I have outlined the historical context in which the *Epistles* must be understood, with particular attention to the changing nature of *libertas* during the early empire. The contention that the collection is the product of and reaction to a particular historical moment does not, however, necessitate that we read the poems as autobiographical documents or mine them for information concerning the lived realities of Horace or the figures addressed therein.[58] The poems offer especially enticing material for those wanting to reconstruct the friendship between Horace and Maecenas or to gauge the degree to which the verses substantiate the theory of Maecenas's fall from imperial favor.[59] Rather than try to lay bare the largely irrecoverable historical realities of the poet's biography, I consider the epistolary Horace to be an artfully constructed persona fashioned for specifically literary goals. Furthermore, the addressees we encounter in these poems, including Horace's grand patron Maecenas, are also meticulously fashioned poetic personae rather than historically accurate representations.[60] As literary constructs, they can stand as symbols and meta-phors for a range of ideas and themes explored in the collection. Even when the addressee is a documented, historical individual, he—as a "character"—has been custom-made by Horace to be the recipient of the specific ethical, philo-sophical, and poetic advice offered to him.

Let me briefly outline my understanding of Horace's epistolary persona. The character "Horace" that we encounter in this collection experiences, as I will argue, a profound spiritual dilemma as a result of his ambivalent feelings toward freedom and dependence.[61] At no point do I mean to suggest that this reflects a real crisis in the life of Horace the historical poet. I cannot know whether the historical Horace felt his autonomy was constrained by his relationship with Maecenas or by his poetic success. For the sake of convenience, however, I will refer throughout this book to this character or persona simply as Horace. The idea that Horace presents in his poems a carefully constructed persona is by no means new, and much work has already been done on Horace's poetic self-fashioning, especially in the *Satires*.[62] What I would emphasize about my under-standing of Horace's epistolary self is that he remains the same "character" throughout, and the letters of which he is the purported author present to us an ethical progression or journey in which he charts and gradually resolves, though perhaps imperfectly, his vacillations, inconsistencies, failures, successes, errors, and revisions.[63] The man giving advice in *Epistles* 1.17 may at first glance be quite different from the one in 1.1, but that does not mean that Horace presents us with a totally different persona for each poem; rather, the epistolary Horace has learned much from his own ethical reflections in the intervening poems. The character "Horace" does a great deal of progressing and changing over the course of the collection, as he learns to redefine *libertas* in light of his ethical considerations, but the actual experiences of the historical Horace simply can-not be retrieved from these poems.

Similarly, the poems do not necessarily provide reliable evidence for the lives and careers of the men to whom they are addressed, nor can they be taken as testimony for the state of literary patronage in general or Horace's own patronal relationships in particular at this stage of his career.[64] In my approach to Hor-ace's addressees I am indebted to socio-poetic approaches to Horace's presenta-tion of patronage and friendship, particularly those of Zetzel and Gold, which recognize that Horace constructs his addressees in order to fulfill poetic goals rather than to hold up a mirror to the realities of Roman *amicitia*.[65] Horace's epistolary addressees, that is, are every bit as fabricated as Horace's own persona. To quote Gold, Horace's friends and patrons can been seen as "raw material for verse, standing as a symbol for important themes and ideas in the poet's work."[66] They are, according to Zetzel, "subject to the same creative transformations that anything else in poetry is."[67] Gold furthermore points out that "while critics often regard the figure of the poet/narrator as a literary construct, they are less willing to depart so far from historical reality where the patron is concerned." This has been especially true in the case of Maecenas, for whose life Horace's poetic corpus has been taken as valuable historical evidence.[68]

I approach Maecenas and Horace's friendship with him as one poetic theme that stands parallel to and elucidates other important themes. Maecenas is associated in the collection with public poetry, the city, and patronage, and Horace often explores his ambivalence toward these spheres in connection with his great friend. When Horace turns down Maecenas's demands in the opening poem, for example, he rejects the whole way of life for which he stands, and it is this rejection that establishes the central thematic antitheses that run through the book: city versus country, public versus private, engagement versus withdrawal, freedom versus slavery.[69] In contradistinction to Maecenas, the narrator Horace aligns himself with private poetry, the country, and disengagement, so the two men stand metaphorically for divergent modes of life. In many ways Maecenas becomes the figure onto whom Horace can project his own desires for public life even as he himself disavows them, and, in bridging the gap in his friendship with Maecenas, Horace simultaneously opens up a path between public and private life. A similar phenomenon occurs with other addressees, such as Aristius Fuscus (1.10) or even the bailiff of his farm (1.14), whom Horace constructs as antitheses to himself (even as he reveals his similarities to them).[70] At other times, however, the addressee is fashioned into an alter ego for the poet that shares his propensities and imperfections. Examples of this are Albius (1.4) and Bullatius (1.11), who take Horace's desire for withdrawal to an extreme. In correcting their behavior, Horace simultaneously corrects his own.

None of this is to suggest, however, that the names of Horace's addressees exist in a historical vacuum and bring nothing to bear on how we are to interpret the poem. Be they illustrious or completely obscure, Horace chooses his addressees for a reason. One example of Horace utilizing the well-known associations of his addressee is *Epistles* 1.5, where Torquatus risks exhibiting the excessive *severitas* to which members of his family are thought to be prone. Again, however, we cannot know whether Horace's addressee really *was* too severe, but Horace exploits stereotypical personality traits of the Torquati in order to construct the persona of his epistolary addressee and to offer him moral advice that accords with his larger ethical and poetic concerns. Horace therefore carefully chooses his addressees for their well-known connotations even if the poems do not reflect their lived realities.[71] Equally important to the collection are the addressees whose names have no real historical significance.[72] Horace creates for these characters a persona every bit as nuanced and colorful as those of their known counterparts, and they too are fashioned so as to illustrate and develop Horace's epistolary themes. So Vinnius Asina's bumbling obsequiousness, for example, amusingly developed by Horace, illustrates the larger theme of excessive servility and its dangers.

Perhaps the most significant theme developed through the inclusion of these friends and patrons, both historical and not, is that of friendship itself. Friendship, particularly as it is manifested as patronage, is one of Horace's central epistolary concerns, and the degree to which Horace wishes to participate in *amicitia* and advises others to do the same will be an important measure of *libertas*. Rigid independence has the undesirable outcome of isolating Horace and his addressees from friendship, and therefore *amicitia* is one of several spheres in which one must find a moderate balance between freedom and slavery. The asymmetrical patron-client relationship, though it brings highly desirable benefits, has the potential to come uncomfortably close to the master-slave relationship, and Horace is at pains to explore and to illustrate how one can participate in patronage without losing entirely one's sense of autonomy. The addressees exhibit a range of attitudes toward freedom and friendship, and these attitudes have been carefully crafted by Horace to reflect and advance his epistolary themes and concerns rather than to reflect the reality of the historical men to whom these personae correspond.

THE *EPISTLES* AND PHILOSOPHY

I take a similar literary approach to Horace's use of philosophy in the collection. Rather than try to uncover Horace's actual philosophical allegiances, I suggest that a more fruitful way of approaching this knotty and much debated question is to consider philosophical study as one of Horace's epistolary themes through which he explores issues of freedom and slavery. Many scholars have debated the degree to which the collection is meant to be formally philosophical and, if so, to which school, if any, Horace adheres. This has in many ways been the primary scholarly approach to the collection.[73] While I will argue that philosophical study is a central theme in the collection, I do not consider formal philosophy to be its primary purpose, nor will I try to solve the thorny issue of Horace's philosophical allegiance, which persistently eludes categorization.[74] Rather, I emphasize the essential importance of his eclectic or adaptable *approach* as outlined in the first poem, which offers us the first glimpse of moderate freedom in the collection, for Horace walks a middle ground between philosophical dependence and independence. Horace's free use of philosophy offers a valuable point of comparison for his approach to freedom in other spheres. In friendship, for example, Horace will gradually recommend a client-patron relationship much like the one he initially looks for in a philosophical guide: a blend of dependence and freedom. Horace's construction of philosophical freedom, in other words, becomes the primary model for freedom generally.[75]

This moderate philosophical *libertas*, though certainly indebted to various philosophical schools, cannot be identified with any one in particular. Horace does, however, provide us with an important model for such freedom in the Cyrenaic philosopher Aristippus, whom Horace presents as exercising restrained independence and adaptability in philosophy and especially in friendship.[76] Aristippus is not the only model for *libertas* presented by Horace, but he is the one whose presence is most pervasively felt across the collection and whose name is invoked more often than any other.[77] Although I argue that the Horatian Aristippus exemplifies ideal freedom, moderation, and adaptability, I do not mean to suggest that these principles, as Horace presents them, are wholly indebted to the historical Aristippus, nor do they mark him as an orthodox Cyrenaic.[78] Aristippus in the *Epistles* in fact provides a model for lack of philosophical orthodoxy, and one of the reasons he may have appealed to Horace is that in the first century B.C. the Cyrenaic school was by no means one of the dominant systems to which one might adhere.[79] It is furthermore unclear how much of Aristippus's writing, if any at all, Horace would even have had access to, though I will make suggestions along the way that he was familiar with certain Aristippean sayings and Cyrenaic ideas.[80] To a large degree Aristippus was available to Horace only as a series of anecdotes of the sort recorded in Diogenes Laertius, in which his adaptability and independence take center stage.[81] One text in which he figures prominently and to which Horace alludes is Xenophon's *Memorabilia*, where Aristippus debates with Socrates the nature of freedom, defining it as a middle path between rule and slavery, and this passage will feature largely in my discussion of the *Epistles*. It is in fact because he is not a well-known philosophical figure that Horace is free to make of him what he will.[82] Horace's Aristippus is in many ways as much a poetic fiction as Horace himself is, and Horace constructs him as his philosophical alter ego who embodies the ethical lessons that the epistolary Horace often still needs to learn before he can espouse them to others. If Aristippus embodies freedom, moderation, and adaptability, it is not because these were the primary tenets of Cyrenaicism, but because they are the chief ethical formulations of the epistolary Horace himself.

Furthermore, I argue that Horace the "philosopher" never takes precedence over Horace the "poet" in the collection. When approaching philosophical material, only the poet who is emancipated from philosophical orthodoxy can exercise the correct degree of freedom in weaving together various strands of ethical thought. The poet bound to the words and ideas of a philosophical master strays too far toward the extreme of servitude. In his independence the poet surpasses his philosophically orthodox counterparts, while at the same time he is free to adapt the lessons of their works into morally beneficial poetry for his readers. Central to Horace's approach to philosophy is the idea of appropriate imitation, which again must accord with moderate *libertas*. A philosophical master must be imitated with a free hand, and Horace applies this method to the spheres of poetry and friendship as well. As in philosophy, proper poetic imitation requires one to depend on the models provided by others while avoiding slavish imitation of them; in other words, to walk a middle path between the extremes of freedom and dependence. Overreliance on poetic forerunners, like dogmatic philosophy, is the mark of slavery. Similarly, the true friend finds a mean between flatterers who imitate powerful friends to an extreme and harsh critics who can find no ground whatsoever for compromise and agreement. In all three spheres Horace strives to set himself apart from the "slavish herd" (*servum pecus*, 1.19.19) that relies too heavily on its models, but at the same time he *does* find benefit in seeking out a useful model (*utile exemplar*, 1.2.18) for guidance.

Organization and Overview

Crucial to my argument is the idea that the collection has been carefully crafted by Horace to work as a unity, with each poem meant to project us backward and forward to the other poems and so to revisit problems and search for solutions. Most recent scholarship on the *Epistles* has taken for granted the careful organization of the collection; Ferri, for example, has stated that "the letters gain enormously from being read one after the other, indeed, they require a continuous reading, in which even backslidings, second thoughts, contradictions are parts of a planned overall effect on the reader."[83] The development of "Horace" as a character is central to the plot of *Epistles* 1. As the plot unfolds Horace moves gradually from an uncompromising view of freedom to one that is characterized by moderation and adaptability. One way he accomplishes this is by taking up the roles of student and teacher simultaneously. We therefore get to watch his progress as he expounds moral lessons to others and progressively adopts them for himself. As he advises his addressees to avoid extremes, he himself relaxes his own immoderate tendencies in favor of flexibility and compromise.

Though I consider throughout the significance of the successive placement of each poem, my discussion is organized thematically in order to chart Horace's adoption of moderate freedom in the spheres of philosophy, location, friendship, and poetry. The first chapter takes up the issue of freedom as constructed in *Epistles* 1.1, focusing especially on the gladiatorial imagery that opens the poem. In chapter 2, I examine Horace's extreme insistence on *libertas* in the first epistle as arising from his persona's highly ambivalent attitude toward public and private life, an ambivalence he continues to develop in 1.8 and 1.15. Chapters 3 and 4, which focus on poems 1.2, 1.4, 1.5, 1.6, and 1.12, take up Horace's role as an ethical teacher extolling to his addressees the benefits of moderation and adaptability, especially in the spheres of philosophy and friendship. In the remaining chapters, I examine how Horace applies these lessons to his own situation and thereby resolves tensions and antitheses established in the opening poem. Chapters 5 and 6, which address poems 1.7, 1.10, 1.11, 1.14, and 1.16, examine the ways in which extreme freedom falls short in the spheres of location and friendship; a moderate approach allows Horace to fulfill his seemingly incompatible desires for the city and country, companionship and isolation. Chapter 7 takes up the paired poems 1.17 and 1.18 and considers how Horace applies the idea of moderate freedom to patronal relationships, those of his addressees and his own as well. Chapter 8 focuses on the formulation of moderate freedom in the poetic sphere, with Horace relating the concept first to Florus's poetry in 1.3 and then to his own in 1.19. In the conclusion, I consider how Horace's adoption of moderate freedom in the poetic sphere affects not only his decision to publish his poetry but also his choice of audience.

The Horace of *Epistles* 1 is a complex character whose ambivalent desires must be accommodated in such a way that he can enjoy participation in poetry, philosophy, friendship, and urban life while retaining his independence. He is not a Horace who is content to remain withdrawn in the countryside away from the elite friends who recognize his poetic talent. At a time when the political environment was making quietude a safer and more attractive option, Horace attempts to find a way for ambitious men—including himself—to obtain distinction while at the same time remaining aloof from intrusion and pressure from above. I read the moderated freedom of the *Epistles* as the heart of an agenda that is meant to benefit Horace and his epistolary friends, many of whom, like him, are either seeking to distinguish themselves in this new imperial world or are drawn toward resistance through nonparticipation. While Horace recognizes that one can no longer insist on Republican *libertas*, he also understands the danger of running to the other extreme: achieving social success by slavishly forfeiting freedom. The path between *libertas* and *servitus* offers a means of cooperating with the emperor as well as a way to retreat when such cooperation becomes impossible, and Horace thus offers to his fellow Romans a way of retaining both their ardent longing for social success *and* their fiercely traditional desire for liberty. While Horace's qualified freedom does not present us with an entirely comfortable or complete resolution, it does allow him to formulate an acceptable compromise founded on the two qualities that are most distinctly and unmistakably Horatian: moderation and adaptability.

The Dilemma of *Libertas*

Epistles 1.1

IN THIS CHAPTER I EXAMINE THE NATURE OF *libertas* as it is presented in the opening lines of the first epistle, where Horace, by figuring himself as a newly manumitted gladiator, puts the theme of freedom front and center. Horace here adopts an inflexible view of *libertas* that leads him to disparage the public role his earlier poetry has given to him as compromising his autonomy. In this formulation there are only two options open to him: *servitus* or *libertas*. Horace therefore rejects any compromise that would place him in a position of dependence and make him a slave. He disavows his public poetry, urban life, and his friendship with Maecenas and looks for independence instead in rural withdrawal and philosophical contemplation. His newfound freedom is reflected in his choice of the epistolary genre, since he has no forerunner in the production of a book of poetic letters in Latin. As further evidence of his desire for *libertas* he states that, although he will turn to ethics and philosophy, he will do so without subjecting himself to the tenets of any one system. Horace's philosophical independence, however, differs fundamentally from the freedom he claims to enjoy in the spheres of poetry, location, and friendship, where his *libertas* is absolute and leads to withdrawal and nonparticipation. His free use of philosophy is more adaptable and flexible and allows him to engage in it without becoming a slave to its orthodoxies. This philosophical approach of independent participation thereby opens up a third path between the extremes of *libertas* and *servitus*. The philosopher Aristippus, who is both mentioned directly and evoked through careful allusions, is the chief exemplar of this third, middle path, achievable through adaptability, and through him Horace hints already in the first epistle that this mean can be applied not only to philosophy but to the other spheres as well.

Horace's Declaration of Independence in *Epistles* 1.1

The first line of the first poem binds Maecenas inextricably to Horace's poetry—past, present, and future—not only as dedicatee but also as subject of his song. The similarity of his name to that of Horace's muse (Camena, Maecenas; note the shared *c, m, n*, and *a* sounds) even suggests that Horace finds in his longstanding friend a source of inspiration: *Prima dicte mihi, summa dicende Camena* ("Sung of by my first muse, to be sung of by my last").[1] From the very opening of the collection, therefore, Horace treats Maecenas as poetic material and aligns him with the public poetic role that Horace has won for himself through his lyric poetry, a role that Horace now rejects in a *recusatio*:

> spectatum satis et donatum iam rude quaeris,
> Maecenas, iterum antiquo me includere ludo?
> non eadem est aetas, non mens. Veianius armis
> Herculis ad postem fixis latet abditus agro,
> ne populum extrema totiens exoret harena.
> est mihi purgatum crebro qui personet aurem:
> 'solve senescentem mature sanus equum, ne
> peccet ad extremum ridendus et ilia ducat.' (2–9)

> Do you seek to enclose me, looked at enough and already granted the sword, back in my old game? My age is not the same, nor my mind. The gladiator Veianius, with his weapons fixed to the door of Hercules' temple, lies hidden in the country, so that he may not repeatedly beg the people at the edge of the sand. Often a voice echoes in my clean ears: "Wisely let loose the aging racehorse at the right time so that he not stumble ridiculously at the end and wheeze."

The relationship here between Horace and Maecenas—and by extension between Horace and his previously published poetry—is tense at best.[2] Maecenas, it seems, wishes Horace to resume a poetic role that no longer suits him due to his changed age and mentality (*non eadem est aetas, non mens*). This former poetry is described as *ludus*, a "game," into which Maecenas wishes once again to "enclose," *includere*, his friend. This gamelike quality, this *ludus*, is precisely what Horace renounces in line 10: *nunc itaque et versus et cetera ludicra pono* ("Now therefore I set aside both verses and other playthings"). Before we turn to the depiction of Maecenas in these lines, let us first consider what kind of poetry Horace is renouncing and why.

The poetry he abandons has two main qualities: it is associated with *ludus* ("play," "game," or "sport"), and it brings Horace into the arena as a public spectacle (*spectatum*, 2). The term *ludus* frequently describes non-epic genres, and Horace uses the word elsewhere to denote both his *Odes* and his *Satires*.[3] Most scholars, however, apply Horace's statement to lyric poetry only. I suggest below that *publication* of any poetry, regardless of genre, is what Horace wishes to avoid, but it stands to reason that his refusal is a reaction in particular to the increased prominence he had recently acquired through the publication of the *Odes*, which were an instant classic.[4] Horace uses two metaphors to describe the poetry he relinquishes: the arena and the racecourse. Pointing to the long-standing metaphor of the chariot race for grand (esp. epic and epinician) poetry, Freudenburg suggests that the lyric Horace has in mind here is restricted to his civic/Aeolic lyric poetry, the "horse-driven strains of grand, public lyric, cast here as a kind of 'public entertainment.'"[5] The emphasis on public spectacle (*spectatum*, 2; *populum*, 6) certainly supports this suggestion, but Horace's changed age, *aetas* (4), implies that he renounces erotic themes as well, as a later passage from *Epistles* 1.14 similarly centered on the rejection of *ludus* makes clear:[6]

> quem tenues decuere togae nitidique capilli,
> quem scis immunem Cinarae placuisse rapaci,
> quem bibulum liquidi media de luce Falerni,
> cena brevis iuvat et prope rivum somnus in herba.
> nec lusisse pudet, sed non incidere ludum. (*Epist.* 1.14.32–36)   → slavery

> The one whom fine togas and shining hair once suited, the one whom you know pleased greedy Cinara even without gifts, whom a drink of flowing Falernian pleased in the middle of the day, [now] a short meal satisfies and a nap on the grass near the riverbank. It does not cause shame to have played, but it does [cause shame] not to make an end of play.

Such erotic play with Cinara was appropriate when Horace was young and dapper, but now it must be given up.[7] The abandonment of *ludus* in poem 1.1 therefore encompasses *all* lyric poetry, whether civic or erotic in theme, for each has contributed to Horace's public poetic success.

The real issue here is not necessarily the *Odes* per se, but rather their *publication*, as we will see more clearly in the discussion of 1.20, when Horace expresses similar anxiety over the publication of the *Epistles* themselves. As the language of spectacle shows (*spectatum*, 2), the chief aspect of this poetry is that it visibly exposes Horace to the whims of the *populus* (6), and all Horace can do is hope— or beg (*exoret*, 1.1.6)—for the public's favor. From the moment of publication the poet opens himself up to the prospect of highly visible success or failure. It is the loss of authorial control over his poems' reception that has reduced him to the level of a slave dependent on popular taste, and in the face of public judgment he reacts by withdrawing from the arena altogether and searching for a type of poetry that brings him *libertas* rather than *servitus*. The servile aspects of his former poetry are brought out by the gladiatorial metaphor running through these lines, where the word *ludus* takes on the more concrete meaning of "gladiatorial school." Horace compares himself to a gladiator who has been given the wooden sword of manumission (*donatum rude*, 2) and now, like his fellow gladiator Veianius, has withdrawn into rural retirement and obscurity (*abditus agro*, 5). When Horace renounces *versus et cetera ludicra* (10), therefore, he means not simply poetry that has a "playful" aspect but poetry (of whatever sort) that through publication might expose him again to public scrutiny as though performing at a gladiatorial spectacle. The connotations of this gladiatorial metaphor are troubling, for public success has brought to Horace not elevated status, but social degradation. To quote Barton, the gladiator was "throughout the Roman tradition, a man utterly debased by fortune, a slave, a man altogether without worth and dignity (*dignitas*), almost without humanity."[8] To be a published poet is a dangerous and humiliating spectacle that makes one dependent on the whims of the crowd, at whose will a gladiator may be spared or put to death. Horace must search for a new kind of poetry that accommodates his desire for freedom. Epistolary poetry, which by its nature enables withdrawal and is sent to one person rather than the multitude, perfectly fulfills these requirements. His epistolary freedom is further enhanced by his originality, for there is no forerunner for this poetry analogous to Lucilius for his *Satires* or Sappho and Alaeus for his *Odes*. The *Epistles* therefore grant Horace an independence and control that his already published poetry does not.[9]

There is, however, another side to this gladiatorial metaphor that suggests Horace's valuation of his public poetic successes is not entirely negative. The gladiator was always a complicated figure since, though he was a slave, he could enjoy a public renown analogous in modern society to that of a celebrity. Hopkins, who fully recognizes their degraded social position, nevertheless refers to gladiators as "glamour figures" and "culture heroes."[10] In the same breath that Horace eschews his servile gladiatorial position he advertises the success it has brought to him, for he has won the *rudis* and thus his freedom. This was a particularly coveted reward for a favorite gladiator and was usually given at the crowd's prompting by the producer of the game.[11] Horace may not like petitioning the *populus* at the arena's edge, but he makes it clear that they have rendered him a highly favorable judgment. Horace's *rudis* is therefore double-edged. It is a potent symbol of his past slavery and degradation while at the same time publicizing his victories in the arena of poetic combat. Horace is therefore torn between his pride over his public poetic accomplishments and his yearning to be free from the dependent position in which they place him. The gladiator offers to Horace the perfect figure for conveying his ambivalence.

In *Epistles* 1.1 Maecenas is directly implicated with Horace's gladiatorial service, for he is the one who has orchestrated this role as Horace's metaphorical *lanista*. Throughout the book the health of Horace's friendship with Maecenas will become a litmus test for his feelings about his public poetry, and vice versa. In 1.1 Maecenas is all too eager for Horace to return to the gladiatorial arena of poetic combat, impatient for his old champion to resume publication.[12] In casting Maecenas as his would-be master, Horace assesses their friendship just as damningly as he does his prior poetry, for it too has brought him into the public eye, thereby diminishing his liberty. Horace rejects not just lyric but Maecenas as well, at least so long as Maecenas would have him resume his poetic role. Horace's prior expressions of loyal friendship with Maecenas, as well as his pronounced earlier pride in his lyric accomplishments, makes this passage highly unexpected and troubling.[13]

The force of the gladiatorial metaphor to depict his friendship with Maecenas in *Epistles* 1.1 should not be understated. With it Horace suggests that *amicitia* with prominent public men holds the potential to threaten our freedom, with the superior friend configured as a potential slave master. For Horace the ex-gladiator, to be free is to have no master at all, and *libertas* is thus given its simplest formulation. Roller, for example, has suggested that Roman *libertas* should be defined at its most basic as being "the condition of being not-a-slave," a definition that allows no shades of gray between *libertas* and *servitus*.[14] In such a formulation any perceived imposition on *libertas* can be taken to the logical extreme of *servitus*. Horace takes such a step. By pressuring his friend to resume his public poetic role, Maecenas is nothing better than a would-be master, and Horace, if he were to yield, would be like an obsequious slave publishing poems to order for Maecenas. No compromise seems possible. In order for Horace to be free he must not take part at all in any activity that might impose a restriction on his freedom. Read in the context of the early principate, this presentation of Horace's friendship with Maecenas is highly problematic, since Maecenas is the link that connects him most directly with Augustus. In Augustus's Rome only two types of men emerge, free men and slaves, and participation in public life brings with it the risk of enslavement. How then can Horace take up a public poetic role without losing his *libertas*? Can he maintain his ties to Maecenas, Augustus, and the city, all the while preserving his independence? These opening lines of *Epistles* 1.1 suggest that he cannot.

The dangers of public life are further brought out by the voice Horace claims is echoing through his ears, which warns him to put aside such contests before he becomes a laughing-stock, like an old racehorse who is no longer able to compete (7–9).[15] This mysterious voice fulfills an important role in the *recusatio*, for refusals of this kind normally entail a poet justifying his adoption of one form of poetry over another by claiming that an intervening deity commanded him to do this (such as, most famously, Apollo in Callimachus, *Aetia* fr. 1.21–30 or Vergil, *Eclogues* 6.1–5).[16] Scholars have made the interesting suggestion that this voice alludes to the peculiar divinity (*daimonion*) that famously acts as a deterrent voice for Socrates in the writings of Plato and Xenophon. Moles, for example, argues that it is just such a *daimonion* that is responsible for Horace's philosophical "conversion."[17] Horace therefore dutifully announces his intention to set aside *versus et cetera ludicra* (10) and turn instead to a pursuit of *verum atque decens* (11), in keeping with his own Socratic *daimonion*. It is more important, however, that this voice turns Horace *away* from the public arena than it is that it turns him *toward* philosophy, for this is precisely what Socrates's deterrent *daimonion* warns him against in Plato's *Apology*:

ἐμοὶ δὲ τοῦτ' ἔστιν ἐκ παιδὸς ἀρξάμενον, φωνή τις γιγνομένη, ᾗ ὅταν γένηται, ἀεὶ ἀποτρέπει με τοῦτο, ὃ ἂν μέλλω πράττειν, προτρέπει δὲ οὔποτε. τοῦτ' ἔστιν ὅ μοι ἐναντιοῦται τὰ πολιτικὰ πράττειν, καὶ παγκάλως γέ μοι δοκεῖ ἐναντιοῦσθαι· εὖ γὰρ ἴστε, ὦ ἄνδρες Ἀθηναῖοι, εἰ ἐγὼ πάλαι ἐπεχείρησα πράττειν τὰ πολιτικὰ πράγματα, πάλαι ἂν ἀπολώλη καὶ οὔτ' ἂν ὑμᾶς ὠφελήκη οὐδὲν οὔτ' ἂν ἐμαυτόν. καί μοι μὴ ἄχθεσθε λέγοντι τἀληθῆ· οὐ γὰρ ἔστιν, ὅστις ἀνθρώπων σωθήσεται οὔτε ὑμῖν οὔτε ἄλλῳ πλήθει οὐδενὶ γνησίως ἐναντιούμενος καὶ διακωλύων πολλὰ ἄδικα καὶ παράνομα ἐν τῇ πόλει γίγνεσθαι, ἀλλ' ἀναγκαῖόν ἐστι τὸν τῷ ὄντι μαχούμενον ὑπὲρ τοῦ δικαίου, καὶ εἰ μέλλει ὀλίγον χρόνον σωθήσεσθαι, ἰδιωτεύειν ἀλλὰ μὴ δημοσιεύειν. (31d2–32a3)

Beginning in childhood I have had this, it arises as a sort of voice, and whenever it occurs it always warns me away from what I was going to do, but it never urges me on. This is what prevents me from taking part in politics, and in my opinion it seems to prevent me altogether well: for know well, men of Athens, that, if I had attempted to take part in political affairs, I would have died long ago and I would have benefitted neither you nor myself. And do not be angry at me as I tell the truth: for there is no man who will survive who genuinely opposes you or any other populace and prevents many unjust and unlawful things from happening in the city, but it is necessary that the one who fights in reality for justice, if he intends to survive even for a brief time, live a private life and not a public one.

The gladiatorial Horace of the *Epistles* is in a similar situation to the Socrates of the *Apology*, for they both find themselves in the dangerous position of placing their future safety in the hands of the multitude. For Socrates and for Horace the world of public participation is dangerous and best avoided, and a greater benefit arises, for the poet/philosopher as well as for the state, from private contemplation of ethical matters.

The metaphor of the racecourse in these lines furthermore raises questions about freedom, slavery, and mastery. At first glance, it is not immediately clear to whom Horace corresponds, the horse or its rider. If he is the one to "free the horse" (*solve . . . equum*), then surely he must be equated with its rider or master. The horse's old age (*senescentem*, 8), on the other hand, clearly connects it with Horace, whose advancing age (*non eadem est aetas*, 4) makes epistolary poetry a more suitable genre than lyric. Horace's choice to identify himself simultaneously with the master and the horse is significant, since it illustrates that to be free is to be one's own master. Maecenas momentarily drops out of the poem as Horace disposes of any potential master other than himself. He will not be like the horse described in the fable of *Epistles* 1.10.34–41, who, in order to defeat his rival the stag, enlists the help of man only to find that he cannot rid himself of his new master. Whereas the horse in the fable cannot dislodge the rein from its mouth (*non frenum depulit ore*, 38), in the opening poem Horace, as both master and horse, unties his own reins (*solve*, 8). This equation between freedom and self-mastery will be important in the collection. Only a few lines later, having just declared that he will swear upon the words of no philosophical master (*nullius . . . in verba magistri*, 14), Horace boldly declares that he will be his own king: *ego me ipse regam* ("I myself will rule myself," 27). One question the *Epistles* will pose is how far Horace can involve himself with potential masters in a variety of spheres (philosophical, poetic, social, and geographical) without losing his freedom like the horse of *Epistles* 1.10.

We have seen thus far that in the opening of *Epistles* 1.1, Horace seeks *libertas* in the poetic and social spheres, but his pose of retirement furthermore sets up an antithesis between urban slavery and rural freedom. The countryside becomes a necessary backdrop for Horace to exercise his independence, and in this sphere too Horace again is unwilling to compromise. Like Veianius, he is in retirement in the country, and the word *abditus* (5) illustrates his concealment. The city is thus associated with enslavement and public poetic exhibition while the countryside evokes freedom, obscurity, and philosophical and ethical contemplation. The equations between *rus* and *libertas* on the one hand and *urbs* and *servitus* on the other will remain operative throughout many of the epistles, and in this first poem no middle path is proposed as a third possible option.

Freedom is at the heart of Horace's approach to philosophy as well. In lines 11–19 he explains that his new project will take up philosophical topics but will not be subjected to the orthodoxy of any one school:

quid verum atque decens, curo et rogo et omnis in hoc sum:
condo et compono quae mox depromere possim.
ac ne forte roges, quo me duce, quo lare tuter:
nullius addictus iurare in verba magistri,
quo me cumque rapit tempestas, deferor hospes.

I care about and ask about what is true and seemly, and I am entirely [absorbed] in this; I am gathering and storing up things from which I may soon be able to draw. And so that you do not by chance ask with what leader or in what house I

> take shelter: I am bound to swear on the words of no master. I am carried as a
> guest wherever the storm takes me.

Horace's epistolary poetry in these lines shows great originality and independence: not only is it free of Maecenas's compulsion and a clear poetic forerunner, it also has no single philosophical model. As we will see in later chapters, imitation is the mark of a slave, and Horace in these opening lines wants to avoid any hint of continued slavery. Horace's philosophical technique has been called eclectic (a term to which I will return below), but I would stress here most of all that it is independent. The continuation of the gladiatorial metaphor in line 18 (*nullius addictus iurare in uerba magistri*) connects his philosophical freedom to his freedom from Maecenas, for gladiators were forced to swear oaths of loyalty to their masters.[18] At the heart of these lines is an unwillingness to repeat or dictate anyone else's words (*iurare in verba*), an activity which again and again in the *Epistles* will be analogous to slavery.[19] Just as Horace is unwilling to write about the poetic topics dictated to him by Maecenas, his would-be gladiatorial *magister*, so too he refuses to copy the teachings dictated by a philosophical *magister*.

Let us pause here to draw a comparison with a passage from *Epistles* 2.2, the letter to Florus, written shortly after *Epistles* 1,[20] in which Horace makes a similar claim to set aside the poetry of *ludus* in exchange for philosophical and ethical topics:

> nimirum sapere est abiectis utile nugis,
> et tempestivum pueris concedere ludum,
> ac non verba sequi fidibus modulanda Latinis,
> sed verae numerosque modosque ediscere vitae. (2.2.141–44)

> Of course it is useful to be wise and to cast aside trifles, and to give up play proper to children, and not to seek out words to be sung in tune with the Latin lyre, but to learn the meters and measures of a true life.

As in the opening of *Epistles* 1.1, Horace rejects the poetry of the lyre, which he describes with the terms *nugae* and *ludus*. In place of this light and playful poetry, as in 1.1, Horace seeks to examine what it means to live a morally sound life (cf. *verae* at 2.2.144 and *verum* at 1.1.11). The "meters and measures" of the lyre are replaced here with the "meters and measures" (*numerosque modosque*) of ethical contemplation. This passage, though stripped of the language of freedom and slavery, has much in common with the opening of *Epistles* 1.1, and Horace surely had the earlier passage in mind when composing it.

This is not, however, the only passage from *Epistles* 1 that Horace recalls in 2.2.141–44, for the language here is found also in *Epistles* 1.18 in a very different context. Read just after *Epistles* 1.1.1–15, this passage from 1.18 comes as something of a shock, since in it the harsh *recusatio* and demand for *libertas* of 1.1 have been inverted.[21] Here Horace offers his young friend Lollius advice on how best to get along with powerful friends. Surprisingly, he tells Lollius to comply with the wishes of his great *amicus* and engage in play, *ludus*, when his patron wishes. As in 1.1, gladiatorial imagery is prominent:

> ac ne te retrahas et inexcusabilis absis:
> quamvis nil extra *numerum* fecisse *modum*que
> curas, interdum *nugaris* rure paterno.
> partitur lintres exercitus, Actia pugna
> te duce per pueros hostili more refertur;
> adversarius est frater, lacus Hadria, donec
> alterutrum velox Victoria fronde coronet.
> consentire suis studiis qui crediderit te,
> fautor utroque tuum laudabit pollice *ludum*. (1.18.58–66)

And so that you do not withdraw and stay away inexcusably: although you take care to do nothing out of tune (*extra numerum modumque*), from time to time you are frivolous on your paternal estate. The army divides the boats, with you as leader the Battle of Actium is staged by your slaves in a hostile manner; your brother is the adversary, the lake is the Adriatic, until swift Victory crowns one of you with a garland of leaves. Whoever believes that you agree with his pastimes will, as your supporter, praise your play with each thumb.

Horace in this poem tells Lollius to do exactly what he himself had refused to do in 1.1: yield to the wishes of a powerful patron, at least sometimes (*interdum*). Though Horace is not explicitly talking about poetry in this passage, the poetic language that echoes *Epistles* 2.2.141–44 (italicized) suggests that this is precisely what Horace has in mind. Now dogged insistence on withdrawal is inexcusable (*retrahas et inexcusabilis absis*), and even while on his country estate (*rure paterno*) he should take time for trifles (*nugaris*) and play (*ludus*). Somewhat startlingly, this *ludus* turns out to be a recreation of the Battle of Actium, with Lollius and his brother (*frater*) acting out the hostile sides in the civil war. Though composed in private on a rural estate, this poetry has an overt public dimension. As Bowditch writes, "the diction suggests the writing of poetry, and specifically political verse, since the *ludus* put on by Lollius is a *naumachia* (mock sea battle) of Octavian and Antony's showdown at Actium."[22] If he were to follow Horace's advice and perform public poetry for his patron while on his estate in the countryside, Lollius would all but erase the line between public and private. Whereas the withdrawn Horace of 1.1 had refused to compose poetry that brought him into the gladiatorial arena, this is precisely what he tells Lollius to do, though here it is not the *populus* but the patron who judges Lollius's performance and signals his approval or disapproval by a movement of his thumb, a gesture that recalls the custom at gladiatorial games of the audience signaling their verdict for or against a gladiator.[23] The dogged insistence on freedom found in 1.1 has been replaced with a recommendation to compromise and adapt. But how can Horace recommend behavior that in 1.1 had been tantamount to slavery, especially to a young man who prides himself on his *libertas* (*liberrime Lolli*, 1.18.1)? How can Lollius comply with a patron without adopting a master and surrendering his freedom? The remainder of this book takes up this question and traces how the collection moves from a stance of rigidity and inflexibility to one that allows compromise without a loss of independence. Whereas the opening lines of 1.1 present us with an either/or proposition between freedom/self-mastery and slavery, a third, middle path is opened up between these extremes as the book progresses. This mean will be enacted in the spheres of poetry, location, and friendship, and it will be Horace's independent philosophical method that will provide the model for such compromise.

Horace's Philosophical *Libertas*

The key to opening up a middle path between the extremes of *libertas* and *servitus* as presented in the opening lines of 1.1 lies in Horace's philosophical technique, in which he exercises a freedom that is much more flexible. Whereas Horace's desire to be free in the poetic and social arenas leads him to withdraw entirely from Rome and Maecenas, Horace's rejection of a philosophical master does not lead to a corresponding refusal to participate in philosophical inquiry. Rather, he sets up an adaptable, independent method whereby he can participate without becoming subject to any particular system:[24]

> ac ne forte roges, quo me duce, quo lare tuter:
> nullius addictus iurare in verba magistri,
> quo me cumque rapit tempestas, deferor hospes.
> nunc agilis fio et mersor civilibus undis
> virtutis verae custos rigidusque satelles,
> nunc in Aristippi furtim praecepta relabor
> et mihi res, non me rebus, subiungere conor. (*Epist.* 1.1.13–19)

> And so that you do not by chance ask with what leader or in what house I take shelter: I am bound to swear on the words of no master. I am carried as a guest wherever the storm takes me. Now I become active and am immersed in the waves of civil life as a guardian and rigid attendant of true virtue, now I slip back secretly into the precepts of Aristippus and try to make things subject to myself, not myself to things.

Horace's lack of philosophical allegiance is illustrated by his assertion to be a *hospes*, a "guest" (i.e., one who seeks *hospitium*, "hospitality"), wherever the storm takes him and by his subsequent claim to alternate between contrasting philosophical traditions. This practice allows him to associate with a variety of philosophical masters (i.e., to stay as a guest in their house) without enslaving himself to any. As mentioned above, Horace's system here has been called "eclectic," in that it conforms to no orthodox system.[25] Yet this is a problematic term, as Rudd has pointed out.[26] The ancient concept of eclecticism is very difficult to define, and modern scholars have used the term "to indicate different philosophical attitudes with a number of different senses."[27] The *locus classicus* for ancient Eclecticism is found in Diogenes Laertius, where he states that Potamo of Alexandria established an eclectic school: πρὸ ὀλίγου καὶ ἐκλεκτική τις αἵρεσις εἰσήχθη ὑπὸ Ποτάμωνος τοῦ Ἀλεξανδρέως, ἐκλεξαμένου τὰ ἀρέσκοντα ἐξ ἑκάστης τῶν αἱρέσεων ("Not long ago a certain eclectic school was introduced by Potamo of Alexandria, who picked out the things which pleased him from each system," 1.21). Diogenes goes on to say that Potamo established criteria of truth (κριτήρια τῆς ἀληθείας), universal principles (ἀρχάς τε τῶν ὅλων), and an end (τέλος).[28] Such a coherent and complete system is in no way evident in Horace's claim to switch from one philosophy to another (1.1.13–19).[29] What I would stress instead is that his approach is above all *independent* and fulfills his need for freedom as professed to Maecenas in the opening lines of the poem, but it is freedom of a different degree, one nicely symbolized by the gladiatorial *rudis* he has received.[30] As a freedman, he would enjoy no absolute *libertas*. It would come with significant strings attached since he would be expected to perform due deference (*obsequium*) to his former master.[31] Horace's philosophical freedom nicely reflects this, for it allows him to occupy a middle position between complete slavery to a master and utter freedom from one. His moderate philosophical freedom therefore accords better with his freedman status than does his uncompromising insistence upon freedom in poetry, friendship, and location.

The two philosophical approaches he claims to switch back and forth between in lines 16–19 tell us a lot about how his outlook toward freedom vacillates and changes over the collection. His first philosophical stance (16–17) is rigid and orthodox (*rigidus*, 17), leads to civic participation (*civilibus undis*, 16), and has as its goal *virtus vera* (17). All of this points to Stoicism and traditional Republican ideals.[32] In Horace's Regulus Ode (3.5), it is precisely *virtus vera* to which the Republican hero appeals in order to dissuade the Romans from paying ransom to his Carthaginian captors, arguing that death is more honorable: *nec vera virtus, cum semel excidit, / curat reponi deterioribus* ("Nor does true virtue, when it has once been lost, care to be restored to inferior men," 29–30).

It is this quality too that the personified *Auxilium* in Plautus's *Cistellaria* exhorts
the Romans to employ against their longstanding enemies, the Carthaginians:

> bene valete et vincite
> *virtute vera*, quod fecistis antidhac;
> servate vostros socios, veteres et novos,
> augete auxilia vostra iustis legibus,
> perdite perduelles, parite laudem et lauream,
> ut vobis victi Poeni poenas sufferant. (197–202)

*wordplay of
a particular
model*

> Fare well and conquer with *true virtue*, as you have done previously; preserve your
> allies, both old and new, increase your auxiliaries with fair laws, destroy your
> enemies, produce praise and the victory laurel, so that the Carthaginians, con-
> quered by you, may suffer the penalty.[33]

Though Nisbet and Rudd see in *vera virtus* a "stock alliterative phrase,"[34] I suggest that Horace has chosen it specifically to evoke Rome's Republican past.
These lines from the first epistle especially recall a fragment of Ennius's *Phoenix*,
which, as Lind points out, forms the first surviving statement in Latin concerning *libertas*:[35]

> Sed virum *vera virtute* vivere animatum *addecet*
> fortiterque innoxium stare adversum adversarios.
> ea *libertas* est qui pectus purum et *firmum* gestitat;
> aliae res obnoxiosae nocte in obscura latent. (fr. 308–11 Warmington)

> But it befits a man to live endowed with true virtue and bravely to stand blameless
> against his enemies. That is liberty, the one who bears a heart pure and steady;
> other matters are subordinate and lie hidden in the dark night.

Though Ennius has adapted this work from a Euripidean original, his coupling
of *virtus* and *libertas* in these lines gives them a distinctly Roman flavor, for *virtus* and *libertas* are ideals of Ennius's Republican Rome as much as they are goals
of Stoicism. Horace's passage contains several verbal parallels to the Ennian
one, especially in its emphasis on decorum (*addecet*; cf. *decens*, *Epist.* 1.1.11) and
the direct echo of *vera virtute* in *virtutis verae* at *Epistles* 1.1.17. Later in the first
epistle Horace urges his reader to follow the advice of one "who encourages you
to defy haughty Fortune free and upright," *qui Fortunae te responsare superbae /
liberum et erectum . . . hortatur* (68–69), where again the focus on *libertas* and
rigidity (*erectum*; cf. *firmum*) calls to mind this Ennian passage. One of Horace's
philosophical modes therefore will be inflexibly focused on *virtus* and implicitly aligned with the Republican pursuit of freedom. The uncompromising
aspect of this philosophical approach aligns with the Horace that we saw in
the opening of the poem, who refuses to let his former poetry or his friendship
with Maecenas render him a slave.

There are, however, some major difficulties with the inflexible "Republican" or "Stoic" Horace of 16–17: whereas Horace's opening *libertas* removes him from public life altogether, this philosophical approach forces him into the public arena, where he is soon drowned in civic waves, *mersor civilibus undis*, 16 (continuing the sea metaphor from *hospes*, 15). Stoic rigidity therefore seems to offer no solution to Horace's trouble with public life, and the only way to prevent being drowned at present seems to avoid these waves altogether. Nor does the pursuit of *virtus vera* render him completely free.[36] No philosophical trailblazer, he is the *custos* and *satelles* of a rigid system, and the latter term in particular can have a contemptuous resonance as the adherent to a tyrant or despot.[37] Although this philosophical approach aims at *virtus* and *libertas*, it does so in an extreme and inflexible fashion that renders its follower the slave of a sect and offers no real solution to anxieties about public participation. Again and again in the *Epistles* the ones who are devoted uncompromisingly to *libertas* will be ultimately revealed as servile or as enjoying only partial freedom.[38] In imbuing one of his philosophical approaches with language that recalls the Republican *libertas* of Ennius, Horace makes us question whether this traditional, rigid pursuit of absolute *libertas* can bring us real freedom after all.

But this is only one side or mood of Horace, for at other times he takes a very different philosophical approach, one characterized by adaptability and in which he does not inflexibly uphold the system of another but adapts it to himself. This approach (18–19) is exemplified by the philosopher Aristippus, founder of the Cyrenaic school, who like Epicurus considered pleasure the greatest good.[39] Aristippus is marked out as particularly important here, for this is the first mention of a philosopher by name in the collection, and in fact he is named more than any other philosopher in *Epistles* 1.[40] Some have found Aristippus a surprising choice to contrast with Stoicism in these lines and have suggested that Epicureanism would be the more natural alternative to the Stoicism of 16–17. The hedonistic Aristippus, they suggest, stands in for Epicurus, and Horace's confession to slipping back "secretly" (*furtim*, 18) into these precepts alludes to the Epicurean tag *lathe biosas*, a lifestyle Horace professes to adopt even earlier in his description of Veianius, who, like him, is *abditus agro* (5), "hidden in the country."[41] Epicureanism, however, would make a poor counterpart to the Stoicism described in 16–17, for as a system it is every bit as rigid and orthodox.[42] What Horace stresses about Aristippus is not his hedonism, but his extraordinary ability to adapt and to make every circumstance suitable to himself without becoming enslaved to it.[43] Line 19 (*et mihi res, non me rebus, subiungere conor*) in particular recalls his famous saying that although he holds the courtesan Lais he is not held (i.e., enslaved) by her: ἔχω Λαΐδα, ἀλλ᾽ οὐκ ἔχομαι ("I hold Lais, but I am not held by her," Diogenes Laertius 2.75). Horace makes

a significant amendment to this Aristippean maxim, replacing Lais with *res*
("things, situations, or circumstances")[44] and through this rephrasing indicating
an ability to bend not sensual pleasure but a whole variety of things to oneself.[45]
This adaptability allows Horace a mastery over philosophical systems that cannot be found in orthodox Stoicism, for here it is he who is doing the "yoking"
or "subjugating," *subiungere*, 19, rather than being subjugated.[46] Instead of reading *furtim* as alluding to *lathe biosas* or, as some have suggested, as "a faintly
guilty admission,"[47] we can see it as pointing rather to Horace's natural inclination.[48] Even when Horace immerses himself in dogmatic Stoicism, this mood
does not last long and Horace soon slips back (*relabor*) into his natural pliancy.
The word *conor* suggests, however, that Horace does not always successfully
live up to this Aristippean ideal; rather, philosophical adaptability is a goal that
Horace sometimes attains while at other times slipping into orthodoxy.[49] In
the two opposing philosophical approaches outlined in 16–20, we are therefore
presented with two options: an inflexible insistence on freedom that is ultimately unable truly to deliver *libertas* and an adaptable, polytropic approach
that gives one greater mastery and control.[50]

One major issue in these lines is the proper degree to which a poet interested in morality and philosophy should adhere to dogmatic teachings. That is,
Horace is contrasting two modes of poetic imitation of philosophical models,
one that remains unquestioningly true to a particular sect and another that
approaches philosophical texts with a free hand. A representative of the first
method of imitation would be Lucretius, who, though he shows great poetic
originality in crafting an Epicurean epic, holds true to the teachings of his master, elevating him to the status of a hero and even a god.[51] Horace's natural inclination is rather toward treating philosophical models with freedom, adapting
them to his own purposes rather than crafting his poetry in faithfulness to them.
Key here is the repeated word *res* in line 19, where it can mean "circumstances"
while hinting also at "subject matter."[52] A similar use of the word *res* can be
found in the *Ars Poetica*, in which Horace outlines the importance for the poet
of using philosophy as source material in composing his poetry, and the language of this passage has many affinities with that of *Epistles* 1.1:

> munus et officium nil scribens ipse docebo,
> unde parentur opes, quid alat formetque poetam,
> quid deceat, quid non, quo virtus, quo ferat error.
> scribendi recte sapere est et principium et fons:
> rem tibi Socraticae poterunt ostendere chartae,
> verbaque provisam rem non invita sequentur. (*AP* 306–11)

> Though writing nothing myself, I will teach [the poet's] duty and job, from where
> his resources are acquired, what nourishes and forms the poet, what is fitting,

what is not, where virtue and error lead. The origin and font of writing well is to
be wise. Socratic writings can show subject matter to you, and words willingly will
follow once subject matter has been supplied.

In each passage Horace demonstratively casts aside poetry (*versus et cetera ludicra pono, Epist.* 1.1.10; *nil scribens ipse*, 306) while also stating the importance of
finding subject matter that befits the poet (*deceat, AP* 308; *decens, Epist.* 1.1.11).
Both poems posit philosophy as poetic source material, and the idea that this
material can be stored away or put aside for later use (*unde parentur opes, AP*
307) is central to *Epistles* 1.1.11–12 (*quid verum atque decens curo et rogo et omnis
in hoc sum; / condo et compono quae mox depromere possim*, "I care about and
ask about what is true and decorous, and I am entirely [absorbed] in this; I
am gathering and storing up things from which I may soon be able to draw").
It is noteworthy that in the *Ars* passage Horace is rather ambiguous about precisely which philosophical materials provide the best raw subject matter for the
poet, for *Socraticae chartae* would cover a wide range, from Plato to Xenophon
to Hellenistic philosophers, almost all of whom saw themselves as the heirs of
Socrates.[53] The very generality of the statement invites the interpretation that
Horace recommends that poets pick and choose from a wide variety of philosophical sources without regard to dogma or orthodoxy. The repetition of *rem*
in 310–11 encourages us to look back on the repeated use of this same word in
Epistles 1.1.19, where philosophical adaptability is front and center. The philosophical freedom of the first epistle is a statement not just about the speaker's non-
adherence to any particular creed but also about how a poet should approach
source material, by freely using and adapting philosophical models. What Horace
will not realize until *Epistles* 1.19, however, is that his previous poetry, especially
his *Epodes* and *Odes*, far from being the source of slavery that they are presented
as in 1.1, exemplify just this type of free imitation.

Two divergent modes of freedom emerge in the philosophical attitudes of
lines 16–19. The first mode finds Horace adhering inflexibly to Stoic and Republican *libertas*, but it fails to resolve his anxiety toward public life and ultimately subordinates him to an orthodox philosophical system. The second is
more in keeping with his innate personality and allows him to master philosophical material by adapting it to himself and his own poetic program rather
than vice versa. Ultimately it will be the latter approach to freedom that will
triumph and that will enable Horace to walk a middle path between *libertas*
and *servitus*. Rather than renounce philosophy entirely he makes use of it but
with a free hand. What Horace will have to do is apply this same adaptable,
moderate approach to friendship, poetry, and location, in which areas only the
two opposing extremes of inflexible *libertas* and slavish dependence have so far

been offered. In the opening of the first poem he is leaning too far in these spheres toward the extreme inflexibility of lines 16–17, an approach that leaves him unwilling to compromise with his famous friend and unable to navigate the waves of public, urban life without being overcome by them.

ARISTIPPEAN SOCIAL *LIBERTAS*

Aristippus provides Horace not only with an exemplar of philosophical freedom and moderation but also with a model of how these can be applied to other spheres as well, especially the social sphere. Already in the first poem Horace provides hints that an Aristippean approach will be taken to overcome his ambivalence toward friendship with the powerful, which in the opening lines jeopardizes autonomy and renders one a slave. The stories that are passed down about Aristippus testify to his tremendous adaptability and independence in dealing with the elite, qualities that allowed him to have rich and powerful friends if he so desired and the opportunity arose, but, if not, to live modestly and privately.[54] With Aristippus as his model for social interaction, Horace can satisfy his desires for social success and friendship with Maecenas without sacrificing his independence and thus can open up a third path between extreme freedom and slavery.

The first clue that Horace's philosophical method can be applied to the social arena comes in his claim to be a guest, *hospes*, wherever the storm takes him (15). As scholars note, Horace here has in mind Aristippus's assertion in Book Two of Xenophon's *Memorabilia* that he belongs to no *politeia*, but is a guest everywhere: οὐδ' εἰς πολιτείαν ἐμαυτὸν κατακλείω, ἀλλὰ ξένος πανταχοῦ εἰμι ("I do not shut myself up in a regime but am a guest everywhere," 2.1.13).[55] Although scholars have acknowledged the parallel, no one has sufficiently considered how the context of the *Memorabilia* passage, especially its focus on freedom and slavery, has more broadly influenced the *Epistles*.[56] In the Xenophon passage, Socrates and Aristippus are discussing what makes men fit to be rulers. Aristippus declares that he himself would not wish to be a ruler, because the responsibility would be too great a burden and would interfere with his pursuit of ease and pleasure. Socrates then redirects the conversation and asks Aristippus whether rulers or subjects live the more pleasant life. To this Aristippus responds that he is no candidate for slavery either:

> οὐδὲ εἰς τὴν δουλείαν αὖ ἐμαυτὸν τάττω, ἀλλ' εἶναί τίς μοι δοκεῖ μέση τούτων
> ὁδός, ἣν πειρῶμαι βαδίζειν, οὔτε δι' ἀρχῆς οὔτε διὰ δουλείας, ἀλλὰ δι' ἐλευθερίας,
> ἥπερ μάλιστα πρὸς εὐδαιμονίαν ἄγει. (*Mem.* 2.1.11)

> I do not, in turn, appoint myself for slavery, but there seems to me to be a certain middle path, which I try to walk, neither through rule nor through slavery, but through freedom, which most especially leads to happiness.

Socrates protests against this "middle path," saying that one cannot follow it while actually living among human beings, whereupon Aristippus makes his claim to be a guest everywhere, which Socrates calls a δεινὸν πάλαισμα, "a clever trick."[57] Aristippus's being a guest pertains to the social arena and refers to the middle path that he walks between being a ruler and being a slave, which he calls freedom. As a "guest" in the houses of the powerful, Aristippus can partake of the good things they offer without coming under their power and suffering a loss of freedom. This Aristippean definition of freedom has important ramifications in the *Epistles* since it aligns freedom not with ruling, as Horace at times does,[58] but as a path between ruling and being ruled. Aristippean freedom enables one to associate with potential rulers without becoming a slave, just as Horace can visit a variety of philosophical houses without staying put in any. Whereas Horace's claim to be a *hospes* ostensibly refers only to his philosophical approach, the allusion to the Xenophon passage suggests that this can be applied to the social arena as well. His refusal to let Maecenas shut him up (*includere*, 3) in any *ludus*, furthermore, can, as Moles has suggested, "be read (retrospectively) as including a (prospective) gloss on Aristippus's refusal to 'shut himself into' any *politeia*."[59] Horace's challenge is how to re-embrace his former poetry and Maecenas without letting them shut him into the servile gladiatorial arena, and he will do so by walking the path of freedom between ruling and slavery that Xenophon's Aristippus has proposed. Rather than insist on the total and absolute *libertas* that brings no ruler whatsoever, this Aristippean freedom allows us to enjoy the benefits of engaging with a variety of potential masters (whether philosophical, poetic, social, or geographical) without swearing on the words of any. It is only through this middle path that Horace will be able to navigate the perils of public life without being overcome by them and to gain possession of the true freedom that, for all his dogged insistence, eludes him in the opening of 1.1.

Horace's *hospes* has a coloring that Aristippus's ξένος does not, since Horace's use of the word is tied to the nautical imagery that runs throughout the first part of the poem (*tempestas*, 15; *mersor*, 16; *undis*, 16).[60] If Horace's rigid philosophical mode leaves him immersed or drowned at sea (*mersor*), it will only be in learning to navigate with adaptability and flexibility that he can achieve the middle path. This combination of nautical imagery with an allusion to the middle path certainly recalls Horace's *Odes* 2.10, where one achieves the *aurea mediocritas* ("golden mean," 5) by steering a middle course: "neither by always pressing the deep nor, when you are cautiously beginning to fear storms, by hugging the uneven shore too much" (*neque altum / semper urgendo neque, dum procellas / cautus horrescis, nimium premendo / litus iniquum*, 1–4). The nautical imagery is continued in the final stanza of the poem, where Horace tells his addressee Licinius to "appear spirited and brave in difficult situations: likewise you will wisely draw in your sails when they are swollen by too favorable a wind" (*rebus angustis animosus atque / fortis appare: sapienter idem / contrahes vento nimium secundo / turgida vela*, 21–24). Here the *aurea mediocritas* is achieved not by adhering strictly to the middle path but by adapting to changing circumstances (*rebus*) and preparing for unpredictable fluctuations. It is the combination of the middle path and adaptability that enables one to avoid life's perils, figured as a shipwreck. Adaptability therefore forms a crucial component to the *aurea mediocritas*, and it is such adaptability that the Aristippus of *Epistles* 1.1.19 exemplifies. In adapting circumstances (*res . . . rebus*) to himself, he—unlike his rigid opposite—finds safety and *hospitium* rather than being drowned (*mersor*, 16) at sea. By adopting such an approach not only to philosophy but to a variety of spheres, Horace will be able to set his own terms for compromise rather than have them imposed upon him.

Adaptability, the middle path, true *libertas*: these will be the central ethical lessons of the *Epistles*. They are the means by which Horace can maintain ties of dependence in philosophy, poetry, friendship, and location without losing his freedom. The subsequent chapters of this book take up these themes in turn and examine the ways in which Horace formulates moderate *libertas*. In each sphere Horace will reject extreme freedom and slavery as incapable of bridging the seemingly incompatible worlds and desires of the poet: the city and the country, poetry and philosophy, friendship and isolation, fame and anonymity. Above all they cannot provide him with an *aequus animus*, ballast against life's constant vacillations. The ethical examinations of *Epistles* 1 all lead to the question of how one can maintain freedom, equanimity, and consistency in the face of circumstances and desires that can spiral out of one's control. The Horace we meet in *Epistles* 1.1 is not just a man who longs for independence for its own sake but one who is searching for a cure for something more troubling and profound, who turns to philosophy for an inner freedom that can overcome the constant wavering and ambivalence of his own soul.

2

Horace the Student

Inconsistency and Sickness in
Epistles 1.1, 1.8, and 1.15

I N THE PREVIOUS CHAPTER, I examined the ways in which the Horatian persona of *Epistles* 1.1 uncompromisingly demands independence in the spheres of poetry, friendship, and location. At the same time, he takes a more flexible and moderate approach to philosophy, where he walks a middle path between the extremes of *libertas* and *servitus*. In this chapter I focus on another aspect of Horace's epistolary persona and examine *why* he longs so strongly for independence, isolation, and ethical contemplation: he is suffering from a spiritual disease produced by his inconsistency and ambivalence. These shortcomings are not new to the *Epistles* and were already leveled against Horace in the *Satires*, especially in reference to his friendship with Maecenas. The goal of Horace's ethical examinations throughout the first book of *Epistles* is to attain an equanimity (*animus . . . aequus*, 1.11.30; *aequum . . . animum*, 1.18.112) that he repeatedly presents himself as lacking or pursuing. This equanimity will arise, however, not by adhering uncompromisingly to one extreme or another, but through moderation and adaptability, which will enable Horace to accommodate different sides of his personality without compromising his inner core. The search for equanimity is one that will unfold over the course of the book, and Horace figures this search as a return to the schoolroom and casts himself in the role of a student whose rocky progress will unfold across the collection.

SELF-CRITICISM IN THE *SATIRES* AND *EPISTLES*

In the introduction I suggested that Horace's interest in freedom carries over from his *Satires* and deepens in the *Epistles*, and I would like to begin this chapter by considering another and complementary way in which the *Epistles* continues a trajectory that took shape over the course of the two books of *Satires*. Horace increasingly turns the satiric lens from others' faults and inconsistencies onto his own, and in the *Epistles* he, first and foremost, is the one who needs ethical guidance and spiritual renewal. While Horace himself takes up the persona of the satirist in *Satires* 1, this role is adopted by a series of others, including Damasippus (2.3) and Davus (2.7), in the second book, and their satire is frequently directed, however inexpertly, against Horace.[1] Chief among the charges leveled at Horace by both Damasippus and Davus are, first, Horace's inconsistent behavior regarding Maecenas, and, second, his hypocrisy in criticizing faults in others that he too possesses. While these accusations meet with Horace's anger in the *Satires*, in the *Epistles* Horace places his own faults front and center, and he examines for himself whether Damasippus's charge of *insania* or Davus's charge of *servitus* holds any weight.

By projecting the mask of satirist onto these speakers in the *Satires* Horace is free to examine his own faults and to hurl painful accusations at himself from a safe distance. He reveals his own inconsistencies through the exposés of Damasippus and Davus. For Damasippus, Horace is far from the unambitious man he has presented himself to be, for example, in *Satires* 1.6. The chief topic of his speech in *Satires* 2.3 is madness, *insania*, a word used twenty-six times throughout the poem. Damasippus has recently been on the verge of suicide and was convinced not to jump from the Fabrician Bridge by the philosopher Stertinius, who has convinced him of the Stoic doctrine that everyone but the wise man is mad. He proceeds to deliver a long speech to Horace on this Stoic precept; the speech culminates in Horace asking Damasippus in what respect he would consider Horace to be mad: *Stoice . . . /qua me stultitia, quoniam non est genus unum, insanire putas? ego nam videor mihi sanus* ("Stoic, in what foolishness, since there is not just one kind, do you think that I am mad? For I seem to myself to be sane," 300–302). Damasippus replies that Horace's desire to be like the great, particularly Maecenas, makes him both mad and an object of ridicule:

>   primum
> aedificas, hoc est, longos imitaris, ab imo
> ad summum totus moduli bipedalis; et idem
> corpore maiorem rides Turbonis in armis
> spiritum et incessum: qui ridiculus minus illo?
> an quodcumque facit Maecenas te quoque verum est
> tantum dissimilem et tanto certare minorem? (307–13)

First of all you are building, that is you imitate the lofty, though from bottom to top all up you measure two feet, and at the same time you laugh at the pride and gait of Turbo when he is in his armor as being too big for his body: how are you less ridiculous than he is? Or is it right that, whatever Maecenas does, you, who are so unlike him and so much less than he is, compete with him?

Damasippus goes on to use one of Horace's favorite satirical weapons against him: the fable. Horace imitating Maecenas is like the frog who tries unsuccessfully to imitate a calf by puffing itself up; it simply will never be able to equal the calf's size (314–19). Though Damasippus's attack on Horace proves, in the words of Bond, to be "clumsy and unconvincing,"[2] it nevertheless hits a sensitive spot in Horace, who reacts first angrily and then dismissively to Damasippus: *iam desine. /. . . . teneas, Damasippe, tuis te. /. . . . o maior tandem parcas insane, minori!* ("Now stop. . . . Mind your own business, Damasippus. /. . . . o at last spare, greater madman, the lesser one," 323–26). The accusation of imitation (*imitaris*, 308) is one that is particularly damning, for it implies that Horace, though he endeavors to rise above his status, is nothing more than a servile imitator of his powerful friend, and in *Epistles* 1.19.19, Horace explicitly connects overly zealous imitation with slavery: *o imitatores, servum pecus* ("o imitators, servile herd"). No matter how hard Horace may try, Damasippus implies, he can never be Maecenas's peer, and all efforts to ignore that fact only reveal his madness, hypocrisy, ambition, and servility. All of these issues will resurface in the first book of *Epistles*.

Davus in *Satires* 2.7 delivers a similar harangue against Horace, and like Damasippus he bases his beliefs on a Stoic precept, this time that only the wise man is free. As in the beginning of *Epistles* 1.1, masters, slaves, and *libertas* are central. Davus, Horace's slave, approaches his master during the Saturnalia, and upon being instructed to make use of the holiday's freedom of speech (*libertate Decembri*, 4), proceeds to adopt the role of the satirist. He begins by taking up a theme that Horace himself had already addressed in the *Satires*, that of inconsistency (6–20), but he quickly turns his criticisms against his master (22).[3] Davus tries to persuade Horace that his adulation of Maecenas, however much he hypocritically tries to hide it by praising the simple life of the country, and his inconstant desires make him no better than a slave. Davus may be a literal slave, but Horace is a spiritual one. Horace professes to prefer the countryside and to be indifferent to the attentions of Maecenas, but his true desires quickly reveal themselves:

> laudas
> fortunam et mores antiquae plebis, et idem
> si quis ad illa deus subito te agat, usque recuses,
> aut quia non sentis quod clamas rectius esse,
> aut quia non firmus rectum defendis, et haeres

nequiquam caeno cupiens evellere plantam.
Romae rus optas, absentem rusticus urbem
tollis ad astra levis. si nusquam es forte vocatus
ad cenam, laudas securum holus ac, velut usquam
vinctus eas, ita te felicem dicis amasque
quod nusquam tibi sit potandum. iusserit ad se
Maecenas serum sub lumina prima venire
convivam: "nemon oleum fert ocius? ecquis
audit?" cum magno blateras clamore fugisque. (23–35)

You praise the fortune and customs of the ancient plebs, and yet if some god suddenly should offer you those things, you would always refuse, either because you
do not think what you extol is more honorable or because you do not consistently
defend what is right and, though you desire to tear your foot from the mud, you
cling in vain. At Rome you want the country, but when in the country you fickly
raise the city to the stars. If by chance you have been called to dine nowhere, you
praise carefree vegetables and, as if you would go anywhere only in chains, you say
this is how you are happy and you love not having to drink anywhere. Should
Maecenas summon you late at night to come to him as a dinner guest: "Will no
one bring the lantern oil more quickly? Is anyone listening?" you blather with a
great shout and rush off.

Throughout his speech Davus uses the language of slavery to describe his master. In addition to condemning his behavior toward Maecenas, Davus accuses
Horace of adulterous affairs, an accusation that does not, however, seem to hit
home quite like those involving Maecenas. As Oliensis points out, there is
throughout Davus's speech a "slippage between sexual and social enslavement,"
and Davus's attacks on Horace's sexual subjugation can be read really as applicable to his relationship with Maecenas.[4] Such passions, Davus argues, make
Horace a slave just as much as if he were to sell himself as a gladiator: *quid refert,
uri virgis, ferroque necari / auctoratus eas, an turpi clausus in arca, / quo te
demisit peccati conscia erilis, / contractum genibus tangas caput?* ("What difference does it make whether you hire yourself out as a gladiator to be burned by
rods and to be slain by a sword, or you touch your crouched head to your knees,
hidden in a disgraceful chest, where your sinful mistress's accomplice has placed
you?" 58–61). An *auctoratus* was a free man who sold himself as a gladiator to a
lanista, and Davus's language directly echoes the oath sworn by such men.[5] To
Davus, Horace's figurative slavery makes him no better than a literal slave,
and the analogy of the gladiator that he uses for one enslaved to passions is
exactly the one that Horace uses in *Epistles* 1.1, where Horace likewise alludes
to this gladiatorial oath. In the epistle Horace makes the same connection
between literal and metaphorical slavery that Davus does; were he to comply

with Maecenas's wishes, as Davus claims he does all too eagerly, he would be no better than one who forfeits his freedom in the service of a master. Horace applies the gladiatorial imagery not to adulterous affairs, as Davus does, but directly to his friendship with Maecenas.

Davus implies in his speech that Horace's spiritual slavery is in fact worse than his own literal slavery because it is self-imposed. Even if he should be freed, Davus says, Horace would return again and again to his enslaved state: *o totiens servus! quae belua ruptis, / cum semel effugit, reddit se prava catenis?* ("O so many times a slave! What perverse beast returns to its broken chains when once it has fled them?" 70–71). Davus incredulously asks how such a slave could possibly be considered the master of another: *tune mihi dominus, rerum imperiis hominumque / tot tantisque minor, quem ter vindicta quaterque / imposita haud umquam misera formidine privet?* ("Are you my master, you who are a slave to countless commands of things and of men, whom in no way ever will the rod of freedom, placed upon you three and four times, free from wretched fear?" 75–77). Like the epistolary Horace, Davus uses imagery of manumission and suggests that no exterior agent can release Horace from his internal desires and that his freedom must ultimately come from within. The same holds true in the *Epistles*; Horace may have received the wooden *rudis* from Maecenas, but it is an inner and self-won freedom that he must achieve in order to reconcile his ambivalence toward his powerful friend. In *Satires* 2.7, Davus's accusations climax in an image of Horace as a puppet whose strings are being controlled by another, implicitly Maecenas: *tu mihi qui imperitas alii servis miser atque / duceris ut nervis alienis mobile lignum* ("You, who command me, are the wretched slave of another, and you are lead around like a wooden puppet by somebody else's wires," 81–82). As Oliensis suggests, "the image of the marionette seems designed to illustrate Horace's 'enslavement' not to sexual desire (Davus's ostensible subject here) but to Maecenas."[6] The final straw for Horace comes when Davus accuses him of such inner turmoil that he cannot bear his own company (*non horam tecum esse potes*, "You are not able to be with yourself for an hour," 111–12); Horace may try to escape his anxiety, but it will pursue him as though he were a runaway slave (*teque ipsum vitas fugitivus et erro, / iam vino quaerens, iam somno fallere curam: frustra; nam comes atra premit sequiturque fugacem*, "And you avoid yourself like a runaway slave and a truant, now seeking with wine, now with sleep to deceive anxiety: in vain, for it presses and pursues you as a dark companion as you flee," 113–15). Freedom can thus only be achieved by an inner restoration, by achieving a state in which one ceases to run from oneself and returns to oneself, as Horace nicely puts it at *Epistles* 1.18.101: *quid te tibi reddat amicum* ("What returns you to a friend to yourself?"). This final accusation by Davus hits Horace a little too close to home, and the satire ends abruptly with an angry Horace threatening to pelt him with stones and ship him off to work on the Sabine farm (116–18).[7] If Horace cannot prove his inner self-mastery to Davus, he can at least reassert his literal mastery over his too outspoken slave.

The Horace of *Epistles* 1.1 is determined not to live up to Davus's accusations. He will not, like a *belua prava*, return to his chains, and, having been "manumitted" from Maecenas's service, he will try to master *res*, "things" or "circumstances," rather than be subjected to them (*Satires* 2.7.75; *Epistles* 1.1.19). Horace's declaration of independence in the first epistle in fact seems carefully designed to respond to *Satires* 2.7, but now it is Horace taking himself to task for these same faults and looking for solutions in philosophy. As Johnson has stated, "What seems . . . to illuminate best what Horace is struggling with in *Epistles* 1 . . . is the ferocious self-criticism of 2.7, where Davus, his slave, symbolizing both Horace's alter and his ideal ego, dissects the poet's character with a hatchet."[8] Yet despite the fact that Davus hits upon the faults of his master, he nevertheless fails to offer a sensible solution to them. For Davus, whose speech reveals that he too suffers from considerable flaws, the answer is to become a Stoic *sapiens* devoid of passions and unflustered by the vicissitudes of fortune:

> quisnam igitur liber? sapiens sibi qui imperiosus,
> quem neque pauperies neque mors neque vincula terrent,
> responsare cupidinibus, contemnere honores
> fortis, et in se ipso totus, teres atque rotundus,
> externi ne quid valeat per leve morari,
> in quem manca ruit semper fortuna. (83–88)

Who then is free? The wise man, who has full command of himself, whom neither poverty nor death nor chains terrify, who bravely withstands his desires and scorns honors, complete in himself, round and spherical, so that nothing external can stick to him on account of his smoothness, against whom fortune always rushes lame.

Davus's solution is very much like that of Damasippus, who, though he seems unlikely ever to achieve the level of *sapiens* himself, proclaims that the sage alone is free from madness:

> quem mala stultitia et quemcumque inscitia veri
> caecum agit, insanum Chrysippi porticus et grex
> autumat. haec populos, haec magnos formula reges,
> excepto sapiente, tenet. (2.3.43–46)

Whomever evil foolishness and ignorance of the truth drives in blindness, the Stoa and herd of Chrysippus says is insane. This principle applies to nations and great kings, all but the wise man.

For Damasippus and Davus the only path to freedom and sanity is to be found in the orthodoxies of Stoicism, in trying to attain an unattainable perfection, and there is no doubt that both Damasippus and Davus fall far short of this high standard. This is not a remedy that Horace will accept, and at the end of the first epistle he rejects the sage as unsuitable for providing the kind of answer he is seeking: *ad summam: sapiens uno minor est Iove, dives, / liber, honoratus, pulcher, rex denique regum, / praecipue sanus, nisi cum pituita molesta est* ("In short: the wise man is inferior to Jupiter alone. He is rich, free, honored, beautiful, finally a king of kings. He is above all sane/healthy, except when he has an annoying cold," 1.1.106–8). As Mayer states, "the perfection of the *sapiens* is ironically guyed in the final line as an unattainable ideal."[9] The solution Horace will propose will not be found in inflexible and uncompromising orthodoxy, but in adapting to every situation so as to remain consistent and true to his inner self in the face not only of his own inconsistencies but also of changing and uncontrollable external circumstances.

HORATIAN INCONSISTENCY AND DISEASE IN *EPISTLES* 1.1

The Horace of the opening lines of 1.1 expresses an unambiguous preference for withdrawal, disengagement, and freedom. His state of mind, he tells Maecenas, is not what it once was: *non eadem est . . . mens*, 4. How has Horace's mind changed, and why has this led him to isolate himself in the countryside to study ethics? I would like to turn now back to the first epistle and examine the ways in which Horace describes his troubled state of mind, which he figures as a disease that prompts him to search for a cure in philosophical contemplation.[10] This disease imagery runs throughout the first book of *Epistles* to express Horace's ambivalence. Despite his seemingly clear preference for separation from Maecenas and Rome in the opening of the first poem, it quickly becomes clear that his desires are far more complex than his initial self-portrait would have us believe. Horace is in fact torn between two worlds he constantly sets against one another that can be expressed through a series of antitheses or dilemmas: friendship versus seclusion, the city versus the country, poetry versus philosophy, freedom versus dependence, and fame versus anonymity. Since his desires vacillate between these conflicting spheres and since he cannot yet find a way to resolve or bridge them, he accuses himself of the same inconsistency with which Davus had charged him, and concludes, à la Damasippus, that he must be mad.

Horace hints at his poor state of mind near the beginning of the poem through an allusion to an earlier poetic *epistula*. *Epistles* 1.1.15–16, in addition to describing his adaptable philosophical technique, contains a clear allusion to Catullus 68a.11–14, in which Catullus writes to his friend Manlius and describes his own weak emotional state, which prohibits him from complying with Manlius's wish for him to send requested "gifts," *munera* (10).[11] Placement of the two passages side-by-side helps to bring out their shared language:

> sed tibi ne mea sint ignota incommoda, Manli,
>   neu me odisse putes *hospitis* officium,
> accipe quis *merser* fortunae *fluctibus* ipse,
>   ne amplius a misero dona beata petas. (Catullus 68a.11–14)

But so that my troubles may not be unknown to you, Manlius, and so that you do not think that I disregard the duty of a guest-friend, learn in what waves of fortune I myself am immersed, so that you may stop asking for happy gifts from a miserable man.

> quo me cumque rapit tempestas, deferor *hospes*.
> nunc agilis fio et *mersor* civilibus *undis*. (Horace, *Epistles* 1.1.15–16)

I am carried as a guest wherever the storm takes me. Now I become active and am immersed in the waves of civil life.

Both Woodman and Moles recognize the allusion to Catullus in Horace's lines, but its significance remains unexamined.[12] Catullus's troubles, *incommoda*, arise from the recent loss of his brother, whose death at sea has cast Catullus into a metaphorical sea of sorrows and has led him to withdraw from Rome to Verona (27–36). This loss has so affected Catullus that he can no longer take pleasure in the erotic and poetic pastimes that used to delight him: *multa satis lusi. non est dea nescia nostri / quae dulcem curis miscet amaritiem* ("I have had enough of lavish play. The goddess who mixes sweet bitterness with cares is not ignorant of me," 17–18).[13] Catullus's state of mind therefore prompts him to isolate himself and prevents him from complying with the wishes of a friend who desires poetic *munera* that require *ludus*. The situation in *Epistles* 1.1 is similar. Maecenas wants Horace to resume his previous poetic *ludus*, but Horace's state of mind bars him from doing so and requires him to remove himself to the countryside. Catullus's inability arises from his grief over his brother's death, while the reasons for Horace's state of mind are revealed only as the poem progresses.[14] The allusion does show, however, that Horace's withdrawal from Maecenas arises not simply from a newfound desire to be free but from a deeply troubled state of mind akin to the one Catullus experiences at the loss of his brother.

The last third of *Epistles* 1.1 focuses directly on Horace himself and elucidates his poor inner health as a product of uncontrollable inconsistency, a fault that he hypocritically criticizes in others. First, in lines 70–93 he takes the *populus Romanus* to task for their fickleness and is at pains to set himself apart from them, to voice his rejection of their vain and erratic opinions:

quodsi me populus Romanus forte roget, cur
non ut porticibus sic iudiciis fruar isdem
nec sequar aut fugiam quae diligit ipse vel odit:
olim quod volpes aegroto cauta leoni
respondit, referam: 'quia me vestigia terrent,
omnia te adversum spectantia, nulla retrorsum.'
belua multorum es capitum. nam quid sequar aut quem? (70–76)

But if by chance the Roman people should ask me why I do not share their judgments just as I share their colonnades and why I neither follow nor flee what they
themselves love or hate, I would respond what once upon a time the wary fox
answered to the sick lion: "Because the footprints scare me, they all are facing
towards you, none back." You are a beast with many heads. For what should I follow or whom?

At issue here is Horace's freedom from the populace, for he twice emphasizes
his refusal to follow them (*sequar*, 72 and 76), and the fable that he cites demonstrates how "following the herd irreversibly compromises independence of
judgment."[15] Above all, the populace is changeable, and nobody is consistent for
very long in the same pursuits: *idem eadem possunt horam durare probantes*?
("Are the same men able to persist in approving of the same things for an hour?"
82). The rich man rushes now to Baiae (83–85), now to Teanum (85–87), and the
married man wishes to be single, and the single married (87–89). Such men are
as changeable and unpredictable as a Proteus: *quo teneam voltus mutantem Pro-
tea nodo*? ("With what knot should I restrain the Proteas changing his faces?"
90). The poor man too is just as open to ridicule (*ride*, 91), for he is as inconstant as his wealthy counterpart (91–93). This whole passage complements the
opening of the poem, in which Horace refuses to be subjected to the judgments
of the *populus* like a gladiator awaiting their verdict (1.1.6). Such dependence on
the crowd is dangerous because their judgment is fickle and based on caprice.

Having criticized the populace for their contradictions, Horace then turns
around to reveal exactly the same quality in himself. Despite his refusal to follow the whims of the Roman people, his judgment seems no sounder than
theirs, and Horace's friendship with Maecenas lies at the heart of his troubles:

si curatus inaequali tonsore capillos
occurri, rides; si forte subucula pexae
trita subest tunicae vel si toga dissidet impar,
rides: quid? mea cum pugnat sententia secum,
quod petiit spernit, repetit quod nuper omisit,
aestuat et vitae disconvenit ordine toto,
diruit, aedificat, mutat quadrata rotundis?
insanire putas sollemnia me neque rides

nec medici credis nec curatoris egere
a praetore dati, rerum tutela mearum
cum sis et prave sectum stomacheris ob unguem
de te pendentis, te respicientis amici. (94–105)

If I have run to meet you when my hair has been tended to by an uneven barber,
you laugh; if by chance there is a worn out shirt beneath my brushed tunic, or
if my toga sits unevenly, you laugh. How do you react when my judgment fights
with itself, spurns what it has sought and seeks again what it has just given up,
when it vacillates and is inconsistent in its whole system of life, it destroys, it
builds, it changes square to round? You think that I am mad in the usual way, and
you do not laugh at me, nor do you think that I need a doctor or a caretaker given
by the praeter, although you are the guardian of my affairs and you grow angry
on account of the badly cut nail of a friend who depends on you and looks to you
for help.

Horace's mind is at war with itself in these lines, and he is suffering from an
intense changeability in his desires. As Mayer notes, Horace's wearing a new
tunic, *pexa tunica*, over a worn-out shirt is "a hint at the theme of hypocrisy," for
what is within does not match that which is without.[16] The medical terminology (*aestuat*, 99; *medici*, 102) figures this inconsistency and hypocrisy as a kind
of disease, and *insanire* (101) especially recalls Damasippus's criticisms in *Satires* 2.3. Whereas the opening of *Epistles* 1.1 shows us a Horace decidedly intent
on freedom, the final image we are left with in the poem is of a Horace who is
subject to desires that vacillate out of his control. Davus's charges appear to have
merit after all, and the claim to independence that opens the poem must now
be viewed with suspicion.[17]

Closely connected with Horace's poor mental state in these lines is his friendship with Maecenas, who laughs at his friend's outer appearance and does not
act to help him where he needs it most, within. Maecenas gets amusement out of
his friend's awkward appearance and goes so far as to grow annoyed (*stomacheris*, 104) when Horace's fingernails are poorly groomed, but he does not understand that Horace's outward disarray is a mirror of his inner turmoil.[18] Horace
very significantly no longer expresses freedom from Maecenas but dependence
on him (*de te pendentis*, 105). As Oliensis states, "the philosopher who earlier
claimed to be his own guardian (*me . . . tuter*, 13) here acknowledges, albeit with
a certain face-saving petulance, that he does after all need his patron's protection
(*tutela*, 103)."[19] Furthermore, while Horace had earlier claimed to have been
looked at enough (*spectatum*, 2), he now looks to Maecenas (*respicientis*, 105) for
help, and whereas he before was actively "caring" (*curo*, 11), he now confesses
to needing a "caregiver" (*curatoris*, 102). Finally, Horace's refusal to be laughed
at (*ridendus*, 9) is now undercut by Maecenas's laughter (*rides*, 95 and 97).[20] The

poem therefore opens and closes with two very different pictures of Horace: first he is independent and in need of no one's protection and patronage, but at the end he is subject to his own desires and dependent on Maecenas's friendship and help. The poem begs the question, which is the "real" Horace:[21] the defiantly independent one at the beginning, or the conflicted and inconsistent one at the end?

The self-portrait of *Epistles* 1.1.94–105 brings Horace's associations with slavery and the turmoil they cause him to the fore. Horace's description of himself as a bumbling buffoon in these lines emphasizes the social disparity between him and Maecenas and again places him in an almost servile relationship to his patron. His running to meet Maecenas (*occurri*, 95) is particularly telling, for a quickened gait or run was considered the mark of a slave and an indication that one lacked moderation.[22] As Oliensis has pointed out, this sort of bumbling behavior is typical of social inferiors toward their superiors, and Horace repeatedly describes himself in this way in the *Satires* to express deference toward Maecenas.[23] She draws on the sociolinguistic work of Brown and Levinson, who write, "In societies all over the world members of dominated groups or lower strata express deference to dominant members by bumbling, by the kinesics, prosodics and language of slow-wittedness or buffoonery."[24] The problem in *Epistles* 1.1, however, is that this submissive behavior is causing Horace great turmoil, and whenever he plays the buffoon for his superior Maecenas his "whole system of life" (*vitae . . . ordine toto*, 99) is turned upside down. He seems to make a thinly veiled warning to Maecenas that so long as such acts of deference are required their friendship will suffer. Horace's badly shorn hair and toga would furthermore evoke the costume of Roman freedmen, who shaved their heads upon being manumitted, at which time they were also endowed with the right to wear the toga.[25] The inelegant fit of the toga suggests that he is slightly uncomfortable in such a garment and unfamiliar with the proper way to wear it. This detail reveals his "servile" origins. The patron-client relationship between Horace and Maecenas has once again become unnervingly close to that of former master-freedman, and this description thus harkens back to his portrait of himself as a manumitted gladiator at the opening of the poem. At its core the anxiety described at the end of the first epistle is bound up with status and the suspicion that his association with this great man has made him somehow less than free. Interestingly, it is Maecenas whose help Horace really needs in navigating the ambiguity of his social position. Rather than help, Maecenas simply laughs at Horace's awkwardness, and Horace has no option but to withdraw from Maecenas and look for relief in isolation, away from the gaze of those who might ridicule him, as we see him do at the poem's beginning.

The strained relationship between Horace and Maecenas is further brought out by an allusion in these lines to *Satires* 1.3, where Horace criticizes those who focus on the exterior faults of friends rather than considering their inner character. In the satire he takes issue especially with the Stoic paradox that all faults are equal, a view that when applied to friendship, Horace suggests, leads ultimately to friendlessness and isolation (137–42). He describes a man who is a buffoon on the outside but whose talent and integrity outweigh those faults and make him worthy of friendship:[26]

> iracundior est paulo, minus aptus acutis
> naribus horum hominum; rideri possit eo quod
> rusticius tonso toga defluit et male laxus
> in pede calceus haeret: at est bonus, ut melior vir
> non alius quisquam, at tibi amicus, at ingenium ingens
> inculto latet hoc sub corpore. (29–34)

> He is a little too irascible, too little suited to the keen noses of today's men; he could be laughed at because he has a rustic haircut and his toga trails down and a loose shoe clings poorly to his foot. But he is a good man, there is none better; but he is your friend, and a great talent lies beneath his uncultivated body.

As Freudenburg has shown, given the correspondences between this passage and Horace's self-description in *Epistles* 1.1, the buffoon of *Satires* 1.3 describes none other than the satiric persona of Horace himself. Thus Maecenas in the satire is praised for his ability to look beyond the low social status of his friend to the heart of the man within, while Horace expresses deference to Maecenas's social standing by describing himself in this way. In the first epistle, however, Maecenas, far from considering what *latet sub corpora*, focuses his attention on Horace's outer faults, and in doing so does not live up to the ideals of friendship set up in *Satires* 1.3. Were he to act as Horace recommends in the satire, he would look beyond his friend's outer eccentricities and see that Horace is in need of help, that this friendship and the acts of deference it entails are causing him distress. Maecenas is so busy amusing himself with Horace's bumbling that he fails to see that what his friend needs is free rein to act independently.

Perhaps neither friend is fully living up to the ideals put forth in *Satires* 1.3, where Horace promotes mutual flexibility and forgiveness:

> amicus dulcis ut aequum est,
> cum mea conpenset vitiis bona, pluribus hisce—
> si modo plura mihi bona sunt—inclinet, amari
> si volet: hac lege in trutina ponetur eadem.
> qui, ne tuberibus propriis offendat amicum

postulat, ignoscet verrucis illius; aequum est
peccatis veniam poscentem reddere rursus. (69–75)

A sweet friend, as is fair, should weigh my good attributes against my faults and
tilt the scale toward[27] the former, which are in greater abundance—provided that
my good attributes *are* in greater abundance—if he desires to be loved. By this
agreement he will be placed on the same scale. Whoever asks that he not offend
his friend with his own boils should pardon the other's warts. It is fair that one
who wants pardon for his sins should render it in turn.

Forgiveness in friendship is here described as a two-way street in which each
party observes a kind of golden rule by treating his friend as he wishes to be
treated. As depicted in *Epistles* 1.1, the friendship of Horace and Maecenas is
failing to live up to this standard, for neither regards the other with moderation
and forgiveness. Maecenas cannot look past Horace's outer faults to provide him
the help he needs, while Horace responds in the extreme by withdrawing from
their friendship entirely and casting Maecenas as a would-be slave master. The
equilibrium between them must be restored. Horace will have to accept some
moderate (in)dependence vis-à-vis Maecenas rather than vacillate between extremes of freedom and slavery as he does in the opening poem, while Maecenas
will have to prioritize his friend's inner well-being and grant him the breathing
space in which to find this balance. This will be an ongoing struggle for both
throughout the collection. While Horace's vacillations and inconsistencies may
never be resolved completely, he can learn to live with them with greater equanimity by finding a way of controlling them rather than being controlled by
them and of thereby hitting upon a mean in his friendship with Maecenas
between the extremes of *libertas* and *servitus*.

Horatian Inconsistency and Hypocrisy in *Epistles* 1.8 and 1.15

Horace's sickness is a refrain that arises repeatedly in the book, which makes
its cure appear elusive and hard to find. Nowhere is his disease more prominently described than in *Epistles* 1.8, written to his friend Celsus Albinovanus.
The poem is directly addressed not to Celsus but to his Muse, an intermediary
between the two men, who act as foils for one another. Celsus is the *scriba Neronis*, and, as such, seems to have met with success, and Horace's challenge, as
Kilpatrick puts it, is "how to tell a friend not to let [this] success go to his head":
"Horace achieves his tact by allowing opprobrium to fall back on himself. He
makes himself the *exemplum*."[28] Rather than directly call Celsus's state of mind
into question, he first catalogues his own list of symptoms and then inquires as
to how Celsus is. If Celsus should answer that he is "well" (*recte*, 15), the Muse

should respond, *ut tu fortunam, sic nos, te, Celse, feremus* ("Just as you tolerate your fortune, Celsus, thus shall I tolerate you," 17). Horace may be suffering, but at least he recognizes his faults. Celsus, on the other hand, does not.

The bulk of the short poem is taken up with Horace's description of his own illness. He starts by telling Celsus that despite his best intentions he is far from reaching his ethical goals: *si quaeret quid agam, dic multa et pulcra minantem / vivere nec recte nec suaviter* ("If he asks how I am doing, say that, though I intend many beautiful things, I am living neither correctly nor sweetly," 3–4). The reasons for this have nothing to do with damage to his crops or herds but are entirely internal:

> . . . quia mente minus validus quam corpore toto
> nil audire velim, nil discere quod levet aegrum,
> fidis offendar medicis, irascar amicis
> cur me funesto properent arcere veterno;
> quae nocuere sequar, fugiam quae profore credam,
> Romae Tibur amem, ventosus Tibure Romam. (1.8.7–12)

> . . . because, less well in mind than in all my body, I want to hear nothing, to learn nothing that may alleviate my illness. I offend my trustworthy doctors, I grow angry at my friends because they hasten to protect me from deadly torpor. I pursue harmful things, and I flee what I think may help. At Rome I love Tibur, while at Tibur, fickle as the wind, I love Rome.

This illness causes him to react angrily and rashly toward the unspecified friends who are trying to help him. His spiritual disease above all leads him to be inconsistent and desirous of what he does not have. He is fickle (*ventosus*), a word that he will later use to describe the capriciousness of the *plebs* (*Epistles* 1.19.37). The self-criticism with which he concludes his list of symptoms echoes that leveled at him by Davus in *Satires* 2.7.28–29: *Romae rus optas, absentem rusticus urbem / tollis ad astra levis*, "At Rome you want the country, but when in the country you fickly raise the city to the stars." For Davus, Horace's inconsistent attitude toward the city and country is closely linked to his friendship with Maecenas, and we can assume that this close association is behind *Epistles* 1.8 as well. The city is where Maecenas is, and 1.7, the letter that immediately precedes 1.8, is a lengthy address from Horace to his powerful friend and patron. It is as though writing to Maecenas has rekindled his ambivalence, and the health that he claims to find in the countryside in the beginning of 1.7 has been undercut by his desire to see—or avoid—his urban friend.

In *Epistles* 1.15 Horace again presents himself as a creature of vacillating desires. Here his inconsistency is directed toward simple and lavish lifestyles, especially when it comes to food and wine, and it is of course proximity to a wealthy patron that enables one to dine on sumptuous fare. In the *Satires* Horace had repeatedly attributed to himself values of simplicity and sufficiency, values symbolized especially by plain food. For example, in *Satires* 1.6.114–18 Horace describes the unpretentious fare of his daily diet as well as the simple table from which he dines:

> inde domum me
> ad porri et ciceris refero laganique catinum;
> cena ministratur pueris tribus, et lapis albus
> pocula cum cyatho duo sustinet; adstat echinus
> vilis, cum patera gutus, Campana supellex.

> Then I take myself home to a plate of leeks, chickpeas, and simple flour pancake. Dinner is served by three slaves, and a white stone holds up two cups along with a ladle. A cheap salt-cellar sits nearby, and a jug with a saucer, equipment from Campania.

In *Satires* 2.6.63–64 Horace laments his absence from his Sabine farm and longs for rustic beans and greens: *o quando faba Pythagorae cognata simulque / uncta satis pingui ponentur holuscula lardo,* "o when will beans, the relatives of Pythagoras, and vegetables greasy with bacon fat be served?" In both *Satires* 1.6 and 2.6 this simple diet is cited as evidence for Horace's lack of ambition and essentially private lifestyle, but at the same time this is surely not how Horace dines every night. As Brown states, "Horace, as *convictor Maecenatis*, obviously did not spend all his evenings in the quiet domesticity described here."[29] In his claim to enjoy only plain fare, Horace is somewhat disingenuous, displaying a quality that Davus is at pains to reveal. As we have seen, he claims that Horace is only too happy to eat "carefree vegetables" (*securum holus, Satires* 2.7.30) when he has not been invited to dine out, but the moment he receives a dinner invitation from Maecenas he is only too eager to attend. In the fifteenth epistle Horace candidly owns up to this hypocrisy when it comes to food and drink.

In this poem he writes to his friend Vala to inquire about possible vacation destinations and asks about the fare that will be available in each. As in 1.1 and 1.8, Horace appears to suffer from an illness and takes this retreat on the advice of the imperial doctor Antonius Musa (3). He takes particular interest in the quality of wine and notes that when he leaves the countryside he likes to enjoy superior vintages:

> rure meo possum quidvis perferre patique:
> ad mare cum veni, generosum et lene requiro,
> quod curas abigat, quod cum spe divite manet
> in venas animumque meum, quod verba ministret,
> quod me Lucanae iuvenem commendet amicae. (17–21)

In the countryside I am able to endure and put up with anything. But when I
have come to the sea I require something superior and mellow that can drive away
cares and drip with rich hope into my veins and my spirit, which serves up words
and recommends me as though a youth to a Lucanian girlfriend.

Horace here exposes his earlier praise for simple food as dishonest. This is only
one side of his personality, and he is as likely to enjoy a glass of fine wine as he
is to drink from modest cups (cf. *Odes* 1.20.1–2: *vile potabis modicis Sabinum /
cantharis*). Such a wine can restore him to his youthful vigor, the loss of which
made him unsuitable for attending to Maecenas in *Epistles* 1.1.4.[30] Horace ends
the poem with a lengthy description of a certain Maenius, whom Damon refers
to as a "quintessential parasite"[31] and who displays the same inconsistency toward food as Horace does:

> hic ubi nequitiae fautoribus et timidis nil
> aut paulum abstulerat, patinas cenabat omasi
> vilis et agninae, tribus ursis quod satis esset,
> scilicet ut ventres lamna candente nepotum
> diceret urendos, correctus Bestius. idem,
> quidquid erat nactus praedae maioris, ubi omne
> verterat in fumum et cinerem, 'non hercule miror'
> aiebat 'si qui comedunt bona, cum sit obeso
> nil melius turdo, nil volva pulchrius ampla.' (33–41)

This man, when he had taken nothing or a little from those who approve of or
feared his wantonness, was dining on plates of tripe and cheap lamb, enough for
three bears, with the result that naturally he, a Bestius converted, said that the
bellies of spendthrifts should be burned with a white-hot blade. The same man,
whenever he had acquired better spoils, when he had turned it all into smoke and
ash used to say, "By Heracles I am not amazed at those who squander their goods,
since there is nothing better than a fat thrush, nothing more beautiful than a large
sow's womb.

The astonishing thing about Maenius is that the same man (*idem*, 37) can hold
such contradictory views, eating both cheap fare and delicacies with equal gusto
and changing his opinion to match his current meal. This seems to be the height
of hypocrisy and inconsistency, yet in the following lines Horace claims that he
is just like Maenius:

> nimirum hic ego sum; nam tuta et parvola laudo,
> cum res deficiunt, satis inter vilia fortis;
> verum ubi quid melius contingit et unctius, idem
> vos sapere et solos aio bene vivere, quorum
> conspicitur nitidis fundata pecunia villis. (42–46)

Of course I am just like him, for I praise small, safe things when my wealth is inadequate, sufficiently austere among cheap goods. But when something better and more luxurious befalls me, I, the same man, affirm that you alone are wise and live the good life whose well-established money is on display in gleaming villas.

Just like Maenius, Horace, though he remains the same man (*idem*, 44), can hold wildly contradictory views. To quote Damon, Horace's "moral ballast . . . has a distressing tendency to shift. But inconsistency is not the only thing he and Maenius share, for it is clear that he, like Maenius, is dependent on others for his access to luxury."[32] It is hard to imagine the Horace of the opening lines of *Epistles* 1.1 saying these lines; for him freedom in the countryside and independence from powerful *amici* is paramount. Yet the spiritually ailing Horace who closes the first poem prepares us for this later description, and it would seem that in the fifteenth epistle the inconsistent and hypocritical Horace has won out over the defiantly independent one of 1.1.1–9.

What then is the solution for such inconsistency, or does it, in the end, even need to be resolved? The opening pose of the collection is not one that Horace seems capable of maintaining, as it is too extreme and would force Horace to repress the very many desires he has that contradict his preference for withdrawal and isolation. The solution will be for Horace not to choose one extreme over another, but to find a way to accommodate both sides of his complex personality. In the fifteenth poem the fact that the same man (*idem*) can vacillate between such different ways of acting and thinking is, I suggested, evidence for hypocrisy and inconsistency, but it could be interpreted more positively. Through being able to adapt himself to different situations at different times, Horace can turn present circumstances to his advantage without destroying his inner consistency. Horace chooses his language carefully in 1.15 so as to emphasize that such circumstances are largely out of his control and that he does not actively seek out such delicacies from the rich; rather, they simply "befall" him (*contingit*, 44). He can make any situation suit himself and in doing so does not so much change his identity as adapt and define the present condition to suit his versatile persona. Inside, Horace remains the same man in every situation (*idem*). In the self-portrait that closes *Epistles* 1.15, we see Horace begin to think differently about his inconsistency, and he does not respond to it with the same anguish as he had in 1.1.94–105 and 1.8. Rather than see in it evidence for a profound spiritual sickness, he is moving closer to his Aristippean goal of adapting circumstances to himself rather than himself to circumstances: *mihi res, non me rebus, subiungere conor*, 1.1.19. By finding what suits him in each situation he does not have to choose between plain and fine fare. He can have both.

ADAPTABILITY AND *AEQUANIMITAS*

Horace hints already in the first epistle that adaptability is the key to his achieving equanimity and accepting his own contradictions. He concludes his list of the inconsistent behavior of the *populus Romanus* (82–93) with the exemplum of the poor man who tries to imitate the wealthy by renting a boat: *conducto navigio aeque / nauseat ac locuples, quem ducit priva triremis* ("In his hired ship he gets just as seasick as the wealthy man whom a private trireme transports," 92–93). McGann has suggested that Horace's use of *triremis* here points to a common source with Plutarch's *De Tranquilitate Animi* 466b–c, and his comments bear revisiting and expanding.[33] Plutarch uses the exemplum of the man who moves from one ship to another to illustrate the problem of discontent with one's present lot, and like Horace (1.1.87–89) he also cites the married and the unmarried:

ἀλλ' ὥσπερ οἱ δειλοὶ καὶ ναυτιῶντες ἐν τῷ πλεῖν, εἶτα ῥᾷον οἰόμενοι διάξειν ἐὰν εἰς γαῦλον ἐξ ἀκάτου καὶ πάλιν ἐὰν εἰς τριήρη μεταβῶσιν, οὐδὲν περαίνουσι τὴν χολὴν καὶ τὴν δειλίαν συμμεταφέροντες ἑαυτοῖς· οὕτως αἱ τῶν βίων ἀντιμεταλήψεις οὐκ ἐξαιροῦσι τῆς ψυχῆς τὰ λυποῦντα καὶ ταράττοντα· ταῦτα δ' ἐστὶν ἀπειρία πραγμάτων, ἀλογιστία, τὸ μὴ δύνασθαι μηδ' ἐπίστασθαι χρῆσθαι τοῖς παροῦσιν ὀρθῶς. ταῦτα καὶ πλουσίους χειμάζει καὶ πένητας, ταῦτα καὶ γεγαμηκότας ἀνιᾷ καὶ ἀγάμους· διὰ ταῦτα φεύγουσι τὴν ἀγοράν, εἶτα τὴν ἡσυχίαν οὐ φέρουσι, διὰ ταῦτα προαγωγὰς ἐν αὐλαῖς διώκουσι, καὶ παρελθόντες εὐθὺς βαρύνονται. (466b–c)

But just like cowards and those suffering from seasickness while sailing, who then think that they would pass the voyage more easily if they should change from a light vessel to a merchant ship and in turn to a trireme, they accomplish nothing, since they bring their bile and cowardice with them. In this way the partaking of different lifestyles does not remove from the soul the things that cause it grief and trouble: and these things are inexperience in affairs, thoughtlessness, and the inability and ignorance of how to make correct use of present circumstances. These are the things that distress, like a storm, both the rich and the poor; these things trouble both the married and the unmarried. On account of these things people avoid the *agora* and then do not endure their quiet; on account of these things men pursue promotions at court, and when they have acquired them immediately are distressed.

According to Plutarch, restlessness and inconsistency are the products of inexperience and the inability to deal rightly with the circumstances at hand, likened to boats of various sizes, while the ability to master one's present situation without distress constitutes εὐθυμία ("tranquility"), a concept that McGann connects to the Horatian *aequus animus*.[34] Equanimity allows one to adapt to any size boat in which one happens to find oneself at any given time and thus to master circumstances. Plutarch significantly a little later in the treatise puts forth Aristippus as an example of a man who was able to do just this:

> καὶ γὰρ οἱ πολλοὶ τὰ χρηστὰ καὶ πότιμα τῶν ἰδίων ὑπερβαίνοντες ἐπὶ τὰ δυσχερῆ
> καὶ μοχθηρὰ τρέχουσιν. ὁ δ᾽ Ἀρίστιππος οὐ τοιοῦτος, ἀλλ᾽ ἀγαθὸς ὥσπερ ἐπὶ
> ζυγοῦ πρὸς τὰ βελτίονα τῶν ὑποκειμένων ἐξαναφέρειν καὶ ἀνακουφίζειν αὐτόν.
> (469c)

> And indeed many men ignore the beneficial and pleasant aspects of their own
> situations and concentrate on what is wretched and annoying. Aristippus was not
> such a man, but he was good at rising up, as if on a scale, toward the better aspects
> of his circumstances and lightening himself.

As McGann suggests, "it is clear that the ability to remember his blessings which Aristippus showed is part of a general adaptability to circumstances,"[35] and Horace perfectly captures such Aristippean adaptability in 1.1.19: *et mihi res, non me rebus, subiungere conor*, "I try to subject things to myself, not myself to things." Attaining such adaptability will not so much free Horace from his inconsistent desires as allow him to conform contradictory circumstances and ways of life to himself without losing his consistent inner core. In other words, it will enable him to enjoy either a small boat or a trireme without being plunged into spiritual despair.

Another important parallel for *Epistles* 1.1.92–93, put forth by Kiessling and Heinze but too readily dismissed by McGann, is a fragment of Aristo of Chios, a third century B.C. Stoic philosopher:[36]

> κυβερνήτης μὲν οὔτε ἐν μεγάλῳ πλοίῳ οὔτε ἐν μικρῷ ναυτιάσει, οἱ δὲ ἄπειροι ἐν
> ἀμφοῖν. οὕτως ὁ μὲν πεπαιδευμένος καὶ ἐν πλούτῳ καὶ ἐν πενίᾳ οὐ ταράττεται,
> ὁ ἀπαίδευτος ἐν ἀμφοῖν. (*SVF* 1. 396)

> A helmsman will become seasick in neither a large nor small ship, but will be
> experienced in both. Likewise the one who has been trained in both wealth and
> poverty will not be troubled [by either], while the untrained [will be troubled] in
> both.

In this passage, experience in various extremes (small boat/big boat and wealth/poverty) enables one to cope with changes in fortune and varying situations. The ability to adapt allows one not necessarily to avoid extremes—as circumstances are often out of our control—but to deal with them more effectively by being prepared for them. Horace himself uses a nautical metaphor to say something very similar in the *aurea mediocritas* ode: *rebus angustis animosus atque / fortis appare; sapienter idem contrahes vento nimium secundo / turgida vela* ("In narrow circumstances appear strong and brave; likewise wisely draw back the sails swollen by too favorable a wind," *Odes* 2.10.21–24; cf. 1–4). Through wisdom (*sapienter*) a person can attain control over extreme situations (*rebus*) insofar as one can understand that they are temporary and prepare oneself for a reversal of fortune. For Horace such mastery of circumstances is at the heart of what it means to "love the golden mean," *auream . . . mediocritatem diligit* (2.10.5–6). As McGann points out, Aristo does not link the adaptability implicit in the above passage to the notion of inner consistency, but in a later passage from the second book of *Epistles* Horace himself does, connecting inner consistency, adaptability, and the mean with the metaphor of large and small boats:[37]

> ego, utrum
> nave ferar magna an parva, ferar unus et idem.
> non agimur tumidis velis Aquilone secundo,
> non tamen adversis aetatem ducimus austris,
> viribus, ingenio, specie, virtute, loco, re,
> extremi primorum, extremis usque priores. (*Epist.* 2.2.200–204)

> Whether I am carried on a large or small boat, I will be carried as one and the same person. I am not driven by swollen sails in a favorable north wind, nor, moreover, do I live my life in adverse south winds: in strength, talent, appearance, virtue, position, and wealth, [I am] behind the first, always ahead of the last.

This passage, especially Horace's claim to be in neither first nor last place perfectly illustrates the *aurea mediocritas*, and the key to achieving it is to adapt to shifting circumstances, thus maintaining inner consistency (*unus et idem*, 201) in the face of change. These lines present Horace as a successful Aristippean, and in *Epistes* 1.1 he carefully hints that this way of living holds the key to overcoming despair over his own inconsistency. Nevertheless, he is still trying (*conor*, 19) to master Aristippean adaptability and moderation. They are goals that he will both seek for himself and endorse for others over the course of the collection.

Horace's Return to the Schoolroom

As the first poem unfolds, two simultaneous roles emerge for Horace: those of student and teacher. For the remainder of this chapter I would like to consider in particular how Horace constructs the former role for himself in the opening poem.[38] We can thereby trace how Horace makes progress—despite frequent relapses—toward his ethical goals, all the while eschewing the perspective of a sage and instead adopting that of a gradual learner whose experience and even failures can ultimately lead to wisdom. Through Horace's missteps, lapses, and often slow progress he indicates how he and his reader together can learn how to master circumstances and attain equanimity.[39]

In order to relieve the malaise his inconsistency and troubled friendship cause him, Horace will have to relearn the basics of moral behavior, and he thus figures his turn to ethics in the first epistle as a return to the schoolroom.[40] This imagery is brought out by an extended allusion to *Satires* 1.1 in the opening lines of *Epistles* 1.1. Just after proclaiming in the first epistle that he is setting aside playthings (*ludicra*, 10) in pursuit of truth and decorum (*verum atque decens*, 11), so that he not become a laughingstock (*ridendus*, 9), Horace immediately casts doubts on his progress:

> ut nox longa quibus mentitur amica diesque
> lenta videtur opus debentibus, ut piger annus
> pupillis quos dura premit custodia matrum,
> sic mihi tarda fluunt ingrataque tempora quae spem
> consiliumque morantur agendi naviter id quod
> aeque pauperibus prodest, locupletibus aeque,
> aeque neglectum pueris senibusque nocebit.
> restat ut his ego me ipse regam solerque elementis. (20–27)

Just as the night seems long for those whom a girlfriend misleads, and the day protracted to those who work for hire,[41] just as the year seems slow for wards whom the harsh oversight of their mothers keeps in check; so for me the time flows by sluggish and unpleasant that delays my hope and plan of doing diligently what benefits the poor and the rich equally, and when neglected will harm the young and the old equally. It remains for me myself to rule and console myself with these ABCs.

Horace goes on to say that one must not put off ethical pursuits simply because one cannot achieve perfection (28–31) and concludes with a brief *sententia*: *est quadam prodire tenus, si non datur ultra* ("One can proceed up to a certain point, even if it is not granted to go farther," 32).[42] Throughout these passages from 1.1 Horace carefully picks up and transforms ideas found in the description of his serio-comic satirical method (*spoudogeloion*) in *Satires* 1.1:

> praeterea ne sic ut qui iocularia ridens
> percurram: quamquam ridentem dicere verum
> quid vetat? ut pueris olim dant crustula blandi
> doctores, elementa velint ut discere prima:
> sed tamen amoto quaeramus seria ludo. (23–27)

Furthermore, so that I do not rush through these things while laughing, like someone rushing through jokes: although what prohibits someone from telling the truth while laughing, as when coaxing teachers give cookies to boys so that they will be willing to learn their first ABCs? But nevertheless let us put play aside and inquire after serious things.

Here Horace's claim temporarily to set aside playfulness (*ludo*, 27) in order to seek serious matters (*seria*, 27) anticipates his similar assertion in *Epistles* 1.1 that he sets aside *ludicra* (10; cf. *ludo*, 3) in favor of ethical topics. This echo of *Satires* 1.1.27 in *Epistles* 1.1.10 simultaneously recalls Horace's satiric method and sets the *Epistles* apart from it by suggesting that, whereas humor is only temporarily suspended in the satire, it is less prominent in the *Epistles*. Furthermore, while it is Horace in the satire who laughs at the moral faults of others (*ridens*, 23; *ridentem*, 24), in the epistle he wants to avoid becoming a laughingstock himself (*ridendus*, 9); in other words, Horace presents himself not as the source but as the potential target of ethical criticism. Whereas in the satire he claims the authority to teach the truth (*verum*, 24) and *elementa* (27), in the epistle he instead proposes to learn the truth (*verum*, 11) and *elementa* (27).[43] In the terms of the simile from *Satires* 1.1 above, the epistolary Horace seems analogous to the student learning the ABCs of ethical life rather than the teacher offering cookies.[44] As we shall see, however, the Horace of the *Epistles* can be best understood as playing both roles, and in line 27 his dual role as teacher and student is nicely illustrated in line 12, where he claims to store up ethical lessons for later use in addressing others: *condo et compono quae mox depromere possim* ("I am gathering and storing up things which I may soon be able to bring out," 12). This "storing up" and "bringing out" of ethical lessons correspond to the roles of student and teacher that Horace will play.

School imagery is especially prominent in *Epistles* 1.1.52–60, where Horace criticizes the young and old men who sit in attendance in the corrupt classroom of Janus, who teaches that money is more important than virtue:

> vilius argentum est auro, virtutibus aurum.
> 'o cives, cives, quaerenda pecunia primum est;
> virtus post nummos': haec Ianus summus ab imo
> prodocet, haec recinunt iuvenes dictata senesque
> laevo suspensi loculos tabulamque lacerto.
> est animus tibi, sunt mores, est lingua fidesque,
> sed quadringentis sex septem milia desunt:
> plebs eris. at pueri ludentes: 'rex eris' aiunt,
> 'si recte facies.' (52–60)

Silver is cheaper than gold, gold cheaper than virtue. "O citizens, citizens, first money must be sought; virtue after cash!" Janus teaches these things from top to bottom, and the young men and old chant back these things that have been dictated to them, with their knapsacks and slate hung over their left arm. You have a mind, you have character, eloquence and trustworthiness, but you fall a few thousand short of the required 400,000: you will be a plebeian. But boys while they play say, "you will be a king if you act rightly."

Whereas earlier Horace had described himself as a man too old for the poetry of *ludus* (4–10), he now aligns himself with children at play (*pueri ludentes*, 59), who have not yet been corrupted and so understand what should be self-evident moral principles. *Ludus* is thus transformed from a negative attribute of his prior poetry and the public sports arena into a positive idea that connotes rejuvenation and the schoolroom. As Oliensis states, "Horace is indeed returning to the *ludus*—not Maecenas's gladiatorial school, but the *ludus litterarum* or 'elementary school' of his own verse letters."[45]

In contrast to these uncorrupted children are the *iuvenes . . . senesque* of Janus's schoolroom (54–56), whom Horace describes by repeating a line from *Satires* 1.6.74: *laevo suspensi loculos tabulamque lacerto* (*Epist.* 1.1.56).[46] In the satire the line describes the boys who attend the regional school of Flavius, to which Horace's father refuses to send his son, enrolling him instead in a prestigious school at Rome and taking charge himself of his son's moral education. The repetition of this line in the epistle reminds us of Horace's early education and signals that he is re-enrolling, not in the gladiatorial *ludus* of Maecenas, but in the moral *ludus* in which his father first enlisted him. Just as Horace contrasts the schooling provided by his father with that at the *Flavi ludus*, in the epistle too he differentiates his education from that offered by Janus in Rome's financial district. These corrupt students are criticized not just because they study immoral lessons but also because they unquestioningly recite back the lessons that have been taught to them by their schoolmaster (*recinunt . . . dictata*, 55). Such recitation stifles free thought, and by slavishly repeating the words of others these men contrast with the independent Horace of line 14 who refuses to swear on the words of a philosophical *magister*. Horace's insistence on educational freedom is stated emphatically in line 27: *his ego me ipse regam . . . elementis* ("I myself will rule myself with these ABCs"). Following the dictates of a teacher would undermine the self-sufficiency and autonomy that Horace the student demands. This independence allows Horace to view the teachings of others with a critical eye before distilling them for others. In the epistolary schoolroom, therefore, Horace's curriculum will be marked by the same freedom that he declares for himself in the poem's opening lines.

One of Horace's primary goals as a student of ethics is to put his newfound wisdom to use as a teacher of them, a role I trace in my next two chapters. He never claims, however, to have achieved perfection in his chosen subject, and his level of expertise varies from one poem to another. Sometimes he stumbles as he proceeds, sometimes he is only slightly more advanced than his addressee, sometimes he approaches the full authority of a didactic master, and sometimes he casts doubt on his teachings even as they leave his pen.[47] The recipients of his verse letters often suffer from the same sorts of spiritual faults as Horace

himself—shifting inconsistencies and a tendency toward inflexible extremes—
and Horace offers himself up as a realistic and pragmatic model for how to proceed toward a sounder and happier way of life. He becomes a guide through
whom his addressees and readers, by tracing his rocky progress, can also attain
to spiritual and mental well-being. As Horace outlines to his students the path
toward equanimity and adaptability, he himself gradually learns these lessons as
well and applies them to his own shifting desires and circumstances. Teaching
others is often a necessary step in Horace's self-education. To quote Seneca the
Younger, *homines dum docent discunt*, "men, while they teach, learn" (*Epist.* 7.8).

3

Horace the Teacher
Poetry and Philosophy in *Epistles* 1.1 and 1.2

WE SAW IN THE PREVIOUS CHAPTER how Horace casts himself as a student in the opening poem, and in this chapter I address how he constructs a complementary role for himself, that of teacher, focusing especially on how Horace formulates the relationship between poetry and philosophy in the first two epistles. I begin by looking briefly at a section of 1.1 in which he promises his reader the same kind of spiritual restoration that he himself hopes to find, but for his reader this will be achieved through reading the quasi-magical words of Horace's own epistolary book. Horace thereby attributes to his poetry the same medicinal charm that had been usurped from it by philosophy. In *Epistles* 1.2, which takes up the bulk of the chapter, Horace combines this charm with another of poetry's traditional attributes that had been appropriated by philosophers, especially the Epicureans: that of moral education. Though he draws extensively on philosophical topics in the *Epistles*, he prioritizes the poet over the philosopher as a *teacher* of moral truths. The primary virtue the poet has over the orthodox philosopher is his freedom to pick and choose from a wide range of systems in order to construct his own unique ethical program.   Lucretius?!

VERBA ET VOCES: HORACE THE TEACHER IN EPISTLES 1.1

In the first epistle Horace clearly aligns his own process of moral study with that of his reader, who he imagines is suffering from a spiritual ailment similar to his own:

> fervet avaritia miseroque cupidine pectus:
> sunt verba et voces, quibus hunc lenire dolorem
> possis et magnam morbi deponere partem.
> laudis amore tumes: sunt certa piacula, quae te

ter pure lecto poterunt recreare libello.
invidus, iracundus, iners, vinosus, amator,
nemo adeo ferus est, ut non mitescere possit,
si modo culturae patientem commodet aurem. (33–40)

The heart seethes with greed and wretched desire: there are words and voices with
which you can alleviate this pain and get rid of a great part of the sickness. Are you
swelling with love of praise? There are certain expiatory rites that can heal you if
you read the little book three times in a ritually pure fashion. A person who is
envious, prone to anger, indolent, an inebriate, love-sick—no one is so wild that
he cannot be tamed, if only he lend a patient ear to training.

These lines are loaded with imagery of disease and healing: *fervet, lenire, dolorem,
morbi, tumes, recreare*. Horace envisions the "you" of these lines, his reader, as
someone in need of the same cure for which he himself is searching, and he
especially connects himself with his reader by alluding to the ears of both. In
line 7 he had drawn attention to his own "cleansed ear," *purgatam . . . aurem*,
which, as I argued in chapter 1, is open to the advice of his Socratic *daimonion*,
and now he urges his reader to have similarly receptive ears (40). This need for
the addressee to pay attention is furthermore a common feature of didactic
poetry, particularly that of Lucretius, who again and again urges Memmius to
have attentive ears.[1] Throughout this chapter we will see Horace repeatedly
mention receptive and non-receptive ears, thereby aligning himself with the
role of didactic *praeceptor*.

   The cure in *Epistles* 1.1, moreover, seems to have magical associations: the
expiatory rites (*piacula*), the words and voices (*verba et voces*), the number
three (*ter*), and the emphasis on ritual purity (*pure*) all evoke magic ritual.[2] The
libellus of line 37 also had a role in magic, for it would have contained the words
of spells. Harrison has suggested that the medicinal imagery of these lines
alludes to the longstanding "idea that philosophy is a cure for the soul just as
medicine is a cure for the body."[3] Horace in this case would be urging his reader
to turn to philosophy with him in search of a cure. Magic and enchantment,
however, were originally associated not with philosophy but with poetry, and
it was poetry's ability to enchant its listeners that philosophers routinely cited
as dangerous. The Platonic Socrates, for example, frequently faults poetry for
its dangerous potential. As Belfiore suggests, "Plato often uses the vocabulary
of magic (for example, *goes, goeteia, kelesis*, and their cognates), spells (*epodai*),
and drugs (*pharmaka*) to condemn an enemy."[4] Among the chief offenders who
are guilty of misusing the seductive charm of language are the poets, whose
destructive magical power Plato repeatedly attacks.[5]

   At the same time that he criticizes poetry's enchanting power, Plato's Socrates
himself is repeatedly described with the language of magic. He is a sorcerer

who, when rational argumentation fails, can seduce his audience into having correct opinions.[6] Socrates thus usurps from the poets what he considers a dangerous weapon and repurposes it as a tool for his own philosophy to win over his interlocutors where reason cannot. Horace's *verba et voces* seem especially to allude to a passage of Plato's *Charmides* in which Socrates tells Charmides that he has learned a certain charm, *epode*, from a Thracian doctor that can engender *sophrosyne* into the soul and thereby relieve both physical and spiritual ailments:[7]

θεραπεύεσθαι δὲ τὴν ψυχὴν ἔφη, ὦ μακάριε, ἐπῳδαῖς τισιν, τὰς δ᾽ ἐπῳδὰς ταύτας τοὺς λόγους εἶναι τοὺς καλούς· ἐκ δὲ τῶν τοιούτων λόγων ἐν ταῖς ψυχαῖς σωφροσύνην ἐγγίγνεσθαι, ἧς ἐγγενομένης καὶ παρούσης ῥᾴδιον ἤδη εἶναι τὴν ὑγίειαν καὶ τῇ κεφαλῇ καὶ τῷ ἄλλῳ σώματι πορίζειν. (157a)

"And the treatment of the soul," he said, dear friend, "is by certain charms, and these charms are beautiful words: and by such words temperance is created in the soul, and when it has been created and is present it is easy to furnish health to the head and the rest of the body."

At the conclusion of the dialogue Charmides states that the charm he really needs is Socrates himself (176b). As Vorwerk states, "We can see that Charmides considers the conversation with Socrates to be a charm, a beautiful speech that renders his soul *sophron*."[8] Horace's allusion to the *Charmides* reveals that his reader too should look for such a charm, through which his soul may be healed and instructed.

The question remains as to whose *verba* and which *libellus* it is that Horace has in mind as being able to perform such a magical rite. Mayer suggests that, though the *libellus* is the booklet of spells used in propitiatory rites, the word also points to other books generally and that Horace "may be hinting at the Epicureans' reliance on tracts."[9] Armstrong develops the latter suggestion and argues that Horace alludes "to the specially Epicurean habit of memorizing things."[10] If Horace's *libellus* refers to works of philosophy, then he holds himself and his reader to two different standards. He encourages his reader to read, repeat, and memorize certain philosophical *verba* (34), while he himself is free from slavishly repeating the words of a philosophical master (*verba magistri*, 14). Horace therefore would be advising his reader to do something that compromises his *libertas*. Harrison hints at what I believe is closer to the mark: "*lecto . . . libello* points to the surprise and the intentional ambiguity—the illness is one of the spirit, and its cure is a book, a text of philosophy, perhaps the very one which the poet is writing. The reader is being encouraged to read on in hope of a cure."[11] The *libellus* that Horace encourages his readers to read and reread is the very book they currently hold in their hands, the *Epistles*, a book of poetry that draws on the teachings of philosophy. Horace the poet is therefore a sort of intermediary between the *Socraticae chartae*, which he scours for ethical subject matter (*AP* 310), and the reader whose soul is suffering. It is Horace who will weave together a seductive poetic song and infuse it with healing power in order to cure not only his own spirit but his reader's as well. In doing so Horace turns the method of Plato's Socrates on its head. He reclaims the "magic" of traditional poetry from Socrates and attributes to his verse the same power to charm and teach that Plato ascribes to Socratic dialogue. Whereas Plato had harnessed the power of traditional poetic magic for his philosophical program, Horace exploits the teachings of philosophy in the service of his poetic goals, in the hope that his seductive poetry will not harm but heal its listeners. The poet who refuses to repeat the words of a philosophical master therefore puts himself forth as a *magister* whose *verba et voces* can be read again and again and, in being read, can heal.

Horace Reads Homer: *Epistles* 1.2

It is not only from philosophy that Horace draws his ethical subject matter in the *Epistles*, for the poetic tradition also offers abundant educational material that he can rework to fit his own particular ethical teachings, and his reading of Homer in 1.2 demonstrates well how he freely adapts his source material, whether poetic or philosophical, in accordance with the technique outlined at *Epistles* 1.1.13–19.[12] In *Epistles* 1.2, Horace continues to reclaim for the poet the healing and educational functions that had been usurped by philosophy, and in this poem Horace again takes on the dual roles of student and teacher. It is because of the independence the poet enjoys over the orthodox philosopher that he ultimately proves to be the more effective didactic guide. Independence, adaptability, and freedom from philosophical orthodoxy are in fact the principal lessons that Horace draws out of the Homeric epics, and his reading of these poems illustrates well how Horace puts his own individual stamp on traditional material. In *Epistles* 1.2 Horace furthermore figures poetry as a wine or elixir that has the potential to heal moral and ethical failings, and this imagery runs throughout not just this poem but the collection as a whole and anticipates well-known passages from the *Ars Poetica* and *Epistles* 2.1 in which the educational role of the poet is central.

Homeric *utilitas* and *planitas*

Horace begins the second epistle by saying that Homer is a better moral teacher than the professional philosophers Chrysippus, a Stoic, and Crantor, an Academic.[13] Although Horace does not explicitly mention any Epicurean by name, his attribution of clarity and utility to Homer conflicts in particular with the

Epicureans, who had criticized Homer's morality and the dangerous seduc-
tiveness of his poetry when used in traditional education. Horace's reading of
Homer recalls and challenges especially the Epicurean philosopher Philodemus, to whose treatise *On the Good King According to Homer* Horace alludes, I
argue, in order to counter the idea that Homer is beneficial only when explicated
by a philosopher.[14] It was of course Lucretius who had most recently bridged
the gap between poetry and orthodox Epicurean philosophy, and Horace adopts
imagery from Lucretius not only to emphasize the beneficial aspects of poetry
but also to counter Lucretius's belief that such poetry is instructive only when
it has a firmly orthodox philosophical foundation. Lucretius uses liquid and
medicinal imagery throughout the *De Rerum Natura* to illustrate the healing
and edifying powers of Epicureanism, and Horace uses just such imagery to
attribute these same powers to Homer's poetry as well as his own.

Apart from Maecenas, Lollius Maximus is the only addressee of more than
one poem in the collection: 1.2 and 1.18. Little is known about his career, but he
is perhaps the son of the Marcus Lollius to whom Horace dedicates *Odes* 4.9 and
who was consul in 21 B.C., the year before the publication of *Epistles* 1.[15] *Epistles*
1.2 falls roughly into two halves: in lines 1–31 Horace gives an interpretation of
the *Iliad* (6–16) and *Odyssey* (17–31), citing the good and bad exempla found in
each, and in lines 32–71 he addresses Lollius directly and encourages his young
friend to devote himself to moral study. The poem's placement in the book is
significant. As we have seen, in the first epistle Horace tells Maecenas not to
expect him to resume his light, playful poetry, for he is now devoting himself to
serious ethical study (1–12), and by the end of 1.1 it becomes clear that Horace
turns to ethics because he himself is experiencing a spiritual sickness arising
from his inconsistency and ambivalent desires (94–105). Horace therefore under-
goes a metaphorical return to the schoolroom to learn the ABCs of moral behavior (*elementis*, 27). Rather than turn to a book of philosophy for instruction, as
one might expect, Horace begins his study in *Epistles* 1.2 with Homer, as would
any young boy embarking on his education.[16] In 1.2, the elder "schoolboy" Horace in turn invites his young friend, now studying rhetoric, to return to the elementary schoolroom with him in order to relearn the basics of moral behavior.

In the opening lines of 1.2, Horace contrasts his current schooling with that
of Lollius. While Lollius studies declamation in the city, he has been rereading
the *Iliad* and *Odyssey* in the countryside:

Troiani belli scriptorem, Maxime Lolli,
dum tu declamas Romae, Praeneste relegi;
qui, quid sit pulchrum, quid turpe, quid utile, quid non,
planius ac melius Chrysippo et Crantore dicit.
cur ita crediderim, nisi quid te detinet, audi. (1–5)

While you, Lollius Maximus, declaim at Rome, in Praeneste I have reread the
writer of the Trojan War, who says what is beautiful, what foul, what useful, what
not, more clearly and better than Chrysippus and Crantor. Hear why I think this,
unless something detains you.

Horace resumes in these lines the antithesis between city and country that
opens the collection in *Epistles* 1.1. As in the opening poem, Horace's retirement
in the countryside aligns him with private life, while his addressee, whose study
of declamation indicates that he is about to embark on a political career, occupies the public sphere. But rather than make a contrast between himself and
Lollius, as he does between himself and Maecenas in 1.1, Horace suggests that
both he and Lollius, despite their differences, have moral insights to gain from
rereading the Homeric epics. The lessons that these epics teach are equally relevant to the private middle-aged Horace in the country and the public young
Lollius in Rome.

In these opening lines, as Mayer suggests, Horace reveals that his allegiance
in the longstanding debate between philosophy and poetry as to which is the
better moral guide is with the poets,[17] and his defense of Homeric utility is emphasized by the repetition of *utile* in lines 3 and 18 of the poem. Both McGann
and Kilpatrick suggest that Horace's use of *pulchrum* and *utile* (3) points to the
influence on the *Epistles* of the Stoic and Academic schools and especially of
the moderated Stoicism of Panaetius as communicated in Cicero's *De Officiis*.[18]
In using these key terms *against* representatives of the Stoic (Chrysippus) and
Academic (Crantor) schools, however, Horace implies that the Homeric epics
reveal more about these key concepts than these philosophies. Whereas Horace
can quickly dismiss these Stoic and Academic philosophers, his refutation of
Epicurean attitudes toward Homer and poetic moral utility is more sustained
and implicit throughout the poem.[19]

Armstrong has recently taken a different approach to the poem, arguing
that Horace's philosophical thought in it and *Epistles* 1 as a whole is deeply Epicurean.[20] He cites as evidence of Horace's Epicurean allegiances the fact that
Horace does not openly mention an Epicurean philosopher by name in these
opening lines of 1.2, as he does Chrysippus and Crantor.[21] Horace implicitly includes the Epicureans in his critique, however, by the very attribution to Homer
of *planitas* and *utilitas*, which specifically recalls Epicurean criticisms of his
poetry. Epicurus's condemnation of Homer, as Asmis has persuasively shown,
involves his use in the traditional education curriculum.[22] As she states: "Epicurus believed that the whole traditional educational system, with its teaching of
Homer and other poets, was a corrupting influence that prevented a person from
achieving happiness. . . . Epicurus aimed to replace . . . education with Epicurean

philosophy."[23] According to the Epicureans, Homeric poetry was harmful not only because, in running counter to Epicurean philosophy, it was fundamentally in error, but also because poetry itself provided a "destructive lure of myths" that entices us away from true knowledge.[24] Diogenes Laertius (10.6) reports that Epicurus urged his friend Pythocles to avoid traditional education as though sailing away from it in a boat (παιδείαν δὲ πᾶσαν, μακάριε, φεῦγε τἀκάτιον ἀράμενος), and Plutarch explicitly connects this Epicurean boat to the avoidance of listening to the Siren-song of poetry.[25] Because poetic language can obscure any potentially beneficial passage, Epicurus urged his followers to use prose rather than poetry for formal instruction because of its greater clarity.[26] The Epicurean Philodemus, who was writing in Horace's own lifetime and associated with Vergil, among others,[27] also promoted the clear style of prose for communicating philosophy.[28] While Philodemus did write playful epigrams that drew on a range of philosophical ideas and schools, his orthodox Epicurean treatises are all written in prose.[29] Horace's use of *planius* (4) to describe Homer's poetry is therefore quite pointed, and with it he rejects the Epicurean view that poetry lacks clarity and that this limits its educational validity.

Lucretius is an obvious exception to the Epicurean belief that poetry obscures what prose can say straightforwardly, for he frequently describes his own poetry as shining *claritas* and *planitas* on obscure philosophical matters. Lucretius links these two concepts at 4.777–78: *multaque in his rebus quaeruntur multaque nobis / clarandumst, plane si res exponere avemus* ("And in these matters many things demand explanation, and we must make many things clear, if we want to expound things plainly").[30] Gale has shown that the reasons for Lucretius's clarity are twofold: his poetry casts light on the difficult concepts found in Epicureanism, while Epicurus himself is said to have enlightened the ignorant minds of man by lifting them from darkness and ignorance to clarity and truth.[31] The philosophy and the poetic form thus work together to produce clear thought and moral benefit. While Lucretius rejects the notion that poetry *necessarily* has an obscuring effect, he still is highly critical of traditional epic poets, including Homer and Ennius (1.117–26). The closest he comes to unambiguous praise of a previous poet is in his eulogy of Empedocles, whose songs expound *praeclara reperta* ("clear discoveries," 1.732), even though they are in error because they do not rest on a true philosophical foundation.[32] Horace follows Lucretius in denying that poems are necessarily obscure and harmful, but he implicitly rejects the idea that moral benefit can only arise from philosophical orthodoxy. This is not to suggest that Horace is less concerned than Lucretius with poetry's ability to instruct; rather, he reasserts the educational role of Homer and assigns to him the same power of illumination that Lucretius finds in Epicurus. Horace's engagement with both Philodemus and Lucretius will continue throughout the poem.

Horace's Advocacy of Morally Useful Poetry

Horace's best-known advocacy of the moral utility of poetry comes in the *Ars Poetica*. In lines 333–34 Horace reviews the differing goals of poets, saying that some want to benefit (*prodesse*, 333), others to please (*delectare*, 333), and some want to say things that are both pleasant and helpful for life (*simul et iucunda et idonea dicere vitae*, 334). Horace thereupon states that the best poet is the one who does both: *omne tulit punctum qui miscuit utile dulci, / lectorem delectando pariterque monendo* ("he wins each vote who has blended together utility with pleasure/sweetness, by delighting and advising the reader equally," 343–44). Thus poetry does not necessarily have to benefit its listeners, but the *best* poetry will do so, and it will combine this utility with the pleasure that to Epicurus and Philodemus risks distracting us from its moral message.[33] Philodemus's belief is that if a poem's content contains any benefit, this benefit is incidental and, more often than not, the words actually prove harmful.[34] Therefore, poems as poems (καθ[ὸ] π[ο]ήματ)[35] are not morally useful and should not be judged good or bad on the basis of their moral content. Many good poems, furthermore, are excellent in quality even though they do not provide moral instruction, and the wise man is able to derive pleasure from listening to such poems without moral harm because he has been properly trained in Epicureanism. It ultimately belongs to the philosopher to uncover what content is morally useful and what is not.[36] Unlike Philodemus, Horace in the *Ars Poetica* clearly promotes utility as a criterion of a good poem and does not suggest that a philosopher is needed to explicate a poem's moral content. Rather, it is the poet who best distills for young and old the teachings of philosophers, a belief that effectively reverses the Epicurean position: *scribendi recte sapere est et principium et fons: / rem tibi Socraticae poterunt ostendere chartae, verbaque provisam rem non invita sequentur*, "The origin and font of writing well is to be wise. Socratic writings can show subject matter to you, and words willingly will follow subject matter that has been provided," 309–11.

The nearest Philodemus comes to assigning morally useful content to a poet is in *On the Good King According to Homer*, and this text has been put forth by Gigante and Armstrong as the model for Horace's interpretation of Homer in *Epistles* 1.2.[37] In this treatise Philodemus elucidates for his patron Piso examples of good and bad kingship in the Homeric poems as "starting points for correction" (ἀφορμαί εἰς ἐπανόρθωσιν).[38] In pointing out beneficial exempla from Homer, Philodemus does not contradict his ideas about poetic utility; he recognizes that the text of a poem may be useful, but only when elucidated by a philosopher. Philodemus in *On the Good King* certainly does not suggest that the whole of the *Iliad* and *Odyssey* are useful. Elsewhere, in fact, he falls in line with the philosophical attacks against Homer that accuse him of impiety and moral harm.[39] As Armstrong states, "The poet is not morally useful *as a poet* and not useful at all until the philosopher points out how he should be read."[40]

I find it convincing that Horace alludes to Philodemus's text in *Epistles* 1.2 and would suggest that he does this not so much to align himself with Philodemus's philosophical reading of Homer, as Armstrong argues, as to draw attention to his participation in the debate over moral utility. Horace's description of Nestor clearly echoes Philodemus's text:

> . . . Nestor componere lites
> inter Peliden festinat et inter Atriden (*Epist.* 1.2.11–12)

> Nestor rushes to settle the quarrels between the son of Peleus and the son of Atreus.

> καὶ τὸν Νέστορα παρεισ[ά-
> γων σπε[ύδ]οντα λύειν τὴν
> στάσιν κὰ[ν τ]οῖς πρὸς Ἀγ[α]μέ-
> μνονα (*On the Good King* col. 28.27–30)

> . . . and introducing Nestor as eager to resolve discord in the disputes with Agamemnon.[41]

While Nestor is cited here as a positive exemplum from the *Iliad*, it is Odysseus, Horace tells us, who furnishes the *Odyssey* with an *utile exemplar* (18). The repeated coupling of Nestor and Odysseus as positive exempla in *On the Good King* could have influenced Horace's interpretation.[42] Armstrong argues that Horace's rereading of the Homeric epics is "exactly the style" of that of Philodemus.[43] In other words, Horace himself would be acting as a philosophical teacher to Lollius, and Homer remains morally harmful unless read with such guidance. However, Horace is not, like Philodemus, a professional philosopher. He is a poet claiming that another poet, the very one about whom the old debate between philosophy and poetry started, is a useful moral guide both for himself and his addressee. The opening words of the poem, *Troiani belli scriptorem*, place Homer in the poem's emphatic primary position. However much steeped in and influenced by Epicureanism—or any other formal school—Horace is, making him an adherent to one system runs counter to his profession of lack of orthodoxy in the opening poem: *ac ne forte roges, quo me duce, quo lare tuter: / nullius addictus iurare in verba magistri* ("and lest by chance you ask under which leader, in which house I take shelter, I am bound to swear on the words of no master," 13–14). A second important objection to the argument that Horace acts as a philosophical teacher in the vein of Philodemus is that in the previous poem, as we have seen, Horace has adopted a persona far from that of the philosophical *sapiens*; he reads Homer not as a sage but as a student who is spiritually sick and in need of the guidance such poetry offers. In the epistle Homer takes pride of place above Horace, whereas in Philodemus the philosopher is superior. Horace offers a protreptic to his young friend to follow his lead in rereading Homer, and he offers his own insights into the moral teachings of the epics, but he is clearly in need of such lessons himself. He urges Lollius not to be his follower but his fellow-traveler on the path of wisdom, in which pursuit Lollius might surpass or lag behind his friend: *quodsi cessas aut strenuus anteis, / nec tardum opperior nec praecentibus insto,* "But if you lag or zealously go ahead of me, I neither wait for the slow nor rush to catch up with those in front," (70–71).

In *Epistles* 1.2, Horace finds utility in Homer's poetry particularly in his use of positive and negative exempla, which of course were an important didactic tool in Roman education.[44] Achilles and Agamemnon, for example, are put forth as negative examples of *ira* (13), while Odysseus is put forth as an *utile exemplar* (18) of wisdom and virtue. This emphasis on exempla looks ahead to *Epistles* 2.1, addressed to Augustus, in which Horace lists the various ways in which poets benefit the state (*utilis urbi*, 124) and cites especially their instruction of the young through *nota exempla*:

> os tenerum pueri balbumque poeta figurat,
> torquet ab obscenis iam nunc sermonibus aurem,
> mox etiam pectus praeceptis format amicis,
> asperitatis et invidiae corrector et irae;
> recte facta refert, orientia tempora *notis*
> instruit *exemplis*, inopem solatur et aegrum. (126–31)

> The poet shapes the tender and stammering mouth of a child, now he turns the ear from obscene language, soon he also molds the heart with friendly precepts; he is a corrector of harshness and envy and anger; he records things done rightly, he furnishes advancing age with *known examples*, and he comforts the poor and sick at heart.

Horace here attributes to poets not only the role of educating the young but also that of checking bad behavior and providing comfort to the ill. In the second half of *Epistles* 1.2 Horace turns from his readings of Homer to directly offering Lollius precepts against such vices as *invidia* (1.2.57–59) and *ira* (1.2.59–63), and the vocabulary and imagery he uses anticipate not only this passage from *Epistles* 2.1 but other passages from the *Ars Poetica* that promote poetic moral utility. Horace figures not only Homeric poetry but by extension his own as a nourishing medicine or wine that can both inculcate moral truths in the young and heal the faults of the spiritually ill. Horace continues his engagement with Epicurean ideas, employing Lucretian metaphors in order to attribute to Homer and to his own philosophically nonconformist poetry the same curative powers that Lucretius bestows upon Epicurus and his heavily orthodox verse.[45]

Horace's Poetic Wine

Throughout Horace's poetry wine has an important symbolic function and can often stand as a metaphor for poetry itself.[46] In *Odes* 1.20, for example, Horace invites Maecenas to drink simple wine at his Sabine farm: *vile potabis modicis Sabinum / cantharis, Graeca quod ego ipse testa / conditum levi* ("You will drink from modest cups the inexpensive Sabine wine which I myself stored away and sealed in a Greek jar," 1–3). Some scholars have read these lines metapoetically, with the Greek jar representing Horace's Greek meter and the Italian wine his Latin poetry; such a reading, as Commager notes, "suggests that Horace's real gift to his patron is not so much the promised wine as the poem itself."[47] Horace similarly uses wine symbolically in the later literary epistles that advocate poetic moral benefit. In *Ars Poetica* 343–44, as we have seen, Horace privileges the poet *qui miscuit utile dulci* ("who blends the useful with the sweet"). Horace here alludes to the practice of mixing dry and sweet wine, as Rudd has pointed out: "The mixture, evidently, is a kind of drink—a blend of dry (and morally beneficial) with sweet (and emotionally attractive)."[48] The advantage that poetry has in espousing the dry wine of ethical and philosophical subject matter is that it can do so by blending in the pleasure that arises from poetry's sweetness— the pleasure that to Epicurus and Philodemus muddles a poem's clarity but that Lucretius finds advantageous for laying out the obscure doctrines of Epicurus. The liquid imagery in these lines of the *Ars Poetica* is made more distinct by what immediately precedes them:

> quidquid praecipies esto brevis, ut cito dicta
> percipiant animi dociles teneantque fideles.
> omne supervacuum pleno de pectore manat. (335–37)

> Whatever you instruct, be brief, so that docile minds may quickly understand and faithfully retain what has been said; each superfluous thing drips from a full chest.

Horace here urges brevity when giving educational precepts (*praecipies*), so that no excess may drip (*manat*) from the sated chest of the listener. Liquid clearly stands as a metaphor for poetry, and the *pectus* (37) of the listener is analogous to an overflowing jar.

At the end of *Epistles* 1.2 Horace uses similar imagery and terminology. He tells Lollius to "drink in" truths (*vera*) while still young, and Lollius's *pectus* is explicitly likened to a new jar (*recens testa*):

fingit equum tenera docilem cervice magister
ire viam, qua monstret eques; venaticus, ex quo
tempore cervinam pellem latravit in aula,
militat in silvis catulus. nunc adbibe puro
pectore vera puer, nunc te melioribus offer.
quo semel est imbuta recens servabit odorem
testa diu. (64–70)

The trainer trains the docile horse with its tender neck to go on the path where the
rider points him. The hunting puppy serves in the forest from the time when it has
barked at a deerskin in the courtyard. Now drink in truths with your pure chest;
now offer yourself to your betters. A jar for a long time will preserve the odor in
which it was first steeped while new.

Horace here emphasizes the importance of early education by comparing Lollius
to a horse and hunting dog whose training must begin at a young age. These
lines contain several important verbal parallels not only with the *Ars Poetica*
passage just cited but also with the passage from *Epistles* 2.1 quoted above. Placing the passages side by side allows us to see these echoes more clearly:

fingit equum *tenera docilem* cervice magister
ire viam, qua monstret eques; venaticus, ex quo
tempore cervinam pellem latravit in aula,
militat in silvis catulus. nunc adbibe puro
pectore vera puer, nunc te melioribus offer.
quo semel est imbuta recens servabit odorem
testa diu. (*Epistles* 1.2.64–70)

quidquid praecipies esto brevis, ut cito dicta
percipiant animi *dociles* teneantque fideles.
omne supervacuum pleno de *pectore* manat. (*AP* 335–37)

os *tenerum* pueri balbumque poeta *figurat*,
torquet ab obscenis iam nunc sermonibus aurem,
mox etiam *pectus* praeceptis *format* amicis,
asperitatis et invidiae corrector et irae;
recte facta refert, orientia tempora notis
instruit exemplis, inopem solatur et aegrum. (*Epistles* 2.1.126–31)

The *exemplum* of the docile horse, *equum docilem*, with a tender neck, *tenera
cervice*, at *Epistles* 1.2.64 is paralleled by both the tender mouth, *os tenerum*, of
Epistles 2.1.126 and the docile minds, *animi dociles*, of *AP* 336. The chest, *pectus*,
of the poet's audience is likewise highlighted in all three passages, and in both
Epistles 1.2 and 2.1 the idea of "shaping" or "molding" is present (*fingit*, 1.2.64;
figurat, 2.1.126; *format*, 2.1.128). By employing in *Epistles* 1.2 the same vocabulary

describing the moral function of poetry that is found in *Epistles* 2.1 and the *Ars Poetica*, Horace anticipates these later statements about poetic utility and shows that both the Homeric poems and his own fulfill these educational ideals. Docility and tenderness emphasize the formative role of the poet in shaping the morals of the young, for they will retain the values they first encounter, just as a new vase (the *pectus*) will retain the odors it first held.[49] In *Epistles* 1.2 Horace calls attention to Lollius's youth by playing on the alliteration and assonance in *puro*, *pectore*, and *puer*, thereby emphasizing the necessity for Lollius to begin his ethical studies straightaway while still young and uncorrupted.[50]

Lucretius similarly uses liquid imagery in urging Memmius to turn to philosophical pursuits. He worries that Memmius may not sufficiently apply himself to the task, in which case he threatens to pour forth an endless stream of *argumenta* from his *pectus* into Memmius's ears:[51]

> usque adeo largos haustus e fontibu' magnis
> lingua meo suavis diti de pectore fundet,
> ut verear ne tarda prius per membra senectus
> serpat et in nobis vitai claustra resolvat,
> quam tibi de quavis una re versibus omnis
> argumentorum sit copia missa per auris. (1.412–17)

> My sweet tongue will pour forth from my rich chest such abundant draughts from great fountains that I fear that slow old age may creep through our limbs and loosen the bolts of life in us before the abundance of proofs about any one thing in all my verses has been sent through your ears.

⌈Whereas Horace uses the analogy of wine in *Epistles* 1.2, Lucretius here figures his poetry as water. Lucretius "pours" water that has been collected from a fountain (the writings of Epicurus) from one jar (his *pectus*) into another (that of Memmius). Memmius's ears, *auris*, evoke the "ears" of a jar, for in Greek οὖς, "ear," denotes a jar's handle.[52] Lollius in the epistle will likewise "drink in" moral lessons by listening with his ears to the poetry of Homer and Horace.[53] Although there are few verbal parallels between these *Epistles* and *De Rerum Natura* passages beyond the *pectora* of Lollius and Lucretius, the liquid imagery used is quite similar, as is the triangle set up between teacher, poet, and pupil. Epicurus, Lucretius, and Memmius are analogous to Homer, Horace, and Lollius, respectively. In *Epistles* 1.2 Homer replaces Epicurus as the font of ethical principles.⌋

Moral guidance of the young is but one aspect of poetry in *Epistles* 1.2, for it also acts as a medicine that can heal the older and already corrupt (cf. *Epistles* 2.1.129: *invidiae corrector et irae*). This is revealed by another jar metaphor at line 54, where the jar is not clean (*purus*), but contaminated, and its dirtiness spoils everything poured into it:

qui cupit aut metuit, iuvat illum sic domus et res
ut lippum pictae tabulae, fomenta podagram,
auriculas citharae collecta sorde dolentis.
sincerum est nisi vas, quodcumque infundis acescit. (51–54)

> House and money please one who desires and fears just as paintings please one
> with sore eyes, just as wrappings please gout, or lyres please ears hurting because
> they are clogged with dirt. If the jar is not clean, whatever you pour in turns sour.

The jar in this metaphor is analogous to the eyes, feet, and ears of those suffering from sore eyes, gout, and clogged ears, respectively.[54] A person's moral failings—the dirtiness of the jar—cause any potentially pleasurable activity, such
as the visual arts (*tabulae*) or music (*citharae*), to be spoiled. Line 54, as scholars
have stated, condenses a passage from Lucretius 6.17–19:[55]

intellegit ibi vitium vas efficere ipsum
omniaque illius vitio corrumpier intus
quae collata foris et commoda cumque venirent.

> Then [Epicurus] understood that the jar itself causes the fault and that by the fault
> of the jar everything inside is corrupted, whatever came into it collected from
> without, even good things.

Here too the jar is a metaphor for the mind or chest, and the cure for the jar's
fault is Epicurean philosophy, for Lucretius goes on to say that Epicurus puri-
fied the jar/chest (*purgavit pectora*, 24), put an end to desire and fear (*finem
statuit cuppedinis atque timoris*, 25; cf. *Epistles* 1.2.51: *qui cupit aut metuit*), and
pointed out the *summum bonum* (26).[56] Armstrong argues that Horace's allusion to this passage further supports his contention that Horace adheres to
Epicureanism in *Epistles* 1.2.[57] However, Horace is very explicit about what he
is consulting for himself and recommending to Lollius: it is not Epicurus, but
Homer, whose healing, liquid poetry (and, by extension, Horace's) can cleanse
the jar, and Horace therefore recasts the vase analogy to stress the therapeutic
power of traditional poetry. In *Epistles* 1.2 Homer has the same restorative power
that Epicureanism has in the *De Rerum Natura*. If the clean new jar represents
Lollius, then the dirty jar must represent Horace, since they are the two readers
of Homer envisioned in the text of *Epistles* 1.2. This fits well with the persona
Horace adopts in the opening poem, where he is far from being a self-sufficient
philosopher and is in need of spiritual healing.
➤ In likening poetry to medicinal liquid, Horace evokes the most famous simile in the *De Rerum Natura*: the cup of wormwood (Epicureanism) smeared with
honey (poetry) (1.936–50 = 4.11–25).[58] In this simile the benefit arises from the
medicinal philosophy alone, while the honey is a trick to make the philosophy

more palatable. As Gale states, "the famous image of the honeyed cup portrays the poetry as something separate from and subordinate to the philosophy of the *DRN*, as a sweet coating which merely covers the surface of the bitter doctrine and so induces the reader to swallow it."[59] In this simile poetry retains the allure that Epicurus found potentially dangerous, and it is precisely this seductive quality that Lucretius hopes to harness to his benefit. For Lucretius the poetry loses all benefit if the philosophical component is removed, and he is at pains to show he does not deviate from his philosophical master.[60] For Horace, poetic form is not a separable component from ethical teaching and is not used to mask an orthodox doctrine that many would find bitter. As we have seen in the *Ars Poetica*, the best poet mixes the useful with the sweet (*miscuit utile dulci*, 343) and thereby produces a single drink, with neither aspect subordinate to the other. The wormwood/honey simile in fact emphasizes Lucretius's lack of philosophical innovation; he provides an original poetic framework as a vehicle for traditional Epicurean orthodoxy. In Horace, however, the poet's task is not just to produce the sweet honey of poetry but to provide original moral advice as well by adapting ethical source material found both in philosophical and poetic sources. Whereas a poet or philosopher writing in service of an orthodox system cannot deviate from that system, a nonconforming poet is free to formulate his own ethical ideas by drawing on a number of sources and mixing them with poetry to create and blend a drink all his own.[61] Horace's rereading and rewriting of the Homeric epics nicely demonstrates the independent approach he takes with source material, whether poetic or philosophical. He picks and chooses examples that he can mold to his own moral program and thus conforms his subject matter to his own purposes rather than conforming himself to his subject matter. His method of adapting Homer thus is in keeping with the eclectic philosophical methodology he put forth in the opening epistle (1.1.12–15); it is also especially in line with the Aristippean approach outlined at 1.1.19: *et mihi res, non me rebus, subiungere conor*, "I try to make things subject to myself, not myself to things." The freedom, adaptability, and avoidance of orthodox extremes that Horace exercises toward his sources are in fact the central ethical lessons at the core of Horace's rereading of the Homeric epics.

Freedom, Adaptability, and Moderation in *Epistles* 1.2

In this section I will look more closely at the specific moral guidance that runs throughout the poem, focusing especially on Horace's readings of the Homeric epics in the poem's first half. The negative exempla from both the *Iliad* and *Odyssey* represent extremes of behavior and the lack of independence that results from enslavement to passions such as anger, erotic love, and pleasure. These are the figures of Agamemnon, Achilles, the companions of Odysseus, the suitors, and the Phaeacians. Opposed to these negative exempla stands the *utile exemplar* Odysseus, who represents *virtus* and *sapientia*. The wise man does not succumb to extremes, be they extremes of passion, circumstance, or orthodoxy. Odysseus is foremost a figure of the independence made possible by adaptability and moderation, and liquid imagery is again used to illustrate his autonomy. Furthermore, Odysseus is a parallel not only for Horace's philosophical independence as described in *Epistles* 1.1.13–19 but also for the general freedom and adaptability associated chiefly in the *Epistles* with Aristippus.

Horace begins his interpretation of Homer by first discussing the *Iliad* (6–16). Paris, Agamemnon, and Achilles are victims of their various passions, and their unwillingness to rein them in extends the long war and throws everything and everyone in and around Troy into madness:

> fabula qua Paridis propter narratur amorem
> Graecia barbariae lento collisa duello,
> stultorum regum et populorum continet aestus.
> Antenor censet belli praecidere causam:
> quid Paris? ut salvus regnet vivatque beatus,
> cogi posse negat. Nestor componere lites
> inter Pelidem festinat et inter Atriden:
> hunc amor, ira quidem communiter urit utrumque.
> quidquid delirant reges, plectuntur Achivi.
> seditione, dolis, scelere atque libidine et ira
> Iliacos intra muros peccatur et extra. (1.2.6–16)

> The story in which it is told how Greece was brought into collision by a protracted war with a barbarian nation contains the furies of stupid kings and peoples. Antenor resolves to cut off the cause of the war, but what does Paris do? He refuses to be compelled to rule in safety and live happily. Nestor hastens to end the quarrels between the sons of Peleus and Atreus. Love burns the former, while anger burns them both jointly. However the kings rave, the Achaeans suffer. Because of dissension, trickery, crime, lust, and anger all goes wrong within the Trojan walls and without.

The Iliadic kings are characterized by their stupidity, which infects not only them but their subjects as well. The only heroes willing to compromise and put an end to war, Antenor and Nestor, are unable to curb these unregulated passions, and the kings' subjection to their emotions is figured as a disease that causes mass suffering (*aestus*, 8; *salvus*, 10; *urit*, 13; *delirant*, 14). Implicit in this passage is the irony that those who are supposed to be in charge (*regum*, 8; *regnet*, 10, *reges*, 14) clearly are not, and their loss of control is well illustrated by the impersonal passive *peccatur* (16). In the second half of the epistle Horace, in exhorting Lollius directly, returns to the subject of unregulated passions, especially pleasure, greed, envy, and anger, the last of which especially recalls his reading of the *Iliad*. Here Horace connects passions with servitude and emphasizes the need to moderate such extremes:

> sperne voluptates; nocet empta dolore voluptas.
> semper avarus eget: certum voto pete finem.
> invidus alterius macrescit rebus opimis;
> invidia Siculi non invenere tyranni
> maius tormentum. qui non moderabitur irae,
> infectum volet esse, dolor quod suaserit et mens,
> dum poenas odio per vim festinat inulto.
> ira furor brevis est: animum rege, qui nisi paret,
> imperat, hunc frenis, hunc tu compesce catena. (1.2.55–63)

> Scorn pleasures: pleasure bought with pain is harmful. The greedy man always wants; seek a fixed limit to desire. The envious man wastes away due to another's riches. Sicilian tyrants have discovered no greater torment than envy. Whoever does not moderate his anger will wish undone what his grief and frame of mind convinced him to do while he was violently hastening to exact penalties because of unavenged anger. Anger is a brief madness. Rule your heart, which, unless it obeys, commands. Check it with reins, check it with the chain.

These lines illustrate the necessity of being the master of one's own emotions, and the chain (*catena*) in particular evokes ideas of slavery. Armstrong has connected these lines, especially their focus on anger, to Epicurean ideas, and certainly he is right that Horace has drawn on Epicurean sources.[62] He suggests that these lines especially recall Philodemus's *On Anger* col. 33.23–27, in which Philodemus argues against what he takes to be the Peripatetics' positive evaluation of anger and claims that such a view results in soldiers giving orders to their generals rather than vice versa. Philodemus's arguments in favor of moderating anger no doubt would have appealed to Horace, who in lines 59–61 condemns the man who does not moderate his anger (*qui non moderabitur irae*).[63] The idea of moderation is found throughout the passage and not only with respect to anger; those who suffer from avarice and envy, for example, have not placed a *certum finem* ("a fixed limit," 56) on their desire.[64] Thus the passions that drive on the Iliadic kings make them negative examples of immoderate extremes.

The Epicureans, however, are not the only philosophical presence lurking in the background of this passage, and Horace simultaneously alludes also to a Stoic source in order to illustrate the slavery of those who possess such extreme passions. In *Paradoxa Stoicorum* 33 Cicero uses very similar language (italicized) to that of Horace to expound the Stoic tenet that only the wise man is free while every fool is a slave, and his advice, like that of Horace, applies to a range of passions, including desire, pleasure, anger, and avarice:

laudetur vero hic imperator aut etiam appelletur aut hoc nomine dignus putetur— imperator quo modo? aut cui tandem hic libero *imperabit*, qui non potest cupiditati- bus suis *imperare*? *Refrenet* primum libidines, *spernat voluptates, iracundiam* teneat, coerceat *avaritiam*, ceteras *animi* labes repellat—tum incipiat aliis *imperare*, cum ipse improbissimis dominis, dedecori ac turpitudini, *parere* desierit. dum quidem his oboediet, non modo imperator, sed liber habendus omnino non erit.

Indeed this man may be praised as a commander or even called one or may be thought worthy of this name—how is he a commander? Or, pray, what free man will he command, who cannot command his own desires? First let him rein in his longings, let him scorn pleasures, let him check his wrath, let him restrain his avarice, let him ward off the other disgraces of the mind. Then let him begin to command others when he himself ceases to obey the most shameless masters: vice and disgrace. Indeed while he obeys them, not only must he not be considered a commander, but he also must not be considered free.

Like Cicero, Horace emphasizes the inability of one to be in command (*imperat*, 1.2.63) who obeys (*paret*, 1.2.62) his passions and urges us to "scorn pleasures" (*sperne voluptates*, 1.2.55).[65] Both writers furthermore mention anger, avarice, the *animus*, and the need to "rein in" such emotions (*frenis . . . compesce*, 1.2.63; *refrenet, Parad*). The lack of freedom that results from such enslavement to the passions is central to the Ciceronian passage, and by alluding to this text Horace makes issues of independence and servitude central to his poem. This exhorta- tion to curb passions in *Epistles* 1.2.55–63 looks back to and expands his reading of the *Iliad* and indicates that the Iliadic *reges* are examples of extremes that re- sult in the loss of autonomy. Horace has thus drawn on both Epicurean and Stoic sources to support his larger ethical agenda of moderation and independence.

In contrast to these so-called rulers from the *Iliad* we have the positive ex- emplum of Odysseus in lines 17–26, who embodies freedom from extremes and Aristippean adaptability to circumstance.[66] He is furthermore described by lan- guage that aligns him with Horace's own lack of philosophical orthodoxy as described in *Epistles* 1.1. Readers of *Epistles* 1.2 have been inclined to identify Horace's Odysseus with one or another school of philosophy. Foremost among recent such interpretations are those of Moles and Armstrong, who have argued that he represents Cynicism and Epicureanism, respectively.[67] Building on an argument of Eidinow, I will suggest, however, that Odysseus represents instead a rejection of just these orthodox systems. Standing in contrast with Odysseus are the suitors of Penelope and the Phaeacians, who, like the Iliadic kings, are subject to immoderate extremes.[68]

Horace begins his reading of the *Odyssey* by stating that Odysseus is an exemplar of *virtus* and *sapientia* who exercises remarkable foresight and endurance:

rursus, quid virtus et quid sapientia possit,
utile proposuit nobis exemplar Vlixem,
qui domitor Troiae multorum providus urbes,
et mores hominum inspexit latumque per aequor,
dum sibi, dum sociis reditum parat, aspera multa
pertulit, adversis rerum inmersabilis undis. (1.2.17–22)

> On the other hand he has put forth for us Odysseus as a useful exemplar of what virtue and wisdom can achieve, the tamer of Troy who observed with foresight the cities and customs of many men and, while throughout the wide sea he was preparing a homecoming for himself and his companions, endured many hardships, unsinkable in the hostile waves of things.

The attribution of *virtus* to Odysseus here might put us in mind of Stoicism, and the coupling of this trait with nautical imagery certainly recalls Horace's description of one pole of his philosophical vacillations found in the opening poem: *nunc agilis fio et mersor civilibus undis, / virtutis verae custos rigidusque satelles*, "Now I become active and am immersed in the waves of civil life as a guardian and rigid attendant of true virtue," (1.1.16–17).[69] In these lines the *virtus* to which Horace stubbornly clings, as we have seen, certainly does recall Stoicism and its uncompromising insistence on *libertas*. On closer consideration, however, the virtue Odysseus displays arises not from his inflexibly adhering to one system of belief or behavior but from his adaptability to a variety of situations with the result that he is not mastered by any. Whereas Horace's inflexibility results in his being "drowned" (*mersor*, 16) in civil waves, Odysseus is "unsinkable" (*immersabilis*) in *rerum undis*, the "waves of things" (i.e., constantly changing and uncontrollable circumstances). In this he is not so much like Horace the Stoic in 1.1 as like Horace the Aristippean, who in 1.1.18–19 tries to make circumstances/things (*res*) subject to himself, not himself to things (*rebus*).[70] Thus the *virtus* that Odysseus displays is not that of uncompromising Cynicism or Stoicism but the virtue of adaptability, and Horace's description of Odysseus indicates that he is already beginning to reject the unbending *virtus* and its concomitant *libertas* outlined in 1.1.16–17 and to embrace instead the freedom that comes through Aristippean flexibility. This description of Odysseus forms an important point in the redefinition of both *virtus* and *libertas* that takes place over the course of the collection: in 1.1 *virtus* is first an attribute of the unbending Stoic, whereas in 1.6.16 it will be a trait that itself can be pursued to an extreme, and finally in 1.18.9 it is redefined as adhering to the mean between extremes: *virtus est medium vitiorum et utrimque reductum*, "Virtue is a midpoint between vices and removed from both." The virtuous mean of 1.18, furthermore, will fall between the extremes of uncompromising *libertas* and obsequious servility.

Horace chooses two episodes from the *Odyssey* to illustrate Odysseus's *virtus et sapientia*, the Sirens and Circe:

> Sirenum voces et Circae pocula nosti;
> quae si cum sociis stultus cupidusque bibisset,
> sub domina meretrice fuisset turpis et excors;
> vixisset canis immundus vel amica luto sus. (23–26)

> You know about the voices of the Sirens and the cups of Circe. If he had stupidly and greedily drunk from them with his companions, he would have lived foully and foolishly under a courtesan mistress; he would have lived like a filthy dog or a pig that loves the mud.

Horace cites the Sirens only briefly and more fully describes Circe's transformative cups, which Odysseus was wise to avoid. The Sirens and Circe episodes are inverses of one another: whereas Odysseus listens to the song of the Sirens and his companions do not, his companions drink the cups of Circe and he does not. Although Odysseus was wise to avoid destruction at the hands of the Sirens, we could nevertheless read the *Sirenum voces* of line 23 positively. As we have seen, the Sirens form an important component in Epicurus's criticisms of Homer as symbols of the lure of traditional poetry, its ὀλέθριον δέλεαρ, and, given Horace's engagement with these Epicurean criticisms in the poem, Horace's Sirens call to mind these attacks against traditional poetry. Horace does not mention the risks posed by the Sirens and focuses instead on the dangerous temptations of Circe. One could of course argue that the Sirens' song and Circe's cups hold similar dangers for Odysseus against which he must take protective measures, but, if we read the episodes as inversions of one another, the *Sirenum voces* and the *Circae pocula* are contrasts; Odysseus was wise to avoid the cups of Circe but was also wise to listen to the song of the Sirens. We must recall that it is because his ears were not clogged by wax that he was able to listen to their song, and Horace in the opening poem makes it clear that his ears too are unblocked: *purgatam . . . aurem* (1.1.7). It is thus with open ears that Horace turns in 1.2 to reading the Siren song of Homeric epic, and he urges his readers as well to follow Odysseus's example in not stuffing their ears against such beneficial poetry. It is furthermore implicitly with his open ears that Lollius will "drink in" (*adbibe*, 67) the truths that Homeric and Horatian verse can teach him, while it is because of clogged ears (*auriculas . . . collecta sorde dolentis*) that one cannot enjoy the music of *citharae* at 1.2.53. We cannot, however, empty the Sirens entirely of their potentially dangerous associations, and even in the realm of poetry one must take care to maintain independence, just as Odysseus remains tied to the ship's mast while listening to their song. Both poetry and philosophy offer to Horace ethical source material, but he must take care not to follow either source slavishly, and therefore his reading of Homer has been tailored to suit his own moral agenda. His approach to the Homeric epics is in fact similar to his approach to philosophical sources in that he partakes of them while transforming them into something uniquely his own.

While the Sirens have associations with poetry, Circe in the epistle has clear links with orthodox philosophy, and the *Circae pocula* that Odysseus is praised for rejecting contrast with the poetic drink that Horace urges Lollius to imbibe (cf. *bibisset*, 24, and *adbibe*, 67). Horace states that these cups have the ability to turn a man into a dog (*canis*) or pig (*sus*). While the transformation of men into pigs is already present in the *Odyssey*, Homer never explicitly mentions dogs on Circe's island.[72] Eidinow has put forth a compelling argument explaining Horace's addition of dogs. He points out the well-known associations between dogs/Cynics and swine/Epicureans, associations to which Horace clearly alludes elsewhere in the *Epistles*.[73] By rejecting the cups offered by Circe, Odysseus rejects both of these orthodox philosophical systems. Eidinow concludes: "The man of virtue, the wise man, is the one who does not allow himself to be seduced by a *domina meretrix*, who therefore does not commit himself to either of the two philosophies." Horace's description of the dog as *immundus* (1.2.26) is significant, since elsewhere in Horace's poetry as well as that of Ovid *munditia* is a quality associated with moderation between extremes.[74]

The *domina* (1.2.25) that Odysseus rejects is analogous to the philosophical *magister* to whom Horace refuses to swear philosophical allegiance in the first poem, and just as Horace would have forfeited his independence had he sworn to an orthodox school, so too does Odysseus's rejection of such extremes render him free. Keane makes the important observation that in the *Odyssey* Odysseus does in fact drink from the cups of Circe after obtaining from Hermes an antidote to her charms: "It is not that he 'did not drink as his companions did,' but that he 'did not drink in the company (or the circumstances) of his companions.'"[75] He did not, that is, drink in such a way that he would be transformed into the slave of a *domina*, but he did in fact drink. In other words, he partook without becoming subjugated, just as Horace can participate in philosophy without swearing to a *magister*.

The *Odyssey* provides Horace with plenty of negative exempla to contrast with Odysseus. Like the heroes of the *Iliad*, they have little interest in moral improvement. Rather than succumb to passion, violence, and war, the suitors and Phaeacians spend their time absorbed in idle amusements and sleep:

> nos numerus sumus et fruges consumere nati,
> sponsi Penelopae nebulones Alcinoique
> in cute curanda plus aequo operata iuventus,
> cui pulchrum fuit in medios dormire dies et
> ad strepitum citharae cessantem ducere somnum. (1.2.27–31)

> We are of no consequence and were born to consume the fruits of the earth, the
> worthless suitors of Penelope and the youth of Alcinous, who busied themselves
> in primping their skin more than is right and to whom it was beautiful to sleep
> until noon and lure delaying sleep with the noise of the lyre.

Like the Iliadic heroes, these figures offer Horace exempla of extreme behavior.
The suitors are significantly called *nebulones*, "good-for-nothings," a word Horace uses elsewhere to describe those who pursue extremes rather than the mean.
In *Satires* 1.2.12–17 he complains about a certain Fufidius, who fears having the
reputation of a *vappa*, "worthless person," or *nebulo* (12) and who consequently
becomes an unforgiving moneylender and miser. The moral, he states, is that
"fools, in avoiding vices, run to their opposites," *dum vitant stulti vitia, in contraria currunt*, 24. In *Satires* 1.1.103–7 Horace makes a similar complaint:

> non ego, avarum
> cum veto te fieri, vappam iubeo ac nebulonem.
> est inter Tanain quiddam socerumque Viselli.
> est modus in rebus, sunt certi denique fines,
> quos ultra citraque nequit consistere rectum.

> I do not, when I prohibit you from becoming a miser, order you to be a worthless
> fellow or a good-for-nothing (*nebulo*). There is a certain difference between
> Tanais and the father-in-law of Visellius. There is a measure in things, there are, in
> sum, fixed limits, beyond and short of which what is right cannot stand.

By using the term *nebulones* to describe the suitors in *Epistles* 1.2, Horace surely
intends his reader to recall these passages from the *Satires*, the only other times
he uses the word, and to recognize the inability of such *nebulones* to hit upon
the correct *modus in rebus*. Horace expounds more fully upon the immoderate
behavior of the Phaeacians. They primp themselves *plus aequo*, "more than is
right," which pointedly contrasts with Horace's self-description in 1.4.15, where
in an Epicurean mood he describes himself as having a "well groomed skin,"
bene curata cute. The Phaeacian youth thus represent a distorted, excessive
hedonism. When not primping they spend their time sleeping until midday to
the sound of the lyre, an extreme of inactivity bordering on lethargy. The mention of *citharae* in line 31 looks ahead to line 53, in which the sound of *citharae*
gives no pleasure or benefit to one whose ears are clogged with dirt. The suitors

are thus like the dirty vase, but the poetry to which they listen cannot penetrate their clogged ears and heal the souls within. Unlike Odysseus or Horace, the suitors' ears are closed to the beneficial aspects of poetry, and their musical entertainment serves only to intensify their hedonism.

Whereas Horace in line 27 lumps himself and Lollius together with the suitors and the Phaeacian youth (*nos numerus sumus*), beginning in line 31 he exhorts Lollius directly and encourages him to distinguish himself from them. He is not to listen to poetry in order to be lulled to sleep but so that he might wake up and take to heart its moral lessons:

> ut iugulent hominem, surgunt de nocte latrones:
> ut te ipsum serves, non expergisceris? atqui
> si noles sanus, curres hydropicus; et ni
> posces ante diem librum cum lumine, si non
> intendes animum studiis et rebus honestis,
> invidia vel amore vigil torquebere. (1.2.31–37)

> Robbers rise in the night to cut a man's throat. Won't you wake up so that you can save yourself? And if you will not do so while healthy, you will have to run with swollen feet. And unless you ask for a book and a lamp before sunrise, unless you apply your mind to studies and honorable pursuits, you will be tormented throughout the night by envy or love.

The only way to avoid the extremes of lethargy (exemplified by the Phaeacians) or of passions (exemplified by the Iliadic kings) is to apply one's mind to studies beginning early in the morning by requesting a *liber* (35). It is left ambiguous which book exactly Horace has in mind, whether it is the same book Horace is reading (i.e., Homer), Horace's book (the *Epistles*), or *any* book (i.e., studies in general).[76] No doubt Horace's *liber* evokes all these various texts simultaneously, and Horace wants Lollius to find moral lessons in literature (and philosophy) generally, including his own *Epistles*, two of which are addressed to him. His exhortation that Lollius read with an eye to moral improvement surely anticipates the later epistle he will address to Lollius (1.18), in which he again urges him to consult written works to learn how to live a good life: *inter cuncta leges et percontabere doctos, / qua ratione queas traducere leniter aevum*, "In the course of everything you will read and investigate the learned as to how you might be able to lead your life moderately," 96–97. This is a process that Horace urges Lollius to begin (*incipe*, 41) in *Epistles* 1.2 and one in which he expects that Lollius will have made progress by the time he—and we—reach 1.18. As Keane puts it, "with books in hand, the young man will have the room to shape his own 'didactic plot,' which will include not just progress, but mistakes, regression, and new revelations achieved through rereading."[77] In this he will be following the example of Horace, his fellow learner, who has already provided him with a model of reading and interpretation in the second epistle, a model through which Horace displays both the benefits to be derived from a moral reading of traditional poetry as well as the freedom he enjoys in adapting these lessons to suit his own individual ethical course. Through this process Horace has distilled traditional material into a new mixture all his own, a blend of the useful and the sweet of which he invites his readers to partake and thereby to learn in turn the lessons of freedom, moderation, and adaptability that run throughout not only this poem but the entire collection.

EPISTLES 1 AND LIQUID IMAGERY

In my reading of *Epistles* 1.2, I have attempted to show how Horace offers a sustained response to philosophers who had denied that traditional poetry has valid moral lessons to teach and that Horace thereby reasserts this morally beneficial function not just for Homer's poetry but also for his own. Horace offers a reading of Homer that affirms its ethical value and at the same time demonstrates the freedom with which he adapts traditional material to suit his own moral agenda. Such morally beneficial poetry is figured as a liquid that heals faults and inculcates truths, and the epistle that Horace has constructed is itself a poetic drink into which he has blended the ethical insights not just of Homer but a wide range of poetic and philosophical sources. This poetic mixture challenges the notion that poetry is instructive only when built upon a solid philosophical foundation. Unlike the orthodox philosopher or poet, the "eclectic" poet is free to choose from and adapt a wide variety of sources, both poetic and philosophical, in order to blend his drink of dry ethics and sweet poetry, and in doing so Horace follows the lessons of freedom and adaptability that he finds modeled by the character of Odysseus. By way of conclusion I would like now to show how this liquid imagery is central to two other passages in *Epistles* 1 and indeed becomes symbolic for the moral value of the book as a whole.

In *Epistles* 1.8 Horace suggests that poetry, again figured as a liquid, can unclog the ears of his addressee and make him receptive to ethical advice. Horace asks his Muse (*Musa*, 2) to take a message to Albinovanus Celsus, who we are told is in the imperial cohort of Tiberius (2). As scholars have pointed out, Horace's advice to Celsus is "not to let success go to his head."[78] At the end of the poem the Muse is told to ask Celsus how he is and, should he answer with a mistaken *recte* ("well," 15), told to "remember to drip this precept into his ears: that as you bear your fortune, so shall we bear you" (*praeceptum auriculis hoc instillare memento: ut tu fortunam, sic nos te, Celse, feremus*, 16–17). Wine and oil are found elsewhere as a cure for deafness or clogged ears, and Horace's language is paralleled in medical writings. Cato at *De Agricultura* 157.16 recommends a mixture of macerated cabbage and wine as a cure for deafness (*auribus si parum audies, terito cum vino brassicam, sucum exprimito, in aurem intro tepidum instillato*, "If you hear poorly, macerate cabbage with wine, squeeze out the juice, drip it warm into the ear"), and the elder Pliny at *Natural History* 27.114 offers similar advice (*sucus et auribus purulentis instillatur*, "the juice is dripped into ears full of pus"). Thus the medicine that Horace's Muse (i.e., his poetry) will drip into the ears of Celsus will unclog them and make him receptive to Horace's advice. As we have seen, the dirty jar of *Epistles* 1.2.54 is compared to clogged ears (53) that derive no enjoyment from the music of *citharae*, and Horace's poetry in 1.8 thus acts as a medicine that can repair such moral defects. Celsus's mind is the faulty jar that through Horace's Muse can be healed, instructed, and delighted.

Horace's poetry is likened to a liquid or wine as early as the programmatic opening of *Epistles* 1.1, where Horace says that he is storing away moral truths for future use: *quid verum atque decens, curo et rogo et omnis in hoc sum: / condo et compono quae mox depromere possim* ("I care about and ask what is true and seemly, and I am totally [absorbed] in this: I am storing up and setting by things which I may soon be able to bring out," 11–12). The verbs *condo* and *compono*, in addition to referring frequently to the act of composing literature, are each commonly used to express storing goods, especially wine.[79] Horace similarly plays with the meaning of *condere* in *Odes* 1.20.3 (*conditum*), in which, as I mentioned above, the wine and vase have been read as representing the Latin words and Greek meter of Horace's poem. Furthermore, (*de*)*promere* is used frequently by Horace for bringing wine out of storage, as Lathière has shown.[80] *Recondere* and *promere* are brought together in this context at *Odes* 3.28.2–3: *prome reconditum, / Lyde, strenua Caecubum* ("quickly bring out the stored Caecubum, Lyde"). Thus in *Epistles* 1.1.12 Horace is composing and storing up (*condo et compono*) moral lessons as though they were wine, and we see this process continue in his reading of the Homeric epics in 1.2. In urging Lollius to drink (*adbibe*) in *Epistles* 1.2.67, Horace fulfills his claim that he will soon draw from his ethical stores (*depromere*, 1.1.12). Bowditch suggests that the wine metaphor in 1.1 stands for "the teachings of philosophy in many of his verse letters" and that the wine is the "philosophical content."[81] Rather, as I hope to have shown, Horace's poetic wine stands not just for the philosophical aspect of his poetry, but for the mixture of both poetic sweetness and moral utility that both delights and heals. It is a symbol for the very best kind of poetry, that which fulfills poetry's traditional function of not only entertaining but also benefiting its listeners. At the same time the morally beneficial component of this drink is freely drawn from a wide range of philosophical and poetic sources. His poetic task is not to adorn another's superior wisdom with his beautiful language but to

use his own authority as a poet to construct a moral program to benefit his listeners. In doing so he follows the example of Homer, who himself blends together the beautiful (*pulchrum*, 3) with the useful (*utile*, 3). In offering a reading
of Homer that is highly selective and heavily targeted to his central teachings
of adaptability, moderation, and independence, Horace shows how his eclectic
philosophical technique (outlined in 1.1.13–15) is applicable also to the use of
poetic models, and we will see him in 1.19 advocate strongly for such "independent dependence" in the imitation of poetic forerunners. In the next chapter
I continue to examine the ethical advice of the didactic Horace with an examination of 1.4, 5, 6, and 12, keeping in mind that Horace the teacher is never fully
distinguishable from Horace the student. As in 1.2, independence, adaptability,
and moderation are at the heart of his moral lessons.

Nil Admirari
The Moral Adviser of
Epistles 1.4, 1.5, 1.6, and 1.12

I N T H I S C H A P T E R I D I S C U S S four closely connected poems: 1.4 and 1.5, 1.6 and 1.12. In each poem Horace presents himself as a moral adviser who prizes moderation and adaptability and invites his addressees to enjoy these qualities with him. *Epistles* 1.4 and 1.5 are invitation poems in which Horace urges his addressee to put an end to extreme pursuits and join him in a welcome change of activity. Albius in 1.4 adheres to the extreme of solitary withdrawal and philosophical contemplation, while in 1.5 Torquatus is a man of the city whom Horace urges to join him for a simple dinner freed from the stresses of clients and business. In each of these poems the addressee is presented as overly somber and in need of pleasure and friendship, and Horace offers himself as a friend who can provide them some greatly needed amusement. In 1.6, a poem much more serious in tone, Horace adopts the didactic mode in addressing a certain Numicius, to whom he stresses the importance of the doctrine *nil admirari* (i.e., the avoidance of zealous adherence to any one pursuit, whether it be philosophy, politics, business, or pleasure). This doctrine emerges as fundamentally important to the moral thought not only of this group of poems but also of the entire collection. In 1.12 Iccius is susceptible to just such *admiratio* and pursuit of extremes, particularly in his desire for wealth, and Horace again urges his addressee to limit his extreme tendencies and look for happiness in friendship. Central to all of these poems are the values of moderation and adaptability, traits that the narrator himself promotes and seems to embody. The Horace of these poems is therefore not the student suffering from inconsistency and spiritual malaise—the Horace to whom we shall return in the next chapter—but the teacher who is drawing on the lessons he has learned and distilling them for those of his companions who need his guidance and help. The self-presentation of Horace in these poems therefore contrasts with that of the opening epistle, where he displays an unwillingness to compromise in the interest of friendship, and we can therefore see in these poems that Horace begins to apply the adaptability and moderation of his philosophical method to the social sphere, even if he has not yet explicitly adopted them in his own friendship with Maecenas. Throughout these poems we see Horace the teacher modeling moral behavior that Horace the student has yet fully to embrace in his own life.

THE EPICUREAN PIG OF *EPISTLES* 1.4

In the letter to Albius (1.4), Horace explicitly cites himself as an example to be emulated in contrast to the extreme behavior of his addressee. Albius is also the recipient of *Odes* 1.33, where we are told that he writes "mournful elegies" (*miserabiles elegos*, 3), and some scholars have suggested that he is the elegist Albius Tibullus.[1] This identification must, however, remain speculative and is not necessary for uncovering the most important aspects of Albius's character. The letter's goals are twofold: to direct Albius away from excessive behavior and to remind him that the means of living well are easily within his grasp if only he focuses on enjoying the present moment among friends. The poem is in many ways a corrective to Horace's own attitude in *Epistles* 1.1, in which his poor mental state causes him to withdraw from friendship and hide himself away in the countryside. Albius emerges as a double for Horace and, in projecting his own behavior onto Albius, Horace gains the distance and perspective required to see its folly. In *Epistles* 1.4 Horace suggests that, in order to achieve well-being, seclusion and seriousness must be balanced by levity and companionship.

Horace begins the poem with a reminder of their past friendship by stating that Albius has been a candid critic of his *Satires*: *Albi, nostrorum sermonum candide iudex* (1).[2] In exercising frankness and candor Albius has been not only an ideal critic of Horace's poetry but also an ideal friend, and Horace often praises literary *amici* for exhibiting this quality. In *Satires* 1.10.86, for example, Horace includes "frank Furnius" (*candide Furni*) in his list of learned friends (*doctos et amicos*, 87) whose readership he desires, and in *Satires* 1.5.41–42 Horace states that the earth has born no more candid souls (*animae candidiores*) than Plotius, Varius, and Vergil and concludes *nil ego contulerim iucundo sanus amico* ("While in my right mind I would compare nothing to a pleasant friend," 44). In *Ars Poetica* 419–52 it is this willingness to offer honest literary criticism that separates the false from the true friend (*mendacem verumque . . . amicum*, 425). By describing Albius as *candidus* in *Epistles* 1.4.1, Horace praises him for proving himself a true friend in the past and prepares him and us for the focus on friendship that is central to the epistle.[3] Furthermore, just as Albius had previously proven himself a friend to Horace with his frank criticism, Horace now gently but candidly evaluates him and offers him advice not on literary matters but ethical ones.

Having reminded Albius of their friendship, Horace inquires about his current activities. Horace is aware that Albius has withdrawn to the countryside but does not know what exactly he is doing there: *quid nunc te dicam facere in regione Pedana? / scribere quod Cassi Parmensis opuscula vincat?* ("What should I say that you are doing now in the region of Pedum? That you are writing something to outdo the little works of Cassius of Parma?" 2–3).[4] Pedum was located east of Rome close to Praeneste and thus in proximity to Horace's Sabine villa, and his rural retreat is therefore evocative of Horace's own. Horace imagines that Albius is busy writing poetry, perhaps the same *miserabiles elegi* Horace attributes to him in *Odes* 1.33, where Horace reveals that he tends to extremes both in his emotions and in his poetic output: *Albi, ne doleas plus nimio memor / immitis Glycerae neu miserabilis / decantes elegos* ("Albius, do not grieve too much as you remember harsh Glycera and do not endlessly sing your miserable elegies," 1–3). This is not a man naturally disposed toward moderation. As Nisbet and Hubbard point out, the preposition in *decantes* "hints that the whimpering has gone on *ad nauseam*."[5] Therefore, the reader familiar with the ode who encounters *Epistles* 1.4 already knows Albius to be prone to excess. Horace knows this too, and in the absence of any concrete information about Albius's activities he can only imagine what extreme behavior his friend is up to. In the epistle it is not love that Horace worries might be consuming Albius but excessive poetic rivalry, for Horace envisions him wanting to "be victorious" (*vincat*, 2) over Cassius.[6] Albius is perhaps then in a competitive mood and anxious about the future reception of his poetry. Horace therefore will urge him to live in the here and now and to focus not on competition but on friendship.[7]

Horace next supposes that Albius might be devoted instead to ethical study as he wanders through the forests of Pedum: *an tacitum silvas inter reptare salubres, / curantem quidquid dignum sapiente bonoque est?* ("or are you strolling quietly among the healthful forests, concerned with whatever is worthy of one who is wise and good?" 4–5). This second option is described at greater length, which suggests that it, in Horace's opinion, is the more likely and preferred scenario. The Albius of these lines in his concern (*curantem*) for ethics looks a lot like the Horace of *Epistles* 1.1.11, who concerns himself with truth and propriety (*verum atque decens curo*). Horace imagines Albius is drawn to the countryside for its healing aspects (*salubres*, 1.4.4), and so Albius, like the Horace of 1.1, may not be in the best spiritual health. Given Horace's own predilection for withdrawal and ethical study, we could imagine that Horace would approve of Albius doing likewise. However, Horace subtly casts doubt on the therapeutic potential of such withdrawal, and the isolation of this retreat serves to intensify

the extreme tendencies of Albius. First, his silence (*tacitum*, 4) as he strolls
through the countryside indicates that he is all alone, hidden from the world.
His isolation is taken a step further than that of Horace in the opening poem,
since he is not, as Horace's ignorance about his activities shows, sending letters
to friends explaining his motives and staying in touch. Secondly, the verb *rep-*
tare figures him as a snake, not so much "strolling" as "slithering" through the
woods. To quote Putnam:

> The implicit comparison with a snake suggests someone who goes slowly along,
> perhaps in circle. . . . The snake is by nature a paradigm of the devious. It lurks
> hidden, out of sight of the world. This would mean, in a person, someone who is
> both unaccounting and unaccountable, even slightly sinister. . . . There is an irony,
> then, in Horace's application of the adjective *salubris* to Tibullus' woods.[8]

Putnam cites as an interesting parallel for Albius's behavior a letter of Cicero,
whose despair at the death of his daughter compelled him to seek comfort in
silence and solitude: *in hac solitudine careo omnium conloquio, cumque mane*
me in silvam abstrusi densam et asperam, non exeo inde ante vesperum. secun-
dum te nihil est mihi amicius solitudine ("In this solitude I do not converse
with anyone, and, when in the morning I have hidden myself in the thick, wild
woods, I do not come out before evening. After you nothing is more friendly to
me than solitude," *Ad Atticum* 12.15). Though Cicero professes to look for comfort in this solitude and find it amicable, his description of it only serves to
intensify his despair. As Dutsch puts it, "the wilderness surrounding Cicero's
remote villa is the landscape of his emotions."[9] This isolation has a major draw-
back in that it prevents him from associating with his friend Atticus, whose
presence would no doubt be an even greater comfort for his grief, as he admits
in the previous letter: *solitudo aliquid adiuvat, sed multo plus proficeret sit tu*
tamen interesses ("Solitude is somewhat helpful, but nevertheless it would be
much more beneficial if I had you as company," 12.14.3). The benefit that Cicero
claims to receive from solitude is undermined by his desire for his friend's company. Friendship, it seems, has much greater therapeutic value than isolation,
and it is this that Horace aims to teach Albius in the epistle.

Horace's first strategy for cheering up his friend is to remind him of the various advantages that he has been given. He has beauty (*formam*, 6) and wealth
(*divitias*, 7), and he knows the proper way to enjoy them (*artem fruendi*, 7).
Horace's praise of Albius's *ars fruendi* has a protreptic function designed to urge
him to make good use of these assets, which he does not now seem to be doing.
Such are his gifts, Horace states, that no nurse could desire more for a child in
her care:

quid voveat dulci nutricula maius alumno,
qui sapere et fari possit quae sentiat et cui
gratia, fama, valetudo contingat abunde
et mundus victus non deficiente crumina? (8–11)

What more could a nurse desire for her sweet nursling than that he can be wise
and say what he thinks and have in abundance popularity, renown, good health,
and a stylish way of life thanks to a never-failing purse?[10]

Horace here exhorts his friend to reconnect with the world. His capacity both
"to be wise and say what he feels" (*sapere et fari . . . quae sentiat*, 9) contrasts
with lines 4–5, where, though Albius is pondering things worthy of a wise man
(*dignum sapiente*), he does so alone and in silence (*tacitum*). His "popularity"
and "renown," moreover, are not being put to good use in his present isolation
and would be better employed in *amicitia* than *solitudo*. The word *mundus* (11)
is especially important since it has strong associations with the mean, and Horace therefore urges Albius to curb his currently extreme pursuits.[11]

In the poem's final lines Horace encourages Albius to focus only on the present and invites him to enjoy his companionship, and the advice of these lines
has an especially Epicurean flavor:[12] *inter spem curamque, timores inter et iras /
omnem crede diem tibi diluxisse supremum: / grata superveniet quae non sperabitur hora* ("Amid hope and anxiety, fear and anger, believe that every day that
dawns is your last; the unexpected hour will be a pleasant surplus," 12–14). Albius's supposed "concern" (*curantem*, 5) about ethical matters is here transformed
by Horace into "anxiety" or "worry" (*curam*, 12). *Spes, cura, timor*, and *ira* are
emotional responses to situations that are largely out of our control, and hope,
worry, and fear are especially concerned with uncertainty about future events.
What we can control and enjoy, Horace stresses, is the present moment, while
hopes about tomorrow can detract from the enjoyment of today. Horace strongly
recalls his *carpe diem* ode in these lines, both with the recommendation to cut
short hope about the future (*spes, Epist.* 1.4.13 and *sperabitur, Epist.* 1.4.14; *spem,
Odes* 1.11.7) and with *crede diem* (*Epist.* 1.4.13) corresponding to *carpe diem* (*Odes*
1.11.8) in both meter and sound.

The best way to stop worrying and "seize the day" is to spend time pleasantly
with friends, and Horace ends the poem by inviting Albius to visit him and, in
order to stir a laugh in his somber friend, paints an amusing portrait of himself
as a sleek, fat Epicurean pig: *me pinguem et nitidum bene curata cute vises, / cum
ridere voles Epicuri de grege porcum* ("When you want to laugh, come see me,
fat and sleek with my hide nicely primped, a pig from the herd of Epicurus,"
15–16). As has been pointed out, Horace is having a joke at his own expense, for

Suetonius describes Horace as short and stout (*habitu corporis brevis fuit atque obesus*), while Horace himself comments on his shortness at *Epistles* 1.20.24 (*corporis exigui*).[13] Whereas Albius's *cura* suggests excessive anxiety, the porcine Horace is *bene curata cute*. His *cura* has been better directed not toward uncontrollable circumstances or concern with the future but toward grooming his "hide" for the amusement of his friend. The description looks back to the Ithacan suitors of 1.2.29 who groom themselves immoderately (*in cute curanda plus aequo*). Horace's *cura* therefore denotes moderation in contrast with Albius's tendency toward excessive worry and with the suitors' overly zealous pursuit of corporeal pleasure. Above all friendship is central to these lines, for, unlike the solitary, serpentine Albius of line 4, Horace prefers to be part of a herd, *grex*. It is because of the high value they place on friendship that Horace aligns himself here with the Epicureans, who were often compared with pigs, especially by their deriders.[14] Horace instead puts a positive and amusing spin on this image and may have in mind Cicero's description of the many friends whom Epicurus welcomed into his house, to whom Cicero refers as *greges*: *at vero Epicurus una in domo, et ea quidem angusta, quam magnos . . . tenuit amicorum greges!* ("But indeed Epicurus in one house, and a small house at that, had so many herds of friends!" *De Finibus* 1.65).[15] The Epicurean Horace that closes *Epistles* 1.4 illustrates well how he can adapt his philosophical teaching to the needs of the moment, for Albius could greatly benefit from adopting this Epicurean tenet and becoming part of the herd. With this invitation Horace urges Albius to balance his seriousness with laughter and his isolation with companionship.

The Horace we are presented with in these lines contrasts sharply with the one we met in the opening epistle, where he demonstrates the same extremes of withdrawal and anxiety that he here attributes to Albius. As we saw in the first two chapters, he there hides himself away in the countryside (*abditus agro*, 1.1.5) from his *amicus* Maecenas because of mental anguish (1.1.94–105) and devotes himself to the same sort of ethical contemplation that he attributes to Albius. Like that of Albius in 1.4, his philosophical devotion in 1.1 is extreme, for he immerses himself entirely in this pursuit: *quid verum atque decens curo et rogo et omnis in hoc sum* ("I care about and ask about what is true and seemly, and I am entirely [absorbed] in this," 1.1.11). These serious ethical contemplations rule out levity and play, which he claims to lay aside (*ludicra pono*, 10), and he especially wants to avoid becoming a laughingstock. Figuring himself as an aging racehorse (*senescentem equum*, 1.1.8), he reports that his inner voice warns him against making an absurd spectacle (*ridendus*, 1.1.9) of himself, and at the end of the poem he is troubled by Maecenas's laughter at his disheveled appearance (*rides*, 1.1.95; *rides*, 1.1.97). Now, on the other hand, he invites Albius to have a laugh (*cum ridere voles*, 16) at his amusing self-portrait as a *porcus*, thus showing that he sees an appropriate place for laughter and amusement as an antidote against unremitting withdrawal and seriousness. The isolation espoused by Horace in the opening poem is now seen as insufficient for providing the well-being that both he and Albius need, and the uncompromising attitude of 1.1 is replaced here by a need to moderate extreme tendencies. It is as though assessing his friend's behavior has enabled him to evaluate his own more clearly, and doing so has provided him with greater equanimity than he had in 1.1, for his well-groomed exterior in 1.4 reflects a healthy interior, which reverses what we saw in the earlier poem, where his disheveled appearance mirrored his troubled mind.

THE OENOPHILE HOST OF *EPISTLES* 1.5

The speaker of *Epistles* 1.5 likewise urges moderation to a friend who, like Albius in 1.4, inclines toward extremes. However, whereas Albius's anxiety leads him to excessive isolation, Torquatus has inherited a natural disposition toward *severitas* and public service, and Horace urges his friend to balance his public duties by joining him in a temporary and relaxing symposium. While Albius clings unremittingly to private *otium* in the countryside, Torquatus is devoted to urban *negotium*, but they share a tendency toward extreme seriousness. Just as Horace had offered himself to Albius as an example of how to balance private withdrawal with pleasant companionship among friends, Horace here becomes a model for incorporating leisure and relaxation into urban life. Nisbet, Eidinow, and Feeney have nicely examined the ways in which Torquatus's family background contributes to our understanding of the poem, and my own reading is indebted to their observations. Horace makes use of the associations of Torquatus's family with, on the one hand, *severitas*, a Stoic and traditionally Roman desideratum, and, on the other, Epicureanism, in order to recommend that he temper his excessively austere disposition. When the situation demands, Torquatus should be able to adapt and incorporate Epicurean relaxation into his life.

The Torquatus to whom Horace addresses the epistle no doubt belongs to the family of the Manlii Torquati, and Livy recounts the well-known deeds of the founder of this line.[16] The first Manlius Torquatus, who had the cognomen *Imperiosus* ("Domineering") and was consul in 347, 344, and 340 B.C., became known for the excessive *severitas* he displayed when putting his son to death for disobedience in battle (Livy 8.7). Livy states that this deed made Torquatus an exemplum of severity to future Romans (*Manlianaque imperia non in praesentia modo horrenda, sed exempli etiam tristis in posterum essent,* "Manlian orders were not only dreadful at that present moment but also were to serve as a stern exemplum for posterity," 8.7.22) and elsewhere reports that *Manliana imperia*

was a proverbial phrase for excessively difficult commands (4.29.6). Feeney
argues that "the rigidly strict discipline meted out by T. Manlius Imperiosus
Torquatus gave the Manlii Torquati a name for old-fashioned harsh severity, so
much so that the episode is demonstrably responsible for projections forward
and backward in time, as Manlian anecdotes were crafted to make other members of the family fit in with the template of rigidly enforced strict discipline."[17]
A later descendent of this Manlius Torquatus shows that he inherited his ancestor's disposition toward excessive *severitas*. T. Manlius Torquatus, consul in 235
and 224 B.C., is described by Livy as having just this quality: *priscae ac nimis
durae, ut plerisque videbatur, severitatis* ("He was, as it seemed to most people,
a man of excessively harsh severity," 22.60.5). Later, upon being voted consul he
refused it, stating *neque ego vestros . . . mores consul ferre potero neque vos imperium meum* ("Neither will I be able as consul to endure your character, nor will
you be able to endure my command," 26.22.9).[18]

Not all of the Torquati, however, fit this mold. L. Manlius Torquatus, a well-
respected orator who was praetor in 49 B.C., is a major speaker in Cicero's
De Finibus, in which he is the spokesman for Epicureanism, and Cicero suggests that his Epicureanism is incompatible with the *severitas* of his line (1.23–
24). The Epicureanism of this Torquatus did not, however, prevent him from
participation in public life, for he died fighting against Julius Caesar in 47 B.C.[19]
In the *De Finibus* he argues that duty, though troubling, often cannot be avoided
because we must sometimes undergo difficulties in order to enjoy greater pleasure in the future (1.33). He therefore seems to have been able to temper and
balance doctrinaire Epicureanism with his sense of duty to the state.[20] The wedding of this Manlius Torquatus is furthermore celebrated by Catullus in an epi-
thalamium (61). Catullus includes a wish that this marriage produce a son who
will grow up to be like his father (*sit suo similis patri Manlio*, 217–18), and this
son is most probably the Torquatus of *Epistles* 1.5. Whereas the elder Torquatus
could fit a place for duty into his devotion to Epicurean pleasure, Horace's Torquatus, conversely, must interject pleasure into his life of old-fashioned duty.

The opening lines of the poem suggest that Torquatus may in fact be actively
avoiding the Epicureanism of his father due to a belief that it leads to dangerous
libidinous excess:

> si potes Archiacis conviva recumbere lectis
> nec modica cenare times holus omne patella,
> supremo te sole domi, Torquate, manebo. (1.5.1–3)

> If you are able to recline as a dinner guest on the couches of Archias and do not
> fear to dine only on vegetables from a modest plate, I will await you, Torquatus, at
> my house at the end of the day.

Eidinow has nicely suggested that the *Archiaci lecti* are associated with excessive pleasure at the expense of duty, which Torquatus is determined to avoid. Taking up a suggestion of Bourgery that had been revived by Kilpatrick, he argues that the "couches of Archias" allude to the story of Archias of Thebes told by Cornelius Nepos.[21] This Archias was sent a letter warning that certain Theban exiles had entered the city in order to overtake it, but Archias refused to interrupt his dining to pay attention to these serious matters. His neglect of duty led to his death:

> quae cum iam accubanti in convivio esset data, sicut erat signata, sub pulvinum subiciens, 'in crastinum,' inquit, 'differo res severas.' at illi omnes, cum iam nox processisset, vinolenti ab exsulibus duce Pelopida sunt interfecti. (*Life of Pelopidas* 3.2–3)

> When this letter had been given to him while he was reclining at a dinner party, placing it unopened beneath his cushion, he said, "I postpone serious matters." But all of those men, when the night had already advanced and they were drunk with wine, were killed by the exiles under the leadership of Pelopidas.

Archias serves as a warning against deferring serious matters in favor of pleasure, but in the epistle Horace invites Torquatus to do just that, to put off the *severitas* of his family and run the risk of enjoying himself for a while. The conditional *si potes* suggests that such deferral of duty does not come easily to Torquatus, and the exemplum of Archias would in fact be a suitable one for Torquatus himself to cite in refusing Horace's invitation to relax. As Eidinow states, "Surely, says Horace, Torquatus does not really believe that finding room in life for having fun is going to kill him."[22] The *patella* (2) points to another excuse that Torquatus might offer: that such feasting is extravagant and even sacrilegious. Eidinow convincingly suggests that Horace here alludes to Cicero's condemnation of Epicurean pleasure in the *De Finibus*, where he tells L. Manlius Torquatus, *atque reperiemus asotos primum ita non religiosos ut 'edint de patella'* ("And yet we shall find profligate men who are first of all so impious that they would 'eat from a sacrificial dish,'" 2.22). Cicero here expresses doubt as to whether one who pursues pleasure can limit his desires: *unum nescio, quomodo possit, si luxuriosus sit, finitas cupiditates habere*, "There is one thing I do not know: how one can, if he gives himself to luxury, have limited desires," 2.23. Cicero's condemnation of Epicurean pleasure is common in anti-Epicurean polemic and seems to be shared by Horace's addressee Torquatus, whom Horace imagines to be afraid (*times*, 2) of succumbing to such decadence. Again, to quote Eidinow:

> Horace urges the pleasures of his dinner-party upon Torquatus by the . . . controverted use of an image derived from (as it were) one of the documents of Torquatus's

family history, a cheeky theft of a counter-example cited by Cicero in his attempt
to bring L. Torquatus up to scratch and dissuade him from his Epicureanism, used
here to suggest relaxation into a pleasure with which neither Epicurus nor Cicero
could properly have found fault.[23]

At the same time that he anticipates Torquatus's possible objections Horace
reassures him by emphasizing the modesty of the proposed dinner. The vegetarian meal will hardly be haute cuisine, and the *patella* is not here a sacred object
but a simple plate. The keyword is *modica* (2). The meal and dinnerware will be
modest, and in partaking of it Torquatus will show himself to be neither a man
of excessive *severitas* (a risk he currently runs) nor a man for whom relaxation
leads to immoderate pleasure and luxury (a risk he currently fears).

Horace furthermore presses Torquatus to compromise by setting aside the
imperious nature of his family and subjecting himself to Horace's directives as
the "master of the feast."[24] Horace carefully describes the wine they will imbibe
as having been pressed from grapes grown "between Minturnae and Sinuessan
Petrinum" (*inter Minturnas Sinuessanumque Petrinum*, 5) and bottled during
T. Statilius Taurus's second consulship (i.e., in 26 B.C.). At only six years old,
this is a modest wine suitable to the simple food Horace will serve. As Nisbet
has convincingly demonstrated, Horace here alludes to the battle fought and
won by Torquatus's ancestor T. Manlius Imperiosus—the one who put his own
son to death for disobedience—in 340 B.C., which Livy states took place *ad
Trifanum*—*inter Sinuessam Minturnasque is locus est* ("at Trifanum—this is a
place between Sinuessa and Minturnae, 8.11.11).[25] Nisbet points out that, while
wine with a sentimental value is commonly offered in invitation poems, "wine
from a battlefield is unique."[26] Horace alludes to this battle, I suggest, not only
to remind Torquatus of his famously severe ancestors but also to emphasize
the ever-changing cycle and rhythm of human affairs. What once was a battlefield is now a vineyard. War gives way to peace, and the ground once nourished
by Roman dead now produces vines meant for pleasure and relaxation. Severity
yields to levity, and Torquatus too must yield. Horace states, however, that if
Torquatus has a superior wine, he should send for it. If not, he must submit to
Horace's command: *arcesse, vel imperium fer*, 6. Nisbet—followed by Eidinow
and Feeney—argues that *imperium* here alludes to the *imperia Manliana*.[27] As
Nisbet states, "Torquatus, though he came of a family which was used to giving
orders, would have to receive them for once." Horace here even echoes the words
of the T. Manlius Torquatus who in 210 B.C. turned down the consulship: *neque
ego vestros . . . mores consul ferre potero neque vos imperium meum* (26.22.9).
Torquatian inflexibility and stubborn imperiousness must, Horace suggests,
give way.

Horace next assures Torquatus that his house has long been prepared for his friend's arrival, and he especially emphasizes its cleanliness: *iamdudum splendet focus et tibi munda supellex*, "for a long time the hearth has been shining for you, and the furniture clean," 7. Cleanliness is underlined again later in the poem:

> haec ego procurare et idoneus imperor et non
> invitus, ne turpe toral, ne sordida mappa
> corruget nares, ne non et cantharus et lanx
> ostendat tibi te. (21–24)

> I willingly command myself, as is appropriate, to see to the following: that no foul coverlet and no dirty napkin make you turn up your nose in disgust, that goblet and plate show you to yourself.

Though Eidinow argues that Horace's emphasis on cleanliness is an amusing transference of the discipline of the Torquati to his own domestic sphere,[28] I suggest instead that this reassuringly illustrates the moderation of Horace's household. Like the *modica patella* of line 2, *munditia* has associations with dining that adheres to the mean.[29] This is especially evident in *Satires* 2.2., which has moderation in dining as its central concern. The satire, in which Horace professes to report the teachings of his old neighbor Ofellus, opens with an attack against luxurious fare, such as peacock and turbot, but Ofellus is equally opposed to overly abstemious dining, such as that practiced by the Cynic Avidienus, who does not allow himself any indulgence even at weddings and on holidays (55–62). Correct dining involves neither self-denial nor luxury but hits upon the mean, and in avoiding decadent fare we should not turn to the opposite extreme: *sordidus a tenui victu distabit, Ofello / iudice; nam frustra vitium vitaveris illud / si te alio pravum detorseris*, "Miserly eating will differ from humble, in Ofellus's judgment; for in vain will you have avoided one fault if you wrongly turn yourself to another," 53–55. Both excesses must be avoided by the wise man: *quali igitur victu sapiens utetur, et horum / utrum imitabitur? hac urget lupus, hac canis, aiunt*, "What sort of eating, therefore, will the wise man employ; and which of these will he imitate? On this side a wolf attacks, on the other a dog, they say," 63–64. The *canis* here looks back to the austere Cynic Avidienus, earlier called *Canis*, 56, while the *lupus* must therefore refer to the opposite extreme of gluttony. Ofellus states that the wise man, in adhering to the mean, will be *mundus*, "clean":

> mundus erit qua non offendat sordibus, atque
> in neutram partem cultus miser. hic neque servis,
> Albuci senis exemplo, dum munia didit
> saevus erit; nec sic ut simplex Naevius unctam
> convivis praebebit aquam; vitium hoc quoque magnum. (65–69)

He will be clean, so that he not offend with his filth, and his way of living will be wretched in neither direction. He will not be harsh to his slaves, like old Albucius, when he allots their duties; nor, like simple-minded Naevius, will he offer his guests greasy water: this too is a great fault.

On the one hand Albucius is too strict and harsh, and on the other Naevius is so laissez-faire that his guests are offered dirty water with which to wash their hands. The wise man hits upon a mean between excessive severity and indulgence, and his dining habits fall at a midpoint between gluttony and abstemiousness. Horace similarly uses the word *mundus* in his great invitation poem to Maecenas, *Odes* 3.29, where humble dinners can soothe the cares of busy men. As in *Satires* 2.2, *munditia* is here associated with moderation and timely rest from activity:

> plerumque gratae divitibus vices
> *mundae*que parvo sub lare pauperum
>   cenae sine aulaeis et ostro
>   sollicitam explicuere frontem. (13–16)

Often changes are pleasant for the rich, and in the house of the poor clean dinners without tapestries and purple have smoothed a worried brow.

In these lines it is the lack of ostentatious display that makes these humble dinners *mundae*, and by partaking of them Maecenas can avoid excessive anxiety (*ultra fas trepidat*, 31–32). In emphasizing the cleanliness of his furnishings in *Epistles* 1.5, Horace suggests to Torquatus both that the dinner he will offer adheres to the correct mean and that the indulgence he urges is in no way dissolute. Torquatus need not fear that in relaxing his *severitas* he will run to the opposite extreme, and the momentary lapse into relaxation will in fact be beneficial.

In order to illustrate further the need for relaxation and Torquatus's potential for excessive severity, Horace reveals that tomorrow is Augustus's birthday and therefore a holiday (9). The occasion demands that Torquatus take a break. Torquatus can stay up late into the night (*tendere noctem*, 11) and spend tomorrow in bed (*somnum*, 10) with impunity (*impune*, 10). He can, for just one day, live like the Phaeacians of *Epistles* 1.2.30, "to whom it was fine to sleep until noon," *cui pulchrum fuit in medios dormire dies*. Torquatus must be willing to adapt himself to the demands of the occasion, and failure to do so will reveal him not only to be immoderately stern but also entirely fettered by his inherited character. Horace now turns his attention to another kind of inheritance, the financial one passed down from one generation to the next. What use is good fortune, he asks, if we do not take time to enjoy it for ourselves (*quo mihi fortunam, si non conceditur uti*, 12) rather than parsimoniously setting it aside for an heir (*parcus ob heredis curam nimiumque severus / adsidet insano*, "Whoever is frugal and overly severe on account of his concern for his heir is like a madman," 13–14).[30] The excessive severity (*nimium severus*) of the one who denies oneself enjoyment points directly to Torquatus's family history, and this is a quality that renders one a madman, *insano*. Torquatus must free himself from his ancestral madness and seize the day.

The climax of the poem comes in lines 16–20, in which Horace sings the praises of wine, which are familiar from several of his odes:[31]

> quid non ebrietas dissignat? operta recludit,
> spes iubet esse ratas, ad proelia trudit inertem,
> sollicitis animis onus eximit, addocet artes.
> fecundi calices quem non fecere disertum,
> contracta quem non in paupertate solutum?

> What does intoxication not unseal? It exposes secrets, bids hopes to be realized, urges the sluggish man to battle, removes the burden from anxious minds, and teaches new arts. Whom have the full cups not made eloquent, whom have they not made free amid narrow poverty?

Wine relaxes us and releases us from anxiety. The "fickle hopes" (*levis spes*, 8) Horace previously urged Torquatus to dismiss are now replaced by "valid hopes" (*spes ratas*, 17). Fickle hopes cause worry about things outside of our control, whereas the hope produced by wine creates optimism and cheer, and in *Odes* 3.21.17 Horace similarly offers convivial hope as an antidote to anxious care: *tu spem reducis mentibus anxiis* ("You [i.e., wine] lead back hope to anxious minds"). Wine especially turns us away from our normal tendencies. It makes the coward brave, the tongue-tied eloquent, and the poor man free. It can, Horace implies, assuage Torquatus's natural severity and induce the *sermo benignus* (11) in which Horace hopes to pass the night and which would not come easily to a man of *severitas*.[32] To quote Kiernan, "Wine brings freedom from the whole realm governed by convention, mechanical duty; it opens a private garden where friends can leave off their masks, and life can be unconstrained."[33] It is just such camaraderie that Horace bids Torquatus to expect: *procurare . . . imperor . . . / . . . ne fidos inter amicos /sit qui dicta foras eliminet, ut coeat par iungaturque pari*, "I bid myself to see to it that among the faithful friends there be no one who may carry outside the things we have said, that equal come together and be joined with equal," 21–26. Just as in *Epistles* 1.4, in which Albius is invited by Horace to join him in laughter and friendship, Torquatus is urged to turn his mind from excessively serious pursuits and cast off his inhibitions among trustworthy friends.

Horace names these friends near the end of his invitation: *Butram tibi Septi-ciumque / et nisi cena prior potiorque puella Sabinum / detinet adsumam. locus est et pluribus umbris* ("I will add to the guest-list for you Butra and Septicius, and Sabinus too, unless a previous dinner engagement and a better girl detain him. There is room as well for a few hangers-on," 26–28). These dinner guests are not otherwise known and certainly are not meant to evoke men of great public importance. As Mayer notes, this gives the impression of "a party of close friends, rather than of celebrities."[34] This will be a party of equals, and no great men of state, such as Maecenas, will be at this party to detract from Tor-quatus's private relaxation and reinforce social hierarchies. Horace emphasizes, furthermore, the need to keep the group small: *sed nimis arta premunt olidae convivia caprae* ("but stinking she-goats oppress overcrowded dinner parties," 29). This amusing reference to body odor is no doubt intended to rouse a smile on the normally stern face of Torquatus and to set the mood for the easygoing atmosphere of the party. At the same time it emphasizes once more the need to avoid excess (*nimis*). In contrast to these *amici fidi et pares* is the client waiting in Torquatus's hall, whom Horace urges Torquatus to give the slip by exiting secretly out his back door: *rebus omissis / atria servantem postico falle clientem*, "lay aside your business and by using the back door elude the client that guards the entrance hall," 30–31. The highly stratified world of business and patronage, with its stuffy rules and responsibilities, is rejected here in favor of the egalitar-ian relaxation of the dinner party.

In advising Torquatus to drop his business (*rebus omissis*) Horace urges him to take charge of his own affairs, to become, in a way, like the Aristippean Horace of 1.1.19, who controls and is not controlled by situations (*res*): *et mihi res, non me rebus, subiungere conor*. He must learn to adapt himself to the situation at hand and not to adhere stubbornly to one extreme. Sternness and levity both have a place in human life, and Torquatus must compromise and become fes-tive when the circumstances demand, even if it is just for the day. Though the two poles Horace plays off each other in the poem are old-fashioned and Stoic *severitas*, on the one hand, and Epicurean pleasure, on the other, the ability to move back and forth between them at different times is particularly Aristippean. Horace himself is not so very different from Torquatus, as he likewise must put aside the serious philosophical pursuits outlined in the first epistle in order to enjoy the day with his friend in the city. He too must adapt himself to the festival day and spend it not in the isolation of the countryside but in the com-pany of friends at his urban *domus* (3). This is the first indication in the col-lection that Horace does not adhere uncompromisingly to rural withdrawal, as the opening poem would lead us to expect, but instead moves back and forth between the city and the country. He seems, at least for the time being, to have overcome the anxiety he describes at the end of the opening poem, but perhaps such equanimity is possible for Horace only because Maecenas, a major source of his anxiety, will not be attending the dinner party with Torquatus. Horace will remain in this adaptable and compromising mood throughout the following poem, *Epistles* 1.6.

MODERATION AND ADAPTABILITY IN *EPISTLES* 1.6

Epistles 1.6 opens with the striking tag *nil admirari* ("marvel at / be surprised by nothing"), and in the rest of the poem Horace seeks to define this concept for his addressee, Numicius, about whom no information survives. This poem has not received the attention it deserves by critics, yet it makes up an important expression of Horace's moral thought in the *Epistles* and develops in particular the adaptability and moderation that the Aristippean Horace of 1.1.19 sets as his goal.[35] Though *Epistles* 1.4 and 1.5 see Horace offering moral advice in the manner of an ethical guide and holding up his own behavior as an exemplum for his friends, *Epistles* 1.6 takes this a step further and presents us with a Horace who approaches a didactic teacher in his confidence and wisdom. To employ the categories outlined by Volk, the poem is written in the "didactic mode" in that it fulfills two of her four requirements for didactic: it "states clearly, or gives other strong indications, that it is first and foremost supposed to teach whatever subject or skill it happens to be treating," and "the speaker of the text teaches a student or students by means of the poem itself."[36] Numicius, though he does not emerge as a strong presence in the poem, takes up the role of both epistolary and didactic addressee. The strongest didactic note is struck at the ending of the poem, where Horace invites Numicius to apply the moral lessons expounded in the poem to his own life, provided that he has learned nothing better himself: *siquid novisti rectius istis, / candidus imperti; si nil, his utere mecum* ("If you have learned anything better than what I have outlined, share it candidly; if not, employ these things with me," 67–68).[37] Although, as McGann suggests, the tone of these lines "is not that of one who, confident that he is right, is unwilling to learn from another,"[38] Horace nevertheless places himself in a position of superior knowledge to Numicius throughout the poem and invites his addressee to learn from his greater experience. In expressing his willingness to listen to better teaching if available, Horace in fact exemplifies the flexibility, detachment, and lack of dogmatic adherence that is the central ethical lesson implied in *nil admirari*.

Horace claims that this lack of astonishment is just about the "one and only thing that can make and keep a man happy" (*prope res una, Numici, / solaque, quae possit facere et servare beatum*, 1–2). The tag *nil admirari* immediately invites the reader to consider to which philosophical school such a thought belongs, but one looking for an easy answer to this question will be disappointed. As both Rudd and Mayer point out, this was a motto associated with many divergent philosophical systems.[39] I will suggest below, however, that the tag does point us toward Cyrenaic and thus Aristippean ideas. This fact does not, however, mark him as an orthodox Cyrenaic. Rather, it connects the ethical positions outlined in 1.6 to the general adaptability ascribed elsewhere in the *Epistles* to Aristippus. The precise definition of *nil admirari* is a difficult one; above all it is the adherence to the mean through the avoidance of extremes, which can arouse in us emotions such as alarm, fear, surprise, grief, and desire that can ultimately paralyze us. Lack of astonishment must be practiced in two major spheres: in our reactions to circumstances beyond our control, and in our attempts to pursue goals that risk holding us in their thrall. If *nil admirari* is correctly applied to these areas, one may achieve autonomy. Issues of control, power, and independence predominate, and, as we shall see, Horace carefully responds to and revises the declaration of freedom that opens the first epistle.

Horace explains the concept of *nil admirari* through a series of examples, many of which demonstrate what *nil admirari* is not. The first exemplum Horace gives is a positive one: the doctrine is exemplified by those who are able to look upon (*spectent*, 5) the sun, stars, and seasons without fear or awe (*formido*, 4). These lines, as Armstrong states, have a strong Epicurean flavor, for Epicurus argued that we can come to an understanding of the universe without succumbing to religious dread. Horace thus employs an Epicurean tenet to underscore the importance of control over emotions. Interestingly, Horace does not suggest that we *not* gaze upon natural celestial phenomena, but suggests instead that we reach a state in which we can do so without becoming so engrossed by our emotional response to the exclusion of all else. Throughout this opening section of the poem the issue of sight is central (*spectanda*, 8; *species*, 11; *vidit*, 13; *oculis*, 14; *spectant*, 19), but the question is not whether or not we should look but *how* we should look at various pursuits and circumstances (*quo spectanda modo*, 8). If they captivate our sight completely, we can see nothing else, and Horace wants Numicius to be able to look without losing himself and thus to hit upon a midpoint between averting his eyes altogether and utter captivation.

Horace in lines 5–7 now passes on to further examples toward which we should have an attitude of detachment: wealth (*munera*, 5), games (*ludicra*, 7), applause (*plausus*,7), and public office (*amici dona Quiritis*, 7). To a large degree these are things beyond our control, and, in the case of applause and public office, given according to the mood of the populace (*amici Quiritis*). *Nil admirari* promotes, therefore, an indifference to circumstances over which we are powerless, and this indifference is a moderate position between the intense desire for certain outcomes and the crippling fear that things will not turn out as we had hoped. Above all, *nil admirari* implies that we should not be surprised or over-whelmed when events turn out contrary to our expectations:

> qui timet his adversa, fere miratur eodem
> quo cupiens pacto; pavor est utrubique molestus,
> improvisa simul species exterret utrumque.
> gaudeat an doleat, cupiat metuatne, quid ad rem,
> si, quicquid vidit melius peiusve sua spe,
> defixis oculis animoque et corpore torpet? (9–14)

> Whoever fears the opposite of these things marvels almost in the same way as the one who desires them; what is troubling in each case is the alarm that results as soon as an unexpected appearance startles either.[40] Whether he feels joy or grief, desire or fear, what does it matter, if, when he has seen something better or worse than he had hoped, he becomes numb and his eyes and mind and body are transfixed?

Joy, grief, desire, and fear are all closely connected in these lines, for each rivets us and renders us impotent in the face of chance. Horace again closely allies desire and fear in the sixteenth poem and states explicitly that these emotions remove our independence: *nam qui cupiet, metuet quoque; porro / qui metuens vivet, liber mihi non erit umquam* ("For whoever will desire will also fear; further-more, whoever will live in fear will never, in my opinion, be free," 1.16.65–66). The only way to maintain control over chance and retain one's independence, as presented in the sixth epistle, is through preparation for any outcome, whether good or bad. The unprepared man is the one who has not foreseen (*improvisa*, 1.6.11) all possibilities and so is utterly crushed when things turn out counter to his hopes. The provident man will have an imperturbability characteristic of the *providus Ulixes* of *Epistles* 1.2.18–19, who, as we have seen, embodies mod-eration and adaptability, qualities that make one capable of experiencing both good and bad circumstances with equanimity.

Horace's thought in these lines comes very close to that of the Stoics, who promoted a detachment from extreme passions through preparation for changes in fortune.[41] Especially relevant here is Cicero's *Tusculan Disputations*, which has many correspondences with these lines of the epistle. At 4.14 Cicero lays out the Stoic belief that passions can be labeled under four basic categories that cor-respond to those in *Epistles* 1.6.9–14: desire, fear, pleasure, and grief:[42]

> itaque eas definiunt pressius, ut intellegatur, non modo quam vitiosae, sed etiam quam in nostra sint potestate. est ergo *aegritudo* opinio recens mali praesentis, in quo demitti contrahique animo rectum esse videatur, *laetitia* opinio recens boni praesentis, in quo ecferri rectum esse videatur, *metus* opinio impendentis mali, quod intolerabile esse videatur, *libido* opinio venturi boni, quod sit ex usu iam praesens esse atque adesse.

And so [the Stoics] define them [i.e. passions, *perterbationes*] more precisely, so that we can understand not only how wicked these are but also to what degree we can control them. And so grief is defined as a fresh notion of present evil, in which it seems to be proper that the spirit be lowered and depressed. Happiness is a fresh notion of present good, in which it seems to be proper for the spirit to be puffed up. Fear is a notion of impending evil that seems to be intolerable. Desire is the notion of approaching good that would be useful already to be present and at hand.

The passions identified by Horace are equivalent to these four posited by the Stoics and outlined by Cicero. Horace's *timet* (9) and *metuat* (12) correspond to Cicero's *metus*, *cupiens* (10) to *libido*, *gaudeat* (12) to *laetitia*, and *doleat* (12) to *aegritudo*. All four emotions are neatly expressed by Horace in line 12, where *gaudeat an doleat* correspond to Cicero's *opiniones recentes* pertaining to present circumstances (good and bad, respectively) and *cupiat metuatne* to *opiniones* of future circumstances (good and bad, respectively).

Furthermore, Horace's promotion of foresight in *Epistles* 1.6 strongly resembles Cicero's suggestion in the third book of the *Tusculan Disputations* about how to diminish the negative impact of unexpected outcomes. According to Cicero, only through considering evils beforehand can one soften their blow: *haec igitur praemeditatio futurorum malorum lenit eorum adventum, quae venientia longe ante videris* ("Therefore this pre-consideration of future evils alleviates their arrival, which you will have seen coming long before," 29). He expands on this a few lines later in language that strongly anticipates that of Horace, especially in his insistence on foresight (*provisio*) and being surprised by nothing (*nihil admirari*):[43]

> ergo id quidem non dubium, quin omnia, quae mala putentur, sint *improvisa* graviora. Itaque quamquam non haec una res efficit maximam aegritudinem, tamen, quoniam multum potest *provisio* animi et praeparatio ad minuendum dolorem, sint semper omnia homini humana meditata. et nimirum haec est illa praestans et divina sapientia, et perceptas penitus et pertractatas res humanas habere, *nihil admirari*, cum acciderit, nihil, ante quam evenerit, non evenire posse arbitrari. (30)

> Therefore there is indeed no doubt that all things considered bad are worse when unforeseen. And although this [i.e., lack of foresight] is not the only thing that causes extreme grief, nevertheless, since foresight and mental preparation are very effective at diminishing grief, a human should consider at all times everything that can befall human beings. And certainly this is that outstanding and divine wisdom: to understand thoroughly and to study carefully human affairs, to be surprised by nothing when it happens, and to think that there is nothing that cannot happen before it has happened.

Cicero's *nihil admirari* champions the same foresight as Horace's *nil admirari*, and Horace intends, I suggest, for us to have Cicero's use of the phrase in our mind. According to both Cicero and Horace, freedom from gripping emotions can only be achieved through a pre-prepared mindset that lets us avoid being surprised when events do not accord with our expectations.

Cicero contrasts these Stoic ideas with those of Epicurus, who believed that anticipation of and preparation for evil detracts from present pleasure:

> qui censet necesse esse omnis in aegritudine esse, qui se in malis esse arbitrentur, sive illa ante provisa et expectata sint sive inveteraverint. nam neque vetustate minui mala nec fieri praemeditata leviora, stultamque etiam esse meditationem futuri mali aut fortasse ne futuri quidem: satis esse odiosum malum omne, cum venisset; qui autem semper cogitavisset accidere posse aliquid adversi, ei fieri illud sempiternum malum; si vero ne futurum quidem sit, frustra suscipi miseriam voluntariam; ita semper angi aut accipiendo aut cogitando malo. (32)

> He [i.e., Epicurus] believes that anyone who considers himself to be in bad situations must necessarily experience grief regardless of whether those evils have been previously foreseen and expected or are of long standing. For evils are neither diminished through long duration nor do they become easier to bear when they have been considered beforehand, and also pre-consideration of evil that may or may not come is foolish. Every evil is hateful enough when it has come. Moreover, evil is occurring all the time for one who constantly expects something bad to happen; but if it never happens, misery is taken up voluntarily and in vain. And so a person always feels anguish because he is either experiencing or pondering something bad.

The Stoics, however, were not the only proponents of the idea that future pains can be diminished through foresight, and throughout this passage in the *Tusculan Disputations* Cicero contrasts the beliefs of Epicurus with those of the Cyrenaics, with whom on this matter the Stoics agree. In section 28 he states, for example, *Cyrenaici non omni malo aegritudinem effici censent, sed insperato et necopinato malo* ("The Cyrenaics believe that grief is produced not by every evil, but by unexpected and unforeseen evil."). A little later Cicero even states that he is taking these ideas about preparation and foresight from the Cyrenaics themselves: *accipio equidem a Cyrenaicis haec arma contra casus et eventus, quibus eorum advenientes impetus diuturna praemeditatione frangantur* ("Indeed I am borrowing from the Cyrenaics these weapons against chance and accidents, with which their force is broken as they arrive through constant pre-consideration," 31).[44] Thus, though Epicureans and Cyrenaics share hedonism as their *telos* they nevertheless have very different views of how to overcome and prevent grief and fear.[45] The founder of the Cyrenaic school was of course Aristippus, whose ability to master circumstances is, as we have seen, put forth by Horace as the

goal to which he himself aspires in *Epistles* 1.1.19. Horace is perhaps drawn to
these Stoic ideas found in the *Tusculan Disputations* because they are simultaneously connected to the Cyrenaics and help him formulate his own Aristippean moderation and adaptability to chance, central to which is the doctrine of
nil admirari.[46]

Horace interestingly applies the idea of *provisio* to potentially good events
as well, for the same *pavor* (10) and *torpor* comes equally to those who desire
and fear, rejoice and grieve. For Horace the goal is not just for us to be free
from unexpected pain but also to buttress ourselves against excessive pleasure
and joy, lest we become surprised and disappointed when circumstances take
an unexpected turn. True enjoyment of our present circumstances comes only
when we free ourselves from anxiety or expectations about the future, and we
do this by preparing for any outcome, whether good or bad. The idea of preparation as a means of adapting to any turn of events is likewise central to the *aurea
mediocritas* ode, for there it is the "well prepared heart" that can handle any
change of fortune: *sperat infestis, metuit secundis / alteram sortem bene praepa-
ratum / pectus*, "the well prepared heart hopes for another lot in bad circumstances and fears another in favorable ones," 2.10.13–15. The *provisio* that enables
one to *nil admirari* in *Epistles* 1.6 is therefore fundamental also to the golden
mean, which involves not only steering a middle course between divergent extremes but also the ability to adapt to these extremes when they are unavoidable
by preparing for them ahead of time.

Beginning at *Epistles* 1.6.15, Horace directs his attention to moderation in pursuits and activities over which we do have control and which we often falsely
believe will make us happy. The first example of excessive pursuits that Horace
gives proves him to be no orthodox Stoic at all. It is possible, he states, to seek
even virtue in excess, which results only in madness and lack of equanimity:
*insani sapiens nomen ferat, aequus iniqui, / ultra quam satis est virtutem si petat
ipsam* ("Let the sane man bear the name of the insane, the tranquil of the un-
balanced, if he should seek virtue itself beyond what is enough," 15–16). It is
of course the Stoics who placed the *summum bonum* in virtue, but here such
behavior is criticized as an extreme. The idealization of virtue is not, of course,
exclusive to the Stoics; it was just as much a quality venerated by traditional
Romans and ranked among the most important of the *mores maiorum*. What
Horace criticizes is not so much virtue as the overly tenacious pursuit of it, and
therefore even seemingly good aspirations can be striven for to excess. The rest
of Horace's examples are more straightforwardly open to criticism. He faults,
for example, those who are dazzled by riches (17–19); those who strenuously
seek financial gain (20–23; 32–48); those who desire pomp, renown, and political

success (49–55); those who pursue gastronomic delights (56–64); and finally those who spend their lives in amorous pleasure (65–66). Horace does not in fact so much criticize these pursuits directly as urge Numicius to consider whether any of them *alone* will make and keep him happy by providing him the means to "live appropriately," *recte vivere*, 29. Each of these options is implicitly rejected by Horace, and we are left with the opening doctrine of *nil admirari* as the only means to live a good and harmonious life. Horace's criticisms do not imply an absolute condemnation of these activities; rather, he is concerned with *how* and *to what degree* we pursue these goals. He repeatedly emphasizes excessive single-mindedness and zeal: *ultra quam satis* ("more than enough," 16); *navus* ("energetically," 20); *virtus una* ("virtue alone," 30); and *res sola* ("wealth alone," 47). None of these pursuits on their own can render us *beatus*, and happiness should be possible with or without them. *Nil admirari* would have us possess these things—or not—without excessive desire (*cupiens*, 10; *cupiat*, 12) or pleasure (*gaudeat*, 12) on the one hand, and fear (*timet*, 9; *metuat*, 12) or grief (*doleat*, 12), on the other. There is a place, then, for virtue, wealth, renown, food, and sensuous pleasure, but each must be approached and valued with moderation and adaptability so that admiration of them does not compromise our control over them and thus over ourselves. Wisdom (*sapiens*, 15) comes from knowing how to deal with every circumstance and pursuit with levelheaded tranquility (*aequus*, 15),[47] which in turn will disable any of these pursuits from incapacitating and enslaving us.

The doctrine of *nil admirari* in many ways looks back to the opening epistle and the two methods of philosophical inquiry Horace outlines in it. As I argued in the first chapter, Horace's ethical pursuits oscillate between rigidity and orthodoxy, on the one hand, and adaptability and flexibility, on the other:

> nunc agilis fio et mersor civilibus undis,
> virtutis verae custos rigidusque satelles,
> nunc in Aristippi furtim praecepta relabor
> et mihi res, non me rebus, subiungere conor. (1.1.16–19)

> Now I become active and am immersed in the waves of civil life as a guardian and rigid attendant of true virtue, now I slip back secretly into the precepts of Aristippus and try to make things subject to myself, not myself to things.

The *rigidus* Horace of these lines, who champions *virtus vera* inflexibly and thus *ultra quam satis*, does not follow the doctrine of *nil admirari* as outlined in the sixth epistle, and this rigidity and lack of compromise characterizes Horace throughout the opening lines of the first poem. He rebuffs Maecenas's desires for more poetry, clings to withdrawal, and refuses to take part in anything connected with "play" or "games" (*ludo*, 3; *ludicra*, 10) for fear that this will compromise his freedom. In the sixth epistle these extreme views are rejected in favor of the flexible Aristippean approach (1.1.18–19) that Horace sets in opposition to inflexible orthodoxy, and this rejection is especially evident in several verbal and thematic parallels between the two poems.

In 1.6.6–7, Horace criticizes those who are overly captivated by *ludicra*, *plausus*, and the *amici dona Quiritis*, "games, applause, and the gifts of the friendly Quirites." The word *ludicra* here immediately recalls the opening lines of the first poem, for this is what Horace emphatically casts aside as making him dependent on the whims of the *populus* (1.1.6). Whereas Horace's attitude toward *ludicra* in the first poem seems unambiguously negative, he here considers them in a different light. Our attitude should instead be detached, and we should not allow ourselves to become enthralled by our "admiration" for them, whether that admiration arises from desire or fear, enthusiastic participation or pointed denunciation. In the first epistle, Horace's view toward *ludicra* is anything but indifferent, and it leads him to adopt an extreme position of aversion and withdrawal. In 1.1, furthermore, he is too closely following the excessive pursuit of *virtus* as described in 1.6, a topic on which Horace elaborates in lines 28–31:

> si latus aut renes morbo temptantur acuto,
> quaere fugam morbi. vis recte uiuere—quis non?:
> si virtus hoc una potest dare, fortis omissis
> hoc age deliciis.

> If your flank or kidneys are disturbed by a sharp disease, seek out the reason for the disease. You wish to live appropriately—who doesn't? If virtue alone is able to provide this, set about this and lay aside delights.

The disease imagery, the focus on *virtus*, and the casting aside of trifles in these lines all recall the first epistle. Horace implies in 1.6 that virtue alone is not sufficient to provide a person with the means to live well, and therefore to pursue it to the total exclusion of pleasurable pursuits, *deliciae*, is foolish. On the other hand, the quest for delights alone is equally objectionable (1.6.65–66), and a moderate stance toward both virtue and frivolities must be established.[48] One who "admires nothing" therefore participates in both without losing his control over either. The Horace of 1.1 who foreswears *ludicra*, devotes himself exclusively to serious pursuits, and attends rigidly to *virtus vera* (17) becomes an object of censure in the sixth epistle, while the Horace who advises Numicius on *nil admirari* in 1.6 is analogous to the Aristippean Horace of 18–19, who is prepared for anything and can adapt accordingly.

Epistles 1.6 occupies an important place in the collection in moving us away from the extreme inflexibility of 1.1.16–17 and toward the adaptable and moderate

Aristippean Horace of 1.1.18–19 who will prevail in the collection's closing poems. The poem also forms a nice conclusion to the thematically linked 1.4 and 1.5 in that it applies the avoidance of extremes recommended in those poems more broadly to a wide variety of pursuits. Both Albius (1.4) and Torquatus (1.5) are victims of the *admiratio* described in 1.6; Albius zealously "admires" contemplative isolation in the countryside and Torquatus *severitas* and duty. In order to disengage them from their admiration, Horace tries to convince them to find balance by participating in activities that will force them out of their currently extreme and inflexible behavior. *Epistles* 1.12 presents us with a similarly captivated, marveling Iccius.

THE ADMIRING ICCIUS OF *EPISTLES* 1.12

Though *Epistles* 1.12 does not immediately follow 1.6, the ethical lessons Horace espouses in it can best be elucidated by the doctrine of *nil admirari*, which the Iccius of 1.12 falls far short of fulfilling. This Iccius, also the addressee of *Odes* 1.29, seems predisposed to extremes and to dissatisfaction with his current lot. In particular his mind is fixated on the acquisition of wealth, and in both the ode and the epistle this hinders his pursuit of philosophical wisdom. Horace suggests that he will be unable to achieve wellbeing until he learns how to curb his appetite for riches by making moderation and contentment his philosophical goals. Though Horace credits Iccius for examining questions of natural philosophy, this pursuit does him no good if he does not also consider how to achieve a happy, sound life. In other words, Iccius's current philosophical pursuits have no practical ethical application. Like Albius in *Epistles* 1.4, Iccius is far removed from the city of Rome and consequently he seems cut off from the world. Horace urges him, just as he does Albius (1.4) and Torquatus (1.5), to seek companionship and benefit in the company of a friend. Finally, Horace informs Iccius of the great abundance of wealth spreading throughout Italy from foreign campaigns, and this information not only is aimed at reconnecting him to society and turning his view from his own individual desires to the needs of the state but also subtly tests Iccius's resolve to lead a contemplative life.

The reader who is already familiar with Iccius from Horace's *Odes* 1.29 will be well-prepared for the description of him in the epistle, and Putnam has uncovered many of the ways in which the two poems can fruitfully be read together.[49] The lyric Iccius is above all motivated by personal desire for wealth, which he hopes to attain through conquest:[50]

Icci, beatis nunc Arabum invides
  gazis, et acrem militiam paras
    non ante devictis Sabaeae
      regibus, horribilique Medo

> nectis catenas? quae tibi virginum
> sponso necato barbara serviet?
>   puer quis ex aula capillis
>   ad cyathum statuetur unctis? (1–8)

Iccius, do you now look with envy on the blessed treasures of the Arabs and prepare harsh warfare for the kings of Sabaea, never before conquered, and do you weave fetters for the frightful Mede? Which of the barbarian maidens, once her betrothed has been killed, will be your slave? What boy from the palace will be made to stand with perfumed hair beside the ladle?

Iccius's mental gaze (*invides*) is directed enviously toward eastern wealth, which he imagines will make him "happy." This word (*beatis*, 1; cf. *beatum, Epist.* 1.6.2) is no doubt focalized through Iccius rather than Horace. Iccius in the ode has succumbed to the same *admiratio* for wealth that is described in the sixth epistle, where Horace casts doubt on the one who marvels at riches: *i nunc, argentum et marmor vetus aeraque et artes / suspice, cum gemmis Tyrios mirare colores* ("Come now, look upon silver and ancient ivory and bronze and arts, admire Tyrian dyes and gems," 17–18).[51] Iccius furthermore is motivated to undertake military service not, it seems, by patriotic duty but by desire for personal gain. Among the spoils he imagines bringing back with him are slaves, whom he desires to fulfill his sexual and sumptuary cravings—the *virgo barbara* and perfumed *puer* are meant, we can infer, to perform not just menial domestic tasks.[52] The young man will be his cupbearer, in a hint at a life of decadence and luxury that also recalls Ganymede, the mythological *eromenos* to Jupiter's *erastes*. *Statuetur* (8), moreover, suggests *statua*, "statue";[53] this young boy is thus envisioned by Iccius as an artistic object that will, like the *beatae gazae* he hopes to acquire, not only enhance but also display his wealth. Iccius's desire for riches in this ode is unbound by moderation and will not easily be satisfied.

In the second half of the ode we discover that Iccius's longing for wealth is both new and completely unexpected:

>   quis neget arduis
>   pronos relabi posse rivos
>   montibus et Tiberim reverti,
>
> cum tu coemptos undique nobilis
> libros Panaeti Socraticam et domum
>   mutare loricis Hiberis,
>   pollicitus meliora, tendis? (10–16)

Who will deny that downward flowing streams can flow back up the lofty mountains and that the Tiber can reverse its course, when you, who promised better things, are now intent on exchanging the books of noble Panaetius, which you bought from all over, and the house of Socrates for Spanish cuirasses?

Iccius was previously so devoted to philosophy that his current abandonment of it in favor of pursuing wealth seems impossible.[54] His previous philosophical dedication seems to have been as extreme as his current desire for wealth, for he has scoured the world (*undique*, 12) for books of philosophy just as he now intends to scour it for plunder and wealth. Though Horace claims that Iccius's dedication to philosophy was intense, his inconsistency and changeability suggest that in reality it was lukewarm at best—he is more a connoisseur of books than a genuine student of philosophy. In conclusion, the Iccius of the ode is fickle, given to extremes, and desirous of riches; his philosophical pursuits are suspect. We must keep all of this in mind when we read the epistle.

Horace opens the epistle by stating that Iccius is currently residing in Sicily as the manager of the estate of M. Agrippa, a position that would bring him great benefits. But Iccius is not satisfied, and Horace presents him as having previously complained about this position, presumably because, although he had the *ususfructus* of the land, he did not own it outright:[55]

> fructibus Agrippae Siculis quos colligis, Icci,
> si recte frueris, non est ut copia maior
> ab Ioue donari possit tibi. tolle querelas;
> pauper enim non est, cui rerum suppetit usus. (1–4)

> If, Iccius, you are enjoying correctly the Sicilian produce of Agrippa that you are collecting, it is impossible that Jupiter could give a greater abundance to you; put aside complaints. For he is not a pauper for whom there is a sufficient use of things.

The keyword here is *recte* (2). Iccius does not know how to enjoy his wealth properly, and his complaints (*querelas*, 3) suggest that he wants more (*maior copia*). Horace urges moderation to him, for a man who considers his stores sufficient (*suppetit usus*) does not need more. Iccius fails to realize that his current situation in fact provides him with the perfect opportunity to achieve happiness through restraint and contentment. As Putnam states, "His economic situation is now . . . in-between. He is neither poor and dependent nor rich and master of his own domain, but the manager of a soldier's estates. He has the ability to enjoy Agrippa's land and the right of usage, but not possession. The epistle forces upon him forms of *mediocritas* which in the lyric he is made to eschew."[56] Such *mediocritas*, however, is not sitting well with Iccius, whose desire for greater wealth intimates that, if he continues upon his current course, he will never be satisfied.

If Iccius could live satisfactorily on a small amount, then it would cease to matter how much fortune smiles upon him:

> si forte in medio positorum abstemius herbis
> vivis et urtica, sic vives protinus, ut te
> confestim liquidus Fortunae rivus inauret. (7–9)

If by chance you were to practice self-restraint through things that are readily available to everyone and live on herbs and nettle, you could continue living in this way without interruption even if the flowing river of Fortune should suddenly enrich you with gold.

The satisfied man remains consistent (*sic vives protinus*) whether fortune favors him with wealth or not, and if Iccius would learn this lesson he could enjoy his current benefits and not unnecessarily suffer because he wrongly thinks he needs more. Contentment makes changes of fortune (whether positive or negative) easily manageable, and it prevents us from being reduced to the paralyzed amazement described in 1.6.9–14. Horace offers Iccius two avenues by which to achieve this contentment: *vel quia naturam mutare pecunia nescit, / vel quia cuncta putas una virtute minora* ("either because money cannot change your nature, or because you consider all things inferior to virtue alone," 10–11). Of these two paths to sufficiency, Iccius, given his Stoic leanings in the ode, would no doubt be drawn to the second option, given the Stoic color of *una virtute*. Horace, however, has already cast doubt on the ability of *virtus una* to make us happy, for in the sixth epistle it itself became an object of *admiratio* to those who pursued it above all else (*si virtus hoc una potest dare*, 1.6.31; cf. 1.6.15–16). The other option is to achieve a consistency that money cannot alter (10), and this, I would suggest, is the preferable option. If our nature stays the same, it does not matter whether we have riches or not so long as what we do have is sufficient. Consistency therefore entails an ability to adapt to changing fortune without changing the inner core of who you are, without being reduced to a state of *admiratio* when circumstances change either for the better or for the worse.

Horace next changes the topic to Iccius's philosophical pursuits. Whereas Democritus's contemplations distracted him from the practicalities of life, Iccius is able to study philosophy and manage Agrippa's estate at the same time:

miramur, si Democriti pecus edit agellos
cultaque, dum peregre est animus sine corpore velox,
cum tu inter scabiem tantam et contagia lucri
nil parvum sapias et adhuc sublimia cures:
quae mare compescant causae, quid temperet annum,
stellae sponte sua iussaene vagentur et errent,
quid premat obscurum lunae, quid proferat orbem,
quid velit et possit rerum concordia discors,
Empedocles an Stertinium deliret acumen? (1.12.12–20)

We find it amazing that the herd of Democritus ate up his fields and crops while his swift mind travelled abroad without his body, whereas you, amid so great a contagious itch for gain, have no small amount of wisdom and still care about lofty things: what checks the movement of the sea, what regulates the year, whether the stars meander and drift of their own accord or under command, what buries the moon in darkness, what brings its orb into the light, what is the meaning and power of "a discordant concord," whether Empedocles or shrewd Stertinius is mad?

Mayer suggests that this comparison to Democritus is meant to be complimentary to Iccius: "Democritus' neglect of his property in favour of scientific speculation is surpassed by Iccius' devotion to study amid the world of affairs, which he handles without contamination."[57] I would argue, however, that Democritus is in reality a foil meant to cast serious doubt on Iccius's philosophical pursuits. Iccius's examinations are devoted to natural philosophy, which is studied not "amid the world of affairs," as Mayer puts it, but in the midst of *scabiem tantam et contagia lucri* ("so great a contagious itch for gain," 14), where greed for lucre is figured as an infectious illness. Given Iccius's prior complaints about his livelihood we can imagine that this image has specific application to him, and his philosophical pursuits are doing nothing to allay his desire for gain. Though Horace compliments Iccius's wisdom in the following line, the language he uses subtly undermines this praise. Iccius's wisdom is *nil parvum* ("not small") and his thoughts are *sublimia* ("lofty"), but *nil parvum* does not necessarily imply that his wisdom is great, while *sublimia* means literally that his philosophical concerns are limited to celestial phenomena (16–20). If his studies had not just scientific but also ethical application, his *scabies et contagia lucre* would not continue to exist in the midst of them.

The story of Democritus's pursuit of wisdom to the detriment of his worldly affairs is first found in Cicero's *De Finibus* 5.86–87. Here Cicero has Piso state that the aim of philosophy is to attain a happy life (*omnis auctoritas philosophiae . . . consistit in beata vita comparanda*). This, he says, is the reason that philosophers such as Plato, Pythagoras, and Democritus traveled abroad to share their teaching and learn from others:

> cur tantas regiones barbarorum pedibus obiit, tot maria transmisit? cur haec eadem Democritus? qui (vere falsone, non quaeremus) dicitur oculis se privasse; certe, ut quam minime animus a cogitationibus abduceretur, patrimonium neglexit, agros deseruit incultos, quid quaerens aliud nisi vitam beatam? quam si etiam in rerum cognitione ponebat, tamen ex illa investigatione naturae consequi volebat, bono ut esset animo; id enim ille summum bonum εὐθυμίαν et saepe ἀθαμβίαν appellat, id est animum terrore liberum.

> Why did [Pythagoras] traverse so many barbarian regions on foot, cross so many seas? Why did Democritus do these same things? He—I will not inquire whether this is true or false—is said to have blinded himself. But it is certain that he, so that his mind might be distracted as little as possible from his contemplations, neglected

his patrimony and left his fields uncultivated, seeking what else except a happy life? Even if he was locating [a happy life] in the contemplation of things, he nevertheless wanted to attain out of that investigation of nature that he have a good state of mind. Indeed he names this highest good *euthumia* and often *athambia*, which means to have a mind free of terror.

According to Piso, Democritus's investigations into nature were done in service to his ethical goals and from them he hoped to discover how to achieve happiness, which he called *euthumia* ("tranquility") or *athambia* ("lack of astonishment"). Horace was no doubt aware of this story from the *De Finibus* and, I suggest, means for us to have it in mind when we encounter the epistle. Iccius, unlike Democritus, does not have a larger ethical purpose to his investigation of nature. Democritean *euthumia* or *athambia* would be just the right antidote to Iccius's discontent, and *athambia* especially recalls the *nil admirari* of 1.6. Central to the acquisition of *euthumia* and *athambia* is moderation, particularly in the desire for wealth, as the fragments that record Democritus's ethical thought show. In the longest fragment on ethics that survives, recorded at Stobaeus 3.1.210, Democritus stresses the importance of μετριότης ("moderation"):

ἀνθρώποισι γὰρ εὐθυμίη γίγνεται μετριότητι τέρψιος καὶ βίου συμμετρίη· τὰ δ᾽ ἐλλείποντα καὶ ὑπερβάλλοντα μεταπίπτειν τε φιλεῖ καὶ μεγάλας κινήσιας ἐμποιεῖν τῇ ψυχῇ. αἱ δ᾽ ἐκ μεγάλων διαστημάτων κινούμεναι τῶν ψυχέων οὔτε εὐσταθέες εἰσιν οὔτε εὔθυμοι. ἐπὶ τοῖς δυνατοῖς οὖν δεῖ ἔχειν τὴν γνώμην καὶ τοῖς παρεοῦσιν ἀρκέεσθαι ... ὅκως τὰ παρεόντα σοι καὶ ὑπάρχοντα μεγάλα καὶ ζηλωτὰ φαίνηται, καὶ μηκέτι πλεινόνων ἐπιθυμέοντι συμβαίνῃ κακοπαθεῖν τῇ ψυχῇ.[58]

For tranquility (*euthumia*) comes about for men through moderation in pleasure and proportion in life. Things in deficiency and excess tend to change suddenly and produce great movements in the soul. And those souls that are moved at great intervals are neither stable nor tranquil. Therefore it is necessary to keep your mind upon what is possible and to be satisfied with what is at hand . . . so that what is at hand and the present circumstances may seem great and enviable, and no longer will suffering in the soul occur for one because he wants more.

In this fragment moderation produces *euthumia* or *athambia* in one's soul and makes it no longer subject to the changes or disturbances wrought either by having too little (deficiency) or having too much (excess). In another fragment Democritus states that the desire for possessions must be limited through satiety, since the more we desire the more we feel we are lacking: χρημάτων ὄρεξις, ἢν μὴ ὁρίζηται κόρῳ, πενίης ἐσχάτης πολλὸν χαλεπωτέρη· μέζονες γὰρ ὀρέξεις μέζονας ἐνδείας ποιεῦσιν ("The longing for money, if it is not limited by satiety, is much more difficult than the utmost poverty, for greater longings produce greater wants").[59] Horace's ethical advice to Iccius in the first eleven lines of

Epistles 1.12 conforms well to these fragments of Democritus. Horace's *pauper enim non est, cui rerum suppetit usus* ("For he is not poor who has a sufficient use of things," 4) is very close in thought to Democritus's πενίη πλοῦτος ὀνόματα ἐνδείης καὶ κόρου· οὔτε οὖν πλούσιος ὁ ἐνδέων οὔτε πένης ὁ μὴ ἐνδέων ("Poverty and wealth are names for lack and surplus. Therefore the one who feels lack is not wealthy, and the one who does not feel lack is not poor").[60] When Horace describes the mental flight of Democritus the initial impression is that he censures Democritus's negligence of practical affairs by his devotion to philosophy, while Iccius is complimented for doing both. By reading the story in light of the version told in the *De Finibus* and by connecting the thought of lines 1–11 to the ethical fragments of Democritus, we realize, however, that the situation is reversed. Democritus's philosophical investigations had the practical goal of improving his life through *euthumia* and *athambia*, while Iccius's currently serve no ethical purpose and do not induce him to limit his desires through satiety.[61]

The antidote that Horace offers to Iccius is the same as the one he offered to Albius (1.4) and Torquatus (1.5): friendship:

> verum seu piscis seu porrum et caepe trucidas,
> utere Pompeio Grospho et, siquid petet, ultro
> defer: nil Grosphus nisi verum orabit et aequum. (21–23)

> But whether you slaughter fish or leeks and onions, be friends with Pompeius Grosphus and, if he asks for anything, offer it without hesitation; Grosphus will ask for nothing except what is true and fair.

Horace further casts doubt on Iccius's philosophical commitment by suggesting that his diet might consist of fish, on the one hand, or vegetables, on the other. In line 20 he implies that the philosophers Iccius studies include Empedocles, who followed Pythagoras in believing in the transmigration of souls and alleged that his soul previously had inhabited, among other things, a fish (Diogenes Laertius 8.77). If Iccius is abstaining from fish and eating only vegetables it would be, Horace implies, because he is currently in one of his philosophical moods and does not want to risk killing an animal into which had gone a human soul, perhaps even that of Empedocles himself.[62] If he is currently eating fish, not only is he violating the precepts of his chosen philosophical guide, but he is also enjoying decadent fare, for fish was widely regarded as a delicacy.[63] Horace's ignorance as to Iccius's current meal of choice suggests, as has already been shown in the ode addressed to him, that he is wildly inconsistent, devoted at times to philosophy and at times to luxury. Regardless of whether Iccius eats fish or vegetables, he can and should turn his mind toward friendship with Pompeius Grosphus, and friendship is ultimately what will enable him to live a better and more satisfying life.

Only in these final lines is it revealed that Horace's purpose all along has been to introduce these two men, both of whom live in Sicily. Pompeius Grosphus is the addressee of *Odes* 2.16, where he is a wealthy Sicilian landowner (33–37), and Horace recommends to him the same contentment and moderation that he does Iccius in *Epistles* 1.12.[64] In the epistle Horace assures Iccius that Grosphus will be a genuine friend who will not ask for excessive favors and that the cost of his friendship will therefore be cheap: *vilis amicorum est annona, bonis ubi quid deest* ("The market price of friends is cheap, when it is good men who need something," 24). Though these lines focus on what Iccius can be expected to do for Grosphus, in reality Horace is more concerned with how friendship with Grosphus can benefit Iccius. Commentators suggest that line 24 adapts a passage from Xenophon's *Memorabilia*, where Socrates urges a certain Diodorus to befriend his companion Hermogenes:[65] οἱ μέντοι ἀγαθοὶ οἰκονόμοι, ὅταν τὸ πολλοῦ ἄξιον μικροῦ ἐξῇ πρίασθαι, τότε φασὶ δεῖν ὠνεῖσθαι. νῦν δὲ διὰ πράγματα εὐωνοτάτους ἔστι φίλους ἀγαθοὺς κτήσασθαι ("Good household managers, moreover, say that one should buy whenever it is possible to purchase something valuable at a small price. And in the current circumstances it is possible for good friends to be acquired very cheaply," 2.10.4). Diodorus responds by asking Socrates to have Hermogenes come to him, which Socrates refuses to do, stating that he should go to Hermogenes himself and that in fact Diodorus has just as much, if not more, to gain from the friendship than Hermogenes: νομίζω γὰρ οὔτε σοὶ κάλλιον εἶναι τὸ καλέσαι ἐκεῖνον τοῦ αὐτὸν ἐλθεῖν πρὸς ἐκεῖνον οὔτ' ἐκείνῳ μεῖζον ἀγαθὸν τὸ πραχθῆναι ταῦτα ἢ σοί ("For I think neither that it would be better for you to summon that man than to go to him yourself, nor that it is a greater good for him than for you that this happen," 2.10.6). By alluding to this passage of the *Memorabilia* Horace not only urges Iccius to seek out the friendship of Grosphus but also implies that this is more for Iccius's benefit than for that of Grosphus, since it is Iccius whose spiritual state is not as it should be. Iccius must get his head out of the heavens and reconnect with what can make him content in the here and now (i.e., friendship). Whereas in *Epistles* 1.4 and 1.5 Horace had offered his own friendship as an antidote to the excessive behavior of Albius and Torquatus, the great distance between Horace and Iccius prevents him from doing the same here, and consequently he urges Iccius to enjoy the friendship of someone closer to him whose character Horace already knows.

Horace ends the poem by telling Iccius what is happening in the world at large and focuses in particular on the imperial family's recent military successes:

ne tamen ignores quo sit Romana loco res:
Cantaber Agrippae, Claudi virtute Neronis
Armenius cecidit; ius imperiumque Phrahates

Caesaris accepit genibus minor; aurea fruges
Italiae pleno defundit Copia cornu. (25–29)

And yet, so that you are not unaware of the condition of the Roman state, the Cantabrian has been felled by the prowess of Agrippa, and the Armenian by that of Claudius Nero; Phrahates has received the justice and rule of Caesar with bended knees; golden Abundance pours forth her produce on Italy from her abundant horn.

By attaching this postscript to the epistle Horace underscores his friend's isolation, as it implies that Iccius is far too removed to have heard about these recent news items and needs to be reconnected with the larger world. At the same time these lines offer yet another corrective to Iccius's lack of contentment. Putnam has nicely shown how words and concepts in these lines look back to earlier parts of the poem.[66] Iccius had seemingly complained that the "fruits" (*fructibus*, 1) he currently enjoys do not provide him with a great enough "abundance" (*copia*, 2), and in line 9 Horace imagines a flowing stream of *Fortuna* suddenly enriching him with gold (*liquidus Fortunae rivus inauret*). As we have seen, Iccius should be indifferent to this personal enrichment, provided that he has a sufficient livelihood. In the closing lines, it is the collective enrichment of Italy to which Horace draws Iccius's attention, again mentioning gold (*aurea*, 28), abundance (*Copia*, 29), and fruits (*fruges*, 28).[67] The question remains, however, as to whether Iccius can hear of such riches without wanting some of them for himself. In this respect these final lines serve as something of a test of and challenge to Iccius to take to heart Horace's recommendation of moderation, satiety, and friendship.

Epistles 1.4, 1.5, and 1.12 are all addressed to men drawn to extremes ranging from isolation to severity to the desire for wealth. In each of these poems Horace advises his addressee both to moderate his behavior and to turn himself to more productive and balanced pursuits, and his recommendations can be well summarized by the doctrine *nil admirari* that is central to 1.6. In each of these poems, inflexibility, rigidity, and extreme behavior are urged to give way to compromise, adaptability, and moderation. In 1.4, 1.5, and 1.12, furthermore, compromise in the name of friendship offers the best antidote for immoderate and inflexible behavior. At the same time that Horace offers this advice, however, we must keep in mind that he too has acted inflexibly and rigidly with his friend Maecenas, with whom he refuses to compromise in the opening poem. Only gradually over the collection will Horace be able to apply to his own situation the same moral lessons he offers to Albius, Torquatus, Numicius, and Iccius. In fact, just after espousing *nil admirari* as the one thing that can make a man happy, Horace returns in *Epistles* 1.7 to his own inflexible and extreme behavior, stripping himself of the confident didactic mask he has worn in 1.4–6 and becoming once again the melancholy and inconsistent student in need of further moral study.

5

Otia Liberrima

Horace, Maecenas, and the Sabine Farm in *Epistles* 1.7 and 1.16

I
N THIS CHAPTER I TURN FROM Horace the teacher back to Horace the student, whose progress I shall be tracing for the remainder of this book, though of course these dual roles are ultimately inextricable. Horace's advice to his friends to yield, bend, and avoid extremes is not something that he easily applies to his own situation, especially when he is faced with demands from Maecenas that he feels compromise his freedom. As we saw in the first chapter, Horace in the opening epistle uses the master-slave relationship as an analogy for his friendship with Maecenas since Maecenas's desire for his friend's attendance and poetry threatens to keep Horace in an overly servile position. There is very little indication in the opening poem that Horace will be willing to compromise his freedom to accommodate Maecenas's wish that he resume his public poetic role in the city. When Horace begins to distill ethical lessons to his various friends, however, it is not defiant inflexibility that he espouses, but moderation, adaptability, and compromise, and as a simultaneous teacher and student, these are lessons that he himself begins to take to heart. In 1.7, we see Horace initiate a renegotiation of the terms of his friendship with his patron in such a way that both Horace and Maecenas will have to compromise in order for the friendship to continue.[1] At the same time, 1.16, in which Maecenas's name is conspicuously absent but the Sabine farm central, provides a powerful caveat that this willingness to bend extends only so far and that genuine *libertas* is an inner possession that can never be removed by any outside force.

MAECENAS AND THE BENEFACTION OF THE FARM IN 1.7

Nowhere is Horace's attitude toward his public role, the city, and Maecenas more challenging and complex than in *Epistles* 1.7.[2] The poem is written as though in response to Maecenas's annoyance at his friend's continued absence, and in it

Horace pointedly and boldly prolongs his withdrawal while at the same time opening up the door to a possible return, a compromise that diverges from Horace's inflexible pose in 1.1 but one that is possible only if both friends agree to certain conditions. Maecenas cannot demand that his friend sacrifice his liberty beyond a certain point and must allow him a sphere in which he exercises autonomy, while Horace must yield to some extent to the wishes of his powerful patron in order to continue enjoying the benefits of the rustic *otia liberrima* that his relationship with Maecenas has made both necessary and possible. The rural *libertas* that Horace desires paradoxically can only be achieved through compromising his freedom vis-à-vis Maecenas. In between the extremes of total compliance (i.e., *servitus* to Maecenas) and absolute refusal (i.e., total autonomy from Maecenas), Horace proceeds to open a third path akin to what Aristippus in the *Memorabilia* called ἐλευθερία, "freedom."[3] It is the Sabine farm itself that symbolizes this third path or mean, for it is simultaneously the seat of his rustic freedom and, in being made possible by Maecenas's generosity, a token of Horace's dependence on his powerful friend.[4]

Horace's tone toward Maecenas in the poem has been difficult to gauge, and interpretations of it have diverged widely. The argument that Horace's tone is harsh goes back to the late-Antique scholia attributed to Pseudo-Acro: *hac epistola asperius ac destrictius Maecenati praescribit libertatem se opibus non vendere,* "In this letter Horace rather harshly and severely writes to Maecenas that he would not sell his freedom for wealth." Others, however, have been hesitant to attribute acerbity to Horace in this poem. Among recent interpreters, Kilpatrick is especially resistant to such a reading, arguing that the poem is entirely complimentary to Maecenas and his propriety in giving gifts.[5] Mayer likewise expresses surprise that some readers have found the tone of the letter harsh.[6] Lyne and Oliensis, on the other hand, offer readings in which Horace's abrasive tone, though tempered by touches of humor and politeness, should nevertheless be taken seriously. Lyne states that the letter as a whole "must have been a testing read for Maecenas, very far from pleasing in all its aspects. It wraps tough messages in humor and diplomacy; but the tough messages are hard to miss."[7] Oliensis suggests that "if Horace stretches the ties of friendship in *Epistles* 1.1, in *Epistles* 1.7 he pulls away with more force—hard enough, indeed, to risk snapping the connection." The poem, she says, is an "exercise in polite rudeness or amicable hostility."[8] Freudenburg similarly has called the tone "edgy and unusually aggressive."[9] My own reading tries to find a mean between these two critical tendencies, between the overly complimentary tone detected by some and the acerbic and hostile tone put forth by others. I suggest that the outcome of Horace's renegotiation with Maecenas is not a pulling away from him, but the conditional renewal of a friendship that in the opening poem was close to the breaking point. Where others have sensed a harsher tone in 1.7 than in 1.1, I find that in 1.7 Horace begins to soften the aggressive stance toward his friend and patron that opened the collection.

Though Horace's focus on freedom throughout the poem certainly can and should be read in light of the solidification of Augustan power and the changing political landscape of the early empire, the poem nevertheless cannot be used as an accurate reflection of Horace's historical friendship with Maecenas in 20 B.C. or as evidence for Maecenas's decline during this period, and I will not attempt to draw any conclusions about such questions.[10] Rather, I am more interested in Maecenas's symbolic value in the poem, for he is closely aligned with public life and the city, and Horace's ambivalence toward him is analogous to his feelings about these two spheres.[11] In many ways, the Maecenas/Horace antithesis functions similarly to the antitheses between city and country, public and private, and dependence and freedom that are central to the *Epistles*. Whereas "Horace" is aligned frequently with the private *libertas* of the country, "Maecenas" stands for the public duties of urban life that can impinge upon one's freedom. In negotiating a middle ground with Maecenas, Horace simultaneously opens the door for compromise in these other spheres as well. "Horace" and "Maecenas" are in many ways conflicting aspects of the poet's complex persona that must be brought into a delicate balance with one another through moderation and adaptability.

The opening lines of the poem, in which Horace explains his continued withdrawal to Maecenas, recall and in many ways revise the opening lines of the first epistle, where Horace had explained his need for retirement by likening himself to a newly freed gladiator and Maecenas to the *lanista* who would re-enslave him. In 1.7 Horace's withdrawal is exposed not to have been the permanent retirement envisioned in 1.1 but a temporary holiday that he has prolonged beyond its initially promised length:

> quinque dies tibi pollicitus me rure futurum
> Sextilem totum mendax desideror. atqui
> si me vivere vis sanum recteque valentem,
> quam mihi das aegro, dabis aegrotare timenti,
> Maecenas, veniam, dum ficus prima calorque
> dissignatorem decorat lictoribus atris,
> dum pueris omnis pater et matercula pallet
> officiosaque sedulitas et opella forensis
> adducit febris et testamenta resignat.

> Although I promised you that I would be in the country for five days, I—liar that I am—have been missed for the whole of August. But if you want me to live soundly and in good health, you will give me the same pardon, Maecenas, when I

fear to become ill that you give me when I am ill, while the first fig and the heat adorn the funeral director with his dark lictors, while every father and mother fears for her children, and while official business and the work of the Forum bring on fevers and unseal wills.

Horace's fear that he may become ill continues the motif of the poet's sickness that was begun in the opening poem (cf. esp. 1.1.94–105), where it necessitated both his withdrawal from the city and his adoption of ethical subject matter. This illness was one not of the body but of the mind (cf. *mens*, 1.1.4), and it arose especially because of Horace's inconsistency and ambivalence. In 1.7 it seems that the time he has spent in the country has done the trick; he is no longer ill, though he fears that his sickness would resume if he were to return to the city during the pestilential summer heat. Rome is associated with disease and death, and the country with healthy and sound living, and we can assume that the disease Horace fears in 1.7 is, as in 1.1, not so much physical as mental. Horace's health here is firmly a matter of location and is predicated upon his remaining ensconced in the countryside. Following upon 1.6, however, in which the doctrine of *nil admirari* warns us against pursuing any extreme too vigorously, Horace's clinging to rural life might be viewed suspiciously. He certainly does not exhibit the indifference to place that in 1.11 will be a quality of one with *aequanimitas* (30). Because it is so conditional, the health Horace currently enjoys in the countryside is somewhat questionable and tenuous.

Whereas in 1.1 it is Maecenas's motives that are thrown into doubt by his desire to re-enroll Horace into his gladiatorial *ludus* and by his inability to recognize Horace's inner turmoil, in 1.7 Horace shifts some of the blame onto himself for having been dishonest to Maecenas about how long he intended to stay away. In accepting some of the responsibility for the tension within their relationship, Horace signals an openness to compromise that was lacking in the first poem. By describing himself as a *mendax*, "liar" (2), he suggests that he perhaps has not been an entirely true friend to Maecenas, and in *Ars Poetica* 425 he will use the same word to contrast the false friend, *mendax*, from the true one, *verus*.[12] By the end of the epistle, Horace will put aside falsehood for truth (*verum nomen*, 93; *verum est*, 98), bringing himself and Maecenas a step closer to reconciliation. One difficulty of interpreting *mendax*, however, is deciding whether this word reflects the thought of Horace or Maecenas. Is Horace reproaching himself or merely "representing Maecenas' complaint in free indirect discourse?"[13] The ambiguity of just whose thought *mendax* reflects problematizes any straightforward interpretation of this passage. If *mendax* echoes Maecenas's complaints, then he is more annoyed with his friend's prolonged absence and false promises than he is concerned for Horace's inner well-being. If Maecenas truly cared about his friend's health he would readily grant him forgiveness for his falsehood. Neither Maecenas nor Horace comes across as entirely innocent or blameworthy in the poem's opening lines; Horace has been less than candid about his intentions, while Maecenas remains unmindful of his friend's real needs.

We might expect Horace to reassure Maecenas that he will return to Rome once the pestilent summer has passed, but instead he says that he will extend his absence through the winter until spring. In the meantime he will make his way to the seaside, where he will pass the season in reading and study:

> quodsi bruma nives Albanis illinet agris,
> ad mare descendet vates tuus et sibi parcet
> contractusque leget: te, dulcis amice, reviset
> cum Zephyris, si concedes, et hirundine prima. (1.7.10–13)

> But if the winter scatters snow on the Alban fields, your bard will go down to the sea and see to himself and, huddled up, will read. He will return to you, sweet friend, with the Zephyrs, if you allow, and with the first swallow.

Horace's description of winter in these lines sheds light on his motives for prolonging his absence and suggests that it is not so much the urban pestilence that is keeping him away from Rome as the myriad duties that go along with being Maecenas's friend. This rather than the weather is the real source of Horace's fear and the cause for any disease or illness that the city might induce. The placement of *bruma nives* in line 10 recalls Horace's complaints in *Satires* 2.6, a satire which we shall see is very much in the background of the epistle, about the incessant tasks this friendship has brought him when he is in the city, which do not abate even in the wintertime: *sive Aquilo radit terras seu bruma nivalem / interiore diem gyro trahit, ire necesse est*, "Whether the north wind grazes the lands or the winter pulls the snowy day in a narrower circuit, it is necessary to go," 25–26. The duties he lists in the satire all have a public dimension: he is a *sponsor* in a court case, he is present at Maecenas's morning *salutatio*, where he is asked not only to attend to a number of duties but also to bring certain business to Maecenas's attention, and his presence even during Maecenas's leisure hours makes him the target of others' envy. He had forsworn just such a public role in the opening epistle, and his continued refusal in 1.7 must result from the same desire to escape the negative aspects of this friendship. As in *Epistles* 1.1, Horace's public role in 1.7 is connected above all to the success his lyric poetry has brought him, and Horace clearly alludes to the public aspect of his poetry by referring to himself as Maecenas's *vates* (11). As Freudenburg states, "Maecenas wants the prompt return of his beloved *vates*, a term that Horace uses consistently in his works to designate . . . his higher 'public' lyric voice. That, it seems, is the role Maecenas is anxious to have him revive."[14] That such a public poetic role is inextricable from his friendship with Maecenas is evident from the possessive phrase *vates tuus*, which, though it "assures Maecenas of his friend's fidelity,"[15] at the same time suggests that this role brings him into a position dependent on Maecenas or even that it makes him in some way Maecenas's possession.[16] Horace's feelings about Maecenas and his public poetry remain as ambivalent as ever. As in 1.1, private withdrawal and contemplation are the preferred alternative.

Despite the anxiety that complying with Maecenas's requests produces in him in 1.7, Horace nevertheless acknowledges the positive aspects of this friendship and in fact explicitly promises a return to the city and to Maecenas, offering a sharp contrast with the intention to withdraw that he outlines in the opening poem. Although his dependence on Maecenas is signaled in *vates tuus*, the phrase simultaneously betrays in Horace a warmth of feeling toward his friend. Horace further softens his refusal by referring to Maecenas as his "sweet friend," *dulcis amice* (12). This is a reminder that despite its inconveniences his friendship with Maecenas is one that has brought him pleasure. In *Satires* 2.6, for example, even in the midst of his urban duties he nevertheless receives delight in being spoken of as Maecenas's associate, and about this he cannot bring himself to be *mendax*: *hoc iuvat et melli est, non mentiar*, "This is pleasant and honeysweet, I will not lie," 32. The phrase *dulcis amice* especially recalls *Satires* 1.3, in which Horace describes the indulgence and forgiveness that an *amicus dulcis* (implicitly Maecenas) should exhibit in his dealings with a friend such as Horace and vice versa, and we have already visited this passage in connection with the friendship of Horace and Maecenas in the chapter 2 discussion of 1.1:

>   *amicus dulcis*, ut aequum est,
> cum mea compenset vitiis bona, pluribus hisce
> (si modo plura mihi bona sunt) inclinet, amari
> si volet: hac lege in trutina ponetur eadem.
> qui, ne tuberibus propriis offendat amicum,
> postulat, ignoscet verrucis illius; aequum est
> peccatis veniam poscentem reddere rursus. (1.3.69–75)

A sweet friend, as is fair, should weigh my good attributes against my faults and tilt the scale toward the former,[17] which are in greater abundance—provided that my good attributes *are* in greater abundance—if he desires to be loved. By this agreement he will be placed on the same scale. Whoever asks that he not offend his friend with his own boils should pardon the other's warts. It is fair that one who wants pardon for his sins should render it in turn.

By referring to Maecenas as a *dulcis amicus* in 1.7, Horace reminds him of this earlier passage, in which forgiveness is a crucial component to friendship. In asking Maecenas for "pardon," *veniam*, at 1.7.5, Horace desires the same sort of indulgence from his friend that he had described in the satire (*veniam*, 1.3.75), and he thereby implies that though his refusal to comply with Maecenas might be counted as a fault (*vitium*), it is a minor one that his friend should overlook. Horace, in turn, as is fair, will pardon the faults of his friend. Rather than being cast as a manumitted gladiator and *lanista*, as they are in *Epistles* 1.1, in 1.7 Horace and Maecenas are described with the language that in *Satires* 1.3 had been used for forgiving and tolerant friends. It is not the master/slave relationship that is the paradigm for Maecenas and Horace in 1.7, but *amicitia*. This tone of possible reconciliation (rather than continued opposition) paves the way for the poem's examination of the friendship between the two men. Horace explores their friendship through a series of exemplary tales that reflect—both positively and negatively—its various aspects, and these tales, which look simultaneously to the past, present, and future of their friendship, place certain provisos on its continuation. Thus Horace compels Maecenas to take stock of the friendship along with him in order for him to understand that the level of compliance he can expect from Horace is fixed and limited and that he must take care to assess whether his demands are in the best interests of his friend and consistent with his personality and desire for independence.

The first exemplary tale is that of the Calabrian host, who too persistently offers unwanted pears to his already satisfied guest:

> non quo more piris vesci Calaber iubet hospes
> tu me fecisti locupletem: 'vescere sodes.'
> 'iam satis est.' 'at tu, quantum vis, tolle.' 'benigne.'
> 'non invisa feres pueris munuscula parvis.'
> 'tam teneor dono, quam si dimittar onustus.'
> 'ut libet: haec porcis hodie comedenda relinques.' (1.7.14–19)

> Not in the same way as the Calabrian host bids his guest to eat pears did you enrich me: "Please, eat." "I am full." "But take all that you want." "No, thank you." "You will take not unwelcome gifts to your small children." "I am as grateful for the gift as I would be if I were being sent away weighed down by them." "As you like: you will leave them to be eaten tomorrow by the pigs."

A complimentary reading of this story runs thus: The emphatic *non* that introduces this story suggests that the Calabrian host is meant as a contrast to Maecenas.[18] Unlike the Calabrian host, who desires to bestow gifts beyond what is necessary, Maecenas's enrichment of Horace has been within proper bounds and is in keeping with a key ethical concept that runs throughout Horace's work, that of satiety (*satis*, 16), a concept that he frequently uses food and dining to illustrate.[19] As scholars have noted, *locupletem* (15) suggests "rich in land" and calls to mind most especially the Sabine farm that Maecenas either bestowed on Horace as a gift or supplied him with the money to purchase on his own.[20] It is his satisfaction with the farm and his desire for nothing more that opens up *Satires* 2.6, often read as a thank you to Maecenas for this benefaction: *nil amplius oro, / Maia nate, nisi ut propria haec mihi munera faxis,* "I ask for nothing more, son of Maia, except that you make these gifts permanent for me," 4–6.[21] If the tale of the Calabrian host is taken *ex contrario*, then Maecenas has acted correctly in bestowing the farm on Horace since the benefaction does not compromise Horace's ethical principles. Maecenas is thus the *vir bonus et sapiens* described in the moral of this tale, who helps those who deserve it with gifts that, unlike the pears offered by the Calabrian host, have genuine value to both giver and recipient:

> vir bonus et sapiens dignis ait esse paratus,
> nec tamen ignorat, quid distent aera lupinis:
> dignum praestabo me etiam pro laude merentis. (1.7.22–24)

> The good and wise man says that he is prepared to help the deserving, and besides he is not unaware of how real coins differ from fake ones. I too will show myself worthy in accordance with the praise of my benefactor.

The Sabine farm is a highly valued and deserved gift, and with it Maecenas has proven himself to be a praiseworthy benefactor. In turn, Horace will in the future continue to show himself worthy of both it and Maecenas.[22]

Such an overtly complimentary interpretation of the tale is not, however, entirely compatible with, nor does it sufficiently enlighten us about, his refusal in the opening part of the poem to return to Maecenas in the city. How exactly does the story expand upon or explain that refusal? What do the unwanted pears of the exemplum correspond to in Horace's relationship with Maecenas? The past tense of *fecisti* (15) suggests that Maecenas's *past* benefactions are what Horace contrasts with the pears of the Calabrian host. Up until now, Maecenas has offered him nothing that might correspond to such unwanted and unsuitable gifts.[23] But what about now? Maecenas's current "offering" meets with Horace's refusal just as the pears do the guest's. This is life in the city and all that it entails: lyric poetry, public renown, and attendance on Maecenas, all of which Horace repudiated in the opening poem and continues to reject in 1.7.25–28:

> quodsi me noles usquam discedere, reddes
> forte latus, nigros angusta fronte capillos,
> reddes dulce loqui, reddes ridere decorum et
> inter vina fugam Cinarae maerere protervae.

But if you are unwilling for me ever to leave you, return my strong flank, my dark
hair on a narrow brow. Return my sweet speech, return my charming laughter and
wine-fueled lamentations over wanton Cinara's flight.

What Maecenas currently wants is the Horace of the *Odes*, who was younger
and better suited to urban life, both the private world of the symposium and the
public world of the civic *vates*.[24] Such a return to his younger self is now impossible for Horace, and new terms for their friendship must be agreed upon. The
chief issue here is that Maecenas, at least according to Horace, wants his friend's
constant attendance. Maecenas offers no compromise, since he does not yet
understand that the Horace of the *Epistles* is different, both in mind and in age
(*Epistles* 1.1.4), from his earlier lyric self. In prevailing upon Horace to take up
a life that does not suit him, Maecenas does not, like the *vir bonus et sapiens*,
distinguish a genuine benefaction from an unwanted and thus counterfeit one.
To quote Freudenburg, "it is clear that Maecenas resembles the pushy Calabrian
in one important sense: he is pushing! He wants *his* poet to take more of the fine
feast he has set before him, and to linger a while longer even though he has by
now fed himself quite full."[25] It is not that Horace wishes to cut himself off from
Maecenas entirely; rather, he wants his friend to recognize that there are limits
to and conditions on the "benefactions" he is willing to receive. The tale of the
Calabrian host thus sets up important stipulations on their continued friendship. Maecenas must continue to act in accordance with the worthiness of his
own past behavior and stop pushing Horace to give in to unwanted demands.
Maecenas must make compromises and learn what will be a true and worthy
benefaction for Horace—the right to attend to his friend on his own terms. If
he does so, Horace will respond in kind by continuing to show himself worthy
of their friendship in the future (24).

Whereas the first tale focuses on Maecenas's behavior and propriety in giving gifts, the second tale examines Horace's past acceptance of benefactions in
light of his current refusal to comply with Maecenas. Central to this story is the
nature of freedom for one who has, like Horace, accepted benefactions, which
ideally should enhance and not restrict *libertas*. While the Calabrian host is a
negative exemplum for bestowing gifts, the fable of the fox in the corn bin illustrates the improper and greedy taking of them:[26]

forte per angustam tenuis vulpecula rimam
repserat in cumeram frumenti, pastaque rursus
ire foras pleno tendebat corpore frustra.
cui mustela procul 'si vis' ait 'effugere istinc,
macra cavum repetes artum, quem macra subisti.'

hac ego si compellor imagine, cuncta resigno:
nec somnum plebis laudo satur altilium nec
otia divitiis Arabum liberrima muto. (1.7.29–36)

By chance a thin fox had crept through a narrow crack into a bin of corn. After he
ate, he was trying to go out in vain because of his full body. A weasel not far off said
to him, "If you want to escape from there, you will have to seek out again while
thin the narrow hole that you entered while thin." If I am accused by this account,
I sign everything back. I do not praise the sleep of the plebs when I am stuffed
with birds, nor do I exchange my very free leisure for the riches of the Arabs.

As a consequence of his greedy eating, the little fox becomes trapped in the
corn bin and loses his freedom. The story is a warning against the indiscriminate acceptance of gifts without considering whether they might ultimately
compromise autonomy. Just as the fox becomes trapped by his eagerness for
more and more, so too can a client have his independence restricted by over-
indulging his appetite for benefactions. The fox, unlike the Calabrian's guest,
does not recognize when enough is enough. An outside observer might claim
that Horace's past friendship with Maecenas has rendered him dependent and
that he, like the *volpecula*, has voluntarily surrendered his freedom. Just as
Maecenas cannot restore Horace's *angusta frons*, so too the fox cannot simply
reclaim his freedom and squeeze himself back through the *angusta rima*. We
could even imagine that this is implicitly Maecenas's own argument for why
Horace should comply with his desires. How does he think he can refuse Maecenas now when his past acceptance of gifts has created certain obligations?

Horace responds to such a charge by denying that he has received any gifts
from Maecenas that might restrict his independence. Line 34, *hac ego si compellor imagine, cuncta resigno*, is simultaneously a denial that the fable applies
to him and a threat that, if it turns out to be a valid charge, he will rid himself
of Maecenas's past benefactions by giving them all back, including the Sabine
farm.[27] If the fox can be freed only by returning to his thin self, Horace will
likewise have to restore himself to his pre-Maecenas condition, but the possibility of such a restoration is highly doubtful and in any case unnecessary, he
suggests, since he has not in fact fed himself fat like the fox. In fact, the Sabine
farm, Maecenas's most significant gift and the one to which Horace clearly
alludes, provides him, he claims, with the greatest *libertas* (*otia liberrima*, 36)
and is in keeping with the principle of satiety that the Calabrian's guest had
espoused.[28] It is not because he is suffering from insomnia brought on by over-
indulging his appetite (*satur altilium*, 35) that he often praises in his poetry the
simple life of the plebs, and thus his praise of *libertas* is not a result of his having sacrificed his independence. Horace therefore denies that he is guilty of the

excessive overindulgence that *satur* implies;[29] he is instead like the Calabrian's guest who accepts only what is sufficient. It is Horace's very possession of such a farm that provides a testament to his character and free status. It reflects and substantiates his freedom rather than detracting from it, and as a mirror for the values of its owner it should readily convey to Maecenas the impossibility that Horace would exchange it for any promise of urban renown he might offer.[30]

By retaining the farm, however, Horace necessarily accepts a measure of dependence on Maecenas, and thus the *libertas* that he attributes to himself through this *exemplum* has an important qualification. The moderated independence symbolized by the farm is a mean between two equally unappealing extremes. On the one hand are the *divitiae* offered by Maecenas that would render him excessively dependent. These obviously must be refused. The other extreme is to repudiate the farm and thus all obligations to Maecenas. Such an act would be the ultimate statement of independence, but paradoxically it would require him to lose the *otia liberrima* that the farm makes possible. It would necessitate a return to the urban life that not only restricts freedom but also produces the spiritual sickness that Horace's retirement is aimed to prevent. As Bowditch has pointed out, the verb *resigno* (34) has already been used in line 9, where the business of Rome "unseals wills." She argues:

> Should Horace give back the Sabine farm, the most prized and prominent of the *donata* or "gifts," the act would be tantamount to unsealing a will, *testamenta resignat*. The echo of this verb in the noun *dissignatorem* (undertaker, 6) further underscores this subtext. Giving back all, *resignare cuncta*, would necessitate returning to the city, a place that causes death.[31]

With the tale of the fox in the corn bin, like that of the Calabrian host, Horace lays out certain terms by which he and Maecenas can continue their relationship. Their *amicitia* will be endangered not only if Maecenas pushes inappropriate gifts onto his friend but also if Horace accepts them. Maecenas must allow Horace a measure of freedom, and in turn Horace will be able to admit a measure of dependence. This qualified freedom and dependence are symbolized by the farm.

As if in acknowledgment of the dependent position in which his acceptance of benefactions has placed him, in lines 37–39 Horace reminds Maecenas that in his past behavior he has exhibited due deference toward his more powerful friend:

> saepe verecundum laudasti, rexque paterque
> audisti coram, nec verbo parcius absens:
> inspice, si possum donata reponere laetus.

Often you have praised my modesty, and you have been called king and father
openly, nor when you are absent have I been more sparing by a word. See if I am
able to return your gifts gladly.

The asymmetrical aspect of their patron/client relationship is at the forefront of
these lines, and Horace thus makes it explicit that he and Maecenas are not, in
the end, egalitarian *amici*. Such a relationship has the potential for both parties
to be treated with respect and exercise autonomy, but it also has the potential
to be pushed to the opposite extreme, and in fact has already been cast as such
by Horace's depiction of himself as Maecenas's freed gladiator in 1.1. Horace's
acknowledgment of and willingness to play a deferential role extends only so
far. In the past the propriety each man demonstrated made it easy and comfortable for Horace to treat Maecenas with *verecundia*, "humility" or "deference."
But if Maecenas pushes beyond what is appropriate Horace has no choice but to
extricate himself from Maecenas entirely, and Horace's general lack of deference
throughout the epistle illustrates his willingness to do just this. He will follow
through on his threat to return all of Maecenas's benefactions, *donata reponere*
(39), but such an action will not come easily. Most scholars interpret *laetus* in
line 39 along the following lines: "I'll return your gifts, and I'll be happy to do
so."[32] However, it seems far more likely, given Horace's obvious love for his
farm, that relinquishing it will in fact be a source of pain that will make such a
gesture of independence difficult. I interpret the line as, "See if I can happily
give them back," with the expected answer of "no, but I will if you compel me to
take on a more dependent role than I already have." If Maecenas pushes Horace
to one extreme or another—to either excessive servility toward him or uncompromising *libertas* from him—Horace makes it clear which extreme he will
choose. Despite its negative consequences, Horace will return the farm rather
than become Maecenas's slave. By far the most preferable option, however, is
for Maecenas and Horace to continue adhering to a mean between these two
extremes that allows Maecenas to receive adequate deference and Horace to
enjoy the necessary degree of freedom.

In the third exemplary tale Horace further justifies his refusal to return to
Maecenas in Rome by appealing to *decorum*. It is the countryside that currently
suits him, but he hints that this has not always been the case and that it may not
always be in the future. With this tale Horace draws a stark antithesis between
Maecenas, the city, and public poetry, on the one hand, and himself, the country, and private poetry, on the other. The tale is taken from *Odyssey* 4.601–8,
in which Telemachus refuses the horses offered to him by Menelaus as being
inappropriate for the terrain of Ithaca:

haud male Telemachus, proles sapientis Vlixei:
'non est aptus equis Ithace locus, ut neque planis
porrectus spatiis nec multae prodigus herbae:
Atride, magis apta tibi tua dona relinquam.'
parvum parva decent; mihi iam non regia Roma,
sed vacuum Tibur placet aut imbelle Tarentum. (1.7.40–43)

Not at all badly did Telemachus, the offspring of wise Odysseus, say, "Ithaca is not
a place suitable for horses since it is neither flat with wide plains nor lavish with
abundant grass. Son of Atreus, I will leave your gifts as more suitable for you."
Small things befit the small. Now it is not royal Rome but quiet Tibur or unwarlike
Tarentum that pleases me.

With this exemplum Horace distances himself from the language of lines 37–38,
in which the asymmetrical nature of his patron-client relationship with Maecenas was emphasized, and instead presents the two in terms of Homeric aristocratic egalitarianism.[33] Telemachus provides for Horace a precedent for the
polite refusal of inappropriate gifts, while Menelaus becomes for Maecenas the
model for how to respond to such a refusal.[34] In the *Odyssey* Menelaus responds
to Telemachus's refusal not by retracting the offer of gifts but by exchanging the
unsuitable gift for an appropriate one of even greater value.[35] The gift that Horace refuses as analogous to the horses of the *Odyssey* passage is *regia Roma*,
"royal Rome," a place that is much more suitable for Maecenas than Horace.
What suits Horace instead is Tibur or Tarentum (i.e., the countryside in which
he is currently ensconced). The more suitable and more valuable gift that Maecenas can exchange for *regia Roma* is his ready acquiescence to Horace's desire
to extend his rural withdrawal until the following spring. Though Horace does
not mention the Sabine farm explicitly in these lines, the implication is that it
is not a new gift at all that Horace desires but the continued enjoyment of the
entirely satisfying one that Maecenas has already given.[36]

As in the opening poem, the city and Maecenas are never entirely separable from Horace's public poetic role. The refused "gift" in this exemplary tale, as
Freudenburg has pointed out, has poetic qualities traditionally associated with
grand, public genres:

Parvum parva decent Horace says in conclusion, in words that strongly recall his
many refusals to write poetry of a certain grand and martial type. And so the language of horses and racing plains, of small things preferred to large, of leisure to
war, and so on, just as the language of "thin" (*tenuis*) versus "corpulent" (*pleno . . .
corpore*) in the story of the over-fed fox above, all conspire in this story to suggest
that the "gift" being refused here, and so aggressively agonized over, is not a basket
of pears, nor even a simple invitation to return home.[37]

Maecenas's "gift" thus has poetic strings attached, and as in the opening epistle it is his public poetic role that he is eager for Horace to resume by writing not epic but more of the lyric poetry that has made him famous. The horses refused by Telemachus as unsuitable for Ithaca's terrain remind us of Horace's earlier comparison of himself to an old horse that is no longer able to compete in the poetic arena without becoming a laughingstock (1.1.8–9). Thus these lines are a continuation of that refusal to resume writing his former poetry and offer further justification for it. Horace would prefer a gift from Maecenas that allows him to persist longer in the genre of private epistolary verse, and the continued enjoyment of the Sabine farm is precisely the gift that makes such poetic output possible. What Horace wants from Maecenas is the freedom to determine for himself the qualities and concerns of his own poetry and the locale that gives rise to it.

Whereas the refusal of Maecenas, the city, and public poetry seemed in the opening poem to be permanent, we again have in 1.7.44–45 hints that Horace's withdrawal is not meant to be final but temporary. Just as Horace earlier had promised the return of *vates tuus* (1.7.11), here too he uses language that suggests that he will not persist forever in his preference for the private poetry associated with rural *otia*. The *iam* of line 44 places his preference firmly in the present, with the implication that it has not always been and may not always be thus. Horace's refusal to return to Maecenas and the city is thus less forceful in 1.7 than it was in 1.1, and Horace leaves the door open to future compromise. Just as Horace had criticized Maecenas for his extreme desire that Horace remain with him constantly (1.7.25–28), so now does Horace give reassurance that he will not be as extreme in his own preference for rural retirement. The reader who recalls the opening epistle, moreover, knows that Horace is plagued by inconsistency, particularly in his attitude toward Maecenas, and the unambiguous preference for the country that he shows in 1.7 is therefore highly suspicious. In the following poem, in fact, we see that Horace's clear-cut predilection for Tibur over Rome is short-lived and quick to change: *Romae Tibur amem, ventosus Tibure Romam*, 1.8.12. For Horace the real solution will come not in trying to choose one over the other but in opting for both *vacuum Tibur* and *regia Roma*. Until then, however, he must stay in the countryside, enjoying that gift that does suit his current poetic pursuits, the Sabine farm.

The final and most vexing tale of *Epistles* 1.7 recounts the friendship gone horribly wrong between Philippus and Mena and takes up roughly the last half of the poem. As Oliensis has put it, "critics have tied themselves into knots attempting to unsnarl its complications."[38] While most scholars agree that the episode must be read in light of Horace's own relationship with Maecenas, especially as depicted in *Satires* 1.6,[39] there is disagreement about the degree to which Philippus corresponds to Maecenas and Mena to Horace.[40] Should the story be read strictly as a contrasting exemplum outlining the ways in which Horace and Maecenas have not behaved and thus illustrating the positive aspects of their friendship? Or does it make the rather uncomfortable suggestion that there is something of Philippus and Mena lurking behind Maecenas and Horace?[41] My interpretation of the tale adopts both of these readings simultaneously. Like the tales of the Calabrian host and the fox in the corn bin, the story offers an alternate version of what might have happened had not Maecenas and Horace behaved properly in the past and at the same time serves as a warning for what could still happen should they act differently now. The most important backdrop to the tale is the story that Horace has previously told about his friendship with Maecenas in *Satires* 1.6 and 2.6, which offers a sharp contrast to that of Philippus and Mena. As different as the story is, however, there are undeniable similarities between Mena and Horace. Most significantly, while both Mena and Horace initially enjoy a simple, pleasant urban life, each ultimately experiences a massive transformation and upheaval as a result of this new friendship. For both men this friendship brings about a move from the city to the country, but for different reasons. For Horace his Sabine farm shields him from the negative consequences of his friendship with Maecenas, while for Mena his Sabine farm *is* the negative consequence of his friendship with Philippus. Whereas Horace's farm allows him to transfer his urban life of contentment and sufficiency to the country, Mena's farm effectively destroys the contentment and sufficiency he previously enjoyed in the city and becomes a locus of anxiety. The most important difference between Horace and Mena is that while Horace does not change himself or his way of life to conform to Maecenas, Mena readily yields to Philippus's desires and adopts behavior that better suits his powerful friend, in the process destroying the very qualities that initially drew Philippus to him. Despite these differences, however, the story of Philippus and Mena serves as a cautionary tale for what the friendship of Maecenas and Horace might become if Maecenas continues to pressure Horace to return to his public poetic role. The strings with which the Sabine farm attaches Horace to Maecenas may make of it a source of anxiety just like Mena's farm. Should Maecenas use the farm as a means to bind Horace more tightly to him, it will become a seat of servitude and dependence rather than freedom and leisure. The story compels Maecenas to consider the consequences if Horace were to comply with him and accept a way of life that does not suit him. Such compliance would, as in the case of Philippus and Mena, do away with the independence and sufficiency at the heart of Horace's identity and ultimately force an irredeemable break between the two friends.

Horace introduces us first to Philippus, whom he describes with words that identify him as a public man of action. As he is returning home from the forum he spies Mena lounging at a barbershop:

strenuus et fortis causisque Philippus agendis
clarus ab officiis octavam circiter horam
dum redit atque Foro nimium distare Carinas
iam grandis natu queritur, conspexit, ut aiunt,
adrasum quendam vacua tonsoris in umbra
cultello proprios purgantem leniter ungues. (1.7.46–52)

Philippus, active and strong and famous for pleading cases, while he was returning from business at around the eighth hour and, since he was of considerable age,
was complaining that the Carinae was too far from the Forum, saw, as they say, a
certain close-shaven man sitting in the idle shade of a barber calmly cleaning his
fingernails with a little knife.

Horace's description of Mena enjoying the idle shade, *vacua umbra* (52), not
only contrasts him with *strenuus et fortis Philippus* (46), but also aligns Mena's
personality with Horace's, since it is Tibur's idle quality (*vacuum Tibur*, 45) that
he finds appealing. The shade of the barbershop furthermore makes it a *locus
amoenus* along the same lines as Horace's Sabine farm, as will be described at
Epistles 1.16.10 (*multa umbra*). They key difference here between Mena and
Horace is that while the epistolary Horace is able to find this idleness and leisure only in the countryside, Mena is able to do so in the city.[42] Mena's contentment and lack of anxiety is emphasized by his calm demeanor (*leniter*, 51) and
especially his attentiveness to his appearance, in particular his fresh shave and
clipped fingernails, for it is Horace's disregard of these same things that out-
wardly reflects his inner turmoil in the opening poem (*inaequali tonsore*, 94;
prave sectum unguem, 104).[43] Mena thus enjoys in the city the same freedom
that Horace enjoys in the country and does so without the spiritual sickness
that plagues the poet.

Philippus, impressed by what he sees,[44] sends his slave Demetrius to find out
more information about Mena. He wants to know specifically about Mena's
familial background, status, and connections of patronage: *quaere et refer, unde
domo, quis, / cuius fortunae, quo sit patre quove patrono* ("Ask and report back
where he is from, who he is, of what status, who is his father and who his
patron," 53–54). Demetrius does as he is told and delivers to Philippus and the
reader a description of Mena's daily life in the city:

it, redit et narrat, Volteium nomine Menam,
praeconem, tenui censu, sine crimine, notum
et properare loco et cessare et quaerere et uti,
gaudentem parvisque sodalibus et lare certo
et ludis et post decisa negotia Campo. (1.7.55–59)

> He goes, returns, and reports that his name is Volteius Mena, an auctioneer, of
> slender means, free of reproach, known both to work hard and to rest, both to
> make money and to spend it, all at the proper time, and that he rejoices in his
> humble companions and settled home and, when his duties have been finished, in
> the games and the Campus.

Mena carries out all of his actions at the appropriate time and in the right proportion (*loco*, 57).[45] As Mayer states, he "fulfills an Horatian ideal of well-balanced
activities."[46] The parallels between Mena and Horace are brought out further by
his slender means (*tenui censu*, 56; cf. *Epist.* 1.20.20: *in tenui re*) and associations
with smallness (*parvis*, 58; cf. *parvum parva decent*, 1.7.44). Mena's profession as
a *praeco*, an auctioneer, coupled with his status as a freedman, has led scholars
to compare him to Horace's father, who, we are told in *Satires* 1.6, was a *libertus*
(6) and held a similar position as a *coactor* (86), the intermediary between buy-
ers and sellers at auctions.[47] In the satire Horace says that neither he nor his
father would have been ashamed had Horace pursued either of these professions
(86–88). Mena is in several ways an alter ego for Horace, a depiction of what
might have been if Horace had made different choices or been given different
opportunities. Mena is furthermore a counterpart to the Calabrian's guest in the
first exemplary tale of the poem. When Philippus makes him a dinner invitation
that he does not desire he issues a polite but powerful "no, thank you," *benigne*
(62; cf. line 16). He thus lives, at least prior to his friendship with Philippus,
according to the important Horatian principles of satiety and contentment.

Scholars have rightly seen in the introduction of Mena and Philippus comparisons and contrasts with that between Horace and Maecenas as described
in *Satires* 1.6.45–64. Like Maecenas in the satire, Philippus seems to look past
Mena's low social status; while he asks about Mena's father (*quo patre*, 1.7.54), just
as Maecenas seems to have asked about Horace's (*non ego me claro natum patre*,
Sat. 1.6.58), this seems not to affect his decision to court Mena as a client. However, Philippus may actually pay too little attention to matters of social standing.
Mena's status as a freedman puts him into a class with whom Maecenas most
likely did not associate, as Horace implies at *Satires* 1.6.7–8.[48] The class difference between Philippus and Mena is further brought out by the surprisingly
free use of the vocabulary of patronage throughout the story (*quove patrone*, 54;
cliens, 75; *patrone*, 92), which Horace avoids in *Satires* 1.6, employing instead
the language of *amicitia* (*amicum*, 50 and 53; *in amicorum numero*, 62). Whereas
Maecenas takes care in the satire that his *amici* are his equals in worth if not
exactly in status, Philippus seems purposefully to be interested in binding
Mena to himself as his socially inferior client. In order to do so, he behaves in a
way radically opposed to Maecenas in *Satires* 1.6. Maecenas is approached by

Horace (*ut veni coram*, 56) after being told about him by Vergil and Varius, whereupon he waits nine months to invite Horace into the company of his *amici* (61–62). Philippus, in contrast, wastes no time in inviting Mena to dinner (60–61) and even approaches him again the following morning (after Mena has refused the first invitation) to issue the initial salutation (66). In trying so hard to woo Mena as a client Philippus behaves in a way anomalous with his superior status, whereas Maecenas acts with a caution and reserve that are in keeping with his high position.[49] Though Mena's way of life has much in common with Horace's, as we saw above, his behavior also offers a contrast to that of Horace in *Satires* 1.6 in that Mena is all too easily swayed from his life of simple contentment. Whereas Horace is able to stammer out only a few words to Maecenas (*singultim pauca locutus*, *Sat.* 1.6.56), Mena, though initially stunned into silence by Philippus's invitation (*mirari secum tacitus*, 62), on the following day nevertheless accepts his invitation to dinner, where he lets down his guard and talks about whatever comes to mind (*dicenda tacenda locutus*). This changeability and lack of restraint does not bode well for the outcome of this friendship.

While scholars have tended to focus on the contrasting introductions of the two sets of friends, the Philippus/Mena story in fact resonates even more fully than this with *Satires* 1.6 as well as with *Satires* 2.6, a poem that Armstrong has called 1.6's counterpart.[50] The most important similarity between Horace in *Satires* 1.6 and Mena in *Epistles* 1.7 is the untroubled lifestyle each enjoys in the city. After describing his introduction to Maecenas in the satire, Horace explains how this high profile friendship has not inspired in him an ambition for political office. In lines 111–29, Horace describes his leisurely daily life in the city, an illustration of contentment usually reserved in Horace's poetry for the countryside. He spends his evenings at leisure strolling around the Circus and Forum (113–14), eats a simple dinner of the sort he would eat in the country (114–18), and goes to bed and wakes when he pleases (119–21) (i.e., he does not have to attend a morning *salutatio*). He lounges in bed reading and writing until midmorning (122–23) before heading to the Campus for some exercise and a game of ball (*Campum lusumque trigonem*, 126). Finally, he goes to the baths (125), eats a light lunch (127), and relaxes at home (128). This description of his lifestyle, as Oliensis has shown, "distinguish[es] Horace not from the political aspirant but from the parasitic social climber."[51] Thus Horace has not cultivated a friendship with Maecenas for financial and social gain. Mena in the epistle initially exhibits a way of life that similarly distinguishes him from a would-be parasite, and he does not actively pursue a friendship so as to enrich himself or gain fame. At first, he seems little interested in taking part in the customary activities of clients, such as attending the morning salutation. When

Philippus approaches him on the morning after his rejected dinner invitation, he somewhat suspiciously cites work as his excuse for not attending the great man's *salutatio* (*excusare laborem et mercennaria vincla, / quod non mane domum venisset*, 67–68). While he does take part in business activity to make his living, which betrays his less secure financial position than that of Horace, he nevertheless balances this with the same sort of leisurely activities that Horace enjoys. Most significantly, both men enjoy spending time at games and the Campus Martius (*Campum lusumque trigonem*, *Satires* 1.6.126; *et ludis et post decisa negotia Campo*, *Epistles* 1.7.59).

For neither Horace nor Mena, however, will this leisurely and contented lifestyle in the city last for very long once they have entered the *amicitia* of a more powerful and prominent man. The dramatic upheaval in Mena's life will be the result of his all too eager willingness to abandon his content life in the city— like the fox, he will feed himself fat on the patronage of Philippus. The changes in Horace's life likewise stem from his friendship with Maecenas, but Horace responds to them with a reluctance to abandon his lifestyle of contentment. Furthermore, whereas Maecenas's benefactions are motivated by a desire to help his friend live as he desires, Philippus seems inclined to remake his friend in his own image, either out of ignorance of Mena's true nature or, even worse, as a bit of amusement to himself. As we will see in chapter 7's discussion of 1.17 and 1.18, Horace is highly critical of the client who slavishly imitates the behavior of his patron. He also criticizes the patron who deliberately ruins his client by exposing him to an unsuitable lifestyle.[52] Philippus and Mena are guilty of both of these faults.

The coupling of *ludus* and *Campus* in *Epistles* 1.7.59 looks back not only to *Satires* 1.6 but to *Satires* 2.6 as well, in which Horace examines the effect that his friendship with Maecenas, now eight years in duration, has had on his life. The urban contentment he described in *Satires* 1.6 is now impossible. If he were to watch games with Maecenas or play ball with him in the Campus, it would incite envy and lead to constant questions concerning the inner workings of government:

> per totum hoc tempus subiectior in diem et horam
> invidiae noster. ludos spectaverat una,
> luserat in campo: "Fortunae filius!" omnes.
> frigidus a rostris manat per compita rumor:
> quicumque obvius est me consulit. (2.6.47–51)

> Through all this time have I been subjected daily and hourly to envy. Had I watched the games or played in the Campus together with [Maecenas]: "Son of Fortune!" all [would say]. A cold rumor drips from the rostra through the crossroads: whoever meets me asks my advice.

Throughout the first half of the satire Horace describes the annoyances he must face in the city because of the high profile his friendship with Maecenas has brought him. It is only because of the possession of the Sabine farm that he is able to escape back to the leisurely life that in 1.6 he had practiced in the city: *o rus, quando ego te aspiciam? quandoque licebit / nunc veterum libris, nunc somno et inertibus horis, / ducere sollicitae iucundae oblivia vitae?* ("O farm, when will I see you? And when will it be allowed for me, now with the books of the ancients, now with sleep and idle hours, to induce sweet forgetfulness of my busy life?" 2.6.60–62). The farm in 2.6, although as a gift from Maecenas it renders him dependent, nevertheless frees him to enjoy the *otium* that is now impossible for him to find in the city, and it can be inferred that Maecenas's benefaction was motivated by his concern for Horace's well-being. *Satires* 2.6 ends with the story of the city mouse and country mouse, a tale that, like the Philippus and Mena story of *Epistles* 1.7, takes up roughly the last half of the poem. In some ways Philippus and Mena recreate the city and country mice, except that now the city mouse (i.e., Mena) has his life destroyed by someone who pulls him into the country.

Whereas Horace in *Satires* 2.6 has his life restored by a Sabine farm, in *Epistles* 1.7 Mena's Sabine farm proves to be his undoing. After Mena finally acquiesces and accepts Philippus's invitation to dinner, Philippus exhorts him to apply himself to increasing his wealth: *nunc i, rem strenuus auge* ("Now go and zealously augment your wealth," 1.7.71). Philippus thus encourages him to take on qualities that suit himself (cf. *strenuus*, 46) rather than the easy-going *praeco*. It is just such augmentation of wealth that Horace in *Satires* 1.6.100 claims he does not have to worry about due to his lack of ambition: *nam mihi continuo maior quaerenda foret res*, "for immediately greater wealth would have to be sought by me." Mena now becomes a regular attendee at Philippus's morning *salutatio* (*mane cliens*, 1.7.75), a duty that Horace avoids in the satire (*salutandi plures*, 1.6.101). Whereas Horace neither becomes more ambitious nor adopts the lifestyle of an obsequious parasite after his introduction to Maecenas, Mena responds in the opposite fashion, drawn to the benefits to be gained from a powerful connection in the way a fish is drawn to a hook (*occultum visus decurrere piscis ad hamum*, 74). He becomes a constant dinner guest at Philippus's house (75) and, when he accompanies his patron to the countryside, his incessant praise of Philippus's Sabine property (*non cessat laudare*, 78) suggests that he is in danger of becoming a flatterer and adopting a way of life that is suitable for his patron but not himself. Likewise Philippus, rather than looking out for the best interest of his new friend, gives him the means to purchase a little farm— by giving half the money as a gift and half on loan—as a source of amusement to himself, as if knowing beforehand the terrible outcome and anticipating humor in it:

> videt ridetque Philippus,
> et sibi dum requiem, dum risus undique quaerit,
> dum septem donat sestertia, mutua septem
> promittit, persuadet uti mercetur agellum. (1.7.78–81)

Philippus sees and laughs, and since he seeks relief and amusement for himself, persuades him to buy a little farm by giving him seven thousand sesterses and promising seven thousand more on loan.

Mena unsuccessfully employs his farm as a way of amassing wealth (*amore senescit habendi*, "he grows old with the love of possessing," 85) and in doing so experiences a reversal of the leisure and peace of mind that he previously enjoyed in the city. His animals are stolen or succumb to illness, while his crops fail and the oxen are worked to death by plowing (86–87). Finally, Mena gives up and asks Philippus to return him to his former way of life:

> offensus damnis media de nocte caballum
> arripit iratusque Philippi tendit ad aedes.
> quem simul aspexit scabrum intonsumque Philippus,
> 'durus' ait, 'Voltei, nimis attentusque videris
> esse mihi.' 'pol, me miserum, patrone, vocares,
> si velles' inquit 'verum mihi ponere nomen.
> quod te per Genium dextramque deosque Penates
> obsecro et obtestor, vitae me redde priori.' (1.7.88–95)

Hurt by his losses in the middle of the night he seizes his horse and angrily sets out for the house of Philippus. As soon as Philippus sees him rough and unshorn, he says, "Volteius, you seem to me to be too hard-worked and stressed." "Truly, patron, you would be calling me wretched," Mena replies, "if you were wanting to place a true name on me. But I beg and entreat you by your guardian spirit, right hand, and household gods, return me to my previous life."

Mena's ambition has led him to be what Horace had no interest in being or pretending to be in *Satires* 1.6, a landowner who rides a *caballus* around his country estate: *non ego circum / Saureiano vectari rura caballo*, "I did not say that I was carried around my rural estate on a Tarentine horse," 58–59; *plures . . . caballi / pascendi*, "more horses would have to be fed," 103–4. Whereas earlier Mena was relaxing freshly shaven in the shade of a barbershop (50), his distress and the reversal of his state of mind are now brought out by his unshaven beard and unshorn hair (*scabrum intonsumque*). By the story's end, therefore, Mena has been brought to the same state of anxiety that Horace attributed to himself at the end of the first epistle, where he similarly has poorly cut hair (*curatus inaequali tonsore capillos*, "with my hair looked after by an uneven barber," 94). As we saw in the opening chapters, Horace's state of mind in the first epistle is brought on by the pressure Maecenas is exerting on him to comply with his demands for attendance, and Mena's crisis is similarly caused by his compliance with and conformity to a patron's way of life that does not match his own. While Horace has the farm to provide him with the solace necessary to calm his mind, Philippus can only ask that he be returned to his former way of life, a return that at this stage is highly improbable.[53]

The Philippus and Mena tale poses the question to Maecenas of whether he truly wants Horace to comply with him after all and outlines for him what might be the consequences if Horace should do so. Does Maecenas want a Horace who conforms to his wishes with disastrous results or a Horace who stays true to himself and the qualities that first drew Maecenas to him and that give rise to the poetry that Maecenas values so highly? The moral Horace draws from this tale is that the only solution for one who has not acted in accordance with his nature is immediately to seek again what he has abandoned:

qui semel agnovit, quantum dimissa petitis
praestent, mature redeat repetatque relicta.
metiri se quemque suo modulo ad pede verum est. (1.7.96–98)

Once someone recognizes how much what has been abandoned excels what one has sought, let him return quickly and seek again what he gave up. It is right that each person measure himself by his own scale and foot-rule.

If Horace should comply with Maecenas's demands and therefore sacrifice his independence, like the overfed fox, or too quickly compromise his character, like Mena, it would ultimately result in not just a pulling away but a final break between the two men in order for Horace to seek again what he gave up. But if both Maecenas and Horace take care not to be like the negative exemplars (the Calabrian host, the fox, Philippus and Mena) outlined in the series of tales in *Epistles* 1.7 and to be instead like the positive ones (the Calabrian guest, Telemachus, and Menelaus), then there is no need for the friendship between the two to be terminated. The stories set out the terms by which a continued friendship is possible. They must first of all treat one another with the compassion and indulgence that dear friends, *dulces amici*, exercise toward one another. Maecenas is welcome to grant benefactions to Horace and to expect gratitude and deference in return, but these benefactions must, like the Sabine farm, be suitable to Horace's needs and personality and should not lead to an expectation that such gifts oblige Horace to comply with or accept unwanted requests. Above all, appropriate gifts should enhance and not threaten independence. If these terms are met, then Maecenas can expect the return of his beloved *vates* in due time. Only by making compromises can Maecenas hope to obtain compromises in turn, whereas extreme demands will meet with an equally extreme response.

The final balancing act Horace assumes is one that mixes obedience with defiance, praise with criticism, and above all dependence with autonomy. Such are the concessions that in the end constitute friendship.

THE UNCOMPROMISING *LIBERTAS* OF 1.16

Epistles 1.16 has been called Horace's "noblest of Epistles," but in many ways it is his most difficult to decipher.[54] Whereas the Sabine farm in 1.7 symbolizes Horace's negotiation of a moderated freedom in that it provides him *libertas* and autonomy at the same time that it necessitates continued dependence on Maecenas, in 1.16 it is celebrated as investing Horace not just with liberty but with rule. The farm gives Horace the power to achieve *libertas* by providing him a place over which he holds sway. The definition of freedom, however, becomes amended over the course of the poem from a possession granted from without (such as by the farm) to one that is an inner state available no matter the exterior circumstances. This inner freedom is in fact greater than and preferable to that provided by the farm, since, while the farm can be taken away, true inner freedom can never be wrested from the one who possesses it, and the speaker of the poem defiantly challenges anyone who would make this attempt. The challenge that the poem poses, therefore, is how to transform the conditional rural independence Horace describes at the poem's beginning into one that is unconditional and transferable anywhere.

The sixteenth epistle is Horace's most pronounced display of his desire for freedom and autonomy and shows him at his most stubborn and inflexible, and this uncompromising stance is expressed throughout the epistle by a pronounced Stoicism.[55] At the same time the epistle reveals the problems that arise from uncompromising liberty and rigidity. Throughout the poem there is a marked emphasis on the private world not only of the farm but also of the soul, and we are left to wonder what place this uncompromising freedom has for one who desires the benefits and enjoyment that arise from friendship and social participation, which require flexibility and make demands on independence. Although Horace endorses adaptability and moderated freedom by the end of the collection, the sixteenth epistle nevertheless offers a profound demonstration that Horace will never absolutely sacrifice his freedom and that he will meet any extreme demands made on him with a defiant and stubborn inner liberty. This inner liberty in fact is a necessary prerequisite for the moderated freedom we will find endorsed elsewhere since it enables one to bend and compromise without forfeiting his internal core of freedom. This limitation that Horace puts on his willingness to bend and adapt is pointedly placed between 1.15 and 1.17, the two poems in which Horace professes and commends adaptability most unreservedly.

In *Epistles* 1.1 Horace asserts that he will vacillate between two poles in the collection, one of rigidity and one of adaptability. I argued in the first chapter that the Horace that opens that poem, in his insistence on withdrawal and freedom, exemplifies the posture of rigidity. The sixteenth epistle sees him take up once again this inflexible stance and insist on absolute freedom and nonparticipation. The opening section of the poem paints a portrait of total rural freedom and shows us a Horace who holds sway over his private farm. From the first lines of the poem Horace underscores his ownership of it:

> ne perconteris, fundus *meus*, optime Quincti,
> arvo pascat *erum* an bacis opulentet olivae,
> pomisne et pratis an amicta vitibus ulmo,
> scribetur tibi forma loquaciter et situs agri. (1–4)

> In case, dear Quinctius, you should inquire whether my farm supports its master with its land, or enriches him with fruits of the olive tree or with apples and meadows or with elm wrapped with vines, the beauty and site of the farm will be described to you.

Horace pointedly calls the farm "mine," *meus*, and he is its "master," *erus*.[56] Not only is the farm in his dominion but so too are the very trees that grow on it: *si quercus et ilex / multa fruge pecus, multa dominum iuvet umbra?* ("Suppose you knew that the oak and ilex please the herd with much fruit, and their master with much shade," 9–10). Whereas in 1.7 Horace had obliquely acknowledged that his acquisition of the farm was due to Maecenas's generosity, here it is presented as belonging to him alone and investing him not just with *otia liberrima* (1.7.36) but with dominion. In 1.7 Horace may have enjoyed independence on the farm, but he nevertheless acknowledged Maecenas as his *rexque paterque* (1.7.37). In 1.16, however, it is clearly Horace who rules, and Maecenas's name is unspoken.[57] For this Horace, to be free means to have no one to whom to defer, to be not just one's own master but to hold mastery over a realm.

Whereas Quinctius, Horace imagines, would be interested in the actual agricultural activity of the farm, Horace finds the farm's value in its pleasantness (*amoenae*, 15) and therapeutic utility (*utilis*, 14). Richard Thomas has nicely examined the idealized nature of Horace's portrait and, drawing on the topoi of ethnographical writing, suggested that, from the brambles that spontaneously produce cornel cherries and plums to the oaks and ilex that provide acorns and shade, Horace has transformed his farm into a marvelous *locus amoenus* and endowed it with attributes of the golden age.[58] The landscape over which Horace holds sway is therefore a poetic one, removed from the realities of farming life. The poetic power of his farm is foremost emphasized in his description of his fountain, *fons*, as cooler and purer than the Hebrus river that runs through Thrace (13–14), which is replete with Callimachean literary associations.[59] For Horace the fountain's poetic value is inseparable from its ethical value, for it brings him not only inspiration but also physical and, by extension, spiritual well-being: *infirmo capiti fluit utilis, utilis alvo* ("It flows useful to the unwell head, useful to the stomach," 14).[60] In this idealized landscape Horace ceases to suffer from the spiritual ailments described at 1.1.94–105, 1.8.3–12, and 1.15. In 1.16 Horace seems to have found the retreat he was seeking in 1.15, where he presents the hot springs of Baiae as being disgruntled by those who seek therapy for their ailing heads and stomachs (*caput et stomachum*, 8) in the fountains (*fontibus*, 8) of the cool countryside (*frigid rura*, 9). There is no need to report to Salernum, Clusium, or Gabii (1.15.1–9) for treatment, since the cure is available to him on his own Sabine farm. It is this spot in 1.16, with its cool and pleasant *amoenitas*, that keeps Horace physically and spiritually sound: *hae latebrae dulces et, iam si credis, amoenae, / incolumem tibi me praestant Septembribus horis* ("This sweet and, if you now believe me, pleasant hiding place keeps me safe and sound in September's season," 16). Horace's farm brings him a wholeness in which his exterior physical health matches his inner spiritual health.

Horace's rural authority and spiritual well-being are, however, limited by being tied so closely to one particular place, which is cut off almost entirely from the real world. The contentment and equanimity that the farm provides Horace should, if we follow the advice that he gives in 1.11, be available to him anywhere: *quod petis hic est, / est Ulubris, animus si te non deficit aequus* ("What you are seeking is here. It is at Ulubrae provided that equanimity does not fail you," 29–30). In no way does Horace suggest in 1.16 that his rustic *aequus animus* is transferable to any other space, and its ability to help him overcome his ambivalence toward public life is therefore suspect.[61] Surrounded by mountains, miraculous brambles, shade trees, and pigs, Horace is the lonely master.[62] Gone are the rural neighbors whose company and conversation he professes to enjoy, for example, in *Satires* 2.6.65–76. The farm is nestled within a valley almost entirely surrounded by *continui montes* (5), which cut it off from the rest of the world. It sees the sun rising (*veniens . . . sol*, 6) and setting (*discedens*), giving the impression that little exists beyond this private world. The isolation and disconnection of his farm are intensified by his calling it *latebrae* (15), a refuge from the world but also a hiding place. Like Veianius in 1.1.5, who is *abditus agro*, "hidden in the countryside," Horace eschews the public eye, but like Albius of 1.4 his search for spiritual renewal is taken to an extreme and leads him to isolation. Horace's *imperium* is over a limited, idealized, and intensely private world and is therefore fragile and open to threat from the city and the people in it.[63]

Horace compares the beauty and foliage of his farm to the southern Italian town of Tarentum, for which it could be mistaken: *dicas adductum propius frondere Tarentum* ("You would say that Tarentum with its foliage had been brought closer," 11). Thomas has convincingly suggested that this is an allusion to Vergil's old man of Tarentum, whose floral garden is described in *Georgics* 4 and who, like Horace, occupies a private world of simple berries and shade trees:

> ille etiam seras in versum distulit ulmos
> eduramque pirum et spinos iam pruna ferentis
> iamque ministrantem platinum potantibus umbras. (*Georgics* 4.144–46)

> He also planted mature elms in a row, and hardy pear and blackthorns that already were bearing plums, and now a plane tree that provides shade for drinkers.

Vergil's *pruna ferentis* (4.145) is clearly echoed in Horace's *pruna ferant* (1.16.9), and, as Thomas (14) suggests, "the sequence is the same in both passages: from berries and fruit to larger trees administering shade." Just as Horace seems to exclude the realities of agriculture from his farm (plowing, 1; the fruits of olive and apple trees, 1–2; vines, 3), the old man of Tarentum spends his time gardening rather than plowing, tending his flocks, or growing vines (4.128–29). When Horace mentions Tarentum, according to Thomas, "he means Virgil's Tarentum; the claim is that his own farm possesses those same qualities which Virgil imputed to the plot of the old man."[64]

The old man of Tarentum, like Horace, enjoys autonomy and even authority in his garden, for, although his plot is small and his food simple, he seems to himself to equal kings in wealth: *regum aequabat opes animis* ("He equaled the wealth of kings in his spirit," 4.132). The old man's garden, like Horace's farm, is a world apart and allows him to enjoy a deeply private existence that contrasts with the political and communal life of the bees that Vergil subsequently describes. Clay has nicely examined the contrast between the old man and the bees, suggesting that "the old man who tends his garden presents that aspect of human nature which is strictly private and individual" and that "by juxtaposing the anonymous old man in the garden against the marvelous society of the bees, Virgil indicates the irreconcilable tension between the demands of the political life and the requirements of the human heart."[65] Vergil's old man therefore throws into contrast private and public life, and Horace's rustic farm points to a similar antithesis between the interior and private world of the individual, on the one hand, and the ties of society and public life, on the other. W.R. Johnson more recently has examined the potentially troubling aspects of the old man's isolation, arguing that his *lathe biosas* is radical and does not provide him with the pleasure of Epicurean friendship: "He is, manifestly—all the signals point to it—an Epicurean. But apart from needing beauty too much, his autonomy is suspiciously extreme. He has, in short, no friends."[66] Horace's farm, I suggest, is similarly extreme and prohibits him from enjoying the beneficial aspects of society and community. Though *latebrae* (1.16.15) is suggestive of the *lathe biosas*, his ensconcing himself in it denies him the enjoyment of Epicurean friendship, the very friendship Horace had urged Albius to enjoy instead of isolating himself in 1.4. The epistolary form itself emphasizes Horace's isolation and separation from his friends, and Quinctius is pointedly not present with Horace to view the farm with his own eyes. Quinctius is not, like the Tyndaris to whom Horace describes his Sabine farm in *Odes* 1.17, invited to visit the farm and experience its recuperative benefits for himself.[67] What Horace must do is find a mean between the private life that gives him authority and the life of engagement that impinges on his autonomy. He must learn to walk an Aristippean middle path between rule and slavery, one that constitutes freedom and leads to happiness.[68]

Horace's emphasis on one's hidden, private life continues when he turns his attention in line 17 from describing his farm to an examination of inner happiness and freedom. The interior health provided by the Sabine farm invests him with the authority to advise Quinctius on the importance of not just seeming but in fact being *beatus* ("happy," 18), an attribute that Horace says belongs only to the wise and good man:

> tu recte vivis si curas esse quod audis.
> iactamus iampridem omnis te Roma beatum;
> sed vereor ne cui de te plus quam tibi credas
> neve putes alium sapiente bonoque beatum. (1.16.17–20)

> You live rightly if you take care to be what you are called. For a long time all of us in Rome have stated confidently that you are happy, but I am afraid that you might believe someone else's opinion of yourself rather than your own or that you might think that someone is happy other than the wise and good man.

It is what is inside, where the eyes of the outside world cannot penetrate, that is of the greatest importance. If people consider you *beatus*, Horace tells Quinctius, then you must take care actually to be so and not ignorantly assume that you are happy simply because you are widely thought to be. By the same token, just because others may falsely accuse you of baseness does not mean that you actually are base (36–40). The opinions of others and judgment of the public is, after all, fickle: *qui dedit hoc hodie, cras, si volet, auferet* ("Whoever has granted this today will take it away tomorrow, if he so desires," 33). Unwarranted praise and groundless blame affect only the person whose inner health is lacking: *falsus honor iuvat et mendax infamia terret / quem mendosum et medicandum?* ("Whom does false honor please and untruthful disgrace terrify except the one who is full of faults and in need of healing?" 39–40). The emphasis here is placed on self-awareness and living an ethically sound life for its own sake and for one's own benefit. The man who is able to achieve this inner happiness is termed the *vir bonus* (40), "good man," the definition of whom takes up the poem's second half. The chief characteristic of the *vir bonus* is the possession of an inner core of freedom and virtue that cannot be compromised, and the absolute independence that he embodies on first consideration undercuts the moderation and flexibility that Horace espouses elsewhere.

In describing the *vir bonus*, Horace draws on the tenets of orthodox Stoicism and especially recalls three of the Stoic paradoxes: a) virtue is sufficient for happiness, b) all sins are equal, and c) only the wise man is free.[69] The *vir bonus* of 1.16 will exemplify Stoic devotion to virtue and freedom and look back to the uncompromising Horace of 1.1.17, who is a *virtutis verae custos rigidusque satelles* ("guardian and rigid attendant of true virtue") and whose rigidity, as I suggested in the first chapter, leads him not to public service (as the Stoics valued) but to uncompromising private withdrawal.[70] *Virtus* and *libertas* are prized by Horace not for their potential to serve the state but instead for their ability to withstand threats made by it, and to the Stoics *libertas* in particular was an inward condition achievable regardless of the exterior political landscape. It is not given or taken away by another but is a state of the soul available to anyone.

In lines 41–43 Horace imagines an interlocutor offering a traditional definition of the *vir bonus* as a man who is devoted to public service:

'qui consulta patrum, qui leges iuraque servat,
quo multae magnaeque secantur iudice lites,
quo res sponsore et quo causae teste tenentur.'

"It is the one who observes the decrees of the Senate, who observes laws and rights, the one who acts as judge when many great quarrels are decided, the one who acts as guarantor when possessions are retained, who acts as witness when cases are won."

This traditional definition is, however, insufficient because public service does not accurately reflect one's inner goodness, and these public duties can be used like a cloak to conceal the faults of one's private life: *sed videt hunc omnis domus et vicinia tota / introrsum turpem, speciosum pelle decora* ("But the whole house and the entire neighborhood see that this guy is ugly on the inside, that his beauty is due to a comely skin," 44–45).[71] Such a man is not prompted to public service because of an inner love of virtue. Horace next turns to an examination of motives and argues that it is less important that we are good than *why* we are good. His *exemplum* here is no longer the tainted public servant but a slave who suffers not only literal slavery but figurative slavery as well. This slave feels he should be commended for neither stealing nor running away, but his master, called by Horace a *Sabellus* (49), feels otherwise:[72]

> oderunt peccare boni virtutis amore;
> tu nihil admittes in te formidine poenae:
> sit spes fallendi, miscebis sacra profanis.
> nam de mille fabae modiis cum surripis unum,
> damnum est, non facinus, mihi pacto lenius isto. (52–56)

> Good men hate to sin because they love virtue, while you will commit no crime
> because you fear punishment. If there is hope of escaping notice, you will mix the
> sacred with the profane. For when you steal just one bean out of a thousand bar-
> rels, the loss, not the crime, is less to me in that case.

Though Mayer downplays the influence of the Stoic paradox that all sins are
equal on these lines, McGann and Kilpatrick are right to emphasize it.[73] Once a
theft has been made a moral boundary has been crossed, and the extent to which
the boundary has been crossed makes no difference. As Cicero puts it, *est pec-
care tamquam transire lineas; quod cum feceris, culpa commissa est; quam longe
progrediare, cum semel transieris, ad augendam transeundi culpam nihil pertinet*
("To sin is like crossing boundary lines. When you have done this, a fault has
been committed. When it comes to increasing the fault of the transgressor it
does not matter how far you advance when you have already transgressed," Cic.
Parad. 20). This is, as Kilpatrick observes, "an extreme Stoic view," and it is one
which elsewhere Horace vehemently censures as not conducive to friendship
due to its unforgiving nature (*Satires* 1.3). Virtue (52), not friendship, is Horace's
chief consideration in *Epistles* 1.16, and according to the Stoics virtue was sufficient for providing happiness, the *beatitas* at the core of the epistle's moral
examinations (18, 20).[74]

Whereas the *servus* of lines 46–56 experiences literal enslavement, Horace's
next target, an *avarus*, "miser," illustrates figurative enslavement due to his greed,
which makes him fall prey to humiliation:

> qui melior servo, qui liberior sit avarus,
> in triviis fixum cum se demittit ob assem,
> non video. nam qui cupiet, metuet quoque, porro
> qui metuens vivet, liber mihi non erit umquam.
> perdidit arma, locum virtutis deseruit, qui
> semper in augenda festinat et obruitur re. (63–68)

> I do not see how the miser is better or freer than a slave, when he bends down in
> the crossroads on account of a penny glued there [as a joke]; for whoever desires
> also fears; further, whoever lives in fear will never be free, as I see it. He has lost
> his defenses, he has abandoned the station of virtue, whoever keeps busy at and is
> overwhelmed by increasing his wealth.

Enslavement to his emotions, particularly his fear, strips the miser of both *libertas* and *virtus*. In outlining the Stoic paradox that every fool is a slave Cicero similarly singles out fear as especially destructive of freedom: *An non est omnis metus servitus?* ("Is all not fear slavery?" *Parad.* 40). To the Stoic true freedom has to do with one's personal inner state rather than with one's exterior circumstances.[75] Interestingly, Davus employed just this paradox in *Satires* 2.7 to condemn his master of moral slavery. According to Davus, only the *sapiens* enjoys perfect freedom:

> quisnam igitur liber? sapiens sibi qui imperiosus,
> quem neque pauperies neque mors neque vincula terrent,
> responsare cupidinibus, contemnere honores
> fortis, et in se ipso totus, teres atque rotundus,
> externi ne quid valeat per leve morari,
> in quem manca ruit semper fortuna. (2.7.83–88)

> Who then is free? The wise man who has full command of himself, whom neither poverty nor death nor chains terrify, who bravely withstands his desires and scorns honors, complete in himself, round and spherical, so that nothing external can to stick to him on account of his smoothness, against whom fortune always rushes lame.

Though Davus's depiction of the Stoic *sapiens* is open to criticism, Horace nevertheless offers a similar portrait of the truly free man at the end of *Epistles* 1.16. This man, the *vir bonus et sapiens*, has such an inner core of freedom and virtue that he obdurately defies any external force that threatens him.

In order to illustrate the *vir bonus et sapiens*, whom he has already claimed is the only man capable of true *beatitas* (20), Horace adapts a scene from Euripides's *Bacchae* 492–98 in which the tyrannical Pentheus threatens the Lydian stranger—Dionysus in disguise—with loss of property and enslavement:

> Δι. εἴφ᾽ ὅτι παθεῖν δεῖ· τί με τὸ δεινὸν ἐργάσῃ;
> Πε. πρῶτον μὲν ἁβρὸν βόστρυχον τεμῶ σέθεν.
> Δι. ἱερὸς ὁ πλόκαμος· τῷ θεῷ δ᾽ αὐτὸν τρέφω.
> Πε. ἔπειτα θύρσον τόνδε παράδος ἐκ χεροῖν.
> Δι. αὐτός μ᾽ ἀφαιροῦ· τόνδε Διονύσῳ φορῶ.
> Πε. εἱρκταῖσί τ᾽ ἔνδον σῶμα σὸν φυλάξομεν.
> Δι. λύσει μ᾽ ὁ δαίμων αὐτός, ὅταν ἐγὼ θέλω.

> Di. Tell me what I have to suffer. What terrible thing will you do to me?
> Pe. First I will cut off your pretty curls.
> Di. My locks are sacred. I let them grow for the god.
> Pe. And then hand over that thyrsus from your hands.

Di. Take it away from me yourself. I carry it for Dionysus.
Pe. We will guard your body in prison.
Di. The god himself will release me whenever I want.

Horace replaces the Lydian stranger with the *vir bonus et sapiens* whose inner freedom cannot be compromised by the tyrant. Dionysus/Bacchus himself was very much associated with freedom, as one of his major titles was *Eleutherios* ("Liberator") and he was called *Liber* among the Romans, and the wise man therefore embodies this freedom.[76] Unlike the Lydian stranger whose Dionysian emblems Pentheus threatens to seize, the *vir bonus et sapiens* risks losing all his possessions, including his life:

vir bonus et sapiens audebit dicere 'Pentheu,
rector Thebarum, quid me perferre patique
indignum coges?' 'adimam bona.' 'nempe pecus, rem,
lectos, argentum: tollas licet.' 'in manicis et
compedibus saevo te sub custode tenebo.'
'ipse deus, simulatque volam, me solvet.' opinor,
hoc sentit 'moriar.' mors ultima linea rerum est. (73–79)

The good and wise man will dare to say, "Pentheus, ruler of Thebes, what unworthy thing will you compel me to suffer and endure?" "I will take away your goods." "You mean, I suppose, my herd, my estate, my couches, and silver; you may take them." "I will keep you under a harsh guardian in handcuffs and fetters." "The god himself, as soon as I want, will free me." I think he means this: "I will die." Death is the finish line for things.

The fearlessness of the *vir bonus et sapiens* as he dares (*audebit*) to defy the tyrant illustrates the inner freedom he possesses, and in expressing his defiance verbally (*dicere*) he further manifests his *libertas*, which encompasses freedom of speech.[77] True freedom cannot be compromised by any outside force and is neither obtained by possessions nor restricted by imprisonment. These lines force us to reexamine the freedom that in the opening part of the poem Horace claims to receive from his Sabine estate, for as an external good it is subject to seizure. As Bowditch states:

This image of Dionysus stripped of his goods suggests more than the poet's characteristic concern with independence of will and thought, for it must be set against the autobiographical image of the author, literally self-present with his farm, at the beginning of *Epistles* 1.16. As a material good the farm is an external *bonum* and thus subject to the same caprices of power as are Dionysus's belongings.[78]

Among the *bona* that Pentheus threatens to take in the epistle are the *vir's pecus* ("herd") and *res* ("estate"). In *Epistles* 1.14.5 Horace refers to the Sabine farm as his *res*, and earlier in 1.16 itself Horace mentions possessing a herd, *pecus* (10), that enjoys the produce of the oak and ilex. As we saw in examining the opening lines of the poem, Horace's independence is granted to him by his possession of the farm, and as formulated there it seems unlikely that Horace could retain this freedom if, like the *vir bonus et sapiens*, he were to lose this most valuable possession. Though Horace does not profess to be himself the *vir bonus et sapiens*, it is nevertheless clear that this is his aspiration in 1.16, and in order to achieve this he will need to develop an autonomy that exists apart from his farm and is transferable to all manner of circumstances.

The figure of Pentheus in the epistle deserves careful consideration. Whom is he meant to evoke, and what are the circumstances that could threaten the *bona* of the wise man or even Horace himself? On the most abstract level he could simply stand in for the capriciousness of *Fortuna*, to whose vicissitudes we are all subject. In *Epistles* 1.1, for example, it is *Fortuna* against whom we are encouraged to stand free and defiant: *isne tibi melius suadet, qui rem facias . . . / an qui Fortunae te responsare superbae /liberum et erectum praesens hortatur et aptat?* ("Does he advise you better, the one who bids you to make money . . . or the one who helpfully exhorts and equips you, free and bold, to defy Fortune?" 65–69). Given the fact that Pentheus is a ruler, however, a political reading of these lines is difficult to avoid. The person who seems to be threatening Horace's independence the most in the collection is Maecenas, and Horace even states that Maecenas's desire for more poetry threatens to "enclose" or "imprison" him in gladiatorial servitude (*includere*, 1.1.3).[79] It is to Maecenas that Horace asserts in 1.7 his readiness to hand over the benefactions he has received if he is pushed (34; 39). Maecenas to an extent can be read as standing in by proxy for Augustus. Though scholars such as McGann resist a political reading of these lines, others such as Johnson and Bowditch have read this closing vignette in the light of growing imperial power, a reading that is hard to avoid and must not be dismissed.[80] To quote Bowditch: "By the time of the *Epistles*, of course, it is unlikely either that Horace will give back or that Augustus, as the supreme authority, will take away, but the consciousness that the latter *could* exercise his power over Horace, should he wish to, appears in the . . . final lines of *Epistles* 1.16."[81] Horace's resistance toward Maecenas's demands, so clearly expressed in 1.1 and 1.7, is taken to its most extreme at the close of 1.16. Association with great men has the potential to be dangerous, and the powerful have to observe limits on the degree to which they impose themselves on others. If not, the only possible outcome for the lesser party is either servitude or, for the one who finds this intolerable, death, the ultimate exercise of freedom.

Horace's *moriar* (79) has most convincingly been understood as a reference to Stoic suicide in the face of unacceptable political infringement on *libertas*.[82] Sedley nicely describes the Stoic approval of suicide in extreme situations: "The wise are free, and remain so under any regime, however repressive. This is partly because the wise are under no obligation to stay alive, and are free to make a 'well-reasoned exit' (εὔλογος ἐξαγωγή) from life—if necessary by suicide—at any time rather than compromise their integrity under political pressure."[83] In the face of extreme political threats to liberty the *vir bonus et sapiens* of *Epistles* 1.16 has recourse to the equally extreme decision to take his own life, and this was an option that, though relatively rare under Augustus, would be put into practice with increasing frequency throughout the early principate, reaching a peak during the reign of Nero.[84] As Hill points out, "in the fifty years covered by the surviving sixteen books of Tacitus' *Annals*, for instance, there are found 74 instances of suicide."[85] These deaths are on the whole modeled on the suicide of Cato Uticensis, who preferred to die rather than be subjected to Caesar's power and consequently became synonymous with Republican and Stoic *virtus* and *libertas*.[86] As Plutarch (*Cato Minor* 67.1–2) reports, prior to his death Cato dined and conversed with friends, during which he vehemently defended the Stoic paradox that only the wise man is free, which made clear his resolve to die. Though Horace by no means seems literally to threaten suicide himself in the epistle he certainly does anticipate what would be the aristocratic response to increasing imperial power as Rome transitioned from Republic to Empire. Roller has argued that in the principate Stoicism, particularly that of Seneca, offered aristocrats a way of dealing with their diminished *libertas* by refashioning it as a mental state impervious to political threats, and Horace's description of the *vir bonus* anticipates such reformulations of traditional liberty.[87] Furthermore, his celebration of the noble suicide of the *vir bonus et sapiens* is a bold illustration—or perhaps warning—that an emperor must respect the *libertas* of his subjects and that men of true freedom will not countenance its loss.

We do not, however, have to read the ending of *Epistles* 1.16 as unambiguously hostile to Augustus. Rather, a Stoic resolve to die, like all extremes, is best avoided as a last resort, provided that those with authority practice moderation in making demands on the freedom of their inferiors. Above all, lack of compromise is not practical. Fowler, for instance, speaks of the ending's "radical Stoicism" and calls into question the practicality of the poem's closing stance:

> There is nothing temperate about the Stoic paradox to which he devotes the epistle. To the orthodox Stoic all human goods are indifferent, and one must be prepared to resign them at any time without regret. Horace embraces this radicalism with enthusiasm—but can one *live* like that?[88]

Though Horace warns Quinctius not to think that anyone other than the *vir bonus et sapiens*, with his inner freedom and inflexibility, can be *beatus* (20), other epistles cast doubt on this assertion, especially 1.6, where Horace claims that *virtus* should not be sought to an extreme (15–16; 30–31) and that *nil admirari*, which promotes adaptability and moderation, is the only thing that can render one *beatus* (1–2). There must be a practical way to maintain inner freedom without reaching the extremes of Stoic inflexibility, particularly if the exterior political environment is not as repressive as that of Pentheus's Thebes. Furthermore, this independence cannot be as tied to place as the one Horace claims to enjoy on his farm in the epistle's opening lines, for such conditional freedom is not the true *libertas* of the *vir bonus et sapiens*. In order for Horace to maintain his freedom regardless of place he will have to internalize his rural independence in order to make it available at all times.

I propose that the Sabine farm in 1.16 is best read not as a literal space but as a symbolic one that reflects Horace's (desired) inner landscape.[89] Read symbolically, the farm is an internal rather than external possession and an expression of ideal inner *libertas*. The farm, like the soul, is shut off from the outside world and intensely private, and it offers one a figurative hiding place, *latebrae*, that is impervious to the capriciousness of fortune or rulers and that renders one spiritually and morally sound. This possession can neither be taken away nor compromised, and in being carried within him it makes spiritual health and equanimity available to him in any situation. As an inner condition Horace's independence can be maintained even amid the complex ties of society and friendship, and he does not have to be present on the farm to enjoy this autonomy. The possession of this symbolic *fundus* enables Horace to return to society in the subsequent poems (1.17–1.20), in which Horace opens up a middle path between the extremes of servility and absolute autonomy. In these poems adaptability and compromise will take center stage, particularly in one's dealings with more powerful *amici*. *Epistles* 1.16 in fact plays a crucial role in Horace's formulation of adaptability and moderated freedom, despite its intense recommendation of unyielding *libertas*. In compromising and adapting it is important that we not yield entirely, that we have an inner core of freedom not subject to negotiation, without which we would indeed be enslaved. Stoic inflexibility is not practical in the new political reality, but complete compromise is much worse. It is this solid and uncompromising core that *Epistles* 1.16 describes, and Horace's *fundus* (1), which he unambiguously claims as his very own (*meus*), becomes not so much the physical space of his farm as the internal "foundation" or "basis" of freedom he possesses which allows him to adapt and bend without compromising himself.[90] The inflexible freedom of 1.16, when read in this way, becomes complementary rather than antithetical to the more qualified independence we will encounter in the poems that follow.

Horace's attitude and solution in many ways look ahead to Tacitus's response to defiant *libertas* and suicide in the face of imperial power. Though Tacitus admiringly describes the Stoic suicides of men such as Seneca, whose final act was to pour a libation to Jupiter the *liberator* (*Annals* 15.64), he nevertheless finds it preferable and more productive for a man to attempt to navigate imperial power by walking a line between excessive displays of *libertas* and servility.[91] In evaluating Marcus Lepidus in *Annals* 4.20, for example, Tacitus clearly promotes such a middle path as a way of dealing productively with a capricious emperor:

> hunc ego Lepidum temporibus illis gravem et sapientem virum fuisse comperior: nam pleraque ab saevis adulationibus aliorum in melius flexit. neque tamen temperamenti egebat, cum aequabili auctoritate et gratia apud Tiberium viguerit. unde dubitare cogor fato et sorte nascendi, ut cetera, ita principum inclinatio in hos, offensio in illos, an sit aliquid in nostris consiliis liceatque inter abruptam contumaciam et deforme obsequium pergere iter ambitione ac periculis vacuum.

> I am discovering that this Lepidus in those days was a dignified and wise man: for he turned very many matters away from the harsh flatteries of others towards a better outcome. Nor, however, was he lacking moderation, since he thrived with consistent authority and favor with Tiberius. From this I am compelled to wonder whether it is because of fate or our lot in being born, as in other matters, that some meet the favor of emperors and others disfavor, or whether there is something in our own judgments that allows us to travel a path free from ambition and danger between uncompromising stubbornness and shameful obsequiousness.

The virtuous behavior described here represents a change from the ideals of the Republic. As Classen states, "The freedom of the Republic is gone, and Tacitus knows that nothing is to be gained by *inanis iactatio libertatis* (*Agric.* XLII 3), as it will neither bring back what is lost nor help the individual under the principate. . . . A new virtue is called for which he designates as *moderatio*."[92] The exemplar *par excellence* of such *moderatio* in Tacitus is Agricola, who was able to achieve success and fame even under the bad emperor Domitian:

> Domitiani vero natura praeceps in iram, et quo obscurior, eo inrevocabilior, moderatione tamen prudentiaque Agricolae leniebatur, quia non contumacia neque inani iactatione libertatis famam fatumque provocabat. Sciant, quibus moris est inlicita mirari, posse etiam sub malis principibus magnos viros esse, obsequiumque ac modestiam, si industria ac vigor adsint, eo laudis excedere, quo plerique per abrupta sed in nullum rei publicae usum ambitiosa morte inclaruerunt. (*Agricola* 42.3–4)

> In truth Domitian's nature was quick to anger, and he was as unrelenting as he was secretive. Nevertheless he was mollified by the moderation and prudence of Agricola, because he was not calling forth fame and death either through obstinacy or through a useless display of liberty. Let those whose custom it is to admire illicit

things learn that it is possible for great men to exist even under bad emperors and that compliance and moderation, if industry and energy are present, result in the same degree of praise as the many who by courses that were dangerous but of no use to the Republic became famous through an ostentatious death.

While such an *ambitiosa mors* is acceptable and even praiseworthy as a last resort, the changed political reality of Rome makes such displays of *libertas* unproductive to the state, and other means of achieving success and renown are preferable and attainable through compromise.[93] In this passage obstinacy in fact has a negative consequence in that it pushes emperors to an extreme, while moderation and compliance mollify and calm their natural tendency toward repressive anger.[94] Central to Agricola's ability to walk this middle path of *moderatio* is his adaptability, which allows him to play varying roles according to the situation: *iam vero tempora curarum remissionumque divisa: ubi conventus ac iudicia poscerent, gravis intentus severus, et saepius misericors: ubi officio satis factum, nulla ultra potestatis persona* ("Truly the times for business and relaxation were distinct: when the assemblies and the courts were demanding, he was serious, stern, and more often merciful. When his duty was sufficiently complete he no longer wore the official mask," *Agricola* 9.3). As Classen maintains, "While Tacitus is anxious to emphasize that Agricola avoided all forms of excess, he stresses that he assumed whatever attitude seemed appropriate according to time, circumstances, and people concerned; in other words, that the avoidance of extremes, the *moderatio*, allowed for a certain range of different attitudes and actions."[95] Moderation and adaptability are therefore closely tied to one another in the *Agricola*, and in the *Epistles* as well they have a synergetic relationship. For Tacitus this adaptable middle ground allows one to achieve prominence and glory under an emperor, while for Horace it allows him to enjoy friendship with the great (1.17 and 1.18) and poetic renown (1.19 and 1.20).

Adaptability and compromise constitute a careful dance between friends of uneven social positions and, by extension, between rulers and subjects. The ideal is one in which the party with more authority takes care not to impinge too forcefully into the *libertas* of inferiors and subjects, while the latter bend and yield without utterly giving up their independence. These are the terms of the contract between Horace and Maecenas that is renegotiated in the seventh epistle, where the Sabine farm symbolizes the middle ground between absolute autonomy and total dependence. *Epistles* 1.16 is, however, a bold warning and illustration for anyone in power that his dominion has limits and that it cannot reach into the hiding places of the human soul, where the truest and most important freedom and rule reside. By internalizing the *regnum* and *libertas* bestowed upon him by the Sabine farm and making them inner possessions, Horace can attain the most lasting kind of freedom that cannot be taken away.

Such an inflexible insistence on freedom seems at first to be incompatible with the more moderate *libertas* Horace promotes elsewhere in the collection since it does not easily lend itself to compromise, adaptability, or moderation. The possession of an inner core of freedom, however, is a necessary prerequisite for anyone who aims to maintain his integrity while bending to the will of another. As such, the freedom that Horace describes in 1.16 makes up an essential component of the redefinition of *libertas* that takes place over the epistolary book.

∞ 6

The Limits of Rural *Libertas*

Epistles 1.10, 1.11, and 1.14

I N THE LAST CHAPTER I EXAMINED the Sabine farm as a symbol of
Horace's independence. In 1.7 the *libertas* of the farm is bought at the price
of some level of dependence on Maecenas, while in 1.16 the farm stands
figuratively for inner liberty that can never be compromised. In this chapter I
turn to *Epistles* 1.10 and 1.14, the poems in which Horace casts himself as an
unambiguous *ruris amator*, "a lover of the countryside," and argue that in these
poems Horace actually reveals the problems involved in rejecting the city, since
this results in an inability to satisfy all the desires of his complex and ambivalent persona. In these poems Horace attempts to resolve the inconsistency
between city and country clearly expressed in the eighth poem (*Romae Tibur
amem, ventosus Tibure Romam*, "At Rome I love Tibur, while at Tibur, fickle as
the wind, I love Rome," 12) by choosing once and for all the countryside. In 1.10
and 1.14 the country is superior because of the freedom it bestows, while the
city threatens to enslave Horace with its duties and obligations, especially in
the realm of friendship. The equations city = slavery and country = freedom
are found as early as the opening lines of the collection, where, as we saw in the
first chapter, Horace figures Maecenas as a would-be slave master and himself
as a manumitted gladiator.[1] *Epistles* 1.10 and 1.14 take up and develop in full
Horace's desire for the liberty found in withdrawal. In both 1.10 and 1.14, however, friendship—as we saw in 1.16 as well—is incompatible with the rural independence of the farm, and this is why this uncompromising rural freedom
must ultimately be rejected. While the farm can make him free, it cannot make
him entirely happy or bring equanimity. In 1.11, written as a corrective to 1.10,
Horace offers a better—though no doubt more arduous—solution for overcoming the vacillations and indecisiveness he attributes to himself in 1.8. Instead of
seeking equanimity in an external place that is not always available, it must be

sought instead within oneself, and only then will it be accessible anywhere. It is our inner state, as in 1.16, that brings true independence and can enable Horace to bridge the gap between his conflicting desires so that he can move freely between the city and country and all that each represents. In 1.11 Horace effectively applies the philosophical adaptability that he outlines in 1.1 to one's physical surroundings and suggests that we—and he—must have the same flexible attitude to place that he claims to enjoy in philosophy. The equanimity of 1.11 is, however, as difficult to sustain as it is to achieve, and we find Horace slip again into the role of *ruris amator* in 1.14, where it is the similarities rather than the alleged differences between Horace and his slave that call into question his claim to find freedom in the countryside.

Horace's strong preference for the countryside in both 1.10 and 1.14 is precipitated in each case by an uncomfortable shift toward the city and especially the imperial family in the poems that precede them. In 1.9 Horace writes Tiberius with a letter of recommendation for a friend named Septimius. As Horace describes it, writing the letter compels him to doff modesty (*pudor*, 12) and adopt "town-bred confidence" (*frontis urbanae*, 11). Horace's discomfort with such a task is apparent throughout the poem, and he is at pains to find the right balance between apologizing for his presumption in writing to the prince and asserting what genuine influence he does have. In 1.13, discussed more fully in the conclusion, Horace gives instructions to a courier named Vinnius, whom he has charged with taking and presenting some of his poetry to Augustus, and his focus on even the most minute details of Asina's delivery betray his anxiety when presenting his work to the emperor. Vinnius's bumbling servility can be read as a projection of Horace's own feelings of inferiority when faced with the approval or disapproval of the *princeps*. In poems 1.10 and 1.14 he appears to fling himself back with full force into rural life, as if in response to his heightened proximity to Rome's epicenter. In the movements from 1.9 to 1.10 and 1.13 to 1.14 we see enacted Horace's vacillations between the extremes of city and country.

THE FUGITIVE SLAVE KING OF 1.10

The tenth epistle is addressed to Aristius Fuscus, a close friend of Horace already familiar from *Satires* 1.9, in which he famously refuses to rescue Horace from an annoying pest, and the *integer vitae* poem, *Odes* 1.22, of which he is the dedicatee. At *Satires* 1.10.83 Horace includes him among his ideal readership, and the scholiasts suggest that he was a schoolteacher, *grammaticus*.[2] Throughout the poem Horace sets up a series of oppositions that at first seem unflattering to Fuscus, who, unlike Horace, is an *urbis amator*, "a lover of the city." While the countryside is associated with *paupertas*, freedom, and leisure, the city is a place of greed, slavery, and business. How, one thinks, can Fuscus bear to live there? By the end of the poem, however, Horace suggests that Fuscus is just as able to live a morally sound life in the city as Horace is in the country, and the oppositions that Horace has been at pains to set up are called into question. The source of Horace's anxiety is not, in the end, the city itself, which corrupts only those who allow it. The antidote to avarice and dependence is not to run away to the countryside but to become satisfied with whatever lot is currently ours by adapting to it. Such satisfaction is presumably available anywhere, even to Fuscus in the city. In fact, Fuscus emerges as an alter ego for Horace on whom Horace can project his own *amor urbis* while exploring the benefits and limitations of rustic life.

The opening lines of the poem set up the antithesis between the city-loving Fuscus and his rustic counterpart, Horace, while emphasizing their similarities rather than their differences:

> urbis amatorem Fuscum salvere iubemus
> ruris amatores, hac in re scilicet una
> multum dissimiles, at cetera paene gemelli
> fraternis animis, quidquid negat alter, et alter,
> adnuimus partier. vetuli notique columbi
> tu nidum servas, ego laudo ruris amoeni
> rivos et musco circumlita saxa nemusque. (1–7)

> I, lover of the country, bid hello to Fuscus, lover of the city. Of course in this matter alone we disagree a great deal, but in everything else we are almost twins with brotherly minds; whatever one refuses, the other does too, and we nod "yes" in unison. A pair of old and friendly doves, you keep the nest, while I praise the streams, moss-covered rocks, and grove of the pleasant countryside.

At first glance their differing preferences seem to be of little consequence to their friendship. The warmth and closeness between the two is given charming expression in Horace's comparison of them to two devoted doves nodding in unison. However, it quickly becomes obvious that the relationship is in fact greatly affected by their different inclinations because it separates these seemingly inseparable "birds of a feather." While Fuscus "keeps the nest" at Rome, Horace runs off to the countryside at the first opportunity, providing a hint that while Fuscus is satisfied with his lot Horace himself discontentedly tends to look for happiness elsewhere. Their separation is enacted in the poem itself in the switch from nominative plurals (*gemelli, columbi*) and the first person plural (*adnuimus*) to the antithetical pairing of *tu . . . ego* in line 6. The unified "we" is separated into "you" and "I," and Horace thereupon sets up a series of oppositions that both call into question his and Fuscus's alleged similarities and cast the *urbis amator* in an unflattering light.

The first and most important of these oppositions is between the freedom of the countryside and the slavishness of urban life. Horace compares himself to a runaway slave who finds not just freedom but—as in 1.16—power and sovereignty in rustic simplicity:

> quid quaeris? vivo et regno, simul ista reliqui
> quae vos ad caelum effertis rumore secundo,
> utque sacerdotis fugitivus liba recuso;
> pane egeo iam mellitis potiore placentis. (8–11)

> In short, I live and reign, as soon as I have left behind those things which you folks raise up to the sky with cries of approval, and just like a priest's runaway slave I refuse cakes; now I want bread more than honeyed cakes.

Horace's preference for the country sets him apart from the majority, a group into which he lumps Fuscus with the second person plural forms *vos* and *fertis*. In the countryside Horace is a king (*regno*), while city-dwellers, according to the implicit contrast, lack independence. Horace figures his move from city to country as an escape from servitude by likening himself to a runaway slave, *fugitivus*. This comparison recalls the gladiatorial metaphor of the opening epistle (1.1.1–15), but whereas Horace the "gladiator" had received officially recognized freedom in the form of the wooden sword (*rude*, 2) bestowed on gladiators upon manumission, the Horace of 1.10 is a runaway whose freedom is stolen and illicit. This switch from freedman to runaway casts doubt on Horace's rural independence, for it is that of a fugitive and therefore under constant threat.[3] His runaway's freedom compels Horace to make an either/or choice: either the city or the country, either honeyed cakes or simple bread. One might wonder, as Johnson imagines Fuscus doing, "Why not . . . eat both?"[4] By setting up such stark antitheses between urban enslavement and rural independence Horace makes compromise and a middle path seem impossible.

Horace next undertakes to persuade Fuscus that it is unnatural to live in the city. As Harrison has shown, this act by Horace plays upon what appears to be Fuscus's allegiance to Stoicism, a primary tenet of which was to live in accordance with nature:[5]

> vivere naturae si convenienter oportet,
> ponendaeque domo quaerenda est area primum:
> novistine locum potiorem rure beato? (12–14)

> If one ought to live in agreement with nature, and firstly a site must be sought for building a house, do you know of a better placed than the happy country?

Horace here transforms the definition of *natura* from "the Stoic principle that a man, as a rational being, should be governed by his reason and accept his place in the universe"[6] into one that denotes the natural beauty of the rustic landscape.

Kilpatrick suggests that we should imagine that Fuscus has proposed to build a house in the city and that Horace here is seeking to persuade him to build in the country instead.[7] Horace's goal, however, is not merely to entice his friend away from the city but to cast doubt on his whole way of life.[8] Horace's use of technical philosophical language and an allusion to Hesiod's *Works and Days* lends this passage a highly didactic tone,[9] and the lesson Horace imparts is that the countryside (rather than the city) truly fulfills the Stoic ideals not only of living in harmony with nature but also of achieving *libertas*.[10] Fuscus could object to Horace's arguments by claiming that true *libertas* is not bestowed by location but found within and that he enjoys independence even while living in the city, which is not in keeping with Horace's definition of nature but nevertheless conforms to his own individual nature.[11] After all, at the end of *Epistles* 1.7 Horace claims that our individual natures should guide our decisions and behavior: *metiri se quemque suo modulo ac pede verum est* ("it is right that each person measure himself by his own scale and foot-rule," 98).

In order to entice Fuscus further Horace proceeds to produce a catalogue of pleasures that are to be found in the countryside, attributing to it the classic features of a *locus amoenus*. It is mild in winter (15) and cool in summer (15–17); it furnishes untroubled sleep (18) and provides purer water than that piped into the city (20–21). The country's fragrant grass, furthermore, is in no way inferior to the expensive mosaics found in the houses of the wealthy (19). This mention of mosaics leads into another antithesis in the city/country divide: riches and greed on the one hand (*urbs*) and contentment and *paupertas* on the other (*rus*). Horace puts forth as proof of the country's superiority the fact that the wealthy try to recreate natural landscapes in their luxurious urban homes: *inter varias nutritur silva columnas / laudaturque domus longos quae prospicit agros* ("Amid the mottled columns a forest is being grown, and the house that looks out on fields far and wide is praised," 22–23). In their attempt to control nature these artificial landscapes are morally dubious, and nature, which is ultimately untamable, will always gain the upper hand: *naturam expelles furca, tamen usque recurret / et mala perrumpet furtim fastidia victrix* ("You can drive out nature with a pitch fork, yet always she will run back and stealthily burst victorious through your wicked scorn," 24–25). Men who try to replicate nature display an inability to distinguish what is real and genuine from what is fake (*vero distinguere falsum*, 29).[12] At this point we must again wonder how Fuscus would respond to such arguments. As Williams puts it, "poor Aristius Fuscus, schoolmaster, now finds himself not only classified with the rich but also with those who cannot distinguish truth from falsehood."[13] Certainly Horace's contention that the city is full of wealthy men and the country full of modest men who enjoy plain fare is rather disingenuous. As Horace himself states in the final line of *Epistles* 1.15, it was in their country villas that the rich often exhibited their wealth (*quorum/conspicitur nitidis fundata pecunia villis*, "whose well-established money is put on display in gleaming villas," 45–46). Volteius Mena, on the other hand, according to the *fabula* recounted in *Epistles* 1.7, is able to live a modest life in the city, whereas in the countryside he experiences ruin and a loss of independence (46–95). Furthermore, by drawing such stark antitheses between city- and country-dwellers Horace risks undercutting his earlier assertion that he and Fuscus are so much alike that they are twins (*gemelli*) or birds of a feather (*columbi*). If what Horace has said is true, and the city is full of wealthy but slavish men and the country full of autonomous men of modest means, there is no way he and Fuscus could in fact possess *fraterni animi*.

Horace carries this contrast between rich and poor through the rest of the poem. A problem that plagues the wealthy, Horace continues, is that they are unable to deal with any change for the worse in their fortunes, and Horace's language especially recalls the *nil admirari* poem (1.6):

> quem res plus nimio delectavere secundae,
> mutatae quatient. siquid *mirabere*, pones
> invitus. fuge magna: licet sub paupere tecto
> reges et regum vita praecurrere amicos. (1.10.30–33)

> The one whom favorable circumstances have delighted too much will be shaken when they change. If you marvel at anything, you will put it aside unwillingly. Flee great things. Although living under a poor man's roof you can outstrip kings and the friends of kings in your way of life.

The *nil admirari* of 1.6 promotes a powerful indifference to circumstances, and the marveling man Horace imagines in these lines is taken aback and upset by changes in his fortunes, *res*. Such a man in no way possesses the adaptability required to master a wide range of situations, like the Aristippean Horace of 1.1.19 (*et mihi res, non me rebus, subiungere conor*, "I try to make things subject to myself, not myself to things"). The solution that Horace gives to such *admiratio* in 1.10, however, falls short because it does not fully enable one to adapt to all circumstances as it compels one to be content only with one: rustic *paupertas*. *Fuge magna*, "flee great things," he tells Fuscus, and instead find a life that equals that of kings—and the friends of kings—through living humbly. *Fuge* especially recalls the *fugitivus* to whom Horace had compared himself in line 10, thus revealing that his preference for the country is motivated by a desire to avoid the excesses of the wealthy, who are enslaved by their own greed. He wants to be neither one of these *reges* nor their *amicus*: friendships with the powerful belong to the *magna* that must be avoided. Fuscus could, however, ask Horace whether in fleeing from one extreme he runs to another,[14] since surely there is a middle ground where one can enjoy success, friendship, and the city without being reduced to *admiratio* and enslavement. The man who truly exemplifies *nil admirari* is adaptable and maintains his imperturbability even in the city amid *magna* and *reges*, and he can enjoy wealth and *amicitia* when it suits him and easily embrace *paupertas* when it does not.[15]

Though Williams denies that *reges* in line 30 is meant to evoke Roman patrons, such an association is unavoidable when the most recent *rex* mentioned in the collection is Maecenas (1.7.37).[16] Williams himself does admit, however, that "the mere mention of *regum amicos* is enough to turn thoughts in the direction of patronage and its servitudes." What causes Horace anxiety and what he flees is the loss of independence that comes when negotiating the complicated world of Roman patronage, from which he has already extricated himself in the opening epistle. In 1.10 Horace places two kinds of kingship in opposition with one another: the superior kingship he experiences while (alone) on his farm (*vivo et regno*, 8) and the inferior one enjoyed by the great men of the city, which they exercise over their lesser *amici*. These *amici*, though their proximity to powerful men increases their social standing, nevertheless are denied sovereignty and thus independence. To the uncompromising Horace, to be free means to have no master other than oneself, and thus *libertas* cannot remain intact for anyone who has cultivated *reges*. These *regum amici* have bought friendship at the price of freedom, and the fable of the stag and horse that immediately follows—although ostensibly about the pursuit of wealth—applies equally to the relationship they have negotiated with their *reges*.

Once upon a time, Horace tells us, a stag and a horse came into conflict over a shared pasture. The horse got the better of the stag by enlisting the help of man, but unfortunately the cost for this help was his freedom:[17]

> cervus equum pugna melior communibus herbis
> pellebat, donec minor in certamine longo
> imploravit opes hominis frenumque receipt.
> sed postquam victor violens discessit ab hoste,
> non equitem dorso, non frenum depulit ore. (34–38)

The stag, which was better in battle, used to drive the horse from their shared grasses, until the lesser in the long contest begged for the help of man and took the bit. But after the violent victor withdrew from his enemy, he could remove neither the horseman from his back nor the rein from his mouth.

Horace thereupon adds the moral:

> sic, qui pauperiem veritus potiore metallis
> libertate caret, dominum vehet improbus atque
> serviet aeternum, quia parvo nesciet uti. (39–41)

> Thus, whoever out of fear of poverty lacks freedom, which is better than mines of gold, will disgracefully convey a master and will be a slave forever because he does not know how to enjoy a little.

Though ostensibly this fable is directed generally against the desire for wealth, it applies nicely to the *reges et regum amici* just mentioned, who correspond to the man and horse respectively.[18] In seeking to get ahead by enlisting the support of powerful friends these *amici* forfeit their *libertas*, which they can retain only through *pauperies* and contentment with a little (*parvo uti*). In 1.10 Horace presents himself as having avoided this particular trap by embracing instead a humble rustic way of life, but Fuscus, his good friend, would have good reason to object to Horace's self-presentation. It was Horace, after all, whom *pauperies* compelled to seek financial security by composing poetry, as he tells us in the roughly contemporaneous *Epistles* 2.2:

> unde simul primum me dimisere Philippi,
> decisis humilem pennis inopemque paterni
> et laris et fundi, paupertas impulit audax
> ut verus facerem: sed quod non desit habentem
> quae poterunt umquam satis expurgare cicutae,
> ni melius dormire putem quam scribere versus? (49–54)

> As soon as Philippi dismissed me from there, bold poverty compelled me, humbled with my wings clipped and lacking paternal house and farm, to make verses. But what hemlock will ever be able sufficiently to cure me, who has enough to be sufficient, if I should ever fail to think that it is better to sleep than to write verses?

In these lines *paupertas* is not something that Horace readily embraced; on the contrary, it compelled him to come up with bold ways of restoring his wealth through writing poetry. It is due to his poetic success that he came into the circle of Maecenas, and this association makes him one of the *regum amici* who in *Epistles* 1.10 have given up their freedom.[19] The claim to embrace liberating poverty free from political and social ties is all well and good now that he has sufficient stores, but this was not always the case, and Horace, like the horse in the fable, had to enlist the help of Maecenas in order to reach this position of security and contentment. Horace's adherence to rural independence in the *Epistles* in many ways illustrates his attempt to shake this rider from his back—and we should bear in mind that in the opening poem, in which Horace refuses Maecenas's demands, he likens himself to an aging racehorse trying to break free of its reins (8–9). However, Horace's loss of *libertas* is irrevocable, and, like Volteius Mena in 1.7.95, he can no longer demand to have his former way of life restored (*vitae me redde priori*). Horace, like the horse, has paid for his success and security by a reduction in freedom, and the *Epistles* enact Horace's gradual coming to terms with this loss. Should we therefore imagine that, if he could do it over again, Horace would act differently and refuse to let the rider on his back? What did Horace gain by compromising his independence? Above all there is the farm, which has more value to him than the most exquisite riches (1.7.36; cf. *Odes* 3.1.47–48) and which enables him to carve out for himself a corner of the world where he does hold sway. And there is the friendship he enjoys with Maecenas, whom he addresses throughout his poetry with great affection. As he confesses in *Satires* 2.6, however many annoyances this relationship has brought to him, he nevertheless derives pleasure in being recognized as Maecenas's *amicus: hoc iuvat et melli est, non mentiar* ("This is pleasing and honey-sweet, I will not lie," 32). To choose uncompromised *libertas* entails undesirable losses. Rustic freedom comes at the price of losing friendship and recognition for his poetic talent. But urban companionship and renown come at the price of dependence. Despite his unambiguous claim to prefer the country and its freedom, Horace nevertheless in 1.10 exposes an ambivalence within himself. To quote Johnson:

> His conflict with Fuscus, which is also, in a different and much more powerful manifestation, a conflict inside himself, is not something that he can argue away, can argue himself out of, or argue out of himself. His identity, particularly in this poem and in the book that is centered on it, is shaped by both the necessity and the impossibility of freedom (as well as by the necessity for—and maybe the impossibility of—the interdependence and fusion of the contrary virtues that city and country represent).[20]

The establishment of a complementary rather than antithetical relationship between these different spheres is ultimately the only solution to Horace's conflict and will be the means by which he can enjoy both the freedom he professes to have in the country *and* the friendship and renown that the city offers. This necessarily will require him both to accept a reduction in *libertas* and to acquiesce in some degree to his own *rex*. In acceding to a moderate degree of freedom rather than total freedom Horace will position himself somewhere between being his own king and being a slave, a compromise that is particularly Aristippean.[21]

Horace in fact already seems to be moving toward such compromise in the second half of the poem, since he now begins to advocate not rustic freedom but a general contentment with one's present lot and adaptability to circumstance, which differs considerably from what has preceded, where happiness is tied to a specific location. In lines 42–43 Horace compares wealth to a shoe and suggests that it is not the size of one's wealth that matters so much as one's attitude toward it:

cui non conveniet sua res, ut calceus olim
si pede maior erit, subvertet, si minor, uret.

If one's wealth is not agreeable, it is like a shoe: sometimes if it is too big for the
foot, it will trip, if it is too small, it will chafe.

Ideally wealth should not be like a poorly fitting shoe, and our peace of mind
should not be affected by the size of our estate, *res*. *Res* here indicates not only
wealth but a whole range of "circumstances" that can negatively affect us if they
do not suit us, and the large and small shoe in the context of the poem suggest
the city (associated with wealth) and the country (associated with *paupertas*).
The best way to make sure one's current lot is amenable is to adapt to it and
by adapting to master it, and *res* recalls again here *Epistles* 1.1.19: *et mihi res, non
me rebus, subiungere conor*. Only through adaptability can any *res*, big or small,
become agreeable (*conveniet*). Horace makes a similar analogy in *Epistles* 2.2
using boats, where he claims that the size of the boat in which he travels makes
little difference to him due to his inner integrity: *ego, utrum / nave ferar magna
an parva, ferar unus et idem* ("Whether I am carried on a large or small boat,
I will be carried as one and the same person," 200–1). This is not, however,
an ability that the Horace clinging to his rustic freedom in the opening of 1.10
seems to possess, since if he were suddenly to find himself in the city his inner
happiness would collapse.

The poorly fitting shoes in lines 42–43 recall a surviving fragment of Aristippus recorded by Stobaeus.[22] Like Horace, he compares wealth to an overly
large shoe but states, as Horace implies, that this is ideally *not* how wealth
should function. Unlike the excess of a shoe, wealth does not have to "trip us
up" if we are adaptable:

οὐκ ὥσπερ ὑπόδημα τὸ μεῖζον δύσχρηστον, οὕτω καὶ ἡ πλείων κτῆσις· τοῦ μὲν
γὰρ ἐν τῇ χρήσει τὸ περιττὸν ἐμποδίζει, τῇ δὲ καὶ ὅλῃ χρῆσθαι κατὰ καιρὸν ἔξεστι
καὶ μέρει.

Wealth that is too great is not like a shoe that is useless when it is too big. For on
the one hand in the use of a shoe a surplus trips the foot, but on the other hand it
is possible to use wealth both in its entirety and in part in accordance with *kairos*.

Aristippus is not so much advocating the unrestricted acquisition of wealth in
this fragment as he is promoting its wise use.[23] The phrase κατὰ καιρόν is especially important in this passage, but a precise translation is difficult to produce.
The word *kairos* suggests ideas of both the "right time" and the "right degree."[24]
Aristotle includes it as an important consideration for those who would observe
the mean, since what is appropriate depends on the particular circumstances in
which we find ourselves: δεῖ δ᾽ αὐτοὺς ἀεὶ τοὺς πράττοντας τὰ πρὸς τὸν καιρὸν

σκοπεῖν, ὥσπερ καὶ ἐπὶ τῆς ἰατρικῆς ἔχει καὶ τῆς κυβερνητικῆς ("It is necessary that those who act always observe what accords with the *kairos*, just as is the case too in the medical and navigational [art]," *EN* 1104a8–10). In the art of sailing, appropriate action must take into account the particular situation (i.e., whether the ship is in harbor or at sea, in calm weather or a storm), and Horace uses similar nautical imagery in his "golden mean" ode, 2.10.[25] Furthermore, *kairos* had associations with moderation going back to Hesiod.[26] Wilson defines the term as "the area between too much and too little" and as "the opposite of excess."[27] In one word, therefore, Aristippus has captured both the adaptability and the moderation that ought to be exercised in every situation. When faced with a surplus or excess of wealth, the only way we can avoid being tripped up is to adapt to that particular circumstance and try to observe due measure in its use.

In the epistle Horace forefronts the idea of moderation that is implicit in the Aristippean fragment.[28] It is only when wealth is too big or too small that it holds the potential to endanger us, so a modest amount of wealth is best. If a person does not adhere too zealously to one extreme (large/small shoe; large/small wealth; city/country), then it is unlikely that he will be daunted when the opposite is unavoidable. Similarly, in the passage of *Epistles* 2.2 involving the small and large ships, cited above, Horace continues by evoking the mean:

> non agimur tumidis velis Aquilone secundo,
> non tamen adversis aetatem ducimus austris,
> viribus, ingenio, specie, virtute, loco, *re*
> extremi primorum, extremis usque priores. (201–4)

> I am not conveyed by swollen sails when the north wind is favorable, nor yet do I pass my life among the hostile south winds. In strength, talent, appearance, virtue, position, and wealth I am behind the ones in front, but always ahead of the ones in back.

Through observing this middle path Horace can adapt to a whole range of situations by observing what is *kairos* in each. In the terms of *Epistles* 1.10, Horace does not have to choose just the country (and all that it entails) over the city (and all that it entails). Adaptability and moderation complement one another and enable even opposites to suit the same individual.

Horace concludes the epistle with the thought that we must master our circumstances rather than let them master us. Both Horace and Fuscus are able to live wisely provided that they are content with their current situation:

> laetus sorte tua vives sapienter, Aristi,
> nec me dimittes incastigatum, ubi plura
> cogere quam satis est ac non cessare videbor.

imperat aut servit collecta pecunia cuique,
tortum digna sequi potius quam ducere funem. (1.10.44–48)

If you are happy in your lot, Aristius, you will live wisely, nor will you send me
away unrebuked, when I seem to collect more than is sufficient and not to cease.
For everyone collected wealth is either a master or a slave, but it ought to follow
rather than to lead the twisted rope.

Here Gigante compares Horace's attitude to wealth with Aristippus's famous
remark about the courtesan Lais: ἔχω Λαΐδα, ἀλλ᾽ οὐκ ἔχομαι ("I possess Lais
but am not possessed by her," Diogenes Laertius 2.75).[29] One can possess wealth
without being possessed by it, but ideally, Horace states, wealth should be kept
within the bounds of satiety (*satis*). A person's relationship not only to wealth
but also to chance (*sorte*) should be like a master over his slave. Horace here
clearly distances himself from the earlier idea that freedom is determined by
place. It is instead one's mentality that determines our degree of independence,
and if we are appropriately content with our current situation, whatever it may
be, we will have not just freedom, but mastery. Fuscus then can be every bit
as much a *rex* in the city as Horace claims to be in the country. One does not
have to flee great things (*fuge magna*)—like a runaway slave—but can instead
adapt and thereby master them.[30] Horace in fact subtly hints that Fuscus may
have the ethical upper hand. Nisbet has suggested that *incastigatum* (45) alludes
to Fuscus's supposed profession as a *grammaticus*, in which capacity he would
have been expected to exercise corporal punishment of poor students.[31] Whereas
Horace begins the poem by making himself Fuscus's moral adviser, by the end
the roles of teacher and pupil have been reversed.

The final lines of the poem leave us with a portrait of Horace that casts into
serious doubt the rustic happiness he claimed to enjoy in the poem's beginning:

haec tibi dictabam post fanum putre Vacunae,
excepto quod non simul esses, cetera laetus. (49–50)

I was dictating these words to you behind the crumbling shrine of Vacuna, happy
in all things except that you are not with me.

As explained in Pseudo-Acro, Varro identified Vacuna with the goddess Victory and etymologized her name as deriving from *vacare* ("to be at leisure"):
*Varro primo rerum divinarum Victoriam ait, quod ea maxime hii gaudent, qui
sapientiae vacant* ("Varro in the first book of *Res Divinae* says that she is Victory,
because those men rejoice in her most especially who have leisure for philosophy"). Picking up on Varro's explanation, Macleod argues that the closing lines
of the poem illustrate the philosophical victory that Horace is enjoying in the
country:

So these words are a . . . rejection of success as commonly conceived, in that the shrine of Victory is "crumbling." At the same time, they suggest that there is a better kind of success, which is indicated by Varro's etymology for the name Vacuna . . .; the leisure and study implicit in the word *vacare*, or the philosophic "victory," is precisely what Horace enjoys in the country, at the shrine of Vacuna.[32]

Macleod does not see Horace's qualification in the final line (*excepto quod non simul esses, cetera laetus*) as detracting from this philosophical victory and suggests instead that this focus on friendship complements the picture of Horace in retirement, as "friendship is a natural and necessary counterpart to freedom."[33] This is, however, a serious qualification that calls into question Horace's philosophical "victory" as he holds sway over his farm. In order to gain this victory, Horace must isolate himself, but this isolation detracts from his happiness and contentment. The repetition of *laetus* in lines 44 and 50 is highly significant. Horace is not completely *laetus sorte* because he cannot currently enjoy his friendship with Fuscus, divided as they are by their different preferences for city and country. True happiness and victory will come only when Horace bridges the gulf between them. The situation also calls his freedom into question. He may be free from Rome, but he is not free to see his friend. Not only is his fugitive freedom precarious, it is incomplete.

   Throughout the poem Horace uncovers the problems involved with being a *ruris amator* even as he purports to extol country life. The neat oppositions he sets up between city and country collapse as the poem unfolds, for the stated similarity between Horace and Fuscus makes such strict antitheses impossible to maintain. In the latter half of the poem a new way of achieving contentment is formulated instead, one that is available to *ruris amatores* and *urbis amatores* alike, provided that they are happy with their current circumstances. But Horace himself is not content, since he has tried to conform to a role that ultimately does not suit him and that does not allow him to enjoy both his sovereignty on the farm *and* his friendship with Fuscus. These two worlds, the *urbs* and the *rus*, must ultimately be brought together and the line between them blurred. Fuscus is in many ways the *urbis amator* within Horace, the part of him that cries out for the absent city (1.8.12), and, despite his best efforts, this part of him cannot be repressed. The *urbis amator* and the *ruris amator* make up two contrasting halves of Horace's psyche, and each needs satisfaction. Instead of suffering because he is torn between the *urbs* and *rus*, he can derive happiness in either as the circumstance demands, and a compromise will have to be struck between the freedom and mastery of rural life, on the one hand, and the ties of dependence that Rome brings, on the other.

EQUANIMITY AT ULUBRAE: *EPISTLES* 1.11

Epistles 1.11 carefully responds to 1.10. It corrects the idea that the countryside can provide us with freedom and happiness, and it expands the idea that these are possible in any situation provided that one is *laetus sorte*. In the eleventh epistle Horace promotes indifference to location and argues that only those with equanimity—a central tenet in the *Epistles* that is expressed clearly here (*animus aequus*, 30) for the first time[34]—can derive true enjoyment from any place in which they happen to be, whether home or abroad. Three major arguments are at the heart of the poem: 1) equanimity cannot be produced by location; 2) permanent withdrawal is undesirable, and when circumstances allow, home is best; and 3) equanimity enables a person to adapt himself to and find happiness in any place. Equanimity is the cure for the inconsistency of spirit that causes us to look for happiness in one place followed by another, such as that which causes Horace to vacillate between the countryside and Rome, now expecting one to make him happy and, on finding his dissatisfaction undiminished, now the other. An *aequus animus* enables a person not only to stay put in one place by removing his false belief that another location holds the cure for his inconsistency but also allows him, if the circumstance demands, to go from one place to another with no negative effect on his psyche. If Horace were to achieve such equanimity he could be happy whether he is in Rome or in the country and travel easily between them.

The addressee of the epistle is a Bullatius who is not otherwise known but appears to be journeying extensively throughout the Greek islands and Asia Minor. Horace asks him how such faraway places compare to the familiar sites of Rome:

> quid tibi visa Chios, Bullati, notaque Lesbos,
> quid concinna Samos, quid Croesi regia Sardes,
> Zmyrna quid et Colophon, maiora minoraue fama?
> cunctane prae Campo et Tiberino flumine sordent? (1–4)

> What sort of place did Chios seem to you, Bullatius, and famous Lesbos? What of elegant Samos, and Sardis, the royal seat of Croesus? What of Zmyrna and Colophon? Are they better or worse than their reputation? Or do they all appear dingy compared to the Campus Martius and the Tiber River?

In these lines Horace reformulates and takes in a new direction the *urbs/rus* antithesis of the preceding poem. Rome is now weighed not against the country but against distant islands and cities, and the contrasts now are between west and east, home and abroad. It is not clearly stated why Bullatius is traveling so extensively but, given Horace's focus on equanimity in the poem, he seems to be suffering from the sort of inconsistency that afflicts the spiritually unwell, such as those described in 1.1.80–93, where the rich man travels now to Baiae, now Teanum, and the poor man likewise sets sail in a hired boat in imitation of the rich man and his private yacht. Horace wonders whether Bullatius feels the desire to continue his travels or if he is ready to settle down, even if in the small town of Lebedus: *an venit in votum Attalicis ex urbibus una? / an Lebedum laudas odio maris atque viarum?* ("Or does one of the cities of Attalus enter your prayer? Or do you exalt Lebedus due to your hatred of the sea and roads?" 5–6). If Bullatius is ready to settle, it is only because his dissatisfaction and constant changes of locale have simply worn him out.

Horace can correctly diagnose Bullatius's lack of equanimity because he has felt such a desire too, and he now confesses that he himself has fantasized about withdrawing to a small town like Lebedus:

> scis, Lebedus quid sit: Gabiis desertior atque
> Fidenis vicus; tamen illic vivere vellem,
> oblitusque meorum, obliviscendus et illis,
> Neptunum procul e terra spectare furentem.[35] (7–10)

> You know what Lebedus is: a village more deserted than Gabii and Fidenae: yet
> I should have liked to live there, forgetful of my friends and forgotten by them,
> and to gaze afar from the land at the raging sea.

We have already seen how in 1.1, 1.7, 1.10, and 1.16 Horace is prone to bouts of escapism in the countryside, but here he takes such a desire to an extreme.[36] In 1.7.11–13 he had proposed a similar, albeit temporary, withdrawal from friendship into the isolation of the seaside:

> ad mare descendet vates tuus et sibi parcet
> contractusque leget: te, dulcis amice, reuiset
> cum Zephyris, si concedes, et hirundine prima.

> Your bard will go down to the sea and be kind to himself and see to himself and,
> huddled up, will read. He will return to you, sweet friend, with the Zephyrs, if you
> allow, and with the first swallow.

Horace will again consider such a seaside retreat for himself in 1.15. In 1.11 it is not just the isolated *rus* of Italy (Gabii and Fidenae) but a place even more deserted and removed from the reach of Rome. To escape to Lebedus would be to fade into oblivion, "the world forgetting, by the world forgot."[37] Such an escape would remove Horace entirely from the realm of friendship, and there would be no more epistles to bridge the gap between him and the abandoned world. This is a radical form of *lathe biosas*, but whereas orthodox Epicureanism promotes friendship Horace's retreats into isolation come into conflict with it. Line 10 seems especially to recall the opening of the second book of the *De Rerum Natura*:[38]

> suave, mari magno turbantibus aequora ventis,
> *e terra* magnum alterius *spectare* laborem.

> It is sweet, when the winds are disturbing the surface of the great sea, to watch the great labor of another from the land.

Lucretius's lines illustrate the freedom from pain and anxiety, or the *ataraxia*, that is at the heart of Epicurean hedonism. Lucretius goes on to provide a vivid and beautiful portrait of groups of people at ease and content relaxing under a tall tree beside a stream (29–33). The delightful fellowship described in Lucretius's passage offers a sharp contrast with Horace's gloomy need to escape into isolation. The raging sea upon which he desires to fix his gaze does not so much contrast with his state of mind (as in the Lucretius passage) as it does reflect it.[39] He may hope to achieve *ataraxia* in such moods, but it would be a perverted type of *ataraxia*, one that is found in oblivion rather than friendship.

Just as Horace seems to become engrossed in this portrait of himself in seaside isolation, he quickly checks himself with an emphatic *sed*, "but." Such avoidance of the world may bring a temporary respite but not true tranquility, and home is not in the end permanently avoidable:

> sed neque qui Capua Romam petit, imbre lutoque
> aspersus volet in caupona vivere; nec qui
> frigus collegit, furnos et balnea laudat
> ut fortunatam plene praestantia vitam;
> nec si te validus iactaverit Auster in alto,
> idcirco navem trans Aegaeum mare vendas. (11–16)

> But whoever seeks Rome from Capua, sprinkled with rain and mud, will not want to live permanently in an inn; nor would one stiff with cold praise stoves and baths as fully offering a fortunate life. Nor, if a strong south wind should toss you on the deep, would you on that account sell your ship on the other side of the Aegean.

The inn in these lines is like Lebedus or any of the other towns visited by Bullatius. Though he might wish to stay there temporarily as a *hospes*, his visit should not be extended into permanent residence. One simply must return home. The sea imagery combined with the idea of *hospitium* in these lines recalls the opening epistle, in which Horace likens his free use of philosophy to the *hospitium* sought by a shipwrecked sailor:

> ac ne forte roges, quo me duce, quo Lare tuter;
> nullius addictus iurare in verba magistri,
> quo me cumque rapit tempestas, deferor hospes. (13–15)

> And so that you do not by chance ask with what leader or in what house I take
> shelter: I am bound to swear on the words of no master. I am carried as a guest
> wherever the storm takes me.

In these lines Horace claims that he will enjoy philosophical *hospitium* by staying as a guest in various houses but swearing allegiance to none. Horace's retreat
into philosophy, however, was simultaneously withdrawal into the countryside
and thus away from Rome. The Horace of 1.1 is in many ways similar to the Bullatius of 1.11, since he too is drawn to escapism. Now Horace argues that such
withdrawal should be temporary, both for Bullatius and, by extension, for himself. Two ideas are thus combined: on the one hand, retreats, like inns on a long
journey, can be pleasing and agreeable but they do not bring a *vita fortunata*; on
the other hand, home offers advantages that withdrawal does not and therefore
holds the potential for greater happiness. For Seneca one of the chief drawbacks
to foreign travel is that while it brings *hospitium* it does not lend itself to *amicitia*: *vitam in peregrinatione exigentibus hoc evenit, ut multa hospitia habeant,
nullas amicitias* ("For those who pass life in foreign travel it often is the case
that they have much hospitality but no friendships," *Epist.* 2.2). The *vita fortunata* is fully available only to those who are able to combine the private contemplation that temporary escape provides with the camaraderie and friendship
that can only be found at home.

If one is already in good spiritual health, moreover, it simply makes no sense
to seek benefits from travel. This would be as useful as wearing a heavy coat in
summer or a loincloth in winter:

> incolumi Rhodos et Mytilene pulchra facit quod
> paenula solstitio, campestre nivalibus auris,
> per brumam Tiberis, Sextili mense caminus.
> dum licet ac voltum servat Fortuna benignum,
> Romae laudetur Samos et Chios et Rhodos absens. (17–21)

> To one who is sound Rhodes and lovely Mytilene do just as much as a coat in sum-
> mer, a loincloth in snowy breezes, the Tiber in the winter, a stove in August. While
> it is allowed and Fortune preserves her kindly face, let Samos and Chios and far-
> away Rhodes be praised while in Rome.

As Mayer notes, *incolumis* has a double connotation. On the one hand it denotes
one who is morally sound, or in possession of the *aequus animus* of the poem's
closing line.[40] For such a person there is no need for escape. At the same time it
suggests a person "whose citizen status was fully operative," and so Horace "has
in mind the exile or voluntary retirement which prominent Romans might have
to endure, often on islands."[41] Horace thus implies that one motive for withdrawal could be political. Horace's use of *incolumnis* here has led some scholars

to conclude that Bullatius is abroad because he was part of the Republican opposition to Augustus and that Horace is encouraging him to take advantage of the amnesty put into effect by Augustus in 30 B.C. and return home.[42] Though the facts surrounding Bullatius's life are irrecoverable, the word does add an interesting political color to the poem, and withdrawal into private life was another of the potential responses to rising imperial power. Just as 1.16 illustrates extreme defiance and assertion of *libertas* in response to this power (for which see the preceding chapter), 1.11 presents us with another extreme: the lure of safety through disengagement.[43] Such retirement, however, is unnecessary if the current climate (*Fortuna*) is kindly (*benignum*) and no threat to one's citizen status is imminent.[44] Unyielding defiance (1.16) and withdrawal (1.11) are options only when the political landscape is equally extreme. Compromise on both sides, by both the rulers and the ruled, is preferable.

The poem ends with an exhortation to seek enjoyment from the present moment and by doing so to make any situation agreeable:

> tu quamcumque deus tibi fortunaverit horam
> grata sume manu neu dulcia differ in annum,
> ut, quocumque loco fueris, vixisse libenter
> te dicas; nam si ratio et prudentia curas,
> non locus effusi late maris arbiter aufert,
> caelum, non animum mutant, qui trans mare currunt.
> strenua non exercet inertia; navibus atque
> quadrigis petimus bene vivere. quod petis, hic est,
> est Ulubris, animus si te non deficit aequus. (21–30)

> You, take with a thankful hand whatever hour the god will have blessed you with, and do not defer pleasant things until next year, so that wherever you have been you may say that you lived gladly; for if it is reason and wisdom that remove cares, not a place that looks upon the widespread sea, they change their climate, not their mind, who rush across the sea. Busy inactivity troubles us; we seek the key to living well in ships and horse-drawn chariots. What you seek is here, it is at Ulubrae, if equanimity does not fail you.

If we can make the most of the present moment (i.e., *carpe diem*) then we can adapt any place or circumstances to suit ourselves and thus acquire equanimity. This is produced from within by reason and wisdom and not provided by a pleasant location, and the sea vista in line 25 is certainly meant to recall "raging Neptune" (*Neptunum furentem*) in line 10. Such equanimity is available in a backwater such as Lebedus or Ulubrae,[45] but it is also available in Rome in the company of friends, whom we should not forget and by whom we should not be forgotten. It is much easier to run away from problems and search for solutions elsewhere than it is to effect a change in our soul, but equanimity alone is the one true key to happiness.

I would like to conclude my discussion of *Epistles* 1.11 by looking briefly at a letter of Seneca (28) that Horace's poem seems to have inspired; in it Seneca warns against the same tendency to look for happiness in a change of location and connects several important ideas running through the *Epistles*.[46] Seneca signals his debt to Horace's epistle early in the letter when, having proclaimed that foreign travel (*peregrinatione*, 1) and changes in location (*locorum varietatibus*, 1) cannot alleviate mental sadness and depression (*tristitiam gravitatemque mentis*, 1), he states that "you ought to change your mind, not your climate" (*animum debes mutare, non caelum*, 1), a clear echo of Horace's *caelum, non animum mutant, qui trans mare currunt* ("they change their climate, not their mind, who rush across the sea," 27). Constant flight only further aggravates the mind of one who is spiritually sick and makes every new place just as disappointing as the last. Only when the mind is healed do all locations become pleasurable:

> at cum istuc exemeris malum, omnis mutatio loci iucunda fiet; in ultimas expellaris terras licebit, in quolibet barbariae *angulo* colloceris, hospitalis tibi illa qualiscumque sedes erit. magis quis veneris quam quo interest, et ideo *nulli* loco *addicere* debemus animum. cum hac persuasione vivendum est: 'non sum *uni angulo* natus, patria mea totus hic mundus est.' quod si liqueret tibi, *non admirareris* nil adiuvari te regionum varietatibus in quas subinde priorum taedio migras; prima enim quaeque placuisset si omnem tuam crederes. Nunc non peregrinaris sed erras et ageris ac locum ex loco mutas, cum illud *quod quaeris, bene vivere*, omni loco positum sit. (4–5)

> But when you remove the evil from there [i.e., the mind], every change of location will be pleasant. Even if you should be driven out into the farthest lands, in whatever corner of a barbarian country you might be placed, that abode, of whatever sort it is, will be hospitable to you. It matters *who* you go as more than *where* you go, and therefore we ought to enslave our mind to no location. One should live with this conviction: "I was not born for one corner of the world, but this whole world is my fatherland." If this were clear to you, you would not be surprised that it is of no benefit to travel into a variety of locales due to boredom with earlier places, since each "first place" would have pleased you if you had believed that it belonged to you entirely. As it is now, you are not traveling but wandering and exchanging one place after another, although what you are looking for, i.e. living well, can be found anywhere.

The final line quoted here strongly echoes in both language and idea the close of Horace's epistle: *navibus atque / quadrigis <u>petimus bene vivere</u>. <u>quod petis</u>, hic est, / est Ulubris, animus si te non deficit aequus*, 28–30. The Horatian echoes in this Senecan passage are not restricted to *Epistles* 1.11. *Non admirareris* strongly echoes the *nil admirari* of 1.6 and thereby connects the quality of soul he is promoting to the imperturbability outlined in that poem. Most interestingly, Seneca echoes Horace's first epistle in his statement that we should "enslave our mind to no location," *nulli loco addicere debemus animum*, where the combination of *nulli* and *addicere* strongly recalls Horace's claim to swear on no philosophical master: *nullius addictus iurare in verba magistri* (1.1.14). This implies that, according to Seneca, an inability to adapt to place renders one every bit the slave that swearing on a philosophical master does to Horace. For Seneca any *sedes* can be *hospitalis*, just as for Horace any philosophical house can be a temporary source of *hospitium* (*hospes*, 1.1.15). Seneca transforms Horace's philosophical cosmopolitanism into genuine cosmopolitanism. Seneca offers in this letter a nice interpretation of *Epistles* 1.11 by suggesting that Horace now applies to physical locations the same sort of adaptability that he exercises in the philosophical arena. To Seneca, and for Horace as well, true freedom cannot be found in devoting oneself exclusively to one place, and the word *angulus* that he uses suggests a place that is private and removed from public life. Seneca's choice of the word recalls *Epistles* 1.14.23, in which Horace puts the same word into the mouth of his *vilicus* to describe the farm, which the slave disdains (*iste angulus*, 23).[47] As we shall see, in that poem Horace is enslaved by his *admiratio* of his farm and in no way enjoys the equanimity he describes in 1.11. This sort of surrender to one isolated location does not to Seneca bring true freedom, and it is fitting that the letter climaxes with a vivid picture of a defiant Socrates enjoying freedom even amid the tyrants of Athens, whereupon Seneca concludes *quod interest quot domini sint? servitus una est; hanc qui contempsit in quanta libet turba dominantium liber est* ("What does it matter how many masters there are? There is only one slavery, and whoever despises it is free no matter how great a throng of masters surround him," 8). As in *Epistles* 1.16 the truest and most important freedom is found within, and the one who is content with where he is—wherever that happens to be—has genuine independence, even in the presence of those who would master him. Whereas Horace began in 1.1 by claiming that only unyielding withdrawal makes him free, he suggests in 1.11 that in fact the opposite is true. If we imagine that a place can make us free or happy or fix our inconsistencies, then we have in fact bound ourselves over to a master.

THE SLAVE MASTER OF 1.14

In 1.14 Horace continues to argue that one should be indifferent to place, but he himself hypocritically fails to practice this advice and instead succumbs to *admiratio* of the countryside. This epistle is addressed to his *vilicus*, the enslaved bailiff tasked with overseeing his farm, whom Horace rebukes both for his current desire for the city and for his inconsistency, since he previously had yearned for the country. Horace's claim in 1.10 to rule (*regno*, 8) while in the countryside is literalized in 1.14: he is now a slave-holding *dominus*. The freedom Horace finds for himself in the country is not universal, for this same farm brings slavery to another. Horace suggests that it is not the bailiff's literal enslavement that makes him a slave but his spiritual slavery to the city and his inconsistency, an argument that we might imagine the *vilicus* (who unlike Horace knows first-hand what *real* slavery is) will find less than convincing. The situation of the epistle reverses the one found in *Satires* 2.7, in which Horace's slave Davus lectures his master on inner freedom and claims that Horace, though free, is a slave to his conflicting desires. In 1.14 Horace argues that the bailiff's condition will improve if only he should become content with his current lot in the country. As in 1.11, location should not matter and one must adapt to the circumstance at hand. Horace, however, utterly fails to live up to his own advice, for he is as dissatisfied with his current location—the city—as the bailiff is with the country. In 1.14, as in 1.11, indifference to place is a quality sorely needed by Horace himself, and the *vilicus* again becomes a figure onto whom Horace can project the less than flattering aspects of his own personality. Horace and the *vilicus* form two halves of the same coin, and it is their similarities rather than their differences that the poem ultimately makes manifest. This poem more than any other begs the question, "Does Horace's attachment to the countryside *really* make him free?"

In the opening lines of the epistle Horace frames the contrasts he draws between himself and the bailiff as a contest to see whether the master or the slave is morally superior to the other:

> vilice silvarum et mihi me reddentis agelli,
> quem tu fastidis habitatum quinque focis et
> quinque bonos solitum Variam dimittere patres,
> certemus, spinas animone ego fortius an tu
> evellas agro, et melior sit Horatius an res.[48] (1–5)

> Bailiff of my forests and the little farm that returns me to myself, which you disdain because it is inhabited by only five families and is accustomed to send five good fathers to Varia, let us compete to see whether I am more robust at removing thorns from the mind or you from the field, and whether Horace or his property is in a better condition.

In the bailiff's opinion, Horace's farm is the same sort of deserted backwater as Lebedus was in the previous poem. With its sparse population it provides him with very few opportunities to socialize, and it is companionship above all that the bailiff seems to desire. Horace proposes to adjust the slave's attitude by "removing the thorns from his mind" and by showing him that rural contentment is within his grasp. By framing this as a contest Horace is able to draw a series of contrasts between himself and the slave which he hopes will prove that he is in a better spiritual condition than his slave (*certemus . . . melior sit Horatius an res*)—the *res* of line 5 points not so much to the farm as to the slave himself as part of Horace's "property."[49] Beginning with *ego . . . an tu* in line 4 Horace shifts his focus back and forth between the two contestants, alternating between first and second person pronouns: *me* (6), *ego . . . tu* (10), *tu* (14), *me* (16), *meque et te* (19), *te . . . tibi* (21), *mea* (37), *tu* (41), and *tibi* (42). The contest proposed here, I will argue, ends not in Horace's clear victory but in a draw.

Horace begins by describing his own situation: his duty, *pietas*, to a grieving friend is keeping him in the city, though he longs to return to his farm:

> me quamvis Lamiae pietas et cura moratur
> fratrem maerentis, rapto de fratre dolentis
> insolabiliter, tamen istuc mens animusque
> fert et avet spatiis obstantia rumpere claustra. (6–9)

> Although I am delayed by duty and care for Lamia, who is mourning his brother and grieving inconsolably about his brother being snatched away, nevertheless my mind and spirit incline to that place and long to break the barricades that block the course.

Whereas in 1.10 Horace is at the farm missing his friend, he is now attending to a friend in the city and pining for his farm, and both situations bring discontent. Horace seems doomed never to be able to reconcile the conflict within himself between friendship and isolation. Kenney has questioned Horace's propriety in complaining in this letter about having to perform this duty for a friend: "If Horace was really Lamia's friend, would he even implicitly have admitted to wanting to be anywhere but at his side at such a time?"[50] Though I do not agree with his suggestion that Lamia's brother has been snatched away not by death but by a love affair, he is nevertheless correct to question Horace's desire to be gone as soon as possible. Horace's attachment to the countryside is preventing him from being as good a friend as he could and should be. Yes, he performs his duty (*pietas*), but he does not seem to like it. The intensity with which Horace longs to return to his farm is akin to that felt by a racehorse that eagerly awaits the opening starting gates (9).[51] One whose *animus* is so keen to be gone certainly does not possess the equanimity that in 1.11 enables a person to be indifferent to place.

What causes the bailiff and Horace to disagree so vehemently is that they have varying ideas about what makes a person happy, and both are equally wrong:

rure ego viventem, tu dicis in urbe beatum:
cui placet alterius, sua nimirum est odio sors.
stultus uterque locum immeritum causatur inique:
in culpa est animus, qui se non effugit umquam. (10–13)

I say that the one who lives in the country is happy, but you say it is the one in the city. Whoever envies another's lot of course will find his own hateful. Each foolishly and unfairly blames the undeserving place. The mind, which never escapes itself, is at fault.

Horace had previously associated happiness (*beatum*, 10) with the countryside at 1.10.14 (*rure beato*). However, we even earlier were advised in 1.6.1–2 that the only thing that produces *beatitas* is "admiring nothing," *nil admirari*, a code of behavior that certainly goes against Horace's current clinging to the countryside and praising it alone. The word *sors* at 1.14.11 recalls the end of 1.10, where Fuscus is told that the key to living well is to be content with whatever his current lot happens to be (*laetus sorte*, 44). In 1.14 neither master nor slave exhibits such contentment or the ability to adapt to his current situation and make it amenable to himself. Instead each suffers from an acute case of μεμψιμοιρία, "envy of another's lot."[52] The language of flight (*effugit*, 13) recalls *fugitivus* and *fuge* in 1.10.10 and 32, and what neither the slave nor Horace can escape is his own lack of equanimity, evoked by the close proximity of *inique* (12) and *animus* (13).[53] Horace seemed momentarily to have overcome his desire for such escapism in 1.11, but it returns powerfully in 1.14 as he imagines that leaving the city behind will bring him contentment. Just as the countryside does not warrant the slave's disapproval, so too, Horace confesses, is the city unworthy to be blamed (*locum immeritum*, 12) for his own lack of equanimity. The *ego* and *tu* of 10 are momentarily brought together in *uterque* (12) in shared censure.

In the next lines Horace attempts once again to gain the moral upper hand over his *vilicus* by claiming that whereas the slave is inconsistent in his desires and always wants a different lot he himself is consistent in his preference for the country:

tu mediastinus tacita prece rura petebas,
nunc urbem et ludos et balnea vilicus optas:
me constare mihi scis et discedere tristem,
quandocumque trahunt invisa negotia Romam. (14–17)

When you were a laborer you used to beg for the countryside in a silent prayer, but now that you are a bailiff you want the city and its games and baths. You know that I am consistent with myself and depart in sadness whenever hateful duties drag me to Rome.

Whereas the slave exhibits μεμψιμοιρία in both the city and the country, Horace, he would have us believe, is guilty of it only when in the city. If he were to read Horace's earlier letter to Celsus (1.8), the *vilicus* would have grounds to question Horace's self-characterization in these lines: *Romae Tibur amem ventosus, Tibure Romam* ("At Rome I love Tibur, while at Tibur, fickle as the wind, I love Rome," 12). We as readers of the whole collection might suspect that Horace has either deluded himself or is being insincere when in 1.14 he claims to be perfectly consistent (*constare*, 16) in his love for the countryside.

In lines 18–19 Horace admits that his disagreement with his *vilicus* stems from their "admiration" of different things: *non eadem miramur; eo disconvenit inter / meque et te* ("We do not admire the same things, and that is why there is disagreement between you and me"). Such *admiratio*, as we know from 1.6, makes one unable to handle changes in fortune or to adapt to a wide range of circumstances. The slave's love for the city makes him see only the bad aspects of country life, while Horace's partiality toward the country blinds him to them:

> nam quae deserta et inhospita tesqua
> credis, amoena vocat mecum qui sentit, et odit
> quae te pulchra putas. (18–20)

For what you consider a deserted and inhospitable wasteland, the one who agrees with me finds pleasant and hates what you think is beautiful.

The slave, who seems chiefly concerned with the isolation (*deserta . . . tesqua*) of the farm, lacks the Aristippean adaptability that would enable him to feel hospitality (*inhospita*, 18) everywhere, while Horace in his constant focus on the farm's *amoenitas* (cf. 1.10.6 and 1.16.15) fails to acknowledge any validity in the *vilicus*'s complaints: there is nobody around with whom to enjoy friendship, levity, or fun.

Throughout the epistle Horace lists what he imagines to be the objects of the bailiff's desire for the city. In line 15 he suggests that it is the games (*ludos*) and baths (*balnea*) upon which the *vilicus*'s heart is set, and in lines 21–26 he expands the catalogue to include brothels, wine, and women:

> fornix tibi et uncta popina
> incutiunt urbis desiderium, uideo, et quod
> angulus iste feret piper et tus ocius uua,
> nec uicina subest uinum praebere taberna
> quae possit tibi, nec meretrix tibicina, cuius
> ad strepitum salias terrae grauis.

The brothel and the greasy cook-house arouse in you a desire for the city, I see, and the fact that that retired spot will bear pepper and incense more readily than grapes, and the fact that there is neither a neighboring tavern which can offer you wine nor a flute-playing prostitute at whose noise you might leap heavily upon the ground.

Toward the end of the poem Horace states with incredulity that the bailiff would rather eat the inferior food allotted to urban slaves when he has use of Horace's firewood, flock, and garden:

> cum servis urbana diaria rodere mauis,
> horum tu in numerum voto ruis: invidet usum
> lignorum et pecoris tibi calo argutus et horti. (40–42)

> You prefer to gnaw on the city's daily rations with the slaves; in your prayers you rush into their number. Meanwhile the shrewd drudge envies your use of firewood and the flock and the garden.

What seems to matter to the bailiff is not the quality of the food but the opportunity to be *cum servis*, in the company of other slaves at what could be called a very modest or crude version of a symposium, many elements of which—wine, companionship, sex—make up the slave's desires. Horace furthermore acknowledges but does not seem fully to take into account that while the farm is a place of leisure and relaxation to him it is a lot of work (*multa mole*, 30) to the bailiff. For the bailiff the country rather than the city is the site of *invisa negotia*.[54]

Horace claims to have given up all the things that the *vilicus* now desires. Instead of enjoying the companionship of a symposium he now prefers a solo lunch and nap while relaxing on the farm:

> nunc age, quid nostrum concentum dividat audi.
> quem tenues decuere togae nitidique capilli,
> quem scis immunem Cinarae placuisse rapaci,
> quem bibulum liquidi media de luce Falerni,
> cena brevis iuvat et prope rivum somnus in herba.
> nec lusisse pudet, sed non incidere ludum. (31–36)

> Now come, hear what splits our agreement. The one whom fine togas and shining hair once suited, the one whom you know pleased greedy Cinara even without gifts, whom a drink of flowing Falernian pleased in the middle of the day, [now] a short meal satisfies and a nap on the grass near the riverbank. It does not cause shame to have played, but it does [cause shame] not to make an end of play.

As Rudd states, "what the city means to the bailiff now (drink and sex) is just a coarser version of what it once meant to Horace (wine and love)."[55] The slave looks a lot like Horace's past self, and it begins to seem as if this is a conversation that Horace is having or has had with himself in an attempt to dissuade himself away from his "slavish" desire for the city. While the slave desires levity and play—*lusisse* and *ludum* (36) look back to *ludos* (15)—Horace has now run to the opposite extreme, and although his younger self enjoyed such indulgences, he has now given them up. The abandonment of *ludi* looks back especially to the opening epistle, where his refusal to partake in *ludi* goes hand in hand with his declaration of freedom (1.1.1–15). To enjoy the lighter aspects of urban life and to go to the city under anything other than duress would, Horace implies, make him no better than his slave and lock him back up in the *ludus* of Maecenas (*iterum antique me includere ludo*, 3). It is no accident that these lines in 1.14 recall Horace's refusal in 1.7 to attend constantly to Maecenas's desires:

> quodsi me noles usquam discedere, reddes
> forte latus, nigros angusta fronte capillos,
> reddes dulce loqui, reddes ridere decorum et
> inter vina fugam Cinarae maerere protervae. (1.7.25–28)

> But if you are unwilling for me ever to leave you, return my strong flank, my dark hair on a narrow brow. Return my sweet speech, return my charming laughter and wine-fueled lamentations over wanton Cinara's flight.

Though Maecenas's name is unspoken in 1.14 the echo of 1.7 places him firmly in the poem's background, and just as his refusal to attend to Maecenas in 1.7 involved his *libertas* so too is his "hatred" of the city in 1.14 motivated by his unwillingness to be made a slave.

In aligning himself so closely with the country—and its lack of *ludus*—Horace in fact is taking an extreme position that is ultimately untenable. In 1.6 Horace had called into question the ability of one way of life alone to produce happiness, and among the list of items that are rejected are included both unremitting seriousness and *virtus*, on the one hand, and constant love and jests on the other:

> si virtus hoc una potest dare, fortis omissis
> hoc age deliciis. (1.6.30–31)

> If virtue alone is able to do this [i.e., enable one to live wisely], do this steadfastly with trifles set aside.

> Si, Mimnermus uti censet, sine amore iocisque
> nil est iucundum, vivas in amore iocisque. (1.6.64–65)

> If, as Mimnermus judges, nothing is pleasant without love and jokes, live in love and jokes.

As we saw in chapter 4, to adhere to only one way of life is to hold it in admiration and thus should be rejected. The implication of the two passages cited above is that, while neither *virtus* nor *deliciae* should be our sole purpose, there is a place in life for both and we should adapt ourselves according to the demands of the situation. This is a lesson that Horace had espoused, for example, in Odes 2.7 and one that he will champion again in Odes 4.12.[56] In *Epistles* 1.14, however, play and seriousness correspond to different phases and ways of life and cannot coexist simultaneously. The pursuit of one necessarily excludes the pursuit of the other (*nec lusisse pudet, sed non incidere ludum*). As Mayer and others note, this line—as well as the focus on his formerly gleaming locks both in 1.14.32 and 1.7.26—and the thought behind it are indebted to an epigram of Philodemus:[57]

> ἠράσθην. τίς δ' οὐχί; κεκώμακα. τίς δ' ἀμύητος
> κώμων; ἀλλ' ἐμάνην ἐκ τίνος; οὐχὶ θεοῦ;
> ἐρρίφθω, πολιὴ γὰρ ἐπείγεται ἀντὶ μελαίνης
> θρὶξ ἤδη, συνετῆς ἄγγελος ἡλικίης.
> καὶ παίζειν ὅτε καιρός, ἐπαίξαμεν· ἡνίκα καὶ νῦν
> οὐκέτι, λωϊτέρης φροντίδος ἁψόμεθα.[58]

> I fell in love. Who has not? I reveled. Who is uninitiated in revelry? But because of whom was I driven mad? Was it not because of a god? Let it go. For now grey hair, which is the messenger of the wise time of life, is rushing in to replace the dark. And when it was the right time to play, we played. And now when it is no longer right, we will attach ourselves to better thoughts.

By evoking this epigram in 1.14 Horace implies that the time of life when such play—the eroticism and companionship of an urban symposium—was appropriate has passed him by and he must now devote himself to wisdom and philosophy, and this is essentially the thought behind the opening of *Epistles* 1.1 as well. Play or philosophize, live in the city or the country, but not both.

However, Horace does not sustain this attitude throughout the entire collection, and we have already seen him urge Torquatus in 1.5 to abandon the unrelenting seriousness of his public life and join him in the temporary enjoyment of an urban *cena*. In this invitation poem Horace reveals none of the same ambivalence we find in 1.14, but instead he adapts himself to his urban situation and encourages Torquatus to adapt to the demands of the festive holiday as well. In a footnote Bowditch makes the interesting suggestion that another well-known saying is lurking behind 1.14.36 in addition to the Philodemus passage. She writes:

> Given the *vilicus*'s own desire for a brothel—*fornix* (21)—perhaps the phrase claiming the speaker's end of "play" echoes the similar comment made by Aristippus and quoted by Montaigne: "Aristippus parlant à des jeunes gens qui rougissaient de le voir entrer chez une courtisane: 'Le vice est de n'en pas sortir, non pas d'y entrer.'"[59]

The saying to which Montaigne refers is found in Diogenes Laertius 2.69: οὐ τὸ εἰσελθεῖν χαλεπόν, ἀλλὰ τὸ μὴ δύνασθαι ἐξελθεῖν ("It is not entering that is the danger, but not being able to exit"). For Aristippus as long as one does not become enslaved by the pursuit of pleasure and play, then there is no need to give up such pursuits entirely. If we apply the exemplum of Aristippus to Horace's situation, this way of life would allow Horace to participate in *ludus* (i.e., city life and all that it entails) without becoming entrapped in it (*includere ludo*, 1.1.3). As an Aristippean Horace can go back and forth between city and country and all that each implies. In 1.14, however, he is trying to conform to a perspective that does not in fact fully suit him.

The real issue behind Horace's withdrawal, as in 1.1, does not in fact seem to be Horace's age but rather the exposure to the public eye that his poetic success has brought him and the judgment and envy that results from it:

> non istic obliquo oculo mea commoda quisquam
> limat, non odio obscuro morsuque venenat:
> rident vicini glaebas et saxa moventem. (1.14.37–39)

> In that place [i.e., the country] nobody detracts from my successes with an envious eye or poisons them with secret hatred and malicious attack. My neighbors laugh as I move clods and rocks.

Horace's past "play" has in fact brought him public success, enough that it has elicited the hateful envy of others. As Mayer notes, the chief of the *commoda* he has obtained through his accomplishments is his friendship with Maecenas,[60] and the resentment this friendship sparked in others drove him into the country as early as *Satires* 2.6 (cf. esp. 20–57). Yet he does not seem to be entirely at home in the country, as his attempts to work his farm bring amusement to his rustic neighbors. A bridge must be formed between these two worlds so that Horace can continue to enjoy the *commoda* he has earned while still maintaining this rustic refuge from the public exposure that urban life brings.

Horace ends the poem by simply taking himself out of the contest and focusing instead upon the μεμψιμοιρία of the *vilicus* and the *calo*, another of Horace's slaves whose status is beneath that of the *vilicus* and who envies the bailiff's access to the goods of Horace's farm (41–42). Rather than envy one another, Horace claims, these two should be content to practice their own skill: *quam scit uterque, libens, censebo, exerceat artem* ("Let each one, I advise, gladly practice the skill which he knows," 44). Horace's clever attempt to elide himself from a contest that he has not proven himself to be winning must not go unnoticed, nor should we be fooled into thinking that Horace himself exemplifies the final moral he has produced. The *ars* at which Horace excels is the composition of poetry that brings him urban renown, exactly the *ludus* he proudly claims to have set aside. Instead, his awkward attempts at farming arouse incredulous laughter from his neighbors, exactly the sort of laughter he had hoped to avoid in 1.1.9. Is this rustic withdrawal really so decorous or suitable after all?

By withdrawing from the contest in this way Horace tacitly acknowledges that he has not won it. The mask that Horace tries to force onto himself in 1.14 simply does not fit him and goes against too many of the lessons Horace has tried to impart to others throughout the poems that precede it. At the heart of the poem, as throughout the *Epistles*, is the issue of freedom. Horace suggests that the *vilicus's* attachment to the city and lack of consistency make him servile in both a literal and figurative sense. But what ultimately comes through the surface of the poem is that Horace's own attachment to the countryside leaves him less than free himself. He and the *vilicus* are equally "enslaved" by their own *admiratio*, which leaves them incapable of adapting to a variety of circumstances. Insofar as he desires friendship and company the *vilicus* in fact gains the upper hand over Horace, for whom the duties of friendship, though he performs them, are hateful (*invisa negotia*, 17). In *Satires* 1.5.44 Horace had proclaimed, "So long as I am in my right mind, I would compare nothing to a pleasant friend" (*nil ego contulerim iucundo sanus amico*). In ranking the country so much higher than friendship in this poem we are left to wonder just how *sanus* Horace the *ruris amator* is.

Throughout these poems two types of freedom are set in opposition with one another. On the one hand the poems carefully articulate the freedom and its concomitant mastery that the country brings to Horace, with its release from all the troubling duties of the city. But throughout 1.10 and 1.14 doubts are cast on this kind of freedom. It is limited, conditional, extreme, and ultimately very fragile. But most importantly, it isolates him from the urban sphere in which *amicitia* flourishes. On the other hand the poems simultaneously express the freedom that comes through being content with our current lot by accepting it and making the most of it, whether circumstances find us in the city or the country. This kind of freedom gives us the adaptability needed to navigate back and forth between these two spheres and keeps us from attaching ourselves too completely to either extreme. Through this kind of adaptability Horace can retain his freedom from the city while also being free to enjoy urban life from time to time. This latter type of freedom is effectively an application to the rural and urban spheres of the type of freedom he claims to enjoy in approaching philosophy in 1.1.13–19, which enables him to participate in philosophy without becoming enslaved to any one system. We have seen indications throughout the poems thus far discussed that Horace associates such adaptability especially with Aristippus, who will take center stage in my next chapter.

Moderate Freedom and Friendship
Epistles 1.17 and 1.18

WE SAW IN THE PREVIOUS CHAPTER that the freedom Horace enjoys in the countryside is limited and conditional and that true equanimity and independence should arise from an adaptability to place that allows enjoyment in any location, whether urban or rural. In the current chapter I examine how Horace applies these same ideas to the social realm in *Epistles* 1.17 and 1.18, each devoted to the topic of friendship.[1] In both poems Horace encourages his young *amici* to cultivate friendships with the great and advises them how best to do so while retaining their virtue and independence. These poems are therefore critical to the reformulation—over the course of the collection—of not only *libertas* but also *virtus*. Freedom and virtue arise not from adhering stubbornly to an extreme but from being adaptable or hitting upon a mean. *Libertas* does not now come from steadfastly resisting the oppressive demands of powerful friends—as Horace's opening stance in 1.1 suggested—but from finding a middle ground through which compromise is possible without a loss of independence. Horace thereby applies his philosophical independence to the realm of friendship. In both philosophy and *amicitia*, it is possible to position oneself between total freedom from and total slavery to a master. This middle ground allows a degree of dependence on others and constitutes a moderate degree of *libertas*, which is preferable to the unyielding independence that results in isolation. Just as Aristippus was the model in *Epistles* 1.1 for this philosophical approach, in these poems he proves the most outstanding exemplar for independence in social relationships, since he can adapt himself to a variety of situations without sacrificing his autonomy or consistency of character. By means of these poems Horace works out a compromise through which he himself can eventually enact a return to the city and to the prominent men therein.

ARISTIPPEAN FREEDOM, VIRTUE, AND
ADAPTABILITY IN *EPISTLES* 1.17

Aristippus takes center stage in *Epistles* 1.17, in which Horace uses the philosopher as an exemplar for instructing his young addressee Scaeva on how one may appropriately interact with the powerful.[2] In the first half of the poem, Horace recounts a well-known incident between Aristippus and Diogenes the Cynic in which the former denies that the latter truly possesses the freedom he claims to enjoy. Whereas Diogenes refuses to interact with the wealthy on any terms and prefers to gain his livelihood from begging, Aristippus can enjoy friendships with the great without becoming distressed at their loss or unavailability. Horace clearly sides with Aristippus and suggests that his path is more virtuous and moderate than the extreme one followed by Diogenes. The successful Aristippean can embrace at times a withdrawn life of isolation and at other times the camaraderie and benefits of friendship and engagement. In other words, he can enjoy friendship without being subjected to it in keeping with the Aristippean philosophical goal Horace set for himself in the opening poem: *et mihi res, non me rebus, subiungere conor*, 1.1.19. Or, to use again the famous phrase of Aristippus: ἔχω Λαΐδα, ἀλλ᾽ οὐκ ἔχομαι, "I hold Lais, but am not held by her." In *Epistles* 1.17, however, Lais is replaced by friendships with the great. In the second half of the poem Horace advises Scaeva generally on how to avoid the extremes, both surprisingly embodied by Diogenes, of nonparticipation and dependent parasitism.

Several scholars have found the poem unsatisfactory and argued that Horace's persona and advice in it are satirical and should not be taken seriously. The chief complaint such readings express is that Horace seems to encourage Scaeva to practice parasitism rather than genuine friendship and therefore his advice is out of keeping with values and practices found elsewhere in his poetry. Fraenkel, who finds the whole poem "upsetting," calls Scaeva "a conceited young careerist" for whom "Horace did not greatly care."[3] Perret considers Horace's advice to be especially distasteful and calls the poem a "true satire, from the first line to the last":

> There Horace assumes in his own name a role analogous to the one he gave the virtuous Tiresias in *Satire* II 5; but now it is not the art of snaring wills but rather the art of success, or, better, the art of parasitism: it is this art that constitutes virtue itself (37–42). Reserve, a spirit of independence—that is, everything that the true Horace made the law of his life—are derided as the ridiculous appurtenances of cowards, the pusillanimous, and weaklings. . . . it is amazing that such outrageous remarks—the bore in *Satire* I 9 did not go so far—have not alerted certain critics who have believed that this caricature represents the true thought of Horace.[4]

More recent readings have similarly taken Horace's tone as ironic and satirical. Damon argues that the behavior Horace outlines in the poem is clearly that of the parasite and calls Perret's reading of the poem as an *ars parasitandi* "not very far from the mark." She concludes that both *Epistles* 1.17 and 1.18 pit "friendship with the great" as a foil against "contemplative withdrawal" and that ultimately the epistolary Horace opts for the latter.[5] Oliensis similarly speaks of Horace's persona in 1.17 as being out of keeping with that found elsewhere, especially in the *Satires*. "What Scaeva's unscrupulous teacher offers here," she argues, "is a Machiavellian reformulation of the admirable principle Horace espoused in the satires: it is crucial for a client (not to be but) to appear uninterested in gifts if he is (not to be but) to appear worthy of them." To Oliensis, the persona Horace exhibits in the poem is not the same one he dons elsewhere in the collection, while in *Epistles* 1.18, also on the topic of friendship, "Horace reverts to his authorial persona, offering sage advice."[6] Armstrong similarly calls the epistle a "sarcastic attack on the pursuit of profit through clienthood" and argues that "the self-serving precepts of Aristippus and the Hedonists lead in the end only to degradation, servitude, and making oneself both notorious and ridiculous."[7]

Not all scholars, however, have been hostile to Horace's advice in *Epistles* 1.17. More favorable interpretations of the poem have been offered by Moles, Traina, Mayer, and Johnson, who take seriously Horace's stated preference for searching out friendships with great men and argue that Horace's advocacy of Aristippean adaptability should not be read as satire.[8] I am indebted to these readings, particularly that of Traina, and agree that Horace's advice in *Epistles* 1.17 must be taken earnestly. Furthermore, the instruction he gives to Scaeva, whereby Cynic inflexibility is rejected in favor of Aristippean adaptability, should be understood in light of the larger collection, in which Horace himself transitions gradually from stubbornly refusing participation in social relationships to conditionally embracing them. As a model for social participation, Aristippus offers a way of accommodating one's longings for public life and friendship with the great without sacrificing one's independence or consistency of character. Horace recommends this system to others at the same time that he progressively adopts it for himself.

Horace's central concern in *Epistles* 1.17 is to illustrate how one can court the powerful while maintaining decorum:

> quamvis, Scaeva, satis per te tibi consulis et scis
> quo tandem pacto *deceat* maioribus uti,
> disce, docendus adhuc quae censet amiculus, ut si
> caecus iter monstrare velit; tamen aspice, siquid
> et nos quod cures proprium fecisse loquamur. (1.17.1–5)

Although, Scaeva, you sufficiently look out for yourself on your own and know in what manner *it is fitting* to associate with the great, learn the opinions of your humble friend, who himself still needs more teaching, as though a blind man wants to point out the path. But nevertheless consider if even I might say something that you may care to make your own.

Horace makes it clear that he himself is still in the process of learning the very lessons that he now aims to teach Scaeva. As he does throughout the collection, he here embraces the roles of student and teacher simultaneously and invites us to consider how the advice he offers Scaeva pertains equally to his own friendships with the great. The idea of decorum has been central to the *Epistles* since the opening poem, where Horace devotes himself to *verum atque decens* (11), and the concept will become particularly prominent in Horace's analysis of Aristippus in the anecdote that follows.

Rather than dive immediately into this exemplum, however, he first offers Scaeva an alternate path, one that especially recalls the *lathe biosas* of Epicurean withdrawal:

> si te grata quies et primam somnus in horam
> delectat, si te pulvis strepitusque rotarum,
> si laedit caupona, Ferentinum ire iubebo;
> nam neque divitibus contingunt gaudia solis,
> nec vixit male, qui natus moriensque fefellit.
> si prodesse tuis pauloque benignius ipsum
> te tractare voles, accedes siccus ad unctum. (1.17.6–12)

> If pleasant quiet and sleep until the first hour delight you, if dirt and the noise of wheels and the tavern bother you, I will bid you to go to Ferentinum. For joys do not befall the rich alone, nor has he lived badly who has escaped notice from birth to death. But if you wish to benefit your friends and to treat yourself a little more generously, approach a rich table when you are thirsty.

One option is to live in rural withdrawal and thus in complete anonymity, and the focus on *quies* and pleasure (*grata, delectat, gaudia*) evokes Epicurean *ataraxia* and *hedone*. This is the kind of lifestyle, away from the taverns and noisy distractions of town, that Horace had adopted for himself as a *ruris amator* in poems 1.10 and 1.14, and several scholars have suggested that to Horace this Epicurean withdrawal is in fact preferable to the engaged Aristippeanism that the remainder of the poem purports to teach.[9] But Horace is clear in the earlier poems and 1.17 that such a lifestyle has its drawbacks, for it removes one from the company of *amici*, which is best enjoyed in the city.[10] As such, it is something of an extreme option if one adheres to it at all times. It is a way of life to which Horace is repeatedly attracted in the *Epistles* (cf., e.g., *latet abditus agro*, 1.1.5), but it is ultimately one that must be balanced by periods of participation. The regular company of friends, particularly in the context of urban symposia (*accedes siccus ad unctum*, 1.17.12; cf. *Epist.* 1.5), has mutual advantages for oneself (*si . . . paulo benignius ipsum te tractara voles*, 1.17.11–12) and one's associates (*si prodesse tuis . . . voles*, 1.17.11–12). Horace adds to these lines, however, an important qualification. One's participation should be conditional and moderate, since only when one is "thirsty" (*siccus*) is a great man's table suitable, and constant attendance upon a patron is an extreme that should be avoided. Horace thus puts forth three possible paths in these opening lines: a withdrawn life of Epicurean *quies*; the constantly engaged life of extreme attendance on the wealthy (i.e., dependent parasitism); and a mean between the two, or a middle path through which one can enjoy Epicurean *quies* and, when the occasion demands, spend time with one's friends in the city. Aristippus exemplifies this middle path in 1.17.[11] As a model for withdrawal, however, the quasi-Epicureanism outlined in this passage is by far preferable to the other philosophical system highlighted in the poem, that of Cynicism, in which rejection of society is coupled with harsh asperity. What Horace ultimately rejects in the collection is not so much the studious and reflective retirement of Epicurean *quies* —indeed, this path is necessary for balancing periods of participation—so much as the inflexible and extreme hostility to engaged life that is embodied in 1.17 by Diogenes the Cynic. In fact, Horace ultimately corrects such Cynic tendencies in himself over the course of the collection.[12]

In 1.17 Horace outlines the benefits of periodic social interaction by recounting an encounter between Aristippus and Diogenes, found also in various forms in Diogenes Laertius:[13]

'si pranderet holus patienter, regibus uti
nollet Aristippus.' 'si sciret regibus uti,
fastidiret holus, qui me notat.' utrius horum
verba probes et facta, doce, vel iunior audi,
cur sit Aristippi potior sententia. namque
mordacem Cynicum sic eludebat, ut aiunt:
'scurror ego ipse mihi, populo tu: rectius hoc et
splendidius multo est. equus ut me portet, alat rex,
officium facio: tu poscis vilia rerum,
dante minor, quamvis fers te nullius egentem.' (1.17.13–22)

"If Aristippus could tolerate dining on vegetables, he would not want to associate with kings." "If the one reprimanding me knew how to associate with kings, he would loathe vegetables." Teach me, out of these two, of whose words and deeds do you approve? Or, since you are younger, hear why the opinion of Aristippus is better. For in this way, as they say, he outmaneuvered the biting Cynic: "I play the *scurra* for myself, you for the people. What I do is better and finer by far. I fulfill obligations so that a horse may convey me, so that a king may feed me. You beg for scraps and become inferior to the giver, although you boast that you need nobody."

Readers familiar with Horace's appreciation of simple vegetarian fare, particularly in his *Satires*, might expect him to approve of Diogenes here. In *Satires* 1.1.74, for example, Horace argues that when used correctly, money can buy basic necessities such as *panis, holus, vini sextarius*, "bread, vegetables, and a pint of wine." In *Satires* 1.6.112 Horace's afternoon stroll involves asking the price of *holus*, and in *Satires* 2.6.63–64 Horace looks forward to eating simply prepared beans and vegetables (*holuscula*) when next at his farm. But this is only one side of Horace, and he is at times accused by others of an almost parasitic attendance at Maecenas's table. In *Satires* 1.6.47 he finds himself the butt of others' envy because he is Maecenas's "constant associate," *convictor*, a word that Gowers suggests "conjures up the world of the *convivium* or dinner-party where parasites scrambled for seats and bit each other's backs."[14] In *Satires* 2.7.29–35 Davus accuses Horace of being all too willing to abandon his plate of vegetables (*holus*, 30) for a seat at Maecenas's table. In the *Satires* Horace therefore casts some doubt on his praise of simple fare and suggests that he also enjoys the occasional plate of fine food provided by his wealthy friend and patron. In *Epistles* 1.17, rather than donning the mask of the simple vegetarian, he aligns himself with the more complex personality of Aristippus, and his approval of Aristippus's *sententia* (17) is emphasized by his repetition, three times, of Aristippus's name (14, 17, 23), while Diogenes is referred to only as *Cynicum* (18). Unlike Diogenes, Aristippus is not content merely to tolerate plain vegetables (*holus patienter*, 13) when finer fare is readily at hand. At the same time, his adaptability—which Horace is about to highlight—suggests that when such fare is unavailable he is content to dine on simple *holus*.

Central to the debate between the two philosophers in the epistle is the issue of freedom. In his rebuttal of Diogenes, Aristippus stresses the fact that both men rely on others for their livelihoods and thus play the role of *scurra*, or "parasite."[15] At issue are two different models of dependency and the question of which one strikes a better balance between liberty and slavery. Diogenes's mendicancy places him squarely at the bottom of the social ladder since it renders him entirely subordinate to the *populus* from whom he begs, and Horace here clearly plays on well-known associations (which run throughout the poem) between needy parasites and Cynic beggars.[16] The self-sufficiency so valued by Cynics is here attributed instead to Aristippus, who claims that he plays the parasitic role for his own sake rather than as a source of exhibitionism to the populace, and his autonomy is underscored by *ego ipse mihi*, a phrase which calls to mind Horace's own professions of self-sufficiency elsewhere in the *Epis-tles*.[17] As a model for dependency, Aristippus is preferable because his friend-ship with the great renders him subordinate to an elite few while Diogenes's begging makes him a slave to the populace at large.

Horace further explains his approval of Aristippus over the Cynic in the fol-lowing lines, explaining that Aristippus's superiority arises from his adaptabil-ity, which enables him to take or leave such friendships with equanimity. Unlike Diogenes, Aristippus—via a theatrical metaphor—easily adapts himself to any role or mask (i.e., *persona*) in which he finds himself, and from this adaptability his true freedom arises:

> omnis Aristippum decuit color et status et res,
> temptantem maiora, fere praesentibus aequum.
> contra, quem duplici panno patientia velat,
> mirabor, vitae via si conversa decebit.
> alter purpureum non expectabit amictum,
> quidlibet indutus celeberrima per loca vadet,
> personamque feret non inconcinnus utramque;
> alter Mileti textam cane peius et angui
> vitabit chlanidem, morietur frigore, si non
> rettuleris pannum. refer et sine vivat ineptus. (1.17.23–32)

Every color and status and circumstance suited Aristippus, who attempted greater things but as a rule was content with what he had. On the other hand I would be amazed if the opposite way of life suited the one whom suffering wraps in a double rag. The one (Aristippus) will not wait for a purple cloak, but clothed in anything will go through the most celebrated spots and will wear either mask not inelegantly. The other will avoid a woven Milesian robe as worse than a dog or snake. He will die of cold if you do not return his rag. Give it back and let him live his foolish life.

Whereas Aristippus can adopt the mask of a pauper or a parasite while main-taining his decorum and elegance, Diogenes conforms to his Cynic *persona* in his every action. As Traina puts it, "The Cynic . . . will always be the prisoner of his own mask."[18] He relies on his outer appearance (i.e., the beggar's cloak) to reflect his inner virtue, while Aristippus's inner virtue remains intact no mat-ter his outward appearance.[19] Whereas Aristippus's donning of beggar's rags is not unbecoming (*non inconcinnus*, 29), Diogenes's insistence on wearing them makes him foolish (*ineptus*, 32). Mayer has pointed out the strong disapproval sounded by *inconcinnitas* and *ineptia*, attributes identified by Cicero at *De Ora-tore* 2.17, as being particularly distasteful to Roman sensibilities:[20]

> nam qui aut, tempus quid postulet, non videt, aut plura loquitur, aut se ostentat,
> aut eorum, quibuscumque est, vel dignitatis, vel commodi rationem non habet,
> aut denique in aliquo genere aut *inconcinnus* aut multus est, is *ineptus* dicitur.

For he is called inept who does not see what the circumstance demands or talks too much or boasts or has no reckoning of the dignity or the convenience of those in his company or finally in some way is either unbecoming or tedious.

In this passage Cicero connects *inconcinnitas* and *ineptia* not only to the inability to recognize and adapt to varying situations (*tempus quid postulet*) but also to an inability to act in accordance with the *dignitas* and convenience of one's friends. Diogenes can thus neither adapt to sudden change nor behave in a socially becoming way.

Horace's approval of Aristippus, on the other hand, is underscored by his insistence that Aristippus maintained decorum no matter which mask he was wearing (*decuit*, 22; cf. *decebit*, 26). His claim that every *res* befits Aristippus recalls in particular *Epistles* 1.1.18–19 (*nunc in Aristippi furtim praecepta relabor /et mihi res, non me rebus, subiungere*), and in each of these passages, Aristippean adaptability is contrasted with rigid inflexibility. The word *color* (1.17.23) alludes to the polyp, an image frequently used to denote adaptability.[21] Such a comparison is often used of parasites and flatterers who adapt themselves to those around them in order to gain favor, but here Horace uses it positively to describe Aristippus's ability not to ingratiate himself with others but to enjoy their company or not with equal facility.[22] Diogenes Laertius describes Aristippus's adaptability in language that echoes Horace's, particularly his use of the theatrical metaphor of the "mask": ἦν δὲ ἱκανὸς ἁρμόσασθαι καὶ τόπῳ καὶ χρόνῳ καὶ προσώπῳ, καὶ πᾶσαν περίστασιν ἁρμοδίως ὑποκρίνασθαι ("he was able to adapt himself to place and time and mask, and to act the part in every circumstance appropriately," 2.66). Diogenes further emphasizes Aristippus's ability to don either rags or a fine cloak by reporting a remark made to Aristippus either by Strato or Plato: σοὶ μόνῳ δέδοται καὶ χλανίδα φορεῖν καὶ ῥάκος ("to you alone has it been given to wear both the fine cloak and the rag," 2.67).[23] Aristippus's adaptability therefore allows him comfortably to enjoy either social withdrawal (the rag) or participation (the nice cloak)—in other words, to play the part of the Cynic pauper or Cyrenaic hedonist equally well. By adapting himself to changing situations, Aristippus does not so much alter his own disposition as adapt the circumstance at hand to suit himself. This adaptability allows him to retain his integrity in the face of change and to stay true to the man behind the mask.[24] Most importantly, Aristippus is able to retain his equanimity (*aequum*, 24) no matter his level of participation or withdrawal. As we have seen, equanimity is the goal that the epistolary Horace works toward consistently, though at times unsuccessfully.

The appreciation of such Aristippean adaptability is not new to the *Epistles*. In fact, in the penultimate poem of *Odes* 1–3 Horace includes a portrait of himself as a successful Aristippean who can praise *Fortuna* while she is present but be content when she departs:

> Fortuna saevo laeta negotio et
> ludum insolentem ludere pertinax
>   transmutat incertos honores,
>   nunc mihi, nunc alii benigna.
>
> laudo manentem; si celeres quatit
> pinnas, resigno quae dedit et mea
>   virtute me involvo probamque
>   pauperiem sine dota quaero. (3.29.49–56)

> Fortune, happy in her savage duty and persistent in playing her insolent game, changes her uncertain honors, kind now to me, now to another. I praise her while she stays; if she shakes her swift wings, I resign what she has given, and I wrap myself in my virtue and seek honorable, undowered poverty.

By claiming to "wrap" himself in his virtue, Horace alludes to the tattered cloak worn by the Cynics,[25] the one that Aristippus dons when there is no elegant one to be had. Horace thus adopts at the end of the *Odes* a persona that in the *Epistles* he attributes to Aristippus, and it is his struggle to enact such adaptability successfully that unfolds over the course of the collection. Again in *Epistles* 1.15, Horace describes himself similarly, comparing his adaptability—though portrayed here as inconsistency—to the seemingly contradictory behavior of a *scurra* named Maenius, who praises simple food when times are tough and expensive food when he has fallen in with a rich friend:

> nimirum hic ego sum; nam tuta et parvola laudo,
> cum res deficiunt, satis inter vilia fortis;
> verum ubi quid melius contingit et unctius, idem
> vos sapere et solos aio bene vivere, quorum
> conspicitur nitidis fundata pecunia villis. (42–46)

> Of course I am just like him, for I praise small, safe things when my wealth (*res*) is inadequate, sufficiently austere among cheap goods. But when something better and more luxurious befalls me, I, the same man, affirm that you alone are wise and live the good life whose well-established money is on display in gleaming villas.

In *Epistles* 1.15, Horace still views this inconsistency with a degree of ambivalence and as symptomatic of spiritual disease, for his impetus for writing the letter in the first place arises from the medical advice he has received from Antonius Musa (3–5). By *Epistles* 1.17, however, Horace has learned to assess such adaptability as something entirely positive and in keeping with Aristippus's (and by extension his own) complex personality. There is no need for him to transform himself to an unchanging and static ideal. The result of such complexity is that he is fully satisfied neither with simple vegetables and a tattered cloak, on the one hand, nor with fine dining and a luxurious robe, on the other. Rather, he wants the freedom to enjoy both when the opportunity and appropriate occasion arise. Though *Epistles* 1 opens with a clear opposition between participation and withdrawal, by 1.17 Horace sets up a complementary relationship between these seeming opposites and progresses from choosing between two extreme paths (either/or) to opening up a middle path between them (both).

In the second half of the poem Horace moves away from the Aristippus/Diogenes episode to advise Scaeva generally about the proper way to interact with the great. Throughout this half he urges Scaeva to embrace moderate behavior and avoid extremes. Scaeva is especially to avoid the two seemingly contradictory extremes that the Cynic Diogenes simultaneously embodies: refusing social participation entirely yet also engaging in parasitic begging. He begins this section by arguing that those who make the attempt to interact with the great exhibit more *virtus* than those who do not:

> res gerere et captos ostendere civibus hostis
> attingit solium Iovis et caelestia temptat:
> principibus placuisse viris non ultima laus est.
> non cuivis homini contingit adire Corinthum.
> sedit qui timuit, ne non succederet. esto.
> quid? qui pervenit, fecitne viriliter? atqui
> hic est aut nusquam, quod quaerimus. hic onus horret
> ut parvis animis et parvo corpore maius,
> hic subit et perfert. aut virtus nomen inane est,
> aut decus et pretium recte petit experiens vir. (1.17.33–42)

To accomplish great exploits and display captured enemies to the citizens is to touch the throne of Jupiter and to attempt heavenly feats. To have pleased the foremost of the city is not the meanest praise. It does not befall just anyone to reach Corinth. He who feared that it might not turn out just sat there and did nothing. So be it. What about the one who accomplished his goal? Did he do this in a manly fashion? And yet here or nowhere is what we seek. This man dreads the burden as too big for his paltry strength and small body, while the other takes it up and carries it to the end. Either virtue is an empty name, or the enterprising man rightly seeks glory and reward.

Horace in these lines not only reformulates the traditional Cynic conception of *virtus* but also places the man who courts the great at a midpoint between nonparticipants at the bottom of the social hierarchy and those of the highest success at the top.[26] While the highest praise goes to those godlike few who have reached the pinnacle of Roman society, the praise enjoyed by those who associate with them is *non ultima*, "not the meanest," and this praise is greater than those who choose not to participate at all, such as Diogenes. It is in this mean position that Horace in *Epistles* 1.20.23 will later place himself with a clear allusion back to this passage that aligns him with the Aristippean social participation outlined in 1.17: *me primis Urbis belli placuisse domique*, "I pleased the foremost of the city in war and in peace" (cf. *principibus placuisse viris*, 1.17.35). Horace envisions the contest between those who court the powerful and those who do not as a race. Those who court the powerful may not "reach Corinth," as the wealthy do, but at least they bother to participate. The image of the race has already been seen at the end of *Epistles* 1.2, where Horace employs it to evoke the mean, positioning himself ahead of the losers and behind the winners: *quodsi cessas aut strenuus anteis, / nec tardum opperior nec praecedentibus insto*, "But if you delay or energetically go ahead, I neither wait for the slow nor rush to catch up with those ahead," 70–71.

The question of *virtus* is central not only to these lines (*viriliter*, 38; *virtus*, 41) but throughout the entire collection. In the opening poem, Horace's intermittent philosophical championing of *virtus vera* was the mark of a rigid and unbending character: *virtutis verae custos rigidusque satelles* (1.1.17), but by the second poem, as we have seen, this view of *virtus* had already begun to be reformulated in the figure of Odysseus, whose adaptability and resistance to orthodoxy made him an *utile exemplar* of *virtus* and *sapientia* (1.2.17–18). In *Epistles* 1.6 Horace labels those who unbendingly pursue *virtus* among the *admiratores* whose devotion to a single goal renders them the slavish followers of an extreme: *insani sapiens nomen ferat, aequus iniqui, / ultra quam satis est virtutem si petat ipsam*, "Let the sane man bear the name of the insane, the tranquil the name of the distressed, if he should pursue Virtue herself beyond what is enough," 15–16. Finally, in 1.18.9 Horace will redefine *virtus* not as an unbending extreme but as a midpoint: *virtus est medium vitiorum et utrimque reductum*, "virtue is a mean between vices and removed from both." *Epistles* 1.17 occupies an important position in the reformulation of *virtus* that has taken place since the opening poem, and his association of virtue with those in the middle anticipates the *virtus est medium* of *Epistles* 1.18. The *virtus* we should pursue is not the inflexible one represented by Diogenes, but the one that comes about through the adaptability and moderation of Aristippus. In *Epistles* 2.2, a passage we have encountered now several times, Horace will paint a portrait of himself as a successful Aristippean that brings together many of the ideas we have encountered in 1.17: adaptability, integrity, the race, the mean, and *virtus*:

ego, utrum
nave ferar magna an parva, ferar unus et idem.
non agimur tumidis velis aquilone secundo,
non tamen adversis aetatem ducimus austris,
viribus, ingenio, specie, virtute, loco, re,
extremi primorum, extremis usque priores. (*Epist.* 2.2.199–204)

Whether I am carried on a large or small boat, I will be carried as one and the
same person. I am not driven by swollen sails in a favorable north wind, nor,
moreover, do I live my life in adverse south winds: in strength, talent, appearance,
virtue, position, and wealth, [I am] behind the first, always ahead of the last.

By including *virtus* among those attributes he possesses in moderation Horace
again aligns himself against those, such as Diogenes, who would advance an
extreme and inflexible notion of what constitutes this prized quality.

In the final section of the poem Horace transitions from urging Scaeva to
choose participation in friendship over nonparticipation to exhorting him to
distinguish himself from a parasitic beggar, and this section of the poem has
most bothered those who argue that Horace's advice must be read satirically.
Foremost in these lines is the idea that the one who is quiet about his need in
fact receives more advantages from friendship than a beggar who makes his
every need known:

coram rege suo de paupertate tacentes
plus poscente ferent. distat, sumasne pudenter
an rapias; atqui rerum caput hoc erat, hic fons.
'indotata mihi soror est, paupercula mater
et fundus nec vendibilis nec pascere firmus'
qui dicit, clamat: 'victum date.' succinit alter:
'et mihi.' dividuo findetur munere quadra.
sed tacitus pasci si posset corvus, haberet
plus dapis et rixae multo minus invidiaeque. (1.17.43–51)

The ones who are silent about their poverty in the presence of their patron will take
more than the one who begs. There is a difference whether you take with restraint
or grasp greedily. Indeed this has always been the head of things, this the font.
"My sister is undowered, my mother poor, and my farm is neither saleable nor
reliable in providing food." Whoever says this shouts, "Give me food!" Another
chimes in, "Me too!" The morsel will be split and the benefaction divided. But if
the crow were able to eat quietly, he would have more of the feast, and there would
be much less quarreling and jealousy.

The acknowledgment that being a *cliens* has a financial motive and the advice for how to maximize benefactions have understandably rested uncomfortably with some critics. What I would emphasize in these lines is how Horace is

careful to distinguish the moderate (*pudenter*, 44) *cliens* from the grasping beggar. One of the criticisms Aristippus lodges against Diogenes in the first half
of the poem is that his begging results only in obtaining *vilia*, "cheap scraps,"
whereas Aristippus enjoys the finer benefactions of a horse to ride or nice meal
to eat. The connection between Diogenes and the beggar parasite is emphasized by the repetition of the verb *poscere* (*poscis*, 21; *poscente*, 44). The one
who begs makes a spectacle of his own need and receives not genuine tokens
of friendship but scraps that serve, however temporarily, to placate him and
keep him quiet. Moreover, by calling attention to himself, the beggar invites the
competition and jealousy of his fellow parasites, and, rather than being singled
out for worthwhile benefactions, the beggar and his competitors are thrown
a few handfuls of food with no distinction as to their moral worth or genuine
need. The Aristippus of the earlier vignette would no doubt find such begging
undignified and servile. As recounted in his poetry, Horace himself has never
displayed such begging, and he has enjoyed in return such valuable benefactions
as Maecenas's companionship and the gift of the Sabine farm.

Horace ends the poem by making two further comparisons. The parasite
that makes a display of his need is like a prostitute or a street beggar who uses
ruses in an attempt to elicit gifts from a customer or passerby. If one complains
constantly while accompanying a patron on a journey with the hope of receiv-
ing better fare, one is no different from a *meretrix*:

> Brundisium comes aut Surrentum ductus amoenum
> qui queritur salebras et acerbum frigus et imbres
> aut cistam effractam et subducta viatica plorat,
> nota refert meretricis acumina, saepe catellam,
> saepe periscelidem raptam sibi flentis, uti mox
> nulla fides damnis verisque doloribus adsit. (1.17.52–57)

> Whoever, when taken as a companion to Brundisium or pleasant Surrentum,
> complains about the poor roads or the bitter cold and rain or cries about a broken
> chest and stolen money reproduces the known tricks of a prostitute, who often
> laments that her necklace, often that her anklet has been stolen, with the result
> that soon there is no credence for her true losses and pains.

Horace's reference to a trip to Brundisium is no doubt humorously self-
referential, since one of his best known satires (1.5) recounts such a trip he took
as a *comes* of Maecenas, and in it he does not fail to complain about a number
of inconveniences experienced along the way. The allusion lends Horace's advice
credibility, since he seems to be speaking from his own experience as a client
of the wealthy, though of course the humorous tone of 1.5 removes some of the
edge from his complaints. To quote Cucchiarelli:

By now from a distance of many years, *Satires* 1.5 confirms itself as a text relevant to the fragile relationship between patron and client: in that poem the young Horace had proved that he could take a humorous view of his adventures and misadventures (e.g., the rain of lines 94–5), that he could complain, but still avoid (though perhaps just barely) the malice of the plaintive *meretrix*.[27]

The comparison of a parasitic beggar to a *meretrix* anticipates the opening of the following poem, *Epistles* 1.18, in which the true friend differs from the obsequious *scurra* to the same degree that a matron differs from a prostitute: *ut matron meretrici dispar erit atque / discolor, infido scurrae distabit amicus*, "Just as a matron will be unlike and differ from a prostitute, so will a friend differ from an untrustworthy *scurra*," 1.18.3–4. One chief difference between a *meretrix* and a *matrona* is the duration of the relationship one enjoys with each. True friendship, like marriage, is of a long duration with rewards spread out over time, whereas a parasite or prostitute, who uses tricks to accomplish his or her goal, can expect only to receive a few rewards before such ruses are discovered and the relationship ceases. Horace makes a similar point with the final exemplum of 1.17, that of the beggar in the crossroads who falsifies an affliction so as to win the sympathy and spare change of a passerby:

nec semel irrisus triviis attollere curat
fracto crure planum. licet illi plurima manet
lacrima, per sanctum iuratus dicat Osirim
'credite, non ludo; crudeles, tollite claudum,'
'quaere peregrinum' vicinia rauca reclamat. (1.17.58–62)

Nor does someone who has been made a fool of once care to lift up an imposter in the crossroads with a broken leg. Although many a tear fall from his face and he swears by holy Osiris and says, "Believe me, I am not deceiving you. Cruel men, lift up a crippled man!" "Seek out a stranger," the hoarse neighborhood shouts back.

This final example calls us back to Diogenes, who practiced his begging on the streets. Such a man has no interest in cultivating a long-term friendship with a powerful man, and the most for which he can hope are one or two transactions based purely on pity and nothing more. Such a man, like Diogenes, relies on society but cannot accurately be called a participant in it and most certainly does not exemplify the virtuous mean to which a would-be *cliens* should adhere.

To some, Horace's advice in 1.17 is disturbingly mercenary, and his argument that one should refrain from parasitic begging in order to gain more (*plus ferent*, 44) from one's friends is unsettling. But what is the "more," *plus*, that a praiseworthy client will receive? He will take part in society, like Aristippus, rather than stand outside of it, like Diogenes. He will gain a friendship of long duration based on trust, unlike the prostitute or street beggar. And the benefits he receives will be motivated by genuine friendship and will be of greater value than the paltry crumbs on which Diogenes survives or the one-time offerings given to the *meretrix* or mendicant. Rather than be disturbed at the inescapably quid pro quo nature of Roman *amicitia* as depicted in this poem and dismiss it entirely, we can try to ascertain why Horace finds Aristippus superior to Diogenes and advises a mode of friendship through which Scaeva can avoid swearing off such friendships entirely, on the one hand, and making himself a subservient beggar, on the other. Read as such the poem becomes a testament to the two most important ethical principles of *Epistles* 1, moderation and adaptability, both of which are exemplified by Aristippus and enable one to participate in friendship with the great without losing one's integrity or independence. After Aristippus's triumph in this poem, the epistolary Horace never returns to his own inflexible and extreme tendencies, and the book's remaining poems more fully examine what constitutes this moderate freedom and how it helps one achieve equanimity.

Virtus Est Medium:
The Moderate Libertas of Epistles 1.18

Lollius Maximus, the recipient of both *Epistles* 1.2 and 1.18, is the only addressee other than Maecenas to receive more than one poem in the collection. As we have seen, in *Epistles* 1.2 Horace recommends to him the avoidance of philosophical extremes and the adoption of Odyssean adaptability. In *Epistles* 1.18, which is the longest poem in the book and has been called its "climax,"[28] these same recommendations of moderation and adaptability, applied now to the social realm, form the heart of the poem.[29] Setting himself up as Lollius's ethical *monitor* (67), Horace exhorts him on the proper way to apply these principles to the world of Roman patronage, and Lollius's worry that such relationships entail loss of freedom must be read in light of Horace's own ambivalence toward his relationship with Maecenas throughout the collection. It is true, as Oliensis states, that Horace offers a voice of experience throughout the letter and reflects back onto his own past with Maecenas in order to advise Lollius, who is his younger alter ego, on the joys and pitfalls of friendship with the great. But whereas Oliensis sees *Epistles* 1.18 as a continuation of his refusal in *Epistles* 1.1 to comply with Maecenas insofar as he offers up a youthful candidate like Lollius as a substitute for his own social participation, I view it as a revision of that earlier refusal in that it sets up new parameters through which his own compliance can conditionally occur.[30] Horace dredges both his past and his present for lessons on patronage for his youthful addressee not only because he is trying to distinguish his current situation from that of Lollius but especially because, despite their difference in age, their present circumstances hold many similarities.

Even now, with his years of experience, Horace has yet to resolve for himself the misgivings toward patronage displayed by his young friend, who has just begun to navigate this tricky social phenomenon, and it is as his addressee's more advanced *condiscipulus*, as it is frequently in the collection, that he mulls over and seeks solutions for the ambivalence of each toward patronal relationships. Like Scaeva of *Epistles* 1.17, Lollius offers Horace a figure onto whom he can project his own fears and apprehensions about freedom and dependence in the social realm.[31] As in 1.17, the approach he recommends looks very much like the one he adopts toward philosophy in the opening poem. Just as there is a third path between devoted loyalty to a particular system and outright rejection of philosophical participation, so too is there a middle route between total slavery to a powerful patron and an uncompromising insistence on freedom from one. This middle path of true freedom is associated not only in *Epistles* 1.18 but throughout the collection with the proper imitation of models; in this poem the model is one's *potens amicus* but elsewhere the model is philosophical (1.1) or, as we shall see in the next chapter, poetic (1.3 and 1.19).

Horace's advice to Lollius comes in three major sections. First, he argues that Lollius's fear of becoming slavish should not lead him to the opposite extreme of insisting on an outspoken *libertas* that in the end renders him no more free or worthy of true friendship than servility. Secondly, he recommends that Lollius adapt to the expectations of his powerful friend (within moderation) and not give in to his inclination to be standoffish and withdrawn. Finally, he reinforces to Lollius the need to balance social engagement with periodic retirement and private contemplation of ethical questions, using his own episodes of withdrawal as an exemplum for his young friend. Although throughout the poem Horace urges Lollius to give public participation its due, he ends by acknowledging the simultaneous importance of private life. As in 1.17 Epicurean *lathe biosas* ranks above the stubborn and harsh aloofness espoused by the Cynics. The key to resolving one's ambivalence over the public versus the private sphere is to be adaptable to each and thus to attain equanimity.

Horace begins the poem by diagnosing a conflict in Lollius. The *libertas* to which he is naturally inclined is at odds with the loss of independence that comes, Lollius fears, with attaching himself to a powerful friend. Above all, Lollius wants to avoid the appearance of a parasitic *scurra*, and Horace reassures him that an *amicus* and a *scurra* are no more similar than a *matrona* and a *meretrix*:

si bene te novi, metues, liberrime Lolli,
scurrantis speciem praebere, professus amicum.
ut matrona meretrici dispar erit atque
discolor, infido scurrae distabit amicus. (1.18.1–4)

If I know you well, most outspoken Lollius, you will be afraid to offer the appearance of a *scurra* when you have professed yourself a friend. Just as a matron will be unlike and differ from a whore, so will a friend differ from an untrustworthy *scurra*.

Horace here quickly identifies Lollius's predicament as one that results from adhering to extremes. In his fear (*metues*) of appearing like a slavish parasite he clings to the extreme of *libertas*, and his lack of compromise is emphasized by the superlative *liberrime*.[32] Lollius fails to recognize that true *amicitia* is a mean between these extremes. In contrasting a *meretrix* with a *matrona* Horace recalls not only the preceding epistle (1.17.55) but also *Satires* 1.2, in which the prostitute and the matron form two sexual extremes that are best avoided.[33] Horace opens this satire by complaining that many people, in fearing one extreme, run to its opposite: *dum vitant stulti vitia, in contraria currunt* ("While the foolish avoid faults, they run to opposite ones," 24). *Nil medium est* (28), "there is no middle," he concludes. In *Epistles* 1.18 Horace delivers to Lollius a lesson in this elusive moderation.

Horace outlines for Lollius how the extreme of *libertas*—with which word he connotes both "freedom" and "frank" or even "hostile" speech—is a vice nearly as bad as that of the parasite's fawning servitude:

est huic diversum vitio vitium prope maius,
asperitas agrestis et inconcinna gravisque,
quae se commendat tonsa cute, dentibus atris,
dum volt libertas dici mera veraque virtus.
virtus est medium vitiorum et utrimque reductum. (1.18.5–9)

There is a vice opposed to this one and almost worse: rustic harshness that is unbecoming and severe, which recommends itself with closely cropped hair and black teeth while wanting to be called undiluted freedom and true virtue. Virtue is a mean between vices and removed from both.

Horace in these lines draws on a host of writing on friendship ranging from Aristotle to Theophrastus to Philodemus to Cicero, as has been well documented.[34] Plutarch would later write a treatise on how to distinguish flatterers from friends, in which he complains of false friends who try to avoid the appearance of servility through adopting to an extreme the frank speech expected of equals. His insistence on finding a mean between flattery and harsh speech closely echoes Horace's advice in *Epistles* 1.18 and is worthwhile to quote at some length:

διὸ δεῖ τὴν παρρησίαν ἤθει κεκρᾶσθαι καὶ λόγον ἔχειν ἀφαιροῦντα τὸ ἄγαν καὶ τὸ ἄκρατον αὐτῆς. . . . πᾶσαν μὲν γάρ, ὦ Φιλόπαππε, κακίαν φευκτέον ἐστὶ δι᾽ ἀρετῆς, οὐχὶ διὰ τῆς ἐναντίας κακίας, ὥσπερ ἔνιοι δοκοῦσιν αἰσχυντηλίαν μὲν ἀναισχυντίᾳ φεύγειν ἀγροικίαν δὲ βωμολοχίᾳ, δειλίας δὲ καὶ μαλακίας ἀπωτάτω τίθεσθαι τὸν τρόπον ἂν ἔγγιστα φαίνωνται λαμυρίας καὶ θρασύτητος. . . . αἰσχίστη δὲ κολακείας ἄρνησις ἀνωφελῶς λυπηρὸν εἶναι, καὶ κομιδῇ τινος ἀμούσου καὶ ἀτέχνου πρὸς εὔνοιαν ὁμιλίας ἀηδίᾳ καὶ χαλεπότητι φεύγειν τὸ ἀγεννὲς ἐν φιλίᾳ καὶ ταπεινόν, ὥσπερ ἀπελεύθερον ἐν κωμῳδίᾳ τὴν κατηγορίαν ἰσηγορίας ἀπόλαυσιν ἡγούμενον. ἐπεὶ τοίνυν αἰσχρὸν μέν ἐστι κολακείᾳ περιπεσεῖν διώκοντα τὸ πρὸς χάριν, αἰσχρὸν δὲ φεύγοντα κολακείαν παρρησίας ἀμετρίᾳ διαφθεῖραι τὸ φιλικὸν καὶ κηδεμονικόν, δεῖ δὲ μηδέτερον παθεῖν ἀλλ᾿ ὥσπερ ἄλλῳ τινὶ καὶ τῇ παρρησίᾳ τὸ καλὸν ἐκ τοῦ μετρίου λαβεῖν. Plutarch, *How to Tell a Flatterer from a Friend* 25 (66b–d)

Therefore it is necessary that frank speech be mixed with politeness and that there be in it language that removes what is excessive and undiluted. . . . For, Philopappus, every evil must be fled through virtue, not through the opposite evil, just as some people think it right to avoid shyness by acting shameless and rusticity by playing the buffoon and to make their character seem very far from cowardly and soft by appearing bold and audacious. . . . But the most disgraceful way of denying flattery is to cause pain uselessly, and it is the mark of one who is entirely unrefined and unskilled in kindness when in company to avoid lowliness and submissiveness in friendship through unpleasantness and severity, just like a freedman in a comedy who considers abuse to be the fruition of equal freedom of speech. And so since it is disgraceful for one trying to please to fall upon flattery, and it is disgraceful for one avoiding flattery to destroy what is friendly and thoughtful by an immoderate amount of frank speech, it is necessary to experience neither, but in frank speech just as in anything else to adopt what is proper from the mean.

The links between Plutarch and Horace are strong. Each uses a wine metaphor to describe speech that is undiluted in its severity; Horace refers to the hostile friend's *libertas* as *mera*, "unmixed," the same metaphor found in Plutarch's κεκρᾶσθαι and τὸ ἄκρατον.[35] Like Horace, Plutarch recommends a mean between extreme fawning and frank speech, which he associates with virtue, ἀρετή, and like Horace in *Satires* 1.3 he suggests that one can fall into one extreme by avoiding its opposite. In each passage, immoderate *libertas* or παρρησία comes from a fear of appearing a slavish flatterer, and Lollius displays precisely this fear in *Epistles* 1.18. But Plutarch makes explicit something that is only implicit in Horace: excessively harsh speech actually exposes the very servility that the speaker was trying to hide. Harshness is the mark of someone with little experience in the polite candor that is at the heart of true friendship. This harshness plays into the stereotype of the recently manumitted, who do not yet fully understand how to employ their new independence properly. Horace's excessively free friend also bears marks of slavery, for his shorn hair (*tonsa cuta*, 7) recalls the practice of newly manumitted slaves donning shaved heads.[36] The attribution to the harsh friend of *mera libertas* furthermore recalls a passage by Livy similarly describing the extreme acerbity of the newly freed. In this passage Philip V of Macedon complains that the Thessalians are acting like bad freedmen toward their Roman liberators:[37]

> insolenter et immodice abuti Thessalos indulgentia populi Romani, velut ex diutina siti nimis avide *meram* haurientes *libertatem*: ita servorum modo praeter spem repente manumissorum licentiam vocis et linguae experiri et iactare sese insectatione et conviciis dominorum. (Livy 39.26.7–8)

> [He claimed that] the Thessalians insolently and immoderately abused the indulgence of the Roman people, just like people who, after a long thirst, drink unmixed freedom too greedily; that, in the manner of slaves manumitted suddenly and unexpectedly, they were testing the license of their voice and tongue and were acting important by abusing and insulting their masters.

Livy explicitly connects *mera libertas* to *licentia*, a vice that the *liberrimus* Lollius currently risks exhibiting. If Lollius were to adopt excessively hostile speech as a strategy for maintaining his independence in patronal relationships, Horace warns, he would only highlight his socially inferior position. The two extremes of *libertas* and slavery simply collapse upon one another.

It is not just Lollius, however, who must learn to avoid the trap of excessive *libertas*, for there are many parallels to the opening poem that suggest that Horace himself was similarly misguided in trying to assert his independence from Maecenas by adopting excessive hostility.[38] *Epistles* 1.18 can therefore be read as a corrective to the earlier behavior displayed by the epistolary Horace. As we saw in the opening chapter, Horace in *Epistles* 1.1.2–6 likens himself to a newly freed gladiator who has retired to the countryside, and his stubborn refusal to compromise with Maecenas can be compared to the behavior of Plutarch's ἀπελεύθερος or Livy's *servi manumissi*, who try to assert their equality by making hostile allegations. There are several concrete echoes of 1.1 in 1.18 that suggest that in the earlier poem Horace is leaning too far toward the extreme of asperity described in the latter. The inflexibly orthodox Horace of 1.1.17 is described as a <u>*virtutis verae*</u> *custos rigidusque satelles*, "rigid guardian and attendant of *true virtue*," just as the truculent *amicus* of 1.18 wants his *libertas mera*, "unmixed freedom," to come across as *vera virtus*, "true virtue." I suggested in the first chapter that the unbending Horace of 1.1.17 evokes Stoicism, but the parallels with 1.18 suggest that he might equally be read as a Cynic. The harsh friend of 1.18 wants to shore up his independence by giving it a philosophical underpinning, particularly a Cynic one, as it is well known that Cynics prided themselves on their use of unrelentingly harsh speech, even—or especially—among friends.[39] Just as *inconcinnitas* had characterized the Cynic Diogenes in

1.17.29–32, here too the truculence of the harsh friend is called *inconcinna* (6). Horace in 1.18.18 refers to the harsh friend as "barking" (*elatrem*), which recalls the connection between Cynics and dogs alluded to by *mordacem Cynicum* ("biting Cynic") at 1.17.18. The truculent friend's bad haircut and rotten teeth (1.18.7) are furthermore meant as outer manifestations of his inner Cynic *libertas*, for shorn hair, in addition to being the hairstyle of newly freed slaves, was a trait especially favored by ascetic philosophers.[40] Horace himself sports just such a neglected appearance at 1.1.94–97:

> si curatus inaequali tonsore capillos
> occurri, rides; si forte subucula pexae
> trita subest tunicae, vel si toga dissidet impar,
> rides.

> If I have run to meet you when my hair has been looked after by an uneven barber, you laugh; if by chance a worn out shirt is under my brushed tunic, or if my toga sits unevenly, you laugh.

While Horace in 1.1 tries to play the part of an independent friend asserting himself to his powerful patron, his poorly cut hair does not, as we have seen, reveal philosophical detachment from the body so much as it manifests the turbulent state of his mind. In fact it is at this moment that he most strongly confesses his reliance on Maecenas:

> insanire putas sollemnia me neque rides
> nec medici credis nec curatoris egere
> a praetore dati, rerum tutela mearum
> cum sis et prave sectum stomacheris ob unguem
> de te pendentis, te respicientis amici. (1.1.101–5)

> You think that I am mad in the usual way, and you do not laugh at me, nor do you think that I need a doctor or a caretaker given by the praetor, although you are the guardian of my affairs and you grow angry on account of the badly cut nail of a friend who depends on you and looks to you for help.

Horace's attempts at independence and philosophical detachment in 1.1 ironically serve only to highlight his dependence on and need for Maecenas. The Cynic characters in the collection—whether Diogenes of 1.17, the truculent *amicus* of 1.18, or Horace himself—are exposed as not truly possessing the freedom which they claim. Their freedom is simply an act designed to hide their servility, like a freedman who tries to assert his independence by attacking those to whom he should to some degree defer.

Horace continues to evoke the world of Roman freedmen when he describes the opposite of *mera libertas* as *obsequium plus aequo*, "obsequiousness more than is right," 10. Though Horace uses the word *obsequium* to describe the behavior of a flatterer, it also indicated the "deference" or "respect" a freed slave was expected to observe toward his former master. Mouritsen describes *obsequium* as representing "a compromise between [a freedman's] emancipated status and the patrons' claim to exercise continued authority."[41] The expectation of *obsequium* therefore marks the freedman as neither completely free nor still enslaved. Both the *mera libertas* and the *obsequium plus aequo* of *Epistles* 1.18 are extremes to which a newly freed slave might incline as he stumbles gradually toward understanding how to exercise his newfound freedom appropriately. Horace applies these ideas not to freedmen, however, but to friendship, and suggests that just as some *obsequium* is necessary in the case of freed slaves, so too should a true friend offer a measure of deference to his elite *amicus*. The freedman comes in many ways to symbolize the moderated freedom Horace embraces in the final poems of *Epistles* 1, a book that significantly opens and closes with portraits of two freedmen: Horace the freed gladiator of *Epistles* 1.1 and the manumitted epistolary book of *Epistles* 1.20.

In *Epistles* 1.18, Horace further calls into question the harsh critic's so-called freedom by suggesting that it is simply a strategy aimed toward ingratiating oneself with the powerful.[42] It mimics the candor of a genuine friend, and as such, it, like flattery, is the mark of a social inferior who is trying to make himself agreeable to a potential patron, as the phrase *se commendat* (7) would suggest, since *commendare* can mean "to bring (a person or thing) to the favorable notice (of another)" (*OLD* s.v. 4). In this case the would-be client uses *libertas* as a strategy to attract the notice of a patron who fears becoming the dupe of an insincere flatterer. Both flattery and frank speech are therefore tools wielded by *amici minores*, and each can therefore be regarded as a sign of inferiority or even servility that the young Lollius would do well to avoid. The metaphor of unmixed wine reemerges in the following poem, but there it describes the slavishness of literary imitators who follow their models too closely, who quaff unmixed wine (*mero*, 11) night and day in their attempt to mimic their poetic superiors. Horace clearly expresses his disdain for these servile imitators, calling them a *servum pecus*, a "slavish herd." The harsh friend of 1.18, like these imitators, is not genuine in his frank speech but simply copies the *libertas* of others in order to pass himself off as a true friend, and he is thus as dependent on a model of behavior as these inferior poets are on a literary model. Proper imitation, which involves a mean between slavishness and utter independence, is, as we will see in the remainder of this chapter and the next, a central concern of the *Epistles* and applies equally to the spheres of philosophy, poetry, and friendship. If either Lollius or Horace wants to achieve genuine independence in his relation with his patron, he will have to avoid the *mera libertas* that is ultimately a poor imitation of the real thing.

The flatterer's extreme imitation is precisely what Horace censures in *Epistles* 1.18:

alter in obsequium plus aequo pronus et imi
derisor lecti sic nutum divitis horret,
sic iterat voces et verba cadentia tollit,
ut puerum saevo credas dictata magistro
reddere vel partes mimum tractare secundas. (10–14)

> The one [i.e., the flatterer], prone to obsequiousness more than is right and the jester on the lowest couch, shudders at the nod of the rich man, repeats his utterances and lifts up his words as they fall in such a way that you would think that a boy were repeating dictation to his harsh teacher or that a mime actor were playing the second part.

This is the behavior that Lollius is so careful not to adopt, and again Horace invites comparisons with 1.1 that suggest that this is the sort of slavish imitation that he too was trying to avoid in the earlier poem. The flatterer echoes his patron's words just like a schoolboy taking dictation from his teacher, *magister*, or like a second mime actor imitating the lead. The use of the words *puer* and *magister* in line 14 evoke the schoolroom and but also hint that the flatterer is nothing but a slave, since *puer* was a word often applied to slaves (*OLD* s.v. 5) and the word "teacher," *magister*, also means "master." The servile aspects of the flatterer are brought out by his dependence on the rich man's *nutus*, "nod," the mark of an obedient slave in *Epistles* 2.2.6.[43] His repetition of his master's every word, combined with the schoolroom imagery, looks back especially to the corrupt teachings of Janus in the first poem, which the young and old men of Rome unquestioningly hear dictated and repeat verbatim: *haec recinunt iuvenes dictata senesque*, "these things, having been dictated, the young and old man sing back," 1.1.55. Horace contrasts himself with these slavish students and aspires instead to proper imitation. His refusal to repeat a master's words is especially evident at 1.1.14, where he rejects swearing an oath to a philosophical *magister*: *nullius addictus iurare in verba magistri*. But in the philosophical realm, unlike the social realm, Horace does not run to the opposite extreme of uncompromising *libertas*. Instead, he does employ philosophical models, but he freely adapts their words to suit his own purposes. The social approach he recommends to Lollius in 1.18 has many similarities to this philosophical approach in that it involves a mean between total slavishness and total freedom and exercises the proper degree of imitation.

Throughout this reading of the *Epistles* I have emphasized the virtue of adaptability as a necessary component of moderation. Horace's description of the slavish imitation of the flatterer, however, illustrates the dangers of taking adaptability to an extreme. Excessive adaptability leads, he suggests in 1.18, not only to slavish *obsequium* but also to a loss of identity, since the flatterer changes himself with radical flexibility to imitate his patron, and his individuality ultimately disappears behind whatever mask he is currently wearing. Horace's description of the flatterer recalls especially a passage from Cicero's *De Amicitia* 92–93, in which he complains of the flatterer's lack of a uniform personality. Cicero quotes the parasite Gnatho's description of his skillful ability to imitate in Terence's *Eunuch*: *quidquid dicunt laudo; id rursum si negant, laudo id quoque. / negat quis, nego; ait, aio. postremo imperavi egomet / mihi omnia assentari* ("Whatever they say, I praise it; if in turn they reject it, I praise that too. If anyone says no, I say no; if one says yes, I say yes. In short, I have commanded myself to agree to all things," 251–53). Gnatho's echoing of his patrons' words looks very much like the flatterer's behavior in Horace's epistle. Cicero strongly criticizes the changeability of such a flatterer:

> nam cum amicitiae vis sit in eo ut unus quasi animus fiat ex pluribus, qui id fieri poterit, si ne in uno quidem quoque unus animus erit idemque semper, sed varius commutabilis multiplex? quid enim potest esse tam flexibile, tam devium, quam animus eius, qui ad alterius non modo sensum ac voluntatem, sed etiam voltum atque nutum convertitur?

> For since it is the strength of friendship that one soul, as it were, is made from multiple ones, how can this happen, if not even in one person there will be a soul always one and the same, but various, changeable, and manifold? For what can be so flexible, so erratic as the mind of one who changes not only his feeling and desire to that of another, but also his countenance and nod?

Cicero complains that such a person cannot maintain a consistent identity, *unus animus*, or remain the same in every situation (*idemque semper*) because he is always imitating another. Horace discredits this extreme flexibility as well, since it renders its practitioner servile and results in a loss of self. Appropriate adaptability is illustrated well by Aristippus in 1.17, who can encounter a range of situations and roles without sacrificing the consistency of his character. In *Epistles* 2.2.199–200, a passage that I have already cited several times as a nice illustration of Aristippean adaptability, Horace shows that the goal of measured adaptability—rather than slavish imitation or extreme flexibility—is to be able to face different circumstances with consistency: *ego, utrum / nave ferar magna an parva, ferar unus et idem*, "I, whether I will be carried in a big or small boat, will be carried as one and the same man." Horace's language here echoes that used by Cicero in the passage above, with *unus et idem* recalling *unus animus* and *idemque semper*. In *Epistles* 1.18.10–14 Horace makes it clear that the midpoint between slavishness and truculence that he champions is at odds with the radical flexibility of the malleable and slavish imitator.

Horace takes it for granted that Lollius will object to such slavish behavior, and in lines 15–20 he returns to the topic of the excessively hostile friend in order to show Lollius that this behavior is just as bad as that of its opposite. Whereas the flatterer will copy his patron's every whim, the harsh friend will disagree over the smallest matters and will refuse to follow his patron's lead in anything:

alter rixatur de lana saepe caprina et
propugnat nugis armatus: 'scilicet, ut non
sit mihi prima fides?' et 'vere quod placet, ut non
acriter elatrem? Pretium aetas altera sordet.'
ambigitur quid enim? Castor sciat an Docilis plus;
Brundisium Minuci melius via ducat an Appi. (15–20)

The other often argues about goat wool and fights in arms over trifles: "If you please, should I not be believed first?" And "Should I not bark out fiercely what I truly think? The prize of a second lifetime is not worth it [i.e., censoring my opinion]. And what is disputed? Whether Castor or Docilis knows more,[44] whether the Minucian or Appian is a better road to Brundisium.

The harsh friend is as quarrelsome as the flatterer is fawning. Horace suggests here that there are simply some topics not worthy of dispute among friends and that the true *amicus* should exercise a certain degree of acquiescence in these matters. The mention of Brundisium is especially interesting because it forms a link between this and the preceding poem, *Epistles* 1.17.52–57, quoted above, where Horace criticizes the friend who goes with his patron to Brundisium only to complain the entire way about the roads. As we have seen, Horace suggests in 1.17 that such complaints are motivated by the desire for financial gain, since the *amicus minor* hopes that he can thereby secure better traveling conditions and accommodations. Horace compares such behavior to the tricks of a *meretrix*, who hopes to acquire gifts for herself by complaining about the loss of various items of jewelry but who ultimately fails to receive gifts of real value that reflect genuine affection. By recalling this passage in *Epistles* 1.18 Horace suggests once again that the harsh critic, like the flatterer, is ultimately motivated by money and benefactions and that his behavior is every bit as meretricious as his servile opposite. The only way for Lollius to avoid such mercenary behavior is to hit upon the mean between these two extremes, that of the true freedom of a genuine friend.

The poem's next section (21–36) expands further upon the theme of imitation of and acquiescence to rich patrons, and Horace recommends a moderate degree of compliance while criticizing those who reproduce not only the personality but also the faults of their patrons. In lines 21–31 Horace states that one who imitates the vices of a *dives amicus* (24), such as sexual passion, gambling, the desire for glory and wealth, and the fear of poverty, will meet either with his patron's severe disapproval or with his desire to correct such faults. The client's imitation of his patron here takes on a competitive quality, and Horace imagines the patron censuring such behavior, telling his client *meae—contendere noli—/ stultitiam patiuntur opes, tibi parvola res est. / arta decet sanum comitem toga*: *desine mecum / certare,* "My wealth—do not compete with it—allows foolishness. Your wealth is very small. A narrow toga befits a sound companion. Cease to contend with me," 28–31.[45] What the patron wants, Horace says, is a client who is wiser and even more virtuous than he is (27–28) and who maintains an identity separate from his own. In trying to mimic the lifestyle of his patron the client behaves in an unbecoming fashion (*decet*), unlike the Aristippus of 1.17, who can adopt the lifestyle of a rich or poor man with equal decorum and without assuming his patron's vices.

A client who imitates the decadent lifestyle of his patron will lose his freedom not only figuratively, like the flatterer, but also literally. Horace illustrates this by telling Lollius about a certain Eutrapelus, who would hasten a greedy client's demise by furnishing him with luxurious garments:

> Eutrapelus cuicumque nocere volebat
> vestimenta dabat pretiosa: beatus enim iam
> cum pulchris tunicis sumet nova consilia et spes,
> dormiet in lucem, scorto postponet honestum
> officium, nummos alienos pascet, ad imum
> Thraex erit aut holitoris aget mercede caballum. (1.18.31–36)

Eutrapelus used to give costly garments to whomever he wanted to harm, for now the happy man will take up new plans and hopes along with the beautiful tunics. He will sleep into the day, he will put honest work after a prostitute, he will feed his debt, and in the end he will wind up a gladiator or drive the horse of a vegetable salesman for pay.

Eutrapelus uses the client's desire to conform to his patron against him. Since such a client has no genuine identity of his own he adapts his behavior to the costly garments he has been given and ultimately ends up losing what little wealth he does possess and forfeiting his freedom. Excessive imitation here leads directly to servitude. The focus on clothing in this passage strongly recalls by contrast the behavior in the previous poem of Aristippus, who is indifferent to the quality of his cloak and instead maintains his personality and behavior no matter what he is wearing. Because he has a strong identity distinct from that of his patron, Aristippus is not subject to the same afflictions that beset Eutrapelus's misguided client, and Aristippus can thus successfully navigate the complex world of friendship with the great that ruins men like Eutrapelus's client in this poem or Mena in 1.7. Thanks to his integrity of character, no patron has the power to remove Aristippus's independence in this way, and he can wear *vestimenta pretiosa* without conforming to the faulty model of his patron. Lollius, like Aristippus in 1.17, must adhere to a mean between the slavish imitator who is ultimately destroyed by such costly vestments and the Cynic critic who, like Diogenes, can tolerate only the lowliest rags.

Lollius's inclination, however, is not so much toward slavishly imitating the faults of his patron as it is toward the opposite extreme of refusing to comply with a patron altogether. Horace now warns Lollius against this extreme in the poem's following section (40–66). Lollius, it seems, is a poet, and his attention to his poetic activity should not be an excuse, Horace warns, against participating in his patron's preferred pastimes, such as hunting: *nec, cum venari volet ille, poemata panges,* "nor when he wants to hunt will you compose poems," 40. Horace's choice of hunting, which Gurval refers to as a "solemn sport for Roman men,"[46] is highly interesting since it constitutes a kind of *ludus*, and it was Maecenas's desire for Horace's participation in *ludus*, with which Horace refuses to comply, that opens *Epistles* 1.1. Such *ludus*, Horace there argues, is incompatible with the philosophical poetic program he currently is undertaking. Now it is Lollius whose intellectual pursuits are at odds with his patron's desire for him to participate in *ludus*, and Horace encourages his young alter ego to put off his poetic contemplations and adapt to the desires of his friend. Furthermore, the playful activities in which Horace urges Lollius to participate, such as hunting, not only involve spectacle, like the gladiatorial imagery of *Epistles* 1.1, but even impinge on the rural world that in the opening poem is presented as discrete from the patron's involvement.[47] Lollius must not only adapt to his patron's wishes but also allow these wishes to influence even his private pastimes. The advice that Horace gives to Lollius therefore provides us with a stance that has fundamentally changed since the first epistle.

Horace offers as an exemplum for compromise the story of Amphion and Zethus as recounted in Euripides's now fragmentary *Antiope*. Lollius must yield to his patron's more social and engaged pursuits just as the musical Amphion yielded to the active character of his brother:

> gratia sic fratrum geminorum Amphionis atque
> Zethi dissiluit, donec suspecta severo
> conticuit lyra. fraternis cessisse putatur
> moribus Amphion: tu cede potentis amici
> lenibus imperiis, quotiensque educet in agros
> Aetolis onerata plagis iumenta canesque,
> surge et inhumanae senium depone Camenae,
> cenes ut pariter pulmenta laboribus empta. (1.18.41–48)

> This is how the esteem between the twin brothers Amphion and Zethus was broken up, until the lyre, which had been viewed with suspicion by the severe one, grew silent. Amphion is thought to have yielded to his brother's character. You, yield to the gentle commands of your powerful friend, and, however often he leads the mules, weighed down with Aetolian nets, and the dogs into the field, rise up and set aside the gloom of the unsociable Muse, so that you may dine together with him on food bought with labor.[48]

This exemplum of Amphion and Zethus is carefully chosen by Horace and demands analysis. Though Euripides's *Antiope* is now fragmentary, its extensive quotation in Plato's *Gorgias* allows us to reconstruct its plot and themes, particularly the content of the *agon* between the two brothers.[49] As scholars point out, this *agon* centers on whether the life of engagement or the life of contemplation is superior, with Amphion arguing for the latter and Zethus the former. Amphion's life of disengagement and poetic and philosophical contemplation aligns with that preferred both by Lollius in 1.18 and Horace himself in 1.1, but now Horace's changed attitude leads him to put forth this exemplum in support of compromise and engagement. Nightingale offers a brief summary of Euripides's play:

> The plot hinges on the rescue of Antiope . . . from her murderous uncle and aunt, Lycus and Dirce, by her long-lost sons, Amphion and Zethus. Before saving the woman that will turn out to be their mother, however, the brothers must put aside their differences. The brothers rehearse these differences in the famous *agon*. In spite of powerful arguments, Amphion is finally worsted in this debate and yields to his brother. They then proceed to engineer their mother's rescue, though they are prevented at the last minute from putting their uncle to death by Hermes, who makes an appearance at the end of the play. Hermes restores order by restraining the angry brothers and establishing them as the rightful rulers of Cadmeia. He also pronounces that the music from the lyre of Amphion will cause the stones and trees to move unaided and form the walls of Thebes. The *deus ex machina* thus not only provides a resolution to the plot but also resolves the question raised in the *agon* between the two brothers: though Amphion lost the argument with his brother, he is nonetheless vindicated by Hermes at the end of the play, for it is his music that will build the walls of Thebes.[50]

This plot outline is useful for our understanding of *Epistles* 1.18, since Horace's advice to Lollius follows very much the same trajectory. In the play, Amphion is convinced to yield to the active life of his brother so that they may work in cooperation with one another, but this compromise is not taken to an extreme. In the end, thanks to Hermes's intervention, the importance of the private life is upheld since it is through Amphion's musical pursuits that the walls of Thebes will be constructed. The play therefore validates both ways of life and suggests that ultimately they are complexly intertwined with one another.[51] For the remainder of *Epistles* 1.18 Horace will outline to Lollius the advantages of yielding to his active patron, but at the end of the poem he will reinforce to Lollius the equal importance of maintaining a private life of ethical and philosophical contemplation. Both spheres are simultaneously important and necessary for a man of moderation and adaptability.

In lines 49–52 Horace expands on why hunting is an appropriate pastime for Lollius, and the reasons he gives draw attention to the hunt as spectacle. The hunt is a traditional pursuit of Roman men, he claims, and Lollius's youthful strength especially qualifies him for this activity. Lollius is, after all, as stout and nimble as a hunting dog or wild boar.[52] What is more, he is splendid to look at while participating in active, manly pursuits, and he has already taken part in the active life of a soldier:

> adde, virilia quod speciosius arma
> non est qui tractet: scis quo clamore coronae
> proelia sustineas campestria. denique saevam
> militiam puer et Cantabrica bella tulisti
> sub duce, qui templis Parthorum signa refigit
> nunc et, siquid abest, Italis adiudicat armis. (1.18.52–57)

> Add the fact that that no one wields manly weapons more splendidly than you. You know how the audience shouts when you face the battles of the Campus Martius. Furthermore, while still a boy you underwent harsh military service and Cantabrian wars under the leader who now unfastens the standards from the temples of the Parthians and, if anything is wanting, assigns it to Italian arms.

Horace's description of Lollius's drills in the Campus Martius invites us to view them as a kind of spectacle, for his beauty and strength attract the eyes and approval of the audience. It is not just this play warfare that qualifies Lollius to take part in hunting and thus to comply with his patron, but his past real military service as well, for he served in Spain under the command of Augustus, a campaign that concluded in 25 B.C.[53] Lollius, it seems, has not always clung to the withdrawal and poetic composition to which he now is attracted, and his past activities have in fact had a sizable public dimension in that they brought him into the sphere of Augustus and his military campaigns. This detail adds a political dimension that must not be ignored to Lollius's desire to keep aloof from the demands of a patron.[54] Here again Lollius's attitude should be compared to that of Horace in 1.1.

Horace's desire for *libertas* in 1.1 and his gradual redefinition of it over the course of the collection must be read in light of the political reality of Horace's day and the solidification of Augustan power. Horace in the opening poem clings to freedom as an extreme reaction to his earlier "slavery" to Maecenas, in whose *ludus* he ably performed but whose desire for continued service he roundly rejects. Horace's formulation of slavery versus freedom in 1.1 was in many ways reflective of a pull toward Republican *libertas* that was born out of a fear that he had previously leaned too far in the opposite direction. Lollius's situation in 1.18 is very much like that of Horace. Like Horace, he has performed previous service to the emperor and now, like Horace, he reacts to his previous compliance by moving toward the other extreme of nonparticipation and insistence on *libertas*. As Bowditch puts it, "The independent nature which Lollius fears losing, his *liberrimus* character, stands metaphorically for the political liberties that suffered erosion under the Principate."[55] As we have seen, Horace's reformulation of *libertas* as a mean, moreover, anticipates in many ways Tacitus's later suggestions for the best way to live under an emperor (i.e., by adopting a middle ground between resistance and slavish compliance). What Horace offers Lollius is therefore a strategy for how best to manage one's public and private life in an age of empire:[56] comply—with moderation—with the new political reality and yield to the *imperia* of one's patron. "The ultimate patron," Bowditch states, "is the emperor, and lands fall into line beneath the protection of Rome, that is, as *clientelae* to its patronage, in much the same way as the speaker advises Lollius to fall in with his friend."[57] But Lollius's compliance should only go so far and should never extend to the subservient behavior of the flattering toady. It is significant that in lines 1.18.54–57, while Horace uses Lollius's past service to Augustus as a justification for participating in the hunt with his patron, he never urges Lollius to reenlist himself in such active military activity. Hunting, though related to *militia*, is hardly its equivalent and takes place not on the field of imperial combat but in the Roman *rus*. Hunting is therefore a nice compromise between the life of nonparticipation to which Lollius is drawn and that of devoted service to the imperial house that military service would suggest. Though the hunt involves spectacle and compromise, it does not lead to a public display of the disparity between patron and client. In line 48, after all, the hunt results not in a public demonstration of Lollius's deference but in a private dinner party in which both patron and client equally (*pariter*) partake of the food they jointly won.

The recommendation of moderate compliance is again given overtones of spectacle and politics in the section that follows:

> ac ne te retrahas et inexcusabilis absis:
> quamvis nil extra numerum fecisse modumque
> curas, interdum nugaris rure paterno.
> partitur lintres exercitus, Actia pugna
> te duce per pueros hostili more refertur;

adversarius est frater, lacus Hadria, donec
alterutrum velox Victoria fronde coronet.
consentire suis studiis qui crediderit te,
fautor utroque tuum laudabit pollice ludum. (1.18.58–66)

And so that you do not withdraw and stay away inexcusably: although you take
care to do nothing out of tune (*extra numerum modumque*), from time to time
you are frivolous on your paternal estate. The army divides the boats, with you as
leader the Battle of Actium is staged by your slaves in a hostile manner; your
brother is the adversary, the lake is the Adriatic, until swift Victory crowns one of
you with a garland of leaves. Whoever believes that you agree with his pastimes
will, as your supporter, praise your play with each thumb.

I have already discussed this passage in chapter 1 as an inverse of the refusal that
Horace offers to Maecenas in 1.1, and my discussion here will necessarily restate
some of my earlier observations. Whereas Horace in 1.1 had refused "gladiatorial" participation, he here urges Lollius to participate in *ludus* in such a way
that his activity will meet with his patron's commendation, and the description
of the patron's thumb alludes to the practice at gladiatorial games of the audience gesturing their approval or disapproval. Uncompromising withdrawal,
such as Horace adopted in 1.1, is no longer appropriate, and compliance with a
powerful patron must be granted. Rather than argue with his patron about trifles, as the truculent friend does (*nugae*, 16), Lollius is praised for such "trifling"
(*nugaris*). The *ludus* in which Lollius participates, although it takes place on his
"paternal estate" (*rure paterno*), has a hugely public dimension in that it recre-
ates none other than the Battle of Actium. Whereas Lollius's "unsociable Muse"
(*inhumanae Camenae*, 47) would seem to preclude public political topics, here
his behavior, which is given poetic overtones (*numerum modumque*), collapses
the distinction between public and private. It is this willingness to combine
withdrawal with participation by integrating public concerns into his private
life that meets with his patron's approval, and by seeking such approval Lollius
takes on the aspects of gladiatorial spectacle that in *Epistles* 1.1 were for Horace
tantamount to slavery. We therefore might think that Horace is urging Lollius
to take on behavior that could undermine the *libertas* to which he aspires, but
Horace makes it clear that Lollius should not carry such conciliatory behavior
to an extreme. At line sixty he adds the important qualification *interdum*; such
acquiescence is only to be occasional and thus moderate.

One important difference between the compliance that Horace urges here
and that he himself had refused in 1.1 is that whereas in 1.1 it was the *populus*
who would decide the fate of the gladiatorial Horace, here it is the patron alone
with whose approval or disapproval Lollius's *ludus* might meet. This places an
important condition on Lollius's compliance. Whereas Maecenas had threatened

to remove Horace completely from the private sphere and subject him to the whims of the urban crowd, Lollius's patron will have to be content with Lollius making space for engagement within his essentially private life. While Horace's situating of Lollius's *ludus* for his patron in the countryside might be taken to suggest the patron's interjecting himself too far within Lollius's private realm and thus threatening Lollius's *libertas*, it nevertheless also places an important restriction on the patron's expectations. Lollius's reenactment of Actium, furthermore, suggests that he is not completely curtailing his *libertas* in this display and that he in fact may be asserting it. As Gurval, Bowditch, and Ahl have shown, there is something uncomfortably subversive about Lollius's depiction of Actium.[58] Whereas Augustan propaganda downplayed the civil nature of the war, Lollius takes no measures to disguise this aspect of the battle, since his reenactment is fought between him and his brother on their *rure paterno*. It is because this *ludus* is restricted to the private realm that Lollius can assert his freedom of speech in a way that would be prohibited publicly. Though his *libertas* has been restricted he is still able to employ it with moderation yet in a way that meets with his patron's official approval.

Following Horace's description of Lollius's rural reenactment of Actium, he goes on to outline a number of rules that the proper client should follow. He should be careful about what he says and to whom, keep secrets faithfully, avoid sexual liaisons with his patron's slaves, and take care about whom he recommends to his *potens amicus* (67–85). So intricate are the rules for proper *amicitia* that Horace issues a warning to Lollius and, by extension, any young man who is considering attaching himself to a wealthy patron: *dulcis inexpertis cultura potentis amici: / expertus metuet*, "the cultivation of a powerful friend is sweet to inexperienced men, but the experienced man will be afraid," 86–87. Though Mayer suggests that this passage "parodies" Pindar, fr. 110, in which it is war rather than *cultura potentis amici* that causes the experienced man to fear,[59] the Pindaric echo nevertheless lends this line significant weight since *amicitia* takes on a level of dangerous activity that is comparable—figuratively if not literally—to that faced by soldiers in battle, and this explains the intense anxiety that both Horace and Lollius experience when considering the role of an *amicus minor*. Calling these "the harshest lines for Maecenas to overread," Oliensis suggests that Horace here "issues a general warning against Lollius' chosen career . . . where the shift from plural to singular singles out Horace as the man who has tried this kind of 'friendship' and found it wanting."[60] Rather than view these lines as a repudiation of *amicitia*, however, we can read them as a call for it to be entered with opened eyes, the same sort of opened eyes that Horace, thanks to his many years of *amicitia* with Maecenas, currently possesses.[61] Nor is Lollius the inexperienced man who thinks that friendship

with the powerful is purely *dulcis*, since the experienced man's fear (*metuet*) is
what Lollius himself exhibits at the poem's opening (*metues*, 1). Through taking
Horace's advice to heart, Lollius will not necessarily assuage his fear, but he will
be more prepared to endure the unpredictable aspects of *amicitia*. To echo the
nautical metaphor of the lines that follow, such preparedness will make him
more capable of navigating the potentially dangerous waters of Roman patronage: *tu, dum tua navis in alto est, / hoc age, ne mutata retrorsum te ferat aura,*
"you, while your ship is on the deep, see to it that a changed breeze not bear you
back," 87–88. Nautical metaphors are one of Horace's favorite ways of illustrating adaptability and moderation,[62] and in these lines it becomes apparent that
by adopting these qualities Lollius will be able not only to conform from time
to time to his patron's activities but also to confront with equanimity this complex system and the potential problems it brings with it. The unexpected difficulties that arise from friendship with the great will not be disturbing enough
to throw him off course.

The final call for the would-be client to adapt himself to his patron comes
in lines 89–95, where Horace takes one last opportunity to offer this perhaps
unwelcome advice to the potentially truculent and outspoken Lollius. Clients
should, he recommends, try to harmonize their personalities to those of their
patrons, since men of disparate characters rarely interact well:

> oderunt hilarem tristes tristemque iocosi,
> sedatum celeres, agilem navumque remissi,
> potores [bibuli media de nocte Falerni
> oderunt] porrecta negantem pocula, quamuis
> nocturnos iures te formidare tepores;
> deme supercilio nubem: plerumque modestus
> occupat obscuri speciem, taciturnus acerbi. (1.18.89–95)

> The gloomy hate the cheerful man, and the jovial hate the gloomy. The hyper hate
> the calm, and the relaxed hate the one who is active and energetic. Tippling drink-
> ers of Falernian in the middle of the night hate the one who refuses the offered
> cups, even if you should swear that [you do so because] you fear nocturnal fevers.
> Remove the cloud from your brow. Generally the restrained man takes on the
> appearance of one who is secretive, and the quiet man of one who is harsh.

These lines might make tough reading for Lollius. He is to adapt himself to the
personality of his patron for the sake of greater harmony between them, but he
might argue that such behavior approaches too closely to the extreme of the
flatterer who mimics or copies his patron's behavior. From what we have gleaned
about Lollius from the poem, it is not unlikely that he might give the impression of being harsher, gloomier, and more aloof than is appropriate and that

this might threaten potential friendships. It is one thing, however, for a flatterer to mimic his patron slavishly, but something else for an *amicus* to accommodate his personality to his companion for the sake of a harmonious friendship.[63] Like the Torquatus of *Epistles* 1.5, for example, he should put off the severity to which he is inclined and adapt himself to the amenable personality that lends itself to companionship and friendship. Such advice might be inappropriate for one who naturally leans too far toward the extreme of flattery, but it is worthwhile for an addressee who leans too far toward the opposite. The exhortation that he "remove the gloom from his brow" especially warns Lollius against excessive severity or *acerbitas*, since a gloomy brow is associated by Martial, for example, with uncompromising and old-fashioned Roman sternness.[64] As Fraenkel says of these lines, Lollius should "not parade the *triste supercilium* of the rigid champion of virtue."[65]

Horace does not, however, expect Lollius to give up his personal contemplation and withdrawal altogether, and he ends the poem by reinforcing just how important private pursuits are to one's well-being and equanimity. Horace's poem therefore very much follows the same trajectory as Euripides's *Antiope*, where, as we have seen, private study and intellectual pursuits must give way to the demands of the active life but where ultimately the life of withdrawal is given its proper due. Just as *libertas* must be balanced by *obsequium* in 1.18, so too must participation with and acquiescence to a patron be balanced by a healthy amount of personal reflection and secluded contemplation:

> inter cuncta leges et percontabere doctos,
> qua ratione queas traducere leniter aevum,
> num te semper inops agitet vexetque cupido,
> num pavor et rerum mediocriter utilium spes,
> virtutem doctrina paret naturane donet,
> quid minuat curas, quid te tibi reddat amicum,
> quid pure tranquillet, honos an dulce lucellum,
> an secretum iter et fallentis semita vitae. (1.18.96–103)

> Among all this you should read and interrogate the wise as to how you can lead your life comfortably; whether needy desire will always harass and trouble you or whether fear and hope for things that are of little use will; whether learning provides virtue or nature bestows it; what diminishes cares; what renders you a friend to yourself; what perfectly produces tranquility, whether it is honor or sweet gain or the secret path and side-road of an unnoticed life.

This final section reassures Lollius that he does not have to—indeed he should not—disavow entirely his individual preferences or put aside his need for the private life of retirement. Though some scholars have suggested that here Horace, in recommending the private life, performs an about-face that undercuts all the foregoing advice on how to engage with patrons, *inter cuncta* makes it clear that this private contemplation is to happen concurrently with participation in *amicitia*.[66] As Mayer states, *inter cuncta* "refers to all the activities . . . that have been discussed hitherto."[67] It is the intellectual activity done in seclusion that will provide Lollius with the inner core necessary to engage with and adapt to patrons without losing his consistency or integrity. Without these tools *inops cupido*, *pavor*, and *rerum spes* might lead him to the destructive behavior of Eutrapelus's client or the slavish behavior of a fawning flatterer. These lines remind Lollius that the most important friendship is the one he has with himself (*quid te tibi reddat amicum*), and this is a friendship that is renewed and built when withdrawn from the demands of a *potens amicus*. This is the same kind of friendship with one's self that Horace too revives by returning again and again to the Sabine countryside, the "little farm that restores me to myself," (*mihi me reddentis agelli, Epist.* 1.14.1). It is an *amicitia* that cannot be provided by a wealthy patron but must be acquired on one's own, not through *honos* or *lucellum* but through the part of life that is inaccessible to another. The ability to be above all a friend to himself is what will enable Lollius to be a genuine friend to others as well. Horace's advice to Lollius to apply himself to ethical study in private in these lines complements rather than undercuts the advice on patronage that has preceded it. By attaining to both spheres of *amicitia*, Lollius will live a well-balanced life equipped with adaptability and moderation.

In the final lines of the poem Horace shifts attention away from Lollius and onto himself as an exemplum for the benefits that come from withdrawal and seclusion. This concluding section invites us to consider Horace's situation and struggles as being parallel to those of Lollius and justifies the idea that Horace's ambivalence toward public participation and private withdrawal can be read behind that of Lollius:[68]

> me quotiens reficit gelidus Digentia rivus,
> quem Mandela bibit, rugosus frigore pagus,
> quid sentire putas, quid credis, amice, precari?
> 'sit mihi quod nunc est, etiam minus, et mihi vivam
> quod superest aevi, siquid superesse volunt di;
> sit bona librorum et provisae frugis in annum
> copia neu fluitem dubiae spe pendulus horae.'
> sed satis est orare Iovem quae ponit et aufert:
> det vitam, det opes: aequum mi animum ipse parabo. (1.18.104–12)

However often I am restored by the cold stream Digentia, which Mandela, a town wrinkled with cold, drinks, what do you think I feel? For what, friend, do you think I pray? "May I have what I have now, even less, and may I live for myself what remains of my life, if the gods desire that anything should remain. May I have a good abundance of books and of grain supplied in advance to last the year, and may I not vacillate and waver with the hope of an uncertain hour." But it is enough to ask Jove for whatever he grants and takes away. Let him give life; let him give resources. I myself will provide equanimity for myself.

These concluding lines demonstrate to Lollius the importance of private contemplation as well as portray the independence that comes from such withdrawal. Horace's focus on himself through the use of the first person illustrates well the self-sufficiency that Horace's rural escapes provide: *mihi . . . mihi* (107), *mihi . . . ipse parabo* (112). Such self-sufficiency was in the preceding poem championed by the adaptable Aristippus (*ego ipse mihi*, 1.17.19), who managed to combine this independence with a life of engagement with wealthy patrons. Horace's retirement to the stream Digentia and the Sabine countryside is not permanent, though it is often repeated (*quotiens*). Rather than make himself a perfect example of equanimity Horace clearly underscores the reason for why such withdrawal is necessary: his tendency to vacillate and experience ambivalence: *neu fluetem dubiae spe pendulus horae*. It is only through the periodic experience of the private life that such inconsistency can be healed and replaced with equanimity (*aequum animum*). This equanimity cannot come from without as a gift from Jove—or from Augustus or a patron—but must come only from within oneself. Lollius too needs to carve out a sphere for himself in which such equanimity can be attained and without which the mean espoused by Horace cannot be reached. At the moment Lollius is asserting his independence through the wrong kind of uncompromising withdrawal and an outspokenness that borders on Cynicism, and Horace urges him to replace this with an adaptable approach that allows him to enjoy simultaneously participation with powerful friends and the private, almost Epicurean, sphere of philosophical reflection.

The prayer that closes the poem furthermore suggests that Horace's private world cannot be completely extricated from his public friendships, since this rural retreat is what most clearly binds Horace to Maecenas, without which such self-sufficiency and autonomy, as we have seen in chapter 5, would be impossible. To quote Oliensis, "Maecenas' name may be missing from this passage. But we can hear, and Maecenas would have heard, the thanks Horace can best express thus indirectly."[69] McGann similarly sees Horace's own *potens amicus* lurking behind this passage: "As the friend of Maecenas and the proprietor of the *Sabinum*, he has combined a life of pleasing the great with one of withdrawal."[70] Even as Horace ends by illustrating the virtues of seclusion and private reflection, his appreciation for his Sabine farm and the independence it bestows illustrates to Lollius the best kind of benefit that he can hope to derive from participating in friendship. If he is lucky, he just might find a Maecenas of his own and acquire a seat of withdrawal and reflection that provides a similar kind of self-sufficiency and independence. Horace's own situation provides an exemplum of the moderated *libertas* that he sketches throughout the poem.

Throughout *Epistles* 1.18 Horace sets up a series of antitheses that one must ultimately bridge through moderation and adaptability. Between *libertas mera* and *obsequium plus aequo* there is a desirable freedom that enables us to keep the ties that bind us to society intact without a loss of autonomy. Between the outright imitation of a rich *magister* and the adoption of excessive harshness there is a midpoint that allows us to bridge the gap between friends of disparate temperaments. The advice that Horace offers to Lollius not only applies to the current situation of the addressee but must be viewed within the collection as a whole and especially as reflective of Horace's own progress throughout the book. The ring composition of addressees—1.1 to Maecenas, 1.2 to Lollius, 1.18 to Lollius, 1.19 to Maecenas—suggests that Horace has come full circle and is now bringing his ethical pursuits and his return to the schoolroom to a close. He began in 1.1 by leaning too close to the same extremes, harsh *libertas* and uncompromising withdrawal, to which Lollius is drawn and mistakenly interpreted these extremes as the source of true freedom. Over the course of the collection, however, Horace has learned the superiority of the mean, which allows one to adapt to and reconcile various spheres and systems without a loss of independence. In 1.17 and 1.18 we see this moderation and adaptability applied to the social realm, but we have also seen it applied to the city and country (chapters 5 and 6) and to the philosophical realm (chapters 1 and 3). In each of these spheres total adherence to one route is rejected, as is the false belief that one must make an either/or choice between two opposing paths. We can *both* write philosophical poetry *and* refuse swearing to one system; we can enjoy *both* the country *and* the city without enslaving ourselves to either; and we can *both* interact with patrons *and* maintain our private sphere without compromising ourselves. In each of these areas Horace opens up a third path between engagement and detachment, and in 1.18 he clearly associates this third, middle path with freedom. In the next chapter we will see him apply these same principles of adaptability, moderation, and free imitation to the poetic sphere.

8

Moderate Freedom and Poetry

Epistles 1.3 and 1.19

A S WE SAW IN THE PREVIOUS CHAPTER, the major theme of *Epistles* 1.18 is the appropriate mean in friendship, particularly as regards imitation. The true friend will neither slavishly ape the words of his patron nor assert his *libertas* through overly harsh speech. This mean aligns closely with that put forth in the opening epistle in the sphere of philosophical study, where Horace adopts a middle course between orthodox philosophical allegiance (slavery) and cutting himself off entirely from all philosophical systems (freedom). In this chapter I examine the ways in which Horace applies this same mean between freedom and slavery to the poetic realm and how he relates this to friendship, both that between his young acquaintances and that between Maecenas and himself.[1] In *Epistles* 1.3 Horace commends his young friend Florus's adherence to the mean in poetic imitation, yet Florus's inability to apply this same sense of compromise and moderation to his friendships and ambitions undercuts his poetic success. In *Epistles* 1.19 Horace describes his own past imitative technique as being in line with the mean and claims that his previous poetry—specifically the *Epodes* and *Odes*—embody this moderated freedom. Whereas in 1.1 his past poetry rendered Horace a servile gladiator dependent upon the whims of the crowd, it is here reconfigured as embodying the best kind of imitation and independence. The shift that we have seen occur over the course of the book from uncompromising freedom to accepting a degree of dependence is now enacted in the poetic realm as Horace transitions from denigrating the slavishness of his former poetry to reassessing it as representing the correct combination of dependence and freedom. Horace's own social standing similarly partakes of both freedom and slavery as he simultaneously declares independence from the common mob of readers and courts the approval and acclaim of the learned elite, thereby accepting a measured degree of mastery by others whose literary judgment he values.

POETIC IMITATION AND COMPETITION IN *EPISTLES* 1.3

Epistles 1.3 is addressed to a friend named Julius Florus, a young poet and the recipient also of *Epistles* 2.2, where again poetic composition is a central concern. In 1.3 Florus is part of a literary cohort accompanying the future emperor Tiberius on campaign in the East, and Horace inquires as to their various poetic pursuits.[2] Horace asks specifically about the literary activity of three of the young men: Titius, Celsus (the recipient of 1.8), and Florus himself. Titius embodies daring novelty in trying to adapt Pindar to Latin, a pursuit onto which Horace casts doubt because, in striving to be the first to succeed in such a daringly original task, Titius ironically shows very little flexibility and independence. Celsus, on the other extreme, makes no attempt at originality and is accused of plagiarism. Horace suggests that Florus's poetic achievements adhere to the proper mean in imitation between slavish dependence on models (Celsus) and the highly original but unattainable task of trying to become the Latin Pindar (Titius). Florus's adherence to the proper mean in imitation, however, is undercut by his inability to compromise in friendship. In the poem's second half Horace combines poetic with moral concerns, telling Florus to pursue *sapientia* (27) and to repair his broken relationship with his friend Munatius. Horace carefully hints that Florus is a man of ambition and that his poetic pursuits are highly competitive and aimed primarily toward achieving glory. He urges Florus to cease vying with his fellow poets for public renown and instead to compose poetry as a source of moral wisdom that benefits individual and state alike. Florus is thus to apply his poetic principles of moderation to the sphere of friendship.

Horace begins 1.3 by asking the location of the cohort accompanying Tiberius, who is on campaign, before turning his attention to their literary endeavors:

> Iule Flore, quibus terrarum militet oris
> Claudius Augusti privignus, scire laboro.
> Thracane vos Hebrusque nivali compede vinctus
> an freta vicinas inter currentia turres
> an pingues Asiae campi collesque morantur?
> quid studiosa cohors operum struit? Hoc quoque curo.
> quis sibi res gestas Augusti scribere sumit,
> bella quis et paces longum diffundit in aevum? (1.3.1–8)

> Julius Florus, I am eager to know on which shores of the earth Claudius [i.e., Tiberius Claudius Nero], the stepson of Augustus, is campaigning. Do Thrace and the Hebrus, bound with a snowy fetter, delay you, or the straits running through

the neighboring towers [i.e., the Hellespont], or the fertile fields of Asia? What works does the eager cohort construct/compose? I care about this too. Who has taken it upon himself to write about the achievements of Augustus and is extending his periods of war and peace into the distant ages?

Horace plays with his reader's expectations throughout this section; he initially seems to inquire about the military works of the *studiosa cohors*, but it gradually becomes clear that *struit* (6) means not to "construct" military works (*OLD* s.v. 2) but to "compose" poetry (*OLD* s.v. 3a).[3] The cohort is therefore *studiosa* not because they are eager to accomplish military tasks but because they are a literary group. In the opening epistle Horace had declared his intention to direct his care exclusively toward philosophical and ethical topics (*quid verum atque decens, curo et rogo et omnis in hoc sum*, "I care about and ask about what is true and appropriate, and I am entirely [absorbed] in this," 11). Here, however, he inquires about the poetic pursuits rather than the ethical concerns of the literary cohort, adding that this too, *quoque*, is a concern, *curo*, for him (6). His *curae* include therefore not only moral study but poetry as well, and by the end of the poem he will carefully have wedded these two concerns with one another. As Trinacty puts it, "for Horace, 'what is right and appropriate' in life and poetry are matters that will turn out to be remarkably similar."[4] Horace's questions concerning the cohort's poetry make up a catalogue of poetic genres that runs the scale from large to small,[5] and he first asks whether anyone has taken up an epic celebrating the achievements of Augustus (7–8). Horace here again playfully uses a word with two shades of meaning simultaneously, since *diffundit* can mean to "extend in time" (*OLD* 3c) as well as to "spread or diffuse a liquid" (*OLD* 1).[6] This introduces a metaphor that will run throughout this section of the poem in which poetic inspiration and composition are likened to water, and this water imagery will deal especially with matters of originality and imitation.[7]

Horace's next inquiry focuses on the work of a specific individual, Titius, whom Horace suspects to be busy writing Pindaric lyric or, though less likely, tragedy:[8]

quid Titius, Romana brevi venturus in ora,
Pindarici fontis qui non expalluit haustus,
fastidire lacus et rivos ausus apertos?
ut valet? ut meminit nostri? fidibusne Latinis
Thebanos aptare modos studet auspice Musa,
an tragica desaevit et ampullatur in arte? (1.3.9–14)

What of Titius, who is shortly to arrive on the mouths of Romans, who was not afraid to gulp at Pindar's fountain and dared to disdain public lakes and streams? How does he fare? How mindful is he of me? Is he eager to fit Theban meters to

the Latin lyre under an auspicious Muse, or does he rage and speak grandilo-
quently in the tragic art?

Several scholars have sensed in these lines Horace's disapproval of Titius's poetic
endeavor, and I too suspect that Titius is not up to the task of successfully imitating his chosen model.[9] It seems that Titius is attempting to do with Pindaric
meter what Horace himself had done with those of Sappho and Alcaeus in the
Odes or Archilochus in the *Epodes*,[10] an enterprise that immediately casts doubt
on Titius since such a task, as Hubbard puts it, is "incapable of realization."[11]
The daringness of Titius's endeavor is expressed through water imagery, since
Titius did not fear to seek inspiration by drinking directly from the Pindaric
font (*Pindarici fontis*, 10) instead of from public water sources (*lacus et rivos . . .
apertos*, 11).[12] The disapproval of public springs alludes both to Pindaric and
to Callimachean aesthetics, for both authors claim to find poetic inspiration in
natural streams and fountains as opposed to artificial pools used to collect rain-
water; as we shall see, throughout the poem Horace combines Pindaric and
Callimachean imagery to illustrate the correct method of poetic imitation.[13]
Here Titius's disdain for public water sources illustrates especially his desire to
achieve originality and produce an entirely new type of Latin poetry, for public
fountains evoke inspiration that has been taken up by many,[14] while no one has
yet dared (*ausus*, 11) to drink from Pindar's poetic fountain.[15] In his desire for
total innovation Titius is an exemplar of *mera libertas*, as he, like Lollius in 1.18,
refuses to mimic slavishly what his fellow Latin poets have already done.

Titius, however, is taking his literary daring to an extreme by adopting an
inimitable model. The inimitability of Pindar would be visited and emphasized
again by Horace in *Odes* 4.2, a poem with many similarities to the epistle, especially its use of water imagery to figure poetics.[16] In the ode Horace likens one
who attempts Pindaric imitation to Icarus, who flew too close to the sun:

Pindarum quisquis studet aemulari,
Iulle, ceratis ope Daedalea
nititur pinnis, vitreo daturus
   nomina ponto.

Monte decurrens velut amnis, imbres
quem super notas aluere ripas,
fervet inmensusque ruit profundo
   Pindarus ore. (*Odes* 4.2.1–8)

Whoever strives to emulate Pindar, Iullus, relies on wings covered with wax by the
art of Daedalus and will give his name to the glassy sea. Like a river rushing down
a mountain, which the rains have swollen beyond its known banks, Pindar swells
and endlessly rushes with a boundless mouth.

Here Pindar *is* the stream, but now his poetic currents are treacherous for the would-be imitator. *Aemulatio* of Pindar is beyond normal human capacity, just as flying was for Icarus, and the one who attempts to negotiate the Pindaric flood is liable, like Icarus, to drown. Later in the ode Horace contrasts his own poetic technique with the imitator of Pindar by comparing himself to a humble bee, whose works are the result of intricate labor and careful selection:[17]

> ego apis Matinae
> more modoque
>
> grata carpentis thyma per laborem
> plurimum circa nemus uvidique
> Tiburis ripas operosa parvus
> carmina fingo. (4.2.27–32)

In the manner and way of a Matinian bee that plucks thyme through very great labor around the grove and the banks of moist Tibur, I, being small, fashion laborious poems.

The arduous activity of the bee in this passage, especially the word *fingere*, is no doubt meant to recall Vergil's descriptions of the bees in *Georgics* 4.179: *daedala fingere tecta*, "they fashion intricate houses." Vergil's word *daedala* immediately calls to mind the great artisan Daedalus.[18] Horace's ode thus offers a contrast between the "Icarian" rival of Pindar, destined to fail, and the more selective and careful "Daedalian" bee. To quote Harrison, "Horace is no Icarus but rather a Daedalus, keeping low, taking fewer risks, and therefore escaping safely."[19] Whereas Icarus's high flight evokes excess, Daedalus's careful artistic endeavors illustrate the mean. This is the lesson at the heart of Ovid's famous treatment of Daedalus and Icarus in the *Metamorphoses*, where he clearly intends his reader to recall Horatian strictures on the mean. Icarus's fall is a direct result of his refusal to heed his father's lessons on moderation:

> instruit et natum 'medio' que 'ut limite curras,
> Icare,' ait 'moneo, ne, si demissior ibis,
> unda gravet pennas, si celsior, ignis adurat:
> inter utrumque vola. nec te spectare Booten
> aut Helicen iubeo strictumque Orionis ensem:
> me duce carpe viam.' pariter praecepta volandi
> tradit et ignotas umeris accommodat alas. (*Met.* 8.203–9)

He equips his son and says, "Icarus, I advise that you go in the middle path, so that if you go lower, the wave will not weigh down your wings and, if you go higher, the fire will not burn them. Fly between each. And I order you not to look at Bootes or Helice and Orion's drawn sword: follow me and seize the way." He hands down the precepts of flying and at the same time fastens the strange wings to his son's shoulders.

Daedalus's *medius limes* certainly recalls the Horatian ideal of moderation, while his *carpe viam* directly puts Horace in mind by alluding to the *carpe diem* of *Odes* 1.11.8. Because of his excessive audacity (*audaci, Met.* 8.223), Icarus flies too high and meets with failure. Horace in *Odes* 4.2, by mentioning Icarus directly in the opening lines and by evoking Daedalus in his description of the bee, similarly plays with ideas of excess and moderation and applies them to the literary realm. Horace has these same ideas in mind in *Epistles* 1.3, where Titius's Pindaric *aemulatio* signals his lack of adherence to the mean.

Horace uses the same water and bee imagery in the epistle that he would later use in the ode to illustrate these literary concepts. Whereas Titius gulps down the Pindaric fountain, Florus, like the Horace of the ode, gathers thyme in the selective manner of a bee: *quae circumvolitas agilis thyma? non tibi parvum / ingenium, non incultum est et turpiter hirtum* ("Around what thyme do you nimbly flit? Your talent is not small, nor is it untended and offensively rough," 21–22).[20] Horace's use of water and bee imagery recalls especially the ending of Callimachus's *Hymn to Apollo*, a text that itself makes extensive use of Pindaric imagery:[21]

> ὁ Φθόνος Ἀπόλλωνος ἐπ' οὔατα λάθριος εἶπεν·
> 'οὐκ ἄγαμαι τὸν ἀοιδὸν ὃς οὐδ' ὅσα πόντος ἀείδει.'
> τὸν Φθόνον ὡπόλλων ποδί τ' ἤλασεν ὧδέ τ' ἔειπεν·
> 'Ἀσσυρίου ποταμοῖο μέγας ῥόος, ἀλλὰ τὰ πολλά
> λύματα γῆς καὶ πολλὸν ἐφ' ὕδατι συρφετὸν ἕλκει.
> Δηοῖ δ' οὐκ ἀπὸ παντὸς ὕδωρ φορέουσι μέλισσαι,
> ἀλλ' ἥτις καθαρή τε καὶ ἀχράαντος ἀνέρπει
> πίδακος ἐξ ἱερῆς ὀλίγη λιβὰς ἄκρον ἄωτον.' (105–112)

> Envy spoke secretly into the ear of Apollo: "I do not admire the singer who does not sing as much as the sea." Apollo struck Envy with his foot and spoke thus: "The flow of the Assyrian river is great, but it draws much filth from the earth and much trash in its water. But the bees do not carry to Demeter water from everywhere, but from whichever small stream, clean and undefiled, creeps up out of a holy fountain, the very best."

As in *Odes* 4.2, the small-scale activity of the bee contrasts with a copious flow of water, and preference is given to the poetic symbolism of the former. In the epistle, too, Florus's bee-like flitting conflicts with the daring quaffs of Titius from the *fons Pindarica*. Horace's water and bee imagery here illustrates inappropriate and appropriate methods of imitation, respectively, and these ideas about imitation echo not only the ending of the Callimachean *Hymn* but Pindar as

well. Titius's uncompromising imitation of Pindar goes against the poetic strictures of both Callimachus and Pindar himself, while Florus's technique is in
keeping with them. Furthermore, Titius's attempts to reproduce Pindar *in toto*
undercut the originality and independence at which he aims.

In his commentary on the *Hymn to Apollo*, Williams has argued that the sea
in line 106 evokes Homer, and Traill has modified this argument to suggest that
the sea alludes specifically to the *Homeric Hymn to Apollo*.[22] In this formulation, Homer is a sea or fountain from which other poets drink for inspiration.[23]
Envy has therefore faulted Callimachus for shortchanging Apollo by not singing as many lines in his praise as were contained in the Homeric hymn, whereupon Apollo replies that quality rather than quantity is what matters. Unlike
the singer that reproduces Homer *in toto*, who is likened to the Assyrian river,
Callimachus offers a more refined, selective song, symbolized by the fine water
gathered by the bees. To quote Williams, "Callimachus' own goal is to emulate
and recreate Homer in a more meaningful and original way than merely to reproduce slavishly the external dimensions of his epics."[24] Though Cameron and
Köhnken have found fault with Williams's argument,[25] Horace's use of water
and bees in *Epistles* 1.3 and *Odes* 4.2 suggests that he saw in the Callimachean
Hymn imagery relevant to ideas of imitation. As Williams and Beer point out,
Callimachus's phrase ἄκρον ἄωτον (112) is a favorite of Pindar (*Isth.* 7.18), who
uses the word ἄωτον twenty times throughout his works; most significantly, he
uses it to describe the best kind of poetry, which flits around like a bee: ἐγκωμίων
γὰρ ἄωτος ὕμνων / ἐπ᾽ ἄλλοτ᾽ ἄλλον ὥτε μέλισσα θύνει λόγον ("The best of
victory hymns flits like a bee now from one theme, now to another," *Pyth.*
10.53–54). Hubbard has suggested that line 21 of *Epistles* 1.3 alludes to this Pindaric passage: "the epithet *agilis* renders the sense of the verb θύνει, the verb
circumvolitas that of the phrase ἐπ᾽ ἄλλοτ᾽ ἄλλον . . . λόγον."[26] Callimachus in
the *Hymn* is indebted to Pindar not only for the idea of the bee as a symbol of
the best kind of poetry but also for the idea that the poet should be selective in
what he chooses to reproduce from his sources. In *Pythian* 9.76–79 Pindar suggests that it is best for the poet to choose from many possibilities a few choice
topics and that by doing so he follows "due measure" καιρός.[27] Horace alludes
to both Callimachus and Pindar in order to show that Titius is not following
such a "due measure" in his imitation of Pindar. Rather than picking and choosing selectively in the manner of a bee, he is "drinking in" (*haustus*) Pindar in his
entirety, much like the poetic imitators of 1.19.11 who compete all night and all
day in drinking their wine "undiluted" (*mero*). Although Titius's intention is for
unparalleled originality and thus unrestrained freedom, his inability to approach
his model with moderation and adaptability ultimately renders him as unorigi-
nal and slavish as his opposite, Celsus, whom we will meet shortly. As he does

elsewhere, Horace calls into question those who claim to enjoy unmitigated independence. For example, in 1.17 Diogenes the Cynic, though he claims to be free, is nevertheless dependent on those from whom he begs, while the truculent friend of 1.18 mimics the *libertas* of a genuine friend in order to ingratiate himself with his superior patron. Throughout the *Epistles* the extremes of total originality/freedom and slavish dependence become indistinguishable.

Florus, unlike Titius, knows how to make correct use of models. He is, as we have seen, like Pindar's bee, flitting around a poetic meadow choosing his topics selectively, and, as Hubbard has shown, Horace peppers his description of Florus's various activities with words and phrases that evoke Pindar:

> seu linguam causis acuis seu civica iura
> respondere paras seu condis amabile carmen,
> prima feres hederae victricis praemia. (1.3.23–25)

> Whether you sharpen your tongue to argue cases or prepare to make pronouncements on civil laws or compose a charming poem, you will take the first rewards of the victorious ivy.

Amabile carmen (24) picks up the Pindaric ἐρατός, which Pindar uses several times to describe poetry, and the image of Florus sharpening his tongue is similarly Pindaric.[28] Horace is therefore enacting the very kind of imitation that he recommends, picking and choosing themes and images from Pindar in order to suggest that it is Florus rather than Titius who hits upon the proper mean between unattainable originality and slavish imitation.[29] Florus's literary pursuits are in fact no less original than those of Titius (*audes* 20; cf. *ausus*, 11) and because he adapts his model more freely he enjoys greater independence than Titius. Like the independently philosophical Horace of *Epistles* 1.1.14, Florus is *nullius addictus iurare in verba magistri*, "bound to swear on the words of no master" and can pick and choose what suits him in keeping with Pindaric and Callimachean poetics.

In contrast to both Titius and Florus, both of whom aim for originality, Horace describes the poetic activity of Celsus, another of Tiberius's literary cohort. Rather than attain to a single excellent poetic model, such as Pindar, he plagiarizes a wide variety of unnamed writings, whichever ones he happens to find in the library in Apollo's temple on the Palatine:

> quid mihi Celsus agit, monitus multumque monendus,
> privatas ut quaeret opes et tangere vitet
> scripta, Palatinus quaecumque recepit Apollo,
> ne, si forte suas repetitum venerit olim
> grex avium plumas, moueat cornicula risum
> furtivis nudata coloribus? (1.3.15–20)

Tell me, what is Celsus doing? He has been warned and must be warned more that he search out his own private wealth and cease to lay his hands upon whatever writings Palatine Apollo has received, so that, if by chance the flock of birds come to demand back their feathers, the little crow, stripped of its stolen colors, not rouse laughter.

As scholars have noted, the bird fable Horace uses here is paralleled in Phaedrus, where a jackdaw steals peacock feathers and is subsequently punished by a flock of peacocks and shunned by his own flock of jackdaws.[30] While the moral of the Aesopic fable is contentment with one's station in life, Horace uses the fable to warn against overly dependent imitation. In plagiarizing the words of others Celsus is analogous to the flatterer of 1.18, who picks up his master's words like a schoolboy reciting dictation (12–13). Rather than differentiate himself from his crowd of fellow poets, Celsus, by plagiarizing and stealing their words, aims to blend in with and make himself indistinguishable from them. He, like the flatterer, has no unique personality of his own but disappears behind the model he is imitating. Whereas Titius aims to stand apart and do what no one else has done before, Celsus wants only to conform. In the middle of these stands Florus, who achieves originality through selectively adapting what is best in his poetic forerunners to suit his own literary goals and by practicing imitation with a free hand. As in the philosophical and social spheres, moderation and adaptability go hand in hand.

Despite Florus's success in following the mean in imitation, Horace makes it clear that he does not hit upon the mean in every aspect of his life. Florus therefore illustrates the negative consequences that come when moderation is only partially applied; in Florus's case he employs the mean in poetic imitation but not in friendship.[31] In the poem's final lines, Horace shifts his focus away from Florus's poetic pursuits and instead concentrates on his relationship with a certain Munatius, in his friendship with whom Florus has suffered a rupture (30–36). Horace does not state directly the reasons for their broken friendship, but in leading up to these lines he does carefully hint that Florus is excessively keen to win renown for himself through his poetry and that this desire for success has ignited in him a competitive spark that may be negatively affecting his friendships.[32] Florus's intellectual pursuits are not limited to the poetic realm but extend also to the sphere of oratory and law, and lines 23–25 bear repeating:

seu linguam causis acuis seu civica iura
respondere paras seu condis amabile carmen,
prima feres hederae victricis praemia. (1.3.23–25)

Whether you sharpen your tongue to argue cases or prepare to make pronouncements on civil laws or compose a charming poem, you will take the first rewards of the victorious ivy.

Although Mayer rightly comments that the ivy wreath in line 25 properly applies only to poetic success, it must extend implicitly to Florus's oratorical and forensic accomplishments as well, since the poetic and the legal realms are closely connected by *seu . . . seu . . . seu*. Both in his poetic endeavors and in his professional ones, Florus hopes to gain a prize, the ivy wreath, that makes him "victorious," *victricis*, an adjective that normally applies to the laurel wreath of the public politician rather than the ivy of the poet. O'Neill recognizes in these lines an allusion to Vergil's *Eclogues* 8, in which he describes a crown of interwoven ivy and laurel to signify the military and poetic accomplishments of his addressee.[33] In this passage, however, Vergil uses the adjective *victrix* to modify the laurel rather than the ivy, indicating that though these spheres are separate it is the public rather than the poetic sphere that properly brings victory:

> a te principium; tibi desinet: accipe iussis
> carmina coepta tuis, atque hanc sine tempora circum
> inter victricis hederam tibi serpere laurus. (*Eclogues* 8.11–13)

> My beginning is from you; with you shall it end. Receive the songs begun at your command, and allow this ivy to creep around your temples between the victorious laurel.

Horace's *hederae victricis* (*Epist.* 1.3.25) is no doubt meant to recall Vergil's *victricis hederam* (13).[34] As O'Neill writes, "The laurel crown designates military glory, the ivy prestige won through Virgil's poem. By juxtaposing *victricis* and *hederam*, Vergil contrasts the political and literary worlds and mingles them in a symbiotic relationship." By applying the adjective *victricis* directly to *hederae*, Horace collapses the distinction between Florus's legal and literary pursuits and suggests that a similar motive lurks behind each: the competitive desire for victory.[35] The competitive nature of Florus's poetic pursuits is further brought out by an allusion to *Eclogues* 7.5, where Corydon and Thyrsis, who are about to enter a competitive amoebean singing match, are called *respondere parati*, "ready to respond," which is echoed closely by Horace's *respondere paras* (*Epist.* 1.3.24). These subtle hints and allusions are the first sign that Florus's success as a poet will be undercut by his inappropriate and excessive competition.

Though in the *Odes* Horace himself seeks to win glory through his poetic accomplishments, in the *Epistles* he expresses distaste for such competitive poetic goals.[36] We have already seen that in 1.1 he likens his former lyric pursuits to a gladiatorial game, and in 1.19 we shall again see Horace's disdain for such competitive poetic displays. Florus's poetic goals, Horace implies, should not be glory and victory so much as the acquisition of an ethically sound life, both for himself and for others:

quodsi
frigida curarum fomenta relinquere posses,
quo te caelestis sapientia duceret, ires.
hoc opus, hoc studium parvi properemus et ampli,
si patriae volumus, si nobis vivere cari. (1.3.25–29)

> But if you were able to abandon the cold compresses for your cares, you would go
> where heavenly wisdom leads. Let us, both small and grand, hasten on this work,
> this pursuit, if we want to live dear to the fatherland and to ourselves.

These are the most hotly debated lines of the poem. While some scholars argue that Horace here urges Florus to abandon poetry altogether and pursue philosophy instead, others suggest that it is only his excessive desire for glory that Horace wants Florus to give up.[37] I am in the latter camp and suggest that Horace in no way urges Florus to abandon poetry but that he is critical of Florus's desire to obtain *victrix hedera* from it. Much rests on the phrases *frigida curarum fomenta* and *caelestis sapientia*, and scholars have disagreed radically about how these are to be taken. First, to what do the "cold compresses" and "cares" refer, and what kind of genitive is *curarum*?[38] I take the *curarum* as an objective genitive (i.e., "foments for your cares") and as referring to Florus's anxieties about glory. The "cold compresses" are the successes that he hopes will assuage these anxieties. Such ambitions, however, are ultimately insatiable, and thus Horace refers to the *fomenta* as *frigida*, "cold."[39] The coldness of the *fomenta*, in fact, may refer specifically back to the victorious ivy crown, as Moles (1995) suggests, pointing out that "victors wear crowns of ivy, things applied from the outside. 'Cold compresses' are also external applications and ivy itself is 'cold.'"[40] The ivy crown is therefore the foment that Florus thinks will assuage his ambitious *curae* and that Horace now urges him to abandon. If Florus could put such cold foments aside, he would attain to *caelestis sapientia*. It is this wisdom, not poetic one-upmanship, that elevates him to the heavens (*caelestis*).

Much ink has been spilled over the question of why Horace calls this wisdom *caelestis*.[41] I suggest that through this word Horace puts wisdom into direct competition with the *victrix hedera* through which Florus hopes to attain a godlike status. In *Odes* 4.2, which, as we have seen, shares much imagery with *Epistles* 1.3, Horace refers to those victorious addressees of Pindar who have won the Olympic palm as *caelestes* (18), "godlike," and in *Odes* 1.1.29–30 he hopes that the ivy crown at which he himself aims will intermingle him with the gods: *me doctarum hederae praemia frontium / dis miscent superis*, "Ivy, the reward of learned brows, intermingles me with the gods above." In the epistle, however, wisdom, not victory, renders one *caelestis*. None of this necessitates that Florus abandon his poetic pursuits, but it does cause him to rethink his motive for them. Rather than compete with his fellow men, he must seek to improve them along with himself: *si patriae volumus, si nobis vivere cari*, 29.[42] The poem emphasizes the importance of reconciliation and concord with one's fellow man rather than competition and rivalry. In healing rifts rather than causing them Florus will gain a different and more valuable kind of distinction from the fatherland, for it will now hold him dear, *carus*.

Horace ends the poem by giving a specific example of ruptured friendship that Florus has experienced and suggests that he dedicate himself to reconciliation. He asks whether his friend Munatius is as great a source of care, *cura*, for him as he should be. Florus's *curae* have therefore been misdirected in seeking glory and should be aimed instead toward friendship:

> debes hoc etiam rescribere, sit tibi curae
> quantae conveniat Munatius. an male sarta
> gratia nequiquam coit et rescinditur ac vos
> seu calidus sanguis seu rerum inscitia vexat
> indomita cervice feros? ubicumque locorum
> vivitis, indigni fraternum rumpere foedus,
> pascitur in vestrum reditum votiva iuvenca. (1.3.30–36)

> You ought to write back about this too: whether Munatius is as great a source of care for you as he ought to be. Or does the esteem between you, which has been badly sutured, close up in vain and tear open again, and does hot blood or ignorance of things harass you both, wild with untamed necks? Wherever in the world you two are, unworthy of breaking your fraternal bond, a votive heifer is being fed for your return.

The medical imagery of *frigida fomenta* is picked up in Horace's likening of the young men's friendship to a poorly sutured wound. Horace blames the quarrel between the two on *calidus sanguis*, "hot blood," thereby suggesting that it is in fact the quick temper of the young men that is in need of cold foments. Florus, rather than using his intellectual pursuits in the service of his ambition, should aim them toward gaining the wisdom (*sapientia*) necessary to heal this rift and overcome his "ignorance of things," *rerum inscitia*. His inappropriate *cura* and ignorance (*inscitia*), both detriments to friendship, are counterbalanced by Horace's own pursuit of knowledge (*scire laboro*, 1.3.2) and concern (*curo*, 6) toward his friends in Tiberius's literary cohort. Florus is therefore meant to follow Horace's lead in directing himself toward ethics in general and friendship in particular.

Horace plants hints about the cause of the rift between the two by using language that looks ahead to the eighteenth epistle, in which he cites as an exemplum for Lollius the ruptured *gratia* between Amphion and Zethus, which was considered in the previous chapter. Quoting the passages side by side reveals the echoes clearly:

> debes hoc etiam rescribere, sit tibi curae
> quantae conveniat Munatius. an male sarta
> *gratia* nequiquam coit et rescinditur, ac vos
> seu calidus sanguis seu rerum inscitia vexat
> indomita cervice feros? ubicumque locorum
> vivitis, indigni *fraternum* rumpere foedus,
> pascitur in vestrum reditum votiva iuvenca. (1.3.30–36)

> *gratia* sic *fratrum* geminorum Amphionis atque
> Zethi dissiluit, donec suspecta severo
> conticuit lyra. *fraternis* cessisse putatur
> moribus Amphion. (1.18.41–44)

Horace uses *gratia* to describe the relationship between both sets of men, and, while Amphion and Zethus literally are *fratres*, he characterizes Florus and Munatius metaphorically as having a "fraternal bond," *fraternum foedus*. As we have seen, the *gratia* between Amphion and Zethus was almost ruptured by the brothers' adherence to opposite ways of life, Amphion preferring the private, intellectual sphere and Zethus the active, public one. It is only when Amphion yielded to the character of his brother that the two were able to mend their relationship. By looking ahead to this passage in 1.3 Horace hints that the problem between Florus and Munatius is their stubbornness and refusal to compromise with one another. Whereas Florus can find a middle ground with poetic models, he has been unable to find one with Munatius, and Horace insists that he align his poetic principles with his practice of friendship. By applying the same mean he exercises in poetry to the social sphere he will be able to repair his broken friendship with Munatius permanently.

Horace further elaborates on the rift between these two friends by describing them as *indomita cervice feros*, "wild with untamed necks," (34). This could, as Mayer points out, refer either to bulls or stallions, but Hubbard makes a good case not only for taking it as the former but also for understanding it as an allusion to the fighting bulls of *Georgics* 3.209–41, who battle with one another over a *formosa iuvenca* (219).[43] An *iuvenca* is central to the closing line of the epistle as well, but here the *iuvenca* does not contribute to their animosity toward one another but is offered as a sacrifice in the hopes that they might reconcile.[44] To quote Hubbard, "Munatius and Florus are or should be a pair, and Horace's relation to them is rather that of the trainer of *Georg.* 3.164ff., teaching young bullocks in light collars to walk in step."[45] In this passage Vergil stresses the importance of beginning the training of bulls while they are still young: *iam vitulos hortare viamque insiste domandi, / dum faciles animi iuvenum, dum mobilis aetas,* "now urge on the bull calves and enter on the path of taming while the minds of the young bulls are easy to handle, while their age is malleable," (3.164–65). At the end of 1.3 Horace is therefore recommending to Florus the same need to apply his mind to ethical training while still young that he had advised to Lollius at the end of the preceding poem, *Epistles* 1.2, by comparing him to a hunting pup just undertaking his training or a docile horse with a tender neck. Florus may have mastered the art of correct poetic imitation, but much learning remains for him in the sphere of friendship. There is, however, great hope for Florus since his poetic practice shows that he has already grasped the importance of the mean in one area of his life. Both he and Munatius may be wild like warring bulls, but, as Horace has already reassured us in the first epistle, *nemo adeo ferus est, ut non mitescere possit, / si modo culturae patientem commodet aurem,* "nobody is so wild that he cannot be tamed, provided that he lend a patient ear to proper training," 39–40.

Horace throughout the *Epistles* offers advice to friends that he is in the process of learning for himself, and this is especially true of the praise and admonition he gives Florus in 1.3. The poem illustrates the dangers of only partially applying a fundamental ethical principle, since Florus's competitiveness not only affects his relationships with his peers but detracts from the benefit that the composition of poetry might bring to him by reducing it to a vehicle to gain glory. Similarly, we also see Horace initially embrace the mean only partially but then gradually apply this principle to a variety of spheres. This process begins with his philosophical method as outlined in 1.1, where he walks a middle path between dependence and freedom. Gradually he applies this same middle path to other aspects of his life; in particular, he uses it as a means to overcome his ambivalence toward the city and country and toward social relationships. In 1.19 we see him apply the same middle path to his own past poetry. At the same time he signals a reconciliation with Maecenas that is parallel to the reconciliation he hopes will take place between Florus and Munatius in 1.3.

POETRY AND FREEDOM IN *EPISTLES* 1.19

Horace returns to the topic of poetic imitation in the penultimate poem of the collection, *Epistles* 1.19, which, like the penultimate poem of the *Odes*, 3.29, is addressed to Maecenas.[46] By addressing both *Epistles* 1.1. and 1.19 to Maecenas, Horace creates a clear ring composition that signals the book's closing, and *Epistles* 1.19 offers a nice summation of and conclusion to many of the ethical threads we have been tracing.[47] Horace picks up especially on the characterization he gave his former poetry in 1.1, where it was a symbol of his past dependence and brought him into the public eye much like a gladiator pleading before the mob. Maecenas, in this configuration, was his *lanista* and, in wanting more poetry, sought to reenlist him in gladiatorial *ludus*. The opening poem thus places Maecenas and Horace in a clear hierarchy, with Maecenas his former slave master and Horace his newly freed slave. In 1.19 Horace offers a massive revision of this opening stance as he applies the ethical principles we have been following—particularly the mean as regards freedom—to his past poetry.[48] Like Florus in 1.3, Horace hit upon the correct mean in relying on poetic models and freely adapting them. *Libertas* is not the uncompromising stance of the opening poem but a middle path between daring originality and following a clear tradition. Freedom, furthermore, is not demonstrated through unmitigated harsh speech, and invective and attack should also be moderated, just as he tamed Archilochean *libertas* in his *Epodes*. At the same time that he reassesses his former poetry Horace's own status is revised from that of the opening poem. Far from being a *libertus* of low standing Horace becomes a poetic model analogous to a *potens amicus* in the social sphere.[49] Like the patron of 1.18.1–20 he becomes the object of both flattery and harsh criticism and calls upon his learned friend Maecenas as a witness to and defender of his poetic practices.[50] The collection's gladiatorial imagery reappears at the end, with Horace still refusing to participate in the slavish *ludus* of public spectacle but adopting instead ideal readers whose noble, free status accords with his own. In courting such ideal readers, however, Horace has to take on some measure of dependence. By refusing to pander to the crowd while simultaneously hoping to gain the approval of the elite few Horace once again forges a delicate middle path between freedom and slavery, one that brings renown rather than degradation.

Throughout 1.19, as in 1.18, imitation and freedom are linked to issues of flattery and harsh speech. Horace opens the epistle by reminding Maecenas of Cratinus's championing of wine as a source of poetic inspiration:

> prisco si credis, Maecenas docte, Cratino,
> nulla placere diu nec vivere carmina possunt,
> quae scribuntur aquae potoribus. ut male sanos
> adscripsit Liber Satyris Faunisque poetas,
> vina fere dulces oluerunt mane Camenae. (1.19.1–5)

> If you believe ancient Cratinus, learned Maecenas, no poems can last for very long which are written by water-drinkers. Ever since Liber enrolled insane poets among his satyrs and fauns, the sweet Camenae generally reek in the morning of wine.

Traditionally poetic frenzy arising from *natura* or *ingenium* was associated with wine, while meticulous artistry, *studium* or *ars*, was associated with water.[51] A few lines later Homer and Ennius are also put forth as representatives of inspiration through wine and thus *ingenium: laudibus arguitur vini vinosus Homerus; / Ennius ipse pater numquam nisi potus ad arma / prosiluit dicenda*, "Homer by his praises of wine is proven a wine-drinker. Father Ennius himself never leapt forth to sing of arms except when drunk," 6–8. Opposed to such wine-drinkers would be Callimachus, who excelled rather in meticulous artistry. In the *Ars Poetica* Horace will call for an alliance—a middle ground—between *ars* and *ingenium*.[52] In *Epistles* 1.19, however, Horace is less concerned with issues of *ars* and *ingenium* than with issues of freedom and dependence. The extremes of wine and water are to be avoided because neither leads to true *libertas*. *Libertas* in 1.19 pertains both to issues of poetic imitation and to the appropriate degree of harsh criticism.

Cratinus, a representative of Old Comedy, is aligned here with the poetics of *Liber*, whose name has strong associations with *libertas*. In *Satires* 1.4 Cratinus is listed as a representative of old-fashioned *libertas*, by which Horace means "free speech" or "frank criticism":

> Eupolis atque Cratinus Aristophanesque poetae,
> atque alii quorum comoedia prisca virorum est,
> si quis erat dignus describi quod malus ac fur,
> quod moechus foret aut sicarius aut alioqui
> famosus, multa cum libertate notabant. (*Satires* 1.4.1–5)

> The poets Eupolis, Cratinus, and Aristophanes, and other men who are exemplars of Old Comedy, censured with great freedom of speech anyone worthy of being marked out because he was an evil thief or an adulterer or a murderer or infamous for some other reason.

Horace does not fault Cratinus and other Old Comic poets in this satire for their use of *libertas* so much as criticize Lucilius, the father of Roman satire, for depending too strongly on them, changing only his meter: *hinc omnis pendet Lucilius, hosce secutus / mutatis tantum pedibus numerisque* ("Lucilius depends entirely on these, having followed them with only his meter and measures having been changed," 6–7). Lucilius therefore made two mistakes: he failed to alter his model sufficiently (*omnis pendet*) and he copied in particular the unrestrained *libertas* of the Old Comic poets. Later in the satire Horace describes the effect of wine, *Liber*, upon one who is predisposed to *libertas*; wine strengthens and exacerbates his harshness of speech:

> saepe tribus lectis videas cenare quaternos,
> e quibus unus amet quavis aspergere cunctos
> praeter eum qui praebet aquam; post hunc quoque potus,
> condita cum verax aperit praecordia Liber. (*Satires* 1.4.86–88)

> Often you can see four men dining on each of the three couches, one of whom loves to besmear in any way everyone except the one who offers water, but afterward he besmears that one as well when he is drunk and truthful Liber reveals his hidden heart.

Horace promises that such *aerugo mera*, "unmixed malice," will be missing from his pages, though he does reserve the right to use a moderate degree of *libertas* in his poetry (1.4.100–105). Horace therefore takes Lucilian transformation of Old Comedy a step further, modifying and taming the *libertas* that Lucilius had left unchanged.[53] In recalling the satire in the epistle Horace signals that here too he is concerned with poetic *libertas*, both the transformation of poetic models and the appropriate degree of "free speech" that poets adopt. Smith also picks up on the associations between Cratinus and harshness in the opening lines of 1.19 and comments that "excessive drinking is connected with combativeness and, on a literary level, with vituperative or 'Archilochean' satire."[54] Cratinus is perhaps singled out in *Epistles* 1.19 because he was especially associated in antiquity with the harsh censure of political figures. As Bakola puts it, "The principle strand of Cratinus' scholarly reception in antiquity portrays him as the representative of the abusive mode of Old Comedy; (suggested already by Aristophanes in *Ec.* 526–28), and especially as a castigator of wrongdoers; accordingly, one source suggests that Cratinus' invective drew on Archilochus (Platon. *Diff Char.* 1 p. 6 Koster)."[55] Rosen similarly suggests that "like Archilochus . . . Cratinus adopted a vigorous, antagonistic, sometimes vituperative style . . . and even Archilochus (so Cratinus may have maintained) could only sustain it by altering his mental state with alcohol."[56] Horace's taming of Archilochean invective in his *Epodes* will be central to *Epistles* 1.19.[57] The focus on wine in the epistle's beginning recalls furthermore the wine imagery from *Epistles* 1.18, where the harsh friend wants his frank speech to come across as *mera libertas* (8) rather than as the slavish imitation of the flatterer. Just as the *libertas* of the harsh critic is called into question in 1.18, so too will the adherents to wine-drinking and its unmoderated *libertas* in 1.19 be criticized for their abusiveness and slavish mimicry.[58]

What Cratinus, Homer, and Ennius have in common, apart from their allegiance to wine, is the primacy they enjoy in their respective poetic endeavors. Cratinus's career flourished in the 450s B.C., and thus he was older than either Aristophanes or Eupolis; Horace highlights his antiquity with the word *prisco*. Homer of course is *the* font of Greco-Roman literature, while Ennius's role as father of Latin poetry is designated by *pater*.[59] Rather than drawing on models, Horace suggests, they are the models for later writers, and thus their poetry has strong associations with *libertas*. The same cannot be said to hold true for those who follow in their footsteps, who, rather than seek out originality for themselves, copy these writers instead by mimicking their wine-drinking. Unmixed wine becomes synonymous not with freedom but with slavishly aping the qualities of another. Interestingly, the poet whom such imitators are said to copy is not Cratinus, Homer or Ennius, but Horace himself:

'Forum putealque Libonis
mandabo siccis, adimam cantare severis';
hoc simul edixi, non cessavere poetae
nocturno certare mero, putere diurno. (1.19.8–11)

"I will commit the forum and the well of Libo to the sober, I will take away singing from the serious." As soon as I passed this edict, poets have not ceased to content with unmixed wine by night and to stink of it by day.

Horace here casts himself in the role of a magistrate who has passed an official edict prohibiting water-drinkers from poetic composition and leaving them to imbibe water at the *puteal Libonis* in the Roman forum.[60] Such a decree is nowhere to be found in Horace's poetry, but by mentioning it Horace seems to align himself with those poets who favor the inspiration to be found in wine.[61] More importantly, however, Horace's edict involves issues of originality. The "dry" and "serious" are relegated to the artificial water sources to be found in public places. As we saw in our discussion of 1.3, the common well, as opposed to the natural, clean stream, represents well-worn poetic pathways, and in 1.19 Horace's edict has less to do with the inspirational merits of wine versus water than with poetic independence and dependence. Whereas water from artificial sources is associated with lack of originality, wine betokens freedom and novelty. Horace's edict, however, falls upon deaf ears. Poets have failed to understand the symbolism of wine and water and instead have taken Horace's words literally; rather than seek out original subject matter, they have taken to drinking wine in massive quantities. They have transformed his cry for originality and independence into a message of immoderate conformity and slavishness.

Horace, on the other hand, associates himself with those poets who, like Homer and Ennius, are highly original, for he is the model that they are imitating, albeit inappropriately.[62] Their imitation of him has a competitive aspect (*certare*); they are competing not only with each other in following his edict but with Horace as well, and their competitive imitation of him is analogous to that experienced by the *amicus potens* in 1.18.28, who advises his client not to compete with him (*contendere noli*). Horace therefore occupies in the poetic sphere the same role as a wealthy patron does in the social sphere, and he is subject to the same kind of flattery as the *amicus potens*. While these imitative poets are *prima facie* analogous to the flatterer of 1.18, in that they copy another, their servility in fact arises from trying to imitate the *libertas* of wine-drinkers. They are thus simultaneously like the harsh critic of 1.18 who tries to ingratiate himself with a wealthy patron by mimicking to an extreme the free speech of a genuine *amicus*.

Horace employs two examples to illustrate the poor attempts of these slavish imitators to mimic the *libertas* of others. The first example is taken not from the poetic realm but the ethical one. In trying to mimic Horace's originality by drinking unmixed wine, these imitators are like one who tries to copy the inner virtue of old Cato by adopting his exterior characteristics, such as his harsh expression, lack of shoes, and threadbare toga: *siquis voltu torvo ferus et pede nudo / exiguaeque togae simulet textore Catonem, / virtutemne repraesentet moresque Catonis?* ("If someone should imitate Cato by being harsh with a fierce expression and shoeless and by wearing a thin toga, would he reproduce the virtue and character of Cato?" 12–14). Few Romans are as closely associated with the idea of *libertas* as Cato, and this quality is lurking behind this passage as well. The imitator of Cato here is like the other figures in the collection that try to pass off external qualities as freedom and virtue but who are ultimately revealed as slavish. The imitator of Cato is like Diogenes in 1.17, who hopes his threadbare cloak will be an outer manifestation of his inner virtue and independence but whose freedom is undercut by his reliance on the mob for his scanty livelihood. The overly harsh critic of 1.18 similarly relies on his rotten teeth and badly shorn hair to communicate his inner autonomy, but he simply mimics the part of a true friend in order to win a seat at a wealthy man's table, just like a parasite. The imitator of Cato in 1.19, Diogenes in 1.17, and the harsh critic of 1.18—like the immoderate wine-drinkers—all share the same fault of trying to attain independence and originality by slavishly copying the attributes of those who have stronger claims to it.

In lines 15–16 Horace offers a further example, taken from the sphere of contemporary literature, of a slavish imitator who tries to outdo his model and suffers for it. Iarbitas tried to imitate Timagenes's eloquence and wit and, in doing so, caused himself to "burst": *rupit Iarbitam Timagenis aemula lingua, / dum studet urbanus tenditque disertus haberi*, "the tongue that emulated Timagenes caused Iarbitas to burst while he was zealous and eager to be considered urbane and eloquent." Although we no longer know who Iarbitas was, some information about Timagenes has survived. A contemporary of Horace, he was a rhetorician and a writer of histories, and he seems to have been known for his excessive outspokenness, especially toward Augustus. This quality, though it did cause him to fall out of favor with the imperial family, nevertheless did not otherwise cause him considerable harm.[63] Seneca the Elder calls him *homine acidae linguae et qui nimis liber erat*, "a man with an acid tongue who was excessively *liber*," *Controversiae* 1.5.22, while the younger Seneca records his *temeraria urbanitas*, "rash wit," Augustus's tolerance of which was a testament to his lack of *ira*, despite his frequent warnings that Timagenes make use of his free speech with greater moderation: *saepe illum Caesar monuit, moderatius lingua uteretur*, "often Augustus advised him that he use his speech more moderately," *De Ira* 3.23.4–5. Mayer ventures that his imitator Iarbitas "perhaps went a step too far,"[64] and Horace's use of *aemula lingua* would suggest that he tried not only to imitate but even to outdo his model's *libertas*. In this exemplum we again have the combination of *libertas* and excessively slavish imitation, and Iarbitas is criticized for reproducing the already faulty *libertas* of his model: *decipit exemplar vitiis imitabile*, "a model that is imitable in its vices is deceptive," 17. Horace's choice of a contemporary figure who was directly associated with Augustus suggests that such imitation of excessive free speech has no place in contemporary Rome. Thus Horace prepares us for his own method of imitation, which is much more in keeping with the changed nature of *libertas* in the political reality of his day.[65]

Both Smith and Oliensis suggest that Horace's description of Iarbitas as "burst," *rupit* (15), alludes to *Satires* 2.3.312–20, where Damasippus accuses Horace of imitating Maecenas like the frog in the fable who nearly caused herself to burst open by imitating a calf:[66]

> an quodcumque facit Maecenas te quoque verum est
> tanto dissimilem et tanto certare minorem?
> absentis ranae pullis vituli pede pressis
> unus ubi effugit, matri denarrat, ut ingens
> belua cognatos eliserit. illa rogare,
> quantane? num tantum, sufflans se, magna fuisset?
> 'maior dimidio.' num tanto? cum magis atque
> se magis inflaret, 'non, si te ruperis,' inquit,
> 'par eris.' haec a te non multum abludit imago.

> Or is it right that, whatever Maecenas does, you, who are so unlike him and so much less than him, compete with him? When a mother frog was absent her young were smashed by the foot of a calf. When one escaped he told his mother how a huge beast had dashed his siblings to pieces. She asked how big he was. She puffed herself up and asked whether he was this big. "Bigger by half." "Bigger by this much?" When she was puffing herself up more and more he said, "You will not be equal even if you should burst yourself." This picture is not very much unlike you.

Horace's relationship with Maecenas, as alleged by Damasippus in the satire, is like that between the imitators and their models in the epistle. Not only does Horace try to be like Maecenas, he puts himself in competition (*certare*, 2.3.313; cf. *certare*, *Epist.* 1.19.11) with him. By alluding back to the satire Horace makes an analogy between the literary and social realms; a poetic model and social patron are subject to the same kinds of slavish imitation and rivalry. In the epistle, however, Horace's role has fundamentally changed, since it is he who is now subject to the imitation and rivalry of others: *quodsi / pallerem casu, biberent exsangue cuminum*, "but if by chance I were to become pale, they would drink cumin, which causes paleness," 1.19.17–18. As Oliensis states, "it is clear that [Horace] is now aligned not with the frog but with the calf."[67] These imitators would drink anything that they think would help them reproduce Horace's literary qualities, but the traits they mimic are simply the exterior ones that have nothing to do with his inner capabilities. Horace finally calls them out for what they are, not aspirants to poetic or ethical independence but merely slavish imitators that rouse both his indignation and amusement: *o imitatores, servum pecus, ut mihi saepe / bilem, saepe iocum vestri movere tumultus*, "o imitators, slavish herd, how often has your commotion roused my anger, how often my laughter," 19–20.

So far we have seen that Horace's concerns in *Epistles* 1.19.1–20 are threefold. First, he criticizes those literary imitators who follow their models to a slavish extreme by reproducing some superficial quality they find in them, such as adhering to wine drinking. Secondly, Horace hints throughout that such imitators try especially to reproduce the originality and *libertas* of their models but, by doing so, demonstrate only their dependence and servility, and poetic *libertas* evokes not only originality of subject matter but also excessive freedom of speech, which should not be mimicked but moderated. Finally, Horace aligns himself with those authors who occupy a position of prestige in the literary realm, such as Cratinus, Homer, and Ennius, and who are subject to the imitation of others, but this imitation is slavish and elicits only Horace's disdain. Having established himself as a model in the poetic sphere analogous to a patron in the social sphere, Horace now will outline his own appropriate use of poetic models. This involves not only employing a mean between freedom and dependence but also taming and correcting the faults of one's models, particularly the fault of excessively harsh criticism. Horace has therefore attained his exalted poetic position not by adhering uncompromisingly to *libertas* but by moderating it. At the same time, he acknowledges that any act of publication, no matter how original the poetry, necessarily involves subjecting oneself to the judgment of others. Horace thus simultaneously occupies two social poles, that of the wealthy patron/model, on the one hand, and that of the poet who must pimp himself out, on the other. Whereas in the opening poem he set up an either/or opposition between freedom and slavery in the poetic realm, he here negotiates a compromise through which he experiences both concurrently.

Unlike the *servum pecus* of bad imitators, Horace in his past poetry, namely the *Epodes*, embraced a technique that exemplifies freedom and brings him primacy:

> libera per vacuum posui vestigia princeps,
> non aliena meo pressi pede. Qui sibi fidet,
> dux reget examen. Parios ego primus iambos

ostendi Latio, numeros animosque secutus
Archilochi, non res et agentia verba Lycamben (1.19.21–25)

I was the first to place free footsteps through an unoccupied space and pressed
with my foot things that belonged to no one else. Whoever trusts in himself will,
as leader, rule the hive. I was the first to show Parian iambs to Latium, having followed the meters and spirit of Archilochus, not the subject matter and the words
that harassed Lycambes.

Horace's poetic technique here combines the three main threads we have been
tracing: a) he approaches his models with a great deal of independence and
originality and in so doing adopts a mean between reliance on and freedom
from them; b) he does not mimic but rather moderates the harsh *libertas*,
"harsh speech," found in them; and c) by adopting qualified *libertas*, he enjoys
an elevated status on par with that of powerful patrons in the social realm.
Horace's claim to press his footsteps into previously unclaimed territory speaks
to his poetic originality and recalls Callimachean and Lucretian imagery.[68] In
the *Aetia* prologue Apollo warns the poet not to drive his chariot on the tracks
of others or on a wide path but rather on roads that are untraversed (ἑτέρων δ᾽
ἴχνια μὴ καθ᾽ ὁμά / δίφρον ἐλᾶν μηδ᾽ οἷμον ἀνὰ πλατύν, ἀλλὰ κελεύθους /
ἀτρίπτους, εἰ καὶ στεινοτέρην ἐλάσεις, 26–28). Lucretius makes similar use of
this imagery to describe the originality of his poetic project, since nobody previously had attempted an Epicurean epic: *avia Pieridum peragro loca nullius
ante / trita solo*, "I wander through places that are off the beaten path and have
been tread upon by no one's foot previously," 1.926–27. Horace's imagery draws
more strongly on that of Lucretius, since both he and Lucretius press the earth
with their feet rather than ride over it in a chariot.

Although Lucretius employs this imagery to show his poetic originality, he
elsewhere uses the same imagery to show not his freedom from but his indebt-
edness to a *philosophical* model:

te sequor, o Graiae gentis decus, inque tuis nunc
ficta pedum pono pressis vestigia signis,
non ita certandi cupidus quam propter amorem
quod te imitari aveo. (3.3–6)

I follow you, glory of the Greek race, and now I place my footprints firmly on the
ones made by you, not because I am eager to compete with you but because I want
to imitate you out of love.

Though Lucretius claims here that his imitation of Epicurus is not out of rivalry,
he nevertheless shows his total dependence on his philosophical guide. Lucretius's total philosophical dependence contrasts sharply with his poetic originality, and the similar imagery he uses to describe each underlines this divergence.

Horace's approach to both philosophical and poetic models, on the other hand, is equivalent. In 1.1 he describes how he will be a *hospes* in various philosophical houses, drawing on them without swearing allegiance to any. In 1.19 his poetic technique is precisely the same. He follows (*secutus*, 24) poetic models, such as that of Archilochus, but he adopts them with a free hand in such a way that he creates something new (*princeps*, 21; *primus*, 23). In other words, in both philosophy and poetry Horace walks a middle path between total independence and slavish adherence, and this middle path is aligned with true freedom, *libera vestigia*, "free footprints," 21. It is analogous to that described by Aristippus in Xenophon's *Memorabilia* 1.2.11, which runs between having no master at all (ἀρχή) and slavishness (δουλεία), since Horace similarly finds freedom by striking the proper balance between ruling (*dux reget examen*, 23) and following (*secutus*, 24). Freudenburg too has suggested that the poetic freedom Horace describes in 1.19 is especially Aristippean: "Thus the freedom vaunted comes packaged with suggestions of following. . . . Still freedom, he insists, but not absolute. . . . The freedom he knows from his dealings with patrons and his precursors in Greek and Latin poetry is of a much more limited, Aristippean kind."[69] Rather than compromising Horace's social standing, this moderated freedom in fact elevates it. He is not only *dux* (23) but *princeps* (21), and thus his poetic position equals that of Augustus's social position. The bee imagery of these lines (*examen*, 23) especially recalls *Epistles* 1.3.21–22, where Florus, who knows how to make proper use of poetic models, is likened to a bee flitting around meadows full of thyme.[70] Horace the bee also knows how to use his models correctly, picking and choosing what is best from them and adapting them to his own unique purposes.

Horace describes what Archilochean features he chose to follow and which to discard. While he adopted the "meter and spirit," *numeros animosque* (24), of Archilochus, he eschewed his *res et agentia verba Lycamben* (25), "subject matter and words that harassed Lycambes."[71] As we have seen, the repetition of another's words is an object of censure throughout the *Epistles* and marks one as a dependent slave, and Horace's refusal to repeat Archilochus's *verba* is analogous to his refusal to swear on the words of a philosophical master (*nullius addictus iurare in verba magistri*, 1.1.14).[72] The specific part of Archilochus's poetry that Horace refused to follow is its harsh invective, which we might call its *mera libertas*, "undiluted harsh speech."[73] According to tradition, Archilochus attacked Lycambes, who broke off his daughter's engagement with the poet, so viciously that both he and his daughter committed suicide. Archilochus's harshness of speech is immoderate, like that of the harsh friend in 1.18, and thus is an extreme to be avoided. Horace's approach to Archilochus reverses that of Lucilius to Cratinus and other Old Comic poets described in *Satires* 1.4, outlined above. Whereas Lucilius changed their meter but kept their subject matter, particularly their freedom of speech, wholly intact (*hinc omnis pendet Lucilius, hosce secutus / mutatis tantum pedibus numerisque*, 6–7), Horace kept the meter but moderated the *multa libertas* of his model. Such outspokenness is a thing of the Republican past and cannot be made to suit the changed political landscape of Augustan Rome. Both Horace's revision of true freedom as a mean and his toning down of the free speech of his predecessors can be read, at least in part, as a reaction to this new political reality. By conforming to such moderate freedom Horace has forged a new path to social distinction that is well suited to the nascent principate.

Horace anticipates that he may be criticized for not changing his poetic model even more (i.e., for not aiming at total independence), and so he cites as precedents for his practice the imitative methods of Sappho and Alcaeus:

> ac ne me foliis ideo brevioribus ornes
> quod timui mutare modos et carminis artem,
> temperat Archilochi Musam pede mascula Sappho,
> temperat Alcaeus, sed rebus et ordine dispar,
> nec socerum quaerit, quem versibus oblinat atris,
> nec sponsae laqueum famoso carmine nectit. (1.19.26–31)

> And so that you do not adorn me with scantier foliage because I was afraid to change the meters and artistry of his song, manly Sappho *temperat* her muse with the meter of Archilochus, and Alcaeus *temperat* his, but he is different in subject matter and arrangement, and he neither seeks out a father-in-law whom he might smear with dark verses nor weaves a noose for his betrothed with defamatory song.

Line 28 is the most difficult of the poem and has caused no shortage of scholarly ink to be spilled. To quote Fraenkel, "we are face to face with one of the most controversial passages in Latin poetry."[74] The interpretation centers around two points of difficulty: a) on what noun does the genitive *Archilochi* depend? and b) what exactly does *temperat* mean? Some, represented especially by Fraenkel, Macleod, and Woodman, have taken *Archilochi* with *musam*, arguing that *Archilochi* by its position cannot depend on *pede*; the meter referred to in *pede* would be Sappho's own, not that of Archilochus. Moreover, they have translated *temperat* as "modify," "soften," or even "dilute."[75] Fraenkel translates the line, "Sappho of the manlike spirit softens the poetry (the form of the poetry) of Archilochus by the way in which she treats the metre." He suggests that Horace, in claiming that Sappho and Alcaeus modified the meter of Archilochus, has in mind the complicated metrical practice of *adiectio* and *detractio*.[76] Macleod rejects the theory of *adiectio* and *detractio* and argues that "what Sappho and Alcaeus do to Archilochus, then, is not take over and modify his meter, but *temperare* his poetry with their meter." He later translates *temperat* as "modify." As Macleod himself points out, however, this would mean that the correspondence between Horace and Alaeus/Sappho would be lost, for they would be writing without Archilochean meter, whereas Horace clearly states that he followed the *numeros* of Archilochus (24).[77] Woodman has tried to solve this problem by claiming that Sappho and Alcaeus are *not* cited as parallels for Horace's own practice but instead as examples of the watered down version of invective that happens when Archilochean meter is not retained. He summarizes Horace's argument thus:

> His argument is: "I reproduced the metre and spirit of Archilochus but not the attack on Lycambes; and if you complain because I failed to change the metre, look at the poetry of Sappho and Alcaeus <who did effect such a change>: they produced only a diluted version (*temperat*) of Archilochus's poetry <and thus failed to reproduce his spirit>, though on the credit side (*sed*) they too avoided the attack on Lycambes [i.e., his *materiae vitium*]." Horace thus draws the lesson, superficially paradoxical, that his metrical "timidity" produced more daring poetry (i.e., truer to the spirit of Archilochus) whereas the metrical originality of Sappho and Alcaeus had the opposite effect.[78]

While Woodman's conclusions would resolve some of the line's interpretive problems, I cannot agree that Sappho and Alcaeus are held up as negative examples of diluted Archilochean verse. They must be analogous to Horace's own practice, and he quotes them to justify his method of imitation.[79]

Other scholars, going back to Bentley, have argued for a different reading of line 28 that allows *Archilochi* to depend on *pede*, so that Sappho and Alcaeus *temperat* their own poetry (*musam*) by retaining the meter of Archilochus.[80] This is a preferable reading of these difficult lines since it allows us to keep the parallelism between Horace, Sappho, and Alcaeus, and the need for Sappho's and Alcaeus's practice to correspond to that of Horace overrides the awkwardness of the genitive *Archilochi* being separated from the noun on which it depends. Mayer translates thus: "Masterly Sappho regulates her poetry with the metre of Archilochus."[81] According to this reading, both Sappho and Alcaeus, like Horace, retained one aspect of Archilochean poetry (the meter) while altering others. Alcaeus in particular changes Archilochus's *res* and *ordo* (29) and did not, like Horace, adopt harsh Archilochean invective. Perhaps most important, however, is the difficult translation of *temperat*, and I do not think that Mayer can be correct in simply translating it as "regulates." Proponents of both readings have connected the word with the idea of "mixing" or "blending," and the word is particularly associated with the sympotic practice of blending together water and wine, an idea that nicely picks up on the water and wine imagery of the poem.[82] A paraphrase of the passage might run as follows: "Manly Sappho blends together her poetry (subject matter) with the meter of Archilochus. Alcaeus likewise blends his with the meter of Archilochus, but he differs from him in *res* and *ordo* and does not adopt his hostile speech." By retaining Archilochean meter (wine) and mixing it with their own subject matter (water), Sappho and Alcaeus create an amalgam that, like Horace's, hits upon a mean in their reliance upon a poetic model and tones down the sharp freedom of speech found in Archilochus.[83] Unlike the slavish imitators Horace decries, they do not guzzle the unmixed wine (*mero*) of their model but create a mixture of water and wine that is both reliant on and independent from him.[84] Sappho and especially Alcaeus, whose method of imitation is more greatly elaborated, thus become models of moderate freedom for Horace to follow in the poetic realm in the same way that Aristippus is a model in the philosophical realm. Both Alcaeus and Aristippus walk a middle path between reliance on and independence from others, and at the same time they easily adapt subject matter to suit their own purposes. The repetition of *res* in 1.19 (*res*, 25; *rebus*, 29) loudly echoes Horace's Aristippean adaptability as outlined in 1.1.19–20: *nunc in Aristippi furtim praecepta relabor / et mihi res, non me rebus, subiungere conor*. This is the same adaptability that Aristippus practices in the social sphere in 1.17.22 (*omnis Aristippum decuit color et status et res*).[85] In philosophy, friendship, and poetry, Horace adopts the same adaptability and middle path between freedom from models/masters and overdependence on them.

It was not just in the *Epodes* that Horace achieved this kind of ideal imitation and independence. Alcaeus, whose imitative lead he followed in the *Epodes*, in turn became his model in the *Odes* and in emulating him Horace again achieved the proper mean between dependence and originality: *hunc ego, non alio dictum prius ore, Latinus / volgavi fidicen*, "I, the Latin lyricist, made him [i.e., Alcaeus] known, spoken by no mouth earlier," 32–33. At this mention of the *Odes*, however, the elevated status that Horace has claimed for himself throughout 1.19 begins to be called into doubt, and the slavish associations he gave his lyric poetry in 1.1 subtly begin to resurface. The word *volgavi* (33) means that he "made Alcaeus famous" or "a household name" (*OLD* s.v. 4), but it also suggests that he brought Alcaeus—and by extension, himself—into the public view of the *vulgus* (*OLD* s.v. 3d) and can even evoke prostitution (*OLD* s.v. 1b). This is the same exposure to the gaze of the *populus* that Horace had foresworn in the opening epistle and likened to slavery (*spectatum satis*, 2), and it therefore seems odd that Horace now boasts about this achievement. Again later in *Odes* 4.3, addressed to his muse Melpomene, he will describe how his role as *fidicen* exposes him to the gaze and pointing fingers of those who pass him in the street: *totum muneris hoc tui est, / quod monstror digito praetereuntium / Romanae fidicen lyrae,* "It is entirely your gift that I am pointed out as the lyricist of the Roman lyre by the finger of those who pass by me," 21–23. In *Epistles* 1.19.33–34 Horace's lyric success exposes him both to the gaze and to the hands of his readers: *iuvat immemorata ferentem / ingenuis oculisque legi manibusque teneri,* "it is pleasing that I, who report things not yet told, am read by freeborn eyes and held by freeborn hands." Horace's relationship with his readers in these lines becomes almost sexual, as he himself becomes the book that his readers will gawk at and fondle, and Horace's experience of this is not humiliating or degrading but pleasurable, *iuvat.* There is an important qualification in these lines, however, that must not be missed. Though publication involves exposure to the *vulgus* it is not their readership—their touch or gaze—that brings Horace pleasure, but rather that of the *ingenui,* "nobles," as becomes clear in *Satires* 1.10.78–91.[86] He auctions himself off not to the common rabble but to those that share his superior status.[87] Horace here therefore enacts a compromise. He does not, as in 1.1, refuse publication completely; rather, he confesses to having submitted his work to the *vulgus,* but rather than focusing on their judgment of him he instead takes pleasure from the approval of the elite. No matter how much freedom one achieves in the *writing* of poetry, the *publication* of poetry always involves some concession of autonomy and some reliance on the judgment of others. The question is whose approval one should court and whose judgment one should value. In order for Horace to achieve the recognition he craves for his poetic independence and originality—in order for him to be a poetic *princeps*—he simply has to compromise himself and to some degree become a slavish prostitute.[88]

In the final section of the poem Horace describes in further detail why he does not court the judgment and approval of the common populace, who in their unwarranted criticisms are like the unnecessarily harsh friend of 1.18. Resuming again his role as a patron in the sphere of poetry, he claims that such courting recalls a candidate canvassing for votes:

> scire velis, mea cur ingratus opuscula lector
> laudet ametque domi, premat extra limen iniquus:
> non ego ventosae plebis suffragia venor
> impensis cenarum et tritae munere vestis;
> non ego, nobilium scriptorum auditor et ultor
> grammaticas ambire tribus et pulpita dignor. (1.19.35–40)

> You wish to know why my ungrateful reader praises and loves my works at home but unfairly disparages them when he leaves his threshold: I do not hunt for the votes of the fickle plebs with expenditures on meals and gifts of threadbare clothes. I do not, as a hearer and avenger of noble writers, deem it worthwhile to entreat the tribes and platforms of the grammarians.

Horace's detractors secretly love his work in private but criticize it unfairly in public, and thus they take their frank criticism, *libertas*, to an insincere extreme. As Lowrie points out, the language of social class runs through these lines.[89] Horace's disdain is directed toward those of lower social standing, particularly the *ventosa plebs* and grammarians, who were often freed slaves.[90] Though Horace is nominally their social superior, courting their favor as a potential candidate would assign him an inferior role in relation to those who occupy the bottom of the social hierarchy since his success or failure would be dependent upon their approval or disapproval. The mention of *grammatici*, professional scholars, brings us into the worlds of the schoolroom and the recital hall, two venues where Horace is especially hesitant to seek approval.[91] A *recitatio*, in contrast to the quiet reading of those *ingenui* who enjoy Horace's work as a physical book, requires Horace's performance and involves a degree of public spectacle that he is hesitant to adopt, just as in the gladiatorial imagery of 1.1.[92]

As the poem ends the recital hall itself becomes a field of gladiatorial combat, as Horace imagines the kinds of battles he would have to wage were he to court the favor of the *vulgus* or the *grammatici*.[93] Such common *ludi* are simply not in line with Horace's poetic selectivity and would compel him to engage to an unacceptable degree with his harsh detractors. In other words, he would have to try to match their harsh criticism tit for tat:

> hinc illae lacrimae. 'spissis indigna theatris
> scripta pudet recitare et nugis addere pondus'
> si dixi, 'rides' ait 'et Iovis auribus ista
> servas; fidis enim manare poetica mella
> te solum, tibi pulcher.' ad haec ego naribus uti
> formido et, luctantis acuto ne secer ungui,
> 'displicet iste locus' clamo et diludia posco.
> ludus enim genuit trepidum certamen et iram,
> ira truces inimicitias et funebre bellum. (1.19.41–49)

> From this arise tears. If I said, "I am embarrassed to recite unworthy writings in crowded theaters and to add weight to trifles," he would say, "You are teasing. You keep those things for the ear of Jupiter, for you believe that you alone drip with poetic honey, beautiful to yourself." In response to these things I am afraid to stick up my nose and, in order not to be scratched by the sharp fingernail of the wrestler, I shout, "I do not like this place!" and demand a break in the *ludus*. For *ludus* has caused anxious rivalry and anger, and anger has caused savage enmities and deadly war.

The critic uses Horace's desire for a selective audience against him and claims that he desires Augustus himself, implied in *Iovis*, for his audience. He is thus accused of being nothing more than an imperial toady, and Horace has no desire to engage in such arguments, perhaps because they involve an element of truth insofar as his ideal readers are among the Augustan elite.[94] Such literary quarreling is like a public spectacle, such as a wrestling match (*luctantis*) or gladiatorial fight, from which Horace quickly tries to disentangle himself, calling for a *diludia*, "a break in the *ludus*." *Epistles* 1.19 thus closes just as 1.1 had begun, with a renunciation of gladiatorial *ludus*, but, whereas in 1.1 his refusal of *ludus* had itself involved a sharp degree of angry harshness toward Maecenas, in 1.19 he is moved by a desire to avoid *ira* and petty squabbling.[95] *Ludus* is competitive and thus leads to escalating violence: *certamen, ira, inimicitia,* and, finally, *funebre bellum.* In *Epistles* 1.3 Horace warned Florus, who seemed all too eager to engage in literary competition, against adhering to the mean in poetry but not in friendship, and Horace in 1.19 appears to practice what he preached earlier. He will not advise would-be poetic imitators to tone down their *libertas* at the same time that he participates in argumentative displays with his fellow poets.[96]

Horace's rejection of *ludus* in 1.19 is therefore not simply a repetition of the refusal he gave in 1.1, for the terms have changed in keeping with the ethical lessons Horace has developed over the collection. The most important change is Horace's characterization of his relationship with Maecenas. In 1.1 Maecenas's interests were aligned with those of the *populus* since he, as Horace's *lanista*, took an active role in exposing Horace to the fickle judgment of the mob. Far from refusing to enter the gladiatorial fray, Horace had been an active participant in it and was only recently manumitted. Like the wrestler of 1.19.46, who wields his sharp fingernail (*acuto ungui*) as a weapon against his adversary, Horace still sports his own badly pared fingernail: *prave sectum unguem,* 104. His harshness toward Maecenas and desire for uncompromising liberty can be read as a reaction to having just come from the gladiatorial arena, which he wants to reenter under no circumstances, and any desire on Maecenas's part for Horace to compromise is nothing more than a wish to re-enslave him. The *ludus* in which Horace has performed has in 1.1 led to the *inimicitia* and *ira* that in 1.19 he warns against.

In 1.19, however, Horace has gained some perspective and rethinks his earlier position, moderating it to suit the ethical lessons he has both learned and espoused throughout the book. Though he refuses to court the *populus* just as adamantly as he did in 1.1, he does not refuse public spectacle and poetic renown entirely. Maecenas is no longer the would-be *lanista,* a position that itself is not high on the social ladder, but one of his ideal, elite readers, as the vocative *Maecenas docte* (1) implies, and he is called upon as a defender of Horace's poetic freedom. Just as he sees Maecenas in a new light, he begins to see himself and his poetry from a different perspective. He eschews the extremes of freedom and slavery that he set out in the opening poem and finds instead a path for himself and his poetry between the two. The elevation in status he thereby enjoys in turn enables him to compromise in some measure with Maecenas. Maecenas and other *ingenui* are the ones for whom he will publish his poetry and to whose gaze he will expose himself while keeping aloof from the mob.[97] Though the *vulgus* reads and judges his poetry, he does not actively court their approval. Just as his poetry occupies a middle point between freedom and slavery, so too will he preserve this mean in relation to his readers, asserting his superiority to those who slavishly copy or harshly censure him while embracing some degree of dependence on those whose literary tastes he values. The hostility that he earlier directed toward Maecenas in 1.1 has thus been checked and moderated in keeping with his toning down of Archilochus's *libertas* in the *Epodes*, but it has not been repressed entirely. There remains a subtle warning to Maecenas: Do not pressure me to participate again in the *ludi* I despise or once again there will be anger and enmity. Your job is to be my ideal reader and recommend me to the *ingenui*, not parade me in front of the *populus* so that through me you might win their applause. I am, after all, your equal in the sphere of poetry, where, like you, I am a patron and model.

In 1.19 the collection has come full circle as Horace successfully applies to his own circumstances the various ethical lessons he has recommended to others. These lessons involve adaptability, compromise, and moderation, and they were recommended to his various addressees along the way, such as Lollius (1.2 and 1.18), Florus (1.3), Albius (1.4), Torquatus (1.5), Numicius (1.6), Bullatius (1.11), Iccius (1.12), and Scaeva (1.17). Horace applies these lessons to four main areas, which I have traced throughout this study: philosophy, location (city versus country), friendship, and poetry. In each area, he stands at a midpoint between being completely free from a master and being entirely dependent on one, and he can therefore involve himself with a number of potential masters without forfeiting his freedom to any. In the final poem of the collection, Horace takes this notion of moderate freedom a step further and problematizes it, fracturing himself into two halves, one that maintains his uncompromising independence and one that slavishly craves the gaze and touch, not of the select few, but of the vulgar mob. In the conclusion we will see that the compromise Horace enacts over the course of the book is not without discomfort; no matter how much freedom it allows him, it also requires him to acknowledge the servile, dependent part of himself. The final poem shows us that, though Horace professes in 1.19 to court only the elite, his ambition for his epistolary book cannot be so easily fulfilled by so small an audience. Perhaps the *vulgus* will have to be wooed after all so that a more enduring fame than that to be found among the Augustan elite can be won.

Conclusion

Freedom and Publication in
Epistles 1.13 and 1.20

T HE CHIEF ETHICAL STANCE OF *Epistles* 1 has been moderation and
adaptability as a means of avoiding extremes, and we have seen Horace
act as both the teacher and student of lessons on this theme. Moderation
and adaptability are the best ways to avoid fawning slavishly on another's words
or showing unrestrained independence, which leads to isolation. Throughout
the collection Horace positions himself in a space between freedom and slavery,
between the total absence of a master and complete subjection to one. Beginning
in the opening poem, he is both dependent on philosophical models and free
from them. As the collection unfolds he gradually applies this same moderate
freedom and slavery to other spheres. He prizes the rural Sabine farm and the
otia liberrima it provides him, but he simultaneously acknowledges it as a gift
from his superior friend. He also must learn to recognize the limitations of such
rural freedom and balance it with periods spent in the city with his friends. His
poetry too comes to occupy a space that is neither entirely free nor completely
servile. Horace never ceases to be something of a dual personality: on the one
hand, he persists in being drawn to the (free) life of withdrawal and private
contemplation, while on the other he is attracted to the (slavish) life of the city
as a source of public poetic acclaim and friendships with influential men. Neither sphere is complete enough to satisfy Horace's multifaceted personality.

In this concluding section I will trace how 1.13 and 1.20, in which Horace
sends forth or publishes his poetry, illuminate the two conflicting sides of the
Horatian epistolary persona. By comparing 1.13 and 1.20 we can better understand Horace's justification for publishing his *Epistles*, particularly since in 1.1
publication had rendered him a slave to the judgment of the *populus* and in 1.19
he had avowed that appreciation of his poetry was meant instead for an audience of the elite, learned few. In these poems Horace effectively reverses these

stances. Publication for the *vulgus* becomes an act of "freeing" and a small, elite audience is rejected as restrictive of independence. In 1.13 having a highly select readership—in this case an audience that consists of Augustus alone—heightens and exaggerates the servility of the poet, and his fears about how this audience of one will receive his poetry render him—or his proxy Vinnius—a bumbling, obsequious fool. In 1.20, it is instead distribution to a wide audience that exposes Horace to the charge of slavery. But as the one who releases (manumits) his book into the world Horace engages in a final act that is one not of enslaving but of freeing both his poems and by extension himself. The wide readership and eventual survival that he predicts for his book justify this act that otherwise compromises his independence and guarantee that his social successes are recorded for posterity. In both 1.13 and 1.20 the desire for publication is the mark of a slave, but in 1.20 Horace, by fulfilling this desire, simultaneously becomes a free patron and master who enjoys social distinction. The final picture we are left with is of a poet who straddles simultaneously the contradictory spheres of freedom and slavery. Though I have suggested throughout this study that Horace's redefinition of freedom reflects his contemporary political situation and Augustus's restricting of elite *libertas*, these two poems nevertheless show that by adhering to a mean of independence—which, in addition to rejecting *mera libertas*, entails eschewing slavish fawning—Horace avoids making the ethical lessons of his poetry mere propaganda for the Augustan regime. It is not Augustus's approval that Horace's poetry will slavishly court but that of a wider audience of both his contemporaries and future generations. In avoiding undiluted *libertas* Horace will not run to the opposite extreme of *obsequium plus aequo*.

Horace and Vinnius: The Bumbling Asses of *Epistles* 1.13

Epistles 1.13 is addressed to a man named Vinnius, who has been charged with taking some of Horace's poems to Augustus.[1] Though scholars have found the poem to be light and humorous, Horace nevertheless exposes in it a deep concern about his relationship with Augustus and the degree to which this relationship and the poetry that makes it possible compromises his independence.[2] The poem advertises Horace's proximity and access to Augustus, but it does so in a way that ultimately emphasizes his social inferiority to the *princeps*.[3] By deferring to the judgment of a single, powerful man Horace reduces himself, through his humorous doppelganger Vinnius, to a bumbling ass whose servility is on display throughout.[4] It is not the quality of the poems that ensures a positive reception, but the messenger's careful obedience to protocol. Such a route for publication is ultimately rejected, and the book of *Epistles* will take a far different path to fame in the final poem. Horace will ensure the survival and success of his epistolary poetry not through fawning on Augustus, which in the end only demonstrates his servility, but through seeking out a larger and longer lasting audience.

Horace opens *Epistles* 1.13 in the didactic mode by taking up the role of teacher: *ut proficiscentem docui te saepe diuque*, "As I advised you, setting out, often and at length," 1. As Oliensis states, "the epistle opens onto a scene of what looks like philosophical instruction, with Horace 'teaching' a Stoic wayfarer (a *proficiens*)."[5] As quickly becomes obvious, however, Horace is not concerned with Vinnius's ethical or spiritual life but with his comporting himself properly when he brings Horace's poetry into the presence of Augustus. Not only did Horace give him ample instructions before he set out on how to behave in Augustus's presence, but he is now sending this letter as a reminder to him en route:

> Augusto reddes signata volumina, Vinni,
> si validus, si laetus erit, si denique poscet;
> ne studio nostri pecces odiumque libellis
> sedulus importes opera vehemente minister. (1.13.2–5)

> Vinnius, you will deliver the sealed scrolls to Augustus if he is well, if he is happy, and, finally, if he asks for them. Do not in your zeal towards me stumble and incur hatred for my little books by being a servant too eager in your service.

In these opening lines Horace urges Vinnius to adopt a posture of deference to Augustus, but he is concerned that such deference might cause him to become awkward and blundering in Augustus's presence. Vinnius has to navigate a very tricky situation by acknowledging Augustus's supremacy without provoking his annoyance. Oliensis has nicely connected Horace's instructions here with the close of the preceding epistle, 1.12, where Horace offers Iccius an update on Augustus's achievements, including the return of the Roman standards by the Parthian king, Phrahates: *ius imperiumque Phrahates / Caesaris accepit genibus minor; aurea fruges / Italiae pleno defudit Copia cornu*, "Phrahates has received the justice and rule of Caesar with bended knees; golden Abundance pours forth her produce on Italy from her abundant horn," 27–29. Horace cleverly alludes to the return of these standards in 1.13.2, where "you will return the standards to Augustus" is encoded into Horace's instructions: *Augusto reddes signata*. To quote Oliensis, Horace's words "show his 'standard-bearer' in a Parthian posture, deferentially bowing before the emperor, and with an oversized bookroll in his outstretched hand."[6] This image sets up a great disparity between Augustus and Vinnius, with Augustus cast as the triumphant master of the known world and poor Vinnius as the lowly messenger who must show appropriate regard for his majesty.

Horace's worry is that in his eager haste to please Augustus Vinnius risks acting like a bumbling fool and turning himself into a laughingstock or, as Horace suggests, punning on his name, an ass:

> si te forte meae gravis uret sarcina chartae,
> abicito potius quam quo perferre iuberis
> clitellas ferus impingas Asinaeque paternum
> cognomen vertas in risum et fabula fias. (1.13.6–9)

> If by chance the heavy package of paper should cause you discomfort, cast it aside rather than wildly throwing down the pack where you are ordered to deliver it and thereby turning your father's cognomen of Asina into a source of derision and yourself into a topic of gossip.

Horace humorously suggests that his slender book of poems might prove too great a burden for Vinnius, in which case he should avoid awkwardly throwing it down in Augustus's presence. He would thereby live up to his father's name, *Asina*, "ass," and Horace plays throughout line 8 on the identification of Vinnius with this particular beast of burden, calling him *ferus*, "wild," and referring to the poems he carries as *clitellae*, "pack-saddles."[7] Horace's particular fear is that Vinnius will become a source of amused gossip (*in risum*; *fabula*) if he acts unbecomingly in front of Augustus. Horace takes pains to instruct Vinnius even on how to carry the book, urging that he not place it rudely under his armpit (which we will learn in line 16 is sweaty, *te sudavisse*):

> sic positum servabis onus, ne forte sub ala
> fasciculum portes librorum, ut rusticus agnum,
> ut vinosa glomus furtivae †Pirria† lanae,
> ut cum pilleolo soleas conviva tribulis. (1.13.12–15).

> You will keep the burden positioned in such a way that you do not happen to carry the packet of books under your armpit as a rustic carries a lamb, as the wine-loving Pirria carries the ball of stolen thread, as a commoner carries his sandals along with his cap when he is a dinner guest.

Vinnius should not, Horace warns, carry the book like someone of the lower classes, such as a *rusticus* carrying a lamb or a *tribulis* invited to his patron's dinner, who carries his own shoes and hat because he has no slave of his own. Pirria, according to Mayer, refers to a character from a mime or comedy, and she no doubt is of similarly low standing.[8] Throughout these lines it is status— that of Vinnius and by extension himself and his poems—that causes Horace anxiety. Deference from an inferior to a superior may all too easily resemble awkward servility. Such behavior might be amusing for others to watch, like a funny play, but it results in a loss of one's dignity. It is highly significant that the particular status in question here is that of the freedman, as the *pilleolus* in line 15 makes clear. This is the diminutive form of *pilleus*, the cap that was associated most especially with freed slaves. It is just this status that Horace adopts in 1.1 when he fashions himself as a freed gladiator and refuses to show deference that might compromise his freedom, and it is just such obsequiousness that Horace describes in 1.13 as he presents his poetry to the *princeps*, the grandest patron of all.

At this point we must ask why Horace describes in such rich detail the bumbling behavior he is so eager for his emissary to avoid and thereby vividly creates the picture of an asinine Vinnius in the reader's imagination.[9] By doing so Horace exposes his anxieties about his own relationship with Augustus and the servility he might be accused of because of it. Vinnius is a projection of Horace and embodies the potentially asinine and slavish aspects of his personality. Oliensis correctly refers to Vinnius as a "carnival-mirror image of the letter-writer" and as Horace's "servile double."[10] Horace paints such a vivid picture of Vinnius's awkwardness because these are the fears running obsessively through his own mind. The language that Horace uses to describe Vinnius's possible gaffes in fact connects him directly with Horace and strengthens the suggestion that Horace is concerned not with Vinnius's behavior, but with his own. Freudenburg points out that Horace and Vinnius share an "asinine cognomen," since "Flaccus" as an adjective can describe the drooping ears of an ass.[11] If Vinnius behaves like a buffoon it will be Horace, not Vinnius, who lives up to the asinine quality of his name. In 1.1 Horace compares himself to another equine, a horse, in language strongly recalled in 1.13.[12] He here describes a voice ringing through his ears that encourages him to put aside lyric for epistolary poetry. If not, the voice threatens, he risks making a laughingstock of himself like an aged racehorse: *solve senescentem mature sanus equum, ne /peccet ad extremum ridendus et ilia ducat*, "Wisely let loose the aging racehorse at the right time, lest he stumble ridiculously at the end and wheeze," 8–9. The *ne peccet* of these lines is picked up in 1.13.4 (*ne studio nostri pecces*) while the idea of stumbling is found also in the final line of the poem (*cave ne titubes*, "take care that you not stagger," 19). The awkward and slavish behavior that Vinnius might display is therefore analogous to that which Horace wants to avoid in the earlier poem, and in each case the one who behaves in this way is exposed to the humiliating laughter of others (*ridendus*, 1.1.9; *in risum*, 1.13.9). Such bumbling deference is the hallmark behavior of a slave toward his social betters, and by so vividly describing it in 1.13 Horace clearly marks himself out as Augustus's servile inferior.[13] Just as such servility toward the *populus* was rejected in 1.1, in 1.13 Horace implicitly illustrates why such obsequiousness toward the *princeps* must similarly be denied.

In both 1.1 and 1.13 it is not the *Epistles* but another text that causes such anxiety in Horace. As we saw in the first chapter, the poetry that in 1.1 compels Horace to parade himself in front of the crowd (*populus*) for judgment is most likely his *Odes* but may simply be any work that has been sent out for publication and so may also include the *Epodes* and *Satires*. Publication in 1.1 was to Horace akin to being enslaved in gladiatorial combat, in which he has to beg for the people's approval (*populum . . . exoret*, 6), and his withdrawal into the countryside signaled his refusal to participate in such slavery and led instead to the writing of epistles that demonstrate his freedom in a number of ways: a) they have no clear model, either poetic or philosophical, b) they contemplate the nature of freedom throughout, and c) they are as yet unpublished and so do not compromise their author's independence. In 1.13 publication similarly leads to an obsequious display of deference, but this time it is to Augustus alone and not the larger *populus*. Horace teasingly does not specify *which* poems Vinnius is to take to Augustus until the very end, where he reveals that it is *carmina*, which most likely refers to odes:[14]

> neu vulgo narres te sudavisse ferendo
> carmina quae possint oculos aurisque morari
> Caesaris. oratus multa prece nitere porro.
> vade, vale, cave ne titubes mandataque frangas. (1.13.16–19)

> Do not tell the common folk that you are sweating because you are carrying *carmina* that may be able to delay the eyes and ears of Caesar. Even if you are entreated by many pleas, press on further. Go and farewell. Be careful not to stumble and break what has been entrusted to you.

Horace here clearly states that his *carmina* are not aimed toward the *vulgus*'s approval, as they are in *Epistles* 1.1, but to the eyes and ears of the emperor alone, a charge that Horace consequently has difficulty defending himself against at 1.19.43–44: *et Iovis auribus ista / servas*, "you are keeping those things for the ears of Jove." Horace's emissary Vinnius is not to speak to the *vulgus* at all, either because the poetry he carries enjoys Callimachean exclusivity[15] or, and this is more probable in the context of 1.13, because such deference toward Augustus, if publicized, would, like Vinnius's bumbling behavior, cause the poet embarrassment by suggesting that his relationship with Augustus is fawning or subservient. Horace does not, after all, deliver the poems himself, and he urges Vinnius to employ the greatest secrecy. In both 1.1 and 1.13 the poetry whose reception causes Horace distress is pointedly not the *Epistles*. The most likely candidate is the *Odes*, but even that is left purposefully vague. The specific identification of this poetry is less important than its symbolic function. It is meant as a foil to the epistolary poetry that makes up the current book. Whatever this poetry is, it leads to slavishness, while the epistles produce freedom. It brings Horace into view of others (*spectatum*, 1.1; *oculos*, 17), while the epistles allow him a hidden escape (*latet abditus agro*, 1.1.5). Through it Horace can explore the issues involved in publication that his epistles have yet to face and prepare us as readers for the route to public view that the epistles will eventually take to reach our own eyes and ears. *Epistles* 1.13 offers one potential path of publication that will ultimately be refused to Horace's epistolary poems, since to follow it would lean Horace too far toward the extreme of slavery and dependence.

Taken together, 1.1 and 1.13 seem to offer little redemption for the idea of publication. Whether one courts the approval of the lowly *populus* or Augustus, the end product is potential degradation and humiliation. We must keep in mind, however, that Horace's attitude does not remain fixed from the beginning to the end of the collection and that again and again he revises his initial opening stance. *Epistles* 1.13 offers one possible revision to the situation of 1.1 as Horace begins to explore a number of alternatives for what audience his poetry should court. *Epistles* 1.1 rules out the *populus*, while 1.13 shows the problems of aiming instead toward the highest-ranking member of Roman society. Not only does this highlight the disparity between the status of poet and *princeps* but it severely limits the fame that a poet might derive from his poetry. The silence that Horace urges Vinnius to keep toward the *vulgus* in 1.13 and his reserving his poetry for Augustus's eyes and ears alone do not allow Horace's poetry to enjoy the wider readership that might bring him renown. In other poems the appropriate audience lies in the middle between these two extremes. In 1.18.65–66 it is Lollius's patron whose approval Horace encourages him to seek by participating in mock-gladiatorial poetic *ludus*. In 1.19.33–34 Horace claims that his ideal audience consists of a few elite readers, in whose company *Maecenas doctus* (1) is no doubt included: *iuvat immemorata ferentem / ingenuis oculisque legi manibusque teneri*. Here the eyes of the *ingenui* allude back to and contrast with Augustus's eyes (*oculos*) in 1.13.17. As an audience at which to aim, the patron is a compromise between the extremes of the *populus* and the *princeps*, both of whom threaten to undermine the poet's freedom. The patron therefore offers the poet a middle ground through which he can seek an audience to approve of his poetry without entirely jeopardizing his *libertas*.

But the approval of one's patron and a select group of readers is simply not enough for someone who, like Horace, *does* have ambition and wants public renown. A wider readership than just the elite few is necessary, and consequently so is some degree of servitude, even an uncomfortable degree of servitude. If Horace has to court one of the extremes in order to ensure his success, which is better? The *populus* or the *princeps*? *Epistles* 1.13 explains why it must be the former. In Augustus's presence, there is nowhere for Horace's own status to go but down. It is not Vinnius but Horace who we ultimately envision stumbling before the emperor's superior eye, and there is no larger acclaim here to redeem his awkward servility. The route to publication that the *Epistles* itself will take will be different from the one imagined in 1.13. It will court instead the *populus*—of which the *princeps* is ultimately a part—and thus will do precisely what Horace had refused to do in 1.1. In the process the book will expose itself to a wide range of readers now and in the future rather than limiting itself to Augustus alone or even an elite few.[16] It is not that publication and courting the *populus* no longer result in slavery, but Horace has learned over the course of the collection how to balance such slavery with freedom and how to walk a middle path between the two extremes. *Epistles* 1.20 will be the final compromise between freedom and slavery made by Horace in the collection and the one that ultimately ensures that his poetic accomplishment is not forgotten.

I have suggested throughout this book that Horace reformulates freedom to make it align not with uncompromising extremism but with the mean as a reaction to the solidification of Augustan power and that this reformulation reflects the transformation of *libertas* in the early principate. But by contrasting 1.13 and 1.20 we see that such a mean, in which one adheres to neither extreme *libertas* nor extreme *servitus*, allows one also to reject simple flattery of Augustus and opens up a path whereby slavishness toward the *princeps* can be avoided. Horace will not take a flatterer's route to publication since this offers him no middle ground, and he will thus ensure that he is no mere toady of the new regime. The path that the *Epistles* will take will instead be between freedom and slavery and will allow Horace to reach well beyond the politics of his own day and age to find a more enduring claim to success.

Publication as Manumission: *Epistles* 1.20

The closing poem of the book contrasts greatly in tone with the victorious and celebratory finales of *Odes* 2 and 3, in which Horace boasts of his poetic achievement and foretells the immortality of his work.[17] *Epistles* 1.20, on the other hand, has a much more ambivalent tone that arises from the problematic associations that have been given in the collection to courting the literary approval of the *populus* (esp. 1.1 and 1.19) and publication in general (esp. 1.1 and 1.13).[18] Publication, whether to an audience of one or many, necessitates that the author cede control of his work and submit himself to the judgment of another, and consequently it places the audience in a position of power over the author. In 1.1 the published Horace is akin to an enslaved gladiator awaiting the verdict of the *populus*, while in 1.13 the act of publication is accompanied by a series of obsequious gestures that illustrate the poet's bumbling servility. And yet, despite the fact that broad publication necessarily compromises his independence, Horace relents in the final poem and sends forth his *liber* first to Rome and, thence, to the world at large and into posterity. This is the final compromise between freedom and slavery that is enacted in the collection, and Horace achieves it by what Xenophon's Socrates might call a "clever trick," δεινὸν πάλαισμα.[19] He separates himself from the book he has been writing and projects all of his own ambitions for publication and success onto the book, which is figured as a slave that Horace then sends or "manumits" into the world. Horace thereby extricates himself from the book's "slavish" desires for publication and casts himself instead as the slave's "master," whose public successes the *liber* will sing to future readers. Whereas in 1.1 it is Horace who stands in front of the *populus* for judgment, in 1.20 it will be the book alone who will venture forth while its master stays safely ensconced in the *libertas* of private withdrawal. Ultimately, however, the book and its author cannot so easily be dissociated from one another. The epistolary Horace and the epistolary book, most importantly, share the status of being a *libertinus*, a "freedman," which casts each as not entirely free and not entirely slave.

The poem is addressed to the *liber* itself, and throughout the poem the book simultaneously is treated literally as a book and metaphorically as a young slave boy. The book/slave belongs to Horace, in whose household he was raised (*nutritus*, 5), but it/he longs to be sent forth to the city. As in *Epistles* 1.14, addressed to Horace's *vilicus*, yearning for the city is a slavish desire from which Horace attempts to distance himself:

> Vortumnum Ianumque, liber, spectare videris,
> scilicet ut prostes Sosiorum pumice mundus;
> odisti clavis et grata sigilla pudico,
> paucis ostendi gemis et communia laudas,
> non ita nutritus. (1.20.1–5)

> You seem, my book, to gaze at Vortumnus and Janus, no doubt so that you might be polished by the pumice of the Sosii and put yourself up for sale (or "prostitute yourself"). You hate the keys and the seals that please the chaste. You groan about being shown to few and praise public places, though this is not how you were raised.

The poem's opening words *Vortumnum Ianumque* point to the area in Rome where the booksellers were located, but they also evoke ideas of changeability and signal that Horace is here doing an "about-face." Vortumnus (or Vertumnus) is a god associated with transformation who traditionally has the ability to take on many forms and disguises. His presence here helps explain Horace's change of mind in allowing his poetry to court the *populus*, which he had refused to do in the opening poem. He is furthermore an appropriate god to name in the closing poem of a book in which adaptability has taken such a prominent role. Janus, as the god of openings and closings, especially invites us to compare this final poem with the first one and to consider the ways in which Horace's attitude has both changed and remained consistent.[20] In both poems Horace is highly critical of the act of publication, comparing it to gladiatorial combat in 1.1 and prostitution (*prostes*, 2) in 1.20. But whereas in 1.1 Horace retreats into rural isolation, in 1.20 he relents and begrudgingly allows his book to go forth and court the kind of public approval that he had earlier rejected. Horace's opening and closing poems expose his contradictory desire for both isolated obscurity and public distinction.

The desires of the book for a large audience furthermore undermine the compromise he made in 1.19.33–34, in which he professes to court a small, elite readership.[21] The sexual overtones of 1.19.33–34, discussed in the last chapter, are in 1.20 taken to an extreme as publication is analogous to indiscriminate prostitution, whereas in the earlier poem Horace had reserved his poetic charms for a small readership. Horace's avoidance of a large audience in 1.19 speaks not only to his reluctance to submit himself to the judgment of the *vulgus* but also to his Callimachean exclusivity since Callimachus was well known for his disdain for poetry that appealed to popular tastes.[22] He famously compares such poetry to a "wandering beloved," a description that well suits the promiscuous erotic desires of Horace's *liber* in 1.20.[23] The *liber* itself, however, does aspire to Callimachean polish and refinement (*pumice mundus*, 2), but he will employ such charms to court a non-Callimachean audience in "public places," *communia* (4), and he resents the fact that Horace reserves him for only a few readers (*paucis ostendi gemisi*, 4). Horace in frustration declares that this is not how he raised the *liber*, thereby suggesting that the book has not been a good student of the lessons contained within it because he wants to do the very things against which Horace has been preaching. One could argue, however, that Horace's ideals *have* rubbed off on the book since the *liber*, like Horace, rejects enslavement and wants independence. As in 1.14 to the *vilicus*, the rural isolation that is freedom to Horace is slavery to the *liber*, and as long as Horace keeps him under lock and key the *līber* (book) cannot be truly *līber* (free).[24] Whereas in 1.1 publication equaled slavery for Horace, in 1.20 publication equals freedom for the book, and Horace, like Maecenas in 1.1, must allow his slave to go free to forge its own path to independence.[25]

As a product of Horace's pen, however, the wishes of the book are not so easily disentangled from those of Horace. If we follow other scholars in reading the book's desire for publication as a projection of Horace's own desire,[26] we see that Horace has dramatically expanded the sphere in which he can exercise freedom; before, freedom was only possible by nonpublication or by courting a very limited audience, but, by allowing the book to leave its master's (i.e., his) control, Horace allows his own desires for wide publication to be fulfilled. Thus, through the book, Horace can yield to his own "slavish" desires for poetic renown, and this is figured paradoxically as an act of liberation or manumission.[27] By manumitting the book and allowing it to seek freedom in what he had heretofore considered slavish, Horace displays, though somewhat grudgingly, his own adaptability to seemingly contradictory stances. This is not an unproblematic freedom, however, since the slave will spend its time in the less than noble profession of prostitution, frequently practiced by slaves. The freedom that the book will enjoy will be significantly limited, and its formerly servile status colors the future that Horace predicts for it.

In 1.20.5–8 Horace explicitly figures the publication of the book as manumission:

> fuge quo descendere gestis.
> non erit emisso reditus tibi. 'quid miser egi?
> quid volui?' dices, ubi quid te laeserit; et scis
> in breve te cogi, cum plenus languet amator.

> Flee where you long to go. You will not be able to return once you have been released. "What have I, a wretch, done? What did I want?" you will say when something has caused you harm and you realize that you have been forced into a small case when your sated lover grows tired of you.

Fuge (5) suggests at first that the only option for freedom open to the book is to run away and become a *fugitivus*, to which Horace had likened himself in 1.10.10 in describing his flight from the city to the freedom of the countryside. With *emisso*, however, Horace suggests that he is in fact willingly releasing the book into the larger world, and such a release is simultaneously an act of "publishing" and "manumitting."[28] The letter in some ways resembles a *manumissio per epistulam*, an informal method of manumission in which a master addressed a letter to a slave granting him freedom.[29] Horace's status has therefore undergone a reversal over the course of the collection from being the freed gladiator of Maecenas in 1.1 to being a master in his own right about to free his own slave. Whereas Maecenas wants his freedman Horace to reenlist in his servitude (presumably by publishing more poetry), Horace in 1.20 warns the *liber* that once he is free (i.e., published), there will be no return. A published text is irrevocable, as Horace reminds us at 1.18.71, using the same word, *emittere: semel emissum volat irrevocabile verbum*, "a word once sent out flies forth and cannot be called back." Nor does publication guarantee the wide audience that the book craves, for the book's sated lover will store him away in a book roll, where he will be shown not even to a few.[30]

Liberation is therefore a risky course for the book with no guarantee for success, and Horace tries to convince it to stay by listing all that could go wrong. Acting as an *augur* he foretells the book's likely fate. The book will enjoy a brief vogue in Rome, being passed promiscuously from one reader/lover to another, but it will end up utterly degraded, food for lice or shipped in chains to the provinces:

> quodsi non odio peccantis desipit augur,
> carus eris Romae donec te deserat aetas:
> contrectatus ubi manibus sordescere vulgi
> coeperis, aut tineas pasces taciturnus inertis
> aut fugies Uticam aut vinctus mitteris Ilerdam. (1.20.9–13)

> But if your fortuneteller has not lost his reason due to his annoyance at your error, you will be dear in Rome until your youth deserts you. When you have begun to grow dirty by being felt by the hands of the mob, either you will silently feed sluggish maggots or you will flee to Utica or be sent in chains to Ilerda.

The book's Callimachean polish is, like youth, only temporary and will necessarily fade as the book is passed around the hands of his vulgar, non-Callimachean readership and becomes tarnished. The book's defilement by vulgar hands recalls by contrast Horace's own delight in being handled by the *ingenui* (*iuvat . . . ingenuis oculisque legi manibusque teneri*, 1.19.33–34) and is at odds with the route to publication he had taken in 1.13 by entrusting his poems to Vinnius, whom he warns to take special care to avoid the curiosity of the *vulgus* (16). In 1.20 Horace's tone is highly ambivalent. He seems to disdain the *vulgus* much as he did in 1.13 and 1.19, but at the same time he nevertheless relents and allows his book to take this path toward publication, and it forms a step necessary for the survival of his text, which in turn will act as a record of his own life and accomplishments. The epistles will not, despite Horace's protestations and hesitance, keep aloof from common readers or be reserved for the elite few.

Horace suggests, however, that such vulgarization will not immediately pay off, for after its bloom has faded nobody will read the book, and it will fall into silence (*taciturnus*, 12). This is a dire prediction indeed for a book that heretofore has been described through verbs that imply speaking (*gemis*, 4; *laudas*, 4; *dices*, 7) and whose desire for liberation betrays its longing to speak out the words it contains to as wide an audience as possible.[31] As the book loses its voice its status becomes little distinguishable from its former servitude and its liberation from Horace seems to have been in vain, since the book's only options will be either to flee (*fugies*, 13) or be shipped in chains (*vinctus*, 13; i.e., bound up as a parcel) to the provinces. Again there is ambivalence in Horace's prediction. Though this is ostensibly a humiliating fate for the little book, it nevertheless holds out hope that Horace's poetry will spread beyond the city of Rome, which will enable it to achieve an audience that is larger than that found within the confines of the city.[32] Such degradation will ultimately expose the book to a larger and more enduring audience, and the loss of the book's Callimachean polish will give way to a more genuine literary value as the book recovers its lost voice.

In lines 14–16 Horace continues to evoke his earlier qualms about publication in 1.1 and 1.13:

> ridebit monitor non exauditus, ut ille
> qui male parentem in rupes protrusit asellum
> iratus; quis enim invitum servare laboret?

> The one who warns you and has gone unheeded will laugh, just like the one who angrily pushed his disobedient ass over the crags. For who would work to save someone who does not want to be saved?

Like Vinnius in 1.13, the book is in danger of making an ass of itself. Horace alludes to the Aesopic fable of the ass and its driver, in which the ass tries to reach its destination by taking a shortcut down a cliff, much to its driver's chagrin and despite his warnings, and pays with its life.[33] Horace here plays the role of the driver and the book that of the ass, and Horace's warnings, like those of the driver, fall on deaf ears. In 1.13 Vinnius's asinine behavior was likened to "erring" or "sinning," (*pecces*, 4), and in 1.20 the *liber* too is accused of the same kind of error (*peccantis*, 9). In both 1.13 and 1.20 the result of such error is humiliating laughter: *vertas in risum*, 1.13.9 and *ridebit*, 1.20.9. In 1.13, furthermore, Horace warns Vinnius that he not *fabula fias*, "become a fable," a fable like the one Horace now uses to dissuade the *liber* from leaving him. The asinine *liber* is also like the Horace of the opening poem, who has his own *monitor* warning him not to pursue such an audience and thereby make himself the butt of laughter: *est mihi purgatam crebro qui personet aurem: 'solve senescentem mature sanus equum, ne / peccet ad extremum ridendus et ilia ducat*, 8–9. Just as his position in 1.20 is now that of the master instead of the slave, he has also become the adviser rather than the advisee. Despite this transformation, the similarities between the Horace of 1.1 and the *liber* of 1.20 nevertheless remain in force, and the publication of his text in 1.20 can be read as an act of disobedience to the admonitory voice of 1.1. He is not, in the end, any better a student of his *monitor* than his book is of him, and he grudgingly allows his epistolary book to run the risk of making an ass of itself—and him.

The similarities between Horace and his book become even more pronounced as the poem unfolds. The next step that Horace foretells in the book's future life shows it no longer as a youthful and polished prostitute but as an aged schoolmaster teaching boys their ABCs: *hoc quoque te manet, ut pueros ele-menta docentem / occupet extremis in vicis balba senectus*, "This too awaits you, that babbling old age seize you as you teach boys their ABCs in the farthest villages."[34] The book in its old age will become a *ludi magister*, a primary school teacher, a position usually taken up by those of lowly status, such as slaves and freedmen.[35] Scholars almost unanimously consider this the worst imaginable fate for the little book. Bonner calls it "the crowning humiliation," while Harrison suggests that the book's "export to a two-bit province, ending up . . . as an aid to the teaching of spelling" undermines the grandiose predictions Horace gives to his lyric poetry in *Odes* 2.20 and 3.30.[36] Oliensis takes the *balba* of line 18 as especially negative, stating that the elderly book "will no longer be under-stood as anything more than a collection of nonsense signifiers of a certain limited educational use."[37] Horace, to be sure, is critical in *Satires* 1.10.73–75 of the poetry taught in such schools since it is not in keeping with his desires for a limited readership:

> neque te ut miretur turba labores,
> contentus paucis lectoribus. an tua demens
> vilibus in ludis dictari carmina malis?

> Nor should you work for the crowd to admire you, but be content with a few read-ers. Or do you foolishly prefer that your songs be dictated in cheap schools?

As we have seen, however, Horace in 1.20 repeatedly contradicts his earlier positions regarding publication, and the book's position as a schoolteacher, though not glamorous, can be read in a positive light. In fact it is when the book's youthful beauty has faded and it takes this educational role that the genuine worth of the book is able to assert itself. The schoolroom imagery from the first epistle reappears here in the last and connects the educational activity of the book with that of Horace in the earlier poem.[38] In 1.1 Horace spent his new freedom in studying the basics of morals and ethics, which he likened to *elementa* (27), "ABCs." Rather than enroll in the corrupt schoolroom of Janus (1.1.52–56), in which *iuvenes senesque* dictate (*dictata*) their *magister*'s morally corrupt lessons, Horace forged an independent educational path dedicated to studying not only various philosophical schools but literary works as well. Horace in turn distills these moral lessons to his various epistolary addressees, acting both as student and teacher throughout the collection. It is just this role of teacher that the book now inherits from Horace, for it teaches the same *elementa* that Horace care-fully had gathered and composed.[39] Such ethical study was especially suitable to Horace's advancing age (*non eadem est aetas*, 1.1.4), just as it will be in its *senec-tus* (18) that the book will take over this educational role. *Balba* indeed can be taken in a positive light, as it evokes the book's slow and careful pronunciation of the words that it contains, which the schoolboys are meant to repeat.[40] We have seen throughout this study that Horace himself refuses ever to repeat a *magister*'s dictation since to do so would compromise his independence; rather, the only teacher whose words should be repeated are his own, and it is these words that the book now carefully pronounces for the benefit of its charges. In *Epistles* 2.1.126 one of the civic virtues of the poet is that he guides the early reading of children in this way, and there the *puer* rather than his teacher is described as *balbus*: *os tenerum pueri balbumque poeta figurat*. Horace had attributed just such an educational role to himself in the *Satires*, likening his poetry to the cookies that teachers give to boys in order to encourage them to learn *elementa*: *ut pueris olim dant crustula blandi / doctores, elementa velint ut discere prima*, "just as coaxing teachers sometimes give cookies to boys, so that they might be willing to learn their first ABCs," *Satires* 1.1.25–26.[41] The *ut pueros elementa docentem* of *Epistles* 1.20.17 no doubt recalls this earlier passage and signals that the *liber* accedes to this educational function from its own former *magister*, Horace.

The word *balba* takes on positive associations in other ways as well. Whereas in line 12 the book had fallen into total silence (*taciturnus*), the stammering speech of the old *liber* signals that it is reclaiming the voice it had lost when its beauty faded.[42] Within three lines the book will once again resume full speech (*loqueris*, 21). Thus the book's position as a schoolteacher is a crucial step in the survival of Horace's text. It is the book's role in memorializing Horace and his voice with which the poem closes, as Horace dictates his own message, which forms a kind of *sphragis* for the book to repeat carefully to its future readers:

> cum tibi sol tepidus pluris admoverit aures,
> me libertino natum patre et in tenui re
> maiores pinnas nido extendisse loqueris,
> ut, quantum generi demas, virtutibus addas;
> me primis Urbis belli placuisse domique,
> corporis exigui, praecanum, solibus aptum,
> irasci celerem, tamen ut placabilis essem. (1.20.19–25)

> When a warm sun has brought a greater audience (literally "more ears") to you, you will say that I, born from a freedman father and in modest estate, stretched out wings too big for my nest, so that whatever you subtract from my birth you add to my virtues. And that I pleased the foremost of the city in war and at peace, that I had a short body, was prematurely gray, fond of the sun, quick to get mad yet easily calmed.

Though several scholars agree that this period of the book's *vita* takes a more positive turn than and thus marks a new movement from what has gone before,[43] I would argue that from the time of its manumission/publication the book has steadily been progressing toward this moment when it can record and proclaim the achievements of its author. It is at this point that the book's desire—and Horace's—for a large audience will be truly fulfilled, and this audience will not be attracted by the book's shiny yet ephemeral glossiness but by the words that it contains. The *plures aures*, "more ears," that will form the book's audience evoke a motif that has run throughout the collection, as Horace has searched out the right "ears" into which to pour his ethical teachings as well as the right ones to hear his published poetry.[44] These *plures aures* contrast especially with those of Augustus in 1.13.16, and Horace thereby rejects restricting his poetry to so exclusive an audience as the emperor. The message that Horace has the book record is one meant for many rather than the few or especially only one.

Central to the *sphragis* that Horace dictates to the book is his social rise, which exposes him as a man proud of his public successes. This provides further justification for his decision to publish his text and court a large audience, for anonymity and obscurity are simply not options for such a poet, just as being confined under lock and key is not enough for his ambitious *liber*.[45] Horace's likening of himself to a bird with outstretched wings will be later recalled in *Epistles* 2.2.49–52, where he looks back to an earlier period of his life when his wings were not stretched wide but clipped due to the social setback he suffered after taking sides with Brutus at Philippi:

> unde simul primum me demisere Philippi,
> decisis humilem pennis inopemque paterni
> et laris et fundi, paupertas impulit audax
> ut versus facerem.

> As soon as Philippi dismissed me from there, bold poverty compelled me, humiliated with clipped wings and without my paternal wealth and estate, to compose poetry.

Horace transformed these humiliatingly clipped wings into the outstretched ones of *Epistles* 1.20.21, which exceed the humble circumstances into which he was born, and publishing poetry is what has enabled Horace to achieve such a daring social climb. Without publication the social success of which Horace boasts in 1.20 is impossible and cannot be recorded for posterity.[46] This again signals a significant reversal from the opening poem, in which Horace chooses a hidden life of freedom (*latet abditus agro*, 5) over a public one that entails submission. In 1.1 his poetic success, far from allowing him to transcend the humble status of his birth, demotes him further into slavery. By leaving a permanent record of his social achievements in 1.20 Horace does not so much divest them of such slavish associations as accept some loss of independence as a requisite for one who has public ambition. Horace's focus on his friendship with powerful men in line 23 (*me primis Urbis . . . placuisse*) connects him above all to the young addressees of 1.17 and 1.18, whom Horace had advised to walk a careful line between outright freedom from and extreme dependence on a powerful patron.[47] This line recalls especially 1.17.35 (*principibus placuisse viris non ultima laus est*), and thus Horace aligns himself in 1.20 with the Aristippean social adaptability he had espoused in the earlier poem. Rather than render Horace a slave to a powerful patron, these friendships enhance his status and position him, as they did Aristippus earlier, at a midpoint between two social extremes, that of the *primi Urbis*, on the one hand, and on the other hand, that of the withdrawn nonparticipant who makes no attempt to engage.

Scholars have shown how the *sphragis* that closes the book in many ways has the appearance of an epitaph.[48] This epitaph marks his status once more as falling somewhere between freedom and slavery, for epitaphs were an act of commemoration associated especially with freedmen and their sons—and of course Horace's own *sphragis* here marks him as just this, the son of a freedman.[49] Horace's rise from obscurity to prominence, inscribed on the book, can be compared, for example, to the epitaph of another social climber, the freedman Trimalchio, who will want his monument to record his meteoric rise: *ex parvo crevit*, "he grew from little," Petronius 71.12.[50] It was in fact during the principate of Augustus that freedmen increasingly employed funerary inscription as a means of recording their accomplishments for posterity and celebrating their elevation from their former slave status.[51] Horace's epistolary epitaph therefore records his social successes in the very same breath that it marks him yet again as not fully free. Whereas in the first half of 1.20 he is his book's liberating master, the inscription marks him as sharing in his *liber*'s freed status. This was exactly Horace's status in the opening lines of the book, when he likened himself to a newly manumitted gladiator. What Horace has learned in the intervening poems is not to bristle against this rank but to accept it as a marker of the moderated freedom he has formulated over the course of the book. In this final poem, Horace is slave, freedman, and master all at once. The enslaved/free dichotomy that opened the collection cannot sufficiently account for the variety of categories he simultaneously embraces.

Horace's very last words in the collection locate him precisely in time and place, tying him not only to the world of Augustan Rome he inhabits but to the irretrievably distant past of his readers:[52]

> forte meum siquis te percontabitur aevum,
> me quater undenos sciat implevisse Decembres,
> collegam Lepidum quo dixit Lollius anno. (26–28)

> If someone by chance will ask my age, let him know that I fulfilled 44 Decembers in the year in which Lollius declared Lepidus his colleague.

Without a memorial, obscurity and oblivion are the only options for any human being. Severing the author from his text therefore serves a greater purpose than simply to distance Horace from the slavish desires of his book. It becomes the means by which, though he will die, his accomplishments and fame can live on and achieve immortality. This is the ultimate loss of control and autonomy, to leave behind a record whose path he can neither fully predict nor regulate.[53] Whereas 1.13 showed us a poet trying desperately to control his reception, in 1.20 the poet gives up such efforts at control as futile. In a collection that again and again advocates for a middle ground between the extremes of independence and slavery, Horace's publication of his epistolary text is at one and the same time an act of freeing himself and his words and an act of irreversibly subjecting himself to the judgment and whims of posterity. Such subjugation is the price that must be paid by one who refuses to live and die in obscurity. What this final poem leaves us with is one last compromise between Horace's freedom and slavery, and the epistolary poetry that was the product and reflection of his independence must itself take on a degree of servitude.

Horace's act of publication reiterates the other concessions to his freedom we have seen him make and recommend to others throughout the book. In philosophy he cannot be totally free, for he draws on various schools even as he foreswears allegiance to any. In poetry he walks a middle path between reliance on models and originality from them. His complicated spirit is drawn as strongly to the ties that bind him to the city as it is to the freedom from them offered by the countryside, while in friendship too he must find the delicate balance between the extremes of slavish submission and overly hostile *libertas*. The book will record, not only in the final lines of 1.20 but throughout itself, Horace's claims both to freedom and to slavery and the concessions he has made between these two competing spheres. The moderate freedom that we find articulated throughout the poems certainly should be read as a reflection of the Augustan era in which Horace lived, and to which the final lines date him, but it also reflects a deeper truth that transcends Horace's historical moment. Total autonomy and utter self-sufficiency are goals that are simply incapable of realization, no matter what one's time and place. They certainly look and sound attractive, and they are far preferable to the alternative, but for anyone who, like Horace, wants to be a part of society as much as he wants to be apart from it, compromise is necessary. What Horace teaches is not an impossible and unbending way of life that only an ideal sage could achieve but one that enables us all, rich or poor, young or old (1.1.25–26)—real flesh-and-blood people—to find a path to equanimity, one that is achievable through moderation and adaptability, qualities that are accessible to anyone, anywhere, at any time.

Notes

INTRODUCTION

1. For recent introductions to the *Epistles*, see Ferri (2007), Cucchiarelli (2010), Johnson (2010), and Fantham (2013).

2. The centrality of freedom in the collection has long been recognized. See, e.g., Ooteghem (1946). Johnson (1993, 70) states that the "poems between 1 and 20 will examine various aspects of the dialectic of freedom/unfreedom." De Pretis (2002, 183) suggests that "we cannot fully understand Horatian poetry if we fail to appreciate the constant redefinition of the limitations of the poet's power that underlines it, redefinition which takes place in the encounter with other antagonistic powers: Maecenas, Augustus, the literary tradition, contemporary poets, the Roman public, posterity. Horace often presents this condition in terms of freedom: freedom of speech, independence, autonomy from the public's requests." Lee-Stecum (2009, 12) writes that "the careful definition and in some cases active re-definition of power and freedom is at the heart of the ethical and social program of Horace's first book of *Epistles*."

3. For an overview of Horace and Augustus, see Lowrie (2007). Moles (2002, 141) also suggests that the poems have a political resonance, stating that "the poems express some tensions, ambiguities and reservations in Horace's attitudes both to public life and to Maecenas and Augustus, tensions which inform a wide-ranging and radical debate about the pros and cons of engagement in, or withdrawal from, that public life." Whereas Moles concludes that Horace ultimately chooses a conditional Epicurean withdrawal, I argue that he chooses instead to pursue a middle path between engagement and withdrawal that partakes of both simultaneously. Freudenburg (2002, 127) similarly writes, "What does it mean to be a high-profile friend of Maecenas now, not in 23 BCE, but in the early days of 19 BCE, as a retired champion of the lyric fray?" On the difficulty of determining Augustus's restriction of *libertas*, see Feeney (1992, 7): "The *libertas* enjoyed even by the highest members of society had suffered irrevocable infringement, as everybody knew, although nobody could pin down quite where the boundaries were." He goes on to say (9) that "what we are dealing with . . . is . . . a developing and shifting relationship, without any precedents, where all the parties involved are feeling their way. . . . Apart from Ovid, the poet who most effectively catches the mood is Horace, in whose

poetry one sees an acute sensitivity to the transformations of *libertas* under the trium-
virate and principate." Noonan (2003, 37) rightly observes that "the truly important
point . . . is not what moderns think, but that Augustan poets sensed that a redefinition
or revaluation of *libertas* was taking place."

4. See, e.g., Highet (1973, 269) ("He wrote a good deal about slaves and slavery: the
subject haunted him") and Anderson (1995, 163) ("Throughout his poetry, Horace shows
concern with the human desire for freedom and the constraints that society and personal needs place upon freedom").

5. On *libertas* in the *Satires*, see, e.g., DuQuesnay (1984), Kennedy (1992, 29–34),
Freudenburg (1993, esp. 52–108), Ruffell (2003), and Welch (2008).

6. See DuQuesnay (1984, 29–30) and Freudenburg (1993, 87). Each points out that
Trebonius, one of the conspirators in Caesar's assassination, wrote an attack on Antony
in May 44 B.C. that was modeled on Lucilius.

7. DuQuesnay (1984, 30). On *licentia/libertas* generally in Roman satire, see Braund
(2004). Freudenburg (2001, 44–51) interestingly connects Horace's restriction of Lucilian *libertas* not so much to political changes as to his lower status: "Horatian *libertas*, the
brand of 'free speech' he shows us in satire, he claims to have learned from a *libertus*, a
man of severely compromised freedom. And that restricted version of free speech must
necessarily *sound* very different from the Grade-A, uncompromised version of it Lucilius
had access to and seems to have used in his *Satires*."

8. See Ruffell (2003, 61): "Both [Horace and Augustus] equally are attempting to
take the public poetry of invective out of politics, and the public politics out of invective.
This re-definition of *libertas* is a response to the chaos of the triumviral years and the
long crisis that preceded it."

9. Kennedy (1992, 31).

10. See Mayer (1985, 44): "What strikes me most in the *Epistles* is the steady, and
often unobtrusive, references to the royal circle. . . . Horace, on my submission, felt the
wind veer. . . . Horace offers his advice on behavior that will suit the altered social pat-
tern, the new reality, and yet preserve the independence, the manliness of an earlier
day." The imperial household is alluded to in 1.3 (addressed to Florus, who is in the
cohort of Tiberius), 1.5 (the occasion of which is Augustus's birthday), 1.8 (addressed to
Celsus, the *scriba* of Tiberius), 1.9 (addressed to Tiberius), 1.12 (to Iccius, the manager
of Agrippa's estates in Sicily; Horace ends the poem by describing Augustus's military
achievements), 1.13 (addressed to Vinnius Asina, who is to take poems to Augustus), 1.15
(in which Horace mentions that he is being treated by the imperial doctor Antonius
Musa), 1.18 (in which Horace describes Lollius's previous military service for Augustus
and celebrates Augustus's military achievements), and 1.19 (in which Horace is accused
of saving his poetry for Augustus's ears).

11. All quotations of *Epistles* 1 are from the text of Mayer (1994) unless otherwise
specified. Quotations from Horace's other works are from the Oxford Classical Text of
Wickham and Garrod (1912). All translations of Greek and Latin material are my own
unless otherwise noted.

12. There is a substantial amount of scholarship on Roman *libertas*. I have found
the following general discussions particularly illuminating: Wirszubski (1950), Hammond (1963), Nicolet (1980, 317–42), Fears (1980), Fears (1981, 869–75), Lind (1986),
Brunt (1988), Patterson (1991, 203–90), Roller (2001, 213–87), Wallace (2009), and Arena
(2012).

13. Wirszubski (1950, 1) refers to freedom as "a somewhat vague notion." Brunt (1988, 283) argues that "there was, and could be, no single Roman . . . idea of freedom." Patterson (1991, 219) confesses that "at first sight, the term *libertas* seems to have conveyed a bewildering variety of meanings to Romans." Johnston (2006, 21) speaks of its "extreme ambiguity." However, Roller (2001, 228) argues that the meaning of *libertas* was never unstable or open to negotiation: "*libertas* does not mean many different things . . . nor . . . is its meaning unstable and mutable. On the contrary, *libertas* means the same thing in all cases: it means 'the (desirable) condition of not being a slave.'" Though I agree with Roller that the simple designation of free/enslaved is at the heart of what *libertas* theoretically means, in practice freedom proves to be elusive and difficult to define.

14. For the enslaved/free dichotomy, see, e.g., Fitzgerald (2000, 1) and Roller (2001, 220–21).

15. Brunt (1988, 281) states that *libertas* "admitted of degrees." Fitzgerald (2000, 71) acknowledges that "theory demanded an absolute polarity between the autonomy of the citizen and the dependency and service of the slave, but in practice social relations might look more like a spectrum of dependencies and obligations." Roller (2001, 221), however, does not admit any in-between status: "These words [*servus* and *liber*] designate complementary social categories: any person not classifiable as a *servus* is necessarily *liber*, and vice versa; no other status is possible within this system of categorization."

16. Roller (2001, 213–87) argues that the idea of freedom and slavery was always a social one for the Romans (i.e., freedom as the status of non-slavery) and was applied only metaphorically to the political sphere. Fitzgerald (2000, 69) similarly states that "slavery provided the free with a metaphor and yardstick for a variety of relationships."

17. Arena (2012, 47).

18. For law as a guarantor of *libertas*, see Wirszubski (1950, 7–30), Nicolet (1980, 320), and Arena (2012, 45–72).

19. Arena (2012) traces this process throughout her book. As she maintains, this definition of political liberty was shared by both *populares* and *optimates*, though the threats to it identified by the two sides differed, as did the methods espoused for guaranteeing it. To the *optimates* the mixed government provided the best guarantee of freedom, while to the *populares* the heavy involvement of the populace, particularly via the tribunate, was key. To the *optimates* the biggest threats to freedom were the granting of *imperia extraordinaria* to individuals, while to the *populares* it was the power wielded by the Senate via the *senatus consultum ultimum*.

20. For a succinct overview of Augustus's extraordinary constitutional position after the Second Settlement of 23 B.C., see Gruen (2005). On the rise of the metaphor of slavery to describe the political situation during the late Republic and early Principate, see Fitzgerald (2000, 71–77) and Roller (2001, 213–87).

21. For the changed nature of *libertas* under Augustus, see Wirszubski (1950, 97–123), Fears (1980), Patterson (1991, 258–63), and Galinsky (1996, 54–57).

22. For the exploitation of the term by various factions in the late Republic, see, e.g., Syme (1939, 154–56), Wirszubski (1950, 31–96), Fears (1981, 869–75), DuQuesnay (1984, 29–31), Lind (1986, 85–91), Patterson (1991, 219), Freudenburg (1993, 86–87), and Roller (2001, 247–53).

23. See esp. *Cat.* 3.14: *virtute, consilio, providentia mea res publica maximis periculis sit liberata,* "By my virtue, advice, and providence, the state has been freed from the greatest dangers."

24. For Clodius's shrine, see von der Osten (2006, 36–37).

25. See esp. *Civ.* 22.5: *ut se et populum Romanum factione paucorum oppressum in libertatem vindicaret*, "in order to liberate himself and the Roman people, who had been oppressed by the faction of a few." For Augustus's use of similar phraseology, see below.

26. Scholars especially cite the coin minted by Brutus in 43 B.C. that commemorates the Ides of March by displaying a *pilleus*, the cap of freedom, between two daggers, which represent Brutus and Cassius. See, e.g., Freudenberg (1993, 86). For the coin, see Crawford (1974) no. 508/3.

27. For the traditional contrast between *licentia* and *libertas*, see, for example, Wirszubski (1950, 7–9) and Lind (1986, 82–83).

28. As Nisbet and Rudd (2004, ad loc.) point out, Horace here connects *licentia* especially with sexual immorality and material avarice.

29. *Ministri* is Cicero's translation for Plato's οἰνοχόοι. In addition to being an attendant at a table (*OLD* s.v. 1a), a *minister* could be a minor official (*OLD* s.v. 2b).

30. See Gregory (1991) and Arena (2012, 167).

31. Gregory (1991, 644).

32. See Arena (2012, 89). For a full discussion of the Greco-Roman tradition of the mixed constitution as a guarantee of liberty, see p. 81–116. Arena argues that this line of thought in Rome was associated especially with "optimate" ideas about maintaining freedom. For the *popularis* tradition, see p. 116–68. See also Arena (2007).

33. Fears (1980, 13).

34. Fears (1980, 16).

35. *RIC* I² 79 no. 476.

36. On this coin, see Fears (1980, 16–17) and Galinsky (1996, 53–54).

37. The *factio* here refers to Antony. See Roller (2001, 214).

38. Galinsky (1996, 54).

39. On Dio's valuation of Augustus, see Reinhold and Swan (1990).

40. Patterson (1991, 258–59).

41. Roller (2001, 214–15). At n. 4 he points out that *vindex libertatis* and *vindicare in libertatem* are used frequently by aristocratic politicians in the late Republican period. Wirszubski (1950, 103) argues that by Augustus's day it was "an outworn phrase that retained little of its original . . . meaning." Roller, however, counters that the phrase was still used frequently during the late Republic and Augustan period to describe manumission and so retains its associations with slavery. He cites Livy 2.5.8–10, 3.45.11, 3.46.7 and Cicero, *Att.* 7.2.8.

42. Mouritsen (2011, 146–47).

43. Mouritsen (2011, 58). On *obsequium*, see also Verboven (2012, 95–696) and Arena (2012, 20–21).

44. See Mouritsen (2011, 59).

45. As Mouritsen (2011, 36–37) points out, the former master, upon manumission of his slave, received the title *patronus*: "As far back as we can trace, the term carried a double meaning, denoting both a person who had freed a slave and the senior partner in a *clientela* relationship."

46. See Mouritsen (2011, 59).

47. Horace repeats the phrase *me libertino patre natum* at *Satires* 1.6.6, 45 and 46.

48. On Tacitus's views of *libertas*, see, for example, Liebeschuetz (1966), Wirszubski (1950, 160–67), Percival (1980), Brown (1981), Classen (1988), Morford (1991), Mellor (1993, 97–105), and Oakley (2009).

49. See Oakley (2009, 184–85).

50. On political suicide, see Plass (1995, 81–134).

51. For a fuller discussion of the relationship between these passages and *Epistles* 1, see chapter 5.

52. See Lee-Stecum (2009, 27): "With the control of public career paths now largely in the hands of the imperial family and their immediate circle (Tiberius, Augustus, Maecenas and Agrippa are the 'powerful friends' who are prominent in the *Epistles*), Horace offers his ambitious young friends a definition of power and value which promises independence and moral authority even within a subordinate social relationship."

53. See Ferri (2007, 125–26): "The *Epistles* do not open up a window into the world and thoughts of the great and good; the addressees of the work, apart from Maecenas, seem to have been mainly second-rank individuals. The book does not include letters to politically influential personages, or to protagonists of the Roman poetic and intellectual stage such as, say, Pollio, Agrippa, Vergil, Varius."

54. Julius Florus (1.3) and Celsus (1.8) are on the staff of Tiberius. Iccius (1.12) is Agrippa's *procurator* in Sicily. Scaeva (1.17) and Lollius (1.2 and 1.18) are depicted as just beginning to navigate the waters of public life. Torquatus (1.5) and Quinctius (1.16) seem to have public careers, but they do not occupy the same position of prominence as members of the imperial family or those closely associated with them.

55. See Freudenburg (2002, 126), who states that Horace's "project involves taking a stand and speaking to Maecenas in uncharacteristically aggressive ways, something we see already in the first lines of *Epist.* 1.1."

56. Freudenburg (2002, 127). For *aetas* as "era," see *OLD* s.v. 8. Horace's new epistolary genre will therefore be in keeping with the changed realities not only of his age but also of the era in which he lives.

57. For the connection between freedom and mastery, see, e.g., *Epist.* 1.1.17, where, after espousing his philosophical independence, he states *ego me ipse regam*, "I myself will rule myself" (27), and *Epist.* 1.10.8, in which his rustic independence is simultaneously mastery: (*regno*, "I rule"). When he celebrates his poetic independence in 1.19.22–23, furthermore, he exclaims that he *dux reget examen*, "as leader rules the hive."

58. For recent overviews of Horace's biography, see Nisbet (2007), Armstrong (2010), and Günther (2013).

59. For an overview of Horace's friendship with Maecenas, based largely on the evidence of the poetry, see Anderson (2010). The question of Maecenas's fall from Augustus's favor has been widely debated. For arguments that he did fall, see Syme (1939, 387–89), Brink (1982, 523–72; 1995), and Williams (1968, 4–5, 86–88), who later (1990) changed his mind. For the argument that he did not fall from favor, see White (1991).

60. Porter (2002, 23) likewise speaks of both the poet and his addressees as poetic constructs: "Just as Horace's arrangement of the poems in his collection is an act of poetic creation, so too are the characters we meet in them, among whom the most memorable, the most central, is Horace himself."

61. On the authorial persona of the *Epistles* in relation to the themes of freedom and power, see especially the article by Lee-Stecum (2009), who writes (14) that "the persona which Horace creates for himself in *Epistles* 1 is intimately involved in the definition of power and freedom in ways which have not yet been fully appreciated."

62. See, e.g., Zetzel (1980), Anderson (1982, 13–49), Armstrong (1986), Freudenburg (1993; 2010), Braund (1996), Oliensis (1998, 17–63), and Schlegel (2005; 2010). For a reappraisal of the autobiographical element in the *Satires*, see Gowers (2003).

63. My approach to Horace's epistolary persona therefore differs from that of Oliensis (1998), who sees Horace adopting and setting aside at every turn a wide variety of personae or, as she terms them, "faces," in response not only to each poem's addressee but also to a variety of other potential readers, whom she terms "overreaders." The faces Horace adopts, according to Oliensis, are largely a reaction to the degree of deference or authority he wishes to project at any given moment. Though I agree that Horace's self-fashioning is subject to constant change and negotiation, in my reading this is because his epistolary persona is prone to contradiction, vacillation, and ultimately evolution. For Horace's epistolary persona, see also de Pretis (2002, 63–88), who argues against the use of the theatrical term *persona* and employs instead the terms "self-image" and "self-representation." Central to Horace's self-representation in the *Epistles*, she suggests (64), are "contradiction, doubt, reiteration of decisions and self-persuasion." She suggests, as do I, that Horace's self-representation must be considered across the entire book: "Horace's creation of a self-image is a lengthy and complex operation that does yet take place in each single letter, but finds its most thorough fulfillment in the effect of amplification, deepening and completion given by the collection in its entirety." Morrison (2007, 129) speaks of the "doubts, backsliding, and progress of 'Horace' in *Epistles* 1" and (2006) connects this fitful progress by the narrator to that of "Callimachus" in the *Iambi*.

64. Of course many fruitful readings of Horace's poetry have focused on patronage and Horace's relationship with Maecenas. On this friendship, see, for example, Reckford (1959) and Gold (1987, 115–72). Bowditch (2001, esp. 161–246) offers a stimulating reading of the *Epistles* based on the economic aspects of patronage in the poems. On Maecenas's role in literary patronage, see Williams (1990) and Byrne (2000). For literary patronage in general, on which there is a substantial bibliography, see, for example, Clarke (1978), White (1978, 1982, and 1993), Williams (1982), and Wiseman (1982). On imperial patronage in Horace, see Bowditch (2010).

65. See esp. Zetzel (1982) and Gold (1987, 115–41). For an overview of socio-poetic approaches to Horace, see White (2007). Gold (2012), though she focuses on the elegists, is nevertheless an excellent introduction to this approach. See also Wasyl (2003), who makes several relevant observations about *Epistles* 1, suggesting (97) that "Horace's relationship with Maecenas as described by him in his poetry must be read first and mainly as a literary, not factual, account."

66. Gold (2012, 305).

67. Zetzel (1982, 98).

68. See for example Fraenkel (1957, 339) on *Epistles* 1.7: "That the letter which was addressed to Maecenas was published in its present form and included in the book of the epistles, which is dedicated to Maecenas, is to the credit not only of Horace but of Maecenas as well. Nothing could show more clearly that Horace's sincere and courageous message left no sting in his friend's heart. We know that Maecenas had many weaknesses, but lack of *magnanimitas* . . . was not among them. Nor did Horace ever waver in his profound attachment to him. The still fashionable talk about a cooling of their friendship in their later years is contradicted by the evidence." The evidence is, of course, the poetry itself.

69. Gold (2012, 305) argues that Maecenas performs a similar function in Propertius's poetry: "Is Propertius describing an historical figure when he addresses Maecenas at some length in poems 2.1 and 3.9, explaining he is unable to write the kind of verse Maecenas is purportedly requesting (epic), or is Maecenas transmuted into a symbol of important ideas in Propertius's poetry, or into a set of values that Propertius is rejecting?" Johnson (2010, 327) suggests that "when Horace composed *Epistles* 1, Maecenas has come to symbolize a conflicted mix of feelings and thoughts (affection, gratitude, resentment, regret among them)."

70. On the role of the addressees in the poems, see esp. de Pretis (2002, 39–61).

71. See Gold (2012, 306): "The patron as chosen for his connotation not his denotation."

72. Allen (1970), a study of the collection's addressees, omits entirely a consideration of the obviously fictitious ones: "We omit 14, addressed to Horace's overseer (*vilicus*), as well as 20, addressed to this book of *Epistles*; nor do we regard Horace's Muse as the true addressee of 8. We can find nothing of value in considering the addressee of 13, who was chosen because his name indicates an appropriate beast of burden to carry the three books of *Odes* to Augustus."

73. For a good overview of the question, see Moles (2007). Rudd (1993, 66) quotes as representing two extreme views Heinze (1957, 370) ("als Philosoph aber vor allem hat Horaz sein Buch der Briefe geschrieben.") and Pasquali (1920, 580) ("Orazio in filosofia non fu mai più che un dilettante di studi morale."). For varying arguments that the *Epistles* are philosophical, see McGann (1969), Macleod (1979), Kilpatrick (1986), Harrison (1995a), Moles (1985, 2002, and 2007), and Armstrong (2004b). Maguinness (1938) remains an excellent discussion of Horace's "eclecticism." For the argument that Horace is not formally philosophical but nonetheless concerned with proper behavior, see Williams (1968, 28–29), Mayer (1985, 1986), and Rudd (1993). Varying philosophical allegiances have been attributed to him, most often Stoicism, Academicism, and Epicureanism. For Stoicism, see Courbaud (1914), Campbell (1924), and Reckford (1969, 9–10). McGann (1969) argues for the more flexible version of Stoicism taught by Panaetius and formulated in Cicero's *De Officiis* as key to Horace's thought. Kilpatrick (1986) suggests rather that the influence of Cicero on the collection lends it a flavor of Academic Skepticism. For Epicureanism, see Heinze (1957, 370–71), Fraenkel (1957, 225), DeWitt (1937, 1939), Porter Packer (1941), and more recently Ferri (1993) and Armstrong (2004b). Moles (2002) argues that Horace prefers an undogmatic version of Epicureanism. For the influence of Lucretius on the *Epistles*, see Ferri (1993, 81–131) and Morrison (2007, 111–23). For an overview of the various philosophical allegiances that scholars have detected in Horace, see Colish (1985, 161–68).

74. The choice of the epistolary genre of course adds to the philosophical color of the book since it was a form associated with important philosophers such as Plato and Epicurus (and which would later be adopted by Seneca). These philosophical letters, however, are in prose.

75. Lee-Stecum (2009, 23) similarly senses the parallelism in Horace's approach to freedom in philosophy, friendship, and poetry: "As a moralist, as a friend and as a poet, Horace claims for himself a position of authority connected to tradition, to his poetic and philosophical models, and to his social superiors (Maecenas, Tiberius, Augustus, the powerful men of Rome), but at the same time independent."

76. For the importance of Aristippus to the collection I am indebted especially to Traina (1991 = 2009), whose arguments I take up and expand. For recent book length studies of the Cyrenaics, see Tsouna (1998), Zilioli (2012), and Lampe (2015). Mayer (1985, 34) also emphasizes Aristippus's place in the collection.

77. Other important exemplars for Horace's epistolary freedom include the philosophical (Epicurus in 1.4, Democritus in 1.12) and the literary (Odysseus in 1.2, Alcaeus in 1.19). Aristippus is mentioned four times in the collection (1.1.18; 1.17.14, 17, and 22). His inclusion in the programmatic opening of 1.1 marks him as especially important to Horace's philosophical technique.

78. The degree to which the Cyrenaics can even be considered a "school" is debated. See Zilioli (2012, 6–10), who points out that "we do not know anything about the structure and organization of the school itself." Furthermore, it is not always clear which Aristippus is responsible for which Cyrenaic teachings, Aristippus the Elder or his grandson, Aristippus the Younger, who, according to Zilioli (2012, 10), "systematized the doctrines elaborated more or less completely by his grandfather." For an overview of the debate concerning Aristippus the Elder's involvement with the foundation of the school, see Zilioli (2012, 11–16).

79. For Horace to present himself as an orthodox Cyrenaic would have been peculiar indeed, given that the last major Cyrenaic figure, Theodorus, died around 250 B.C.

80. For a list of possible writings by Aristippus, see Diogenes Laertius 2.83–85. However, whether Aristippus wrote at all is the subject of some debate; for an overview of the issue see Zilioli (2012, 31–36).

81. Diogenes Laertius in fact provides our chief source of evidence about Aristippus. For an examination of this evidence, see Zilioli (2012, 17–46). On Diogenes's life of Aristippus, see also Steiner (1976) and Mann (1996).

82. Cf. Steiner (1976, 37), who writes of Diogenes the Cynic and Aristippus, "In most ancient contexts Diogenes and Aristippus, it appears, are remembered and used rather like figures from myth, not for what they ever actually were, but for what they can represent."

83. Ferri (2007, 125). For readings of the collection that argue for the emergence of a progressive narrative, see, for example, Maurach (1968); McGann (1969, 33–87); Armstrong (1989, 117–35); Ferri (1993, 127–31); Johnson (1993, 66–71); Porter (2002); de Pretis (2002, 135–44); and Morrison (2006, 44–61; 2007, 123–31).

CHAPTER 1. THE DILEMMA OF LIBERTAS

1. Pointed out by Oberhelman and Armstrong (1995, 241 n. 42).

2. My reading of the opening lines of Epistles 1.1 is admittedly dark, but this does not discount the self-deprecating humor present in Horace's depiction of himself as an aging gladiator or a wheezing racehorse. As he himself states in Satires 1.1.24–25, *ridentem dicere verum / quid vetat*, "What prevents someone who is laughing from telling the truth?"

3. See, for example, Odes 1.32.1–4 (*si quid vacui sub umbra / lusimus tecum . . . barbite*) and Satires 1.10.37 (*haec ego ludo*).

4. Some scholars read Horace's renunciation of *versus* as a blanket refusal to write any poetry at all. Such a reading suggests that Horace treats the Epistles as something less than formal verse (as he does the Satires at 1.4.56–62). Mayer (1986, 69–70), for example, writes that "Horace never lets go the fiction that his letters are *not* poems. . . . Nowhere does Horace hint that his letters are in verse. . . . When Horace claimed to have put verse

aside at 1.10, he meant it after a fashion." Moles (2002, 145) argues that *versus* should embrace all poetry, which he sets aside in favor of philosophy. Perhaps we should keep in mind a statement from *Epist.* 2.1.111–12: *ipse ego, qui nullos me affirmo scribere versus / invenior Parthis mendacior* ("I myself, who claim that I am writing no verses, am found to be more untruthful than the Parthians"). In my reading, the issue has more to do with publication than any other consideration. The *Epistles* do not bring him before the judgment of the *populus* because, as of 1.1, they are not yet published and will not be until the final poem of the book, where Horace will express similar apprehensions about public display and slavery.

5. Freudenburg (2002, 126). Harrison (1995a, 49) suggests that Horace's depiction of himself as a "clapped-out nag" is "clearly a comic and low-life version of the chariot of poetry." As he points out (n. 10), the topos is common in Greek lyric poetry (e.g., Pind. *Ol.* 6.23, *P.* 10.65, *Isth.* 8.68), "and Horace may be exploiting this here in making a renunciation of lyric."

6. Some scholars argue that Horace's renunciation is only of *erotic* lyric poetry. See, e.g., Gigon (1977, 477) and Traina (2009, 306 n. 82).

7. For the connection between *ludus* and youthful poetry, especially in Ovid, see Wagenvoort (1956, 30–31). Cf., for example, Cat. 68a.17–19, Verg. *Georg.* 4.565, Ov. *Am.*3.1.27–28, *Trist.* 1.9.61.

8. Barton (1993, 12).

9. On the poetic genre of literary epistles, see, for example, Dilke (1981, 1844–47), Mayer (1994, 1–5), and Ferri (2007, 121–25).

10. See Hopkins (1983, 20–27). For the ambivalence toward gladiators, see Tertullian, *De Spectaculis* 22.2–4: *ex eadem arte, qua magnifaciunt, deponunt et deminuunt, immo manifeste damnant ignominia et capitis minutione, arcentes curia rostris senatu equite ceterisque honoribus omnibus simul et ornamentis quibusdam. quanta perversitas! amant quos multant, depretiant quos probant, artem magnificant, artificem notant. quale iudicium est, ut ob ea quis offuscetur, per quae promeretur?* ("They degrade and lessen them because of the same skill for which they esteem them. Indeed they plainly condemn them to disgrace and to the loss of their civil rights, keeping them from the senate house, the speaker's platform, the senate, the equestrian rank, and all other offices as well as certain honors. What great perversity! They love those whom they punish, they denigrate those whom they commend, and they admire the art though they stigmatize the artist. What sort of judgment is it that someone can be made obscure by the very things through which he is prominent?")

11. See Dunkle (2008, 71–72).

12. See, e.g., Freudenburg (2002, 124).

13. See, e.g., the opening and closing poems of the *Odes*. In 1.1.2 he calls Maecenas *et praesidium et dulce decus meum* ("both my protection and sweet adornment"), and in 3.30.1–2 he celebrates the *Odes* as a *monumentum aere perrennius / regalique situ pyramidum altius* ("monument more lasting than bronze and loftier than the regal structure of the pyramids"), an accomplishment for which he asks the muse to crown his hair with triumphant Delphic laurel, *Delphica lauro* (15–16).

14. Roller (2001, 221). See also, for example, Wirszubski (1950, 1), who states that "*libertas* primarily denotes the status of a *liber*, i.e., a person who is not a slave," and Arena (2012, 14), who writes that "all Romans shared a basic understanding of the value of liberty: they agreed that fundamentally *libertas* referred to the status of non-slavery."

15. For laughter as a motif in the book, see Porter (2002, 32–33).

16. For *recusationes*, see Nisbet and Hubbard (1970) on *Odes* 1.6 and Wimmel (1960). For Apollo in *recusationes*, see also Prop. 3.3.13 and 4.1.133; Ovid *Ars* 2.493.

17. Moles (2002, 146). See also Mayer (1986, 66; 1994, ad loc.), and Morrison (2007, 116). For Socrates's *daimonion*, see the volume of essays edited by Destrée and Smith (2005).

18. See Mayer (1994, ad loc.). Cf., e.g., Petronius 117.5: *legitimi gladiatores domino corpora animasque religiosissime addicimus* ("As legitimate gladiators *we bind over* our bodies and souls to our master in a most sacred fashion"). Soldiers too swore oaths of loyalty to their *duces*. Furthermore, as Dilke (1954, ad loc.) points out, *addictus* was "originally a technical term, of a debtor enslaved under his creditor by the praetor's order." Cf., e.g., Livy 34.56.8 (*qui liberum corpus in servitutem addixisset*, "who had bound over his free body into slavery").

19. *Iurare in verba* suggests swearing at another's dictation, for which see *iurare*, OLD s.v. 5.

20. On the dating, see Brink (1982, 552) and Rudd (1989, 13).

21. Porter (2002, 21–23) also takes the drastic change in tone from the beginning to the end of *Epistles* 1 as the starting point for his important article: "Why does Horace, who always takes such pains to shape the endings of his books, create in 17–20 so seemingly strange a concluding quartet to *Ep.* 1? Why does he build such sharp divergences between the opening pair of poems and the two final pairs? How does he move from where he begins to where he ends?" Porter, as do I, finds a progression from withdrawal to engagement over the course of the book.

22. Bowditch (2001, 174).

23. The exchange of patron for *populus* is an important point to which I will return in chapter 7. Lollius's hypothetical patron is playing not a *lanista* parading him before others to be judged, but literary judge himself. Lollius is therefore not subjected to the fickle *populus* but to his patron alone, whose literary tastes are presumably more refined. On this gesture, see Corbeill (2004, 52–64), who points out that in reality it was not the *populus* who gestured with their thumbs but rather the *editor* who put them on and whose decision may have taken into account the reactions of the spectators.

24. My reading of these lines is indebted to that of Traina (2009, 292–98).

25. The best discussion of Horace's eclecticism remains Maguinness (1938). Brucker, the 18th c. author of the *Historica Critica Philosophiae*, published from 1742 to 1767, and proponent of eclecticism, would echo Horace's words when criticizing the eclecticism of Alexandrian Neoplatonists, whom he did not consider genuine eclectics but *syncretistae*, syncretists: *In hoc tamen uno eclecticum quid in iis deprehenditur, quod nullus inter eos . . . in magistri verba iuraverit* ("Nevertheless in this alone is something eclectic detected in them: that no one among them has *sworn on the words of a master*," vol. 2 190. Leipzig). See Donini (1988, 21–22).

26. Rudd (1993, 67).

27. Donini (1988, 31).

28. Potamo's dates are unclear. According to Diogenes Laertius, he lived around the 2nd c. A.D., but the *Suda* suggests that he lived during the Augustan era, which would make him Horace's contemporary. If the *Suda* is correct, Horace may have been familiar with Potamo's Eclecticism. For Potamo, see Zeller (1883, 109–11), Donini (1988, 16), and Kelley (2001, 579–80).

29. See Rudd (1993, 67). See also Mayer (1986, 64–65).

30. The Royal Society of London would adopt its motto, *Nullius in verba*, from the epistle. As the Society's current website (royalsociety.org/about-us/history/) explains, the motto was selected "as an expression of the determination of Fellows to withstand the domination of authority," a sentiment with which Horace's epistolary persona would certainly agree.

31. On *obsequium*, see Mouritsen (2011, 58), Verboven (2012, 95–696), and Arena (2012, 20–21).

32. For the emphasis on Stoic inflexibility, see Moles (2002, 150): "Lines 16–19 institute a complex polarity between orthodox Stoicism/virtue/consistency and Aristippus/ adaptability/pleasure."

33. Cf. also Plaut. *Cas.* 87–88: *vincite / virtute vera, quod fecistis antidhac* ("conquer with true virtue, as you have done previously").

34. Nisbet and Rudd (2004) on *Odes* 3.5.29–30.

35. Lind (1986, 81).

36. For *virtus* in the *Epistles*, particularly Horace's questioning of its traditional Republican association with *libertas*, see Johnson (1993, 49–53). He writes, "Horace has begun to see that *virtus* and the freedom that it tokens no longer exist, and he has begun to wonder if they were ever, in Rome, or in their Greek versions, anything more than, anything other than, hopes, wishes, aspirations, ideals, dreams. He has begun to wonder what happens when human beings realize that . . . the human condition and the facts of political behavior seem to preclude anything resembling the kind of freedom that Cato praises or that Demosthenes and Cicero exhort us to defend to the death."

37. *OLD* s.v. 2. See, for example, Livy 34.36 and 34.41; Seneca, *De Tranquilitate* 5.1; and Tacitus, *Annals* 16. 22. Fowler (2008, 100) similarly points out that Horace's depiction of Stoicism here would not please a Stoic, noting that *satelles* is "a word often used insultingly of the minion of a foreign king."

38. This will be the case, for example, with Diogenes the Cynic in 1.17 or with Horace's claim to enjoy unrestricted freedom (*otia liberrima*) on the Sabine farm in 1.7.36.

39. For Aristippus's importance in *Epistles* 1, see Traina (2009).

40. He will be mentioned three more times in *Epistles* 1.17.

41. See, for example, Nadjo (2002, 121) ("l'épicurisme, symbolisé, ici, par l'hédoniste Aristippe de Cyrène") and Moles (2002, 150) ("Partly in their own right [5], partly through Aristippus, the Epicureans 'lurk' . . . in the background. Aristippus himself represents both a certain conception of pleasure and philosophical flexibility"). I would argue that the latter is at the forefront of Horace's passage. Mayer (1985, 34) similarly objects to the suggestion that Aristippus here stands for the Epicureans: "Horace never mentions Epicurus in the first epistle, but he does speak of Aristippus. It is a pity that commentators from the time of Porphyrio disregard the choice of name and make of Aristippus a counter or token, to serve as a substitute for his successor in hedonism. If Horace had wanted Epicurus here, the name would have fitted into his verse."

42. See Traina (2009, 298).

43. Gibson (2007, 132–33) connects the Aristippean adaptability in these lines with *decens* at 1.1.11. Propriety, he argues, changes depending on circumstances. He points out that Aristippus is also associated with *decorum* at 1.17.23–24.

44. For *res* as an important concept connected with Aristippus in the book, see Porter (2002, 33).

45. See Traina (2009, 297–98): "But especially important is the substitution of the object: in numerous Greek and Latin sources the object is, explicitly or implicitly, Lais, the prostitute, and therefore the pleasure (ἡδονή) with which Aristippus himself . . . glosses his epigrammatic saying. In Horace it is neither a woman nor pleasure that he claims to have renounced in his opening letter. . . . Rather it is the bare, generic res, his 'circumstances'. . . . And therefore the antithesis between virtue and pleasure, which is initially caught sight of, in actuality turns out to be a contrast between the rigidity of Stoic ethics, tightly focused on virtus, and the flexibility of Aristippus, who adapts himself to, but is not subordinated to, res. This is a flexibility that a more rigid branch of Epicurean dogmatism, the dogmatism of ipse dixit, could not provide to Horace."

46. See Traina (2009, 297), who points out that Horace replaces Aristippus's ἔχω with a verb of domination and suggests that "this was perhaps suggested by what Aristippus follows with in the version cited by Diogenes Laertius: ἐπεὶ τὸ κρατεῖν καὶ μὴ ἡττᾶσθαι ἡδονῶν ἄριστον, 'since the best of pleasures is being in charge and not being worsted/subjected,' D.L. 2.75."

47. Rudd (1993, 83).

48. See Mayer (1985, 34; 1994, ad loc.), Nadjo (2002, 121), and Traina (2009, 295–96).

49. See Traina (2009, 297).

50. We might even view the two philosophical modes of Horace in terms of Achillean and Odyssean heroics. Whereas Achilles is inflexible and unbending, Odysseus, like Aristippus, is polytropic and adaptable. Odysseus will emerge as a chief exemplar of virtue and wisdom in Epistles 1.2, while Achilles, like Paris and Agamemnon, is subject to emotions such as love and strife.

51. For the argument that Lucretius takes poetic inspiration from Empedocles but adheres strictly to the philosophy of Epicurus, see Sedley (1998). Lucretius clearly claims poetic originality (1.921–30) and simultaneous dependence on Epicurus (3.1–17). For the heroic treatment of Epicurus, see 1.62–79, and for Epicurus as a deus, see the proem to Book 5 (1–54).

52. For "circumstances," see OLD s.v. 17. For "subject matter," see OLD s.v. 9.

53. See Rudd (1989, ad loc.), who calls this a "vague phrase" that indicates "in general, 'works on moral philosophy.'" On the reception of Socrates in later philosophy, see, e.g., Long (1988) and the essays in Waerdt (1994). Mayer (1986, 73), who downplays the role of formal philosophy in the Epistles, himself emphasizes the importance of Socrates: "In a word, Horace is a Socratic. With that Roman sense of the value of the original he goes back to the source of interest in ethics, Socrates. He may well borrow from the derived schools, as need prompts. . . . But his sense of the classic drove him back ad fontem. . . . Horace's approach to ethics therefore is a throwback to earlier, untrammeled days of wide enquiry." For Horace's Socratic persona in the Satires, see Anderson (1982, 13–49).

54. Many of the anecdotes found in Diogenes Laertius's life of Aristippus involve his interactions with Dionysius of Syracuse. See, e.g., 2.82, where Dionysius, quoting Sophocles, says to Aristippus ὅστις γὰρ ὡς τύραννον ἐμπορεύεται / κείνου 'στὶ δοῦλος, κἂν ἐλεύθερος μόλῃ ("For whoever travels to a tyrant is his slave, even if he comes as a free man"), to which Aristippus quotes Sophocles in reply, οὐκ ἔστι δοῦλος, ἂν ἐλεύθερος μόλῃ ("He is not a slave, if he comes as a free man").

55. On this passage, see Blanchard (1994), Tsouna (1994, 385–86), Urstad (2008), and Johnson (2009).

56. For the parallel, see Mayer (1994, ad loc.) and esp. Traina (2009, 297). Nickel (1980) offers the fullest consideration of Xenophon's passage in relation to Horace, reading Aristippus's middle path as one between ἡδονή ("pleasure") and πόνος ("pain").

57. In the *Memorabilia* Socrates goes on to elaborate to Aristippus the allegory of Hercules, in which he must choose between two paths, one of vice and one of virtue. Socrates therefore rejects Aristippus's three-path model for one that involves only two. In the *Epistles* the trajectory is the opposite, since a two-path model (*libertas* and *servitus*) is rejected in favor of one that incorporates a middle path. For the middle path in the Xenophon passage, see esp. Gibson (2007, 74–76).

58. See, as already noted, 1.1.27. Another important example of this is 1.10.8, where Horace, who figures himself as a fugitive slave, claims to live as a king in the country: *vivo et regno*, "I live and I rule."

59. Moles (2002, 143).

60. On the connection between shipwreck and *hospitium/hospes*, see Woodman (1983b, 101–102).

CHAPTER 2. HORACE THE STUDENT

1. For the argument that the Horatian persona of *Satires* 1 is itself an object of satire, see Zetzel (1980, 69): "the book, in short, is filled with contradictions, of Horace making fun of himself." Also see Freudenburg (1993, 21), where he argues that "[Horace's] shortcomings, obvious at every turn, suggest that he is himself the chief target of satire."

2. Bond (1998, 106).

3. Cf. esp. *Satires* 1.3.1–20, where Horace criticizes a certain Tigellius for his inconsistency. When his interlocutor asks whether he is himself free of faults, Horace explicitly states that his faults are not the same and perhaps less significant ones than those of Tigellius: *immo alia et fortasse minora*, 20. By pointing out Horace's inconsistency Davus seeks to expose what he considers to be the hypocrisy of such statements.

4. Oliensis (1997, 94; 1998, 55). See also Bernstein (1992, 47): "Horace . . . uses sexual motifs as a sublimation of, and disguise for, political anxieties, not the other way around."

5. On *auctoratus*, see Long and Macleane (1874, ad loc.) and Muecke (1993, ad loc.). For the language of the oath, see Petronius, *Sat.* 117 (*in verba Eumolpi sacramentum iuravimus uri, vinciri, verberari, ferroque necari, et quicquid aliud Eumolpus iussisset; tanquam legitimi gladiators domino corpora animasque religiosissime addicimus*, "We swore an oath on the words of Eumolpus to be burned, to be bound, to be beaten, and to be slain with a sword, and whatever ever else Eumolpus ordered; just like legal gladiators we bound our bodies and souls to our master in a most sacred fashion.") and Seneca, *Epist.* 37.1 (*eadem honestissimi huius et illius turpissimi auctoramenti verba sunt uri, vinciri, ferroque necari*, "the words of this most honorable contract and of that most foul one are the same: to be burned, bound, and slain by the sword").

6. Oliensis (1997, 94; 1998, 55).

7. See Evans (1978, 308): "The slave's final remark in his sermon, that Horace cannot live with himself, arouses the poet's anger. . . . Davus appears to have touched a sore point, and Horace reveals some sensitivity to this charge." Also see Ruffell (2003, 63): "The claims he makes about 'Horace' are close to the mark: we may ask then whether it is because he has hit a nerve that Horace shuts Davus up."

8. Johnson (1993, 3).

9. Mayer (1994, ad loc.).

10. For Horace's inner turmoil or sickness and its relationship to freedom, see also Johnson (1993, 1–17).

11. *Muneraque et Musarum hinc petis et Veneris*, "you ask for gifts both of the Muses and of Venus," 10. It is outside the scope of this chapter to get into the various proposals about how to interpret *munera* in the context of the phrase *munera Veneris*, but the expression has been subject to three main interpretations: a) Manlius wants Catullus to send him a girl, b) Manlius wants to kindle a homosexual affair with Catullus, or c) Manlius wants Catullus to send him love poetry. For an overview of these opinions, see Theodorakopoulos (2011, 316–18), who convincingly suggests that the *munera Musarum* and *munera Veneris* correspond to Catullus's poetic talent and *venustas* respectively. The gifts consist therefore of poetry, and Manlius, like Maecenas in 1.1, wants poems that neither Catullus nor Horace is emotionally prepared to give.

12. Woodman (1983b, 102) and Moles (1995).

13. There is some disagreement as to whether *lusi* refers to erotic or literary pursuits. I would suggest that it alludes to both, just as it does in 50.2.

14. Though Horace's philosophical vacillations in these lines, as Johnson (1993, 86) suggests, already offer hints of it: "His claim to autonomy (I'm my own man) is ironically (but not insincerely and not quite untruly) phrased as if his inability to stick to one school were the result of his radical instability of character."

15. Mayer (1994, ad loc.).

16. Mayer (1994, ad loc.).

17. Again, this dark reading does not negate the potential humor in these lines that results from the comic exaggeration of Horace's spiritual crisis.

18. For groomed fingernails as a sign of artistic or intellectual refinement in Horace, see D'Angour (1999).

19. Oliensis (1998, 157).

20. For these verbal correspondences, see Moles (1995).

21. Not, of course, historically, but within the world of the collection.

22. See, e.g., Plaut. *Poen.* 522–23: *liberos homines per urbem modico magis par est gradu / ire, servile esse duco festinantem currere*, "It is more appropriate that free men walk through the city at a moderate pace, and I consider it slavish to rush in haste." For the ideology of walking in Roman thought, see O'Sullivan (2011, esp. 11–22).

23. Oliensis (1997, 96).

24. Brown and Levinson (1987, 186).

25. On the costume of the freedman, see Arena (2012, 33–34). She cites Polybius's description (30.18) of King Prusias II of Bithynia, who in 167 B.C. appeared to Roman envoys with his head shorn and wearing a toga, *pilleus*, and *calcei* to show not only that he had been freed by Rome but that he now enjoyed Roman citizenship. On shorn hair as a mark of freedman status, see also Livy 34.52.12 and Plut. *Flam.* 13.6. See esp. Petronius *Sat.* 32, where Trimalchio's shorn hair coupled with his ornate robes illustrates his comically confused social standing.

26. The correspondences between Horace's self-description at the close of *Epistles* 1.1 and *Satires* 1.3.29–34 and their connection to the buffoon of the comic stage have been explored by Freudenburg (1993, 27–33).

27. For the translation "tilt the scale toward," see Gowers (2012, ad loc.).

28. Kilpatrick (1986, 37–38).

29. Brown (1993, 162).

30. Cf. *Epistles* 1.7.25–28, where Horace tells Maecenas that he will have to restore Horace's youth if he expects constant attendance.

31. Damon (1997, 126).

32. Damon (1997, 127).

33. McGann (1969, 22–23).

34. McGann (1969, esp. 9–32).

35. McGann (1969, 22).

36. See Kiessling and Heinze (1957, 518) and McGann (1969, 22 n. 2).

37. Brink (1982, ad loc.) also connects this passage with *Epist.* 1.1.92–93.

38. I focus on Horace as a teacher in the next two chapters.

39. For the argument that Horace's slow progress marks him as a Stoic *proficiens* or προκόπτων in the vein of Panaetius, see McGann (1969).

40. On the schoolroom imagery, see Mayer (1994, 110) and especially Reckford (2002, 7–9).

41. "Work for hire" is Fairclough's (1929, ad loc.) translation for *opus debentibus* (21).

42. McGann (1969, esp. 10–15) has connected Horace's views here with those of Panaetius, who advocated moral progress with the figure of the προκόπτων or *proficiens*, and certainly such a flexible philosophical approach would appeal to the adaptable Horace of lines 18–19.

43. The nature of these *elementa* in the epistle has been disputed. Dilke (1954, ad loc.) sees this as a technical philosophical term corresponding to the Greek στοιχεῖον, "which was used by Zeno, founder of the Stoa, as a term for 'principle.'" Mayer (1994, ad loc.) suggests that Horace "has something more straightforward and generally appealing in mind." Both Oliensis (1998, 157) and Reckford (2002, 8) translate *elementa* simply as "ABCs," as do I. Rendering it this way nicely takes Horace's schoolroom imagery into account and illustrates how he begins his moral education at the very beginning.

44. For the function of teaching in Roman satire, see Keane (2006, 105–36).

45. Oliensis (1998, 157).

46. Mayer (1994, ad loc.) argues that this line is an "inept repetition from *S.* 1.6.74." "Old men," he writes, "have no use for satchels and writing-tablets which were anyway not carried in the classroom and not employed during recitation; nor did boys in Rome tote their own equipment, which was the job of the *capsarius*." The objections here seem overly literal; the line can be read quite well as an intentional self-repetition, as Dilke (1954, ad loc.) and Kiessling and Heinze (1957, ad loc.) suggest.

47. See Johnson (2010, 323): "Instead of offering himself as infallible guru, he mostly presents himself throughout these verse-letters to his correspondents as no more than a fellow-seeker, a companion on the road to wisdom and happiness."

CHAPTER 3. HORACE THE TEACHER

1. For Memmius's ears, see 1.50–51 (*vacuas auris*); 1.417 (*per auris*); 2.1024 (*ad auris*); 4.912 (*tenuis auris*), and 6.920 (*attentas auris*). For Horace's didacticism in the *Epistles* in relation to that of Lucretius, see esp. Ferri (1993, 81–131), who argues that Horace's chief didactic model is Lucretius but that Horace softens his confident and sublime tone; in doing so he follows the teaching model of Epicurus himself. Though I disagree with the extent of Epicureanism that Ferri finds in Horace, I certainly agree that as a teacher Horace depicts himself as his addressee's fellow traveler toward wisdom. Cf. Ferri (2007, 126):

"Horace's attitude as a teacher is that of a more advanced fellow student." On Horace's Lucretian didacticism, see also Morrison (2007).

2. See Dilke (1954, ad loc.) and Mayer (1994, ad loc.). As commentators point out, the *verba et voces* of line 34 almost certainly alludes to Euripides's *Hippolytus*, in which the Nurse tells Phaedra that there are certain "incantations and enchanting words" (εἰσὶν δ᾿ἐπῳδαὶ καὶ λόγοι θελκτήριοι, 478) that can act as a "drug for her sickness" (φάρμακον νόσου). The nurse has in mind here love spells that will either free her from her erotic distress or—more likely—enchant Hippolytus and make him return Phaedra's desire. See Segal (1993, 102).

3. Harrison (1995a, 54)

4. Belfiore (1980, 128).

5. See, for example, *Republic* 572e–573a, 598d, 602d.

6. See, for example, *Meno* 80a: γοητεύεις με καὶ φαρμάττεις καὶ ἀτεχνῶς κατεπᾴδεις ("You are bewitching and charming me and absolutely casting a spell over me"). Cf. also *Symposium* 215c–d. As Belfiore (1980) points out, the myth at the end of the *Phaedo* is called an *epode* (114d). On the relationship between Socrates and magic see, for example, de Romilly (1975, 25–43), Belfiore (1980), Gellrich (1994), and Welton (1996).

7. See Mayer (1994, ad loc.) and Armstrong (2004b, 275).

8. Vorwerk (2001, 36).

9. Mayer (1994, ad loc.).

10. Armstrong (2004b, 275). For memorization in Epicurean education, see Asmis (2001, 216–22).

11. Harrison (1995a, 55).

12. On *Epistles* 1.2, see Skalitzky (1968), McGann (1969, 37–40), Kilpatrick (1986) 25–32, Edwards (1992), Ferri (1993, 102–10), Taisne (2002), and Keane (2011).

13. Crantor is reported by Diogenes Laertius to have been an especial admirer of Homer (and Euripides, 4.26), while Chrysippus is known to have drawn on Homer in his Stoic writings, for which see Long (1992, 48–50, 58–59). Though Long (1992) challenges and reformulates this view, the Stoics are especially associated with allegory of the Homeric epics, for which see Feeney (1991, 5–56), Gale (1994, 19–26), and the introduction to Russell and Konstan (2005).

14. For Horace and Philodemus in the epistle, see especially Armstrong (2004b), whose conclusions, which I address more fully below, differ sharply from my own.

15. On Lollius Maximus's identity, see Mayer (1994, 8–9).

16. Mayer (1994, ad loc.).

17. See Mayer (1994, 124): "Horace . . . takes a stand in the old battle between philosophy and poetry. Without altogether repudiating the study of philosophical texts he belittles them and reestablishes the poet as the superior moral guide by reason of his unmistakable lessons and useful illustrations."

18. See McGann (1969, 12) and Kilpatrick (1986, 26–31). According to Cicero (*Off.* 1.9 and 3.7–10), it was central to Panaetius's Stoicism to consider whether an action would be honorable (*kalon, honestum, pulchrum*) and whether it would be expedient (*utile*). Though Horace's terms certainly do evoke this terminology, I would argue that *utile* in the epistle has more the sense of "morally beneficial" rather than "expedient." Horace of course also has in mind here Lucilius's well-known definition of *virtus* (fr. 1199–1200 Warmington): *virtus scire homini rectum utile quid sit honestum, / quae bona quae mala item, quid inutile turpe inhonestum* ("virtue is knowing what is right and useful and

honorable for a human being, and likewise what is good and what is bad, what is useless, foul, and dishonorable").

19. By suggesting that Horace refutes Epicurean attitudes about poetic moral utility, I am not arguing against what are Horace's frequent and well-known Epicurean leanings, though I would strongly disagree with any argument that makes him an orthodox Epicurean in the *Epistles*. Nor, in arguing that Horace prioritizes poetry's educational value above that of orthodox philosophy, am I claiming that his poetry is devoid of philosophical content, for he draws heavily from a variety of philosophical schools, including Epicureanism. Much of Horace's poetic theory in fact aligns with that put forth by Philodemus in *On Poems*, especially his ideas on the interconnectedness of form and content, for which see Freudenburg (1993, 139–45) and esp. Oberhelman and Armstrong (1995). On the relationship between form and content in Philodemus, see esp. Porter (1995), Asmis (1995b), and the introduction to Janko (2000). Where Horace does disagree with Philodemus, as I explain below, is in the idea that a poem's quality is divorced from its ethical content and that philosophical prose is a better vehicle for teaching moral truths.

20. Armstrong (2004b) says of *Epistles* 1.2 (281) that "Epicurus and Lucretius and Philodemus . . . turn out to have the field entirely to themselves as philosophical models," and of the collection as a whole (293) he says that "nothing in the poems contradicts any fundamental doctrine of Epicureanism; many of these are explicitly or implicitly affirmed. If an eclectic, Horace can be seen clearly to be an eclectic of the Garden."

21. Armstrong (2004b, 277): "Horace says that Homer teaches . . . better than Chrysippus and Crantor, better than the Stoics and the Academy. The choice of names is not accidental. Would Horace ever have said *Epicuro melius*, better than Epicurus? He could hardly have said *Philodemo melius*, better than Philodemus, since it is from Philodemus that he is borrowing his interpretation." I will address his arguments more fully below.

22. For the Epicurean attitude toward Homeric poetry, see Asmis (1991, 1995a, and 1995b) and Gale (1994, 14–18). For Epicurean education, in which memorization and a teacher's frank guidance were central, see Asmis (2001). Negative views of Homeric moral utility are not of course unique to Epicureanism. For Plato's criticisms of poetry, see the introduction in Murray (1996). For the earlier disapproval of Homer by the Presocratics, particularly Xenophanes, see Feeney (1991, 6–8), Gale (1994, 10–11), and Russell and Konstan (2005, xiv–xv).

23. Asmis (1995a, 19).

24. For Epicurus's view of poetry as an ὀλέθριον μύθων δέλεαρ, see Heraclitus, *Homeric Problems* 4.1.

25. At *Mor.* 15d Plutarch asks whether it is better to prohibit the young from reading poetry by stuffing their ears with wax and "setting sail in an Epicurean boat," Ἐπικούρειον ἀκάτιον ἀράμενους, or to allow them to read it, though carefully guiding them lest they be overwhelmed by pleasure. For the Siren imagery of Epicurus's boat, see Asmis (1995a, 18–19).

26. See Asmis (1995a, 21). Diogenes Laertius reports that clarity was the main feature of Epicurus's style: σαφὴς δ' ἦν οὕτως, ὡς καὶ ἐν τῷ Περὶ ῥητορικῆς ἀξιοῖ μηδὲν ἄλλο ἢ σαφήνειαν ἀπαιτεῖν ("he was so clear that in his work *On Rhetoric* he thinks it fit to demand nothing other than clarity," 10.13). Epicurus furthermore states that the wise man will leave behind writings but will not compose poems energetically (ποιήματά τε ἐνεργείᾳ οὐκ ἂν ποιῆσαι, D.L. 10.120). Thus the writings that he leaves behind for

instructional purposes should be written in prose. For the translation of ἐνεργείᾳ as "energetically" rather than "in practice," see Asmis (1995a, 22).

27. Philodemus seems to have dedicated at least three works to Vergil (*On Flattery*, *On Frugality*, and *On Vices*), along with Plotius, Varus, and Quintilius. Until the identification of Plotius in the dedication of *On Vices*, his name was misidentified as Horace's in the two other works. There is no evidence to suggest that Horace ever studied with Philodemus, though he certainly knew his work. See Tsakiropoulou-Summers (1998).

28. See *On Music* 4 col. 20.11–17 and col. 28.24–35. In *On Music*, Philodemus argues that music distracts the listener from any moral benefit that the words could impart. As Asmis (1995a, 155) states: "Although Philodemus deals only with musical form, the same considerations apply to poetic form without music: it weakens the force of the thought by pleasure, distraction, unnatural diction, and so on. For these reasons, prose is more suited to imparting a benefit than poetry." See Gale (1994, 17), Asmis (1995b, 155), and Armstrong (2004a, 9).

29. See Sider (1995).

30. For other examples of *planus* in Lucretius, cf. 2.934 and 6.653–54.

31. See Gale (1994, 143–45). For poetry's illuminating effect, see *DRN* 1.136–45, 921–22, and 933–34; for Epicurus's, see 2.14–19, 3.1–2, and 5.9–12.

32. For Empedocles's influence on Lucretius, see Sedley (1998, 1–34, 201–2).

33. Horace's advocacy of moral utility was probably influenced by the Hellenistic theorist Neoptolemus of Parium, whose views on poetry survive in Philodemus's *On Poems*, in which he records and criticizes the ideas of various theorists concerning the moral value of poetry. See Asmis (1991, 1995a, and 1995b). For a very useful translation of Book Five based on the text of Mangoni (1993), see Armstrong (1995).

34. See Gale (1994, 17) and Asmis (1995a, 26).

35. *On Poems* 5. col. 32.17–19; see Asmis (1995b, 154).

36. See Asmis (1995a, 31), who states that it is the philosopher who can distinguish "what is morally valuable from what is morally harmful." See also Gale (1994, 17–18). Diogenes Laertius (10.121b) reports Epicurus's belief that only the sage will converse correctly about music and poetry: μόνον τε τὸν σοφὸν ὀρθῶς ἂν περί τε μουσικῆς καὶ ποιητικῆς διαλέξεσθαι.

37. Gigante (1995, 75–78) and Armstrong (2004b, 276–81).

38. Col. 43.16–19 Dorandi (1982). On this "correction," Asmis (1991, 21) states that, "According to Philodemus, Homer himself indicates the difference between good and bad. However, his indications are embedded in a poetic representation that contains much that is ethically reprehensible. Homer's starting points, therefore, must be sorted out from representations of the wrong kind; and this is the job of the philosopher."

39. See Asmis (1991, 17; 1995a, 30 with n. 82). As she points out, these attacks are particularly prominent in the *On Piety*.

40. Armstrong (2004b, 277).

41. This text and translation are those of Fish (2002). Fish reads κὰ[ν τ]οῖς where Dorandi (1982) reads [Ἀχιλλέω]ς; the latter reading would actually be closer to Horace. This parallel has been noted by various scholars, including Dorandi (1982, ad loc.), Asmis (1991, 20–21 n. 95), Gigante (1995, 76), and Armstrong (2004b, 277).

42. See Armstrong (2004a, 277–78), who points out that Odysseus and Nestor are repeatedly coupled as positive exempla. In col. 29.22–26 they are called φρονιμ[ώτα][τοι] τῶν [Ἑλλ]ήνων, "the wisest of the Greeks," who are not subject to their passions (τοσού|τω[ι

καὶ ἀφει]τήδεσαν τῶν | παθ[ῶν τού]των). In *On the Good King* col. 32.16–35 Nestor is again coupled with Odysseus, and both are held up as examples of wise men; in col. 41.21–23 Philodemus highlights Agamemnon's trust of Nestor and Odysseus.

43. Armstrong (2004b, 277). He suggests, furthermore, that Horace's reading of Homer is an Epicurean response to Stoic allegorization of Homer: "That is the first part of the epistle, 1–31, Philodemean to the core, and without a touch of such Stoic specialties as the allegorizing of the gods as elements and natural forces: thus, an Epicurean reply to such Stoic interpretations" (279).

44. For the use of exempla in Roman education, see Skidmore (1996, 13–21). Horace in *Sat.* 1.4.105–29 recounts his own father's use of good and bad exempla to teach his young son proper behavior.

45. Of course that Lucretius writes Epicurean verse at all is somewhat unorthodox. For the justification of Lucretius's use of verse, see Gale (1994, 138–55) and Asmis (1995a, esp. 33–34).

46. The best discussion of wine in Horace remains Commager (1957).

47. See Commager (1962, 325–26), Putnam (1969), and Race (1978). Though I find this argument persuasive, Nisbet and Hubbard (1970, ad loc.) suggest that "[t]his kind of interpretation ought to be rejected without hesitation."

48. Rudd (1989, 232). In *Sat.* 1.10.23–24 Horace refers to this same practice of mixing wines as a metaphor for using both Greek and Latin words in poetry: *at sermo lingua concinnus utraque / suavior, ut Chio nota si commixta Falerni est,* "but speech blended with each language is sweeter, just as when a brand of Falernian has been mixed with Chian." See Brown (1993, ad loc.): "an analogy from blending wines, in which the drier, native Falernian is sweetened with the imported Greek variety."

49. It is not always clear which liquid Horace has in mind; both wine and olive oil would fit the metaphor.

50. For the play on *puer* and *puro*, see Mayer (1994, ad loc.). The metaphor of the clean jar is used again later by Quintilian (*I.O.* 1.1.5) and Philo, *Quod omnis probus liber est* 15, to emphasize the importance of early education. See Skalitzky (1968, 449–50).

51. For Memmius's ears in the *DRN*, see above, note 2.

52. See *LSJ* II.1.

53. The image of ears "drinking" poetry is not uncommon. See, e.g., *Odes* 2.13.32, where Horace describes the scene of Sappho and Alcaeus in the Underworld: *densum umeris bibit aure vulgus,* "the crowd, packed shoulder to shoulder, drinks [the poetry] with its ear."

54. The interpretation of *fomenta podagrum* is vexed. Mayer (1994, ad loc.) suggests that fomenta are "foot-warmers used to alleviate gout." Dilke (1954, ad loc.), on the other hand, says that "*fomenta* cannot here be fomentations, which would give some relief for gout. Sen. *de Prov.* iv.9 and *de Vita Beata* xi.4 uses *fomenta* of wrappings for the feet or body worn by healthy but pampered people; and this must be the sense here." Whether they are therapeutic or luxurious wrappings, the *fomenta* must be analogous to the *pictae tabulae* (51) and *citharae* (52), i.e., potential sources of pleasure that are ineffectual because of disease (i.e., gout).

55. See Dilke (1954, ad loc.), Kiessling and Heinze (1957, ad loc.), and Armstrong (2004b, 280). Cf. Plato. *Protag.* 314a and Epictetus fr. 10. In the latter passage Epictetus is said to have compared the *litterae atque doctrinae* of philosophy to a liquid that when poured into an unclean vessel (*vas spurcum atque pollutum*) is turned into urine or something worse than urine (*si quid est urina spurcius*). See Bowditch (2001, 180).

56. The metaphor of the body as a jar is found in the *DRN* also at 3.440, 3.555, and 3.793.

57. Armstrong (2004b, 280).

58. See Ferri (1993, 99), who also sees this simile behind lines 67–68.

59. Gale (1994, 2).

60. See especially 3.1–17.

61. Even Armstrong (2004b), who states (276) that in the poem "the Epicureans appear to have the whole show to themselves from beginning to end," recognizes (280) that Horace weaves together many ideas that were not particular to any one school: "Of course I do not want to argue that some of these thoughts were unavailable to a Stoic or Academician, or are not to be found in the vast literature of protreptic teaching by other schools here and there; still less to diminish the relevance of the lines cited in the commentaries from Menander and Alexis and other comedians that contain the same thoughts."

62. Armstrong (2004b, 280–81). He connects, for example, line 55 (*sperne voluptates: nocet empta dolore voluptas*) to a statement of Epicurus (fr. 442 Usener): συμφέρει τῶνδέ τινων ἀπέχεσθαι τῶν ἡδονῶν, ἵνα μὴ ἀλγῶμεν ἀλγηδόνας χαλεπωτέρας ("It is beneficial to abstain from certain pleasures so that we not suffer more difficult pains").

63. For Philodemus's views on anger, see esp. Tsouna (2007, 195–238), Armstrong (2008), and Asmis (2011). On the Epicureans in general, see for example Fowler (1997) and Procopé (1998).

64. Cf. *Sat.* 1.1.106: *est modus in rebus, sunt* certi *denique* fines, *quos ultra citraque nequit consistere rectum*, "There is a measure in things, there are, in sum, certain fixed limits, beyond and short of which what is right cannot stand."

65. Mayer (1994, ad loc.) cites the echo of Cicero's *spernat voluptas* at *Epist.* 1.2.55, but he does not take into account the other verbal parallels between the passages.

66. For an analysis of the philosophy of the *Odyssey*, see Rutherford (1986).

67. Whereas Armstrong (2004b, 278) sees Horace's positive valuation of Odysseus as indebted to Philodemus's *On the Good King*, Moles (1985, esp. 34–39) has argued that Odysseus represents the idealized Cynic *vir* whose inflexibility Horace ultimately rejects by the poem's end. He suggests that Odysseus's remarkable sight (*providus*, 19; *inspexit*, 20) "evokes the Cynic notion of the philosophical 'examiner' (ἐπίσκοπος) and 'spy' or 'scout' (κατάσκοπος)." The waves in which Odysseus cannot drown (22) represent to Moles the waves of moral adversity to be confronted by the Cynic *vir*. Whereas some previous scholars have seen Odysseus as symbolic of Stoic *virtus*, Moles argues that he is "not the orthodox Stoic, who takes part in public life, but the Cynic, who rejects public life, courts adversity, and cannot be sunk by it." He concludes that the Cynic Odysseus represents one extreme, while the Epicurean Phaeacians, suitors, and companions represent the other, Epicurean extreme and that at the poem's end Horace positions himself between these extremes in lines 70–71 by evoking the Panaetian *proficiens* and the mean. While I agree with Moles that Horace favors moderation in the poem, I think it is Odysseus himself who represents this mean, which is attainable through adaptability. Ferri (1993, 109–10) also sees Epicureanism behind Horace's Odysseus, whose wisdom, he suggests, is in fleeing the city in favor of a private *angulus*. For Odysseus in Cynicism and Stoicism, see Montiglio (2011, 66–94) and for Epicureanism (especially Philodemus's portrait of him in *On the Good King*), see Montiglio (2011, 95–123). For the reception of Odysseus in the post-Homeric tradition, see especially Stanford (1954).

68. As Keane (2011, 439) points out, the *Odyssey* seems to have "special meaning" to Horace throughout *Epistles* 1: "There are numerous allusions to Odyssean episodes and themes throughout *Epistles* 1. The poet's description of himself at 1.15 as an itinerant philosophical *hospes* could be seen as obliquely evoking Homer's traveling hero; more explicit references come at 6.63–64, where Horace cites the weak companions of Odysseus as negative exemplars, at 7.40–43, where he compares the exchange between Telemachus and Menelaus in *Odyssey* 4 to his own relationship with Maecenas, and at 15.24, where he self-deprecatingly likens himself to the pleasure-loving Phaeacians. And in 1.2, Horace claims to be writing from Praeneste, a town that according to one ancient tradition was founded by Odysseus's son Telegonus."

69. Moles (1985, 35–36) also notes the similarities between the two passages, but with conclusions different from my own.

70. For the Aristippean Odysseus of *Epist.* 1.2, see esp. Traina (2009, 301–2). We cannot forget that the adaptability of Odysseus was traditional, and some of the traits attributed by various authors to Odysseus are identical with those attributed by Horace to Aristippus in *Epist.* 1.17. Atheneus (*Deipnos.* 12.513), for example, likens Odysseus to a polyp, citing Theognis 213–18. In Epictetus fr. 11 Odysseus is said to be able to wear rags or a purple cloak equally well. Epictetus furthermore compares the actor Polos, who is able to play any part ("mask") well (πρόσωπον ὑποκρίνασθαι καλῶς) to Odysseus. Cf. *Epist.* 1.17.23–29 (discussed in more detail in chapter 7 below):

> omnis Aristippum decuit color et status et res,
> temptantem maiora fere, praesentibus aequum,
> . . .
> alter purpureum non expectabit amictum,
> quidlibet indutus celeberrima per loca vadet
> personamque feret non inconcinnus utramque

> Every color and status and circumstance suited Aristippus, who attempted greater things but as a rule was content with what he had. . . . The one (Aristippus) will not wait for a purple cloak, but clothed in anything will go through the most celebrated spots and will wear either mask not inelegantly.

71. The one other time that Horace mentions a Siren can be read positively as well. At *Sat.* 2.3.14 Damasippus accuses Horace—who has been in the countryside reading the dramatists Plato (the comedian), Menander, and Eupolis, but writing little poetry himself—of *desidia*, which he calls an *improba Siren* that should be avoided. Anderson (1961) has interpreted this passage in light of the Epicurean associations between Sirens and intellectual pursuits. Connecting the heightened dramatic element in Book Two to Horace's reading list, he states that "Horace's Siren becomes a symbol of his whole poetic approach in this Satire and book" (107) and that "he has found a Siren which is suspect to the Stoics as *desidia* and to the Epicureans as useless *disciplina* or *doctrina*: an impersonal appeal to the reason through dialogues worthy of Plato and Menander. Most of his readers have felt the powerful lure of such a Siren" (108). The ancient attitude toward Sirens was ambivalent. While to the Epicureans they represented the danger of poetic speech, they were often presented in a more positive light. As Anderson points out (108 n. 1–2), Socrates (*Symp.* 216A), Aristotle (Julian *Orat.* 7.237c), Ariston (Diog. Laert. 7.160), and even Epicurus (Diog. Laert. 10.9) were all compared to Sirens. An anonymous poet is quoted in Suet. *Gramm.* 11 who refers to Cato as a Latin Siren, and Ovid refers to the

Sirens as *doctae* (*Met.* 5.555). Holford-Strevens (2006, 22) similarly discusses the ambivalence toward the Sirens.

72. See Eidinow (1990, 566).

73. Eidinow (1990, 567). In *Epist.* 1.4.6, Horace famously calls himself an *Epicuri de grege porcum*, "a pig from the herd of Epicurus," in a hedonistic moment. In 1.17.18 he calls Diogenes the Cynic a *mordacem Cynicum*, "biting Cynic." The Greek κυνικός of course means "doglike."

74. For a fuller analysis of *munditia* and the mean, see my discussion of 1.5 in chapter 4, and for *munditia* and the mean in the *Ars Amatoria*, see Gibson (2007, 99–104). In *Sat.* 2.2.65–69, for example, Ofellus states that the wise man, in adhering to the mean between abstemiousness and gluttony, will be *mundus*, "clean." Interestingly, in the context of this passage abstemiousness is represented by a *canis* (2.2.63–64), which looks back to the austerity of the Cynic Avidienus (2.2.55–62).

75. Keane (2011, 444).

76. Mayer (1994, ad loc.) states that "Homer is in H[orace]'s mind, not a philosophical text."

77. Keane (2011, 448–49). She continues, "Horace's advice will be one source of aid— analogous to the cures for the man with infected eyes or blocked ears, who cannot enjoy paintings or hear the cithara (51–53). This poet will help Lollius to get what he needs from poetry."

78. Kilpatrick (1986, 37).

79. For *condo* (used of literary composition), see *OLD* s.v. 14a, and for *compono*, see *OLD* s.v. 8a. For *condo* (of "storing"), see *OLD* s.v. 2, and s.v. 2b for specifically of storing wine, and for *compono*, see *OLD* s.v. 2.

80. See Lathière (1997, 148). For *depromere* (of bringing out wine) in Horace, cf. *Epod.* 2.47 (*dulci vina promens dolio*, "bringing out wine from a sweet jar"), *Odes* 1.9.7–8 (*deprome quadrimum Sabina/ . . . merum diota*, "bring out the four year old wine from the Sabine jar"), 1.36.11, 1.37.5 (*antehac nefas depromere Caecubum*, "before it was an offence to bring out the Caecubum"), 3.21.7–8 (*Corvino iubente / promere languidiora vina* ("with Corvinus urging me to bring out mellower wine").

81. Bowditch (2001, 178–80). See also Dilke (1954, ad loc.), who also points out the storing imagery, but does not suggest what it is supposed to symbolize.

CHAPTER 4. *NIL ADMIRARI*

1. Nisbet and Hubbard (1970, ad loc.) state that "there can be no reasonable doubt that this ode is addressed to the poet Albius Tibullus." The identification of Albius with Tibullus was challenged by Postgate (1903, 179–84; 1912) and subsequently defended by Ullman (1912a; 1912b). The identification has more recently been supported by Ball (1994).

2. Mayer (1994, ad loc.) suggests, however, that *sermonum* includes all of Horace's hexameter writing.

3. For the centrality of friendship to the epistle, see Kilpatrick (1986, 56–61).

4. The reference to Cassius of Parma in the epistle is difficult. As commentators note, he was one of the conspirators against Julius Caesar and was long dead when the epistle was written. While some, esp. Otis (1945, 187–88), have seen this comparison as less than complimentary to Albius, it is unclear exactly what its tone is. The late-Antique scholia attributed to Pseudo-Acro note on this passage that Cassius wrote in a number of genres and that his epigrams and elegies were particularly admired (*hic aliquod*

generibus stylum exercuit: inter quae opera elegiaca et epigrammata eius laudantur). If he was an elegist, it would be appropriate that Albius strives to outdo him.

5. Nisbet and Hubbard (1970, ad loc.). On the mean in *Odes* 1.33, see especially Lowrie (1994).

6. For the argument that his melancholy has been brought on by a love affair, see Kilpatrick (1986, 60–61).

7. The poem therefore forms an appropriate follow-up to *Epistles* 1.3, in which Florus is likewise urged not to be excessively competitive with his poetry but instead to focus on friendship. See chapter 8.

8. Putnam (1972, 87).

9. Dutsch (2008, 141).

10. I adopt the translation of line 11 from Mayer (1994, ad loc.).

11. As Mayer (1994, ad loc.) notes here, *mundus* is "used often by Horace to suggest a mean between luxurious superfluity and sordid lack." For the associations between *munditia* and the mean, see below on *Epistles* 1.5.7.

12. See, for example, Usener fr. 490: ὁ τῆς αὔριον ἥκιστα δεόμενος ἥδιστα πρόσεισι πρὸς τὴν αὔριον ("Whoever needs tomorrow least will approach it with the most pleasure."). Armstrong (2004b, 283) cites Philodemus *On Death* col. xxxviii.13–24 as a parallel.

13. See Tsakiropoulou-Summers (1998, 26).

14. See especially Cic. *Pis.* 37.

15. Cited by Kilpatrick (1986, 138 n. 16).

16. On this family history in relation to *Epistles* 1.5, see Nisbet (1959), Eidinow (1995), and Feeney (2010).

17. Feeney (2010, 206). On inherited character among Roman *gentes*, see Wiseman (1979, 25).

18. See Feeney (2010, 212).

19. See Fish (2011, 100–111).

20. On the public service of Roman Epicureans, see Fish (2011), who argues that public service was not incompatible with Epicureanism in every instance.

21. Eidinow (1995, 193). See Bourgery (1935, 130–31) and Kilpatrick (1986, 62).

22. Eidinow (1995, 193).

23. Eidinow (1995, 194).

24. See Mayer (1994) at 1.5.6.

25. Nisbet (1959, 74).

26. For sentimental wine, cf. *Epodes* 13.6, *Odes* 1.20.2, and *Odes* 3.21.1.

27. Nisbet (1959, 73), Eidinow (1995, 194), and Feeney (2010, 218).

28. Eidinow (1995, 195).

29. On *mundus* and *munditia* as evocative of the mean, see Gibson (2007, esp. 19–30 and 93–104).

30. The reference to an heir is especially pointed in the case of Torquatus, who seems to be the last of his line. His frugality and severity do not even serve his own family. Horace similarly exhorts Torquatus to enjoy the present moment in *Odes* 4.7.19–20 (*cuncta manus avidas fugient heredis, amico / quae dederis animo,* "All which you will have granted to your spirit will escape the greedy hands of your heir."). See Eidinow (1995, 197) and Feeney (2010, 221–23).

31. On wine in the *Odes*, see Commager (1957) and Kiernan (1999, 110–16). Cf. esp. 3.21.13–20.

32. See Putnam (2006, 399): "*Severitas* is incompatible with *ebrietas*."

33. Kiernan (1999, 111).

34. Mayer (1994, ad loc.).

35. On the poem, see esp. McGann (1969, 46–48), Musurillo (1974) and Kilpatrick (1986, 65–71).

36. Volk (2002, 36–43). Volk distinguishes between true didactic poems, which fulfill all four of the requirements she outlines, and those that are written in the "didactic mode," which only partially satisfy them. She writes that "a text in the didactic mode is reminiscent of a didactic poem by virtue of exhibiting characteristics typical of didactic poetry, most often by casting a speaker, at least temporarily, in the role of teacher." On the "didactic mode" of *Epistles* 1, see Morrison (2007).

37. *Istis* and *his* have caused some problems of interpretation. McGann (1969, 48) understands *istis* as referring to the rejected pursuits of 28–66 and *his* to Horace's doctrine of *nil admirari*. Dilke (1954, ad loc.) and Mayer (1994, ad loc.) both argue that *istis* and *his* refer to Horace's advice throughout the poem, and I follow their interpretation.

38. McGann (1969, 48).

39. See Rudd (1993, 70), who asks, "When we read the phrase *nil admirari*, are we supposed to think of the Pythagoreans' τὸ μηδὲν θαυμάζειν or of Democritus' ἀθαμβίη, of Epicurus' ἀταραξία, or of the Cynics and Stoics with their ἀπάθεια? The question is misconceived. Avoiding the appearance of dogmatism by the insertion of *prope*, Horace wants the principle to have the widest possible acceptance. He does *not* want to be tied to this or that school." See also Mayer (1994, ad loc.). Armstrong (2004b, 284–85) offers an interesting analysis of the doxography of 1.6 and suggests that Horace, though appearing neutral throughout, actually reveals a preference for Epicureanism. While I think this reading is attractive (though I hesitate to agree that this is a "parody" of Philodemus's didactic methodology), I am interested rather in issues of flexibility and dogmatism and how throughout the poem Horace rejects rigid adherence to extremes. His use of Epicurean strategies of argumentation and even promotion of Epicurean ethical principles does not detract from his stated preference for adaptability and lack of orthodoxy. He is able to use Epicurean thought in the service of his own brand of philosophical independence. The correspondences with *Epistles* 1.1, I will suggest, mark the poem's thought as especially Aristippean insofar as Aristippus through the collection exemplifies adaptability, lack of dogmatism, and the avoidance of extremes.

40. "As soon as an unexpected appearance startles either" is adopted from Dilke (1954, ad loc.).

41. See Kiessling and Heinze (1957, ad loc.). The identification of Horace's thought with Stoic *apatheia* has been deemphasized by Musurillo (1974, 196). On the Stoic tenet of forethought and preparation, see Mayer (1994, ad loc.), Nisbet and Hubbard (1978) at *Odes* 2.10.14, and esp. Newman (1989).

42. See Long (2006, 381). The Greek terms are ἐπιθυμία, φόβος, ἡδονή, and λύπη.

43. Mayer (1994, ad loc.) also cites this passage as a parallel to *Epistles* 1.6.

44. On Cicero's possible sources for this Cyrenaic view, see Graver (2002a, 157–58).

45. On the Cyrenaic *praemeditatio mali futuri*, see Holloway (2002, 434–38) and Graver (2002b, esp. 161–70). On the Epicurean avoidance of pre-rehearsal and instead directing the mind away from pain and ahead to future pleasures, see Graver (2002b, 170–77). For an overview of the differences between the Cyrenaics and Epicureans, see Graver (2002a, 195–201). Asmis (2001, 222) offers a succinct synopsis: "One type of

spiritual exercise that the memorized core of doctrine will not permit is the anticipation (*praemeditatio*) of misfortune. Other philosophers, especially the Cyrenaics, proposed that a person can eliminate present distress by contemplating the possibility of misfortune in advance; for in this way one will not be caught off guard. Epicurus thought that this type of contemplation was wholly useless, or rather harmful: it was to add pain unnecessarily."

46. It is unclear, however, whether Aristippus himself introduced this principle into the Cyrenaic school. Zeller (1868, 325–26 and n. 3) attributes this to his successor Theodorus. Mannebach (1961, 96) does not accept the principle as genuinely Aristippean. Graver (2002a) outlines the reasons that scholars have been hesitant to associate the tenet with Aristippus or with the Cyrenaics at all: "Most accounts of Cyrenaic ethics understand a central text in Diogenes Laertius to say that for these hedonists, the proper goal of human existence is simply the pleasure of the present moment, while the long view which considers one's life of pleasure as a whole is of little concern. This reading is usually combined with passages in later sources which attribute to Aristippus the view that one should live exclusively for the present. An ethics whose sole effort is to maximize the pleasure of the present moment can hardly support a recommendation of the kind Cicero describes; consequently, Cicero's account must be regarded with suspicion." Graver goes on to defend the association of pre-rehearsal of future ills with the Cyrenaics and to contrast their beliefs with those of the Epicureans. Striker (2002, 179) agrees with Graver that "the disagreement probably reflects an actual controversy between the schools, and not just the habit of later historians to set the hedonistic schools side by side to point out the differences." Whether or not Aristippus himself originated this principle, the ideas of the later school could certainly have been associated with him by later writers, and Cicero's testimony certainly shows that the tenet was associated with the Cyrenaics in the Roman era. Lampke (2015, 56–100) argues against the idea that the Cyrenaic focus on present circumstances contradicts with the practice of premeditating future evils.

47. See Musurillo (1974, 202): "We are led to suspect that what must be applied to all five options offered to Numicius is the *modus*, or, as it is here expressed, the *ultra quam satis est* (16). This, for Horace, is the natural corollary of the doctrine of *nil admirari*."

48. Musurillo (1974) points out that in his *Odes* Horace promotes frivolous delights with moderation: *misce stultitia consiliis brevem: / dulce est disipere in loco* (4.12.27–28).

49. Putnam (1995).

50. Although Nisbet and Hubbard (1970, ad loc.) suggest that Horace "teases his earnest young friend with a cultivated humour worthy of his epistles," others have read his tone in the ode as more critical. See Goar (1972/3) and Wright (1974), who sense in the ode a sympathy for the hypothetical girl and boy Iccius intends to enslave that casts doubt on Iccius's motives.

51. See Goar (1972/3, 116): "The former student of philosophy, instead of clinging to the precept *nil admirari*, has succumbed to *invidia divitiarum*."

52. For the suggestion that these slaves will be expected to serve Iccius sexually, see Wright (1974, 49). Nisbet and Hubbard (1970, ad loc.) call the tone of the passage "erotic."

53. Goar (1972/3, 117).

54. The *libri Panaeti* suggest that Iccius was a Stoic philosopher, though of course *Socratica domus* would embrace other systems as well. Santirocco (1986, 68) suggests that his Stoicism seems to have a Pythagorean bent: "The coupling of the Stoic Panaetius

with the Socratics (14), for instance, probably reflects the degree to which contemporary Stoicism was influenced by Platonism. One result of this was a widespread belief in the transmigration of souls, which had been taught by Pythagoras. . . . But it is also attested in the fragments of Panaetius, and it is very interesting that in the only other poem Horace addresses to Iccius, *Epistles* 1.12, the jests concerning that doctrine clearly presuppose Iccius's adherence to it."

55. See Mayer (1994) at 1.12.2: "*Frueris* pointedly echoes *fructibus* and both hint at the legal concept of *ususfructus*, which went beyond *usus* (4) 'the legal right to use another's property' in allowing a right to receive profits from it as well."

56. Putnam (1995, 199).

57. Mayer (1994, ad loc.).

58. Fr. D55 in Taylor (2010) = fr. 211 in Graham (2010).

59. Stobaeus 3.10.43. Fr. D83 in Taylor (2010) = fr. 288 in Graham (2010).

60. Stobaeus 4.33.23. Fr. D147 in Taylor (2010) = fr. 261 in Graham (2010).

61. Morrison (2007, 118–21) reads Horace's advice to Iccius in Epicurean terms. According to Morrison, Horace expresses in the poem "a desire to shift from a Lucretian concern for physics toward ethics." Morrison further argues that "the regular stress throughout the *Epistles* on asking 'what should I/you do,' 'what is right?,' etc. is a corrective to the concentration in the *De Rerum Natura* on physics." Though I agree that Horace urges Iccius to derive ethical lessons from his natural inquiries, this does not automatically suggest Epicureanism, though Epicureanism did of course base its ethics on scientific explanations of the physical universe.

62. See Dilke (1954, ad loc.) and Mayer (1994, ad loc.).

63. See Wilkins (1993).

64. Cf. esp. line 13 of the ode: *vivitur parvo bene* ("one lives well on a little").

65. See, e.g., Dilke (1954, ad loc.) and Mayer (1994, ad loc.).

66. Putnam (1995, 203–4).

67. Barker (1996, 443–44) argues that the personified *Copia* at the end of *Epistles* 1.12 is morally dubious: "The *fruges* which golden Copia pours into Italy from her full horn may be as ambiguous as the *fructus* of the earlier part of the poem—either the agricultural fruits, whether of Italy itself or of its empire, or, metaphorically, the luxurious spoils of the imperial successes Horace lists, the mineral, monetary nature of which is reflected in the goldenness of the Plenty who pours them. In the light of the *Epistle* and of the wider Horatian discourse on luxury and gold, the goldenness of Copia may be taken to imply moral danger." I agree that gold is morally dubious throughout the poem, but the main issue Horace emphasizes in the epistle is how individuals respond to and undertake the enrichment of Italy. The spread of empire brings with it the potential for corruption and greed, and Horace's appeal to Iccius is to avoid such temptation.

CHAPTER 5. OTIA LIBERRIMA

1. My language of "renegotiation" is indebted to Oliensis (1998, 157–58): "An exercise in polite rudeness or amicable hostility, the poem at once (re)creates and averts a crisis by renegotiating a contract that Horace can no longer honor in its original form."

2. *Epistles* 1.7 is perhaps the most discussed poem in the collection. For treatments of it, see Büchner (1940), Gunning (1942), Fraenkel (1957, 327–39), Hiltbrunner (1960), Drexler (1963), Peterson (1968), Williams (1968, 19–23), McGann (1969, 92–96), Wimmel (1969), Kilpatrick (1973a; 1986, 7–14), Riikonen (1977), Hayward (1986), Gold (1987,

126–30), Berres (1992), Horsfall (1993), Lyne (1995, 150–55), Oliensis (1998, 157–64), Thurmond (1998), Bowditch (2001, 181–210), and Freudenburg (2002, 128–31).

3. εἶναί τίς μοι δοκεῖ μέση τούτων ὁδός, ἣν πειρῶμαι βαδίζειν, οὔτε δι᾽ ἀρχῆς οὔτε διὰ δουλείας, ἀλλὰ δι᾽ ἐλευθερίας, ἥπερ μάλιστα πρὸς εὐδαιμονίαν ἄγει, "There seems to me to be a certain middle path, which I try to walk, neither through rule nor through slavery, but through freedom, which most especially leads to happiness" (*Mem* 1.2.11). For a discussion of this passage in relation to *Epist.* 1.1, see chapter 1.

4. See Oliensis (1998, 165): "The Sabine farm is at once the clearest reminder of Horace's dependence and the site and figure of his independence." Most, though not all, scholars have found freedom to be a key theme in the poem. See, e.g., Ooteghem (1946, 186), who calls the poem "une protestation d'indépendance"; Peterson (1968, 313) ("The whole poem sounds the theme of independence"); Williams (1968, 19) ("Horace seems to be asserting his independence"); Shackleton Bailey (1982, 56) ("Independence is almost aggressively asserted"); Gold (1987, 127) ("The main subject is freedom"); Lyne (1995, 150) (The poem's "particular function . . . is to allow Horace to assert the measure of liberty he feels he should possess"); and Nadjo (2002, 144) ("l'épître I, 7 qu'on pourrait intituler 'L'indépendance d'Horace'"). Kilpatrick (1973a, 53; 1986, 14) disagrees that freedom is a central concern: "The theme of the Epistle is not independence, but rather the fitness of one's aspirations as measured by one's proper nature."

5. Kilpatrick (1973a; 1986, 7–14).

6. Mayer (1994, 175). For assessments of Horace's tone as friendly and complimentary, see also Büchner (1940). Fraenkel (1957, 333–39) suggests that Horace begins "with his tongue in his cheek" and finds it "difficult to believe that he could have been wholly in earnest." The threat to return Maecenas's gifts, he states, "may have made Maecenas wince," but the story of Philippus and Mena "could not fail to delight Maecenas." He concludes that "the letter . . . is to the credit not only of Horace but of Maecenas as well. Nothing could show more clearly that Horace's sincere and courageous message left no sting in his friend's heart." Thurmond (1998, 845) speaks of a "tone of bemused irony." Bowditch (2001, 181–210) focuses on Horace's claim to be *mendax* (1.7.2) and suggests that throughout the poem he is "duplicitous," with the result that divergent interpretations are simultaneously possible.

7. Lyne (1995, 155).

8. Oliensis (1998, 157).

9. Freudenburg (2002, 129). Cf. also Shackleton Bailey (1982, 56): "At the beginning of the first Epistle Horace intimates that he is his own man, able to decline a request from Maecenas, but he does it inoffensively. In the seventh independence is almost aggressively asserted." For the argument that Horace's tone is harsh, see also, e.g., Gunning (1942).

10. On Augustus and *libertas*, see the introduction. Several scholars have argued that Maecenas fell out of favor with Augustus right around the time Horace was writing the *Epistles*, basing their arguments on a) Tacitus *Ann.* 3.30.4, where Tacitus suggests that Maecenas held only the appearance of power in his later years, b) Suetonius *Aug.* 66.3, where Maecenas is said to have told his wife, Terentia, that her brother Murena's conspiracy had been discovered, and c) Horace's later poetry, esp. Maecenas's absence from the second book of *Epistles* and the single mention of Maecenas in the fourth book of *Odes* (4.11.19). This view was first promulgated by Syme (1939, 387–89), and is supported by Brink (1982, 523–72) and Williams (1968, 4–5, 86–88). Williams later (1990) changed

his mind, arguing that while the evidence does not support the idea that Maecenas suffered a political fall, he nevertheless ceded to Augustus the lead role in literary patronage. See also White (1991), who argues not only that Maecenas did not fall out of favor, but also that there was no great change to his role in literary patronage and that Augustus played a primary role all the time. Brink (1995) later restates his position. While I agree with those who see little evidence for a political fall, it is beyond doubt that, for whatever reason, Maecenas played a lesser role in Horace's later poetry, which does not necessarily support the idea that there was a personal falling out between the two. As Suetonius reports in his life of Horace, in his will Maecenas requested that Augustus "be as mindful of Horace" as of him himself (*Horati Flacci ut mei esto memor*). The first book of *Epistles*, at any rate, certainly does not prove that Horace is distancing himself from Maecenas, for he is the dedicatee of three of the twenty poems, and his presence colors the entire collection.

11. For this socio-poetic approach to Maecenas, see the introduction.

12. For the suggestion that *mendax* marks Horace as a "duplicitous" speaker throughout the poem, see Bowditch (2001, esp. 182–84).

13. Oliensis (1998, 158). In *Epist.* 2.1.111–12 Horace freely accuses himself of mendacity whenever he professes not to be writing anything (*ipse ego, qui nullos me adfirmo scribere versus / invenior Parthis mendacior*, "I myself, who claim that I am writing no verses, am found to be more untruthful than the Parthians"). In *Epist.* 2.2.24–25 he again refers to himself as *mendax*, but in this context it is clear that he is echoing his addressee Florus's own words (*quereris super hoc etiam, quod / exspectata tibi non mittam carmina mendax*, "In addition to this, you complain because I—liar that I am—do not send the poems that you have been expecting").

14. Freudenburg (2002, 128).

15. Oliensis (1998, 158).

16. See Bowditch (2001, 194): "In his capacity as public poet—as a *vates*—Horace (or at least his labor) would . . . quite literally belong to Maecenas and justify the use of the possessive pronoun."

17. For the translation "tilt the scale toward," see Gowers (2012, ad loc.).

18. E.g., Oliensis (1998, 158).

19. Cf. esp. the end of *Epist.* 2.2: *lusisti satis, edisti satis atque bibisti: / tempus abire tibi est, ne potum largius aequo / rideat et pulset lasciva decentius aetas*, "You have played enough, you have eaten and drunk enough. It is time for you to go away, so that youth, which is more suitably mischievous, may not laugh at you and beat you since you have drunk more than your fair share."

20. See Mayer (1994, ad loc.). Bradshaw (1989, 177) argues that *locuples* here "suggests money." Bradshaw takes issue with the assumption, going back to the ancient scholia, that the farm was a gift from Maecenas, although he does not rule out the argument that Maecenas furnished Horace with the means to purchase the farm on his own. Whether or not Maecenas provided Horace with the farm itself or with the means to purchase it, it remains nevertheless the central symbol of their relationship in his poetry. For the argument that Horace would have been financially independent without Maecenas's help, see Zetzel (1982) and Armstrong (1986). This of course does not prevent Horace from constructing a poetic persona whose self-sufficiency and independence has been enabled by Maecenas's generosity. Zetzel (90) speaks of the financial dependence of poets such as Catullus and Horace as a "literary conceit," while Armstrong (284) urges care in distinguishing between "poetic self-portraiture and fact."

21. For the argument that *Maia nata* is a play on the name Maecenas, see Reckford (1997, 594–95) and Oliensis (1998, 48). For the argument that Mercury here clearly stands for Maecenas and that Maecenas is the Etruscan equivalent of the Greek Μαιαγενής, see Morgan (1994).

22. *Epistles* 1.7.24 is notoriously difficult to translate. For the variety of possible interpretations, see Thurmond (1998), who calls it "one of the most delightfully vexatious lines of any of his works." The possible translations he offers vary from "I will prove myself worthy in accordance with the praise my benefactor so generously bestows on me" to "I will fulfill my part of the deal by praising my benefactor and eliciting public acclaim for him."

23. Oliensis (1998, 159) suggests that the obligations entailed by Maecenas's past benefactions are what troubles Horace: "It is Horace who is feeling obliged, Horace who is feeling 'weighed down,' not by Maecenas's gift but by the continuing obligations it carries with it."

24. The language of 1.7.25–28 recalls both Horace's private, sympotic lyric and his public, civic lyric. As Bowditch (2010, 70) points out, "sweet speech and elegant laughter in a sympotic context imply the lyric Odes—we hear the echo of 'sweetly laughing Lalage' (*dulce ridentem Lalagen*, 1.22.23)—and the erotic odes metonymically imply the political lyric as well. But the adjectives 'sweet' and 'decorous' (*dulce . . . decorum*) conjure up civic lyric on their own, alluding to the memorable line of military sacrifice in the second Roman Ode, 'it is sweet and fitting to die for one's country' (*dulce et decorum est pro patria mori*, *Odes* 3.2.13)."

25. Freudenburg (2002, 129).

26. For fables in the *Epistles*, see Nadjo (2002). For the connections between fable and slavery in Horace, see Marchesi (2005). For ancient fables in general, including those of Horace, see Holzberg (2002).

27. Kilpatrick (1973a, 51; (1986, 12) offers a translation of this line as "If I am the man impugned by this fable, I refute it all!" He explains, "Horace is defending his past conduct as consistent with his own and Maecenas's views, not admitting a fault or taking drastic measures to reform." I agree that this line can be read as a denial that this tale applies to him, but the threat to return all of Maecenas's gifts if he is proven guilty cannot entirely be removed. I agree with Bowditch (2001, 185) that both readings are simultaneously possible. Some scholars have suggested that Horace here threatens to return only Maecenas's city gifts. Macleod (1979, 20), e.g., says that "what Horace would give back is the luxury and grandeur of city life."

28. As commentators note, the line strongly recalls *Odes* 3.1.47–48, where it is explicitly the Sabine property that Horace refuses to exchange for *divitiae*: *cur valle permutem Sabina / divitias operosiores*? "Why would I exchange my Sabine valley for more troublesome riches?"

29. *OLD* s.v. 1.

30. As Leen (2000–2001, 143) writes, "Domestic space served . . . as a barometer of individual character and a statement of moral worth."

31. Bowditch (2001, 125).

32. See, e.g., McGann (1969, 51: "He will find that Horace is able to restore the gifts which he has received and to do this with joy because of the greater good which he has thereby chosen"), Mayer (1994, ad loc.:"Restoration must not cost a pang"), and Freudenburg (2002, 129: "And watch me do it with a smile").

33. See Bowditch (2001, 205): "The aristocratic world of gift exchange is thus the model in which the poet chooses to inscribe his own experience, likening the institution of *amicitia* to the guest-host relations of Homeric *xenia*." He "identifies good patronal relations with the aristocratic equals of Homeric *xenia* and gestures toward a shared elite culture."

34. Lyne (1995, 154) and Bowditch (2001, 202–3) suggest that Telemachus is here committing a social faux pas by refusing the offered horses. Lyne: "The point is, I think, that Telemachus' refusal is a gaffe, a social blunder—a very funny episode in the *Odyssey*. . . . Haud male, 'not badly,' says Horace, pretending not to see the social ineptitude. The social ineptitude that amused Menelaus will, it is hoped, amuse Maecenas." Bowditch: "For although the wise man should give appropriately to the merits of the recipient, the code of Homeric gift exchange and particularly of guest-host relations lays an obligation on the recipient to accept what is offered. Hence, by displaying his own lack of decorum, Telemachus in fact matches the indecorousness in the extravagant giving on the part of Menelaus. In matching gaff for gaff, Telemachus may very well illustrate Horace's ability to requite Maecenas on the level of indecorous behavior." Horace, however, places the episode in a context that is highly influenced by Aristotelian and Hellenistic discussions of gift exchange, in which the appropriateness of the gift is significant. For a discussion of this background see esp. Fraenkel (1957, 330–31).

35. τοιγὰρ ἐγώ τοι ταῦτα μεταστήσω· δύναμαι γάρ. / δώρων δ᾿ ὅσσ᾿ ἐν ἐμῷ οἴκῳ κειμήλια κεῖται, / δώσω ὃ κάλλιστον καὶ τιμηέστατόν ἐστι. / δώσω τοι κρητῆρα τετυγμένον ("And so I will exchange these presents for you, for I am capable of doing so. Of all the presents that lie in store in my house, I will give what is the most beautiful and honored. I will give to you a well-wrought mixing bowl," 4.612–15).

36. There is some dispute as to whether these lines indicate the Sabine farm at all. For example, Mayer (1994, ad loc.) suggests that "at some time H. acquired a villa [at Tibur]; he is not referring to the *Sabinum* which Maecenas gave him." Lyne (1995, 154 n. 40) writes, "I suspect that Horace refers to properties of his own at Tibur and Tarentum." Oliensis (1998, 161) argues that "were the Sabine farm named here, Horace would find himself in the uncomfortable position of at once refusing Maecenas's request and clinging wholeheartedly to Maecenas's most famous and eminently suitable gift. By substituting Tibur and Tarentum, Horace reminds his patron that he does, after all, have other retreats available to him." I find, however, that this "uncomfortable position" is precisely the one in which Horace places himself. Tibur and Tarentum, I suggest, indicate the countryside in general terms, and Horace is saving an explicit reference to a Sabine farm for the final exemplary tale of the poem. Bowditch (2001, 189–90) similarly argues that the Sabine farm is meant as the countryside that contrasts with *regia Roma*: "Since the self-restoring Sabine estate figures in so many of the *Epistles* as the *rus*, the place removed from Rome that creates epistolary distance, the association here is hardly far-fetched. Also, as Catullus 44 suggests, the more fashionable way of referring to the Sabine territory was by the name of Tibur, the town closest to that region."

37. Freudenburg (2002, 129–30).

38. Oliensis (1998, 164).

39. For the comparison with *Sat.* 1.6, see, esp., McGann (1969, 54–55) and Oliensis (1998, 163–64).

40. As Oliensis (1998, 163) points out, these identifications are further problematized by the fact that Mena's name "distantly echoes" that of Maecenas and Philippus's name that of Flaccus.

41. Reckford (1959, 206) says that Horace implies, "This could so easily be us—but it won't be." Kilpatrick (1973a, 53) states that the "apparent resemblances to the events of Horace's and Maecenas' relationship are intended only to intensify the contrasts." Gold (1987, 128) likewise argues that "Horace presents both characters in an exaggerated form in order to satirize by distortion the worst kind of patronage." Harrison (2007, 241) suggests that "this is a negative parable for the relationship of Horace and Maecenas." I tend to agree with scholars who see the tale as at once complimentary and a warning. For example: Macleod (1979, 20) writes that "the bad relationship of patron and dependent is represented only by the two men in the story, not by Maecenas and Horace. But it also shows with painful clarity and blunt humor what could go wrong between them." Lyne (1995, 155) suggests that while there are many differences between Philippus and Maecenas, those differences are not as clear-cut as they were in the story of the *Calaber hospes*. He concludes, "It is up to Maecenas and to us therefore to judge how much of the biting tale of Philippus and Mena does apply to Horace and his great friend." Oliensis (1998, 163–66) argues that "the tale cannot be read strictly *e contrario* as a model of bad patron-client relations and unhappy gifts designed to bring the righteousness of Maecenas and Horace and the rightness of Maecenas' gift into sharper relief" and that "Mena . . . is less the antithesis than a caricature of the virtuous Horace portrayed in *Satires* 1.6." Freudenburg (2002, 131) suggests that the story "helps us imagine what that relationship has the potential to become in 19 B.C.E., describing what that once famous friendship will look like if Maecenas persists in pushing Horace too hard to accept a gift that is much too big for his talents."

42. Like Aristius Fuscus and Horace in *Epist.* 1.10, the urban Mena and epistolary Horace will hold similar values but will uphold them in opposing physical locations.

43. Cf. Oliensis (1998, 163), who suggests that his concern with his physical appearance aligns Mena rather with Maecenas, who was "famously fastidious" about these matters. Bowditch (2001, 189) argues that Mena's clean nails indicate his aesthetic principles, which will be compromised by "the benefactions of the state."

44. Oliensis (1998, 162) nicely says that Philippus is "seduced by this portrait of humble contentment."

45. For a similar use of *loco*, cf. *Odes* 4.12.28: *dulce est desipere in loco*, "it is sweet to be silly on the right occasion."

46. Mayer (1994, ad loc.).

47. For the professions of *coactor* and *praeco*, see Brown (1993, ad loc.) and Gowers (2012, ad loc.). For the identification of Mena as a freedman, see Mayer (1994) on line 55: "His name betrays a freedman, once simply Mena (from Menas, a shortened form of Menodoros . . .). On manumission the *nomen* of his previous owner, Volteius, was added, slaves having no legal father."

48. *Referre negas quali sit quisque parente / natus, dum ingenuus*, "you deny that it makes a difference from what sort of parent someone was born, provided that he is free-born/honorable." See Mayer (1994) at line 54. Brown (1993, ad loc.) and Gowers (2012 ad loc.) point out that *ingenuus* is ambiguous. It can refer to someone that is either freeborn or "noble in nature." To quote Gowers: "The ambiguity here is typical of the poem, which reflects contemporary questioning of aristocratic values and recent attempts . . . to redefine virtue in terms of inner worth." Though I agree that the term is ambiguous in the satire, I find the meaning "freeborn" impossible to remove entirely.

49. For the difficulty of getting an introduction to Maecenas, see *Sat.* 1.9.56 (*difficilis aditus primos habet*).

50. Armstrong (1986, 280): "It might be said that 1.6 and 2.6 are counterparts to each other in the two books of *Satires*. Both portray Horace's relationship to Maecenas, to Roman society, and to the ideal of the simple life, but 2.6 updates the information in 1.6."

51. Oliensis (1998, 34–35).

52. For the imitation of a patron by a client, see 1.18.10–14 and 21–31. For the patron who deliberately ruins his client by giving him access to finery, see 1.18.31–36.

53. The *redde* of line 95, as scholars have pointed out, looks back to the triple anaphora of *reddes* in lines 25–28, where the impossibility of Maecenas's restoration of Horace's youth is implied. Philippus too, it seems cannot return Mena to his former life. See, e.g., Bowditch (2001, 207).

54. Foster (1971). Fowler (2008, 92) suggests that in 1.16 Horace is "at his most devious and hard to decode."

55. See McGann (1969, 74–75): "The terms *sapiens bonusque* (20), *stulti* (24), *sapiens emendatusque* (30), and *vir bonus et sapiens* (73), the statement that all good hate sin because they love virtue (52), and the passages which recall the paradoxes that all sins are equal (55f) and that only the wise man is free (63ff.), all these elements give the epistle a strong flavour of the Stoicism of ἀρετή, κατορθώματα and the σοφός and set it apart from the rest of the book, which expresses the less arduous ideals of *decorum, carpe diem, nil admirari* and *aequus animus*."

56. See Kilpatrick (1986, 97) and Mayer (1994, ad loc.).

57. See Bradshaw (1989, 180).

58. Thomas (1982, 8–34). See also Voit (1975) and Bowditch (2001, 240–41). Leach (1993, 281), however, suggests that Horace's hexameter descriptions of his property are given a more "practical cast" than his lyric descriptions.

59. See Thomas (1982, 19) and Leach (1993, 281–82).

60. See Bowditch (2001, 241–42).

61. In *Epistles* 1.2.47–49 Horace explicitly includes *fundi* among the items that cannot cure spiritual ailments: *non domus et fundus, non aeris acervus et auri / aegroto domini deduxit corpore febris / non animo curas* ("Neither house and farm, nor a heap of bronze and gold has removed fevers from the sick body of a master, nor cares from his mind").

62. See McGann (1969, 74). The *pecus* in line 10 must refer to pigs since acorns, as Dilke (1954, ad loc.) and Mayer (1994, ad loc.) note, were turned into mash for pig feed.

63. Johnson (2010, 327) aptly speaks of the farm as an "illusory sanctum" and suggests that the farm "has failed to provide permanent solutions to enduring problems and has masked them rather than resolved them."

64. Thomas (1982, 13–15).

65. Clay (1989, 190).

66. W.R. Johnson (2004, 81). As he points out, line 146 (*iamque ministrantem platinum potantibus umbras*) suggests that he may occasionally enjoy company: "C. Day Lewis misrenders this as 'the plane that already offered a pleasant shade for drinking,' but L.P. Wilkinson extends the connotation of *potantibus* perhaps a bit too far in a Horatian direction (see *Odes* 1.22.13017): 'And planes already / providing welcome shade for drinking parties.' Perhaps, once in a while, someone else, a thirsty wayfarer maybe, happens to join the Corycian for a cup of wine under the plane tree, out of the summer's heat, but it is hard to imagine this reclusive fellow organizing *convivia*."

67. For the protective qualities of the farm in the ode, see esp. lines 14–28.

68. Xenophon, *Mem.* 1.2.11.

69. On Stoicism in the epistle, see esp. Kilpatrick (1986, 96–102).

70. Seneca of course defended the notion that the Stoic could withdraw from public life in the *de Otio*, arguing that by devoting himself to philosophy he provides a valuable service to his fellow men. On the views concerning *otium* and public participation among the Roman Stoics, see Reydams-Schils (2005, 83–113); on Seneca, see Classen (1988, 103–4).

71. As Mayer (1994, ad loc.) notes, this is an allusion to the fable of the ass in the lion's skin.

72. The *Sabellus* of line 49 has been thought to refer either to one of Horace's Sabine neighbors or to Horace himself, as his birthplace of Venusia was in Samnite (i.e., Sabellian) territory. I think the lines are more pointed if we are to imagine Horace rebuking his own slave and thereby literalizing the authority he describes in the opening lines.

73. Mayer (1994, ad loc.), McGann (1960, 209), and Kilpatrick (1986, 99). Dilke (1954) is noncommittal in his commentary: "Here he is not quite, as Porphyrion thinks, agreeing with the Stoic view, and certainly not, as Ps.-Acron thinks, attacking it. He is saying that if a man, through fear of being detected and punished, steals only one out of a thousand bushels, he is just as much a thief as if he stole a thousand."

74. See, e.g., Cic. *Parad.* 16–19.

75. See Sedley (1997, 50), who writes that "for a Stoic, freedom is first and foremost a personal matter, exclusive to the wise."

76. See McGann (1960, 211) and Fowler (2008, 90).

77. Horace's emphasis on the boldness of the *vir*'s speech is based on the *Bacchae* as well, where Pentheus is particularly taken aback by the boldness of Dionysus's skillful speech: ὡς θρασὺς ὁ βάκχος κοὐκ ἀγύμναστος λόγων ("How bold is this bacchant and not unpracticed in speech," 491).

78. Bowditch (2001, 150).

79. For *includere* of "imprisonment," see *OLD* s.v. 2.

80. For the apolitical reading, see McGann (1960, 211–12). For the political reading, see Johnson (1993, 46) and Bowditch (2001, 150–51).

81. Bowditch (2001, 151).

82. Some scholars are hesitant to associate these lines with Stoic suicide. Dilke (1954, ad loc.), for instance, suggests that Horace "*may* be touching upon the Stoic view" (italics mine). Mayer (1994, ad loc.) denies the reference to Stoic suicide, suggesting that Horace is concerned not with suicide but with "death, sooner or later, as the end of all." Fowler (2008, 90–91) makes a similar suggestion. If read in this way, however, the closing vignette loses much of its intensity and power. *Moriar* is, however, admittedly ambiguous. As Hill (2004, 188) points out, many of the suicides described by Tacitus (over a quarter) are carried out at the command of the emperor. Horace's *moriar* may point either to suicide or to the wise man's composed willingness to be put to death by the tyrannical Pentheus figure, who, once he has taken away the wise man's goods and imprisoned him, has only his life left to take. Kilpatrick (1986, 101) makes the latter argument.

83. Sedley (1997, 50).

84. See Griffin (1986b) and Hill (2004, 184).

85. Hill (2004, 185).

86. See Sedley (1997, 50) and Hill (2004, 186–87). On political suicide in Rome, see Griffin (1986a, 1986b), Plass (1995, 81–134), and Hill (2004, 183–212). On suicide in general, including political suicide, see Grisé (1982) and van Hooff (1990).

87. Roller (2001, 272–86). He argues furthermore that while *libertas* is depicted by Seneca as available to aristocrats through mental serenity, this same freedom is not available to the would-be tyrant subject to the emotions of anger, cruelty, and desire. In this way Stoicism inverts the idea that the Empire brought traditionally free aristocrats into the servitude of the emperor.

88. Fowler (2008, 91).

89. McGann (1969, 74) comes closest to such an interpretation: "More a retreat than a farm, it derives from the vagueness of the language in which it described an aura of otherworldliness so that it is seen not merely as the setting of a simple life, but, when taken in conjunction with the search for the *vir bonus* that follows (41ff.), as a kind of symbol of a life devoted to wisdom." Fowler (2008, 91) speaks of the farm as an "objective correlation of its owner." Leach (1993, 300) suggests that Horace "identifies this property with his social personality, as a Roman aristocrat identifies with his *domus*." In assessing the Corycian farmer in a way equally applicable to the Horace of *Epistles* 1.16 Johnson argues that the garden acts as a "refuge from history, from its grandeurs and its nightmares" and that "in this place of refuge one forgets—wants not to remember?—that Epicurus, and then Lucretius, and then Philodemus, and now Horace had, all of them, found that you could have a garden inside a city, even inside a cosmopolis and its empire, that you could be a part of the process and not part of it, that you could, indeed that you must, emigrate internally and lay out your garden in the invisible here-but-also-elsewhere."

90. For *fundus* as "basis" or "foundation," see *OLD* s.v. 2.

91. For Horace's anticipation of the Tacitean passage in the *Epistles*, see also the introduction.

92. Classen (1988, 116).

93. See Percival (1980, 132).

94. Classen (1988, 98–100) suggests that traditionally *moderatio* (with which Cicero translates *sophrosyne*) was a desirable trait of rulers to possess. As he points out, Cicero used *moderatio* to describe his governance of Cilicia (*Att.* 4.2.4) and that Valerius Maximus illustrates *moderatio* by the exempla of Cincinnatus, Scipio Africanus or L. Scipio Asiaticus. Tacitus, however, he shows, applies the principle not just to rulers but to subjects as well. On these Tacitean passages, see also Percival (1980).

95. Classen (1988, 97).

CHAPTER 6. THE LIMITS OF RURAL *LIBERTAS*

1. On the city/country antithesis in *Satire*, where again it often symbolizes dependence and independence, see Braund (1989) and Bond (2001). For the antithesis throughout Horace's poetry, see Harrison (2007).

2. See Pseudo-Acro on *Epist.* 1.10 and Porphyrio at *Sat.* 1.9.60. See Nisbet (1959, 74–75).

3. In *Satires* 2.7.113 Davus uses the term *fugitivus* negatively to illustrate Horace's inability to be content with his own company: *teque ipsum vitas fugitivus et erro*, "and you avoid yourself, a runaway and vagabond." Though in the epistle Horace uses the term to illustrate his move from urban slavery to rural freedom, the echo of Davus's accusation suggests that discontent is the cause of Horace's failure to stay put.

4. Johnson (1993, 78).

5. Harrison (1992). Harrison convincingly argues that Fuscus must be understood to be a Stoic in *Odes* 1.22 as well.

6. Macleod (1979, 25).

7. Kilpatrick (1986, 73–76).

8. Harrison (1992, 545–46) sees humor and affectionate teasing in Horace's redefinition of what it meant to live in accordance with nature but nevertheless finds a serious purpose behind it: "The serious moralizing use in the poem of Stoic doctrines about the wise man's ability to tell true from false and his resistance to the slavery of wealth points to the greater didactic programme of the first book of *Epistles*."

9. As Harrison (1992, 545) points out, Horace's *vivere naturae si conveniter oportet* echoes Cicero's translation of the Stoic precept ὁμολογουμένως τῇ φύσει ζῆν (*SVF* iii.3.4–7.12) at *Off.* 3.13: *quod summum bonum a Stoicis dicitur, convenienter naturae vivere*. Williams (1968, 594) suggests that line 13 of the epistle (*ponendaeque domo quaerenda est area primum*) echoes Hesiod, *Works and Days* 405: οἶκον μὲν πρώτιστα.

10. Harrison (1992, 546).

11. One of Horace's chief complaints about the city is that his independence is constantly compromised by people who approach him to make demands and ask favors (cf. esp. *Sat.* 2.6.20–39). Nowhere is this better illustrated than in *Sat.* 1.9, in which Horace is accosted by a man who pesters him for an introduction to Maecenas. While Horace becomes extremely agitated and is unable to extricate himself from the pest, Fuscus approaches the two and easily—and amusingly—steers clear of becoming involved (60–74). Fuscus, unlike Horace, is therefore able to maintain his sense of control and autonomy in the crowded streets of Rome.

12. Harrison (1992, 545–46) again finds Stoic argumentation behind Horace's concern with the ability to distinguish the truth from falsehood, a particularly Stoic concern (cf. *Cic. Acad.* 2.67). Thus, in order for Fuscus to experience real truth, Horace suggests, he must retire to the countryside.

13. Williams (1968, 596).

14. Cf. *Sat.* 1.2.24: *dum vitant stulti vitia, in contraria currunt* ("While foolish people avoid vices, they run to opposite extremes").

15. Cf. esp. the successfully adaptable Horace of *Odes* 3.29.49–56, which I consider in more detail in the following chapter.

16. Williams (1968, 597).

17. The fable itself connects Horace to the world of slaves and freedmen, as Marchesi (2005) has suggested, arguing that (308) "fable, insofar as it connects animal characters and human behaviors, performs as a freed genre—that is, it situates itself in the same ambiguous cultural space defined by the intersection of freedom and servitude in which Roman society located the freedmen." She shows how Horace puts fables into his own mouth only gradually over the course of his poetic career and that (322) "the language of fable appears to accompany Horace's growing confidence in his position as a self-appointed moralist poet" as the "personal stigma" of his "familial association with slavery" "receded into the past." It is interesting, however, that Horace's use of fables is more pronounced in the *Epistles*, a collection in which he presents himself not just as the son of a freedman but metaphorically as a freedman (an ex-gladiator) himself.

18. The earliest recounting of this fable is from Stesichorus and is recorded in Aristotle, *Rhetoric* 1393B, where Aristotle reports that it was composed with the aim of dissuading the population of Himera from granting the tyrant Phalaris a bodyguard. Though Horace's version is not overtly political, Ahl (1984, 54) maintains that a political reading is unavoidable: "Rome is Octavian's horse."

19. Ahl (1984, 56) puts a political spin on these lines as well: "The cups of hemlock mentioned evoke memories of Socrates' death. . . . It was Socrates' refusal to come to terms with his accusers and with the city of Athens that brought him to the draught of hemlock. Horace has, of course, compromised himself in the past, when in need. Now he would deserve the hemlock if he compromised himself again."

20. Johnson (1993, 81).

21. See Xenophon, *Mem.* 2.1.11, addressed fully in chapter 1.

22. For the fragment, see Stobaeus 4 31d, 128 = fr. 67 Mannebach (1961).

23. Gigante (1993, 268) first suggested the parallel for the Horatian passage. He too suggests that Aristippus is promoting *un uso razionale della ricchezza . . . secondo le circostanze.* He continues: *Orazio varia la formula aristippea: il possesso non dev'essere né troppo grande né troppo piccolo, dev'essere adatto allo status, alla condizione, alle circostanze.*

24. See Kinneavy (2002, 58), who defines it as "the right or opportune time to do something, or right measure in doing something."

25. For Aristotle's use of *kairos*, see Shew (2013, 49–55). In *Odes* 2.10, observance of the mean necessitates different actions in different circumstances: hope when things are bad, fear when they are good, bravery in adversity, and caution in prosperity.

26. *Works and Days* 694: μέτρα φυλάσσεσθαι· καιρὸς δ᾽ ἐπὶ πᾶσιν ἄριστος, "observe due measure: *kairos* is best in all things."

27. Wilson (1980, 186 and 179). He nicely outlines the use of the term as indicating "due measure."

28. Cf. Gigante (1993, 269): *adattare il possesso ai bisogni della vita significa non disprezzo assurdo della richezza né sordid avarizia: un possesso appropriato, conveniens, impedisce un eccesso in una o nell'altra direzione.* I disagree, however, with Gigante's assertion (268) that Horace's reformulation of this Aristippean comparison points necessarily to Epicureanism. At the heart of these lines of the epistle are adaptability and the mean, and throughout the collection these are attributes primarily associated with Aristippus. Whereas Gigante (272) states that the Aristippean color of the poem is due to Fuscus's personality, I would suggest, with Traina (2009), that it is in keeping with the larger concerns of *Epistles* 1. Gigante in fact takes major issue with Traina's arguments and suggests that what Traina calls Aristippean in the collection is in fact Epicurean. I agree with Traina's arguments and find in Aristippus an illustration of Horace's own lack of dogmatism (including Epicurean dogmatism). This is not to say, of course, that Horace is an orthodox Cyrenaic either. Traina (1994) defends his arguments against the protests of Gigante.

29. Gigante (1993, 269–70).

30. The image of the rope in line 48 has been variously interpreted. Dilke (1954, ad loc.) offers a number of possibilities: "(1) a man leading an animal; cf. *Sat.* ii.7.20 *qui iam content, iam laxo fune laborat*, though that may have wider application; (2) a conqueror leading a captive; (3) a tow-rope; (4) a pulley; (5) a tug-of-war; (6) a dance (Ter. *Ad.* 752 *restim ductans saltabis*); (7) Ocnus, who kept twisting a rope while a donkey gnawed it apart (Reid)." I like the animal imagery in 1, especially given the fable of the horse and stag that precedes. Whereas the horse is mastered by wealth (the rider), the proper configuration of power is for wealth to be the horse and we the riders.

31. Nisbet (1959, 74).

32. Macleod (1979, 27).

33. Cf. also Ferri (1993, 112), who connects the shrine of *Vacuna* in 1.10 with the Lucretian *sapientum templa serena* (2.8).

34. See Maurach (1968, 105). But of course ideas of balance/imbalance are found in the earlier epistles. Cf., e.g., 1.6.15: *aequus iniqui*.

35. Scholars have extensively debated whether lines 7–10 should be attributed to Horace or if they are Bullatius's imagined response to his question. For instance, Kiessling and Heinze (1957, ad loc.) and Mayer (1994, ad loc.) attribute the lines to Horace, while Wickham (1891, ad loc.) inserts them in quotation marks and McGann (1969, 61) places them in Bullatius's mouth. Skalitzky (1973, 318) calls the attribution of these lines to Horace "strange," but others have defended it. Kilpatrick (1986, 77) emphasizes the past potentiality of *vellem* and suggests that "in order to advise friends with problems it helps first to convince them that you understand how they feel—ideally because you have gone through it yourself." Mayer (1994, ad loc.) argues that "the addressee cannot speak in an epistle, as he can in a *sermo*." My reading of the poem supports the attribution of the lines to Horace and suggests that the escapism he expresses accords with the desire to withdraw that he expresses in many places in the collection. See Ferri (2007, 127): "Horace endeavors to cure the elusive Bullatius of his compulsive travel mania by showing that he sometimes feels the same drive to get away from it all."

36. See Johnson (1993, 135), who speaks of Lebedus as "stir[ring] in him thoughts of his persistent inclination to try to escape, to escape into the wilderness, into the 'desolation of reality.'"

37. Pope, *Eloisa to Abelard* 208.

38. Mayer (1994, ad loc.).

39. Cf. Johnson (1993, 135): "So exact is the image it presents to him of what he finds within himself."

40. Horace uses *incolumis* in this fashion also at 1.16.16.

41. Mayer (1994, ad loc.). Cf. *Sat.* 1.4.98.

42. See esp. Kilpatrick (1986, 80–83).

43. On the phenomenon of withdrawal as political resistance, see most recently Dewar (2014).

44. For the image of "kindly fortune," cf. *Odes* 3.29.49–56. There Horace embraces *Fortuna* when she is *benigna* and adapts accordingly when she is not.

45. Ferri (1993, 113), who outlines the Epicurean influence on the book, particularly that of Lucretius, connects the sound of Ulubrae with *latebrae* and thus *l'idea epicurea del vivere nascostamente*. Ulubrae, like the temple of Vacuna of 1.10, represents *uno dei lontani* templa sapientum *delle* Epistole.

46. Seneca devotes two of his *Epistulae Morales* (28 and 104) to the inability of travel to bring happiness, and he devotes *De Tranquilitate* 2.13–15 to the same theme. Skalitzky (1973) mentions the letter in passing but does not pursue in any detail the links between it and Horace's epistle. For Seneca's attitude toward travel in general, see Montiglio (2006).

47. Cf. *Odes* 2.6.14, where he refers to Tarentum as a beloved *angulus*. On the concept of the *angulus* in the *Epistles* and its Epicurean associations, see Ferri (1993) *passim*.

48. I disagree with Mayer's emendation of *res* to *rus* in line 5. Starting in 1.1.19 *res* is an important word running through the *Epistles*. *Res* also covers not just the farm but the *vindex* himself.

49. See Bowditch (2001, 234). As Gardner (2011, 416) points out, slaves belonged to the category of *res mancipi*.

50. Kenney (1977, 233).

51. Kenney (1977, 233–34) compares Lucretius's description of the horse eagerly bursting forth from the starting gates at *DRN* 2.263–65 and also his description of Epicurus "shattering the narrow gates of Nature" (*effringere . . . arta /naturae . . . claustra*) at 1.70–71: "Horace's longing for the country is so intense that it can only be conveyed in words that recall the daemonic urge that sent Epicurus on his mental voyage of discovery around the cosmos." He strengthens his argument by pointing out that *mens animusque* (*Epist.* 1.14.8) is a Lucretian tag. The comparison of himself to a racehorse again evokes *Epistles* 1.1.8–10, where his *daimonion* urges him to stop running and turn to ethics.

52. See Fraenkel (1957, 311–12).

53. In Lucretius 3.1060–70 a similar desire to escape one's own anguished mind is what leads men to be inconsistent and seek now the city, now the country. This is a refrain running through Seneca's epistles on travel as well (28 and 104).

54. See Rudd (1986, 133) and Bowditch (2001, 234–35).

55. Rudd (1986, 133).

56. Cf. *Odes* 2.7.26–28: *non ego sanius / bacchabor Edonis: recepto / dulce mihi furere est amico* ("I, no saner than the Edonians, will play the Bacchant: to me it is sweet to rave when a friend has been regained"). In these lines it is friendship that makes such temporary relaxation and revelry appropriate. This is the case too in 4.12.26–28, an invitation poem: *nigrorumque memor, dum licet, ignium / misce stultitiam consiliis brevem: dulce est desipere in loco* ("Mindful of the dark fires, while it is allowed, mingle temporary foolishness into your plans. It is sweet to act silly when the occasion calls for it").

57. Mayer (1994, ad loc.).

58. Sider (1997) epigram 5 = Gow and Page (1965) epigram 18.

59. Bowditch (2001, 226 n. 39).

60. Mayer (1994, ad loc.).

CHAPTER 7. MODERATE FREEDOM AND FRIENDSHIP

1. McGann (1969, 78) suggests that these poems are "more closely connected than any other pair of juxtaposed epistles in the book."

2. Nothing else is known about Scaeva, who is most likely an invention of the poet. The meaning of his name is disputed. To some it calls to mind the adjective *scaevus*, "awkward" or "inept." For example, Oliensis (1998, 168) refers to him as "Mr. Inept," while Rudd in his Penguin translation calls him "Gauche." Mayer (1995, 285), however, points out that the Latin noun *scaeva* means "a favorable omen."

3. Fraenkel (1957, 321–23). He continues, "Why did Horace write such an extraordinary letter, something that has seemed to many critics unworthy of him? Scaeva had apparently informed him rather complacently of his intention of attaching himself to some great man, and this letter is Horace's reply. But, owing to the way in which his mind worked, he could not and would not keep his thoughts within the narrow compass of a special case. Scaeva's base ambition appeared to him as a typical instance of a moral disease of which he had seen much in the society of his day. Vividly recalling the humiliation to which men's greed often subjects them he grew angry, and his anger was not tempered by any regard for Scaeva." I fail, however, to sense the same anger in the epistle that Fraenkel finds.

4. Perret (1964, 104).

5. Damon (1997, 136–40). See also Morrison (2006, 54).

6. Oliensis (1998, 168–70).

7. Armstrong (2004b, 286–87). See also de Pretis (2002, 45), who refers to Horace's tone in 1.17 as "ironical and superior."

8. Moles (1985, 43–53), Traina (2009), Mayer (1995, 284–90), and Johnson (1993, 99–109).

9. See esp. Damon (1997, 135–40) and Armstrong (2004b, 286–87).

10. In this regard Horace's description of the *lathe biosas* here is at odds with orthodox Epicureanism, for Epicurus and his followers promoted friendship. Horace's language of mutual benefit (*prodesse tuis . . . benignius ipsum / te tractare*) might even be indebted to Epicurean discussions of utility in friendship. For an overview of Epicurean friendship, see Konstan (1997, 108–13).

11. Johnson (1993, 100) says of 1.17 that "the emphasis is on the balance, on the virtue between rival extremes: which moral balance is here incarnated by Aristippus, who . . . comes as close to being a paradigm for behavior as anyone in the *Epistles*."

12. For Cynicism in *Epistles* 1, see esp. Moles (1985), to whose observations I am indebted even though my conclusions are quite different. I do not wish to make the philosophical categories of Epicureanism and Cynicism too neat here. It is not the systems *in toto* that Horace embraces or rejects so much as the degree of engagement that each recommends.

13. Cf. Diog. Laert. 2.68: Παριόντα ποτὲ αὐτὸν λάχανα πλύνων Διογένης ἔσκωψε, καί φησιν, "εἰ ταῦτα ἔμαθες προσφέρεσθαι, οὐκ ἂν τυράννων αὐλὰς ἐθεράπευες." ὁ δὲ, "καὶ σύ," εἶπεν, "εἴπερ ᾔδεις ἀνθρώποις ὁμιλεῖν, οὐκ ἂν λάχανα ἔπλυνες ("Diogenes, washing his vegetables, saw Aristippus going by and said, 'if you knew how to eat these things, you would not be attending the courts of kings.' And the other said, 'And you, if you knew how to interact with men, would not be washing vegetables'"). Cf. also 2.102, where the anecdote is repeated, but attributed to the Cyrenaic Theodorus and the Cynic Metrocles. In the life of Diogenes (6.30) the story is again repeated, but between Plato and Diogenes, with Diogenes gaining the upper hand.

14. Gowers (2012, ad loc.). She points out, furthermore, that "Augustus also framed his request for close companionship with Horace in convivial terms," *sume tibi aliquid iuris apud me, tamquam si convictor mihi fueris* (Suet. *Vita Horati*).

15. The precise meaning of *scurra* is difficult. For an overview of the concept, see Corbett (1986). Damon (1997, 109–10) suggests that the word had a complicated history. As she points out, "Horace appears to have been the first to use *scurra* in a sense approaching that of *parasitus*."

16. The similarities between parasites and Cynic beggars, as Freudenburg (1993, 33) has shown, would have been particularly well-known from the comic stage. The parasite Saturio in Plaut. *Pers.* 123–26 points directly to these similarities: *cynicum esse egentem oportet parasitum prope: / ampullam, strigilem, scaphium, soccos, pallium, / marsuppium habeat, inibi paullum praesidi, / qui familiarem suam vitam oblectet modo* ("it is necessary that the parasite almost be a needy Cynic: let him have a flask, a scraper, a bowl, slippers, cloak, and his purse, in it a little bit of protection, with which may please only his household"). For the similarities between *scurrae* and Cynics, see Corbett (1986, 24, 40–42, 56, 59, and esp. 62–64) and Kinney (1996, 299).

17. See 1.1.27 (*restat ut his ego me ipse regam solerque elementis*, "it remains for me to rule and comfort myself with these ABCs") and 1.18.112 (*aequum mi animum ipse parabo*, "I myself will provide equanimity for myself").

18. Traina (2009, 301).

19. See especially Mayer (1995, 289). Pseudo-Acro says that Horace is here alluding to another story in which Diogenes accompanied Aristippus to the baths, whereupon Aristippus took Diogenes's worn cloak, and Diogenes preferred to remain cold rather than put on Aristippus's purple one. Cf. the exchange between Socrates and Diogenes's teacher, Antisthenes, in Diogenes Laertius 2.36, where Antisthenes, upon adjusting his cloak to show its tears, is rebuked by Socrates and told that his vanity is visible through the cloak (διὰ τοῦ τρίβωνος τὴν κενοδοξίαν). A similar story is told in 6.8, where Plato tells him that his love of glory (φιλοδοξία) is visible through his cloak.

20. Mayer (1985, 36).

21. For the most famous example, see Theognis 213–18. The image is a favorite of Plutarch. Cf., e.g., *How to Tell a Flatterer from a Friend* 52f–53a, *On Having Many Friends* 96f–97a, and *Alcibiades* 23.6 (chameleon).

22. For the image of the octopus or polyp used of flatterers, see Glad (1995, 27–30). For the octopus as a symbol of *metis*, adaptability, and Odyssean cunning, see Hawkee (2004, 53–57).

23. For Aristippus's famous indifference to the quality of his clock, see also Plutarch, *On the Fortune of Alexander* 330c (καίτοι γ᾽ Ἀρίστιππον θαυμάζουσι τὸν Σωκρατικόν, ὅτι καὶ τρίβωνι λιτῷ καὶ Μιλησίᾳ χλαμύδι χρώμενος δι᾽ ἀμφοτέρων ἐτήρει τὸ εὔσχημον, "And indeed people admire Aristippus because, furnished either with a plain threadbare cloak or a Milesian robe, he kept his decorum in both"); *Gnomologium Vaticanum* 493 (ὁ αὐτὸς θεασάμενος Ἀρίστιππον ἠμφιεσμένον πολυτελῶς ἐμόλυνεν τὴν καθέδραν, ἐφ᾽ ἣν καθίζειν ἔμελλεν· τοῦ δὲ Ἀριστίππου κατὰ τὸ ἀσφαλὲς καθίσαντος εἶπε ‘νενόηκα ὅτι ἔχεις τὸ ἱμάτιον καὶ οὐκ ἔχῃ ὑπ᾽ αὐτοῦ,’ "And he [i.e., Socrates] seeing Aristippus clothed expensively dirtied the seat upon which he was about to sit. And when Aristippus sat down upon it without hesitation he said, ‘I knew that you possess the cloak and are not possessed by it.’").

24. See Traina (2009, 300): "The contrast between the flexibility of the Cyrenaic, Aristippus, and the rigidity of the Cynic, Diogenes, is captured in the symbol . . . of clothing (lines 26–32): no matter what mantle Aristippus dresses in, whether it is luxurious or stitched together from rags, he will always be himself."

25. See Nisbet and Rudd (2004, ad loc.).

26. For Horace's strategy of appropriating and reversing Cynic terms in the epistle, see Moles (1985) 44–45.

27. Cucchiarelli (2010, 303).

28. Johnson (1993, 88).

29. For studies of 1.18, see Fraenkel (1957, 316–21), McGann (1969, 77–82), Rohdich (1972), Hunter (1985), Kilpatrick (1986, 49–55), Bowditch (1994), Gurval (1995, 162–65), Damon (1997, 138–40), Oliensis (1998, 170–72), and Krebs (2002).

30. Oliensis (1998, 170–71). She refers to Horace as "passing the clientary baton" and suggests that Lollius is "almost a mirror image of his own youthful self." Though she acknowledges that Lollius's situation is connected to that of Horace in the opening epistle, she suggests that "whereas Horace can claim to be too old for the 'sporting life' of Rome and lyric, Lollius has no comparable pretext for refusing to comply with his patron's demands. . . . The epistle thus helps Horace formulate his excuses to Maecenas, completing his earlier *recusationes*, as it were, by proposing a more suitable candidate (not Lollius himself, but a Lollius: a younger, more energetic man) in his stead."

31. Johnson (1993, 68–69) sees in Lollius a version of Horace's past of which Horace is not proud: "One is tempted to think that Lollius represented for Horace, at least in part, an aspect of himself, an *instantanea* of himself taken when he was this young man's age and one he'd like to forget—a faded portrait of the young artist on the make. For Horace, Lollius represented a 'negative identity fragment' seen in the rearview mirror." I do not sense the same negativity toward Lollius that Johnson finds, though I agree that Lollius is in many ways a reflection of Horace.

32. The superlative recalls the *otia liberrima* Horace enjoys at the Sabine Farm in *Epist.* 1.7.36 and hints not only that Lollius and Horace share an inclination toward this extreme but also that Lollius's current freedom is as fragile as that of Horace's rural freedom, for which see chapters 5–6.

33. Whereas in *Satires* 1.2, however, the *matrona* and *meretrix* are the two extremes, in *Epist.* 1.18 the *matrona* corresponds to the *amicus* who stands at the mean between the slavish *scurra* and uncompromising *libertas*.

34. Horace in these lines draws especially on several Aristotelian passages in which friendship (*NE* 2.1108a) or something very much like it (*NE* 4.1126b) hits upon the mean between obsequious people or flatterers (ἄρεσκοι/κόλακες), on the one hand, and quarrelsome and truculent people (δύσεροι/δύσκολοι) on the other. Theophrastus *Characters* 2 is a sketch of the flatterer; Cicero devotes *de Amic.* 88–100 to the topic of flattery; Philodemus wrote the treatises *On Flattery* and *On Frank Criticism*. For the philosophical background to Horace's ideas in this passage, see esp. Hunter (1985) and, for the connections between Horace and Philodemus, Kemp (2010a). Though I find Kemp's argument compelling that Horace's views on flattery and frankness are indebted to Philodemus, I cannot agree with Armstrong (2004b, 287) that *Epistles* 1.18 constitutes one of Horace's "literary imitations" of Epicurean "philosophical *therapeia*" through the use of frank speech. Concerns with frankness, flattery, and friendship were not exclusive to Philodemus, and Horace's discussion of flattery and *libertas* in these lines of 1.18 lacks the therapeutic dimension so important to Philodemus. For Philodemus's views of these issues, see Glad (1996) and the introduction to Konstan, Clay, Glad, Thom, and Ware (1998). For Epicureanism and frank speech in general, see Glad (1995, 101–81), and for a survey of the various ancient attitudes toward flattery, friendship, and frankness, see Konstan (1996).

35. Cf. *Satires* 1.4.78–105, where Horace also criticizes those who are excessively harsh in their use of frank speech and calls such casting of aspersions *aerugma mera*, "unmixed malice." On the connections between *Epistles* 1.18 and *Satires* 1.4, see Hunter (1985). On *Satires* 1.4, see also Muecke (1979) and Kemp (2010b). For the significance of the wine metaphor in *Epistles* 1.18 in relation to discussions of political liberty in the late Republic, see the introduction.

36. On the cropped hair of the freedman, see Arena (2012, 33–34). She cites Polybius's description (30.18) of King Prusias II of Bithynia, who in 167 B.C. appeared to Roman envoys with his head shorn and wearing a toga, *pilleus*, and *calcei* to show not only that he had been freed by Rome but that he now enjoyed Roman citizenship. On shorn hair as a mark of freedman status, see also Livy 34.52.12 and Plut. *Flam.* 13.6. See especially Petronius *Sat.* 32, where Trimalchio's shorn hair coupled with his ornate robes illustrates his comically confused social standing. See also my discussion of Horace's shorn hair in chapter 2.

37. For the significance of this passage to the moderate freedom espoused by Horace here, especially in relation to the political sphere, see also the introduction.

38. McGann (1969, 79) similarly sees 1.18 as a rejection of Horace's own pull toward extreme *libertas*: "Horace is describing an extreme case of that *libertas* to which it is reasonable to suppose that Lollius is prone. But these lines have an important function in the book as a whole. They are a final indication of Horace's disapproval of the would-be *sapiens*. And they introduce by implication a clarification of an issue raised by some parts of the book. The supreme importance of philosophy in his life, as he portrays it in the *Epistles*, his regarding details of dress and haircut as unimportant, his claim in *Epi*. 7 to *otia liberrima*, and his expressed willingness to return the gifts of Maecenas might be taken as evidence that a certain *asperitas* accompanied this pursuit of wisdom. Already there has been much in the book to show that this is not so, but now in this, the last of the ethical epistles, the pursuit to excess of *libertas* is firmly rejected."

39. See Konstan (1996, 12). As he points out, Stobaeus (3.13.44) attributes to Diogenes the following statement: Ὁ Διογένης ἔλεγεν, ὅτι οἱ μὲν ἄλλοι κύνες τοὺς ἐχθροὺς δάκνουσιν, ἐγὼ δὲ τοὺς φίλους, ἵνα σώσω, "Diogenes used to say that other dogs bite their enemies, but I bite my friends in order to save them."

40. See Mayer (1994, ad loc.) and cf. esp. Juvenal 2.15. For the Cynic aspects of the harsh friend in 1.18, see Hunter (1985, 481) and Freudenburg (1993, 80).

41. Mouritsen (2011, 58). On *obsequium*, see also Verboven (2012, 95–696) and Arena (2012, 20–21).

42. See Roller (2001, 152–53): "Horace in *Epistula* 1.18.15–20 describes a guest who makes a show of quarreling with his host to prove his candor and independence—yet he disagrees only on trifling matters, never on important ones. . . . Guests ostentatiously employ convivial 'free' speech in order to leave the impression that, when they elsewhere express agreement, they are not being complaisant flatterers, but really do agree; thus they actually exploit the host's resistance to complaisant speech as part of a complex strategy to flatter."

43. *Verna ministeriis ad nutus aptus erilis*, "a homebred slave ready for service at the nods of his master." See Mayer (1994, ad loc.). For the voluntary slavery, "freiwillige Knechtschaft," of the flatterer, see Ribbeck (1884, 1–2) and Glad (1995, 26–28).

44. As Mayer (1994, ad loc.) points out, Castor and Dolichus may be actors, gladiators, or *grammatici*. Whatever their profession they are not well known, and the degree of their knowledge is not worthy of contentiously disputing.

45. This is the same kind of competition Damasippus had accused Horace of in *Satires* 2.3.307–20, an accusation that met with Horace's *horrenda rabies* (323). See Mayer (1994, ad loc.).

46. Gurval (1995, 163).

47. On the connections between hunting for sport and hunting in the arena, see Kyle (1998, 187–90). He suggests (188), "Hunts in the wilds and in the arena may have been at opposite ends of the spectrum of Roman hunting, but they were related in the minds and customs of the Romans. Although studies influenced by modern notions of hunting have down-played native Roman hunting traditions . . . Rome knew the overlapping development of subsistence hunting, sport hunting, and hunting as a spectacle. The same Latin words, *venator* and *venatio* (hunter and hunt), cognates of the verb *venorari* and the noun *vena* (blood vessel), were used of sporting hunts in the countryside and spectacular hunts in the arena." And (189), "In later art the analogy of rural hunts to urban beast spectacles is undeniable: mosaics intermingle scenes of farming, sporting hunting, rural meals, and the capturing of beasts for the arena."

48. On the possible anti-Callimacheanism of Lollius's poetic activity, see Macleod (1976).

49. As Hunter (1985) points out, in the *Gorgias* Callicles "uses the dispute between Amphion and Zethus from Euripides' *Antiope* in his attempt to persuade Socrates to abandon 'childish philosophy' in favour of pursuits which are more socially and politically advantageous (*Gorgias* 484c–6c)." On the use of the play in the *Gorgias*, see esp. Slings (1991) and Nightingale (1992).

50. Nightingale (1992, 123).

51. Morrison (2006, 59) analyzes Horace's exemplum here with conclusions different from mine. Focusing on Socrates's refusal to repeat Amphion's yielding in the *Gorgias*, he states, "There is in the *Gorgias*, in contrast to the *Antiope*, no *deus ex machina* to resolve the clash between the different sorts of lives of Zethus and Amphion, and vindicate Amphion's. The echo of the Socrates of the *Gorgias* suggests that the choice 'Horace' presents between different lives, between the life of philosophical detachment and the life of cultivating the great is a stark one—there can be no easy compromise as in the *Antiope*. The lives are incompatible and the choice must be made. And the correct choice is also clear—Socrates was right, not Callicles." At the same time, he recognizes that "the life of (complete) philosophical independence cannot be achieved. This is the central paradox of the *Epistles*."

52. In *Epistles* 1.2.64–67 Horace had similarly compared Lollius to a young horse or a hunting dog in order to illustrate the importance of the impressions made upon him while a *puer*. The comparisons of Lollius to a dog and boar in 1.18 are at the heart of Oliensis's (1998, 171) argument that Horace offers up Lollius as substitute for his own participation. Noting that in 1.1 Horace had compared himself to an aging racehorse, she states, "If Horace is an aging horse, Lollius is as swift as a hunting-dog and as tough as a boar. . . . [I]f Horace is a retired gladiator (*E.* 1.1.2), Lollius is an able performer whose mock-battles earn the applause of the spectators. . . . The epistle thus helps Horace formulate his excuses to Maecenas, completing his earlier *recusationes*, as it were, by proposing a more suitable candidate (not Lollius himself, but a Lollius: a younger, more energetic man) in his stead." Though Oliensis's insights here are valuable and persuasive, I would emphasize, however, that the animal comparisons and allusions to spectacles draw Lollius and Horace together as would-be clients who must "perform" in accordance with the wishes of a patron. In 1.1, furthermore, the depiction of Horace's age is subject to obfuscation, since he is simultaneously an old man refusing gladiatorial *ludus* and a youth reenlisting in the *ludus* of the ethical and philosophical schoolroom. It is as though his ethical pursuits serve to rejuvenate him and make him simultaneously young and old. We will see that in 1.20 Horace's poetry takes on youthful associations that enable it to return to the city in compliance with Maecenas's desires.

53. See Mayer (1994, ad loc.).

54. Bowditch (1994) pays particular attention to the political dimension of the poem. Though my conclusions and argument are different from hers, I am indebted to her for many observations that helped shape my thinking about the poem.

55. Bowditch (1994, 422).

56. See Mayer (1995, 290–91): "Horace seems to sense that Roman society is being turned into a royal court, centred upon a single princely family. [Lollius] has the problems not of one on the rise, but of the courtier. . . . Lollius seemed to need advice on treading the narrow path of true independence within a hierarchical aristocracy now transforming itself into a royal court."

57. Bowditch (1994, 418).

58. Ahl (1984, 52–53), Bowditch (1994, 418–25), and Gurval (1995, 162–65).

59. See Mayer (1994, ad loc.) with Pindar fr. 110 S-M: γλυκὺ δ᾽ ἀπείρῳ πόλεμος· πεπειραμένων δέ τις ταρβεῖ προσιόντα νιν καρδίᾳ περισσῶς, "to the inexperienced war is sweet, but someone with experience fears it exceedingly in his heart as it approaches."

60. Oliensis (1998, 171).

61. Though Oliensis (1998, 171) suggests that "Horace elsewhere depicts his relations with Maecenas as essentially harmonious," as early as *Satires* Horace had been frank about the downside to this friendship—from accusations of being ambitious (1.6) to being accosted by social climbers in the street (1.9) to charges of a slavish dependence on Maecenas (2.7).

62. Cf. esp. *Odes* 2.10 and *Epistles* 2.2.199–204.

63. Aristotle (*NE* 1124b30–1125a2) significantly makes a distinction between the slavishness of a flatterer and the appropriate acquiescence of a friend: καὶ πρὸς ἄλλον μὴ δύνασθαι ζῆν ἀλλ᾽ ἢ φίλον (δουλικὸν γάρ, διὸ καὶ πάντες οἱ κόλακες θητικοὶ καὶ οἱ ταπεινοὶ κόλακες), "[it is a mark of the μεγαλόψυχος, 'great-souled man'] not to be able to live according to another, unless a friend (for this is slavish, because all flatterers are servile, and lowly people are flatterers)."

64. Cf. Martial 1.24.2: *Aspicis incomptis illum, Deciane, capillis, / cuius et ipse times triste supercilium, / qui loquitur Curios adsertoresque Camillos? / Nolito fronti credere: nupsit heri* ("Do you see, Decianus, that man with messy hair and whose gloomy brow you fear, who speaks of the Curii and Camilli, the liberators? Do not believe his forehead: he was a bride yesterday."). Although the masculinity of the man described in this poem is ultimately undercut, Martial nevertheless shows the connections in thought between a *triste supercilium*, messy hair (displayed also by Horace's *asper amicus*), and the veneration of old-fashioned Republicans, champions of *libertas*. In 11.2.1–2 Martial refers to the *triste supercilium durique severa Catonis / frons*, "gloomy brow and stern forehead of harsh Cato."

65. Fraenkel (1957, 319).

66. See especially Damon (1997, 138–40). She writes that the poem's "opening would seem to betoken a poem concerned with finding a behavior midway between flattery and rudeness. But the argument has shifted by the end of the poem, where the poet desires solitude, with books his only companions" and that "careful attention to the precepts of lines 21–95 may make a man a successful companion to a *dives* or *potens amicus*, says Horace, but it will leave him no good friend to himself." Armstrong (2004b, 286) suggests that Horace promotes here at the end of the poem not just withdrawal but specifically Epicurean withdrawal: "once more the Epicurean maxim . . . *lathe biosas*, 'live hidden,' is in pride of place at the *end* of the epistle. Horace makes it clear that all one gets from clienthood is a greater appreciation of *lathe biosas*." Williams (1968, 19) describes the hidden life that closes the poem as "the antithesis of the life with which the letter is concerned." I concur with Fraenkel (1957, 320), however, when he states that "it would be a mistake to regard all else in this epistle as a dark foil to a shining finale." McGann (1969, 80–81), though he argues that the private life is here presented as superior, presents an argument closer to my own by suggesting that Lollius is exhorted to find a balance between these two spheres: "He is not advised to embrace the hidden life, but merely to consider the answers to this as to the other questions. The whole passage is after all introduced by *inter cuncta*. Lollius is to bear in mind the superiority of the

hidden life, refreshing himself (so we must understand) at that source when he is able and eventually perhaps turning to it completely."

67. Mayer (1994, ad loc.).

68. Mayer (1994, ad loc.) suggests, however, that *me* is placed first in the line in order to bring a contrast between Horace and Lollius. I would emphasize, however, the parallelism between Horace and Lollius, but I would agree there is a contrast between the two. Horace is, after all, more advanced than Lollius in the pursuit of wisdom. Several scholars have suggested that Horace here clearly shows that, although he advises Lollius on patronage and interaction with the great, his own personal choice is clearly that of the quiet life of withdrawal. Hunter (1985, 486) says that "Horace offers himself as a model and an example of the superiority of the *secretum iter et fallentis semita vitae*" and that "it is withdrawal from [public] life, symbolized by Ferentinum (*Epist.* 1.17.8) and Mandela (*Epist.* 1.18.105) that leads to contentment." Fraenkel (1957, 320) calls Horace's present situation "a practical fulfillment of the ideal of λάθε βιώσας." Mayer (1994, ad loc.) suggests that the *semita* in line 103 "points to H.'s own circumstances and paves the way to the personal conclusion." McGann (1969, 82) writes that "though *quotiens* shows that he has not retired completely, the life of withdrawal is finally confirmed as his choice." My reading suggests rather that in his own life too Horace aims to find balance between engagement and withdrawal. In other words, he works toward practicing the same ethical lessons he preaches and that he has been learning over the course of the collection.

69. Oliensis (1998, 172).

70. McGann (1969, 81). See also Kilpatrick (1986, 54): "The similarities between this prayer and those found in *Satire* 2.6 and *Ode* 1.31 (15–20), petitions for no more than his present wealth, life, and health, and for poetry and books, give proof of years of a contentment related to the Sabine farm and Maecenas. When Horace defines the ideal *amicitia* he must always think of his own."

CHAPTER 8. MODERATE FREEDOM AND POETRY

1. Lee-Stecum (2009, 27–29) likewise notes the connections between philosophical, poetic, and social freedom in the collection. Porter (2002, 47) notes that "his description of how he has used his poetic models suggests the same blend of respect and independence that 19 embodies in the poet's relationship toward Maecenas."

2. On *Epist.* 1.3, see esp. McGann (1969, 40–42), Foster (1972), Macleod (1977, 362–63), Kilpatrick (1986, 33–37), Hubbard (1995), O'Neill (1999), and Trinacty (2012).

3. See Hubbard (1995, 219).

4. Trinacty (2012, 61).

5. Mayer (1994, ad loc.).

6. Hubbard (1995, 220).

7. For Horace's use of liquid imagery to figure *Epistles* 1, see chapter 3.

8. Hubbard (1995, 220) suggests that Horace includes tragedy here as a possible "escape route" for Titius. The word *ampullatur* can hardly be flattering and, as Macleod (1977, 362) points out, it has an anti-Callimachean resonance: "*ampullatur . . .* recalls the contemptuous word ληκυθίουσα used of tragedy by that very Callimachus (frg. 215) whose precepts Titius had seemed to be obeying."

9. For scholars who have sensed disapproval, see McGann (1969, 40), Macleod (1977, 362), Moles (1995), Hubbard (1995, 220–21), and Race (2010, 151). As Race points out, Horace's declaration that Titius is *Romana brevi venturus in ora* is double-edged, since

this can mean either "famous" or "notorious." Others, however, have detected no censure of Titius in these lines; see Mayer (1994, ad loc.), O'Neill (1999, 84 n. 17).
Trinacty (2012, 62–63) senses not so much disapproval as a warning to Titius that such *aemulatio* "takes guts" and that "if he goes about it, he had better have a 'propitious Muse.'" Kilpatrick (1986, 32–33) offers varying assessments, suggesting that Titius "has the foolhardy courage to imitate the inimitable Pindar" but at the same time "is spoken of with admiration as a daring poet in the high lyric style."

    10. Cf. *Odes* 3.30.10–14 (*dicar . . . princeps Aeolium Carmen ad Italos deduxisse*, "I will be called the first to have led down Aeolian song to Italian melodies") and *Epist* 1.19.23–24 (*Parios ego primus iambos / ostendi Latio*, "I first showed Parian iambs to Latium").

    11. Hubbard (1995, 220). On Horace and Pindar, see Race (2010).

    12. Pindar's spring, as Hubbard (1995, 220) has shown, most likely alludes to the Theban spring Dirce, from which Pindar claims at *Ol.* 6.85–87 to drink while singing: τᾶς ἐρατεινὸν ὕδωρ / πίομαι, ἀνδράσιν αἰχματαῖσι πλέκων / ποικίλον ὕμνον ("I drink its lovely water, weaving for spearmen a many-colored hymn").

    13. For Callimachus in these lines, see Macleod (1977, 362), Mayer (1994, ad loc.), and Trinacty (2012, 62). For artificial versus natural water sources, see also *Epistles* 1.15.15–16.

    14. As Hubbard (1995, 220) points out, Horace alludes to a Pindaric saying cited by Quintilian (10.1.109): [*Cicero*] *non enim pluvias, ut ait Pindarus, aquas colligit, sed vivo gurgite exundat*, "for Cicero does not collect rain water, as Pindar says, but flows forth with a living stream." Hubbard suggests that the spring to which Pindar refers is the Dirce. Callimachus is especially disdainful of public water sources, as he expresses most famously in his epigram 28:

> ἐχθαίρω τὸ ποίημα τὸ κυκλικὸν οὐδὲ κελεύθῳ
>   χαίρω, τίς πολλοὺς ὧδε καὶ ὧδε φέρει·
> μισῶ καὶ περίφοιτον ἐρώμενον οὐδ' ἀπὸ κρήνης
>   πίνω· σικχαίνω πάντα τὰ δημόσια.
> Λυσανίη, σὺ δὲ ναίχι καλὸς καλός· ἀλλὰ πρὶν εἰπεῖν
>   τοῦτο σαφῶς, ἠχώ φησί τις· ἄλλος ἔχει.

> I hate the cyclic poem, nor do I rejoice in whichever road carries many to and fro.
> And I hate a wandering beloved, nor do I drink from a well. I hate all public
> things. Lysanies, you are beautiful, yes, beautiful, but before I say this clearly, some
> echo says, "Another holds him."

In this epigram the cyclic poem, the frequented path, the promiscuous lover, and the public fountain can all be read programmatically as topics that have been repeatedly taken up by others and thus lack innovation and originality. Cameron (1995, 387–99), however, argues that the poem is not so much about poetic as erotic exclusivity. Nevertheless, he does cite a later 1st/2nd c. epigrammatist, Pollianus, who certainly did understand Callimachus's reference to cyclic poetry in light of literary originality:

> τοὺς κυκλικοὺς τούτους, τοὺς "αὐτὰρ ἔπειτα" λέγοντας
>   μισῶ, λωποδύτας ἀλλοτρίων ἐπέων.
> καὶ διὰ τοῦτ' ἐλεγίοις προσέχω πλέον· οὐδὲν ἔχω γὰρ
>   Παρθενίου κλέπτειν ἢ πάλι Καλλιμάχου.
> 'θηρὶ μὲν οὐατόεντι γενοίμην, εἴ ποτε γράψω
>   'εἴκελος,' 'ἐκ ποταμῶν χλωρὰ χελιδόνια.'

οἱ δ᾽ οὕτως τὸν Ὅμηρον ἀναιδῶς λωποδυτοῦσιν,
ὥστε γράφειν ἤδη ᾽μῆνιν ἄειδε, θεά.᾽ (*AP* 11.130)

I hate these cyclic poets, the ones who say, "but then," thieves of others' words. And because of this I devote myself instead to elegy. For I have nothing I can steal from Parthenius or Callimachus. I would become "like the long-eared wild beast" if ever I write, "yellow celandines from rivers." But they steal from Homer so flagrantly that they write, "Sing, goddess, the wrath."

This epigram speaks simultaneously to the originality of Callimachus, since he is inimitable, and to the lack of originality practiced by the Cyclic poets, who slavishly mimic Homer's words. This is the same kind of slavish imitation that Horace takes to task in *Epist.* 1.3.

15. For *audere* used for stylistic boldness, cf. *AP* 10 with Brink (1971, ad loc.). For the word used of innovation and originality, cf. *AP* 125 and 287 with Brink (1971, ad loc.).

16. On *Odes* 4.2, see esp. Putnam (1986, 48–62), Harrison (1995c), and T. Johnson (2004, 45–51).

17. For the connections between bees and poets, see Waszink (1974), Williams (1978, 93), and Crane (1987).

18. See Harrison (1995c, 111 n. 8). On the connections between bees and Daedalus, see Fitzgerald (1987, 83).

19. Harrison (1995c, 111).

20. As West (1967, 30–39) has shown, Horace's use of bee imagery to describe Florus is not restricted to *quae circumvolitas agilis thyme* (21) but runs throughout this section. His name evokes the *flores* around which bees flit, the word *condis* (24) suggests the "storing up" of honey, and the description of his *ingenium* as *non incultum et turpiter hirtum* especially recalls the superior bees of Vergil, *Georgics* 4.96–98. As Hubbard (1995, 221) puts it, Titius is not the dirty and shaggy bee, but "the bright and shiny one, from whom in due season one gets sweet honey." See also Trinacty (2012, 65–66).

21. For Callimachus's use of Pindaric imagery, see Poliakoff (1980) and Beer (2006).

22. For the connection between Homer and the sea, see Williams (1978, 87–89, 98–99) and Traill (1998, 216–18).

23. Traill (1998, 216).

24. Williams (1978, 89). See also p. 4: "The basis of Callimachus' style is the constant interplay between imitation and variation of Homer, and in the *Hymn* he attempts to answer both in practical and theoretical terms the question of how a learned modern poet could appropriately draw on the riches of Homeric poetry in order to create a new idiom."

25. Cameron (1995, 403–9) and Köhnken (1981). Williams's argument is defended and supplemented by Traill (1998) and Beer (2006).

26. Hubbard (1995, 221).

27. ἀρεταὶ δ᾽ αἰεὶ μεγάλαι πολύμυθοι· / βαιὰ δ᾽ ἐν μακροῖσι ποικίλλειν, / ἀκοὰ σοφοῖς· ὁ δὲ καιρὸς ὁμοίως / παντὸς ἔχει κορυφάν ("Great excellence is always of many words, but to elaborate a few things among many is a hearing for the wise. But due measure occupies the head of everything equally"). Throughout this discussion of Callimachus and Pindar I am indebted to Beer (2006). For καιρός as relates to moderation, see my discussion in chapter 6 and esp. Wilson (1980).

28. Hubbard (1995, 221–22). For ἐρατός see, e.g., Pindar *Isth.* 2.31. For the image of the whetstone, see *Ol.* 6.82.

29. See Hubbard (1995, 221), who writes that Horace is "teasingly showing how to make use of Pindar, and by no means in Titius's way."

30. See Mayer (1994, ad loc.). The fable is Phaedrus 1.3.

31. On the centrality of friendship in the epistle, see Kilpatrick (1986, 32–37).

32. Similarly O'Neill (1999, 88): "Florus . . . has taken a healthy competitive urge to an extreme. By alienating those around him, Florus impedes his success instead of fostering it."

33. O'Neill (1999, 86).

34. Horace's allusion to Vergil is actually more extensive than O'Neill suggests, with *Epist.* 1.3.23–27 echoing words throughout *Ecl.* 8.6–14. Vergil's *seu* and *sive* (6–7) are picked up by Horace's *seu . . . seu* (23), and *frigida caelo* (*Ecl.* 8.14) is echoed in *frigida . . . caelestis* (*Epist.* 1.3.26–27).

35. O'Neill (1999, 86) comes to a similar conclusion, but she does not sense that Horace's tone is as sharply critical as I do: "The poetic ivy can be *victrix* not only because poetry, like public life, is a competitive activity, but also because its best practitioners can win glory." She does, however, recognize in Florus a "competitive preoccupation" and suggests (82) that "the poem presents us with a young man who wants to be first, regardless of his companions."

36. For the *Odes*, see 1.1.29–30: *me doctarum hederae praemia frontium / dis miscent superis* ("Ivy, the reward of learned brows, intermingles me with the gods above"). The *hederae praemia* of the ode is clearly echoed in the *hederae victricis praemia* of the epistle. O'Neill (1999, 85–86) also recognizes this allusion and suggests that "Florus is encouraged to follow his mentor's example of seeking the elevation that the ivy crown bestows." I would suggest, however, that Horace's attitude toward such accomplishment has changed from *Odes* to *Epistles* and that Florus is encouraged instead to take Horace's epistolary lead and seek to achieve not just glory but wisdom from his poetic pursuits. See also 3.30.15–16: *mihi Delphica / lauro cinge volens, Melpomene, comam* ("Favorably, Melpomene, encircle my hair with Delphic laurel"). The laurel of the ode is picked up in the *victricis* of the epistle.

37. For those who understand Horace as urging Florus to give up poetry for philosophy, see McGann (1969, 41), Foster (1972), and Macleod (1977, 363; 1979, 22). For those who, like me, take Horace as censuring Florus's excessive ambition, see esp. Hubbard (1995) and O'Neill (1999).

38. Macleod (1977, 363) does not attempt to identify the genitive use of *curarum*, but he takes *fomenta* as referring to poetry: "it [i.e., poetry] is merely, like other worldly cares, a cold compress which stops a man moving to his true goal under the guidance of philosophy. Here, then, Horace depreciates poetry by setting it against philosophy." This argument would work best with *curarum* taken as the defining genitive; in other words, the ineffective cold compresses are equivalent to Florus's *curae*—i.e., poetry and oratory. Mayer (1994, ad loc.) takes the genitive as defining but offers a much vaguer explanation, identifying the *curae* as "public business, perhaps love and the pursuit of gain." Foster (1972, 305) also takes the genitive as defining and suggests that both the *fomenta* and the *curae* are "anxious or ambitious preoccupations about his career. . . . They are, metaphorically speaking, things which you expect to warm (or help) your life, but which in fact chill (or harm) it. Therefore Florus should give them up and seek what is purely beneficial, namely a philosophical *securitas*."

39. Others similarly take Florus's *curae* to refer to his competitive ambitions and understand the *curarum* as objective. See, esp., Hubbard (1995, 222–24), O'Neill (1999, 87), and Moles (1995).

40. He cites *Serv. auct.* on *Ecl.* 8.12. Here Servius explains that the coolness of ivy was considered an antidote to the heat of wine, and this is why poets, devotees of Bacchus, wear ivy wreaths: *hedera autem ideo coronantur poetae quoniam poetas saepe vino plurimo manifestum est uti . . . et haec herba nimium frigida est et vini calorem temperat,* "moreover poets are crowned with ivy since it is clear that poets enjoy great amounts of wine, and this plant is excessively cold and tempers the heat of wine." For ivy used in cold foments, see Celsus 8.10.7: *cicatrix inducta fovenda frigida aqua est, in qua myrtus, hedera, aliaeve similes verbena decoctae sint,* "the wound must be fomented with cold water, in which myrtle, ivy, or similar branches have been cooked."

41. McGann (1969, 41) equates *caelestis sapientia* with philosophy. Foster (1972, 304) argues that it "suggests Stoicism." Moles (1995) connects it with a variety of philosophical ideas, particularly in Cynicism and Stoicism. Kilpatrick (1986, 34–35) connects the idea to "the bonds of friendship." O'Neill (1999, 89–93) connects it to several Ciceronian ideas from the *De Officiis* and defines it (90) as "the ability to rise above the drives inherent in outstanding men and look down on and attach little value to the trappings of success."

42. The ability of poetry, particularly Horace's epistolary poetry, to improve one's fellow man has been implicit since the opening epistle and is central to the second. See the end of chapter 2 and all of chapter 3.

43. Mayer (1994, ad loc.) and Hubbard (1995, 226–27). Trinacty (2012, 66), however, understands this as a reference to stallions.

44. See Mayer (1994, ad loc.) and O'Neill (1999, 94).

45. Hubbard (1995, 227).

46. *Epist.* 1.19 has received a large degree of scholarly attention. On the poem, see, e.g., Fraenkel (1957, 339–50), McGann (1969, 82–85), Kilpatrick (1975; 1986, 18–24), Macleod (1977), Woodman (1983a), Smith (1984), Calboli (1999), Freudenburg (2002, 133–40), Peponi (2002), Hardie (2008, 129–32), Lowrie (2010), and Trinacty (2012, 68–72).

47. Although McGann (1969, 82) suggests that the poem stands apart "as the only epistle concerned exclusively with literary matters," other scholars, especially Macleod (1977) and Freudenburg (2002), have convincingly shown that Horace's comments about poetry resonate with the larger moral concerns of the collection. See, on the other hand, Smith (1984, 255), who states, "I read the epistle as essentially a statement of literary criticism, not an ethical treatise." Despite my difference of approach, many of Smith's observations have informed my reading of the poem.

48. See Porter (2002, 28): "Where 1 begins with Horace seeking freedom from the writing of lyric verse, 19 proudly associates his freedom . . . with the creation of that same type of poetry."

49. On Horace as a patron in the poem, I am indebted to Oliensis (1998, 173–74).

50. Fraenkel (1957, 350) takes seriously Horace's claim in the poem that his *Odes* were poorly received with undue criticism and calls the poem "the only thoroughly bitter document that we have from Horace's pen." Few scholars nowadays read the poem so autobiographically, and I suggest that the description Horace gives of his harsh critics is instead indebted to the themes of flattery and harsh criticism that run throughout the book, esp. in 1.18.

51. On wine and water as sources of poetic inspiration, see Crowther (1979) and Knox (1985).

52. *Ars* 408–11: *natura fieret laudabile carmen an arte / quaesitum est: ego nec studium sine divite vena, / nec rude quid prosit video ingenium; alterius sic / altera poscit opem res et coniurat amice*, "It has been asked whether a praiseworthy poem is made through nature or through art. I see neither what benefit *studium* has without a rich vein of *ingenium*, nor do I see what benefit untrained *ingenium* has. Thus the one demands the help of the other and makes a friendly pact." Ovid too, as Rudd (1989, ad loc.) points out, finds a mixture of these two qualities desirable, judging that Ennius excelled in *ingenium* but was deficient in *ars* (*Trist.* 2.424). Elsewhere Ovid judges Callimachus in the opposite way, as deficient in *ingenium* but outstanding in *ars* (*Am.* 1.15.24).

53. On Horatian and Lucilian *libertas*, see esp. Freudenburg (2001, 44–51).

54. Smith (1984, 257).

55. Bakola (2010, 4–5).

56. Rosen (2000, 34). For the connections between Cratinus, wine, and Archilochus, see Biles (2002; 2011, 138–44). On Cratinus's poetics, see Rosen (2000) and Bakola (2010, 13–80).

57. On Horace's taming of harsh speech in the poem I am indebted to Smith (1984).

58. On the connections between these imitators and the flatterer, see Macleod (1977, 366).

59. See Mayer (1994, ad loc.), who writes that *pater* "suggests Ennius' originality within an imitative tradition."

60. Cf. Smith (1984, 256), who argues that Horace here is adopting the role of a *magister bibendi*. I find this interpretation convincing as well; in either case Horace is a *magister* whose words are subject to slavish imitation.

61. Horace does repeatedly praise the beneficial aspects of wine in his poetry. In the *Epistles*, see esp. 1.5.16–20, where he hopes that drinking wine will dispel some of Torquatus's *severitas*.

62. See Kilpatrick (1975, 120): "He does want us to know . . . that he *has* a rabid following among the *mali poetae*, even if it falls very short of the ideal!"

63. See esp. Seneca the Elder *Controversiae* 1.5.22 and Seneca the Younger *De Ira* 2.32.4–8. On Timagenes's life, see esp. Fear (2010, 429–30).

64. Mayer (1994, ad loc.).

65. For Augustus's associations with moderate freedom, see the introduction.

66. Smith (1984, 261) and Oliensis (1998, 173). See also Macleod (1977, 366).

67. Oliensis (1998, 173).

68. Many scholars have made the connection between Horace's imagery and that of Callimachus and Lucretius. See, e.g., Smith (1984, 263), Mayer (1994, ad loc.), and Trinacty (2012, 69). On the Lucretian parallel, see esp. Hardie (2009, 53–56).

69. Freudenburg (2002, 135–36), where he similarly describes the middle path opened up in this poem: "The poet makes a (hard to make) case for *leading by following*, to suggest that middle way his critics could not abide. . . . And thus, in a poem obsessed with the rival inspirational merits of water and wine, he opens a middle way between the ungainly extremes considered in the poem's opening lines."

70. Trinacty (2012, 68–71) also draws attention to the shared bee imagery in 1.3 and 1.19. For the interesting suggestion that Horace's *dux reget examen* is a Latin calque of Ἀρχί-λοχος (literally "rule-swarm"), see Katz (2008).

71. As Woodman (1983a, 77 n. 5) points out, the *et* in line 25 is explanatory. In other words, the subject matter that Horace did not copy was specifically the *agentia verba Lycamben*.

72. Cf. his criticism of those who repeat the words taught in Janus's corrupt schoolroom (*haec recinunt iuvenes dictata senesque*, 1.1.55) and the flatterer, who repeats his patrons' *voces et verba* (1.18.12).

73. On Horace's imitation of Archilochus in the *Epodes*, see esp. Johnson (2012, 35–76).

74. Fraenkel (1957, 342). For a detailed history of the dispute, see Calboli (1999).

75. Fraenkel (1957), Macleod (1977), and Woodman (1983a). See also Kilpatrick (1975, 121 n. 16).

76. Fraenkel (1957, 346–47).

77. Macleod (1977, 368–69).

78. Woodman (1983a, 78–79).

79. Clay (2010, 131–33) has also recently jumped in the fray over these lines. She too argues that *Archilochi* is dependent on *musam* and translates, "manly Sappho tempered Archilochus' Muse with her meters; Alcaeus did too . . ." She similarly recognizes that to do so breaks down the analogy between Horace and Sappho/Alcaeus: "Alcaeus, and presumably Sappho too, changed the subject matter of Archilochus' iambus, as did Horace. But whereas Horace kept both the iambist's meter and his spirit, the Lesbians did not. Therefore, they cannot, at least on the surface, offer a model for what Horace did . . . there seems no reason to mention them at all, and doing so leaves Horace's defense in shambles. But not if we understand why Horace appeals to his Lesbian models here: they understood an essential principle: that a change in spirit (*Archilochi Musam*) correctly entails a change in form (*pede*)."

80. This is the argument of, e.g., Mayer (1994, ad loc.) and Calboli (1999). Mayer furthermore points out that Horace most likely shares the view laid out later by metricians that "Archilochus was deemed the father of all lyric thanks to his metrical diversity, which inspired imitation, rivalry and the production of yet more verse patterns by his successors." He cites Marius Victorinus *GLK* 6.141, 143.

81. Mayer (1994, ad loc.).

82. Fraenkel (1957, 344 n. 2) cites the meaning of *temperare* given in Ernout and Meillet, *Dict. Etym. Lat.*: "trans. correspond au grec κεράννυμι 'mélanger, mêler,' en particulier mêler de l'eau au vin ou à un liquid pour l'adoucir, couper." Woodman (1983a, 79 n. 14) also points to this definition. See especially Calboli (1999, 61–64) and Peponi (2002, 24–47).

83. Calboli (1999, 61) observes that one method of mixing wine and water was to put the water into the *krater* first and then add the wine, which would align nicely with what Sappho and Alcaeus might be doing in 1.19, where "Archilochus' *pes* (wine) was put into Sappho's and Alcaeus' *Musam* (water)." This concurs with Fass (1994, 91): "In all circumstances the water was poured into the *krater* first, followed by the wine."

84. Calboli (1999, 61) also suggests that Horace has the mean in mind here, but a mean between *ingenium* and *ars*: "We have a kind of Horatian ideal poetry, composed (*temperat*) of both Dionysian inspiration and Callimachean precision and elegance. What has been begun by Sappho and Alcaeus has been perfected and improved by Horace who wisely mixed both essences of poetry, both the Dionysian and Callimachean methods." Peponi (2002, 36) argues similarly: "Archilochus' iambic aggressiveness and dithyrambic

drunkenness have to be moderated through the intervention of Sappho and Alcaeus. Wine does not get replaced by water, but gets moderated by it. . . . Thus, if Callimachean aesthetics expects the poet to control his *ingenium* with the moderating action of his *ars*, the two representatives of Aeolic song seem to undertake here the role that a supporter of Callimachean disposition would have."

85. Another model for moderation and adaptability, as we saw in chapter 3, is Odysseus (*Epist.* 1.2). He too refuses to drink from cups that would make him an adherent to various extremes (24–26) and easily adapts to a variety of *res* (*adversis rerum immersabilis undis*, 22).

86. In *Satires* 1.10.78–91 Horace's ideal readers include Plotius, Varius, Maecenas, Vergil, Valgius, Octavius Musa, Aristius Fuscus, the Visci, Pollio, Messalla, Bibulus and Servius, and Furnius. In the satire he similarly warns against courting the admiration of the crowd (*neque te ut miretur turba labores, / contentus paucis lectoribus*, "do not labor so that the crowd may admire you but be content with a few readers," 72–73). On the connections between the satire and *Epist.* 1.19, see Kilpatrick (1975, 123–24).

87. Cf. Macleod (1977) 373: "Horace is a free man who writes for free men."

88. Many of the issues involved in Horace's likening of himself to a prostitute here are the same ones we will find in 1.20. On prostitution in 1.20, see Oliensis (1995; 1998, 74–81). As Oliensis points out, in 1.20 the book wants an even larger audience and will not limit itself to a few exclusive readers, a topic I take up in the conclusion. On the use of this prostitution trope in elegy, see Fear (2000).

89. Lowrie (2010, 256).

90. Mayer (1994, ad loc.). Likewise in *Satires* 1.10.76–80 Horace names those whose approval he does not seek, and again these are men from the lower classes. Horace wants instead the applause of the equestrian class.

91. For Horace's disdain of the schoolroom, see Gowers (2012) on *Satires* 1.10.74–75: "A fate worse than death for literary works: to become school dictation texts, the most extreme form of promiscuity and ignominy for the Callimachean poet." For Horace's hostility toward recitations, see Markus (2000, 152–55) and, for 1.19 in particular, Lowrie (2010).

92. See Lowrie (2010, 253): "The end of *Epistles* 1.19 contrasts reading with recitation. The poem as a whole sets social performance against literary imitation."

93. Most scholars writing on the poem have picked up on the gladiatorial imagery of these final lines. See, e.g., Mayer (1994, ad loc.), Porter (2002, 27), Lowrie (2010, 257), and Trinacty (2012, 71).

94. For Horace's guilty conscience here, see Williams (1968, 27), McGann (1969, 84), Macleod (1977, 375), Freudenburg (2002, 138), Lowrie (2010, 257). Smith (1984, 268) argues against such a suggestion.

95. Larmour (2010–11) interestingly focuses on Juvenal's adoption of gladiatorial imagery from the *Epistles* and argues (170) that Juvenal "deploys certain reminiscences of Horace—not only of his *Satires*, which we might expect, but also of the *Epistles*—as he reformulates the *libertas* that Lucilius enjoyed in the republican era to a variety of speech more suited to his own imperial circumstances." This process, as I hope to have shown, is already very much underway in the *Epistles*.

96. See Smith (1984, 256): "Horace's withdrawal at the end after confrontation with an unnamed speaker . . . wins our applause for the poet's failure to match the aggressive and combative behavior which the poet has condemned in others and which is a traditional

by-product of drunkenness." See also 269: "By his retreat Horace refuses to serve the demands of the public . . . and also shows that he will not resort to Archilochean lampoon to answer his critics; their very hostility (even if their accusations should be true) condemns them." Horace's refusal to "use his nose," *naribus uti* (45) refers not to the modern practice of being "stuck up" but to the nose as an organ expressive of anger (*OLD* s.v. 4). Smith 269 connects it to the use of "satiric scorn." In *Satires* 1.3.35–36 Horace describes someone who is *iracundior*, "too prone to anger," as having *acutis naribus*, "a sharp nose."

97. Cf. Macleod (1977, 373): "His declaration of independence vis-à-vis his public also corresponds to his claim of originality vis-à-vis his models."

Conclusion

1. For 1.13, see esp. Fraenkel (1957, 350–56), McGann (1969, 65–66), Clarke (1972), Kilpatrick (1973b; 1986, 14–18), Connor (1982), Deroux (1992), Ferri (1993, 67–71), Oliensis (1998, 185–91), and Putnam (2003). The most convincing identification of Vinnius has been put forth by Nisbet (1959) and defended and expanded by McGann (1963), who suggest that he is Vinnius Valens, a member of Augustus's praetorian guard renowned for his feats of strength, as recorded by Pliny the Younger at *NH* 7.82. As seems clear from the epistle, either he or his father carried the *cognomen* Asina or Asellus, for which see McGann (1963). It has been debated what route Vinnius is to take and whether Augustus is in Rome or elsewhere, and much of this has rested on the date of the poem's composition and whether the poems referred to are epistles or odes. See, e.g., Clarke (1972, 158–59), Kilpatrick (1986, 17), and Putnam (2003, 110–11). The poem's precise date and the whereabouts of Augustus are ultimately irrecoverable. Given the strong antithesis between *rus* and *Roma* in the collection, it is best to imagine Vinnius making his way from Horace's country estate to Augustus in Rome. Horace's *liber* will take a similar path to publication in 1.20, though it will end not at the palace of Augustus but the bookstore of the Sosii.

2. For the view that the poem is light and humorous, see Kilpatrick (1986, 17), who calls the poem "a completely light-hearted piece," and Deroux (1992, 321), for whom it is "a good-natured fiction meant to make Augustus laugh, or at least smile." McGann (1969, 66) refers to it as "the first poem in the book in which *ridiculum* predominates" while at the same time suggesting that "the bracketing . . . of the main part of the epistle by *Augusto* (2) and *Caesaris* (18) underlines the fact that it has something to say about Horace's attitude to Augustus." Though I too recognize and appreciate the humorous aspects of the poem, I would argue that its humor verges on the uncomfortable and serves in the end to highlight Horace's anxiety when faced with presenting poems to Augustus. My view of its tone is close to that of Connor (1982), who suggests (148) that "the poem . . . is fraught with nervous tension—rather than the light-hearted joking that has been suggested as its tenor" and (151) that "it is the poet's apprehensiveness that throughout shapes the material of the poem, checks and dampens all the potentially comic situations."

3. See Freudenburg (2002, 139): "The precise nature of the friendship imagined, if friendship can be imagined between *princeps* and this letter-writer, is quite out of keeping with the direct and egalitarian relationships imagined elsewhere in the book."

4. This is not to suggest that Vinnius is actually a slave. If he is Vinnius Valens, he is a free praetorian who presumably has access to the emperor. Kilpatrick (1986, 15–16)

points out that his family's possession of a cognomen rules out slave status. At the same time, however, the behavior Horace fears he will display belongs to one of low social standing: "His social standing is suggested by the satirical and superior tone of the poet . . . and also by the suspicion that he will gossip with the *vulgus* (16) and exaggerate the hardship of this mission." Kilpatrick concludes that he is meant to evoke "a soldier belonging to the lower ranks." Ferri (1993, 69–70) connects his bumbling behavior with that of the *servus currens* in comedy, and Putnam (2003, 104–7) expands on the connections between the poem and comedy, a genre to which Horace directly alludes with *fabula fias* in line 9.

5. Oliensis (1998, 185).

6. Oliensis (1998, 189).

7. See Putnam (2003, 104), who points out that *sarcina* (6) can also "refer to the pack of either man or beast."

8. Mayer (1994, ad loc.).

9. Connor (1982, 149): "By proceeding along such a vivid series of pictures, the reader is in fact constantly impelled to think of Vinnius behaving exactly in that manner in front of the emperor, creating an embarrassing scene and ruining everything." See also Oliensis (1998, 186): "the letter displays the very overzealousness against which it warns and broadcasts the very information it purports to censor."

10. Oliensis (1998, 187).

11. Freudenburg (2001, 139). Horace plays on this association of his cognomen in *Satires* 1.9. Upon being bested by the pest, Horace lets his ears droop like an ass upset by too heavy a load on its back: *demitto auriculas, ut iniquae mentis asellus, / cum gravius dorso subiit onus*, 20–21.

12. See Putnam (2003, 104).

13. To quote Oliensis (1998, 190), "the epistle to Vinnius is . . . in effect the poet's own act of 'surrender' to Augustus."

14. So Mayer (1994, ad loc.). Cucchiarelli (2010, 302) points out that "the plural nouns *volumina* and *libellis* leave no doubt . . . that we are not dealing here with one book of the Epistles," though he admits (315 n. 35) that *carmina* on its own can denote "poetry" in general and need not exclude the *Epistles* entirely. Putnam (2003, 110) limits Vinnius's package to only the first book of odes, an approach that I do not find entirely convincing. Clark (1972) argues that Vinnius delivers epistles—not odes—to Augustus. My argument rests on the idea that the poetry offered to Augustus in 1.13, though only vaguely identified, is not the *Epistles* but acts as a foil to them and their publication in 1.20.

15. Cf. *Odes* 3.1.1 (*odi profanum vulgus et arceo*) with Nisbet and Rudd (2004, ad loc.).

16. My argument here is indebted especially to Oliensis (1998, 190–91): "The epistle to Vinnius can be read as an alternate end-poem, one that Horace chose to displace rather than discard. . . . But Horace's epistles are not, any more than are his odes, designed exclusively or even primarily for an imperial audience. The emperor may be a privileged overreader, like Maecenas. But neither man has proprietary rights over Horace's poems. This is why the epistle to Vinnius has to make way for a very different kind of end-poem, one that releases Horace's work to the general public and to posterity."

17. Harrison (1988).

18. On 1.20, see esp. Fraenkel (1957, 356–63), McGann (1969, 85–87), Bonner (1972), Kilpatrick (1986, 103–9), Harrison (1988), Ferri (1993, 75–80, 131–40), Pearcy (1994), Oliensis (1995; 1998, 174–81), Citroni (2000), Trinacty (2012, 72–75).

19. This is what Socrates calls Aristippus's claim in *Mem.* 1.2.11 to walk a middle path of freedom between rule and slavery. See chapter 1.

20. As Cucciarelli (2010, 311) points out, Janus himself appears in both the opening and closing poems (cf. 1.1.54), a fact that further invites us to consider them together. Porter (2002, 44) similarly connects Vertumnus and Janus here with Horace's tendency to shift and vacillate.

21. See Trinacty (2012, 74).

22. For Horace's rejection of Callimacheanism in the poem, see Pearcy (1994).

23. See Oliensis (1995, 217). Cf. esp. epigram 28:

ἐχθαίρω τὸ ποίημα τὸ κυκλικὸν οὐδὲ κελεύθῳ
  χαίρω, τίς πολλοὺς ὧδε καὶ ὧδε φέρει·
μισῶ καὶ περίφοιτον ἐρώμενον οὐδ' ἀπὸ κρήνης
  πίνω· σικχαίνω πάντα τὰ δημόσια.
Λυσανίη, σὺ δὲ ναίχι καλὸς καλός· ἀλλὰ πρὶν εἰπεῖν
  τοῦτο σαφῶς, ἠχώ φησί τις· ἄλλος ἔχει.

I hate the cyclic poem, nor do I rejoice in whichever road carries many to and fro. And I hate a *wandering beloved*, nor do I drink from a well. I hate all public things. Lysanies, you are beautiful, yes, beautiful, but before I say this clearly, some echo says, "Another holds him."

24. For the pun on *liber* as "book" and "free," see Kilpatrick (1986, 104 and 154 n. 8).

25. See Johnson (1993, 69): "In 1, Horace asks Maecenas for his freedom, for release from service. . . . In 20, the tables are turned. Here as in *S.* 2.7, he is faced with a request for freedom from *his* slave, this young (new) poetry book, which he irritably and grudgingly yields to." See also Porter (2002, 25): "Where the opening of 1 moves toward withdrawal, seclusion, and the country, that of 20 moves toward entry, participation, and Rome; where the gladiator seeks freedom *from* involvement, public exposure, and ridicule, the *puer* of 20 seeks freedom *to* jostle and be jostled."

26. See, e.g., Macleod (1979, 24) ("In criticizing the book/slave, Horace is criticizing a part of himself, the vain author, anxious for publicity and admiration"); Connor (1982, 148) ("In one sense, he is singleminded and the issue is uncomplicated: that kind of life is foul and he will never forgive. On the other hand, in a very real sense, it is about himself that he is speaking, about his own lurking desires; for this is his book, these are his poems"); Mayer (1994, 274) ("The poem artfully discloses a final inconsistency of the poet's. All along he claims to want only the approval of a few and compose with their opinion in view. Yet publication belies this attitude and no one can deny that he secretly wants the widest possible renown"); and esp. Oliensis (1995, 216) ("In this miniature envoi, *i, puer*, the slave is an instrument or an extension of the master's conflicting impulses toward elitism and popularization. In the more elaborate conceit of the epistles, the *puer*, now identified with the *libellus*, acquires a will of his own, enabling Horace to distance himself from his own "vulgar" ambitions while simultaneously fulfilling them").

27. For the idea that publication is here equivalent to manumission in 1.20, see Oliensis (1995, 211–12) and Fitzgerald (2000, 30).

28. For *emittere* as "to publish," see *OLD* s.v. 1c and as "to manumit" see *OLD* s.v. 2b. When it means "to manumit," *manu* usually is present but does not have to be. Cf., e.g., Ter. *Adelph.* 976 (*haud dubiumst quin emitti aequom siet*, "there is no doubt that she ought to be freed").

29. For *manumissio per epistulam*, see, e.g., Buckland (1908, 444–46). See Gaius, *Inst.* 1.5.1: *Multis autem modis manumissio procedit. . . . aut vindicta aut inter amicos aut per epistulam aut per testamentum aut aliam quamlibet ultimam voluntatem*, "Manumission occurs in many ways. . . . either by *vindicta* or among friends or through a letter or through a will or another final testament."

30. Oliensis (1995, 224) makes the nice observation that the sated lover here "is a figure for the reader who has read through to the end—a figure of closure, like the full-fed dinner guest (*conviva satur*, *S*. 1.1.119) at the end of Horace's first satire."

31. Fraenkel (1957, 362) even hints that Horace's play on the *liber* (book) as *liber* (free) evokes the idea of free speech. The book is "talkative by nature (*liber!*), to whom prolonged *taciturnitas* (12) would be pain and grief."

32. In *Odes* 2.20 Horace clearly connects his poetic immortality to his being circulated throughout distant lands beyond Rome. See Macleod (1979, 24) and Oliensis (1998, 177).

33. *Aes.* 186. See Marchesi (2005, 322).

34. Bonner (1972) makes a compelling case for translating *extremis in vicis* as "in the end of the streets," i.e., of Rome. The problem with this interpretation, however, is that Horace has already foretold that the book will be exported from Rome to the provinces, and there is no indication that he will have returned to Rome. It seems best, therefore, to take the phrase as referring to small provincial towns.

35. On the book as *ludi magister*, see Bonner (1972, 516). For the status of such teachers see Vioque (2002, 375–76) on Martial 7.64.7–9.

36. Bonner (1972, 509) and Harrison (1988, 474).

37. Oliensis (1995, 220).

38. On the reappearance of the schoolroom imagery, see Mayer (1994, ad loc.). He, however, sees the schoolroom scene of 1.20 in a negative light: "The theme of education is ironically resumed from the beginning of the collection. But H's epistles will not have the grand moral function of Homer, rather they will be used as a cheap text for the first reading lessons (*elementa*) of poor children." See also McGann (1969, 85), who sees no reference here to the ethical content of the collection.

39. See Trinacty (2012, 73), who suggests that *elementa* here is "a reformulation of the 'simple lessons' that Horace hoped would guide him in his behavior" in 1.1.27.

40. See Bonner (1972, 513).

41. See Trinacty (2012, 73 n. 43).

42. See Pearcy (1994, 462).

43. See Bonner (1972, 510) and Oliensis (1995, 221; 1998, 178).

44. See chapter 3. At 1.1.7 Horace's own ear receives ethical advice, and at 1.1.40 he states that "no one is so wild that he cannot be tamed if only he lend a patient ear to education, *si modo culturae patientem commodet aurem*. In 1.2.52 the mind of one with moral shortcomings cannot enjoy good things, just as clogged ears cannot enjoy music. At 1.8.16 he asks the *Musa* to drip a *praeceptum* into Celsus's ears. At 1.19.43–44 Horace is accused by a harsh critic of reserving his poetry for the ears of Jupiter (i.e., Augustus).

45. See Oliensis (1995, 221): "Like his book, the author is ambitious, eager to rise above his humble origins; and as the book hopes to improve its fortunes by catering to the pleasures of the populace, so Horace boasts of having won the favor (*placuisse*, 23) of eminent men."

46. In *Odes* 2.20.1–3 Horace also figures his poetic ascendency via a bird metaphor: *non usitata nec tenui ferar / pinna biformis per liquidum aethera / vates*, "Not on a common or weak wing will I, a biform poet, be carried through the clear air." For the connection between this passage of *Odes* 2.20 and *Epistles* 1.20, see Kilpatrick (1986, 104).

47. On 1.20.23, see esp. Citroni (2000).

48. See esp. Ferri (1993, 131–37) and Pearcy (1994, 462–63). Pearcy, however, suggests that this epitaph is "appropriate to a member of the governing class," whereas I will suggest that it marks him yet again as a freedman.

49. It has been well documented that epitaphs were a mode of commemoration associated especially with freedman. Mouritsen (2005, 38) reports that "in the city of Rome it has been estimated that at least three quarters of those commemorated in funerary inscriptions were former slaves, while most of the freeborn appear to be first generation *ingenui*." On this phenomenon see Taylor (1961), Zanker (1975), Mouritsen (2005), and Borg (2012).

50. For Trimalchio's concern with his epitaph as a mark of his freedman's status, see Ramsby (2012).

51. See esp. Borg (2012, 26–27): "These tomb reliefs . . . are first attested c. 80 B.C.E. Their heyday of production is the second half of the first century B.C.E., when freedmen profited increasingly from the stabilizing political situation and the economic upturn under Augustus. . . . Foremost they were meant to showcase the deceased's pride on his ascension from his former slave status and from the restrictions associated with slavery."

52. See Oliensis (1995, 223): "No other Augustan poetry book dates itself so precisely."

53. See Oliensis (1995, 213): "Before the book is released to the public, before the speech is committed to writing, the author can act as its chaperone, limiting its encounters and intervening, when necessary, in its defense; once it has begun to circulate on its own he can do very little to control its reception."

Bibliography

Anderson, William S. 1961. "Horace's Siren (*Serm.* II. 3. 14)." *CP* 56: 105–8.

———. 1982. *Essays on Roman Satire*. Princeton: Princeton University Press.

———. 1995. "*Horatius Liber*: Child and Freedman's Free Son." *Arethusa* 28: 151–64.

———. 2010. "Horace's Friendship: Adaptation of a Circular Argument." In *A Companion to Horace* (Blackwell Companions to the Ancient World), edited by Gregson Davis, 34–52. Chichester: Wiley-Blackwell.

Ahl, Frederick 1984. "The Rider and the Horse: Politics and Power in Roman Poetry from Horace to Statius." *ANRW* 2.31.1: 40–110.

Allen, Walter. 1970. "The Addressees in Horace's First Book of *Epistles*." *SPh*: 67: 255–66.

Arena, Valentina. 2007. "*Libertas* and *Virtus* of the Citizen in Cicero's *De Republica*." *SCI* 26: 39–66.

———. 2012. Libertas *and the Practice of Politics in the Late Roman Republic*. Cambridge: Cambridge University Press.

Armstrong, David. 1970. "Two Voices of Horace." *Arion* 9: 91–113.

———. 1986. "*Horatius Eques et Scriba*: Satires 1.6 and 2.7." *TAPA* 116: 255–88.

———. 1989. *Horace*. New Haven: Yale University Press.

———. 1995. "Philodemus, *On Poems* Book 5." In *Philodemus and Poetry*, edited by Dirk Obbink, 255–69. Oxford: Oxford University Press.

———. 1997. "Some Recent Perspectives on Horace." *Phoenix* 51: 393–405.

———. 2004a. "Introduction." In *Vergil, Philodemus, and the Augustans*, edited by David Armstrong, Patricia A. Johnston, and Marilyn B. Skinner, 1–22. Austin: University of Texas Press.

———. 2004b. "Horace's *Epistles* 1 and Philodemus." In *Vergil, Philodemus, and the Augustans*, edited by David Armstrong, Patricia A. Johnston, and Marilyn B. Skinner, 267–98. Austin: University of Texas Press.

———. 2008. "'Be Angry and Sin Not:' Philodemus Versus the Stoics on Natural Bites and Natural Emotions." In *Passions and Moral Progress in Greco-Roman Thought*, edited by John T. Fitzgerald, 79–121. London: Routledge.

———. 2010. "The Biographical and Social Foundations of Horace's Poetic Voice." In *A Companion to Horace* (Blackwell Companions to the Ancient World), edited by Gregson Davis, 7–33. Chichester: Wiley-Blackwell.

Asmis, Elizabeth. 1991. "Philodemus's Poetic Theory and *On the Good King According to Homer*." *ClassAnt* 10: 1–45.

———. 1995a. "Epicurean Poetics." In *Philodemus and Poetry*, edited by Dirk Obbink, 3–14. Oxford: Oxford University Press.

———. 1995b. "Philodemus on Censorship, Moral Utility, and Formalism in Poetry." In *Philodemus and Poetry*, edited by Dirk Obbink, 148–77. Oxford: Oxford University Press.

———. 2001. "Basic Education in Epicureanism." In *Education in Greek and Roman Antiquity*, edited by Yun Lee Too, 209–39. Leiden: Brill.

———. 2011. "The Necessity of Anger in Philodemus' *On Anger*. In *Epicurus and the Epicurean Tradition*, edited by Jeffrey Fish and Kirk R. Sanders, 152–82. Cambridge: Cambridge University Press.

Bakola, Emmanuela. 2010. *Cratinus and the Art of Comedy*. Oxford: Oxford University Press.

Ball, Robert J. 1994. "*Albe, Ne Doleas*: Horace and Tibullus." *CW* 87: 409–14.

Barker, Duncan. 1996. "'The Golden Age is Proclaimed'? The *Carmen Saeculare* and the Renascence of the Golden Race." *CQ* 46: 434–46.

Barton, Carlin A. 1993. *The Sorrows of the Ancient Romans: the Gladiator and the Monster*. Princeton: Princeton University Press.

Becker, Carl. 1963. *Das Spätwerk des Horaz*. Göttingen: Vandenhoeck and Ruprecht.

Beer, Andrew. 2006. "Tradition and Originality in Callimachus' *Hymn to Apollo*. *Frankfurter elektronische Rundschau zur Altertumskunde* 1. http://s145739614.online.de/fera/ausgabe1/Beer.pdf.

Belfiore, Elizabeth. 1980. "*Elenchus, Epode*, and Magic: Socrates as Silenus." *Phoenix* 24: 128–37.

Bernstein, Michael A. 1992. *Bitter Carnival: Ressentiment and the Abject Hero*. Princeton: Princeton University Press.

Berres, Thomas. 1992. "'Erlebnis und Kunstgestalt' im 7. Brief des Horaz." *Hermes* 120: 216–37.

Biles, Zachary P. 2002. "Intertextual Biography in the Rivalry of Cratinus and Aristophanes." *AJP* 123: 169–204.

———. 2011. *Aristophanes and the Poetics of Competition*. Cambridge: Cambridge University Press.

Blanchard, Kenneth C. 1994. "The Middle Road of Classical Political Philosophy: Socrates' Dialogues with Aristippus in Xenophon's *Memorabilia*." *The Review of Politics* 56: 671–96.

Bond, Robin P. 1998. "Horace on Damasippus on Stertinius on. . . ." *Scholia* 7: 82–108.

———. 2001. "*Urbs Satirica*: The City in Roman Satire with Special Reference to Horace and Juvenal." *Scholia* 10: 77–91.

Bonner, Stanley F. 1972. "The Street Teacher: An Educational Scene in Horace." *AJP* 93: 509–28.

Borg, Barbara E. 2012. "The Face of the Social Climber: Roman Freedmen and Elite Ideology." In *Free at Last!: The Impact of Freed Slaves on the Roman Empire*, edited by Sinclair Bell and Teresa Ramsby, 25–49. London: Bloomsbury.

Bourgery, A. 1935. "A propos d'Horace." *RPh* 9: 130–2.

Bowditch, Phoebe Lowell. 1994. "Horace's Poetics of Political Integrity: Epistle 1.18." *AJP* 115: 409–26.

———. 2001. *Horace and the Gift Economy of Patronage.* Berkeley: University of California Press.

———. 2010. "Horace and Imperial Patronage." In *A Companion to Horace* (Blackwell Companions to the Ancient World), edited by Gregson Davis, 53–74. Chichester: Wiley-Blackwell.

Bradshaw, A. 1989. "Horace *in Sabinis.*" *Latomus* 206: 160–86.

Braund, Susan H. 1989. "City and Country in Roman Satire." In *Satire and Society in Ancient Rome,* edited by Susan H. Braund, 23–47. Exeter: University of Exeter Press.

Braund, Susanna Morton. 1996. *The Roman Satirists and Their Masks.* Bristol: Bristol Classical Press.

———. 2004. "*Libertas* or *Licentia*? Freedom and Criticism in Roman Satire." In *Free Speech in Classical Antiquity,* edited by Ineke Sluiter and Ralph M. Rosen, 409–28. Leiden: Brill.

Brink, C.O. 1963. *Horace on Poetry: Prolegomena to the Literary Epistles.* Cambridge: Cambridge University Press.

———. 1971. *Horace on Poetry: Ars Poetica.* Cambridge: Cambridge University Press.

———. 1982. *Horace on Poetry: Epistles Book II.* Cambridge: Cambridge University Press.

———. 1995. "Second Thoughts on Three Horatian Puzzles." In *Homage to Horace,* edited by Stephen Harrison, 267–78. Oxford: Oxford University Press.

Brown, Irene. 1981. "Tacitus and a Space for Freedom." *History Today* 31.4.

Brown, P. Michael. 1993. *Horace: Satires I.* Warminster: Aris and Philips.

Brown, Penelope, and Stephen C. Levinson. 1987. *Politeness: Some Universals in Language Usage.* Cambridge: Cambridge University Press.

Brunt, P.A. 1988. "*Libertas* in the Republic." In *The Fall of the Republic and Related Essays,* edited by P.A. Brunt, 281–350. Oxford: Oxford University Press.

Buckland, William W. 1908. *The Roman Law of Slavery.* Cambridge: Cambridge University Press.

Büchner, Karl. 1940. "Der siebente Brief des Horaz." *Hermes* 75: 64–80.

Byrne, Shannon N. 2000. "Poets and Maecenas." *JAC* 15: 1–12.

Calboli, Gualtiero. 1999. "On Horace's *Epist.* 1.19." In *Papers on Rhetoric II,* edited by Lucia Calboli Montefusco, 35–68. Bologna: University of Bologna.

Cameron, Alan. 1995. *Callimachus and His Critics.* Princeton: Princeton University Press.

Campbell, Archibald Y. 1924. *Horace: A New Interpretation.* London: Methuen and Company.

Citroni, Mario. 2000. "The Memory of Philippi in Horace and the Interpretation of *Epistle* 1.20.23." *CJ* 96: 27–56.

Clarke, M.L. 1972. "Horace, *Epistles* i.13." *CR* 22: 157–59.

———. 1978. "Poets and Patrons at Rome." *G&R* 25: 46–54.

Classen, C.J. 1988. "Tacitus: Historian Between Republic and Principate." *Mnemosyne* 41: 93–116.

Clay, Jenny S. 1989. "The Old Man in the Garden." In *Old Age in Greek and Latin Literature,* edited by Thomas M. Falkner and Judith de Luce, 183–94. Albany: State University of New York Press.

———. 2010. "Horace and Lesbian Lyric." In *A Companion to Horace* (Blackwell Companions to the Ancient World), edited by Gregson Davis, 128–146. Chichester: Wiley-Blackwell.

Colish, Marcia L. 1985. *The Stoic Tradition from Antiquity to the Early Middle Ages*. Vol. 1. Leiden: Brill.

Commager, Steele. 1957. "The Function of Wine in Horace's *Odes*." *TAPA* 88: 68–80.

———. 1962. *The Odes of Horace: A Critical Study*. New Haven: Yale University Press.

Connor, P.J. 1982. "Book Despatch: Horace *Epistles* 1.20 and 1.13." *Ramus* 11: 145–52.

Corbeill, Anthony. 2004. *Nature Embodied: Gesture in Ancient Rome*. Princeton: Princeton University Press.

Corbett, Philip B. 1986. *The Scurra*. Edinburgh: Scottish Academic Press.

Courbaud, Edmond. 1914. *Horace, sa vie et sa pensée* à l'époque *des* Épîtres. Paris: Hachette.

Crane, Gregory. 1987. "Bees without Honey, and Callimachean Taste." *AJP* 108: 399–403.

Crawford, Michael H. 1974. *Roman Republican Coinage*. 2 vols. Cambridge: Cambridge University Press.

Crowther, C.D. 1979. "Water and Wine as Symbols of Inspiration." *Mnemosyne* 32: 1–11.

Cucchiarelli, Andrea. 2010. "Return to Sender: Horace's *sermo* from the Epistles to the Satires." In *A Companion to Horace* (Blackwell Companions to the Ancient World), edited by Gregson Davis, 291–318. Chichester: Wiley-Blackwell.

Damon, Cynthia. 1997. *The Mask of the Parasite*. Ann Arbor: University of Michigan Press.

D'Angour, Armond J. 1999. "*Ad Unguem*." *AJP* 120: 411–27.

Deroux, Carl. 1992. "From Horace's Epistle I, 13 to Maecenas's Epigram to Horace." In *Studies in Latin Literature and Roman History* 6, edited by Carl Deroux, 317–26. Brussels: Collection Latomus.

Destrée, Pierre and Nicholas C. Smith, eds. 2005. *Socrates' Divine Sign: Religion, Practice, and Value in Socratic Philosophy*. Kelowna: Academic Printing and Publishing.

Dewar, Michael. 2014. *Leisured Resistance: Villas, Literature and Politics in the Roman World*. London: Bloomsbury.

DeWitt, Norman. 1937. "The Epicurean Doctrine of Gratitude." *AJP* 58: 320–28.

———1939. "Epicurean Doctrine in Horace." *CP* 34: 127–34.

Dilke, Oswald A.W. 1954. *Horace: Epistles I*. London: Methuen.

———. 1973. "Horace and the Verse Letter." In *Horace*, edited by C.D.N. Costa, 94–112. London: Routledge.

———. 1981. "The Interpretation of Horace's *Epistles*." *ANRW* II 31.3: 1837–65.

Donini, Pierluigi. 1988. "The History of the Concept of Eclecticism." In *The Question of "Eclecticism:" Studies in Later Greek Philosophy*, edited by J.M. Dillon and A.A. Long, 15–33. Berkeley: University of California Press.

Dorandi, Tiziano. 1982. *Filodemo: Il Buon Re Secondo Omero*. Naples: Bibliopolis.

Drexler, H. 1963. "Zur Epistel I,7 des Horaz." *Maia* 15: 26–37.

Dunkle, Roger. 2008. *Gladiators: Violence and Spectacle in Ancient Rome*. Harlow: Pearson/Longman.

DuQuesnay, Ian M. Le M. 1984. "Horace and Maecenas: The Propaganda Value of *Sermones* 1." In *Poetry and Politics in the Age of Augustus*, edited by Tony Woodman and David West, 19–58. Cambridge: Cambridge University Press.

Dutsch, Dorota M. 2008. *Feminine Discourse in Roman Comedy*. Oxford: Oxford University Press.

Edwards, M.J. 1992. "Horace, Homer and Rome: *Epistles* 1.2." *Mnemosyne* 45: 83–88.

Eidinow, John S.C. 1990. "A Note on Horace, *Epistles* 1.2.26 and 2.2.75." *CQ* 40: 566–68.

———. 1995. "Horace's Epistle to Torquatus (*Ep.* 1.5)." *CQ* 45: 191–99.

Evans, Harry B. 1978. "Horace, *Satires* 2.7: Saturnalia and Satire." *CJ* 73: 307–12.

Fairclough, H. Rushton. 1929. *Horace: Satires, Epistles, Ars Poetica* (Loeb Classical Library). Cambridge, MA: Harvard University Press.

Fantham, Elaine. 2013. "The First Book of Letters." In *Brill's Companion to Horace*, edited by Hans-Christian Günther, 407–30. Leiden: Brill.

Fass, Patrick. 1994. *Around the Roman Table: Food and Feasting in Ancient Rome*. Chicago: The University of Chicago Press.

Fear, Trevor. 2000. "The Poet as Pimp: Elegiac Seduction in the Time of Augustus." *Arethusa* 33: 217–40.

———. 2010. "*Interdictiones Domo et Ingenio*: Timagenes and Propertius: A Reading in the Dynamics of Augustan Exclusion." *Arethusa* 43: 429–38.

Fears, J. Rufus. 1980. *Roman Liberty: An Essay in Protean Political Metaphor*. Distinguished Faculty Research Lecture. Bloomington: Indiana University Press.

———. 1981. "The Cult of Virtues and Roman Imperial Ideology." *ANRW* I2.17.2: 827–948.

Feeney, Dennis. 1991. *The Gods in Epic: Poets and Critics of the Classical Tradition*. Oxford: Oxford University Press.

———. 1992. "*Si licet et fas est*: Ovid's *Fasti* and the Problem of Free Speech Under the Principate." In *Roman Poetry and Propaganda in the Age of Augustus*, edited by Anton Powell, 1–25. Bristol: Bristol Classical Press.

———. 2010. "Fathers and Sons: the Manlii Torquati and Family Continuity in Catullus and Horace." In *Ancient Historiography and its Contexts: Studies in Honor of A.J. Woodman*, edited by Christina S. Kraus, John Marincola, and Christopher Pelling, 205–23. Oxford: Oxford University Press.

Ferri, Rolando. 1993. *Il dispiacere di uno epicuro: uno studio sulla poetica della epistole oraziane (con un capitolo su Persio)*. Pisa: Giardini.

———. 2007. "The *Epistles*." In *The Cambridge Companion to Horace*, edited by Stephen J. Harrison, 121–31. Cambridge: Cambridge University Press.

Fish, Jeffrey. 2002. "Philodemus' *On the Good King According to Homer*: Columns 21–31." *Cronache Ercolanesi* 32: 187–232.

———. 2011. "Not All Politicians Are Sisyphus: What Roman Epicureans Were Taught About Politics." In *Epicurus and the Epicurean Tradition*, edited by Jeffrey Fish and Kirk R. Sanders, 72–104. Cambridge: Cambridge University Press.

Fitzgerald, William. 1987. *Agonistic Poetry: The Pindaric Mode in Pindar, Horace, Hölderlin, and the English Ode*. Berkeley: University of California Press.

———. 2000. *Slavery and the Roman Literary Imagination*. Cambridge: Cambridge University Press.

Foster, Jonathan. 1971. "Horace, *Epistles*, 1.16.35ff." *CQ* 21: 214.

———. 1972. "Horace, *Epistles* I 3, 25ff." *Mnemosyne* 25: 303–6.

Fowler, Don P. 1997. "Epicurean Anger." In *The Passions in Roman Thought and Literature*, edited by Susanna Morton Braund and Christopher Gill, 16–35. Cambridge: Cambridge University Press.

———. 2008. "Lectures on Horace's *Epistles*." *PCPS* 54: 80–114.

Fraenkel, Eduard. 1957. *Horace*. Oxford: Oxford University Press.

Freudenburg, Kirk. 1993. *The Walking Muse: Horace on the Theory of Satire*. Princeton: Princeton University Press.

———. 2001. *Satires of Rome: Threatening Poses from Lucilius to Juvenal*. Cambridge: Cambridge University Press.

———. 2002. "*Solus Sapiens Liber Est*: Recommissioning Lyric in *Epistles* I." In *Traditions and Contexts in the Poetry of Horace*, edited by Tony Woodman and Dennis Feeney, 124–40. Cambridge: Cambridge University Press.

———. 2010. "*Horatius Anceps*: Persona and Self-revelation in Satire and Song." In *A Companion to Horace* (Blackwell Companions to the Ancient World), edited by Gregson Davis, 271–90. Chichester: Wiley-Blackwell.

Gale, Monica. 1994. *Myth and Poetry in Lucretius*. Cambridge: Cambridge University Press.

Galinsky, Karl. 1996. *Augustan Culture: An Interpretive Introduction*. Princeton: Princeton University Press.

Gardner, Jane F. 2011. "Slavery and Roman Law." In *The Cambridge World History of Slavery* 1, edited by Keith Bradley and Paul Cartledge, 414–37. Cambridge: Cambridge University Press.

Gellrich, Michelle. 1994. "Socratic Magic: Enchantment, Irony, and Persuasion in Plato's Dialogues." *CW* 87: 275–307.

Gibson, Roy K. 2007. *Excess and Restraint: Propertius, Horace, and Ovid's Ars Amatoria*. London: Institute of Classical Studies.

Gigante, Marcello. 1993. "Quel che Aristippo non aveva detto." *PP* 48: 267–80.

———. 1995. *Philodemus in Italy: the Books from Herculaneum*. Translated by Dirk Obbink. Ann Arbor: University of Michigan Press.

Gigon, Olof. 1977. *Die antike Philosophie als Maßstab und Realität*. Zürich: Artemis Verlag.

Glad, Clarence E. 1995. *Paul and Philodemus: Adaptability in Epicurean and Early Christian Psychagogy*. Leiden: Brill.

———. 1996. "Frank Speech, Flattery, and Friendship in Philodemus." In *Friendship, Flattery, and Frankness of Speech: Studies on Friendship in the New Testament World*, edited by John T. Fitzgerald, 22–59. Leiden: Brill.

Goar, R.J. 1972/3. "Horace and the Betrayal of Philosophy: *Odes* 1.29." *CJ* 68: 116–18.

Gold, Barbara K. 1987. *Literary Patronage in Greece and Rome*. Chapel Hill: University of North Carolina Press.

———. 2012. "Patronage and the Elegists: Social Reality or Literary Construction." In *A Companion to Roman Love Elegy* (Blackwell Companions to the Ancient World), edited by Barbara K. Gold, 303–17. Chichester: Wiley-Blackwell.

Gow, Andrew S.F. and Denys L. Page. 1965. *The Greek Anthology*. Cambridge: Cambridge University Press.

Gowers, Emily. 2003. "Fragments of Autobiography in Horace *Satires* 1." *ClAnt* 22: 55–91.

———. 2012. *Horace: Satires Book I*. Cambridge: Cambridge University Press.

Graham, Daniel W. 2010. *The Texts of Early Greek Philosophy: The Complete Fragments and Selected Testimonies of the Major Presocratics*. Part 1. Cambridge: Cambridge University Press.

Graver, Margaret. 2002a. *Cicero on the Emotions: Tusculan Disputations 3 and 4*. Chicago: University of Chicago Press.

———. 2002b. "Managing Mental Pain: Epicurus vs. Aristippus on the Pre-Rehearsal of Future Ills." *Proceedings of the Boston Area Colloquium in Ancient Philosophy* 5: 155–77.

Gregory, Justina. 1991. "Cicero and Plato on Democracy: A Translation and its Source." *Latomus* 50: 639–44.

Griffin, Miriam. 1986a. "Philosophy, Cato, and Roman Suicide: I." *G&R* 33: 64–77.

———. 1986b. "Philosophy, Cato, and Roman Suicide: II." *G&R* 33: 192–202.

Grisé, Yolande. 1982. *Le Suicide dans la Rome Antique*. Montreal: Bellarmin.

Gruen, Erich S. 2005. "Augustus and the Making of the Principate." In *The Cambridge Companion to the Age of Augustus*, edited by Karl Galinsky, 33–51. Cambridge: Cambridge University Press.

Gunning, J.H. 1942. "Der siebente Brief des Horaz und sein Verhaltnis zu Maecenas." *Mnemosyne* 10: 303–20.

Günther, Hans-Christian. 2013. "Horace's Life and Work." In *Brill's Companion to Horace*, edited by Hans-Christian Günther, 1–62. Leiden: Brill.

Gurval, Robert A. 1995. *Actium and Augustus: The Politics and Emotions of Civil War*. Ann Arbor: University of Michigan Press.

Haight, Elizabeth H. 1948. "*Epistula item quaevis non magna poema est*: A Fresh Approach to Horace's First Book of Epistles." *Studies in Philology* 45: 525–40.

Hammond, Mason. 1963. "*Res Olim Dissociabiles*: *Principatus ac Libertas*: Liberty under the Early Roman Empire." *HSCP* 67: 93–113.

Hardie, Philip. 2008. "Horace's Sublime Yearnings: Lucretian Ironies." *PLLS* 13: 119–72.

———. 2009. *Lucretian Receptions: History, the Sublime, Knowledge*. Cambridge: Cambridge University Press.

Harrison, Stephen J. 1988. "Deflating the Odes: Horace, *Epistles* 1.20." *CQ* 38: 473–76.

———. 1992. "Fuscus the Stoic: Horace *Odes* 1.22 and *Epistles* 1.10. *CQ* 42: 543–47.

———. 1995a. "Poetry, Philosophy, and Letter-Writing in Horace, *Epistles* I." In *Ethics and Rhetoric*, edited by Doreen Innes, Harry Hine, and Christopher Pelling, 47–61. Oxford: Oxford University Press.

———. 1995b. "Some Twentieth-century Views of Horace." In *Homage to Horace: A Bimillenary Celebration*, edited by Stephen Harrison, 1–16. Oxford: Oxford University Press.

———. 1995c. "Horace, Pindar, Iullus Antonius, and Augustus: *Odes* 4.2." In *Homage to Horace: A Bimillenary Celebration*, edited by Stephen Harrison, 108–27. Oxford: Oxford University Press.

———. 2007. "Town and Country." In *The Cambridge Companion to Horace*, edited by Stephen Harrison, 235–47. Cambridge: Cambridge University Press.

Hawkee, Debra. 2004. *Bodily Arts: Rhetoric and Athletics in Ancient Greece*. Austin: University of Texas Press.

Hayward, Thomas A. 1986. "On Measuring a Horatian Epistle (*Epist.* 1.7)." *CW* 80: 15–23.

Heinze, R., see Kiessling.

Highet, Gilbert. 1973. "*Libertino Patre Natus*." *AJP* 94: 268–81.

Hill, Timothy. 2004. *Ambitiosa Mors: Suicide and Self in Roman Thought and Literature*. London: Routledge.

Hiltbrunner, Otto. 1960. "Volteius Mena: Interpretationen zu Horace *Epist.* 1.7." *Gymnasium* 67: 289–320.

Holford-Strevens, Leofranc. 2006. "Sirens in Antiquity and the Middle Ages." In *Music of the Sirens*, edited by Linda Phyllis Austern and Inna Naroditskaya, 16–51. Bloomington: Indiana University Press.

Holloway, Paul A. 2002. "*Nihil Inopinati Accidisse*—'Nothing Unexpected Has Happened': A Cyrenaic Consolatory *Topos* in 1 Pet 4.12ff." *NTS* 48: 433–48.

Holtzberg, Niklas. 2002. *The Ancient Fable*. Bloomington: Indiana University Press.

van Hooff, Anton J.L. 1990. *From Autothanasia to Suicide: Self-Killing in Classical Antiquity*. London: Routledge.

Hopkins, Keith. 1983. *Death and Renewal*. Sociological Studies in Roman History 2. Cambridge: Cambridge University Press.

Horsfall, Nicholas. 1993. *La villa Sabina di Orazio: il galateo della gratitudine: Una rilettura della settima epistola del libro primo*. Venosa: Osanna Venosa.

Hubbard, Margaret. 1995. "*Pindarici Fontis Qui Non Expalluit Haustus*: Horace, *Epistles* 1.3." In *Homage to Horace: A Bimillenary Celebration*, 219–27. Oxford: Oxford University Press.

Hunter, Richard L. 1985. "Horace on Friendship and Free Speech (*Epistles* 1.18 and *Satires* 1.4). *Hermes* 118: 180–90.

Janko, Richard. 2000. *Philodemus: On Poems Book One*. Oxford: Oxford University Press.

Johnson, David M. 2009. "Aristippus at the Crossroads: The Politics of Pleasure in Xenophon's *Memorabilia*." *Polis* 26: 204–22.

Johnson, Timothy. 2004. *Symposion of Praise: Horace Returns to Lyric in Odes IV*. Madison: University of Wisconsin Press.

———. 2012. *Horace's Iambic Criticism*. Leiden: Brill.

Johnson, W.R. 1993. *Horace and the Dialectic of Freedom*. Ithaca: Cornell University Press.

———. 2004. "A Secret Garden: *Georgics* 4.116–148." In *Vergil, Philodemus, and the Augustans*, edited by David Armstrong, Jeffrey Fish, Patricia A. Johnston, and Marilyn B. Skinner, 75–83. Austin: University of Texas Press.

———. 2010. "The Epistles." In *A Companion to Horace* (Blackwell Companions to the Ancient World), edited by Gregson Davis, 319–33. Chichester: Wiley-Blackwell.

Johnston, Patricia A. 2006. "Turnus, Horses, and *Libertas*." *Vergilius* 52: 20–31.

Katz, Joshua T. 2008. "*Dux Reget Examen* (*Epistle* 1.19.23): Horace's Archilochian Signature." *MD* 59: 207–13.

Keane, Catherine. 2006. *Figuring Genre in Roman Satire*. Oxford: Oxford University Press.

———. 2011. "Lessons in Reading: Horace on Homer at *Epistles* 1.2.1–31." *CW* 104: 427–50.

Kelley, Donald R. 2001. "Eclecticism and the History of Ideas." *JHI* 62: 577–92.

Kemp, Jerome. 2010a. "Flattery and Frankness in Horace and Philodemus. *G&R* 57: 65–76.

———. 2010b. "A Moral Purpose, A Literary Game: Horace, *Satires* 1.4." *CW* 104: 59–76.

Kennedy, Duncan F. 1992. "'Augustan' and 'Anti-Augustan': Reflections on Terms of Reference." In *Roman Poetry and Propaganda in the Age of Augustus*, edited by Anton Powell, 26–58. Bristol: Bristol Classical Press.

Kenney, E.J. 1977. "A Question of Taste: Horace, *Epistles* 1.14.6–9." *ICS* 2: 229–39.

Kiernan, V.G. 1999. *Horace: Poetics and Politics*. New York: St. Martin's Press.

Kiessling, Adolf and Richard Heinze. 1957. *Horaz, Briefe*. 5th Edition. Berlin: Weidmannsche Verlagsbuchhandlung.

Kilpatrick, Ross S. 1973a. "Fact and Fable in Horace, *Epistles* 1.7." *CP* 68: 47–53.

———. 1973b. "Mentioned in Despatches: Hor. *Epist.* 1.13." *Humanities Association Review* 24: 294–9.

———. 1975. "Horace on his Critics: *Epist.* 1.19." *Phoenix* 29: 117–27.

———. 1986. *The Poetry of Friendship: Horace, Epistles I*. Edmonton: University of Alberta Press.

Kinneavy, James L. 2002. "*Kairos* in Classical and Modern Rhetorical Theory." In *Rhetoric and* Kairos: *Essays in History, Theory, and Praxis*, edited by Phillip Sipiora and James S. Baumlin, 58–76. Albany: State University of New York Press.

Kinney, Daniel. 1996. "Heirs of the Dog: Cynic Selfhood in Medieval and Renaissance Culture." In *The Cynics*, edited by R. Bracht Branham and Marie-Odile Goulet-Cazé, 294–328. Berkeley: University of California Press.

Knox, Peter. 1985. "Wine, Water, and Callimachean Polemics." *HSCP* 89: 107–19.

Köhnken, Adolf. 1981. "Apollo's Retort to Envy's Criticism." *AJP* 102: 411–22.

Konstan, David, Diskin Clay, Clarence E. Glad, Johan C. Thom, and James Ware, eds. 1998. *Philodemus: On Frank Criticism*. Atlanta: Scholars Press.

Konstan, David. 1996. "Friendship, Frankness, and Flattery." In *Friendship, Flattery, and Frankness of Speech: Studies on Friendship in the New Testament World*, edited by John T. Fitzgerald, 7–19. Leiden: Brill.

———. 1997. *Friendship in the Classical World*. Cambridge: Cambridge University Press.

Krebs, Christopher. 2002. "Das Problem der *amicitia* in der 18. Epistel des Horaz. *Hermes* 130: 81–99.

Kyle, Donald G. 1998. *Spectacles of Death in Ancient Rome*. London: Routledge.

Lampe, Kurt. 2015. *The Birth of Hedonism: The Cyrenaic Philosophers and Pleasure as a Way of Life*. Princeton: Princeton University Press.

Larmour, David H.J. 2010–11. "Tracing Furrows in the Satiric Dust: Echoes of Horace's *Epistles* in Juvenal 1." *Iowa Classical Studies* 35–6: 155–73.

Lathière, Anne-Marie. 1997. "*Nunc itaque et versus et cetera ludicra pono*: Horace poète des Épîtres." *REL* 75: 141–54.

Leach, Eleanor W. 1993. "Horace's Sabine Topography in Lyric and Hexameter Verse." *AJP* 114: 271–302.

Lee-Stecum, Parshia. 2009. "Persona and Power in Horace's First Book of *Epistles. Antichthon* 43: 12–33.

Leen, Anne. 2000–2001. "*Clodia Oppugnatrix*: The *Domus* Motif in Cicero's *Pro Caelio*." *CJ* 96: 121–62.

Liebeschuetz, W. 1966. "The Theme of Liberty in the *Agricola* of Tacitus." *CQ* 16: 126–39.

Lind, Levi R. 1986. "The Idea of the Republic and the Foundations of Roman Political Liberty." In *Studies in Latin Literature and Roman History* 4, edited by Carl Deroux, 44–108. Brussels: Latomus.

Long, A.A. 1988. "Socrates in Hellenistic Philosophy." *CQ* 38: 150–71.

———. 1992. "Stoic Readings of Homer." In *Homer's Ancient Readers*, edited by Robert Lamberton and John J. Keaney, 41–66. Princeton: Princeton University Press.

———. 2006. *From Epicurus to Epictetus: Studies in Hellenistic and Roman Philosophy*. Oxford: Oxford University Press.

Long, George and Arthur J. Macleane. 1874. *Quinti Horatii Flacci Opera Omnia*. London: Whittaker and Co.

Lowrie, Michèle. 1994. "Lyric's *Elegos* and the Aristotelian Mean: Horace, *C.* 1.24, 1.33, and 2.9." *CW* 87: 377–94.

———. 2007. "Horace and Augustus." In *The Cambridge Companion to Horace*, edited by Stephen Harrison, 77–89. Cambridge: Cambridge University Press.

———. 2010. *Writing, Performance, and Authority in Augustan Rome*. Oxford: Oxford University Press.

Luria, Solomon. 1970. *Democritea*. Leningrad: Soviet Academy of Sciences.

Lyne, R.O.A.M. 1995. *Horace: Behind the Public Poetry*. New Haven: Yale University Press.

Macleod, Colin. 1976. "Callimachus, Virgil, Propertius, and Lollius. *ZPE* 23: 41–3.

———. 1977. "The Poet, the Critic, and the Moralist: Horace, *Epistles* 1.19." *CQ* 27: 359–76.

———. 1979. "The Poetry of Ethics: Horace, *Epistles* I." *JRS* 69: 16–27.

———. 1986. *The Epistles: Translated into English Verse with Brief Introductions and Notes*. Rome: Edizioni dell'Ateneo.

Maguinness, W.S. 1938. "The Eclecticism of Horace." *Hermathena* 52: 27–46.

Mangoni, Cecilia. 1993. *Filodemo, Il Quinto Libro della Poetica*. Naples: Bibliopolis.

Mann, Wolfgang-Rainer. 1996. "The Life of Aristippus." *Archiv für Geschichte der Philosophie* 78: 97–119.

Mannebach, Erich. 1961. *Aristippi et Cyrenaicorum Fragmenta*. Leiden: Brill.

Marchesi, Ilaria. 2005. "Traces of a Freed Language: Horace, Petronius, and the Rhetoric of Fable." *CA* 24: 307–30.

Marcucci, Silvia. 1993. "Ac ne forte roges quo me duce, quo lare tuter (Hor. *epist.* I 1,13)" *Maia* 45: 147–60.

Markus, Donka. 2000. "Performing the Book: The Recital of Epic in First-Century C.E. Rome." *CA* 19: 138–79.

Maurach, Gregor. 1968. "Der Grundriss von Horazens erstem Epistelbuch." *AClass* 11: 73–124.

Mayer, Roland. 1985. "Horace on Good Manners." *PCPS* 31: 33–46.

———. 1986. "Horace *Epistles* I and Philosophy." *AJP* 107: 55–73.

———. 1994. *Horace, Epistles Book I*. Cambridge: Cambridge University Press.

———. 1995. "Horace's Moyen de Parvenir." In *Homage to Horace: A Bimillenary Celebration*, edited by Stephen Harrison, 279–95. Oxford: Oxford University Press.

McGann, Michael J. 1960. "The Sixteenth Epistle of Horace." *CQ* 10: 205–12.

———. 1963. "Vinnius Valens, Son of Vinnius Asina?" *CQ* 13: 258–59.

———. 1969. *Studies in Horace's First Book of Epistles*. Brussels: Latomus.

Mellor, Ronald. 1993. *Tacitus*. New York: Routledge.

Moles, John. 1985. "Cynicism in Horace *Epistles* I." *PLLS* 5: 34–39.

———. 1995. Review of Roland Mayer (1994). *Bryn Mawr Classical Review* 95.02.37.

———. 2002. "Poetry, Philosophy, Politics and Play: *Epistles* I." In *Traditions and Contexts in the Poetry of Horace*, edited by Tony Woodman and Dennis Feeney, 141–57. Cambridge: Cambridge University Press.

———. 2007. "Philosophy and Ethics." In *The Cambridge Companion to Horace*, edited by Stephen Harrison, 165–81. Cambridge: Cambridge University Press.

Montiglio, Silvia. 2006. "Should the Aspiring Wise Man Travel? A Conflict in Seneca's Thought." *AJP* 127: 553–86.

———. 2011. *From Hero to Villain: Odysseus in Ancient Thought*. Ann Arbor: University of Michigan Press.

Morford, Mark. 1991. "How Tacitus Defined Liberty." *ANRW* 2.33.5: 3420–50.

Morgan, Gareth. 1994. "Horace's Two Patrons." *LCM* 19: 139–45.

Morrison, Andrew D. 2006. "Advice and Abuse: Horace, *Epistles* 1 and the Iambic Tradition." *MD* 56: 29–61.

———. 2007. "Didacticism and Epistolarity in Horace's *Epistles* 1." In *Ancient Letters: Classical and Late Antique Epistolography*, edited by Ruth Morello and Andrew D. Morrison, 107–31. Oxford: Oxford University Press.

Mouritsen, Henrik. 2005. "Freedmen and Decurions: Epitaphs and Social History in Imperial Italy." *JRS* 95: 38–63.

———. 2011. *The Freedman in the Roman World*. Cambridge: Cambridge University Press.

Muecke, Frances. 1979. "Horace the Satirist: Form and Method in *Satires* 1.4." *Prudentia* 11: 55–68.

———. 1993. *Horace: Satires II*. Warminster: Aris and Phillips.

Murray, Penelope. 1996. *Plato on Poetry: Ion; Republic* 376e–398b9; *Republic* 595–608b10. Cambridge: Cambridge University Press.

Musurillo, Herbert. 1974. "A Formula for Happiness: Horace *Epist*. 1.6 to Numicius." *CW* 67: 193–204.

Nadjo, Léon. 2002. "La Fable dans le Livre I des Épîtres d'Horace." In *Epistulae Antiquae II*, edited by Léon Nadjo and Élisabeth Gavoille, 135–48. Leuven: Peeters.

Newman, Robert J. 1989. "*Cotidie Meditare*: Theory and Practice of the *Meditatio* in Imperial Stoicism." *ANRW* 2.36.3: 1473–1517.

Nickel, Rainer. 1980. "Xenophon und Horaz." *Gymnasium* 87: 145–50.

Nicolet, Claude. 1980. *The World of the Citizen in Republican Rome*. Translated by P.S. Falla. Berkeley: University of California Press.

Nightingale, Andrea W. 1992. "Plato's *Gorgias* and Euripides' *Antiope*: A Study in Generic Transformation." *ClAnt* 11: 121–41.

Nisbet, Robin G.M. 1959. "Notes on Horace, *Epistles* 1." *CQ* 9: 73–76.

———. 1961. *Cicero, in L. Calpurnium Pisonem Oratio*. Oxford: Oxford University Press.

———. 2007. "Horace: Life and Chronology." In *The Cambridge Companion to Horace*, edited by Stephen Harrison, 7–21. Cambridge: Cambridge University Press.

Nisbet, Robin G.M. and Margaret Hubbard. 1970. *A Commentary on Horace, Odes, Book I*. Oxford: Oxford University Press.

———. 1978. *A Commentary on Horace, Odes, Book II*. Oxford: Oxford University Press.

Nisbet, Robin G.M. and Niall Rudd. 2004. *A Commentary on Horace, Odes, Book III*. Oxford: Oxford University Press.

Noonan, J.D. 2003. "Re-valuing Values at the End of the *Aeneid*: *Dignitas, Libertas*, and *Maiestas*. *CB* 79: 33–45.

Oakley, Stephen P. 2009. "*Res Olim Dissociabiles*: Emperors, Senators, and Liberty." In *The Cambridge Companion to Tacitus*, edited by A.J. Woodman, 184–94. Cambridge: Cambridge University Press.

Oberhelman, Steven and David Armstrong. 1995. "Satire as Poetry and the Impossibility of Metathesis in Horace's *Satires*." In *Philodemus and Poetry*, edited by Dirk Obbink, 233–54. Oxford: Oxford University Press.

Oliensis, Ellen. 1995. "Life after Publication: Horace, *Epistles* 1.20." *Arethusa* 28: 209–24.

———. 1997. "*Ut Arte Emendaturus Fortunam*: Horace, Nasidienus, and the Art of Satire." In *The Roman Cultural Revolution*, edited by Thomas Habinek and Alessandro Schiesaro, 90–104. Cambridge: Cambridge University Press.

———. 1998. *Horace and the Rhetoric of Authority*. Cambridge: Cambridge University Press.

O'Neill, Jeanne Neumann. 1999. "Florus and the *Commendatio ad Gloriam*." *Phoenix* 53: 80–96.

Ooteghem, J. Van 1946. "Horace et l'indépendance." *Latomus* 5: 185–88.

O'Sullivan, Timothy M. 2011. *Walking in Roman Culture*. Cambridge: Cambridge University Press.

Otis, Brooks. 1945. "Horace and the Elegists." *TAPA* 76: 177–90.

Pasquali, Giorgio. 1920. *Orazio lirico*. Florence: Le Monnier. Reprinted 1966.

Patterson, Orlando. 1991. *Freedom in the Making of Western Culture*. New York: Basic Books.

Pearcy, Lee T. 1994. "The Personification of the Text and Augustan Poetics in *Epistles* 1.20." *CW* 87: 457–64.

Peponi, Anastasia-Erasmia. 2002. "Fantasizing Lyric: Horace, *Epistles* 1.19." In *Horace and Greek Lyric Poetry*, edited by Michael Paschalis, 19–45. Rethymnon: The University of Crete.

Percival, John. 1980. "Tacitus and the Principate." *G&R* 27: 119–33.

Perret, Jacques. 1964. *Horace*. Translated by Bertha Humez. New York: New York University Press.

Peterson, R.G. 1968. "The Unity of Horace, *Epistle* 1.7." *CJ* 63: 309–14.

Plass, Paul. 1995. *The Game of Death in Ancient Rome*. Madison: University of Wisconsin Press.

Poliakoff, Michael. 1980. "Nectar, Springs, and the Sea: Critical Terminology in Pindar and Callimachus." *ZPE* 39: 41–47.

Porter, David H. 2002. "Playing the Game: Horace *Epistles* 1." *CW* 96: 21–60.

Porter, James. 1995. "Content and Form in Philodemus: The History of an Evasion." In *Philodemus and Poetry*, edited by Dirk Obbink, 97–147. Oxford: Oxford University Press.

Porter Packer, M.N. 1941. "The Consistent Epicureanism of the First Book of the *Epistles* of Horace." *TAPA* 72: xxxix–xl.

Postgate, J.P. 1903. *Selections from Tibullus and Others*. London: Macmillan and Co.

———. 1912. "Albius and Tibullus." *AJP* 33: 450–55.

de Pretis, Anna. 2002. '*Epistolarity*' *in the First Book of Horace's Epistles*. Piscataway: Gorgias Press.

Procopé, John. 1998. "Epicureans on Anger." In *The Emotions in Hellenistic Philosophy*, edited by Juha Sihvola and Troels Engberg-Pedersen, 171–96. Dordrecht: Kluwer Academic Publishers.

Putnam, Michael C.J. 1969. "Horace c. 1.20." *CJ* 64: 153–57.

———. 1972. "Horace and Tibullus." *CP* 67: 81–88.

———. 1986. *Artifices of Eternity: Horace's Fourth Book of Odes*. Ithaca: Cornell University Press.

———. 1995. "From Lyric to Letter: Iccius in Horace *Odes* 1.29 and *Epistles* 1.12." *Arethusa* 28: 193–207.

———. 2003. "Horace *epi.* 1.13: Compliments to Augustus." In *Gestures: Essays in Ancient History, Literature, and Philosophy Presented to Alan L. Boegehold*, edited by Geoffrey W. Bakewell and James P. Sickinger, 100–12. Oxford: Oxford University Press.

———. 2006. "Horace to Torquatus: *Epistle* 1.5 and *Ode* 4.7." *AJP* 127: 387–413.

Race, William H. 1978. "*Odes* 1.20: An Horatian *Recusatio*." *California Studies in Classical Antiquity* 11: 179–96.

———. 2010. "Horace's Debt to Pindar." In *A Companion to Horace* (Blackwell Companions to the Ancient World), edited by Gregson Davis, 147–73. Chichester: Wiley-Blackwell.

Ramsby, Teresa. 2012. "'Reading' the Freed Slave in the *Cena Trimalchionis*." In *Free at Last! The Impact of Freed Slaves on the Roman Empire*, edited by Sinclair Bell and Teresa Ramsby, 66–87. London: Bloomsbury.

Reckford, Kenneth. 1959. "Horace and Maecenas." *TAPA* 90: 195–208.

———. 1969. *Horace*. New York: Twayne Publishers.

———. 1997. "Horatius: The Man and the Hour." *AJP* 118: 583–612.

———. 2002. "*Pueri ludentes*: Some Aspects of Play and Seriousness in Horace's *Epistles*." *TAPA* 132: 1–19.

Reinhold, M. and P.M. Swan. 1990. "Cassius Dio's Assessment of Augustus." In *Between Republic and Empire: Interpretations of Augustus and His Principate*, edited by Kurt A. Raaflaub and Mark Toher, 155–73. Berkeley: University of California Press.

Reydams-Schils, Gretchen. 2005. *The Roman Stoics: Self, Responsibility, and Affection*. Chicago: University of Chicago Press.

Ribbeck, Otto. 1884. *Kolax: Eine Ethologische Studie*. Leipzig: Teubner.

Riikonen, H. 1977. "City and Country in Horace's *Epistle* 1.7." *Arctos* 11: 87–101.

Rohdich, H. 1972. "Die 18. Epistel des Horaz." *RhM* 115: 261–88.

Roller, Matthew B. 2001. *Constructing Autocracy*. Princeton: Princeton University Press.

de Romilly, Jacqueline. 1975. *Magic and Rhetoric in Ancient Greece*. Cambridge, MA: Harvard University Press.

Rosen, Ralph M. 2000. "Cratinus' *Pytine* and the Construction of the Comic Self." In *The Rivals of Aristophanes*, edited by David Harvey and John Wilkins, 23–40. Swansea: The Classical Press of Wales.

Rudd, Niall. 1966. *The Satires of Horace*. Cambridge: Cambridge University Press.

———. 1986. *Themes in Roman Satire*. Bristol: Bristol Classical Press.

———. 1989. *Epistles: Book II and Epistle to the Pisones (Ars Poetica)*. Cambridge: Cambridge University Press.

———. 1993. "Horace as a Moralist." In *Horace 2000: A Celebration*, edited by Niall Rudd, 64–88. Ann Arbor: University of Michigan Press.

Ruffell, Ian A. 2003. "Beyond Satire: Horace, Popular Invective and the Segregation of Literature." *JRS* 93: 35–65.

Russell, Donald A. and David Konstan. 2005. *Heraclitus: Homeric Problems*. Atlanta: Society of Biblical Literature.

Rutherford, Richard B. 1986. "The Philosophy of the *Odyssey*." *JHS* 106: 145–62.

Santirocco, Matthew. 1986. *Unity and Design in Horace's Odes*. Chapel Hill: University of North Carolina Press.

Schlegel, Catherine. 2005. *Satire and the Threat of Speech: Horace's Satires Book 1*. Madison: University of Wisconsin Press.

———. 2010. "Horace and the Satirist's Mask: Shadowboxing with Lucilius." In *A Companion to Horace* (Blackwell Companions to the Ancient World), edited by Gregson Davis, 253–270. Chichester: Wiley-Blackwell.

Sedley, David. 1997. "The Ethics of Brutus and Cassius." *JRS* 87: 41–53.

———. 1998. *Lucretius and the Transformation of Greek Wisdom*. Cambridge: Cambridge University Press.

Segal, Charles. 1993. *Euripides and the Poetics of Sorrow*. Durham: Duke University Press.

Shackleton Bailey, David R. 1982. *Profile of Horace*. Cambridge, MA: Harvard University Press.

Shew, Melissa. 2013. "*The* Kairos *of Philosophy*." *The Journal of Speculative Philosophy* 27: 47–66.

Sider, David. 1995. "The Epicurean Philosopher as Hellenistic Poet." In *Philodemus and Poetry*, edited by Dirk Obbink, 42–57. Oxford: Oxford University Press.

———. 1997. *The Epigrams of Philodemus*. Oxford: Oxford University Press.

Skalitzky, Rachel. 1968. "Good Wine in a New Vase (Horace, *Epistles* 1.2)." *TAPA* 99: 443–52.

———. 1973. "Horace on Travel (*Epist.* 1.11)." *CJ* 68: 316–21.

Skidmore, Clive. 1996. *Practical Ethics for Roman Gentlemen: The Work of Valerius Maximus*. Exeter: University of Exeter Press.

Slings, Simon R. 1991. "The Quiet Life in Euripides' *Antiope*." In *Fragmenta Dramatica: Beiträge zur Interpretation der griechischen Tragikerfragmente und ihrer Wirkungsgeschichte*, edited by Heinz Hofmann and Annette Harder, 137–51. Göttingen: Vandenhoeck and Ruprecht.

Smith, Warren S., Jr. 1984. "Horace Directs a Carouse: *Epistle* 1.19." *TAPA* 114: 255–71.

Snell, Bruno. 1964. *Scenes From Greek Drama*. Berkeley: University of California Press.

Stanford, William B. 1954. *The Ulysses Theme: A Study in the Adaptability of a Traditional Hero*. Oxford: Oxford University Press.

Steiner, Grundy. 1976. "Diogenes' Mouse and the Royal Dog: Conformity in Nonconformity." *CJ* 72: 36–46.

Striker, Gisela. 2002. "Commentary on Graver." *Proceedings of the Boston Area Colloquium in Ancient Philosophy* 17: 178–82.

Syme, Ronald. 1939. *The Roman Revolution*. Oxford: Oxford University Press.

Taisne, Anne-Marie. 2002. "Lecture d'Homère dans l'Épître d'Horace à Lollius Maximus." In *Epistulae Antiquae II*, edited by Léon Nadjo and Élisabeth Gavoille, 149–59. Louvain: Peeters.

Taylor, C.C.W. 2010. *The Atomists: Leucippus and Democritus*. Toronto: University of Toronto Press.

Taylor, Lily Ross. 1961. "Freedmen and Freeborn in the Epitaphs of Imperial Rome." *AJP* 82: 113–32.

Theodorakopoulos, Elena. 2011. "Poem 68: Love and Death, and the Gifts of Venus and the Muses." In *A Companion to Catullus* (Blackwell Companions to the Ancient World), edited by Marilyn B. Skinner, 327–52. Chichester: Wiley-Blackwell.

Thomas, K.M. 1981. "Horace's *Epistularum Liber Primus*: A Structured Whole?" *CB* 57: 49–53.

Thomas, Richard F. 1982. *Lands and Peoples in Roman Poetry: The Ethnographic Tradition*. Cambridge: Cambridge Philological Society.

———. 2011. *Horace: Odes Book IV and Carmen Saeculare*. Cambridge: Cambridge University Press.

Thurmond, David L. 1998. "Horace, *Epistles* 1.7.24: the Ambiguity of *Amicitia*." *Latomus* 57: 842–45.

Traill, David A. 1998. "Callimachus' Singing Sea (*Hymn* 2.106)." *CP* 93: 215–22.

Traina, Alfonso. 1991. "Orazio e Aristippo. Le Epistole e l'arte di convivere." *RFIC* 119: 285–305.

———. 1994. "*In Aristippi praecepta relabor*." *Eikasmos* 5: 243–46.

———. 2009. "Horace and Aristippus: The *Epistles* and the Art of *Convivere*." In *Horace: Satires and Epistles* (Oxford Readings in Classical Studies), edited by Kirk Freudenburg, 287–307. (English translation of Traina 1991).

Trinacty, Christopher. 2012. "The Fox and the Bee: Horace's First Book of *Epistles*." *Arethusa* 45: 57–77.

Tsakiropoulou-Summers, Anastasia. 1998. "Horace, Philodemus and the Epicureans at Herculaneum." *Mnemosyne* 60: 20–29.

Tsouna, Voula. 1994. "The Socratic Origins of the Cynics and Cyrenaics." In *The Socratic Movement*, edited by Paul A. Vander Waerdt, 367–91. Ithaca: Cornell University Press.

———. 1998. *The Epistemology of the Cyrenaic School*. Cambridge: Cambridge University Press.

———. 2007. *The Ethics of Philodemus*. Oxford: Oxford University Press.

Ullman, B.L. 1912a. "Horace and Tibullus." *AJP* 33: 149–67.

———. 1912b. "Rejoinder to Mr. Postgate." *AJP* 33: 456–60.

Urstad, Kristian. 2008. "Aristippus and Freedom in Xenophon's *Memorabilia*." *Praxis* 1: 37–51.

Usener, Hermann. 1887. *Epicurea*. Leipzig: Teubner.

Verboven, Koenraad. 2012. "The Freedmen Economy of Roman Italy." In *Free at Last! The Impact of Freed Slaves on the Roman Empire*, edited by Sinclair Bell and Teresa Ramsby, 88–109. London: Bloomsbury.

Vioque, Guillermo G. 2002. *Martial, Book VII: A Commentary*. Translated by J.J. Zoltowski. Leiden: Brill.

Voit, Ludwig. 1975. "Das Sabinum im 16. Brief des Horaz." *Gymnasium* 82: 412–26.

Volk, Katharina. 2002. *The Poetics of Latin Didactic*. Oxford: Oxford University Press.

Von der Osten, Dorothee Elm. 2006. "The Cult of the Goddess *Libertas* in Rome and Its Reflection in Ovid's Poetry and Tibullan Love Elegy." *Vergilius* 52: 32–44.

Vorwerk, Matthias. 2001. "Plato on Virtue: Definitions of *Sophrosyne* in Plato's *Charmides* and in Plotinus *Enneads* 1.2 (19)." *AJP* 122: 29–47.

Waerdt, Paul A. Vander, ed. 1994. *The Socratic Movement*. Ithaca: Cornell University Press.

Wagenvoort, Hendrick. 1956. *Studies in Roman Literature, Culture, and Religion*. Leiden: Brill.

Wallace, Robert W. 2009. "Personal Freedom in Greek Democracies, Republican Rome, and Modern Liberal States." In *A Companion to Greek and Roman Political Thought*, edited by Ryan K. Balot, 164–77. Chichester: Wiley-Blackwell.

Wasyl, Anna Maria. 2003. "Poet's Freedom and Its Boundaries: Literary Patronage in the Eyes of Roman Authors of Late Republican and Augustan Period." In *Freedom and Its Limits in the Ancient World*, edited by Dariusz Brodka, Joanna Janik, and Slawomir Sprawski, 91–111. Krakow: Jagiellonian University Press.

Waszink, Jan Hendrik. 1974. *Biene und Honig als Symbol des Dichters und der Dichtung in der griechisch-römischen Antike*. Opladen: Westdeutscher Verlag.

Welch, Tara. 2008. "Horace's Journey Through Arcadia." *TAPA* 138: 47–74.

Welton, William A. 1996. "Incantation and Expectation in *Laws* II." *Philosophy and Rhetoric* 29: 211–24.

West, David. 1967. *Reading Horace*. Edinburgh: University Press.

———. 1995. *Horace Odes I: Carpe Diem*. Oxford: Oxford University Press.

White, Peter. 1978. "*Amicitia* and the Profession of Poetry in Early Imperial Rome." *JRS* 68: 74–92.

———. 1982. "Positions for Poets in Early Imperial Rome." In *Literary and Artistic Patronage in Ancient Rome*, edited by Barbara K. Gold, 50–66. Austin: University of Texas Press.

———. 1991. "Maecenas' Retirement." *CP* 86: 130–38.

———. 1993. *Promised Verse: Poets in the Society of Augustan Rome*. Cambridge, MA: Harvard University Press.

———. 2007. "Friendship, Patronage, and Horatian Socio-Poetics." In *The Cambridge Companion to Horace*, edited by Stephen Harrison, 195–206. Cambridge: Cambridge University Press.

Wickham, Edward C. 1891. *Horace II: The* Satires, Epistles, *and* De Arte Poetica. Oxford: Oxford University Press.

Wickham, Edward C., and H.W. Garrod, eds. 1912. *Q. Horati Flacci Opera*. Oxford: Oxford University Press.

Wilkins, Augustus S. 1888. *The Epistles of Horace*. London: Macmillan and Co.

Wilkins, John. 1993. "Social Status and Fish in Greece and Rome." In *Food, Culture, and History* I, edited by Gerald Mars and Valerie Mars, 191–203. London: London Food Seminar.

Williams, Frederick J. 1978. *Callimachus: Hymn to Apollo*. Oxford: Oxford University Press.

Williams, Gordon. 1968. *Tradition and Originality in Roman Poetry*. Oxford: Oxford University Press.

———. 1982. "Phases in Political Patronage of Literature in Rome." In *Literary and Artistic Patronage in Ancient Rome*, edited by Barbara K. Gold, 3–27. Austin: University of Texas Press.

———. 1990. "Did Maecenas 'Fall from Favor'? Augustan Literary Patronage." In *Between Republic and Empire: Interpretations of Augustus and His Principate*, edited by Kurt A. Raaflaub and Mark Toher, 258–75. Berkeley: University of California Press.

Wilson, John R. 1980. "*Kairos* as 'Due Measure.'" *Glotta* 58: 177–204.

Wimmel, Walter. 1960. *Kallimachos in Rom*. Wiesbaden: Franz Steiner.

———. 1969. "*Vir bonus et sapiens dignis ait esse paratus*. Zur horazischen Epistel 1.7." *WS* 82: 60–74.

Wirszubski, M.A. 1950. Libertas *as a Political Idea at Rome During the Late Republic and Early Principate*. Cambridge: Cambridge University Press. Reprinted 1968.

Wiseman, Timothy P. 1979. *Clio's Cosmetics: Three Studies in Greco-Roman Literature*. Leicester: Leicester University Press.

———. 1982. "*Pete nobiles amicos*: Poets and Patrons in Late Republican Rome." In *Literary and Artistic Patronage in Ancient Rome*, edited by Barbara K. Gold, 28–49. Austin: University of Texas Press.

Woodman, Anthony J. 1983a. "Horace, Epistles 1, 19, 23–40." *MH* 40: 75–81.

———. 1983b. "A Reading of Catullus 68a." *PCPS* 29: 100–6.

Wright, J.R.G. 1974. "Iccius' Change of Character: Horace, *Odes* 1.29." *Mnemosyne* 27: 44–52.

Zanker, Paul. 1975. "Grabreliefs römischer Freigelassener." *JDAI* 90: 267–315.

Zeller, Eduard. 1868. *Socrates and the Socratic Schools*. Translated by Oswald J. Reichel. London: Longmans, Green, and Co.

———. 1883. *A History of Eclecticism in Greek Philosophy*. Translated by S.F. Alleyne. London: Longmans, Green, and Co.

Zetzel, James E.G. 1980. "Horace's *Liber Sermonum*: The Structure of Ambiguity." *Arethusa* 13: 59–77.

———. 1982. "The Poetics of Patronage in the Late First Century B.C." In *Literary and Artistic Patronage in Ancient Rome*, edited by Barbara K. Gold, 87–102. Austin: University of Texas Press.

Zilioli, Ugo. 2012. *The Cyrenaics*. Durham: Acumen.

Index

Achilles, 76, 81–82, 286n50
admiratio. See *nil admirari*
aequus animus. See equanimity
Agamemnon, 75, 76, 81–82, 286n50, 292n42
Agricola, 16, 158–59
Albius, 93, 94–99, 105, 115, 121, 122, 255; as Horatian alter ego, 20, 123, 148, 150
Alcaeus, 229, 249–51, 282n77, 293n53
amicitia. See friendship; patronage
Amphion, 215–17, 237–38
Antenor, 82
Antonius Musa, 57, 198, 276n10
Archias of Thebes, 100–101
Archilochus, 229, 242, 246–51, 255
Aristippus: decorum of, 196, 197, 214, 297n43; in Diogenes Laertius, 22, 37, 172, 188, 194, 197, 286n54; as embodying key ethical principles in the *Epistles*, 17, 22, 82, 119, 189; in *Epistles* 1.1, 25, 34, 37, 40–42, 60–62; in *Epistles* 1.10, 170–71, 172; in *Epistles* 1.14, 184, 187–88; in *Epistles* 1.17, 190–204, 212, 214–15, 224; equanimity of, 60–62, 196–97, 204; as exemplum of moderate *libertas*, 40–42, 150, 169, 248; as exemplum of philosophical freedom/adaptability, 22, 37–38, 81, 106, 251; as exemplum of social freedom/adaptability, 40–42, 190–204; Horace as, 38, 59, 62, 171,

198–99, 200–201, 212, 272; and Lais, 37–38, 172, 191; and mastery of *res*, 37, 42, 61–62, 85, 118, 263; and *nil admirari*, 111–12, 113–15, 118, 166; and Odysseus, 82, 84–85, 286n50, 295n70; in Plutarch, 61; as poetic *persona*, 22; in Xenophon's *Memorabilia*, 22, 40–41, 125, 150, 248, 287n57. *See also* Index Locorum
Aristius Fuscus, 20, 162–73, 183, 305n42, 326n86
Aristotle, 170, 206, 295n71, 309n18, 318n63. *See also* Index Locorum
Augustus, 5, 15, 17–18, 104, 122–23, 224, 228, 272–73; amnesty of, 178; Horace as equal of, 248; and *libertas*, 4–18, 29; Lollius's service under, 217–18; Maecenas's possible fall from favor with, 279n59, 301n10; Maecenas as proxy for in the *Epistles*, 29, 155; as patron, 15, 217–18, 260; as Pentheus, 155–56; as potential audience, 162, 253–54, 257–63, 271; and Timagenes, 244–45
aurea mediocritas, 3, 41–42, 61–62, 112, 171

Bacchus, 153–54, 241
bailiff. See *vilicus*
beatitas: as aim of philosophy, 119; Iccius's misunderstanding of, 115–16; and *nil admirari*, 107, 113; as possession of the

beatitas (*continued*)
  vir bonus et sapiens in *Epistles* 1.16, 150,
    152–53, 156–57; produced by the
    countryside, 183
bees, 149, 230–33, 248, 321n20
boats. *See* nautical imagery
Bullatius, 20, 174–79, 255

Calabrian host, 130–32, 133, 134, 138, 140,
  145
Callimachus: poetic aesthetics of, 148,
  229, 231–33, 241, 247, 261, 265, 267–68,
  320n14; *recusatio* of, 29. *See also* Index
  Locorum
carpe diem, 97, 178, 231
Cassius of Parma, 95, 296n4
Cato Uticensis, 156, 244
Catullus, 49–50, 100, 288n11. *See also*
  Index Locorum
Celsus Albinovanus: in *Epistles* 1.3, 227,
  232–34, 279n54; in *Epistles* 1.8, 55–56,
  90–91, 184, 276n10, 330n44
cena. See food
Charmides, 69
Chrysippus, 48, 70, 72
Cicero, 96, 119–20, 196–97, 206; Epicure-
  anism in, 98, 100–102, 111; on flatterers,
  212, 315n34; on *libertas*, 6, 8, 9–10, 14,
  18, 83–84, 153; *nil admirari* in, 109–12;
  Stoicism in, 72, 83–84, 109–11, 152, 153,
  309n9. *See also* Index Locorum
Circe, 86–87
Crantor, 70, 71–72
Cratinus, 240–42, 246, 248
Cremutius Cordus, 16
Cynicism: of Avidienus, 103, 296n74; as
  dogs, 87, 209, 296n73; Epicurean
  withdrawal as preferable to, 193–94,
  205, 224; and the harsh friend of
  Epistles 1.18, 208–9, 224; of Horace,
  194, 208–9; inflexibility of, 196–97, 215;
  and Odysseus, 84–85, 87, 294n67; and
  parasitism, 195–96, 199, 202, 244,
  316n16; rejection of, 194–204, 208–9.
  See also Diogenes the Cynic
Cyrenaics, 22, 37, 108, 111–12, 197, 322n28,
  313n13

Daedalus, 229–31
Damasippus, 44–45, 48, 49, 52, 245, 295n71
Davus, 44, 45–49, 52, 56, 57, 153, 181, 195,
  308n3
decorum: of Aristippus, 192–93, 196–97,
  214; in gift-giving, 132, 135–36; in
  Horace's turn to philosophy, 36, 193
Democritus, 118–21, 282n77
dining. *See* food
Diogenes the Cynic, 191–204, 208–9, 215,
  233, 244, 282n82
Dionysus. *See* Bacchus
drinking, 77–81, 86–87, 90–91, 229, 232.
  See also liquid imagery; wine

ears: of Augustus, 261, 271; of Celsus,
  90–91; of future audience, 271; of
  Horace, 29, 68, 86; of Lollius, 86, 79;
  of Memmius, 68, 79; as motif, 271,
  330n44; of Odysseus, 86; of readers, 68,
  271; of suitors, 88–89
eclecticism, 32, 35, 90
elementa, 63–64, 269–70
Empedocles, 73, 118–19, 121
Ennius, 36–37, 73, 240–41, 242–43, 246.
  See also Index Locorum
Epicureanism: *ataraxia* of, 176, 193; in
  Cicero, 98, 100–102, 111; debates about
  Horace's allegiance to, 281n73, 291n19;
  in *Epistles* 1.4, 97–98; and friendship,
  98, 149–50, 175–76, 313n10; inflexibility
  of, 37; *lathe biosas* of, 37, 149–50, 193,
  175, 193, 205; Lucretius's orthodox allegiance to, 38, 71, 73, 81, 247; Odysseus's
  avoidance of, 87; on *praemeditatio
  mali futuri*, 111–12; as preferable to
  Cynicism, 193–94, 205, 224; role of in
  debate between poetry and philosophy,
  67, 70–81; and swine, 87–88, 97–98;
  Torquatus's avoidance of, 99–102, 106;
  Vergil's old man of Tarentum as, 149–
  50. *See also* Epicurus
Epicurus, 37, 38, 98, 111–12, 247. *See also*
  Epicureanism
equanimity (*aequus animus*): of Aristippus, 60–62, 196–97, 204; attained via
  moderation and adaptability, 43, 60–62,

109, 113, 204, 205; as ethical goal of the
Epistles, 42, 43, 66, 197, 273; Horace's
gradual realization of, 15, 99, 107, 182–
83, 223–25; and indifference to place,
127, 148, 157, 161–62, 174–80, 190; and
periodic withdrawal, 223–25
Euripides, 153–54, 215–17, 222, 290n2. *See
also* Index Locorum

fable, 309n17; ass and driver, 268; ass and
the lion's skin, 307n71; fox in the corn
bin, 132–35; frog and calf, 44–45, 245–
46; jackdaw and peacocks, 233–34; stag
and man, 167–69
flatterers (flattery): Horace as object of,
240, 243; Horace's avoidance of, 263;
imitation by, 211–15, 234; Mena as, 143;
as opposite of *mera libertas*, 206–15; in
Tacitus, 15–17
Florus, 24, 32, 226–39, 248, 254, 255
food: Horace's inconsistent attitude
toward, 56–59, 195, 198–99; as locus of
friendship, 105–6, 185, 194, 218; as mark
of moderation, 102–4; and satiety,
130–31
foresight, 109–12
frankness, 94–95, 206–10, 213
freedman: appearance of, 53, 207–9,
288n25, 315n36; Augustus's subjects as,
12–14; the epistolary *liber* as, 264, 266–
73; epitaphs of, 272, 331nn48–51;
Horace as, 14, 28, 35, 53, 164, 240, 260,
264, 266, 272; Horace as son of, 4, 15,
272, 276n7; and *libertas*, 12–15, 207–10;
as symbol of moderate freedom in the
Epistles, 14–15, 21
freedom. See *libertas*
friendship: in Epicureanism, 98, 149–50,
175–76, 313n10; in *Epistles* 1.3, 227, 234–
39; in *Epistles* 1.4, 94–99; in *Epistles* 1.5,
105–6; in *Epistles* 1.10, 163, 166–69, 173;
in *Epistles* 1.11, 175–77; in *Epistles* 1.12,
121–23; in *Epistles* 1.14, 182, 184–85, 189;
in *Epistles* 1.17, 190–204; in *Epistles* 1.18,
204–25; Horace's isolation from, 150,
161, 169, 173, 175–76, 182, 189; as major
theme, 12, 31, 93–94; and moderate

freedom, 21–23, 24, 190–225; in *Satires*
1.3, 54–55, 152. *See also* Maecenas;
patronage
fugitivus. *See* runaway slave
Fuscus. *See* Aristius Fuscus

gladiators and gladiatorial imagery: in
Epistles 1.1, 27–29, 32, 35, 46–47, 51, 53,
130, 135, 164, 210, 219, 239–40, 254, 266,
272; in *Epistles* 1.18, 33–34, 219, 262; in
Epistles 1.19, 240, 253–54; in *Satires* 2.7,
46–47
golden mean See *aurea mediocritas*
Grosphus. *See* Pompeius Grosphus

happiness. See *beatitas*
Homer/Homeric epics, 70–92, 136, 232,
240, 242–43, 246
hospes (*hospitium*), 35, 37, 40–42, 50, 176–
77, 179–80
hypocrisy. *See* inconsistency

Iarbitas, 244–45
Icarus, 229–31
Iccius, 93, 115–23, 255, 258
imitation: as mark of slavery, 22–23, 32,
45, 65, 69, 210, 240–46, 248; of philosophical models, 32, 38–39, 80–81, 84,
87, 91–92, 205, 210–11, 226, 248, 256; of
poetic models, 39, 87, 91–92, 205, 226–
55; of powerful *amici*, 45, 142–43, 145,
205, 210–25, 226, 243, 245
inconsistency: of Bullatius, 174–75; of
Horace, 43, 45–59, 127, 137, 161, 183–84,
198–99, 224; of Iccius, 117–18, 121; of the
vilicus, 181, 183, 189
insania, 44–45, 52, 105

Janus, 64–65, 211, 264–65, 269
jar, 77–80, 91

kairos, 170–71, 232

lathe biosas, 37, 149–50, 175, 193, 205
laughter: Albius's need for, 97–99; epistolary *liber* as object of, 268; of Horace,
63–64, 268; Horace as object of, 29,

laughter (*continued*)
52–54, 64, 188–89, 260, 268; Vinnius as
object of, 259–60, 268

Liber. *See* Bacchus

libertas: and Aristippus, 22, 37–38, 40–42,
81, 150, 169, 190–204, 248, 251; in
Cicero, 6, 8, 9–10, 14, 18, 83–84, 153;
and the country, 31, 125–26, 133–35, 143,
146–60, 161–89; definition of, 6,
277nn13–19; and epistolary poetry, 28,
32, 273; in the *Epodes*, 246–51; and
freedmen, 12–15; as free speech, 4,
14–17, 45, 206–10, 213, 240–49, 253; in
Livy, 10, 14, 208; as mastery, 18, 30–31,
41, 146–50, 159, 164, 167, 169, 172, 180,
279n57; *mera*, 4, 5, 8–10, 12, 14, 17, 206–
8, 210, 225, 229, 241–42, 248, 257; of
Odysseus, 85–90; in patronage, 166–69,
190–225, 248; and the *pax Augusta*,
11–12; and the philosophical approach
of Horace, 21–23, 25, 31–32, 34–40; as
poetic originality, 28, 32, 227–34, 240,
242–51; of poets over philosophers,
67–92; as Republican ideal, 6–7, 24,
35–37, 39, 158; in the *Satires*, 4–5, 241–
42; Stoic conception of, 35–37, 48–49,
83–84, 151–59; and suicide, 16, 155–56,
307n82; in Tacitus, 7–8, 15–17, 157–59;
as theme in the *Epistles*, 5, 275n2; in
transition from Republic to Empire,
4–18

licentia, 4, 6–11, 13–14, 208

liquid imagery, 71, 77–81, 90–91, 228–33.
See also drinking; wine

Livy, 10, 14, 99–100, 102, 208. *See also*
Index Locorum

locus amoenus, 139, 147, 165, 184

Lollius, 71; as addressee of *Epistles* 1.2,
71–92, 239, 255; as addressee of *Epistles*
1.18, 5, 33–34, 204–25, 237, 255, 262

Lucilius, 3, 4, 28, 241–42, 248–49. *See also*
Index Locorum

Lucretius, 68, 176; philosophical orthodoxy of, 38, 71, 73, 81, 247; use of poetry
by, 73, 81, 247; liquid and medicinal
imagery in, 71, 79–81. *See also* Index
Locorum

ludus: as gladiatorial combat, 27–28,
33–34, 253–55; Horace's renunciation
of, 26–28, 32, 50, 63–64, 114, 254;
Lollius's need for, 33–34, 215, 219–20;
Mena's enjoyment of, 141–43; and *nil
admirari*, 114, 186–87; as schoolroom,
65; the *vilicus*'s enjoyment of, 184–89

Maecenas: as benefactor of Sabine farm,
131, 133–37, 143, 147, 202, 224–25; in
Epistles 1.1, 26–29, 31, 32, 49–55, 98,
208–9; in *Epistles* 1.7, 56, 124–46, 167; in
Epistles 1.19, 239–40, 254–55, 262; fall
from imperial favor, 59, 301n10;
Horace's gradual reconciliation with,
41, 94, 123, 124–46, 168–69, 225, 239,
254–55; Horace's initial hostility
toward, 17, 26, 28–29, 32, 36, 51–55, 98,
123, 124, 208–9, 218, 225, 254–55; as
Horace's would-be master, 28–29, 31,
55, 65, 155, 186; in the *Odes*, 29, 77, 104;
as parallel to poetic and philosophical
models, 17, 18, 32; as poetic persona,
18–20, 126; as proxy for Augustus, 29,
155; in the *Satires*, 5, 43–49, 56–57, 128,
129, 140–43, 195, 202–3, 245

Maenius, 58–59, 198

magic, 67–70

manumission: Augustus's restoration of
the state as, 13–15; in the gladiatorial
metaphor of *Epistles* 1.1, 28, 48, 53,
164; and harsh speech, 207–10; the
publication of the *Epistles* as, 257, 263–
64, 266, 270

medical imagery, 68–70, 71, 77–81, 90–92,
237

Marcus Lepidus, 16, 158

Mena. *See* Volteius Mena

Menelaus, 135–36

meretrix. See prostitute (prostitution)

munditia, 87, 97, 103–4

nautical imagery: and moderation/
adaptability, 41–42, 60–62, 85, 171, 201,
212, 221; and Odysseus, 85; in the
philosophical approach of Horace, 37,
41–42, 176–77

Nestor, 75, 82
nil admirari: in *Epistles* 1.6, 93, 107–15, 123, 156–57, 180, 200; Horace's inconsistent adherence to, 127, 166–67, 184, 189; and Iccius, 115–16, 118, 120–21; and the *vilicus*, 184, 189
Numicius, 93, 107, 108, 255

obsequium, 8, 13–14, 16–17, 209–10, 212, 222, 225
Odysseus: and Aristippus, 82, 84–85, 286n50, 295n70; in *Epistles* 1.2, 75, 76, 81–82, 84–90; in Philodemus's *On the Good King*, 75
Ofellus, 103
Old Man of Tarentum, 149–50

Panaetius, 72, 116, 289n39, 281n73, 290n18
parasite (parasitism): Aristippus as, 195–96; Diogenes the Cynic as, 195–96, 199, 202, 244, 316n16; in *Epistles* 1.17, 191–92, 194–97, 199, 201–4; as flatterer, 212; Lollius's fear of becoming, 205–6; Maenius as, 58; Mena as, 141, 143
Paris, 82
patron: Augustus as, 15, 217–18, 260; client's imitation of, 45, 142–43, 145, 205, 210–25, 226, 243, 245; Horace as, 18, 240, 243, 246–47, 252, 255, 257. *See also* patronage
patronage: ambivalence of Horace toward, 20–21, 204–5, 220–21; analogy with master-slave relationship, 21, 29, 53; in *Epistles* 1.7, 124–46; in *Epistles* 1.10, 166–69; in *Epistles* 1.17, 15, 190–204; in *Epistles* 1.18, 5, 14, 33–34, 204–25; and free speech, 14–15, 206–10; as major theme, 20–21; and moderate freedom, 21, 205, 248, 262, 272. *See also* friendship; Maecenas; patron
pectus. *See* jar
Pentheus, 153–55
persona(e): the addressees as, 18–21; Horace as, 18–19, 23, 192, 280n63; Maecenas as, 18–20, 126
Phaeacians, 84, 87–89, 104
Philippus, 137–46

Philodemus, 71, 73, 74–76, 83, 187, 296
pilleus, 260, 278n26, 288n25, 315n36
Pindar, 220, 227–33, 236
Plato, 8–9, 30, 39, 68–70, 197, 216. *See also* Index Locorum
Plautus, 36. *See also* Index Locorum
play. *See* *ludus*
Plutarch, 60–61, 73, 156, 206–8. *See also* Index Locorum
Pompeius Grosphus, 121–22
populus: in the gladiatorial metaphor of *Epistles* 1.1, 27–28, 34, 219–20; Horace's disdain for, 27–28, 50–51, 114, 219–20, 251–52, 254–55, 261–63, 267; Horace's gradual courting of as audience, 251–52, 262–63, 263–64, 267–68, 271
prostitute (prostitution): Circe as, 86–87; parasite/beggar as, 202–4, 205–6, 213; publication as, 246, 251–52, 265–67; *vilicus*'s desire for, 184–85, 187–88
Pseudo-Acro, 125, 172, 296n4, 314n19. *See also* Index Locorum
publication, 27–28, 246, 252, 256–73, 283n4
Pythagoras, 57, 119, 121

Quinctius, 147, 150, 156

recusatio, 26, 29, 33
rudis, 28, 35, 47, 164
runaway slave, 47, 164, 166, 183, 266, 308n3

Sabine farm, 48, 95, 154–55; as antidote to urban anxieties, 138, 143; as gift from Maecenas, 131, 133–37, 143, 147, 202, 224–25; as *locus amoenus*, 139, 148; of Mena, 138, 143–44; as realm, 146–50; simple fare at, 57, 77; as source of anxiety, 138; as symbol of inner freedom, 157, 159; as symbol of moderate freedom, 125, 146; therapeutic aspects of, 147–48, 223; *vilicus*'s disdain for, 180–89
Sappho, 28, 229, 249–51
satiety, 117–21, 123, 130–31, 133–34, 140, 172
Scaeva, 191–204, 255, 312nn2–3

schoolroom imagery, 63–66, 71, 211, 268–70

scurra. *See* parasite (parasitism)

Seneca the Younger, 66, 156, 158, 177, 179–80, 244. *See also* Index Locorum

severitas, 20, 99–102, 104–6, 115, 222

sickness: countryside's ability to heal, 147–48, 223; of Horace, 49–55, 56, 126–27, 134, 139; of the reader, 67–70

Sirens, 86–87, 295n71

Socrates, 9, 122, 180; and Aristippus, 22, 40–41, 264, 287n57, 314n23; *daimonion* of, 30; as enchanter, 68–70; as font of philosophy, 39

spoudogeloion, 63

Stoicism: in Cicero, 72, 83–84, 109–11, 152, 153, 309n9; of Damasippus, 44–45, 48–49; of Davus, 45, 48–49; of Fuscus, 164–65; in Horace's philosophical vacillations, 35–37, 38, 39, 85; and *libertas*, 35–37, 48–49, 83–84, 151–59; of Panaetius, 72; paradoxes of, 54, 83–84, 151–53; and *praemeditatio mali futuri*, 109–12; pronounced presence of in *Epistles* 1.16, 146, 151–60; rigidity of, 35–37, 38; and suicide, 155–59; and *virtus*, 35–37, 85, 112, 118, 152

suitors (*Odyssey*), 84, 87–89, 98

symposium. *See* food

Tacitus, 7–8, 15–17, 156, 157–59. *See also* Index Locorum

Telemachus, 135–37

Terence, 212. *See also* Index Locorum

Theophrastus, 206

Timagenes, 244–45

Titius, 227–34

Torquatus, 20, 93, 99–107, 115, 122, 187, 222

Vala, 57

Veianius, 26, 28, 31, 37, 148

Vergil, 29, 73, 94, 141, 149, 230, 235, 238. *See also* Index Locorum

vilicus, 20, 180–89, 264, 265

Vinnius Asina, 21, 162, 257–63, 268, 327n1, 327n4

virtus: as extreme, 35–37, 112–13, 118, 152, 186–87, 200, 208; as mean, 190, 199–200; Odysseus as exemplar of, 85–86; reconfiguration of, 85–86, 190, 199–201; and Stoicism, 35–37, 85, 112, 118, 152

Volteius Mena, 137–46, 168, 215

Vortumnus, 264

vulgus. *See populus*

water, as symbol of poetic originality, 228–32, 240–41, 243, 250–51

wine: in *Epistles* 1.5, 102, 105; in *Epistles* 1.14, 184–85; the *Epistles* figured as, 70, 77–81, 90–92; extreme freedom figured as, 4, 5, 8–10, 12, 14, 17, 206–8, 210, 225, 229, 241–42, 248, 257; extreme slavery figured as, 210, 232, 243, 246, 250–51; inconsistency of Horace toward, 56–59; and poetic inspiration, 240–41, 243. *See also* drinking; liquid imagery

Zethus, 215–17, 237–38

Index Locorum

Aristippus (Mannebach)
    Fr. 67 (=Stobaeus 4 31d, 128): 170
Aristo of Chios
    SVF
        1.396: 61
Aristotle
    Nichomachean Ethics
        1104a8–10: 170–71
        1124b30–1125a2: 318n63
Augustus
    Res Gestae
        1: 11
Caesar
    De Bello Civili
        22.5: 278n25
Callimachus
    Aetia
        Fr. 1.21–30: 29, 247
    Epigrams
        28: 320n14, 329n23
    Hymn to Apollo
        105–12: 231
Cassius Dio
    56.43: 12
Cato
    De Agricultura
        157.16: 90–91
Catullus
    61.217–18: 100
    68a.10–18: 49–50, 288n11

Celsus
    De Medicina
        8.10.7: 323n40
Cicero
    Ad Atticum
        12.14.3: 96
        12.15: 96
    Catilinarians
        3.14: 277n23
    De Amicitia
        92–93: 212
    De Finibus
        1.33: 100
        1.65: 98
        2.22–23: 101
        5.86–87: 119–20
    De Officiis
        3.13: 309n9
    De Oratore
        2.17: 196
    De Re Publica
        1.66–69: 9–10
        2.43: 18
    Paradoxa Stoicorum
        20: 152
        33: 83–84
        40: 153
    Pro Flacco
        16: 10

Cicero (*continued*)
  Pro Plancio
    94: 10
  Tusculan Disputations
    3.28–32: 110–11
    4.14: 109
Cornelius Nepos
  Life of Pelopidas
    3.2–3: 101
Democritus
  Fr. D55 (Taylor) = 211 (Graham): 120
  Fr. D83 (Taylor) = 288 (Graham):
    120
  Fr. D147 (Taylor) = 261 (Graham):
    121
Diogenes Laertius
  1.21: 35
  2.36: 314n19
  2.66–67: 197
  2.68: 313n13
  2.69: 188
  2.75: 37, 172, 191, 286nn45–46
  2.82: 286n54
  2.102: 313n13
  6.8: 314n19
  6.30: 313n13
  8.77: 121
  10.6: 73
  10.13: 291n26
  10.120: 291n26
Ennius
  Tragedies (Warmington)
    Fr. 308–11: 36
Epictetus
  Fragments
    10: 293n55
    11: 295n70
Epicurus
  Fragments (Usener)
    442: 294n62
    490: 297n12
Euripides
  Bacchae
    491: 307n77
    492–98: 153–54
  Hippolytus
    478: 290n2

Gaius
  Institutiones
    1.5.1: 330n29
Gnomologium Vaticanum
    493: 314n23
Heraclitus
  Homeric Problems
    4.1: 291n24
Hesiod
  Works and Days
    405: 165, 309n9
    694: 171, 310n26
Homer
  Odyssey
    4.601–8: 135
    4.612–15: 136, 304n35
Horace
  Ars Poetica
    306–11: 38–39, 70, 74
    333–44: 74, 77, 78
    408–11: 324n52
    419–52: 94
  Epistles
    1.1: 17, 25–42, 46–47, 48, 49–55, 58,
      59, 60–65, 67–70, 85, 91–92,
      98–99, 106, 113–15, 139, 148, 151,
      155, 166, 170, 176–77, 180, 186, 188,
      193, 197, 200, 208–9, 211, 228, 233,
      239, 248, 251, 260–63, 268–69,
      313n17
    1.2: 70–92, 109, 200, 204, 306n61,
      317n52
    1.3: 226–39
    1.4: 88, 93–99, 296n73
    1.5: 20, 99–107
    1.6: 107–15, 116, 156–57, 166, 180, 183–
      84, 186–87, 200
    1.7: 56, 124–46, 147, 155, 165, 166, 167,
      168, 169, 186, 187
    1.8: 55–56, 90–91, 161
    1.9: 162
    1.10: 31, 161–73, 183, 184, 266, 287n58
    1.11: 148, 174–80, 181
    1.12: 115–23, 258
    1.13: 162, 256–63, 268
    1.14: 27, 154, 180–89, 223
    1.15: 56–59, 166, 198

1.16: 139, 146–60, 184

1.17: 190–204, 272, 295n70, 296n73, 313n17

1.18: 5, 13–14, 32–34, 47, 85–86, 89, 200, 203, 204–25, 237–38, 266

1.19: 45, 232, 239–55, 261, 262

1.20: 140, 200, 256–57, 263–73

2.1: 76, 78, 270, 282n4

2.2: 32, 62, 168–69, 170, 171, 200–201, 211, 212, 271, 302n19

Odes

1.1: 236, 283n13, 322n36

1.11: 97, 231

1.17: 150

1.20: 77

1.22: 162

1.29: 115–17

1.32: 282n3

1.33: 94–95

2.7: 187, 312n56

2.10: 3, 41–42, 112, 171, 310n25

2.16: 122

2.20: 263, 269, 330n32, 331n46

3.1: 169, 303n28

3.5: 35

3.24: 7

3.29: 104, 197–98, 239, 309n15, 311n44

3.30: 263, 269, 283n13, 320n10, 322n36, 328n15

4.2: 229–31, 236, 305n45

4.3: 251–52

4.7: 297n30

4.12: 187, 312n56

4.15: 7

Satires

1.1: 63–64, 88, 195, 270, 282n2, 294n64

1.2: 88, 206, 309n14

1.3: 54–55, 129–30, 152

1.4: 241, 248–49, 315n35

1.5.41–42: 94, 189, 202–3

1.6: 15, 44, 57, 65, 137, 138, 140–44, 195, 305n48

1.9: 162, 305n49, 309n11, 328n11

1.10: 94, 162, 252, 269, 282n3, 293n48, 326n86

2.2: 103–4, 296n74

2.3: 44–45, 48, 49, 245, 295n71

2.6: 57, 128, 131, 141, 142–43, 148, 169, 188, 195

2.7: 45–49, 56, 57, 153, 181, 195

Livy

4.29.6: 100

8.7.22: 99

22.60.5: 100

24.25.8: 10

26.22.9: 100

34.49.8: 10

34.56.8: 284n18

39.26.7–8: 14, 208

Lucilius

Fragments (Warmington)

1199–1200: 290n18

Lucretius

De Rerum Natura

1.117–26: 73

1.412–17: 79

1.732: 73

1.926–27: 247

1.936–50 (=4.11–25): 80–81

2.1–2: 176

3.3–6: 247

3.1060–79: 312n53

4.777–78: 73

6.17–26: 80

Martial

Epigrams

1.24.2: 318n64

11.2.1–2: 318n64

Ovid

Metamorphoses

8.203–9: 230–31

Petronius

Satyrica

71.12: 272

117: 284n18, 287n5

Philodemus

Epigrams

5 (Sider) = 18 (Gow and Page): 187

On Poems 5

Col. 32.17–19: 74, 292n35

On the Good King According to Homer

Col. 28.27–30: 75

Col. 43.16–19: 74, 292n38

Pindar
  Fragments (S-M)
    110: 220, 318n59
  Isthmian Odes
    7.18: 232
  Olympian Odes
    6.85–87: 320n12
  Pythian Odes
    9.76–79: 232, 321n27
    10.53–54: 232
Plato
  Apology
    31d2–32a3: 30
  Charmides
    157a: 69
  Meno
    80a: 290n6
  Republic
    8.560e5–564a3–4: 8–9
Plautus
  Casina
    87–88: 285n33
  Cistellaria
    197–202: 36
  Persa
    123–26: 313n16
  Poenulus
    522–23: 288
Pliny the Elder
  Natural History
    27.114: 91
Plutarch
  Cato Minor
    67.1–2: 156
  De Tranquilitate Animi
    466b–c: 60
    469c: 61
  *How the Young Man Should Study
      Poetry*
    15d: 291n25
  How to Tell a Flatterer from a Friend
    25 (66b–d): 206–7
  On the Fortune of Alexander
    330c: 314n23
Pollianus
  AP
    11.130: 320n14

Pseudo-Acro
  ad Hor. *Epist.* 1.4.3: 296n4
  ad Hor. *Epist.* 1.7: 125
  ad Hor. *Epist.* 1.10.49: 172
Publilius Syrus
  Sententiae
    48: 13
Quintilian
  10.1.109: 320n14
Seneca the Elder
  Controversiae
    1.5.22: 244
Seneca the Younger
  De Ira
    3.23.4–5: 244
  Epistles
    2.2: 177
    3.1: 287n5
    7.8: 66
    28: 179–80
Servius Auctus
  ad *Eclogues* 8.12: 323n40
Stobaeus
  3.13.44: 316n39
Tacitus
  Agricola
    2.3: 15
    9.3: 159
    42.3–4: 16–17, 158–59
  Annals
    1.1: 15
    1.2: 15–16
    1.7: 16
    4.20: 16, 158
    15.64: 158
  Dialogus
    40.2: 7–8
Terence
  Adelphoi
    976: 329n28
  Eunuch
    251–53: 212
Tertullian
  De Spectaculis
    22.2–4: 283n10
Vergil
  Eclogues

6.1–5: 29
7.7: 235
8.6–14: 235, 322n34
Georgics
3.164–65: 238–39
3.209–41: 238
4.128–29: 149

4.132: 149
4.144–46: 149
4.179: 230
Xenophon
Memorabilia
2.1.11–2.1.14: 40–41, 125, 264, 301n3
2.10.4–2.10.6: 122

Wisconsin Studies in Classics

PATRICIA A. ROSENMEYER, LAURA MCCLURE,
MARK STANSBURY-O'DONNELL, AND MATTHEW ROLLER
Series Editors

Romans and Barbarians: The Decline of the Western Empire
E. A. THOMPSON

A History of Education in Antiquity
H. I. MARROU
Translated from the French by George Lamb

Accountability in Athenian Government
JENNIFER TOLBERT ROBERTS

Festivals of Attica: An Archaeological Commentary
ERIKA SIMON

Roman Cities: "Les villes romaines" by Pierre Grimal
Edited and translated by G. MICHAEL WOLOCH

Ancient Greek Art and Iconography
Edited by WARREN G. MOON

Greek Footwear and the Dating of Sculpture
KATHERINE DOHAN MORROW

The Classical Epic Tradition
JOHN KEVIN NEWMAN

Ancient Anatolia: Aspects of Change and Cultural Development
Edited by JEANNY VORYS CANBY, EDITH PORADA,
BRUNILDE SISMONDO RIDGWAY, and TAMARA STECH

Euripides and the Tragic Tradition
ANN NORRIS MICHELINI

Wit and the Writing of History:
The Rhetoric of Historiography in Imperial Rome
PAUL PLASS

The Archaeology of the Olympics:
The Olympics and Other Festivals in Antiquity
Edited by WENDY J. RASCHKE

Tradition and Innovation in Late Antiquity
Edited by F. M. CLOVER and R. S. HUMPHREYS

The Hellenistic Aesthetic
BARBARA HUGHES FOWLER

Hellenistic Sculpture I: The Styles of ca. 331–200 B.C.
BRUNILDE SISMONDO RIDGWAY

Hellenistic Poetry: An Anthology
Selected and translated by BARBARA HUGHES FOWLER

Theocritus' Pastoral Analogies: The Formation of a Genre
KATHRYN J. GUTZWILLER

Rome and India: The Ancient Sea Trade
Edited by VIMALA BEGLEY and RICHARD DANIEL DE PUMA

Kallimachos: The Alexandrian Library and the Origins of Bibliography
RUDOLF BLUM
Translated by Hans H. Wellisch

Myth, Ethos, and Actuality: Official Art in Fifth Century B.C. Athens
DAVID CASTRIOTA

Archaic Greek Poetry: An Anthology
Selected and translated by BARBARA HUGHES FOWLER

Murlo and the Etruscans: Art and Society in Ancient Etruria
Edited by RICHARD DANIEL DE PUMA and JOCELYN PENNY SMALL

The Wedding in Ancient Athens
JOHN H. OAKLEY and REBECCA H. SINOS

The World of Roman Costume
Edited by JUDITH LYNN SEBESTA and LARISSA BONFANTE

Greek Heroine Cults
JENNIFER LARSON

Flinders Petrie: A Life in Archaeology
MARGARET S. DROWER

Polykleitos, the Doryphoros, and Tradition
Edited by WARREN G. MOON

The Game of Death in Ancient Rome: Arena Sport and Political Suicide
PAUL PLASS

Polygnotos and Vase Painting in Classical Athens
SUSAN B. MATHESON

Worshipping Athena: Panathenaia and Parthenon
Edited by JENIFER NEILS

Hellenistic Architectural Sculpture:
Figural Motifs in Western Anatolia and the Aegean Islands
PAMELA A. WEBB

Fourth-Century Styles in Greek Sculpture
BRUNILDE SISMONDO RIDGWAY

Ancient Goddesses: The Myths and the Evidence
Edited by LUCY GOODISON and CHRISTINE MORRIS

Displaced Persons: The Literature of Exile from Cicero to Boethius
JO-MARIE CLAASSEN

Hellenistic Sculpture II: The Styles of ca. 200–100 B.C.
BRUNILDE SISMONDO RIDGWAY

Personal Styles in Early Cycladic Sculpture
PAT GETZ-GENTLE

The Complete Poetry of Catullus
CATULLUS
Translated and with commentary by David Mulroy

Hellenistic Sculpture III: The Styles of ca. 100–31 B.C.
BRUNILDE SISMONDO RIDGWAY

The Iconography of Sculptured Statue Bases in the Archaic and Classical Periods
ANGELIKI KOSMOPOULOU

Discs of Splendor: The Relief Mirrors of the Etruscans
ALEXANDRA A. CARPINO

Mail and Female: Epistolary Narrative and Desire in Ovid's "Heroides"
SARA H. LINDHEIM

Modes of Viewing in Hellenistic Poetry and Art
GRAHAM ZANKER

Religion in Ancient Etruria
JEAN-RENÉ JANNOT
Translated by Jane K. Whitehead

A Symposion of Praise: Horace Returns to Lyric in "Odes" IV
TIMOTHY JOHNSON

Satire and the Threat of Speech: Horace's "Satires," Book 1
CATHERINE M. SCHLEGEL

Prostitutes and Courtesans in the Ancient World
Edited by CHRISTOPHER A. FARAONE and LAURA K. MCCLURE

Asinaria: The One about the Asses
PLAUTUS
Translated and with commentary by John Henderson

Ulysses in Black: Ralph Ellison, Classicism, and African American Literature
PATRICE D. RANKINE

Imperium and Cosmos: Augustus and the Northern Campus Martius
PAUL REHAK
Edited by John G. Younger

Ovid before Exile: Art and Punishment in the "Metamorphoses"
PATRICIA J. JOHNSON

Pandora's Senses: The Feminine Character of the Ancient Text
VERED LEV KENAAN

Nox Philologiae: Aulus Gellius and the Fantasy of the Roman Library
ERIK GUNDERSON

New Perspectives on Etruria and Early Rome
Edited by SINCLAIR BELL and HELEN NAGY

The Image of the Poet in Ovid's "Metamorphoses"
BARBARA PAVLOCK

Responses to Oliver Stone's "Alexander": Film, History, and Cultural Studies
Edited by PAUL CARTLEDGE and FIONA ROSE GREENLAND

The Codrus Painter:
Iconography and Reception of Athenian Vases in the Age of Pericles
AMALIA AVRAMIDOU

The Matter of the Page: Essays in Search of Ancient and Medieval Authors
SHANE BUTLER

Greek Prostitutes in the Ancient Mediterranean, 800 BCE–200 CE
Edited by ALLISON GLAZEBROOK and MADELEINE M. HENRY

Sophocles' "Philoctetes" and the Great Soul Robbery
NORMAN AUSTIN

Oedipus Rex
SOPHOCLES
A verse translation by David Mulroy, with introduction and notes

The Slave in Greece and Rome
JOHN ANDREAU and RAYMOND DESCAT
Translated by Marion Leopold

Perfidy and Passion: Reintroducing the "Iliad"
MARK BUCHAN

The Gift of Correspondence in Classical Rome:
Friendship in Cicero's "Ad Familiares" and Seneca's "Moral Epistles"
AMANDA WILCOX

Antigone
SOPHOCLES
A verse translation by David Mulroy, with introduction and notes

Aeschylus's "Suppliant Women": The Tragedy of Immigration
GEOFFREY W. BAKEWELL

Couched in Death: "Klinai" and Identity in Anatolia and Beyond
ELIZABETH P. BAUGHAN

Silence in Catullus
BENJAMIN ELDON STEVENS

Odes
HORACE
Translated with commentary by David R. Slavitt

Shaping Ceremony: Monumental Steps and Greek Architecture
MARY B. HOLLINSHEAD

Selected Epigrams
MARTIAL
Translated with notes by Susan McLean

The Offense of Love: "Ars Amatoria," "Remedia Amoris," and "Tristia" 2
OVID
A verse translation by Julia Dyson Hejduk, with introduction and notes

Oedipus at Colonus
SOPHOCLES
A verse translation by David Mulroy, with introduction and notes

Women in Roman Republican Drama
Edited by DOROTA DUTSCH, SHARON L. JAMES, and DAVID KONSTAN

Dream, Fantasy, and Visual Art in Roman Elegy
EMMA SCIOLI

Agamemnon
AESCHYLUS
A verse translation by David Mulroy, with introduction and notes

Trojan Women, Helen, Hecuba:
Three Plays about Women and the Trojan War
EURIPIDES
Verse translations by Francis Blessington, with introductions and notes

Echoing Hylas: A Study in Hellenistic and Roman Metapoetics
MARK HEERINK

Horace between Freedom and Slavery: The First Book of "Epistles"
STEPHANIE MCCARTER

The Play of Allusion in the "Historia Augusta"
DAVID ROHRBACHER